GW01336063

ARABIAN PERSONALITIES
OF THE EARLY TWENTIETH CENTURY

is a primary sourcebook of British intelligence material gathered by such authorities as T.E. Lawrence, Ronald Storrs, Boyle, Craufurd, Bray, Garland, Parker, Davenport, Cox, Douglas Carruthers, C.E. Wilson, and Gertrude Bell.

Amir Abdulaziz of Najd, later to be King of a unified Saudi Arabia, "is a man of about 40 years of age, six feet high and broad in proportion, of kindly face and simple manners; intelligent, energetic and warlike."

Lesser personalities are the subjects of equally fascinating profiles, and sketches of more than three thousand seven hundred other individuals, with their social, political, local and tribal affiliations, make *Arabian Personalities of the Early Twentieth Century*, first published in 1917 in a strictly limited and confidential edition, an indispensable biographical reference work for anyone concerned with the Middle East or Arab politics.

Sections are devoted to Hejaz, Asir, Yemen, Aden and Hadhramaut, the Gulf Coast, Central Arabia, the Syrian Desert and Sinai, the Bedouin tribes, and sedentary tribes of the northwest, west, south and centre of the Arabian Peninsula. With a map and highly detailed index of names.

ROBIN BIDWELL, who has provided a new introduction, is Secretary of the Middle East Centre at Cambridge University. He has also written valuable introductions to Hogarth's *Hejaz before World War I*, Maurizi's *History of Seyd Said, Sultan of Muscat*, and *Arabian Gulf Intelligence*, compiled and edited by Robert Hughes Thomas.

Arabia Past & Present, vol. 19

ISBN 0 906672 39 2

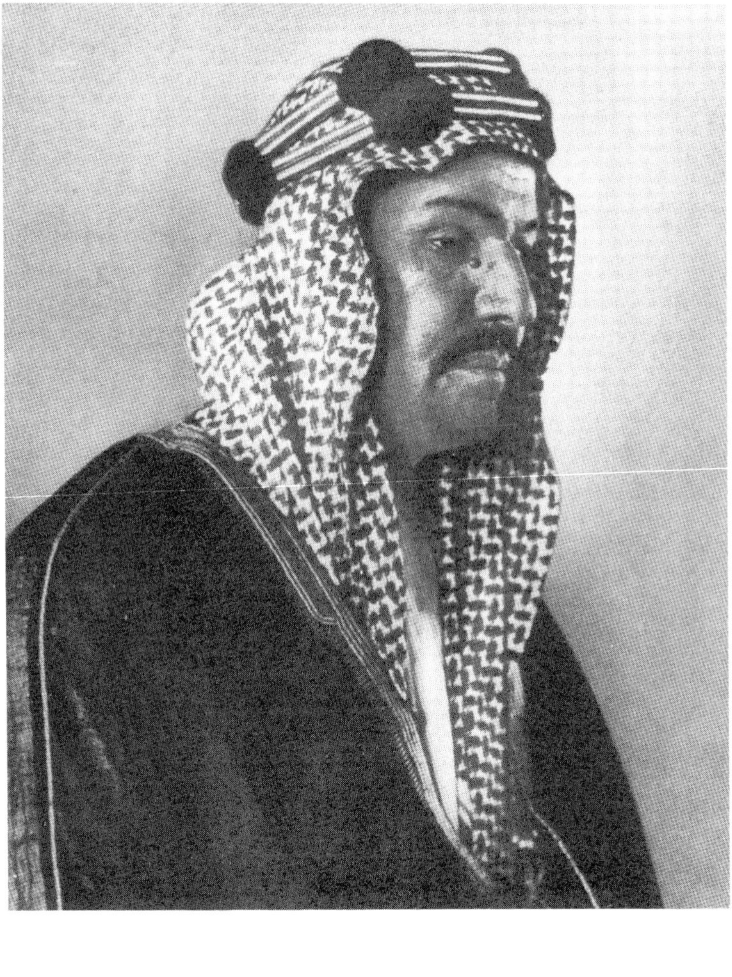

ARABIAN PERSONALITIES OF THE EARLY TWENTIETH CENTURY

with a new Introduction by Robin Bidwell

THE OLEANDER PRESS

The Oleander Press Ltd
17 Stansgate Avenue
Cambridge CB2 2QZ
England

The Oleander Press Ltd
210 Fifth Avenue
New York, N.Y. 10010
U.S.A.

First published 1917
© 1986 additional matter The Oleander Press
and R.L. Bidwell

British Library Cataloguing in Publication Data
Arabian personalities of the early twentieth century.
—(Arabia past and present; v. 19)
1. Politicians—Arabian Peninsula—Biography
I. Series
953'.009'92   DS222

ISBN 0–906672–39–2

Illustrations

Frontispiece: His Majesty King Abdulaziz ibn Sa'ud when Amir of Najd, about 1917.
Map: Tribal Map of Arabia, about 1917.

Printed and bound in Great Britain

INTRODUCTION
Robin L. Bidwell

This is a most interesting and important document which has never before been available outside British official archives. It is in part a selection and in many cases an up-dating of handbooks previously issued but compiled in 1917 with the needs of political and intelligence officers in mind, rather than those concerned on the ground with military operations.

The Hejaz section contains much that has been reprinted from the *Handbook* published a year previously by the Arab Bureau [The Oleander Press, 1978] but it omits much of the purely topographical information and detailed itineraries which took up almost half of the original. Once again in the accounts of the personalities we can catch the accents of T.E. Lawrence and Ronald Storrs but at other times they reflect the less romantic views of Colonel C.E. Wilson, the British representative who had the daily task of dealing with King Husain. The dynastic ambitions of the King and of Sharif Abdullah have become apparent and there are changes in the sketches of other Jiddah personalities. There is also much new information about the tribes, particularly about those such as the Harb and the Billi with whom officers had come into contact, particularly during the period of the Rabigh crisis. Amongst these the most important were N.N.E. Bray, R.G. Garland, A.C. Parker, W.A. Davenport and Henry Cox.

The section on Asir also owes much to the *Handbook* compiled in the Arab Bureau by Kinahan Cornwallis [The Oleander Press, 1976] before the Arab Revolt actually began. In his preface Cornwallis had pointed out that for 80 years no European had visited the interior but in 1916–17 the British made vigorous attempts to persuade the Idrisi Sayyid not to oppose King Husain or to make things easy for the pro-Turkish Imam of Yemen. Incidentally, the material gathered during these negotiations was a major source for the *Handbook* as can be seen from the report of Colonel H.F. Jacob and other officers printed in Faruq Osman Abaza's *Siyasah Britani fi 'Asir* recently published in Cairo. These had resulted in the decision, a month before the publication of this document, to subsidise the Idrisi to the extent of £7500 a month at a time when Ibn Sa'ud received only £5000. Much of the information was collected and some of the diplomacy done by officers of the Royal Navy's Red Sea Flotilla, particularly by "Ginger" Boyle (later Admiral of the Fleet, the Earl of Cork and Orrery) and C.E.V. Craufurd. One has only to look at some of the tribal sections, for example those on the Rijal al-Ma' or the Bani Abs to see how much had been learned.

The Arab Bureau also published a *Handbook of Yemen*, which incidentally has never been reprinted, and this was used as a basis for the present document. At this time no European had met the Imam Yahya – or indeed any Imam for about a century. Sana'a itself was well-known, having been visited by two men who were later to serve in the Arab Bureau, Aubrey Herbert and Leland Buxton, as well as by George Wyman Bury who was serving with Naval Intelligence and Captain Wavell, cousin of the future Field Marshal. However very little was known of some parts of the interior – no European had visited the Yam since Joseph Halévy in 1870. The tribes of the Tihamah and those on the route to Sana'a were well known as a result of the efficient G.A. Richardson, Vice-Consul in Hudaidah and the railway surveyor A.J. Beneyton. A dangerous gap in knowledge was in the crucial Shafai districts north of Aden from which the Turks had advanced catching Aden completely by surprise, for all intelligence work in that area had been left in the hands of the Sultan of Lahej who had used money and arms provided for the purpose for his own private ends. This had enraged Wyman Bury and also left Wingate who was in overall charge of the Arab Revolt deeply dissatisfied. He wrote acidly about the "soi-distant intelligence people in Aden" and tended to rely more upon his own agent there, Khan Bahadur Abd al-Qadir al-Makkawi.

The section on Aden and the Hadhramaut is full of useful information. The British had been in Aden for three-quarters of a century and had acquired a reasonable knowledge of the tribes, whose chiefs used to visit Aden in quest of subsidies. They doubtless exaggerated their own importance but some of the information had been checked on the ground by Wyman Bury, whose famous book *The Land of Uz* had been published under the name of Abdullah Mansur in 1911, and by officers who had participated in the survey of the North Western section of the Protectorate–Yemeni frontier that followed the clash between British and Turkish troops at al-Darayjah in 1901. No westerner had, however, visited Hadhramaut since the Bents in 1893. Much of the tribal information available had been collected by the Assistant Political Resident, Colonel F.M. Hunter, an up-dated version of whose *Arab Tribes in the Vicinity of Aden* had been issued in Bombay in 1909. Some of the accounts of personalities in this document, such as those dealing with the Subeihi chiefs, are paraphrases of that book.

Information about South Eastern Arabia in this document is largely derived from J.G. Lorimer, whose famous *Gazetteer* had been printed in 1908. Indeed, some of the adjectives applied to the tribes, the well-merited "peculiar" for the Shihuh for example, are taken straight from that work. Lorimer had himself been Political Resident in the Gulf since 1914 and presumably updated some of the entries for this document himself, probably with the aid of the veteran Residency Agent in Sharjah – Abd al-Latif bin Abd al-Rahman who had known everyone on the Trucial Coast since 1890.

The section on the realm of Ibn Sa'ud is of particular interest as it comes at the period when he was just starting to become known to British officials. Possibly with some exaggeration he used to claim that he had never spoken to an Englishman before 1910 when at the age of 30 he met Captain W.H.I. Shakespear. Since then he had encountered Gerald Leachman, Trevor the Political Agent from Bahrain, Sir Percy Cox and Gertrude Bell, but had yet not received the two men who came to know him best – H. St John Philby and Dickson. His father, the Imam Abd al-Rahman bin Faisal had graciously received the Dane Barclay Raunkiaer the account of whose journey had been translated by the Arab Bureau. The reports on some subordinate officials also came from Raunkiaer while the tribal information owes much to Shakespear and Leachman.

The section on the personalities of the Rashidi state of Jabal Shammar obviously owes most to Gertrude Bell and indeed no other westerner had been in Ha'il since Hajji Abdullah Williamson twenty years before. Only Miss Bell could have known of the influential slave-girl Turkiyah mentioned on page 97 and she had indeed already spoken of her in a letter home dated 7 March 1914.

The hand of Gertrude Bell can also be seen in the pages dealing with the tribes of the North Western Desert and their leaders. The legendary Auda Abu Tayi of the Huwaitat had unfortunately been absent on a raid when she visited his encampment in February 1914 so, despite the fact that he had robbed Shakespear, he does not emerge as the vivid figure that we meet in the pages of Lawrence. The full importance of Nuri Shaalan of the Ruwala also seems to have been underestimated. In the reports on the tribes we can also see information derived from Douglas Carruthers whose work was used by the Arab Bureau and from the Bohemian scholar Alois Musil whose writings were used both by the Arab Bureau in Cairo and its German rival in Istanbul.

It will be seen, therefore, that practically all the most famous travellers of the first twenty years of this century have contributed to this volume. It will also be seen how haphazard had been the collection of knowledge of the Arabian Peninsula and how much there was still for succeeding generations to do.

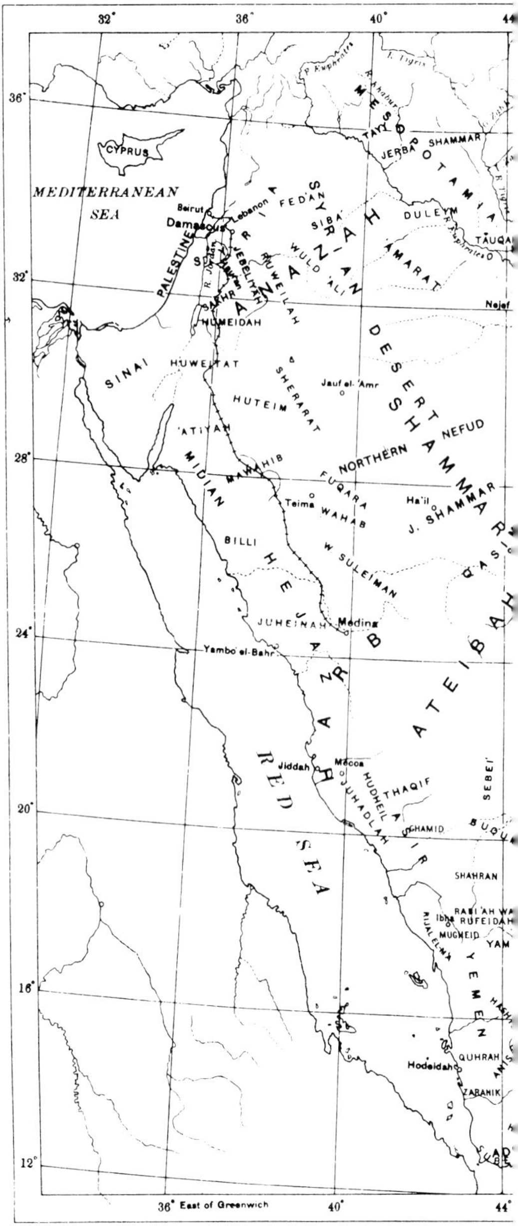
32°
36°
40°
44°
36°
32°
28°
24°
20°
16°
12°
36° East of Greenwich
R. Euphrates
R. Tigris
MESOPOTAMIA
TAYY
JERBA
SHAMMAR
CYPRUS
MEDITERRANEAN
SEA
Beirut
Lebanon
Damascus
FED'AN
SIBA'
DULEYM
TAUQA
SYRIAN
PALESTINE
R. Jordan
JEBELIYAH
RUWEILAH
WULD 'ALI
'AMARAT
ANAZAH
SAKHR
HUMEIDAH
Nejef
SINAI
HUWEITAT
SHERARAT
Jauf el-'Amr
HUTEIM
DESERT
SHAMMAR
NORTHERN NEFUD
'ATIYAH
MIDIAN
MAWAHIB
FUQARA
Teima
WAHAB
Ha'il
J. SHAMMAR
BILLI
W. SULEIMAN
HEJAZ
JUHEINAH
Medina
HARB
Yambo' el-Bahr
ATEIBAH
RED SEA
Jiddah
Mecca
HUDHEIL
THAQIF
SEBEI'
UHADLAH
GHAMID
'ASIR
SHAHRAN
RABI'AH WA
Ibha
RUFEIDAH
MUGHEID
RIJAL EL-MA
YAM
YEMEN
QUHRAH
Hodeidah
ZARANIK

TRIBAL MAP OF ARABIA

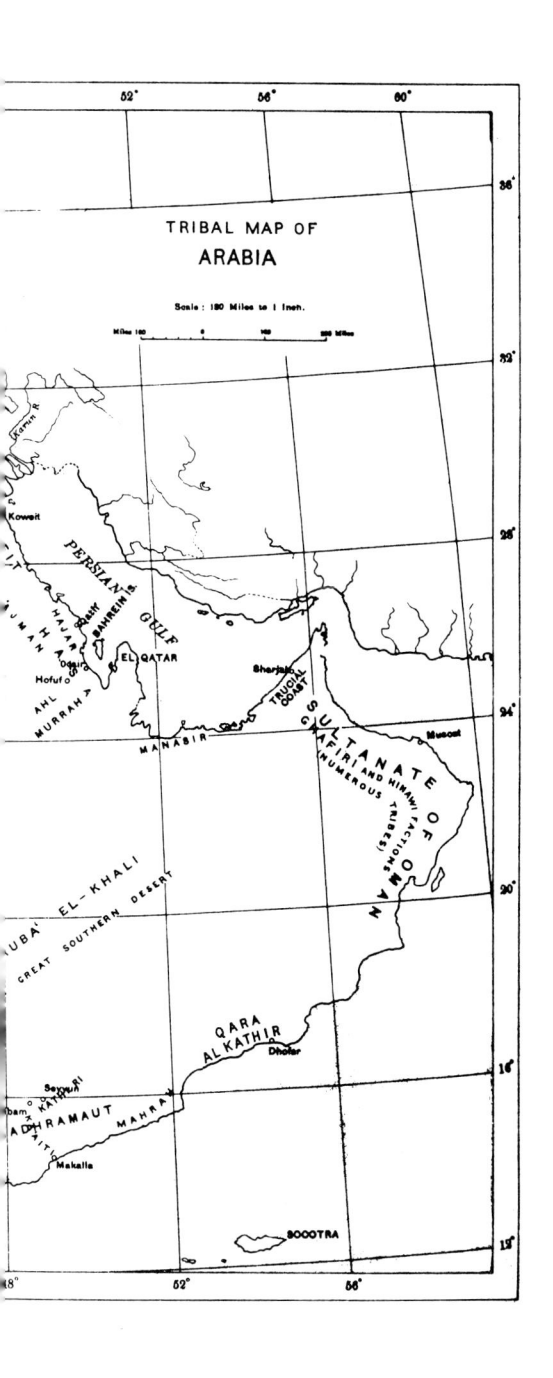

Scale: 180 Miles to 1 Inch.

CONTENTS

Region	Page
I. HEJAZ	3
II. ASIR	22
III. YEMEN	42
IV. ADEN AND HADHRAMAUT	61
V. GULF COAST	70
VI. CENTRAL ARABIA	83
VII. SYRIAN DESERT AND SINAI	97
THE BEDOUIN TRIBES	102
SEDENTARY TRIBES OF THE NORTH-WEST	149
SEDENTARY TRIBES OF THE WEST	157
SEDENTARY TRIBES OF THE SOUTH	246
SEDENTARY TRIBES OF THE CENTRE	327
INDEX	335

PERSONALITIES

ARABIA

REGION I

HEJAZ

EMIRATE OF MECCA.

The Emirs of the 'ABĀDILAH clan are of the Qoreish tribe and directly descended from Hasan, son of the Caliph 'Ali and of Fātimah, the Prophet's daughter.

The present ruling family dates its power to Sherif Mohammed " ibn 'Aun ", who displaced in 1827 the Dhawi Zeid house represented by his predecessor, Ghālib. He was a friend of Mohammed 'Ali of Egypt. The latter presented the Emir with 5,700 feddans of land in Upper Egypt, of which 2,000 were constituted *waqf*. This property is now administered for the Emir. The family has also about 500 feddans at Dawākhilah, near Mahallah, divided between the Emir, his brother Nāsir (q. v.), his sisters and his mother ; 100 feddans at Bahtīn, and properties at Mecca, Tā'if, W. Fātimah, W. Leimūn, and W. Rayyān. The principal residences of the Emirs are at Mecca (winter) and Tā'if (summer). They maintain a princely state and are the most civilized as well as the wealthiest of Arabian potentates.

HUSEIN IBN 'ALI.

Ruling Emir since 1908, when, after twenty-five years' residence in Constantinople, he was nominated, by Kiamil Pasha, to succeed his uncle, 'Abdillah, who had died on his way to Mecca. Of a little over middle height, with fairish complexion and white chin-beard, carefully but not closely clipped. Dignified manners. Intelligent. He is now approaching 70 years of age ; of pacific temper, and popular in Hejaz. Headed the revolt in June 1916, commanding at Mecca, which he took June 13, the fort and barracks surrendering later.

The only sign of ambition which he had given before the present crisis was in 1910, when he sent a force under his son, 'Abdullah, to Qasīm, nominally to assert the rights of the Ateibah tribe, but really to wrest the district from Ibn Sa'ūd, and subject it again to that dependence on Hejaz in which the

A 2

EMIRATE OF MECCA, *continued*.

Egyptian forces had left it in the middle of the nineteenth century. 'Abdullah seized Sa'd, Ibn Sa'ūd's brother ; but disappointed by Ibn Rashīd, who respected a recently concluded peace, readily came to terms with Ibn Sa'ūd as soon as the latter appeared in the field, and retired, saving his face by making certain stipulations about the Ateibah being tax-free, and the Qasīm towns paying an annual subsidy of £4,000 to Mecca, and being at liberty to elect their own Emirs, whether Ibn Sa'ūds or others. Throughout this affair Husein posed as the close ally and representative of the Ottoman Government. In its interest also, as well as his own, he took other action in 1910, partly through his son 'Abdullah (q. v.), against Idrīsi (q. v.), and detached the latter's strongest supporters, as well as saved Ibha for the Turks ; but latterly he has shown some inclination to compromise this feud, and to unite Idrīsi and the Imam of Yemen with himself. Since 1913 he has taken up a distinct anti-Ottoman attitude. He opposed the prolongation of the Hejaz Railway from Medina, supporting the Harb tribesmen, and he refused to call out Hejazi recruits for the Ottoman armies. In order, however, to save himself from heavy requisitions, he allowed a battalion of irregulars to be enrolled at Medina, in 1915, for service with the Turks in Sinai.

In the summer of 1915 he approached us with a view to establishing his independence, and, after being assured of our support, made arrangements with the Harb, Ateibah, and other Hejaz tribes, as well as with some of the Anazah group, and raised the standard of revolt near Medina on June 5, 1916. On June 9 he attacked also Mecca, Jiddah, and Tā'if. The first two surrendered quickly, but Tā'if held out for nearly four months. Both there and at Medina his Arabs (about 15,000 armed men in all) proved little able to deal with fortified positions and artillery. Yambo' surrendered to him at the end of July, and Līth a little earlier. Though he had concluded an agreement with Idrīsi, he was aggrieved at the latter's occupation of Qunfudah in July, and sent an expedition to turn his force out ; but Idrīsi subsequently withdrew without fighting. He appears to have a good hold on the Hejaz tribes except the Zobeid Harb under Husein ibn Mubeirik of Rābugh, whose ambitions conflict with his. While the Juheinah obey him, the Billi are uncertain, and there has not yet been proof of the effective adhesion of any tribes farther north, except the southern Wuld 'Ali. He aspires to a wide suzerainty, extending over not only the Syrian desert but Syria itself. Ibn Sa'ūd has observed a friendly, but watchful, neutrality ; Ibn Rashīd has sided with the Turks ; the Imam of Yemen has not actively assisted Husein, but is inclined to negotiate ; Nūri Sha'lān (q.v.) is allied with him.

EMIRATE OF MECCA, *continued.*

Emir Husein's reputation is that rather of a politician than of a leader of men ; but he has much influence among desert tribesmen (e.g. Harb all sections, Ateibah, Juheinah, Billi, Hudheil, Juhadlah, and some smaller S. Hejazi groups). He keeps in touch with the Pan-Arabists in Syria, &c., and wields a wide local influence extending south to W. Bīshah in Asir and inland through Qasīm to Sedeir.

He has four sons :

'ALI.

His father's favourite and Grand Vizier. Short and slim, looking a little old already, though only thirty-seven. Slightly bent. Skin rather sallow, large deep brown eyes, nose thin and a little hooked, face somewhat worn and full of lines and hollows, mouth drooping. Beard spare and black. Has very delicate hands. His manners are perfectly simple, and he is obviously a very conscientious, careful, pleasant, gentleman, without force of character, nervous and rather tired. His physical weakness makes him subject to quick fits of shaking passion with more frequent moods of infirm obstinacy. Apparently not ambitious for himself, but swayed somewhat too easily by the wishes of others. Is bookish, and learned in law and religion. Shows his Arab blood more than his brothers. At Medina from March to June, 1915, and mediated between the Harb tribesmen and Ghālib Pasha, the incoming Vali of Hejaz, obtaining leave for the latter to proceed, on swearing that he had no Germans with him. He is said to have gone north towards Syria in January 1916, with a few followers, most of his escort having been detained by a tribal disturbance near Medina, apparently provoked expressly to detain him. Originally three clans of the Harb (the 'Auf, Beni 'Amr, and Zeid el-'Alauni) had proposed to follow him to the Canal. In June 1916 he took command of the force destined to blockade Medina, and defeated a Turkish sortie at Ghadīr-Rābugh in August. Habitually represents his father at Medina.

'ABDULLAH.

Minister for Foreign Affairs and President of the Legislative Council. Aged 35, but looks younger. Short and thick built, apparently as strong as a horse, with merry dark-brown eyes, a round smooth face, full but short lips, straight nose, brown beard. In manner affectedly open and very charming, not standing at all on ceremony, but jesting with the tribesmen like one of their own sheikhs. On serious occasions he judges his words carefully, and shows himself a keen dialectician. Is probably not so much the brain as the spur of his father. He is obviously working to establish the greatness of the family, and has large ideas, which no doubt include his own particular advancement. The Arabs consider him a most astute politician, and a far-seeing statesman : but he has possibly more of the former than of the latter in his composition. Has visited Egypt. Formerly Deputy for Mecca in the Ottoman Parliament, and not on good terms with the Committee. Quarrelled with Enver. An experienced warrior and capable leader, who has seen a deal of fighting. Sent in March 1915 with a large escort on a mission to Ibn Sa'ūd and Ibn Rashīd to negotiate peace between the Central Emirates and collect arrears of dues from Qasīm and Sedeir. In this he was successful. Late in 1915 he went to Syria with a considerable following, but returned early in 1916, and took command of the force besieging Tā'if. Led it in many impetuous assaults and took the place after four months. Is reputed to aim at the Caliphate for his House.

FEISĀL.

Minister of the Interior. Age 31. Tall, graceful, vigorous, almost regal in appearance. Very quick and restless in movement. Far more imposing personally than any of his brothers ; knows it and trades on it. Is as clear-skinned as a pure Circassian, with dark hair, vivid black eyes set a little sloping in his face, strong nose, short chin. Looks like a European. He is hot tempered, proud and impatient, sometimes unreasonable, and runs off easily at tangents. Possesses far more personal magnetism and life than his brothers, but less prudence. Obviously very clever, perhaps not over scrupulous. Rather narrow-minded, and rash when he acts on impulse, but usually with enough strength to reflect, and then exact in judgement. A popular idol, and ambitious ; full of dreams, and the capacity to realize them, with keen personal insight, and a very efficient man of business. Went to Constantinople in March 1915, as Deputy for Hejaz, nominally to protest against the enrolment of Hejazis, but really to spy out the strength of the Turks. On his return tried to see Nūri Sha'lān at Damascus, but on repeated orders of Jemāl Pasha, had to leave before Nawwāf, son of Nūri, arrived. Said to have more influence with tribesmen than 'Abdullah. Late in 1915 went up to Syria with a small following, on (it is said) a secret mission from his father. Returned February 1916 with Enver and Jemāl to Medina, but again went to Syria till May. In June 1916 took command of the Arab force on the Hejaz railway, but effected little and returned to operate with 'Ali before

RULING SHERIFIAL ('ABÂDILAH) FAMILY OF MECCA[1]

MOHAMMED IBN 'ABD EL MU'ÎN IBN 'AUN
(Emir, 1827–51 and 1856–8).

- ABDULLAH (Emir, 1858–77).
  - 'ALI (= Rahmah) (Emir, 1905–7. Dismissed. Lives in Egypt).
    - Son, died young.
  - Mohammed.
  - 'Abd el-Muhsin (Lives at Cairo).
    - 'Abdullah.

- 'Ali.
  - HUSEIN (Emir 1908–).
    - 'Ali.
    - 'Abdullah.
    - Feisal.
    - Zeid.
  - Nâsir.
  - Rahmah (= 'Ali).

- HUSEIN (Emir, 1877–80. Murdered).

- 'AUN ER-RAFÎQ (Emir, 1882–1905).
  - Mohammed 'Abd el-'Azîz (Interdicted: resides at Cairo and Constantinople).

- 'ABDILLAH (Emir, 1907–8).

- Sultân.

[1] A member of the rival Dhawi Zeid clan which was in power before 1827, viz. 'AHD EL-MUTALLIB, son of the Emir GHÂLIB and grandson of the Emir MESÂ'ID, was appointed Emir 1851–6, and again in extreme old age, 1880–2, after the murder of Emir HUSEIN.

Medina. Met Col. Wilson at Yambo' in August. A fiery soldier without fanaticism, who admires modern military methods.

ZEID.

Aged about 20. Is quite overshadowed by the reputation of his half-brothers. His mother was Turkish and he takes after her. Is fond of riding about, and playing tricks. Has not, so far, been entrusted with any important commission, but is active. In manner a little loutish, but not a bad fellow. Humorous in outlook, and perhaps a little better balanced, because less intense, than his brothers. Shy. The least important of the four sons. Sent on a peace mission to Asir in March 1915. Met a British delegation on the Hejaz coast on June 6, 1916, immediately before the revolt broke out. Afterwards represented his father at Jiddah, and commanded reserve troops.

NĀSIR IBN 'ALI.

Younger brother of the ruling Emir. Age 54. Was a member of the Ottoman Upper House, and has lived mainly at Constantinople. He has three (or four ?) sons. He is said to support his brother's policy, and shares with him an interest in some of the Egyptian property of the family (see above, p. 3). Was still in Constantinople with his family when his brother's revolt broke out.

'ABD EL-MUHSIN EL-BARAKĀTI.

Son of a sister of the ruling Emir, and used to be the latter's official agent in Egypt. Owns land at Saft el-Laban (Jīzah) and Tarūt (Miniyat el-Kamh). Now at Mecca, where he is (or was) Kaimmakam (Civil Governor) under his uncle.

'ALI HAIDAR PASHA (or HAIDAR 'ALI), Sherif.

Of the Dhawi Zeid clan, and the house of Emir 'Abd el-Mutallib. He has lived at Constantinople for many years as Naqīb el-Ashrāf or official representative of the Sherifial clans, and he has been Minister of Evkaf. Is a member of the C.U.P., and an ex-member of the Ottoman Upper House. Married, as his second wife, an Irishwoman, by whom he has three children ; his eldest boy was educated in England. Pan-Islamist, but inclines to the British interest. Maintains relations with Indian Moslems. Has been proposed as titular Caliph with a small territorial reservation at Damascus or elsewhere, on the analogy of the Papacy ; but it is not known if such is his own desire. His agent at Jiddah, Ahmed el-Hezāzi (q. v.), was convicted of plotting against Emir Husein in 1916, and his house was looted by order on the capture of Jiddah in June. 'Ali Haidar, himself, was nominated Emir by the Porte after the outbreak of the revolt, and ordered to repair to Medina if he could get there, and use his influence with the tribes. He arrived on July 26 and issued a proclamation.

JA'FAR PASHA, SHERIF.
Younger brother of 'Ali Haidar (q.v.). Like him, was kept by 'Abd el-Hamīd at Constantinople ; joined C.U.P. But, while a strong Nationalist and Pan-Islamist, he has been pro-British, in the hope of gaining Arab independence. Has acted as agent for the Committee in Syria and Yemen. Married a daughter of the Sultan.

SA'D ED-DĪN PASHA, SHERIF.
Of the Dhawi Zeid ; cousin of Sherif 'Ali Haidar. Sent by the latter to Ibn Rashīd and the tribes in August 1915. Went to Hā'il with Mumtaz and Eshref Beys ; but said to have secretly opposed them, being a pan-Arab.

'ABDULLAH ABU ZENĀDAH.
Of Jiddah. Ex-slave of the Dhawi Zeid Sherifial family of Mecca. Small broker. Pro-Sherif and anti-Turk.

'ABDULLAH 'ALI RIDHA (RIZA).
Of Jiddah. One of the most influential town councillors, but meddlesome. Well off (*see* Zeini 'Ali Ridha).

'ABDULLAH SARRĀJ (SARĀJ), SHEIKH.
Minister of Justice (Grand Qādhi) and Acting Minister of Education under the Emir. Ex-Hanafi Mufti ; Sheikh el-Islām. Personal friend of the Emir. On April 29, 1916, on the occasion of the Friday visit of notables to the Imarat at Mecca, he brought forward the question of the imminent British blockade and called for action, saying that the Hejaz population must perish if an arrangement was not made with Great Britain. He is a man of about 46, very tall and spare, with long face and nose, and beard clipped close. Enjoys a very high reputation, and is entrusted with very wide powers by the Emir.

'ABDULLAH TAWĀ'D, SHERIF.
Of Yambo'. Friend of Sherif Feisāl, and recruited for the latter's forces. Accompanied Col. Wilson to meet Feisāl in August 1916.

'ABDULLAH ZAWĀWI, SEYYID.
Shafei Mufti at Mecca, and one of the representatives of the Ashrāf on the Emir's Legislative Council. About 65. Friend of the Emir. Good repute ; rich and influential with Arabs.

'ABDULLAH IBN THAWĀB, SHERIF.
Of the Ateibah Ashrāf; Emir of El-Miqātah. About 40. Enlisted troops for Sherif Feisāl. Well educated and of much influence. At Yambo' in October 1916.

'ABD EL-'AZĪZ TAYYĀR, SHEIKH.
Of Medina. Chief of the Shawahlah clan of the Masrūh Harb. Lives always in the town, where he enjoys much influence, but has little outside. A rich merchant. Now very old.

'ABD EL-LATĪF MIZEINI.
Of Jiddah; a Harbi tribesman (Mizeināt). Sheikh of Nuzlat el-Yemenīyah, and has influence with Arabs. Short; grizzled beard; pleasant appearance. Is now Emir el-Bahr (Harbour-master), though ignorant and unable to write. Leads the anti-Muhsin party. Not of good repute.

'ABD EL-MĀLIK EL-KHOTIB.
Javanese of Mecca. Well educated, and used to be Meccan correspondent of the *Mokattam*. Much influence with the Emir. Owns property at Mecca.

'ABD EL-MUHSIN IBN ASSĪM, SHEIKH.
Chief of the 'Usum Section of the 'Auf under Sheikh Furn (q.v.). Lives at Khuleis (Khālis). Hereditary standard-bearer of the Harb. About 55. A noted warrior, and reputed just.

'ABD EL-MUHSIN SUBHI, SHEIKH.
Chief of the Subh clan of the B. Sālim (Harb). Lives at Mastūrah. Of good repute, but not a strong man or of much influence.

'ABD ER-RAHMĀN BA JUNEID.
Of Jiddah. Merchant; owns dhows and runs arms-cargoes.

'ABD ER-RAHMĀN BISHNA'Q, SHEIKH.
Of Mecca. President of the Municipality (Ra'is el-Baledīyah) under the Emir.

'ABD ER-RAHMĀN, SEYYID.
Of Ru'eis, one hour north of Jiddah. Important trader in arms. Anti-Turk (has had two dhows confiscated by the Turks).

'ABD ER-RA'ŪF JAMJŪM.
Of Jiddah. Of Egyptian origin. General merchant. Member of Town Council; stupid, obstinate. About 30.

ABU BEKR KHUKŪR (OR SHAKIR?), SHEIKH.
Member of the Emir's Legislative Council, representing the secular population.

ABU JERĪDAH.
Of Mecca. Leader of the Emir's forces after the latter's sons. Had Ottoman rank of *Bimbashi*. Devoted to Emir Husein. Ex-slave of the Shahrān tribe from Bīshah, whence come most of the Emir's bodyguard.

AHMED BA HĀRŪN.
Of Jiddah. Member of Town Council. About 60. Well off. Devout and stupid.

AHMED EL-HEZĀZI.
Of Jiddah. A Moor. Agent of the Dhawi Zeid and of Sherif 'Ali Haidar. Intrigued actively against the Emir two years ago. On the fall of Jiddah, the latter ordered his house to be looted.

AHMED EL-MULLAH.
Of Jiddah. Before the War, Agent of the Ottoman Steamship Company. A Bokhariote dealer in carpets. Pro-Turk, but of very little influence.

AHMED IBN MANSŪR EL-KERĪMI, Sherif.
Of the Zobeid Harb and brother of Sherif Muhsin (q.v.); is also styled "Emir of the Harb". About 54. Brave and influential; well educated. With Sherif 'Ali at Rābugh. Came with Sherif Zeid to Qadhīmah in September, to receive Husein ibn Mubārak's submission.

AHMED IBN MOHAMMED ABU TOQEIQAH.
Chief of the clan of the Huweitāt which occupies the Midian coast; head-quarters at Dhaba. Pro-Turk and subsidized. Displaced the rightful chief, Shadhli el-'Alyān (q.v.).

AHMED SĀFI, Seyyid.
Of Medina. About 45. Belongs to the most important family in the town next to the Medāni (q.v.). Rich, with much influence in the town, but not outside it.

AHMED TAL'ĀT.
Secretary of Sherif Muhsin at Jiddah. Trustworthy and pro-British.

'ALI EL-HIBSHI, Seyyid.
Of Medina. A rich grain and wood merchant. His cousins, 'Abdullah, Ja'far, and Hāshim are also in the business.

'ALI YŪSUF IBN SĀLIM EL-MĀLIKI.
Of Mecca. Minister of Public Works in the Emir's Council.

'ALI IBN 'ABDULLAH, Sheikh.
Chief of the Beni 'Ali, a Shiah clan of the 'Auf. Is at perpetual odds with the Government, and his tribesmen cut the roads and rob caravans. About 70. A trader.

'ALI IBN 'ABDULLAH, Sherif.
Emir of the Juheinah. Resides at Yambo' el-Bahr. Related to the Emir of Mecca, and his partisan. Left in independent control of the tribesmen by the Ottoman Government, whose authority he acknowledged up to 1914; then superseded, at Ottoman instance, by Mohammed 'Ali el-Bedāwi (q.v.). But when the Emir of Mecca got the upper hand in June 1916, 'Ali returned from Suakin. He expelled Von Stotzingen and Neufeld from Yambo', and led the Sherif's forces sent up from Jiddah, to which the Turkish garrison surrendered late in July.

'ALI LATĪFAH.
Of Jiddah. Of Syrian origin. Town Councillor; meddlesome, obstinate. Large grain merchant. About 65.

'ALI SHARKĀSI, Sheikh.
Of Mecca. Member of the Emir's Legislative Council, representing the secular element.

'AMĀN EL-MUQADDAM, Sheikh.
Of Yambo'. Recommended as likely to favour us and be useful (July 1915). Pro-Sherif.

ANWAR ESHJI.
Of Medina. Of a Turkish family long domiciled there. Ra'is el-Belediyah.

ASAD DHĀN IBN AHMED, Sheikh.
Of Mecca. A favourite Councillor of the Emir. A man of medium height and pale round face, with dark eyes and white beard. About 60.

'ATAS HADHRAMI.
Of Jiddah. One of the chief *ulema* and a merchant, owning dhows and trading in grain with Mīdi. Age about 40. Pro-Sherif and anti-Turk.

'AWAD SALĪMI, Sheikh.
Chief of the Rahalah section of the B. Sālim (Harb). Lives between Medina and Bir Raha. Age about 60. An active opponent of the Turks, in alliance with the Huwāfah, 'Useidi and Beni 'Ali. Popular.

BA LA RĀJ.
Of Līth. The chief merchant and contractor to Government for all military supplies.

BA NĀJI' HADHRAMI, House of.
Of Mecca and Jiddah. Engaged in Indian and coastal trade, owning dhows and running arms-cargoes (e.g. to Qunfudah in the Turco-Italian War). Important members are :—

'ABD ER-RAHMĀN, Sheikh. Of Jiddah. The foremost merchant, and an old man over sixty; white hair and beard. Has resided in Cairo, where he is well known. Was imprisoned about eight years ago at Jiddah by the Turks.

'ABDULLAH, Pasha. Brother of the above. Now at Mecca.

AHMED IBN 'ABD ER-RAHMĀN. Son of the first-named, with whom he was not on very good terms. He broke off and went to Mecca, and did business for the Sherifial family. About 35. Now Minister of Finance in the Emir's ministry.

BARAKĀT ANSĀRI, Seyyid.
Of Medina. A rich man, with much influence in the town. About 65.

BA SABREIN HADHRAMI.
Of Jiddah. Of the 'Amūdi tribe from Hadhramaut. *'Ālim* at Jiddah for the past twenty years. Formerly of Musawwa'. Age about 80; educated at Zebīd. Of good repute and popular.

BA ZĀ'ZA, House of.
Trading at Jiddah, Suez, and Alexandria. AHMED BA ZĀ'ZA used to be deputy harbour-master at Jiddah; he owns dhows and ran arms-cargoes during the Turco-Italian War. The family is of Upper Egyptian origin.

FĀ'IZ EZ-ZOGHEIBI.
Of the Beni 'Amr section of the Harb. Messenger from Sherif 'Ali to his father before the revolt, June 1916.

FITIM IBN MUHSIN, Sherif.
Of Mecca. Representative of the Ashrāf on the Legislative Council.

FURN, Sheikh.
The most important Harb Sheikh. Chief of the 'Auf. Lives at Suweirqīyah, on the Eastern road. An old man of 75, but still vigorous. Never comes to Medina. Wide influence.

GHĀLIB EL-BEDĀWI (locally pronounced BEDEIWI), Sherif.
Brother of Mohammed 'Ali el-Bedāwi (q.v.). Occupied Umlejh for the Sherif in late July or August 1916, and seems to have brought in the Juheinah to the latter's cause.

HAMZAH EL-FEIR, SHERIF.
Of the Ateibah (Berqah section) Ashrāf. Lives at Mecca and serves on the Legislative Council, as a representative of the Ashrāf.

HASAN EDH-DHI'ĀB.
Of Medina ; of the Dhi'āb house. A man of great influence with both the Turks and the Harb ; mediates between the two. Rather anti-Sherif.

HASAN NĀSIR IBN DHI'ĀB, PASHA.
A chief of the Ahamda section of the Beni Sālim (Harb). Inherited his title, and, like his father, is " Bāb-'Arāb " or mediator between the Government and the tribes. Receives £60 *per mensem* from the Turks. Age about 45. Friendly with the chief Harbi Sheikhs and popular with tribesmen. Just and tactful. Dèlegate from Medina to C.U.P. Congress at Constantinople, September 1916. His son, Husein, is in Government employ.

HAZEM, SHEIKH.
Controller of camel transport under the Emir of Mecca ; arranged for the Hajj, 1916. Reported to be secretly anti-Sherif. A friend of the ex-Khedive. Not of good reputation.

HĀZIR EL-'ABĀDILAH, SHERIF.
Of Mecca, chief of the desert police charged with the protection of the caravan roads to Medina. Of great influence.

HUSEIN IBN FUZĀN.
Chief of the Sihāf section of the 'Auf (Harb). Lives at Asfān, on the Mecca-Rābugh road, and is, with his clan, responsible for most robberies in the Mecca-Jiddah district, though he himself tries to restrain his men. About 50, and a Shiah.

HUSEIN IBN MUBĀRAK (pronounced locally MUBEIRIK).
Chief of the Zobeid section of the Masrūh Harb. One of the most powerful Harbi sheikhs ; resides at Rābugh. Formerly anti-Turk, but not necessarily pro-British. " A man of much power, who likes to be addressed by high-sounding titles." Owns dhows, and has had correspondence and other communications with the Red Sea Patrol about seizures ; but has not yet been visited by a political officer. To be treated with distinction and caution. In 1916, raised about 4,000 men and captured a very large sum of money on its way from Medina to Mecca for Ottoman official use. Joined the Emir's revolt in June 1916, but half-heartedly, and opposed the landing of the Egyptian battery at Rābugh. Corresponded with the Turks and accepted their bribes. Detained and

diverted the Emir's supplies. In August he withdrew inland when the Emir occupied Rābugh in force. Later, made his way to Medina and definitely joined the Turks. Not to be trusted to serve any ambition but his own.

IBRĀHĪM NĀ'IB EL-HARĀM, SEYYID.
Of Mecca. Member of the Emir's Legislative Council, representing the secular element.

ISMĀ'ĪL IBN MUBĀRAK.
Brother of Husein of Rābugh. Lives at Bir el-Māshi.

JĀBIR EL-AYĀSHI, SHERIF.
Chief Sheikh of the Juheinah Ashrāf. Lives at Yambo' en-Nakhl. About 44. Pro-Sherif; sent to Suleimān Afnān Rufādah by Sherif Feisāl in September 1916. Has many settled Juheinah under him.

MAHMŪD ASHŪR.
Of Jiddah. Egyptian from Luxor. Grain merchant and dhow owner. Town Councillor; of good repute; sound but not brilliant. About 65.

MANSŪR IBN 'ABBĀS, SHEIKH.
Chief of the Dhuwāhir, the largest section of the Beni Sālim (Harb), living at Hamra. About 60; generous, just, and popular with the tribesmen. His brother, Nāsir, is also of importance.

MEDINA, SEYYIDS OF.
The four important families are: 1. MEDĀNI; 2. JEMĀ-LILEIL; 3. HIBSHI (q.v.); 4. SĀFI (q.v.). All intermarried, and all with the Sherif, except the Sāfi.

MOHAMMED 'ĀBID, SHEIKH.
Of Mecca. Maliki Mufti. Representative of the Ashrāf on the Legislative Council of the Emir. About 65; of good repute, but not clever. Friend of the Emir.

MOHAMMED 'ALI EL-BEDĀWI (locally pron. BEDEIWI), SHERIF.
Emir of the Juheinah at Yambo', who superseded 'Ali ibn 'Abdullah in 1914. Age about 55. Pro-Turk and pro-German; summoned to Mecca early in 1916, and reprimanded by the Emir. Returned to Yambo' and was in his turn superseded in June by 'Ali ibn 'Abdullah (q.v.), but still wields local power and was corresponding with the Turks in August.

MOHAMMED 'ALI LĀRI.
Of Jiddah. Rich carpet-merchant. Persian Consul. A Behai and pro-English. Well educated and intelligent.

MOHAMMED EFFENDI AMĪN EL-MEKKI, SHERIF.

Of Mecca. Minister of Waqf and the Holy Places (Haram): controls contributions and dues for religious purposes. A man of medium height and fair complexion, with a reputation for fair dealing and pleasant character.

MOHAMMED EFFENDI HUSEIN NESĪF.

Honorary agent of the Emir at Jiddah; Anglophile and trustworthy. Owns much property in Jiddah; has a good house and is well educated. Member of Council, but takes no part at present. Anxious to acquire British citizenship. Opposed to the Ashrāf. A son of 'Omar Nesīf, of Egyptian origin. About 32. Merchant trading on a considerable scale. A portly, benevolent-looking, spectacled man.

MOHAMMED ET-TAWĪL.

Of Jiddah. Director of Customs and an adherent of Sherif Muhsin and of the Emir of Mecca.

MOHAMMED IBN 'ARIF 'AREIFĀN, SHEIKH.

Of Qadhīmah in Wādi Ithwel. A sheikh of the Zobeid section of the Masrūh Harb, living about one hour inland from Ras 'Arab (Makhlukh). In the confidence of the Emir of Mecca, but not quite to be trusted where the interests of his paramount chief, Husein ibn Mubārak (q.v.), are involved. Used by us in most of our preliminary communications with the Emir, and has arranged the transit and landing of arms and supplies. Arranged the meeting between Sherif Zeid and the British envoys on June 6, 1916, and also the withdrawal of Idrīsi's garrison from Qunfudah in August. Has seven sons. Claims influence with the Zobeid, and a share in the brutal and treacherous murder of six Germans, about three hours south of his village, in May 1916. A party leader in Jiddah.

MOHAMMED IBN HAMĀD, SHEIKH.

Chief of the Lehābah clan of the 'Auf (Harb). Lives at Rābugh, and is a friend of Husein ibn Mubārak. His family has ruled the 'Auf since the Prophet's day. Age about 45. Rich, but mean and unpopular. Hires out camels to the Hajj, and acquiesces in his tribesmen's raids on it, taking his share of the spoil.

MOHAMMED IBN JIBĀRAH ES-SIRĀSĪRI, SHEIKH.

Chief of the settled non-Sherifial Juheinah tribes. Lives at Yambo' en-Nakhl (formerly at Medina). About 40. Well educated, liberal, intelligent, brave, influential, and popular. Used to be in Turkish pay, but now active for the Emir of Mecca. Sent on a mission to Suleimān Afnān Rufādah, September 1916.

MOHAMMED IBN KHAILĀN ABU TAYY.

Cousin of the late 'Audah Abu Tayy, chief of the Tawāyah section of the Huweitāt, who was killed in autumn 1915. Mohammed is Sheikh ed-Daulah, i. e. he collects sheep and camel-tax for the Ottoman Government from the Huweitāt. He stands in considerable awe of official authority, having been imprisoned for some months in Damascus in 1911 by Sāmi Pasha. Since that time he has ceased to lead raids, contenting himself, no doubt, with the profits of tax-collecting. He has considerable authority with the Huweitāt, and is just and upright, with a strong hand. A man of about 35 ; of magnificent physique. Shakespear met him in 1914 in 'Audah's camp, and arranged with him his further journey towards Akaba.

MOHAMMED IBN SĀLIH.

Former chief of the Beni Ghaneim sub-tribe of the Juheinah, and " Emir of the Arabs " at Umlejh. With his son, Sa'd, his successor as chief, he revolted from the Turks at the end of 1915 and cut up food-convoys between Wejh and Umlejh (where he lives). Sent his son to Medina, where the latter saw Sherif 'Ali, and on his return cut up two Turkish posts. In September 1916, when the Turks had re-occupied Umlejh, he was reported to have retired inland and to be collecting his tribesmen to oppose them. (See Sa'd ibn Mohammed Sālih.)

MOHAMMED NŪR.

Of Jiddah ; chief *tawwāf* of pilgrims. Supports Sherif Muhsin.

MUHSIN IBN MANSŪR EL-KERĪMI, Sherif.

A sheikh of the Masrūh section of the Harb. Follows the Emir of Mecca. Is commonly spoken of on the coast as "Emir of the Harb " (hereditary title). Took command, June 1916, of the Arab force which attacked the Turks at Jiddah. A tall energetic and resolute man, of a little over 40, with grizzled hair and beard and keen eyes. Military commandant of Jiddah under the Emir, but not fitted by character or training for civil administration (he cannot read or write well). Feared and disliked by the townspeople, who intrigue against him, but the best of the Ashrāf there. Pro-British.

MUHARRAJ BAISHI HADHRAMI.

Of Jiddah. In sole charge of camel arrangements for the Hajj, an office which has been in his family for generations. Has influence with the Harb. About 50 ; white, fat, and spectacled.

MURSHID IBN HAMÅD EZ-ZOGHEIBI.
Of the Beni 'Amr section of the Harb. Agent of Ibn Sa'ūd in Medina (November 1914) ; refused to receive Sheikh Shāwīsh, when the latter visited Medina to preach *Jihād* on the occasion of the opening of the Islam University.

MUSTAFA DERWĪSH.
Of Jiddah. Town Councillor, but uninfluential. Small trader. About 40.

NĀSIR IBN MOHAMMED.
Sheikh of Līth and pro-Emir. Took Līth for the latter in June 1916, and led the expedition destined for Qunfudah in July. Dispatched again to Qunfudah in October, after the Turks had re-occupied and withdrawn again. Co-operated with British ships there.

NĀSIR IBN SHĀKIR EL-'ABĀDILAH, SHERIF.
Hākim under the Emir, and charged with the settlement of tribal disputes. A representative of the Ashrāf on the Legislative Council. A man of about 60, notoriously corrupt and unpopular with the tribes. Dark, and closely resembles Sheikh Mohammed ibn 'Ārif 'Areifān (q.v.). Went to Rābugh on H.M.S. *Anne* to arrange the difficulty about the landing of the battery; but seemed powerless with Husein Mubārak (q.v.).

NŪR JUKHĀDIR.
Of Mecca. Chief 'Ālim of the Persians, and superintendent of the Persian Hajj. Keeps out of politics, but is (or was) unfriendly to the Emir.

RASHĪD REFA'ĀYA.
Of the Refa'i ('Ārfu'a) sub-tribe of the Juheinah. Used by Red Sea Patrol Political Officers as an envoy. Tried in 1915 to get the Beni Ghaneim Sheikhs to make a compact with us against the Turks. Greedy old man, strongly anti-Turk. Sent by us on a mission in February 1916 to Mohammed ibn Sālih (q.v.), but is not to be trusted far.

SA'D EL-HUWEIFI, SHEIKH.
Chief of the Huwāfah sub-tribe of the Beni Sālim (Harb). Lives near Medina, and opposes the Turks in every way. About 55. Popular with the tribesmen, and not a robber.

SA'D IBN 'ARUBEIJ, SHEIKH.
Paramount chief of the Beni 'Amr section of the Masrūh (Harb). Lives at Modhiq (Medeiq), between Rābugh and Medina. A notorious robber of the Hajj.

SA'D IBN MOHAMMED SĀLIH.

A typical fighting Bedouin Sheikh. Superseded his father (q. v.) as Chief of the Beni Ghaneim sub-tribe of the Juheinah at Umlejh in 1915. Age about 32. Formerly Emir of the Juheinah at Umlejh, and paid by the Turks; but broke with them early in 1916 and joined the Sherifial revolt. He has since energetically fought the Turks. Met Colonel Wilson at Yambo' in August 1916.

SALĪYAH, Sheikh.

Of Mecca. In charge of the Armoury. A tall man of about 60, with shifty eyes and broken teeth. Dark complexion and short white beard.

SĀLIH MUHSIN IBN 'ALI 'ABD EL-QĀDIR.

Leading merchant at Yambo'. Pro-Sherif, and used by Emir Husein as consignee of supplies for his Medina force in 1916. Later reported to him on military situation, and received reports from Sheikh As'af.

SAQĀF, Seyyid.

Of Mecca. Of the Hadhramaut Seyyids. A merchant, trading in Indian goods, and said to have Singapore connexions. Has an agent at Jiddah. Reported pro-British.

SHADHLI EL-'ALYĀN.

Rightful, but dispossessed, chief of the Midianite Huweitāt. (See Ahmed ibn Mohammed Abu Toqeiqah.)

SHĀKIR IBN ZEID IBN FAWWĀZ EL-'ABĀDILAH, Sherif.

Of Mecca. Hereditary Emir of the Ateibah at Mecca. Related to, and a personal friend of the Emir, and sent on confidential missions, e. g. accompanied Sherif Zeid to meet British envoys on June 6, 1916. About 35; heavily pock-marked; medium height; wears hair Bedouin-wise, in tails.

SHEIBI, House of.

Of Mecca; of the Qoreish. Hereditary openers of the Ka'bah door on the third day of the Hajj. The leading members are:

MOHAMMED SĀLIH SHEIBI, Sherif.

Holder of the key of the Ka'bah, Vice-President of the Legislative Assembly, and representative for the Harām el-Mekki. A short, dark man, of about 70.

'ABD EL-QĀDIR SHEIBI, Sherif.

Member of the Legislative Council and representative for the Harām el-Mekki.

SULEIMĀN AFNĀN RUFĀDAH.

Paramount chief of the Billi tribe; resident at Wejh, where he keeps an armed guard. His cousin is *omdah* of a section of the same tribe near Baliana, Upper Egypt. The latter was sent by us on a mission to the former in April 1915, but without result. Suleimān is said to have come to blows, in 1915, with the Ottoman Governor of Wejh, and to have detached himself and his tribe from the Turks, refusing to allow his two sons to serve in the Ottoman Army. Our ships have had difficulties with his dhows in the Red Sea. In June 1916, he was understood to be favourable to the Emir's revolt, and was recommended by Sherif 'Ali as a channel whereby stores might be sent up to the force besieging Medina. He was won over, however, by the Turks, and in August visited Damascus and received various attentions. Later, he pleaded *force majeure* and was stated to be sitting on the fence, keeping in with the Turks. Declared himself an ally of the latter, but favourable to the Sherif.

SULEIMĀN IBN SA'ĪD, SHERIF.

Of Mecca. Representative of the Ashrāf on the Legislative Council.

SULEIMĀN QĀBIL.

Of Jiddah. Tall and thin, with dark, pleasant face and intelligent eyes. Grain merchant. *Ra'is el-Belediyah* under the Turks. Main agent in inducing the surrender of the Turks in June 1916. The Emir has reappointed him *Ra'is*, and in this capacity he received the Egyptian "Mahmal", making a good impression on the Admiral. Honest and intelligent. Age about 40.

SURŪR ES-SABĀN.

Of Mecca. Chief hide-merchant in Hejaz. An ex-slave. Has agencies at Jiddah, Qunfudah, and Mīdi. Pro-Turk and anti-British.

TAHAR IBN MOHANNAH, SHERIF.

"Chief of the Controlling Department" at Jiddah. Sides with 'Abd el-Latīf Mizeini. Ordered by the Emir of Mecca to accompany his agent in receiving the "Mahmal" from a British ship (October 1915). Member of Town Council. Ignorant and troublesome. Has been described as a "bottle-nosed bandit". The Emir (his relative) is said to have sent him to Jiddah to be rid of him.

WASLALLAH IBN WASIM, SHEIKH.

Lives about two hours south of Jiddah. Of the Zobeid sub-tribe of the Harb. Chief arms-dealer in Hejaz, and against all authority, whether Turkish or Sherifial.

YŪSUF IBN SĀLIM QAHTĀN.

Of Mecca. Minister of Public Works. Has long controlled the cleansing and supplying of the town, and the distribution of oil to mosques by government gift. The Emir has great faith in his judgement. A man of about 65, of medium height, fair complexion, with round face, sparse whitening beard and narrow eyes. (Javanese type.)

ZEINI 'ALI RIDHA (RIZA), House of.

Of Mecca and Jiddah. Merchants in grain and general goods, with most of the Indian trade in their hands; but they do not go in for coastal trade. Shipping agents. Of Persian origin, and good reputation. Leading members are:

'ABDULLAH. Of Mecca; on the Emir's Legislative Council as a representative of the secular element.

HUSEIN. Of Jiddah; head of the firm. Age about 60.

MOHAMMED. His son, age about 32; was M.P. for Jiddah in the Ottoman Chamber.

QASIM. Another son; partner in the firm, and foreign agent. Has also been M.P., and was an active member of the Arab Party, interesting himself in the question of Arab education.

REGION II

ASIR

IDRĪSI PRINCIPATE.

The fortunes of the Idrīsi family began with Seyyid Ahmed, the great-grandfather of the present ruler. Ahmed founded a *tarīqah* (fraternity) at Fez, and in 1799 went to Mecca, where he opened a school and propagated his *tarīqah*. Among his adherents was one Mohammed el-Morghāni, with whom in 1813 he migrated to Zeinia, near Luxor, afterwards (1815) sending him to the Sudan (v. 'Ali el-Morghāni). Having returned to Mecca in 1817, he received (1823) into his *tarīqah* the original Sheikh Senussi, Mohammed 'Ali, who came from Fez. In 1829, after a visit to the famous Seminary of Zebīd in Yemen, where Sherif Husein, the son of Sherif 'Ali, the ruler of Abu 'Arīsh, was powerful, he went to the latter district and fixed his residence at Sabia (Sabīyah), bringing all his family from Mecca. There he died in 1837, having acquired much land and reputation for sanctity, and his tomb became a holy centre, upon which, and the family owning it, was focussed gradually the spirit of independence which has always moved the Abu 'Arīsh district to keep itself detached equally from the Turks, the Sherif of Mecca, and the Imam of Yemen.

Seyyid Ahmed's second son, 'Abd el-'Āl, joined the Senussi in Cyrenaica, and remained with him until the latter's death at Jaghbūb in 1859. The elder son, Mohammed, with his son 'Ali, stayed at Sabia, increasing the wealth and influence of his family. After the final defeat, in 1849, of Sherif Husein of Abu 'Arīsh, who had overrun most of the Yemen Tihāmah, the Idrīsis seem to have succeeded to the local headship, and to have kept Husein's conquerors, the Turks, at a distance. 'Ali's son, Mohammed, is the present head of the family.

MOHAMMED IBN 'ALI EL-IDRĪSI, SEYYID.

Born in 1876. Independent ruler of the Abu 'Arīsh district of S. Asir, and suzerain of a considerable tribal confederacy, embracing the tribes of the Asir coastlands as far north as Qunfudah, and south towards Loheia (Lahīyah), together with some of the inland 'Aqabah. His own ports are Jeizān and Mīdi, and his capital is Sabia, about 20 miles inland ESE. from Jeizān. He claims the coast as far south as Habil (lat. 16.9 N.) or Wādi 'Ain.

In 1896, when he was just twenty, he left Sabia and went to stay in Upper Egypt with his relations at Zeinia. Thence he proceeded to the Azhar in Cairo, where he married, and in 1899 he remained nine months with his cousin, the Senussi, at Jaghbūb and Kufra. After marrying a second

IDRĪSI PRINCIPATE, *continued.*

wife and spending some time with his relatives at Argo (Ārju), in the Sudan, he returned to Asir and began to organize an anti-Turkish power in a district which had been conquered by Ra'ūf and Mukhtār Pashas (1869–72) but had resumed active revolt since 1892. In 1910 he took up arms against both the Turkish Governor of Ibha and the Sherif of Mecca. He failed, however, before Ibha, to whose relief the Sherif sent his son, 'Abdullah, with a considerable force ; the latter succeeded in detaching most of Idrīsi's tribal following. During the Tripolitan War he kept up his recalcitrant attitude, relying on Italian supplies of arms and money ; but, on these failing and his tribesmen beginning to fall away from him, he tried to come to terms with the Imam, whose ambitions had received a definite check by the relief of San'ā. A treaty was signed at Rijāl ; but its subsequent violation by the Imam has led to a more irremediable breach.

In 1914 he was negotiating for Ottoman recognition through 'Izzet Bey el-Ghindi, but, not able to get any better terms than a mere Kaimmakamship of Abu 'Arīsh and Sabia, came over to us definitely, signed an anti-Ottoman treaty with the Resident at Aden in May 1915, and was supplied with arms and munitions, with which he has had moderate success against unfortified positions, but has not yet captured Loheia, his main objective. Pleading lack of ammunition and other means, he withdrew to his own territory at the end of the year, made a truce with the Imam, and undertook no further hostilities against the Turks, except in border squabbles with the Wa'zāt and with some of his own federation, e.g. the 'Abs, and Marwān, until after the Hejaz Revolt had broken out in June 1916.

Meanwhile, the exemption from blockade which we had conceded to his ports, proved a means for the enrichment of himself and his immediate followers, notably his vizier, Mohammed Yahya Ba Sāhi (q.v.), and led to an unsatisfactory position which engaged the continual attention of Aden. The Resident constantly urged him to positive anti-Turk action, but he still pleaded lack of means. After being assured of the fall of Jiddah, in June 1916, he was induced to write a letter to the Sherif of Mecca, promising co-operation and offering to subordinate his own interests, while at the same time he did not abate his claim to all Asir ; and he collected a small tribal force and moved north. When Qunfudah surrendered the place was at once occupied on Idrīsi's behalf by the sheikhs of Birk, and his flag was hoisted. This seriously displeased the Sherif, who sent a force towards the town from Līth. Idrīsi refused, however, to withdraw his garrison, although the Sherif's demand was supported by us,

IDRĪSI PRINCIPATE, *continued.*

and threatened to go over to the Turks, whom he was reported to be blockading in Muhā'il and Ibha ; but in August he consented to evacuate the place and at the same time raised the blockade of Muhā'il and Ibha. Since then he has kept quiet, but is in a discontented, if not actively disloyal, frame of mind towards us.

He is a man of 40, tall, broad, of dark, almost negroid, type. He is of courteous, suave, and polished manners and great energy ; loud-voiced, histrionic, and reputed possessed of magical powers by his adherents. Distinctly intelligent. He is to be reckoned with, and may be trusted so long as his interest is also clearly ours. But he is out for his personal ambition, wherein he is handicapped by lack of noble lineage. Among Arabs he is *parvenu.*

Idrīsi has connexions not only with Zeinia in Egypt (*v.* Mustafa el-Idrīsi), but with the Sudan through a branch of the family formerly settled in Argo Island, but now in Yemen, and through the Morghāni family. The Somali Mullah is a member of the Idrīsi *tarīqah.* Idrīsi is said to desire to bind himself more intimately to the Senussi by marriage ; but in any case the connexion, based on past events, as related above, and on various intermarriages, is close. Idrīsi, however, is not himself a fervent Pan-Islamist, or over fond of a religious character and its restrictions.

MUSTAFA IBN 'ABD EL-'ĀL EL-IDRĪSI, SEYYID.

Cousin of el-Idrīsi (see Idrīsi family), resident at Zeinia, near Luxor, Upper Egypt. Used as a trustworthy go-between and visited his relative in May 1915, being conveyed on one of H.M.'s ships to Jeizān. On the request of the Idrīsi, he was sent again to Asir early in 1916 and accompanied Colonel Jacob and Capt. Crawford (of H.M.S. *Minto*) to a conference with Idrīsi in January. Later, in May and June, he was of service in inducing Idrīsi to resume hostilities. The best of the family.

'ABBĀS, IBN.

Formerly Sheikh of Shuqaiq, but received three years' imprisonment at Sabia for conspiracy against Idrīsi. Now out on guarantee. Is the richest and most important man in Shuqaiq and influences the neighbouring tribesmen.

'ABD EL-'AZĪZ IBN MUSHEIT.

Paramount chief of the powerful tribe of Shahrān. Lives in state at Dhahbān, and owns a house in Khamīs Musheit and many date-groves in Bīshah. A friend of the Sherif of Mecca and of the

IDRISI FAMILY

AHMED EL-IDRIS (of Fez; at Mecca, 1799; at Sabia, 1830; *ob.* October 21, 1837).

- **'Abd el-'Āl** (Mecca till 1847, where educated by Senussi as Khalifah: then with Senussi in Africa till 1859: then Zeinia; *ob.* November 24, 1878, at Dongola). (=daughter of 'Abd er-Rahim of Zeinia and three other wives.)
- Mustafa el-Hasan (*ob.*).
- 'Abd el-Jebba (*ob.*).
- 'Abd el-Hakk (*ob.*).

MOHAMMED (of Sabia).

- 'ALI (of Sabia).
- Idris el-Hersi (of Jiddah).
- Moh. esh-Sherif (of Argo, 1877–87, and since reoccupation; has been our emissary to Senussi).
- Mustafa (of Zeinia).
  - Sa'id.
- Moh. el-Mamūn.
- Senussi.
- Moh. el-Kortadi.
- Moh. el-'Arabi.
- Moh. Abu el-Hasan.
- Ahmed (of Sabia).
- el-Hasan (of Sabia).
- Husein (*ob.*).

MOHAMMED (=daughter of Mustafa Araki, of Dongola, 1901).
(*b.* 1876)
(=daughter of Khalifah 'Arūn, of Dongola, 1903).

- Fātimah (=Sa'id Mustafa of Zeinia)[1] (*b.* 1902).
- 'Ali Mustafa[1] (*b.* 1904).
- 'Abd el-Wahhāb (*b.* 1911).
- 'Abd el-'Aziz (*b.* 1912).

[1] Left at Argo till 1913; then brought to Sabia by Mustafa ibn 'Abd el-'Āl.

A.

D

25

Turks. Levies his own taxes. About 60, and in his old age has taken to drink, leaving the active management of the tribe to his son Sa'īd ibn 'Abd. (See also p. 205.)

'ABD EL-HĀDI.

Chief Sheikh of the Beni Bishr (Qahtān). Pro-Idrīsi, and under Mohammed ibn Dhuleim (q.v.).

'ABD EL-KHALĪFAH, SEYYID.

About 35, educated at Zebīd. Second Mufti of Asir (see Zein el-'Ābidīn) and well spoken of for justice.

'ABDĪYAH BINT 'AMR.

Sister of Mohammed ibn 'Amr (q.v.) and accustomed to rule the Āl ed-Dureib when he is absent. Was married to a Turkish officer named 'Ali Bey Ridha, now dead.

'ABDULLAH IBN 'ALI.

Brother of Hasan ibn 'Ali Mohammed ibn 'Ā'idh (q.v.); a young man of about 20, who disagrees with his brother and is said to favour Idrīsi secretly.

'ABDULLAH IBN HAMŪD.

Sheikh of the Sha'af Rashhah and Āl Yinfa'ah sections of the Shahrān. A tall man of about 55, with a long white beard. Formerly with the Turks, but broke with them and 'Abd el-'Azīz ibn Musheit (q.v.) about eight years ago because his son was murdered by the Beni Wahhāb while a guest at Dhahbān. Now supports Idrīsi and pays him taxes.

'ABDULLAH IBN MILHEM.

Paramount Sheikh of the settled Balahmar and of the nomads with exception of the Āl 'Asla (see 'Ali ibn 'Abshān). A young man about 25 years old, generous and popular with his tribe. A warm supporter of Idrīsi, for whom he collects taxes.

'ABDULLAH BEY IBN MUFARRIH.

Of the Āl Yazīd section of the Beni Mugheid. About 45. Outwardly on good terms with the Turks because he has a large estate near Ibha, but said to be secretly in communication with Idrīsi. There is bitter hatred between his house and that of Hasan ibn 'Ali ibn Mohammed ibn 'Ā'idh (q.v.). Head-quarters, the strong fortress of Sijah, twelve miles south-west of Ibha.

'ABDULLAH IBN MUGHĀTHIL.

Of the Aulād Ibn Mufarrih clan of the Āl Yazīd section of the Beni Mugheid. Rebelled against the Turks nine years ago and defeated a force sent against his fortress at Sijah. Now outwardly loyal to the Turks, but secretly in communication with Idrīsi.

'ABD ER-RAHMĀN BA MUHARREM EL-HADHRAMI.

Of Qunfudah. Merchant on a smaller scale than Ba Jubeir, but owns four sambuks ; used to run arms during the Turco-Italian war. Is pro-Turk and probably engaged in cargo-running now.

ABU 'ALLĀMAH, SEYYID.

Of Sabia ; of the Na'āmi house. About 32 ; adviser of Idrīsi ; poor and reported honest. Has a birthmark covering one side of his face.

ABU HALĪM.

A Sheikh of the Masārihah. Partisan of Idrīsi.

AHMED 'ABDULLAH EL-MEKKI.

Messenger employed in November 1914 to communicate between the Egyptian Government and Idrīsi.

AHMED IBN HĀMID.

Chief Sheikh of the 'Alqam es-Sahil. A prosperous man of about 45, and a member of the *Mejlis Belediyah* at Ibha.

AHMED IBN MUTA'ĀLI.

Of the Jeis Ibn Mas'ūdi section of the Rijāl el-M'a. Eldest son of the paramount chief, Ibrāhīm ibn Muta'āli (q.v.), and virtual ruler of the tribe. A tall fair-skinned man of about 30. Won his fighting reputation in Mikhlāf el-Yemen before the rise of Idrīsi. Supported the latter against the Sherif of Mecca and the Turks in 1910, but, owing to jealousy of Seyyid Mustafa (q.v.), withdrew his forces at a critical moment. Now in chief command of the Rijāl el-M'a. (See also p. 199.)

AHMED IBN UMM SHI'BAH.

Of Ibha. Of the Aulād Ibn Mufarrih clan of the Beni Mugheid. M.P. for Asir. About 50 ; fat, dark, and of medium height ; strong pro-Turk, keen politician and eloquent speaker, with marked bias against the Seyyids. On the *Mejlis Belediyah* at Ibha. Rich, but mean and unpopular.

AHMED JANĀH.

A Sheikh of the Beni Nashar. Adherent of Idrīsi.

AHMED MASĀWAH.

A Sheikh of the Masārihah. Partisan of Idrīsi.

AHMED SHERĪF.

Of Sabia ; joined Mohammed 'Ali Pasha against Idrīsi in 1910. Idrīsi, accusing him of peculation, cut off both his hands. He went to Constantinople, where he had artificial hands fitted. Now lives at Hodeidah on a pension from the Turks of £T. 50 *per mensem*.

AHMED ZEILAH.
Merchant; relative of Mohammed Sālih (q.v.) of Jeizān. He trades with Musawwa', &c., in his own sambuk. Used by Ahmed 'Abdullah el-Mekki (q.v.) to transmit a letter and presents to Idrīsi in autumn 1915. Regarded as a reliable go-between. (See 'Īsa Zeilah.)

'Ā'IDH IBN JABBĀR.
Chief of the wild and truculent Nahās section of the Shahrān. Age about 50. A noted fighter, independent of outside influences.

'ALI, IBN.
Sheikh of the Aulād el-'Alaunah, and, by appointment of Idrīsi, Emir of the tribes of the Hali district, viz. Aulād el-'Alaunah, Kinānah, Ghawānimah, and 'Ābid el-Emīr. Age about 55. Formerly with the Turks, but deserted to Idrīsi on his first revolt, and fought for him in 1910.

'ALI BEDĀWI.
Chief of the Beni Aslam. Has been fighting for Idrīsi.

'ALI BEY IBN DHĀFIR, WALAD DHĀFĪR IBN JĀRI.
Of Namas. Chief of the Beni Shihir el-Yemen. Strong pro-Turk. A man of strict morals, liked and respected by his tribesmen. His mother is a Circassian.

'ALI EL-QAHM.
A Sheikh of the Beni Nashar. Was allied to Hādi ibn Ahmed el-Heij, but submitted to Idrīsi two years ago.

'ALI IBN 'ABDU.
Of the Beni Hilāl tribe and Sheikh of Birk. Was recently reported to be in the pay of the Turks, and to be smuggling mails through to Ibha. But has always been anti-Government, and in 1910 sent a Mauser cartridge to the Sherif of Mecca in reply to the latter's offer of £T. 3,000 if he would desert. Occupied Qunfudah with his tribesmen on Idrīsi's behalf in July 1916. Brother of Mohammed ibn 'Abdu (q.v.).

'ALI IBN 'ABSHĀN, ('ALI GHĀLIB BEY).
Paramount chief of the Balahmar nomads, but only powerful with the Āl 'Asla division; about 55; brave, intelligent. Trained in Army at Constantinople for five years, and returned as Bimbashi to Ibha, where he is chief tax-collector. Remained there when the Balahmar joined Idrīsi. Seyyid Mustafa (q.v.) razed his house at Melāhah in the Beni Mālik country. His son, 'Ali, M.P. for Asir, was captured by Idrīsi on returning from his first session at Constantinople, and died in captivity about 1910. (See also p. 163.)

'ALI IBN FAYY.
Of the Munjahah tribe, living at Wasm ; warlike and powerful and leagued with Idrīsi. About 45.

'ALI IBN HAMŪD.
Chief of the Āl 'Asimah section of the Rabī'ah wa Rufeidah. Fought for Idrīsi in 1910 and was captured by Turks, but after a year's imprisonment was released and reinstated.

'ALI IBN 'ITEIJ.
Sheikh of the Āl Rusheid section of the Shahrān. Lives at Khamīs Musheit. Pro-Turk, and a fighter of repute.

'ALI IBN JABBĀR.
Chief of the Rabī'at el-Yemen. About 45, and a noted warrior who has his tribe well in hand. Pays only a nominal allegiance to Idrīsi.

'ALI IBN KHANFŪR.
Of the Āl Umm Wādi Malah clan of the Beni Mugheid, and middle-class, being the son of a small hide merchant ; M.P. for Asir since 1905. About 40, small, pock-marked, intelligent ; but lost religion in his visits to Constantinople, and is unpopular with his tribe. Used to be chief-accountant (*bāsh-kātib*) at Ibha.

ALI IBN MA'ADDI.
Chief of the settled portion of the Beni Mālik (Asir). Age about 60. Said to be mean and avaricious. A member of the *Mejlis Belediyah* of Ibha.

'ALI IBN MEDĪNI.
Formerly paramount Sheikh of the Belā'ir ; was bribed by the Sherif of Mecca in 1910, and his desertion of Idrīsi lost him the support of all his tribe except the Firshah and Sa'dah clans of the Nawāshirah and the inhabitants of Jōz (Jauz) Belā'ir. Age about 50. (See also Ibn Kheirah.)

'ALI IBN MUBHI.
Sheikh of Shuqaiq, appointed by Idrīsi in place of Ibn 'Abbās (q. v.).

'ALI IBN MOHAMMED.
Paramount Sheikh of the Balasmar. A tall and powerfully built man of about 50 years of age, with a scar over the right eyebrow. Favours Idrīsi and collects taxes for him. His fortress is at Madfa'ah.

'ALI IBN RÁ'IH.
Chief Mufti of the Balasmar, a dark-skinned man of about 55, with a long flowing beard. Sound in his judgements and generous and popular with his tribe. Is said to have Turkish leanings, and is on bad terms with the paramount Sheikh, 'Ali ibn Mohammed (q.v.).

'ALI IBN RUKWÁN.
Of Dahrān. Chief of the Wadā'ah (Qahtān). Goes on pilgrimage nearly every year, and acts as *Emīr el-Hajj* for the Asiri Qahtān. Supports Mohammed ibn Dhuleim (q.v.) and Idrīsi.

'ARÁR, HOUSE OF.
Of Sabia ; partisans of Idrīsi. Prominent members are :

YAHYA 'ARÁR IBN NÁSIR, SEYYID.—About 45, a tall, thin, swarthy man. *Muqdami* over the Beni Jumā'ah and other tribes in the district of Jebel Razah. Joint Commander, with Mohammed ibn Dhuleim (q.v.), of Idrīsi's army in the war with Mohammed Abu Nuweibah in 1912, and greatly distinguished himself. Jointly commanded Idrīsi's forces in May 1915.

'ABD ER-RAHMÁN 'ARÁR IBN NÁSIR, SEYYID.—About 35, brother of the above, whom he resembles ; second to Mohammed ibn Dhuleim (q.v.) in command of the Asiri Qahtān tribes. Fought the Sherif in 1910 at Darajah and Meswar, but was defeated. Considered as able a general as his brother, and popular.

'AZIZ IBN MUSHEIT.
A young man of about 25 ; paramount Sheikh of the settled portion of the Ghāmid. A friend of the Sherif of Mecca and frequently visits him. On bad terms with the Sheikh of the Ghāmid nomads, Mohammed ibn 'Abd er-Rahmān (q.v.).

BADWEILÁN, FIRM OF.
Includes BUKR BADWEILÁN at Mīdi and 'ABDULLAH BADWEILÁN at Jiddah. They have an agent at Qunfudah. Exporters of *semn* and skins, and do general trade. Of good repute and unlikely to smuggle arms or do anything illicit.

BAHRÁN.
Sheikh of Shija'fah. Of the pro-Turkish tribe of Beni Ya'lah. He himself favours Idrīsi.

BAKRI, IBN.
Chief of the Beni Marwān. Has been discontented with Idrīsi ever since the latter accepted Italian help ; revolted in November 1915, and a punitive expedition was sent against him.

BEIT-'ALI ABU 'ATANAH.
Sheikh of the Beni Ya'lah and a supporter of the Turks in Qunfudah.

DERWISH, Seyyid.
Of Qunfudah ; Mufti. Belongs to the Ahdal house. Has a salary of £T. 4 *per mensem* only, but is corrupt and makes a good income out of bribes.

DHAKĪR IBN SHA'R.
Chief of the Āl Mūsa nomads and of the villagers who have broken loose from Turkish authority. Now lives at Jannah in Bahr Ibn Sekeinah country and wages guerilla warfare against the Turks.

FĀ'IZ IBN SA'ĪD.
Younger son of Sa'īd ibn Fā'iz, paramount Sheikh of the Beni Shihir esh-Shām and brother of Faraj Bey ibn Sa'īd (q. v.). Age about 25. Is steadier than his brother and takes a greater interest in tribal affairs, but, like the rest of his family, visits Ibha, Mecca, and Constantinople.

FARAJ BEY IBN SA'ĪD.
Elder son of Sa'īd ibn Fā'iz. Paramount chief of the Beni Shihir esh-Shām. Lives at 'Asābili. About 38. Tall, fair (Circassian mother) ; M.P. Has a Circassian wife at Constantinople. Rich and to be reckoned with, but a drunkard and a libertine. Formerly Kaimmakam of Qunfudah, Muhā'il, and Hali districts and was a terror in his cups. Owns property in Constantinople and Mecca as well as in Ibha, and is much abroad. Distantly related to the Emir of Mecca—Sherif 'Aun having married a girl of his house ; visits the Emir and would join him against the Turks and take his tribe, one of the strongest in Asir, with him. Speaks Turkish and French and wears Stambuli dress. Said to have entertained two German officers at 'Asābili four years ago for many months.

FERDĀN IBN DHULEIM.
Of Rāhat es-Senhān. Chief of the Senhān el-Hibāb (Qahtān). About 35. Warlike, and follows Mohammed ibn Dhuleim (q. v.) and Idrīsi.

HAIDAR BEY, Miralai.
Of Ibha. "The Butcher." Best known Turkish officer in Asir, popular and respected. About 60 ; tall ; used to drink, but has reformed. Came to Asir about thirty years ago, and has seen much fighting all over the country.

HALÍM, ABU.
A Sheikh of the Masárihah. Partisan of Idrīsi.

HAMŪD SIRDĀB, SHERIF.
Of the Khawāji Ashrāf of Sabia. *Muqdami* over the Ja'āfirah, Masārihah, and Beni Hasan tribes. Age 38. Brave, hot-tempered, obstinate; rash general, disliked for risking his men needlessly. Joint-commander in 1911-12 of Idrīsi's force and fought Turks unsuccessfully round Qunfudah, Hali, and Barak.

HASAN ABU MANDÍL, SHERIF.
Sheikh of the Dhawi Barakāt, a man about 45 years old. Completely independent and lives chiefly by raiding coasting dhows between Līth and Qunfudah.

HASAN ES-SA'ĪD.
A Sheikh of the Beni Hasan. Partisan of Idrīsi.

HASAN IBN 'ALI IBN MOHAMMED IBN 'Ā'IDH.
Of Ibha; grandson of the Emir who ruled Asir before the Turks. About 26; a distinguished fighter. Civil Governor of Asir. By birth, paramount chief of the Beni Mugheid. Of good repute. Has the Turkish title of Bey. Owns the strong fortress of Qasr 'Ali ibn Mohammed, about 15 miles south-west of Ibha.

HASAN IBN KHIDHR.
Sheikh of the Beni Zeid. An adherent of the Turks at Qunfudah and rendered a good account of himself against Idrīsi in 1910.

HASAN IBN MATAR.
Chief of the Shamrān esh-Shām, with head-quarters at Balūs. Age about 30. A good fighter and tribal leader. Partisan of Idrīsi.

HUSEIN EN-NA'ĀMI, SEYYID.
Of the house of Na'āmi, settled with the Rijāl el-M'a for generations. A rich man and the chief leader of the tribe in war after Ahmed ibn Muta'āli and Ahmed el-Hayyāni (q. v.).

HUSEIN IBN HEIF.
Of Mudhīq. Chief of the Rufeidat el-Yemen (Qahtān). About 40. His father was a Mudir and died fighting for the Turks in the Ghāmid country, but he himself joined Idrīsi on his first revolt. Is a close friend of Mohammed ibn Dhuleim (q. v.), who married his sister.

HUSEIN IBN MEKKI, Seyyid.

Muqdami over the Munjahah, Beni Hilāl, and Belā'ir. Sheikh of Malhah, near Sabia. Poor tactician, harsh, unfair; said to be corrupt; unpopular. Joint commander with Hamūd Sirdāb (q. v.) in unsuccessful campaigns against Turks, 1911–12.

HUSEIN EFFENDI WALAD MUZEIQAH JULAS.

Of Ibha. M.P. for Asir. Of Turkish origin, son of a N.C.O. About 30; tall; blood-brother of the Beni Mugheid, and influential in all Asir, even with the Rijāl el-M'a. Represented Suleimān Shefīq Pasha and the Emir of Mecca at the abortive peace-conference with Idrīsi in 1910 at Rijāl. Is *persona grata* even to Idrīsi. Eloquent, patriotic, rich in lands near Ibha, and of good repute. *Sandūq Amīni* (Finance Minister) of Turkish Asir.

IBHA, Sherifs of.

HASAN, YAHYA, and AHMED ESH-SHERIF of the Ghalbah (Huseiniyah) house; influential with the Beni Mugheid. Cultivators of old standing at Ibha and secretly pro-Idrīsi. Hasan is Mufti of the Turkish garrison.

'ABDULLAH and MOHAMMED ESH-SHERIF; of the Sherīf Ibn 'Izzedīn house of the 'Abādilah Ashrāf in Rijāl el-M'a. Influential, and friends of the Ghalbah house.

IBRĀHĪM ABU MU'AMMED.

Sheikh of the Beni Shi'bah tribe and a partisan of Idrīsi. Headquarters at Darb.

IBRĀHĪM EL-HUFDHI.

Of the Beni Qutābah section of the Rijāl el-M'a. Sheikh of Athālif. His father helped the Turks in 1872 and was made a Kaimmakam, subsequently being granted a pension of £T. 15 *per mensem* which was paid to his family until the tribe revolted. Ibrāhīm went to Constantinople in 1914 to press his claim to the pension and to assert his loyalty. His influence in the tribe is small.

IBRĀHĪM IBN MUTA'ĀLI.

Of the Jeis ibn Mas'ūdi section of the Rijāl el-M'a and paramount Sheikh of the tribe. Has a good fighting record and is much respected for his wisdom in tribal matters. Now an old man of over 70, he has surrendered most of the administration to his son Ahmed (q. v.). Is leagued with Idrīsi, but as an equal rather than a subject. His fortress is at Umm Jallah.

IBRĀHĪM IBN FAT-HI ED-DĪN, Seyyid.

Of Jeizān; *Muqdami* over the Naj'u and Southern Shahrān (Āl Yinfa'ah). About 45; tall, stout, and fair. Defeated Mohammed

'Ali Pasha at Jeizān in 1912 and captured the town. Popular with and trusted by the people.

IBRĀHĪM SIRHĀN.
A *Muqdami* in the Sabia district, partisan of Idrīsi, and commands a corps of Sabia *fellāhīn* or slaves in war-time.

'ĪSA ZEILAH.
Of Sabia and the Ahl Wādi Jeizān. Brother and partner of Ahmed Zeilah (q. v.); chief arms dealer, who buys for Idrīsi, of whom he is a staunch partisan.

IS-HĀQ IBN MUZELLAF.
Chief of the Shamrān et-Tihāmah (or el-Yemen), living at Marwa'. A supporter of the Idrīsi.

JUHEISH IBN 'AQAD.
Sheikh of the Khath'am; living at Lastar. Age about 60. Pro-Idrīsi. Was a good warrior in his prime.

JIFRI, Seyyid el-.
Of Qunfudah; the leading merchant, trading in hides, gums, and *semn*. Of good repute and trusted.

JUBEIR, BA (Firm of).
Important house, including, as partners, Mohammed Ba Jubeir at Mīdi, 'Abdullah Ba Jubeir at Qunfudah, and Sālim and 'Omar Ba Jubeir at Jiddah. They have agents at Jeizān and Aden and own about twenty *sanbūqs* or dhows.

SĀLIM BA JUBEIR.—Head of the firm; lives at Jiddah. Strongly pro-Turk and smuggled arms through Qunfudah during the Turco-Italian War, for which action Mohammed Yahya Ba Sāhi (q. v.) called the firm to book in 1913.

KHADĀN IBN MOHAMMED.
Chief of the nomad portion of the Beni Shihir et-Tihāmah. Supports Idrīsi.

KHEIRAH, IBN.
Sheikh of the Nawāshirah section of the Belā'ir, and profiting by the unpopularity of 'Ali ibn Medīni (q. v.), virtual leader of all the tribe. Pro-Idrīsi.

MASH'AD IBN BAHRĀN.
Chief Sheikh of the Bulqarn esh-Shām, living at 'Alāyah. A rich landowner, possessing property round 'Alāyah and also in Bīshah; favours Idrīsi, for whom he collects taxes.

MATĪR, ABU.
Chief sheikh of the 'Alqam el-'Alein, about 65 years old. Said to have pro-Idrīsi tendencies.

MUJARRI IBN SA'ĪD.
Sheikh of the Bulqarn el-Yemen. Favours Idrīsi and pays him taxes.

MISMĀR, ABU.
Chief of the settled portion of the Beni Shihir et-Tihāmah; outwardly pro-Turk, but is said to favour Idrīsi secretly.

MOHAMMED ABU SALĀM.
Sheikh of the Beni Qeis section of the Rufeidat el-Yemen (Qahtān). About 75, and deaf. Always sides with the strongest party. At present pro-Turk.

MOHAMMED IBN 'ABD EL-QĀDIR.
Of Qunfudah; an Indian of good repute. Rich grain merchant, and the principal trader of the port. Said not to engage in contraband trade.

MOHAMMED IBN 'ABD ER-RAHMĀN.
Sheikh of the Āl Seyah, the nomad division of the Ghāmid. Age about 45. A noted warrior and entirely independent of outside influences. On bad terms with the Sheikh of the settled Ghāmid, 'Azīz ibn Musheit (q. v.).

MOHAMMED IBN 'ABDU.
Sheikh of the Ahl Birk section of the Beni Hilāl and nominally paramount chief of the tribe; age about 35. A staunch adherent of Idrīsi.

MOHAMMED IBN 'ALI.
Of the Beni Kebīr sub-tribe of the Ghāmid; was chosen to represent Asir in the Ottoman Parliament about ten years ago and went to Constantinople for one session. Disliking the life, he resigned his seat, but still keeps up Turkish connexions.

MOHAMMED 'ALI, Sherif.
Sheikh of the Ja'āfirah, living at Jōz el-Ja'āfirah. Said to be secretly disaffected to Idrīsi.

MOHAMMED IBN 'ALI WALAD 'ALI IBN MURĀ'I.
Of the Bīshat Ibn Salīm section of the Rufeidat el-Yemen (Qahtān). About 45. Shifty and cowardly. Receives a stipend from the Turks.

MOHAMMED IBN 'AZĪZ.

Of Ibha ; of the Umm Manādhir clan of Beni Mugheid. Brother-in-law of Husein Effendi Walad Muzeiqah Julas (q. v.) and assistant *Sandūq Amīni*. Assesses crops for *'ushr*. About 25 ; small, dark ; well reputed and intelligent. His brother, Mansūr ibn 'Azīz, represented Asiri grievances at Constantinople some years ago and obtained redress.

MOHAMMED IBN DHULEIM.

Emir of the Asiri Qahtān tribes (i. e. 'Ābidah, Senhān el-Hibāb, Shereif, Rufeidat el-Yemen, Beni Bishr, and Wadā'ah), being himself of the Shereif tribe. The most important of Idrīsi's lieutenants after Seyyid Mustafa (q. v.) and the only one not a Sherif or a Seyyid. Son of a famous Dhuleim ibn Sha'r, who died about 1900, having been Mudir of the Asiri Qahtān for the Turks. Mohammed succeeded at a stipend of £T. 25 *per mensem*, but seceded to Idrīsi. The Turks raided his stronghold of Harajah, but had to retire, and have left him alone since. He commanded his tribes against the Sherif in 1910 and against Mohammed ibn Nuweibah in Sahār in 1912 ; also against Loheia, 1915. Age 35 ; rich ; good leader in war, and administrator of tribes in peace. (See also pp. 187, 193.)

MOHAMMED IBN 'AMR.

Chief Sheikh of the Āl ed-Dureib. Age about 35. Has been to Mecca and frequently visits Idrīsi, whose confidence he enjoys. During his absence the tribe is ruled by his sister 'Abdīyah (q. v.).

MOHAMMED IBN HAYĀZAH.

Emir, by appointment of Idrīsi, of Barak district and the tribes of Humeidah, Āl Isba'i, Āl Mūsa ibn 'Ali, and Āl Jebāli. A man of about 45 with a reputation for wisdom and moderation.

MOHAMMED IBN HASAN.

Chief of the Āl Ikhtarsh section of the Beni Hilāl. A notorious highwayman with an unenviable reputation for treachery and cunning.

MOHAMMED IBN HASAN IBN EL-'AUD, SHERIF.

Sheikh of the Dhawi Hasan. A notorious freebooter and pirate. Is forced to pay a certain allegiance to the Turks, who have a garrison at Līth, and to the Sherif of Mecca. Communicates with Idrīsi.

MOHAMMED IBN KHIRSHĀN.

Of Hali, of the Khirshān house ; son of the general of the Ahl Hali, who fought the Sherif in 1910 and died soon after. Age 22.

MOHAMMED IBN MUHARRAK.
Of Muhā'il, of the Muharrak house. General of Idrīsi under Seyyid Mustafa (q. v.). Age about 30; a brave soldier. Commands the serfs of Muhā'il (Āl Mūsa) with 'Abd Sa'd 'Abd Nāsir 'Adāwi as his lieutenant.

MOHAMMED IBN MUSA'I.
Chief of the Naju' nomads and leagued with Idrīsi.

MOHAMMED IBN MUSALLAT.
Of Ibha. President of the *Mejlis Belediyah*. Sheikh of the Āl Umm Wādi Malah of the Beni Mugheid. About 30; a good man with a fine fighting record, not popular. Rich; has visited Mecca.

MOHAMMED IBN MUZHAR.
Chief of the Reish. Was badly worsted by the Sherif of Mecca in 1910, and his son was killed while fighting for Idrīsi.

MOHAMMED SA'ID BA HAIDAR.
Of Ibha. The leading merchant. Of Hadhrami origin. Government contractor for all military supplies. Has a brother, Hamād, as partner at Qunfudah, and a son, 'Omar, who manages the business. About 60; of good reputation and influential with tribesmen.

MOHAMMED SĀLIH.
Merchant of Jeizān, friend of Idrīsi, and used as a go-between by Egypt.

MOHAMMED IBN SHĀHIR.
Chief of the Āl Hārith of the Rabī'ah wa Rufeidah. Violently anti-Turk and frequently cuts the Ibha–Muhā'il road in Wādi Tayya. Has a bad reputation for treachery.

MOHAMMED IBN 'URŪR.
Sheikh of the Āl Ghamar section of the Shahrān. On bad terms with 'Abd el-'Azīz ibn Musheit, the paramount chief, and favours Idrīsi.

MOHAMMED TAHAR, SHEIKH.
A chief of the Sabia district, partisan of Idrīsi. Joint Commander, May 1915, of Idrīsi's army at Jeizān and in subsequent operations.

MOHAMMED YAHYA BA SĀHI.
Of Hadhrami family. Emir of Mikhlāf el-Yemen (i. e. Tihāmah between Shuqaiq and Mīdi). Chief Vizier, councillor and minister of Idrīsi, and most important man in Asir. Big merchant. Idrīsi married his daughter in 1913. Sent to buy arms at Jibuti in April

1915. Co-signatory of the agreement with the Resident of Aden on behalf of Idrīsi. Idrīsi's foreign, and even home, policy is in his hands, and he is more than suspected of feathering his own nest with the profits of the shipping permits for Jiddah sanctioned by us. Has been accused of acting in partnership with two brothers, Jubeir (q.v.), at Jeizān and Jiddah in the contraband trade, but Idrīsi has protested warmly against this and other imputations on his vizier. Was present at the conference between Idrīsi and Col. Jacob and Capt. Crawford, on January 6, 1916.

MŪSA HASAN.
A Sheikh of the Beni Hasan. Partisan of Idrīsi.

MU'ĀDI IBN KHAIR.
Chief of the Zobeid. Supports Idrīsi and pays him taxes. Strongly opposed to the Turks.

MUHARREM EFFENDI.
Of Qunfudah. Ex M.P.; of Baghdad origin. Chief Inspector of Customs. About 30; popular.

MUHĀSIN EFFENDI.
M.P. for Asir. At Constantinople, but of Beiruti origin. Qādhi; married into the Qahtān. Reputed a just judge.

MUHYI ED-DĪN BEY.
Turkish military Governor of Asir, and Commandant of the 32nd division of Ottoman troops; age 40; tall and fair. Apparently a capable, politic man. Formerly Governor of Pera, and sent on a special mission to Ibha in August 1913. Has been there ever since.

MUNĪSH, Firm of.
Of Ibha. Partners Mohammed and Suleimān ibn Hasan, chief arms dealers. Agents of the Idrīsi and suspected by the Turks.

MUSTAFA, Seyyid.
Of Jannah in the Bahr Ibn Sekeinah country. Age about 45; fair skin, black beard. Generalissimo of Idrīsi's forces opposed in 1910 to the Sherif, but worsted rather by the latter's financial measures than by any fault of his own. The Rijāl el-M'a, resenting subordination to him, deserted and later tried to murder him. But he still keeps the confidence of Idrīsi and commands Northern Asir, except Rijāl el-M'a. Collects taxes for Idrīsi on 25 per cent. commission and has become rich. (See also p. 162.)

MASTŪR, Sherif.
Representative of the Sherif of Mecca at Līth and responsible for collecting what taxes he can from the Dhawi Hasan.

NĀSIR IBN HEIF.
Sheikh of the Beni Wahhāb section of the Shahrān. Won his position by his sword and is a notorious raider. Recognizes no power but his own.

NĀSIR IBN KURKMĀN.
Of the Beni Wahhāb section of the Shahrān and agent of Idrīsi at Bīshah. Has little influence.

'OTHMĀN SIWĀDI.
A Sheikh of the Masārihah. Partisan of Idrīsi.

RĀSHID IBN JUM'ĀN.
Sheikh of the settled Zahrān. A large, fat man of 55, living at Dūs. Married to Nafalah of the Aulād el-Emīr Mohammed ibn 'Ā'idh family of the Beni Mugheid. Formerly supported the Turks and was made a Bey, but raised a successful revolt 12 years ago and has barred the country to them ever since. Is leagued with Idrīsi.

SA'D IBN DHUH.
Chief of the nomad sections (Āl Habashi, Āl Rumei'ān, and Beni Minbah) of the Beni Mālik (Asir). A brave old warrior of over 70. Anti-Turk. Is supported by seven sons.

SA'D IBN HUSEIN.
Nephew of 'Abd el-'Azīz ibn Musheit (q.v.). Of the Āl Musheit section of the Shahrān. Has been won over by Idrīsi with a promise of the Chief Sheikhship if he can oust his uncle and cousin. Mean, overbearing, and disliked by his tribe.

SA'D IBN SULEIM.
Chief Sheikh of the 'Abidah (Qahtān): About 40. Lives in Khamīs 'Abidah. A rich man, popular with the tribe and a noted warrior. Seceded to Idrīsi on his first revolt. Under Mohammed ibn Dhuleim (q.v.).

SA'ĪD EFFENDI ABU RAS.
Turk, born at Ibha and educated at San'ā. Late Kaimmakam of Qunfudah. About 50; in Government service for thirty years. Efficient, brave, and popular.

SA'ĪD IBN 'ABD.
Eldest son of 'Abd el-'Azīz ibn Musheit (q.v.) and virtual chief of the Shahrān. Age about 32. Has a good fighting record and is popular. Supports the Turks and is a friend of the Sherif of Mecca, but is also said to correspond with Idrīsi.

SA'ĪD IBN 'ASEIDĀN.
Chief of the nomad division of the Zahrān. A well-known warrior; leagued with Idrīsi.

SA'ĪD IBN FĀ'IZ WALAD FĀ'IZ IBN QURŪM.
Paramount chief of the Beni Shihir esh-Shām. An old man who has resigned most of his power to his two sons, Faraj Bey ibn Sa'īd and Fā'iz ibn Sa'īd (q.v.). Owns a fortress at 'Asābili and houses at Ibha, Constantinople, and Mecca, which place he often visits. A great friend of the Emir of Mecca and related to him, Sherif Mohammed ibn 'Abd el-Mu'īn ibn 'Aun having married into his family. Is friendly with the Turks, but would support the Emir in the event of trouble between the two. Has no sympathy with Idrīsi. A rich man and a large landowner. (See also p. 211.)

SA'ĪD IBN HASHBAL.
Sheikh of the Beni Bijad section of the Shahrān. Rich and popular with his tribesmen. Has seceded to Idrīsi and only pays a nominal allegiance to his paramount chief, 'Abd el-'Azīz ibn Musheit (q.v.).

SA'ĪD IBN 'OTHMĀN.
Paramount Sheikh of the Beni 'Amr. Pro-Idrīsi. Defeated a strong Turkish column under Mohammed Amīn Pasha about ten years ago. Lives at Shij on the Ibha-Tā'if road.

SĀLIH IBN 'AJALAH.
A rich merchant who controls most of the trade between the Ghāmid and Mecca. Has a monopoly of the export of tobacco, of which a considerable amount is grown in the Ghāmid country.

SARWI.
Sheikh of the Beni Thuwwah. One of the most noted raiders in Asir, who has given a great deal of trouble to the Ottoman Government.

SHANBAR, Sherif.
Of the Shenabrah clan of Ashrāf; of Qunfudah, where he represents the Sherif of Mecca. About 65; corrupt and of bad repute.

SULEIMĀN IBN 'ALI.
Hereditary Sheikh of the Āl Mūsa, but has lost the support of half the tribe by helping the Turks. Lives in Muhā'il.

TAHAR IBN 'ALI, Sheikh.
Sheikh of Mīdi, with courtesy title, "Sheikh of Sheikhs". Partisan of Idrīsi.

YAHYA 'ALI IBN AHMED HĀDI THAWĀB.
Chief of the Beni 'Abs tribe. Partisan of Idrīsi ; joint commander of his "second army" (May 1915) at Jeizān, and operated subsequently against the Turks and their allies in Northern Yemen, especially against Hādi ibn Ahmed el-Heij (q.v.). Hostilities were reported suspended in November. (See also p. 159.)

YAHYA IBN FĀ'IZ.
Of the Beni Wahhāb section of the Shahrān and represents the Sherif of Mecca at Bīshah. His influence is considerable.

YAHYA MIHAH.
Sheikh of the Masārihah. Partisan of Idrīsi.

YAHYA SAGHĪR.
Chief of the Beni Nashar. Partisan of Idrīsi.

ZEIN EL-'ĀBIDĪN.
Chief Mufti of Asir, of the Beni Dhālim section of the Rijāl el-M'a. Educated at Zebīd and much reputed for learning in the pre-Idrīsi period. Said to be a wise judge and in request to settle tribal disputes. Has the Rijāl el-M'a solid with him. His son was at El-Azhar, Cairo. Lives at Sabia and in Rijāl. Age about 50. (See also p. 200.)

REGION III
YEMEN

IMAMATE OF YEMEN.

THIS principate, now mediatized under Ottoman suzerainty, has a very long history of intermittent independence. Originally its seat was at Sa'dah, in the extreme north of the Yemen highlands, where a Zeidist [1] dynasty (known as the Rassite) was founded at the beginning of the tenth century by Yahya el-Hādi, a direct descendant of Hasan, son of the Caliph 'Ali and Fātimah. When the Turks were expelled from the highlands, in 1639, Mansūr el-Qasīm, a descendant of Yahya, obtained power over all inland Yemen from Sa'dah to Ta'izz, and made San'ā his capital. There his successors reigned till past the middle of the nineteenth century, the Egyptians never succeeding in establishing themselves on the highlands. The latter withdrew from Yemen altogether in 1840; but after a few years of anarchy, tempered by the dominion of Sherif Husein of Abu 'Arīsh in the Tihāmah, the Turks succeeded in gaining a footing once more in the country, and even in reaching San'ā. Though they could not hold the highlands, their firm establishment in Hodeidah, and the incompetency of the Imam Ghālib, led to a decline in the prestige of the Imamate. Native rule went from bad to worse, until at last, in 1872, the notables of San'ā itself invited the Turks to occupy the place. The Imam was pensioned, and the titular ruler relapsed into obscurity for twenty years. After much unrest, the northern tribes broke out into definite revolt in 1891, proclaiming their allegiance to a member of the Rassite family, Yahya Hāmid ed-Dīn, of the Qasīm house of Shehārah, not directly descended from any recent Imam. On this outbreak Yahya Hāmid ed-Dīn fled to Sa'dah, and there remained, leaving the lead of the fighting forces to his cousin, Ahmed esh-Sherā'i, who was finally defeated by Ahmed Feizi Pasha. Yahya himself appears never to have been recognized as Imam, but his son, Mohammed el-Mansūr, was accepted as such by the tribes. He died in 1904, and his son, Yahya, succeeded.

The influence of the Imams is confined almost entirely to the Zeidist districts of Yemen, that is, the central highlands and the inland central part of the Tihāmah. In Asir, on the Tihāmah coast, and in the Aden hinterland, where the population is predominantly Sunnite of the Shafei school, it goes for little or nothing. The office is elective, like the Ibadhi

---

[1] Zeidism is a modified form of Shiism, a sort of opportunist "trimming" between Shiism and Sunnism. Zeidists hold that a true Leader of the Faithful must be of the Prophet's own seed, in order to have the esoteric knowledge and supernatural qualities of Infallibility, &c., which their instinct for Incarnationism and desire to worship their ruler as semi-divine demand. The first three Caliphs were not such true Leaders. But they are accepted by Zeidists as legitimate Caliphs on the principle that Leaders, worthy of reverence but not worship, can be appointed now and then for reasons of expediency. There may, therefore, be at one and the same time an Imam who is a true Leader, and also a Caliph, acting as political Leader.

IMAMATE OF YEMEN, *continued*.

Imamate in Oman ; but, in practice, a lineal descendant of the last Imam is usually, and a scion of the original Rassite stock is invariably, preferred. There are, however, a number of rival houses of that stock, some being not sherifial but seyyid (e.g. the Shehāri house to which the two Imams before the present ruler's father belonged) ; and there has been much chopping and changing among them in past elections, and rivalry and jealousy exist, other houses, e.g. the Hādi Lidin Allah (of which was the Imam 'Ali el-Mansūr, three times elected in the last century) and the Shehāri, considering themselves better entitled to the Imamate than the Qasīm at present in power. The Imam is essentially a sacred personage, and for some generations back the holders of the title have lived more or less in seclusion, mysterious beings, little seen by the people, though sometimes addicted to very profane vices. To this Shiite conception of their office the Imams owe it that they have never obtained the recognition and the dominant position among Moslems accorded to the Sherifs of Mecca.

YAHYA IBN MOHAMMED HĀMID ED-DĪN EL-MUTAWAKKIL.

Sherif, of the Qasīm house at Shehārah. Imam since 1904, when he succeeded his father, who had been elected some time after the Yemenite revolt of 1891. The latter lived an ascetic life in Sa'dah, making no terms with the Turks.

Yahya, who is now about 45 years of age (1916), headed a fresh outbreak in 1904 and captured San'ā. Driven out after a few months he held on in Khamir, and in 1910 besieged San'ā again for three months, but was driven off by 'Izzet Pasha. He was then closely pressed, and in 1912 (on representations made, it is said, by the Sherif of Mecca and the Sheikh Senussi) agreed, in view of the *jihād* proclaimed against the Italians, to an arrangement to which 'Izzet during a visit to Constantinople had, with some difficulty, persuaded the Porte. He accepted a mediatized status with residence in the fortress of Shehārah (about forty miles (?) N. of 'Amrān) and a subsidy since raised to £T.30,000 (£T.12,000 for himself, and the balance for his vassal chiefs). Both Shehārah and Khamir were, however, garrisoned by the Turks. Yahya had become friendly with Mahmūd Nāzim Pasha (q. v.), who had acted for 'Izzet during the latter's absence at Constantinople, and, when 'Izzet left Yemen, and Mahmūd Nāzim succeeded him (1913), this friendship stood the Turks in good stead. After Mahmūd Nāzim's supersession, in 1914, the Imam began to raise difficulties, and he expressed disapproval of the attack on Aden in 1915, as an infringement of his prerogative.

Mahmūd Nāzim returned to power in October 1915, and the Imam wrote a complimentary letter to Enver in November praying for the success of the Ottoman armies. In the earlier part of 1916 he sent a mission under strong escort into the Beida and 'Aulaqi districts of the Aden Hinterland, and made advances to the Hadhramaut chiefs, especially to the Kathīri: but was not very successful. Bitterly opposed to Idrīsi, whom he betrayed in 1912, he has, however, kept a truce with him since the end of 1915. His Turkish sentiments seem on the wane, and he has shown lately some desire for an understanding with the Emir of Mecca, though he had taken no notice of the latter's offer to reconcile him with Idrīsi in the earlier summer of 1916.

Though bound by his position to administer the Sherī'ah and maintain a religious character, Yahya is more lax in observance than his father, and lives less in religious seclusion. He is said to be an intelligent man of honest, but somewhat weak and yielding, character, and owing to his closeness in money matters, and inconstancy to friends, not to have much hold over the Zeidist tribesmen of Hāshid and highlanders of Central Yemen. In fact the tribesmen of Hāshid and Bekīl have largely gone over to Idrīsi; while the Ashrāf, to which body the Imam belongs, are deeply disaffected. He is unlikely either to head another revolt or to enter into relations with us. But he could, on occasion, marshal and arm a large force, and he has guns and munitions of his own and could procure more from the Turks.

Under his agreement with the Turks, Yahya is free to enforce the Sherī'ah, according to Zeidist practice, in all Zeidi districts of Yemen; and he has power to appoint and remove judges and magistrates in such districts (including the city of San'ā), with the approval of the Porte. These districts were to be exempt from tithe for ten years from 1912, and the Imam's adherents were to be amnestied, on condition of good behaviour.

'ABD EL-BĀRI IBN AHMED, SEYYID.

Of the Ahdal house (q.v.) of Marwah, a town inhabited chiefly by Seyyids. The most important Seyyid in the Turkish Tihāmah, of a family exempt from taxation by an old firman. Greatly respected and much sought after in tribal disputes. Accompanied Mahmūd Nāzim and Ragheb Bey (q.v.) on an unsuccessful mission to Idrīsi in June 1913. In January 1916 Idrīsi asked us to allow supplies to go through to 'Abd el-Bāri, who is said to be anti-Turk and in league with the Zaranik. Reputed to have called down lightning on a mosque at Marwah where the Turks had stored ammunition from Hodeidah in spring 1916. In any case there was an explosion.

GENEALOGY OF THE IMAMS OF SAN'Ā PREVIOUS TO THE REIGNING DYNASTY

(Ruling Imams in capitals, and living persons in heavy type.)

MOHAMMED
(Last Imam of Sa'dah only : *ob. c.* 1620).

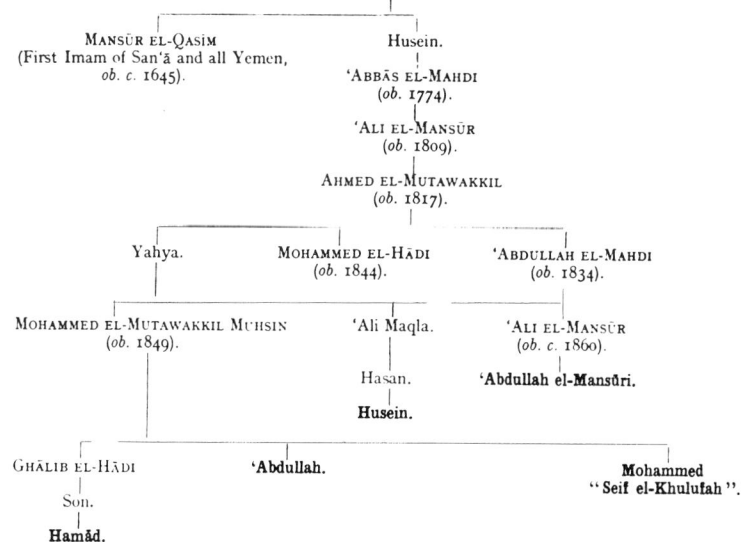

```
            ┌──────────────────────┬──────────────────────┐
    MANSŪR EL-QASIM                                 Husein.
 (First Imam of San'ā and all Yemen,                   │
         ob. c. 1645).                         'ABBĀS EL-MAHDI
                                                 (ob. 1774).
                                                      │
                                               'ALI EL-MANSŪR
                                                 (ob. 1809).
                                                      │
                                             AHMED EL-MUTAWAKKIL
                                                 (ob. 1817).
                                                      │
         ┌────────────────────┬───────────────────────┐
       Yahya.        MOHAMMED EL-HĀDI        'ABDULLAH EL-MAHDI
         │              (ob. 1844).               (ob. 1834).
         │                   │                        │
 ┌───────┴──────┐             │                        │
MOHAMMED EL-MUTAWAKKIL MUHSIN  'Ali Maqla.      'ALI EL-MANSŪR
      (ob. 1849).                │                (ob. c. 1860).
                                 │                    │
                              Hasan.           **'Abdullah el-Mansûri.**
                                 │
                             **Husein.**
  ┌───────────┬─────────────┐                              │
GHĀLIB EL-HĀDI   **'Abdullah.**                        Mohammed
     │                                              "Seif el-Khulufah".
    Son.
     │
  **Hamâd.**
```

The ruling Imam, YAHYA, does not appear in the above Tree, and, on our present knowledge, cannot be affiliated to it. His genealogy is known to us only as far back as his grandfather, the nominal leader of the revolt of 1891.

Yahya Hāmid ed-Din.
│
MOHAMMED EL-MANSŪR
(*ob.* 1904).
│
YAHYA HĀMID ED-DIN EL-MUTAWAKKIL.

'ABD EL-QĀDIR AMBĀRI, Seyyid.
Of Zebīd. Principal of the great Shafei Madrasah or College, the main educational centre in Yemen and of wide repute outside.

'ABD EL-WADŪD.
Notable of Loheia. Instructed to arrange for the journey of Turkish officers by sea to Hejaz " without the knowledge of Idrīsi's tribesmen ", in October 1915.

'ABDULLAH 'ABD EL-QĀDIR, Seyyid.
Of San'ā, of the 'Abd el-Qādir house ; head of the Town Council (*Mejlis beledīyah*) ; together with his brothers, 'Ali and Husein, he enjoys much influence in San'ā.

'ABDULLAH EL-BADRI, Seyyid.
Of Hūth, of the Badri house ; an influential adviser of the Imam.

'ABDULLAH IBN GHAZEILĀN.
Chief of the Dhu Ghazeilān section of the Bekīl ; joined Nāsir ibn Mabkhūt in 1911 against the Imam, and has been in close alliance with him ever since.

ABDULLAH IBN MUHSIN, Seyyid.
Of Hūth, of the Qasīm house, a brother of Mohammed el-Mutawakkil Seif el-Khulufah (q.v.) and son of the Imam Mohammed el-Mutawakkil Muhsin. Has commanded one of the Imam's armies and is trusted by him.

'ABDULLAH EL-MANSŪRI, Seyyid.
Of San'ā, of the Hādi Lidin Allah house and a son of the Imam 'Ali el-Mansūr; supports the Imam and the Turks, receiving a pension from the latter.

'ABDULLAH PASHA EL-BŌNI.
Chief sheikh of the Beni Suleil and Kaimmakam of Zeidīyah under the Turks. His rule extends from Wādi Maur to Hashābiri, and embraces the Beni Qeis, B. Mohammed, Za'līyah, Manāri, and Hashābirah.

ABDULLAH EL-QASĪM, Sherif.
Of Ayyam in Qā' el-Harf, of the house of Qasīm el-Ayyam. Has much influence with the Dhu Fāri' section of the Hāshid under Ahmed ibn Yahya (q.v.), and supports both the Imam and the Turks.

AHDAL, House of.

The ruling house of Seyyids in the district between Beit el-Faqīh, and Zeidīyah; its influence reaches to Idrīsi's tribes and over most of the Yemen Tihāmah. Guardians of the shrine of 'Ali ibn 'Omar el-Ahdal, a saint who died at Marwah some 400 years ago. It is visited by Arabs from all the Tihāmah. The House is reputed pro-Arab and anti-Turk; but Ottoman subsidies and a firman of Sultan 'Abd el-Majīd, exempting it from taxation, tend to keep it on terms with the occupying Power. The following are the chief Seyyids of the House:

    'ABD EL-BĀRI IBN AHMED (q.v.) of Marwah.
    MOHAMMED 'ABD ER-RAHMĀN of Hashābiri, Mufti and local Sheikh el-Islam; M.P.
    HASAN EL-HIJAM of Quti'.
    AHMED EL-AHDAL of Dhahi.
    MOHAMMED IBN YAHYA EL-AHDAL of Munīrah.
    IBRĀHĪM EL-MAQBŪL of Doreihimi.
    'ALI IBN QASĪM of Hadādīyah.
    IBN HIKMI of 'Awajah.
    'ALI EL-AHDAL of Muqfa' and 'Ubāl.
    AHMED YAHYA BAHR of Mansūrīyah.

AHMED BEY KHOBAMI, Seyyid Miralai.

M.P., and Colonel in the Ottoman Army. Educated at Constantinople, and, having lived most of his life in Turkey, is very pro-Turk; but he is unfriendly to the Imam. He now lives at Khobami, being the principal member of its House of Seyyids. Another influential member is Seyyid Ahmed Khobami, merchant in San'ā.

AHMED ED-DAHYĀNI, Seyyid.

Formerly of Dahlān, west of Sa'dah; a staunch partisan of Idrīsi, having quarrelled with the Imam eight years ago. He has lived ever since with the Beni Jumā'ah.

AHMED IBN HUSEIN, Sherif.

One of the chief Sheikhs of the Dhu Husein of Jauf. A firm supporter of the Imam, who fought for him in 1911 against the Turks.

AHMED JĀHIZ, Seyyid.

Of Hūth, of the Jāhiz house. A noted warrior who left the Imam for Idrīsi and for Nāsir ibn Mabkhūt, of whom he is a great friend. He has the Dhu Mohammed section of the Hāshid solidly behind him.

AHMED NA'MĀN, Sheikh.

Sheikh of the Shujeifi district near Ta'izz, made Kaimmakam of Hajarīyah by the Turks. Keeps a Zeidist levy of 500 men, and raised a larger force to help 'Ali Sa'īd Pasha in his expedition against Aden. Eight Sheikhs, acting under his influence, attacked us at Sheikh Sa'īd late in 1914. He attacked Jebel Habashi and Sh. Moh. Hasan (q.v.) early in 1915, and was reported killed (June 1915) and succeeded by his son Mohammed, who was formerly A.D.C. to 'Ali Sa'īd Pasha at Ta'izz, and is energetic and anti-British. But in an Aden communication, dated November 1915, Ahmed Na'mān himself was mentioned as still alive and active on the Turkish side.

AHMED NĀSIR.

General of the Imam sent to the 'Aulaqi country, in spring 1916, with Mohammed el-Mutawakkil Seif el-Khulufah (q.v.)

AHMED EL-QASĪM, Seyyid.

Emir of Jemīmah near Qufl; of the Qasīm house of San'ā. A connexion and friend of the Imam.

AHMED IBN EL-QASĪM, Seyyid.

Of San'ā, of the Qasīm house. The first general in Yemen and a trusted adviser of the Imam. His residence is in Wādi Zohir near San'ā, but he attends constantly on the Imam at Sehārah. A man of about 45; very popular in Yemen.

AHMED NĀSIR ER-RASŪL.

Imam's general sent to the 'Aulaqi and Hadhramaut in spring 1916 with Seyyid Mohammed el-Mutawakkil Seif el-Khulufah (q.v.). Virtually failed in his mission, and returned to Sehārah in June.

AHMED TEWFIK PASHA.

G.O.C. the Ottoman troops in Yemen (VII Army Corps), who sent 'Ali Sa'īd Pasha against Aden.

AHMED IBN YAHYA FĀRI'.

Brother of Dirhem (q.v.), the Chief of the Dhu Fāri' section of the Hāshid. Quarrelled with his brothers and retired from 'Unqān to a village NE. of Khamir. A man of about 45, connected with the Imam, and used by him on business at Mecca during the Pilgrimage, 1915. Has no longer any influence with the Dhu Fāri', who have gone over secretly to Idrīsi.

AHMED IBN YAHYA, Seyyid.

Of Kibs; has been M.P. for San'ā and is strongly pro-Turk and pro-Imam, though with his two brothers, Husein and Ismā'īl, he was exiled to Rhodes for 17 years by Ahmed Feizi Pasha. Much respected in Khaulān et-Tawāl.

'ALI IBN 'ABBĀS, Sherif.

Of the Rusās house of Hūth; Emir of Kaukebān.

'ALI IBN EL-HĀDI, Sherif.
Of Sa'dah ; of the important Hādi house. The family is paid by the Imam to be friendly to himself, and anti-Turk.

'ALI IBN ISMĀ'ĪL, Sherif.
Of Hūth; of the 'Abd el-Kerīm house of Kaukebān, and son of an Emir of Kaukebān, La'ah, Shibām, Thalah, and Tamlah, who died as a prisoner of Mukhtār Pasha. The son moved to Hūth. He leads the Ashrāf of Hūth in hostility to the Imam.

'ALI IBN ISMĀ'ĪL, Seyyid.
Of Dhur'ān ; of the Yahya ibn Hamza house ; now the Imam's agent with the local Emir. Formerly exiled to Rhodes for seventeen years by Ahmed Feizi Pasha.

'ALI NĀSIR EL-KAMARĀNI.
Of Māwiyah ; a holy man of much religious influence, and friend of Sheikh Moh. Nāsir Muqbil (q. v.) ; used by the latter and the Aden Government as intermediary ; was instrumental in making an agreement between the Sheikh and Aden in February 1915.

'ALI SA'ĪD PASHA.
Commander of the 39th Ottoman Division at Ta'izz, and now O.C. the expeditionary force in the Aden Hinterland. Formerly acting commandant at Hodeidah. Has been in great difficulties in his attempt to blockade Aden, and has summoned tribes, e.g. the Fadhli, to his help, and then had to expel them again and recall the arms served out. But has shown himself a stout-hearted soldier, who was in no way dismayed by the Sherifial Revolt or his own isolation. Not on good terms with Mahmūd Nāzim Pasha (q. v.) or the Imam.

'ALI YAHYA EL-YEMENI, Sheikh.
Of Port Sudan ; recommended by Khartoum as a suitable emissary to the Imam, should occasion arise (December 1914).

BA HAKĪM.
Wealthy Hadhrami in business at Hodeidah, and a British subject. Influential and wealthy ; knows Hodeidah and neighbourhood well ; shrewd, active, and loyal. Has lost an eye and two fingers of his right hand. Might be made use of.

BAIRĀM BEY.
Appointed Secretary to Mahmūd Nāzim Pasha, Vali of Yemen, in August 1913. A Syrian, who maintains good relations with the natives, but is weak. Formerly Acting Governor of Menākhah.

BEIT EL-FAQĪH, Seyyids of.
EL-AMĪN BAHR, decorated and subsidized by the Turks.
HASAN 'ALAWI.
MŪSA MOHAMMED.
'ABDU MOHAMMED.
HĀDI RIZK.

CAPROTTI, GIUSEPPE.
Italian merchant, survivor of two brothers in business in Yemen; long the only genuine European resident in San'ā, and entertainer and protector of several foreign visitors (e. g. Wavell 1910, and Bury 1912). He left San'ā in November 1913, and has not returned. Was created *cavaliere* for his geographical and archaeological services, but deprived for writing a socialist article in a German paper, and speaking against the Tripoli expedition. Refused to help the Governor of Eritrea to open relations with the Imam, but mediated for 'Izzet Pasha, and accepted the order of the Mejidieh (third class). About 55 years of age.

COCCALI, DEMETRIUS.
Chief Agent and Inspector of the Red Sea Lighthouse Administration; resident, with his wife, at Mocha. Of Greek race, but Ottoman nationality. Said to be willing to help us.

DAGHSHAR, Sheikh.
Chief of the 'Amarīyīn, living at Beit Jashīsh; has much influence both locally and with the Imam, whose differences with Idrīsi he has made several attempts to settle. Age about 55.

DANĀN, Seyyids of.
AHMED YAHYA KARĀT, favours the Imam, and works the Hāshid for him.
MOHAMMED ABU SHIHA, favours the Imam, and works the Hāshid for him.

DIRHEM IBN YAHYA FĀRI'.
Chief of the Dhu Fāri' section of the Hāshid and one of the most important Hāshid Sheikhs; a firm supporter of Nāsir ibn Mabkhūt. (See Ahmed ibn Yahya Fāri'.)

GHARBI, Seyyid of.
YAHYA IBN MOHAMMED EL-MUSHĀDI, a powerful partisan of Idrisi. Lives north of the Wādi Ahnum in the Hāshid district, and has influence with the tribe.

GHURBĀN, Seyyids of.
YAHYA IBN AHMED and 'ALI, his brother, of the Jebāli house; anti-Imam, owing to an old grudge for deprivation of power after the Imam took Ghurbān fort and installed Seyyid 'Abbās there.

HÁDI IBN AHMED EL-HEIJ.
Chief of the Wa'zāt (3,000 fighting men). Lives at Mu'luq, at the foot of the hills, five hours inland from Loheia. Pro-Turk and Shafei. Raided Idrīsi country, summer 1915, and was shot in the shoulder; applied to the Imam Yahya for help. Now quiescent. Made a Pasha. Took Italian subsidies during Tripolitan War. Controls the country from the Beni 'Abs border to Wādi Maur and is the most influential man in the district after Sherif Hamūd. He wrote a letter of congratulation and submission to the Emir of Mecca in late summer, 1916. (See also p. 243.)

HAJAR, Seyyids of.
AHMED IBN YAHYA, of the Mutakir house; cultivator.
'ALI IBN QASĪM, of the 'Alawi house; merchant.

HAMĀD IBN GHĀLIB, Sherif.
Of San'ā; grandson of the Imam Ghālib el-Hādi. Disaffected to both the Imam and the Turks, and a claimant of the Imamate.

HAMŪD PASHA, Sherif.
Kaimmakam of Loheia under the Turks. A Sherif from Sabia, who has thrown in his lot with the Ottoman régime. Controls the Wa'zāt and Beni Jāmi'. Lives at Mu'taridh.

HASAN IBN QASĪM ZEID, Sherif.
Of Hūth, of the Zeid house. Has much power with the Hāshid, and is a secret friend of Nāsir ibn Mabkhūt and of Idrīsi.

HIJRA (in Hajūr), Seyyids of.
'Ali, Ahmed, and Yahya Fad'il, merchant brothers; agents of the Imam and anti-Idrīsi.

HILMI PASHA.
Colonel commanding (as *Bāsh-mudīr*) the Arab gendarmerie at San'ā. Age about 43; speaks French, and is an able policeman and bureaucrat, but not in touch with the native population. His subordinate, Halīl Bey, however, supplies his defect.

HODEIDAH, Seyyids (Chief Munsībs) of.
 'ABDU 'ALI EL-'ABDAL.
 AHMED MARWA'I.
 'ALI 'AISH.

HUSEIN BEY (TAL'ĀT HUSNI).
Bimbashi on the Staff of the San'ā military district. Was trained at Mainz and, after service at Mosul, volunteered for Yemen. Is Teutophil and Francophobe, and speaks German and French. He

came to Aden in October 1913, with a credit of Rs. 40,000 and a letter to the Sultan of Lahej, ostensibly in order to pay arrears for flour supplied by Messrs. Hasan 'Ali of Aden, and to arrange further credit. He avoided the Aden authorities, and started back via Māwiyah and Ta'izz (the route afterwards taken by the Turkish invaders), alleging that the Mocha-Ta'izz route was closed to him by the tribes; but there are grounds for doubting his ostensible reason for choosing the more arduous road.

HŪTH, SHERIFS OF.

ZEID House:
ZEID IBN YAHYA (q.v.).
HASAN IBN QASĪM ZEID (q.v.).
HUSEIN IBN MOHAMMED, nephew of Hasan ibn Qasīm; advises the Imam at Shehārah.

RUSĀS House:
AHMED IBN 'ABD ER-RAHMĀN, friend and ally of Hasan ibn Qasīm.
'ALI IBN 'ABBĀS, Emir of Kaukebān (q.v.).
'ALI IBN AHMED HIMĀDI, merchant.
IBRĀHĪM MUHSIN, Hâkim Sherā'i at Khabb in Bekīl.
MOHAMMED IBN 'ABDULLAH EL-KHOTIB, *Mu'āwin Idara* of the Imam and a trusted envoy.
YAHYA IBN AHMED EZ-ZAWARI; travels widely in the Ottoman Empire (for the Imam?).

HUSEIN IBN THAWĀBAH.

A'SHISH House:
HUSEIN IBN 'ALI SHERĀ'I, *'Ālim*.

AZAH House:
ISMĀ'IL IBN AHMED, cultivator.

BADRI House:
'ABDULLAH EL-BADRI (q.v.).

HŪTH, SEYYIDS OF.

DIDI House:
HĀDI 'ĪSA, Qādhi.

EL-JINNI House:
HUSEIN EL-JINNI, merchant.

EL-QŪS House:
HUSEIN IBN AHMED, cultivator.

HUNEISH House:
MAHDI, merchant and cultivator.

Is-hāq House:
>MOHAMMED IBN IS-HĀQ, '*Alim*.
>YAHYA IBN MOHAMMED, Hākim Sherā'i at Sheradra.

Jāhiz House:
>AHMED JĀHIZ (q.v.).

Jeilāni House:
>'ALI IBN MOHAMMED, merchant.

Jibāla House:
>'ABDULLAH JIBĀLA, cultivator.
>'ALI JIBĀLA; represents the Imam at Razah.

Luqwa House:
>MUHSIN IBN HASAN (q.v.).

Qudāsh House:
>YAHYA, cultivator.

Sara' House:
>HUSEIN, cultivator.

Sāri House:
>'ALI IBN HASAN, Qādhi Sherā'i.
>LUTF IBN 'ALI, Emir of Suleimah; about 70; represents the Imam.

Serāji House:
>'ABDULLAH SERĀJI, '*Alim*.

Sherāri House:
>LUTF IBN 'ABD ER-RAHMĀN, merchant.

KABSI, Seyyid.
>M.P. for San'ā; reported anti-Turk.

KAUKEBĀN, Sherifs of.
'Abd el-Kerīm House:
>HAMĀD of San'ā; pensioned by the Turks, but anti-Turk and anti-Imam.
>'ALI IBN ISMĀ'ĪL (q.v.).

Sherīf ed-Dīn house:
>'ABD ER-RAHMĀN IBN AHMED, of San'ā.
>AHMED IBN AHMED, of San'ā, brother of above.

Hāfiz ed-Dīn house:
>'ABDULLAH; pensioned by the Turks.

KHAMIR, Seyyids of.
AHMED
'ALI
MOHAMMED
} Of the Ghaili house; all rich and anti-Imam and supporters of Nāsir ibn Mabkhūt (q.v.).

KHARTŪM, Seyyids of.
MUJĀHID house:
HUSEIN IBN AHMED, cultivator.

LUTF SĀRI, Seyyid.
Representative of the Imam with the Suleimah, one of the pro-Imam sections of the Hāshid. A man of influence.

MAHMŪD NĀZIM (NĀDIM) PASHA.
Vali of Yemen, who acted for 'Izzet Pasha in 1912 and succeeded him in 1913. A man of 48, who is disliked by the military element as a civilian risen from the Secretariat; but *persona grata* to the Imam. A swarthy Syrian, corpulent, but energetic and a good administrator. Quarrelled with Idrīsi in 1912, and renounced further relations with him. His son, Shehat Effendi (by his first wife, a Syrian), is, or was, a Lieutenant in the 39th Nishanji at Sūq el-Khamīs. He has no children by his second (Circassian) wife. He was superseded in the summer of 1915 by Sa'īd Pasha (q.v., or by Ahmed Tewfik Pasha?) on account of his disapproval of the attack on Aden. But in early autumn he was reinstated and awarded the War medal in gold, his maintenance in the governorship having proved a condition of friendly relations between the Turks and the Imam. He is not on good terms with 'Ali Sa'īd Pasha (q.v.) or, probably, with the O.C. Yemen.

MAKRAMI, ISMĀ'ĪL EL-.
Chief of the Beni Yām and Emir of Nejrān. Has two brothers, Mohammed and Hasan. All are of the Ismā'īliyah sect of the Shiah, and own, in theory, the supremacy of the Āgha Khān, with whom they maintain some communication. The family, which is descended from Sheikh Makrami, the Nejrān reformer of the eighteenth century, formerly held the Emirate of Heima, Harāz, and Menākhah, but it lost these places to the Turks in 1872. Ismā'īl, with his tribe, favours Idrīsi and is opposed to the Imam.

MĀREB, Sherifs of.
The place, rather than the ruler, governs the policy. The actual Sherif is MOHAMMED IBN 'ABD ER-RAHMĀN IBN HUSEIN, a man of about 50, an Ottoman vassal with the courtesy title of Emir. He comes of the same stock as the Sherifs of Harib and Beihān el-Jezāb. He is said to be Anglophil. He was at San'ā in August 1913, receiving treatment for two gunshot wounds received in a skirmish with the local Seyyid faction, with whom the Māreb Sherifs are at constant feud.

MAS'ŪD EL-BARAK.
One of the chief Sheikhs of the Dhu 'Udhrah section of the Hāshid. A rich man aged about 60. Supports Nāsir ibn Mabkhūt, but reputed a trimmer and coward.

MESWAR, SEYYIDS OF.
'ABD EL-'AZĪM house :
    'ALI 'ABD EL-'AZĪM, cultivator.
EL-HĀDI house :
    MOHAMMED IBN EL-HĀDI, Emir of the 'Udhāqah.
    YAHYA IBN EL-HĀDI, friend of the Imam : represents the Turks at Meswar.
HĀSHIM house :
    QASĪM IBN MOHAMMED ; pensioned by the Imam but opposed to him and the Turks. Influential.

MOHAMMED 'ABD ER-RAHMĀN ESH-SHĀMI, SEYYID.
Of San'ā. Married to one of the two daughters of the Imam, and one of his chief advisers. Usually in attendance at Shehārah.

MOHAMMED ABU NUWEIBAH, SEYYID.
Of the Hāfiz ed-Dīn house, descended from an Imam of that name at Sa'dah. Emir of Sa'dah, Dahyān, Ammān and Heidān. Strongly pro-Turk. A harsh and tyrannical governor, against whom the townspeople protested to Idrīsi in 1911 ; and the Imam's failure to interfere, on Idrīsi's representations, provoked the split between them in 1912.

MOHAMMED 'ALI ESH-SHĀMI, SEYYID.
Vizier of the Imam and used by him as an intermediary with the late Sultan of Lahej and the Aden Government, early in 1915. Visited Aden and saw the Resident on the Imam's behalf.

MOHAMMED EL-MUTAWAKKIL SEIF EL-ISLĀM, SEYYID.
Of San'ā ; of the Qasīm house. Relative of the Imam and his most intimate friend and adviser. After the peace with the Turks in 1911, his son married the Imam's daughter, and the Imam's son married his daughter. An intelligent man of fine presence, and medium height ; wears a long beard. Used to be a confidant of 'Othmān Pasha el-A'rāf, when the latter was Vali ; but, on his departure, he joined the Imam and was given his title, " Seif el-Islām."

MOHAMMED EL-MUTAWAKKIL SEIF EL-KHULUFAH, SEYYID.
Son of the Imam Mohammed el-Mutawakkil Muhsin ; of the Shehāri house. Favours the Imam, and led his expedition into the 'Aulaqi country in spring, 1916. Has been Emir of Sa'dah.

MOHAMMED HASAN, Sheikh.

Chief of a religious fraternity at Ta'izz; lives in Jebel Habashi near the latter town. Active ally of the Turks, who exhorted the Arabs to the attack on Aden. Attacked by Sh. Ahmed Na'mān (q.v.), in 1915, for refusal to pay tithe in Hajarīyah.

MOHAMMED NĀSIR MUQBIL (" MĀWIYAH ").

Sheikh of Māwiyah, Qa'tabah, and Shurmān. Formerly a tax-farmer; subsequently made Kaimmakam of Shurmān and Kameirah by the Turks. In 1901 he fortified Dareija and fought against us, but after a success against the Haushabi Sultan, he was defeated by a British column which blew up his tower. On our protest to the Ottoman Government, he was officially degraded, but promoted later. In February 1915 he signed an agreement with the Resident at Aden that, on condition of a subsidy, he would expel the Turks and recalcitrant chiefs from the district of Ta'izz. He has had relations with Idrīsi. Is Anglophobe, but wishes to be rid of the Turks. Reported well of by M. Beneyton, of the French Railway Survey, in 1913. Capable of stirring up the Haushabi tribesmen. He has kept peace with the Turks since their advance to Lahej, but apparently under constraint, the Aden authorities not having been able to fulfil their side of the agreement. Understood still to wish to act with us.

MOHAMMED NŪRI BEY.

Kaimmakam of Menākhah at the end of 1913, and late officer of *Nizām*. Was sent in the spring of 1913 to Vienna, Paris, Rome, Berlin, and London. He is about 45 years of age, awkward, and of poor nerve, but intelligent and discreet. Slovenly in attire and wears glasses.

MOHAMMED SULEIMĀN FAKHĪRAH.

Of Beit el-Faqīh. Mufti of the Hanafi school.

MOHAMMED YAHYA EL-HIBAH FASHĪK.

Paramount chief of the lowland section of the Zaranik tribe. Lives at Huseinīyah, nine miles north of Zebīd, and controls the country between Zebīd and Beit el-Faqīh from the sea to the hills. Wrote to the Resident at Aden early in 1915 asking for money, arms, and transport for himself to Aden with a view to action against the Turks; offered to accept British protection. He can and does close all communication through the Tihāmah between north and south. In November 1915 he and his half-tribe made common cause with Idrīsi in attacking the Turks; but a highland section of the Zaranik, north of Beit el-Faqīh, sided with the latter. Moh. Fashīk attacked Beit el-Faqīh in May 1916, looted the Turkish *Serai*, and sent mails, &c., to Aden, writing to Colonel Jacob.

MUHSIN IBN 'ABDULLAH, Sherif

A chief of the Dhu Husein at Jauf. Trusted friend of the Imam and sent by him to Aden in August 1914 on a political mission. Previously had commanded a force operating against Idrīsi.

MUHSIN IBN HASAN, Seyyid.

Of Hūth, of the Luqwa house; one of the richest merchants and an active politician who sympathizes with Nāsir ibn Mabkhūt (q.v.) against the Imam.

MUNĀSAR SAGHĪR, Sheikh.

Chief of the northern division of the lowland Zaranik; joint signatory, with Moh. Yahya el-Hibah Fashīk, of a letter to Colonel Jacob offering assistance to us in May 1916.

NĀSIR IBN MABKHŪT.

Paramount chief of the great Hāshid tribe. Tall, powerfully built; fair skin, small white beard. Age about 75. Ambitious, unscrupulous; rules chiefly by fear. Rich from taxes levied on his people. His chief sons are HAMŪD IBN NĀSIR, aged about 35, and NĀSIR IBN NĀSIR, aged about 25. His chief strongholds are at Hamri, Habūr, and Dhōfir. He was an ally of the Imam in his early struggles with the Turks, and up to 1911 fought for him. In 1912 he deserted to Idrīsi in disgust at the Imam's compact with the Turks, and in 1913 was fighting for Idrīsi. He rejoined the Imam in 1914, but is said to have become disaffected again and to be now in league with Idrīsi and the Beni Yām. He is a very powerful chief who can call up 10,000 well-armed men. (See p. 225 f.)

NĀZIM BEY.

Chief of Staff at Hodeidah in 1913; Captain in 3rd Battn. 120th Regt. 40th Div. Volunteered for Yemen. Trained by the Germans, but Anglophil. Able, energetic, fine horseman, and popular with the soldiery. Speaks French, German, and a little English. A very keen soldier.

QUFL, Seyyids of.

HUSEIN IBN AHMED, of the Haddād house; trader and cultivator in Wādi Sadān.

YAHYA IBN AHMED (q.v.).

RAGHEB BEY.

Mutesarrif of Hodeidah in 1913. Declared to the Captain of the *Desaix*, in 1914, that he could not be responsible for the conduct of the Arabs. Commands 40th Div. VII Army Corps. For his mission to Idrīsi in 1913 see 'ABD EL-BĀRI.

A. H

SA'DAH, SHERIFS OF.
    'ALI IBN EL-HĀDI (q.v.).
    SEYYIDS OF.
    MUSEILIHI house :
        'ALI, cultivator.

SA'ID 'ABBĀS, SEYYID.
    Of San'ā ; of the 'Abbās house. Emir of Ghurbān, west of Khamir.

SA'ID PASHA.
    A Turkish soldier of the old school. Formerly Commandant at Smyrna, and entrusted with the suppression of brigandage in the Aidin vilayet. Later was in command of the forces on the Loheia line, and (?) acted Vali of San'ā for some months in 1915 during the disgrace of Mahmūd Nāzim Pasha (q.v.).

SĀLIH, QĀ'ID.
    Sheikh and Kaimmakam of Qa'tabah ; friendly with the Turks and an enemy of Moh. Nāsir Muqbil (q.v.).

SĀLIH IBN MA'ID EL-MOGHRABI.
    Important Sheikh of the Dhu 'Udhrah section of the Hāshid, who follows Nāsir ibn Mabkhūt. Has a good fighting reputation. About 40 years old. Lives at Khartūm.

SĀLIH IBN MUSLIH.
    Of Hamri. Important Sheikh of the Himrān section of the Hāshid ; nephew of Nāsir ibn Mabkhūt and his most trusted lieutenant. Aged about 40. Rich, generous, and popular.

SĀLIH SHADLI.
    Broker of Hodeidah, who claims British nationality on occasion. Sent on a secret service mission by the Turks to Loheia in 1913. A man of about 44, whose eyelids are heavily lined with antimony. Of somewhat insolent bearing, unreliable, shifting, and dissolute. A bad man. Keeps in touch with Aden natives.

SAN'Ā, SHERIFS OF.
    GHĀLIB House :
        HAMĀD IBN GHĀLIB (q.v.).
    SEYYIDS OF.
    QASĪM House :
        AHMED IBN EL-QASĪM (q.v.).
        MOHAMMED EL-MUTAWAKKIL SEIF EL-ISLĀM (q.v.).
        'ABDULLAH IBN MUHSIN (q.v.).
        AHMED IBN EL-QASĪM (q.v.).
        MOHAMMED YAHYA, Emir of Madān in Hāshid ; pro-Imam.

SHĀMI House :
MOHAMMED 'ABD ER-RAHMĀN (q.v.).
MOHAMMED IBN 'ALI ESH-SHĀMI (q.v.).
'ABD EL-QĀDIR House :
HUSEIN (q.v.).
'ABDULLAH (q.v.).
'ALI (q.v.).
'ABBĀS House :
SA'ID 'ABBĀS (q.v.).
HIMĀZI House :
'ALI EL-HIMĀZI ; the Imam's representative among the Hāshid at Hūth.
HĀFIZ ED-DĪN House :
MOHAMMED ABU NUWEIBAH (q.v.).
SHEHĀRI House :
MOHAMMED IBN EL-MUTAWAKKIL, "SEIF EL-KHU-LUFAH" (q.v.).
ABU EL-MEJD House:
'ALI IBN HASAN ABU MEJD ; anti-Imam since he was deprived of the Governorship of Sheradra. Pensioned by the Turks.
MAQLA House :
'ALI MAQLA, brother of the Imam Mohammed el-Mutawakkil Muhsin (dead ?).
HUSEIN IBN HASAN IBN 'ALI MAQLA ; pro-Imam ; pensioned by the Turks.

SHĀMI, SHEIKH ESH-.
Chief of the southern section of the lowland Zaranik. Joint signatory, with Mohammed Yahya el-Hibah Fashīk (q.v.), of a letter to Colonel Jacob offering assistance, in May 1916.

YAHYA 'ABDULLAH MUKARRAM.
Of Beit el-Faqīh. Mufti of the Shafei school.

YAHYA IBN AHMED.
Of the Sherā'i house. Head of the Municipality at Hodeidah.

YAHYA IBN AHMED, SEYYID.
Of Qufl ; of the Fadhā'il house. Hākim Sherā'i and representative of the Imam. An upright and honest man, much respected.

YAHYA IBN MUHSIN EL-MUNTASER, SEYYID.
Of Dhibin ; of the house of Muntaser. Belongs to a house which ruled Hajūr before 1872. Has a following of about 5,000 men among the Hāshid, and great influence.

YAHYA EL-JEBÂLI, SEYYID.
Of Yerīm ; of the Jebāli house. Qādhi Sherā'i of Sadda, but resides at Yerīm.

YAHYA EL-MO'AYYADI, SEYYID.
Of Medīnat esh-Shāhid in Hajar ; of the Mo'ayyad house. *'Ālim* in the Imam's pay and strongly anti-Turk.

YAHYA IBN YAHYA ESH-SHĀ'IF. ——
Chief of the Shā'if section of the Bekīl. A close friend and ally of Nasīr ibn Mabkhūt, and joined in the latter's rebellion against the Imam in 1911.

ZEID IBN YAHYA, SHERIF.
Of San'ā ; of the Qasīm family ; Hākim Sherā'i at San'ā and friend of the Imam. Honest and straightforward ; both feared and respected for the severity of his judgements ; has great influence.

ZUFAR, SEYYIDS OF.
'ABDULLAH, Emir of Zufar. Like his brother, AHMED, he is pro-Imam.

REGION IV

ADEN AND HADHRAMAUT

'ABD EL-KERĪM IBN FADL IBN 'ALI.

Sultan of Lahej and Chief of the 'Abdāli tribe since July 13, 1915, when he succeeded his cousin, accidentally shot. At present, during the Ottoman occupation of Lahej, he lives in Aden. A man of 35, of sedentary habit; fairly well educated as an Arab, but without knowledge of any European language. Was at the Delhi Durbar, 1911. Has shown no marked personality.

AHMED IBN FADL.

Brother of the above; age about 33; knows a little English, and was at Delhi in 1902 and 1911. Married two daughters in succession of Sultan Ahmed.

MUHSIN IBN FADL.

Third brother; age about 31; of delicate physique; knows a little English and was at Delhi, 1902. All three brothers own considerable estates in the 'Abdāli country.

'ALI IBN AHMED FADL.

Eldest son of Sultan Ahmed and distant cousin of the present ruler; age about 36. Tried, in 1914, to assert a claim to the succession, but failed; not popular. Is a good man of business, but knows no European language.

FADL IBN AHMED FADL.

Younger brother of the above; age about 33; knows some English and was at Delhi, 1902 and 1911.

'ABD EL-MAJĪD FADL.

Younger brother of Sultan Ahmed and distant cousin of the present ruler; age 55. Used to command his brother's forces; an amiable gentleman.

MAHMŪD IBN MOHAMMED.

Cousin of the Sultan; age about 55. Hypochondriacal and partly insane. Appears to have been deprived of his estates.

'ABDĀLI SULTANS

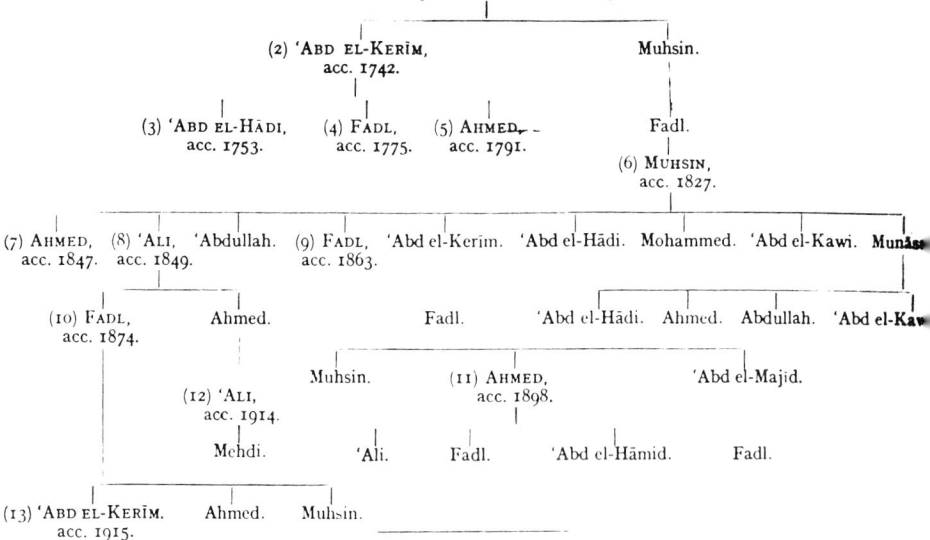

(1) FADL,
acc. 1728,
first independent Sultan of Lahej.

- (2) 'ABD EL-KERĪM, acc. 1742.
  - (3) 'ABD EL-HĀDI, acc. 1753.
  - (4) FADL, acc. 1775.
  - (5) AHMED, acc. 1791.
- Muhsin.
  - Fadl.
    - (6) MUHSIN, acc. 1827.
      - (7) AHMED, acc. 1847.
        - (10) FADL, acc. 1874.
      - (8) 'ALI, acc. 1849.
        - Ahmed.
          - (12) 'ALI, acc. 1914.
            - Mehdi.
      - 'Abdullah.
      - (9) FADL, acc. 1863.
        - Fadl.
        - Muhsin.
        - (11) AHMED, acc. 1898.
          - 'Ali.
          - Fadl.
      - 'Abd el-Kerim.
      - 'Abd el-Hādi.
        - 'Abd el-Hādi.
        - Ahmed.
        - Abdullah.
        - 'Abd el-Kaw
      - Mohammed.
      - 'Abd el-Kawi.
        - 'Abd el-Majid.
          - 'Abd el-Hāmid.
      - Munāss
        - Fadl.
- (13) 'ABD EL-KERĪM. acc. 1915.
- Ahmed.
- Muhsin.

'ABD EN-NEBI HUSEIN.

Important chief of the Ahl Bunyar ; lives at Dhimrah near Soma (Sauma'ah) on the Dahr Plateau, beyond the Kaur. Influential with the 'Audillah tribe and with the Beida tribes, and also with the Upper 'Aulaqi. About 50 years of age. Has had relations with the Imam of Yemen.

'ABD EL-QĀDIR EL-MEKKAWI, KHĀN BAHĀDUR.

Influential merchant, and Arabic scholar of Meccan origin, resident in Aden. Author of a good book, *The Overflowing River of the Science of Inheritance and the Rights of Women*, very favourably received by German Oriental jurists. Shrewd, intelligent, and well versed in both native and European politics. Has been in the habit of reporting on local affairs to the Governor-General of the Sudan, and is in close touch with the native staff of the Aden Government. Speaks and writes English well.

'ABD ER-RU'B SHABEIN.

Chief of Waht, a town on the Lahej plain, which, owing to local fanaticism, has shown anti-British spirit for more than half a century, and is now held in force by the Turks. He is reported to have seized an 'Abdāli caravan of foodstuffs intended for Aden (August 1915), and generally to have obstructed Aden supplies.

'ABD ER-RAHMĀN IBN QASĪM.
Chief of the Maflahi of Upper Yāfa'. Subsidized and loyal. Lives at Jurba.

'ABD ER-RAZZĀQ IBN 'ABD ER-RAHMĀN, SEYYID.
Of Jebel Harīr; influential with the Amīri and has helped to settle trouble with the Sheiri clan. Pro-British. A learned Arab and Koranic scholar.

'ABDULLAH IBN 'ĪSA.
Of the Ahl Afrir. Sultan of Qishn, Socotra, and the Mahrah tribes. Unenlightened, inexperienced, and suspicious, but inclined to keep in with us. Subsidized by Aden.

AHMED IBN MUHSIN.
Of Hakaba. Sherif of Beihān; resident at Jezāb. A man of about 56, crafty and Anglophil, but less powerful than he pretends. At feud with the Seyyids. Signed the Aden Treaty in 1904. On bad terms with the Sherif of Māreb (q.v.), but popular with the Bal Hārith, with whom he spends much of his time in Wādi Behari.

AHMED IBN 'AWAD BUDUS.
Sheikh of Irka; age about 60. Has a subsidy and visits Aden annually. Illiterate, but pleasant and friendly.

AHMED MUTHANNA.
Sheikh of Āl Beishi; of the Sheiri clan of the Amīri and a friend of the Emir of Dhāla. He has been superseded in influence with the tribes by the chief of Melāhah. He has a customs-house at the foot of the Khoreibah pass.

'ALI 'ASKAR (NĀJI).
Joint chief of the Mausata section of the Upper Yāfa' with his brother Muhsin (q.v.). His father signed the Treaty with the Bombay Government in 1904. Age about 50. He comes of a family of intriguers, but undoubtedly has influence in Upper Yāfa'. Has joined the Turks (?)

'ALI IBN 'ALAWI.
'*Aqil* of Khaura and the most powerful 'Aulaqi Chief on the Nisāb road between Soma (Sauma'ah) and Nisāb. A vassal of the Sultan of Upper 'Aulaqi. Elderly.

'ALI IBN 'ALAWI.
Sheikh of Elhīn, a section of the Ahl Armān, the principal tribe in the Oleh federation. Has some influence with the other sections.

'ALI BA HAIDARAH.

Uncle of the chief of the 'Aqrabi tribe, and failed in an attempt to succeed. Age about 70; a shrewd but unpopular old man.

'ALI JA'FAR.

Chief native clerk at the Aden Residency, and Superintendent of the Arabic Department, dealing with confidential native correspondence. Relative of Moh. Sālih Ja'far, native resident, who was attainted of bribery at the instance of the Sultan of Lahej in 1901 (died among the Subeihi since); but 'Ali was not implicated in that matter.

'ALI IBN MANI.

Sultan of the Haushabi. Nephew of his predecessor, who was a very bad ruler. Is not well advised, but was loyal up to the Turkish advance; forced to accompany their advance. Has influence with his tribe.

'ALI IBN NĀSHIR IBN SHĀ'IF.

Chief of the 'Alawi tribe; succeeded in 1898. A man of middle age, having much influence despite long disputes and trouble with the Quteibi. Loyal hitherto, but raised difficulties before the Ottoman invasion. Lives at Kasha'. In 1916 said to have joined the Turks and attacked the Fadhli. (See also p. 249.)

'ALI IBN 'ALI EZ-ZINDĀNI.

Of Sarīr; a chief of the Deiri Muflahi section of the Amīri. Loyal to us, but has not much influence.

'AWAD IBN HAIDARAH.

'*Āqil* of the Ahl Ba Leil in the Oleh federation. He himself is of the Ahl Hanash.

FADL IBN 'ALAWI.

Sheikh of Radfān; popular and influential with the tribes, but a hypocrite.

FADL IBN 'ABDULLAH BA HAIDARAH.

Chief of the 'Aqrabi tribe since 1905; age about 31. A man of fair intelligence; subsidized. Now said to be a prisoner of the Turks.

FADL IBN 'ALI HUMĀDI.

Vizier and adviser of 'Ali ibn Mani, Sultan of the Haushabi (q.v.). A bad man and very corrupt. Led his master to throw in his lot with the Turks in 1915.

GHĀLIB IBN AHMED HIDIYĀN, Naqīb.

A chief of the Deiri Muflahi section of the Amīri ; resides at Jebel Kifa, south of Jebel Jihāf. Loyal to us, but on bad terms with the Emir of Dhāla.

HĀMID IBN NĀSIR BU KATEYYAN.

'*Aqil* of Shabwah, the farthest permanent settlement beyond Nisāb in the direction of the Ruba' el-Khāli, and chief of the Ahl Karab. Vassal (nominally) of the Sultan of Upper 'Aulaqi.

HARIB, Sherif of.

See MĀREB (p. 54). Harib is completely independent of both Ottoman and British influence. The actual Sherif is HĀMID IBN EL-'UTEIR. The Seyyids are strong in this district.

HASAN IBN AHMED.

Chief of the Azraqi section of the Amīri, under the Emir of Dhāla (but considers himself independent). A loyal and sound man. Owns a fertile district.

HASAN 'ABD EL-HĀDI.

Broker at Aden, and Agent to the Sultan of Lower Yāfa'. Knows natives and their life thoroughly. Will be loyal if adequately rewarded ; very shrewd, but not of high character. To be used with caution.

HASAN 'ALI, Firm of.

Business house in Aden, named after its founder, now dead. The present head is his son, MOHAMMED 'ABDULLAH, about 40 years of age ; an enlightened man, in touch with affairs throughout the Middle East. Has connexions with Hodeidah, South Yemen (he contracted for flour for Ottoman troops up to 1913), and the Persian Gulf. In constant relations with Lahej. His house, in the Crater, is a rendezvous for native officials and clerks. Has a country house at Sheikh 'Othmān, in the eastern suburb near the shrine and the British frontier. The firm has been loyal to the British Raj, but is in too close touch with native elements to be used except with discretion.

HUSEIN ABU AHMED.

'*Aqil* of the Ahl Hammām, a section of the Mehājir, who again belong to the 'Aulaqi. Has not much control over the tribesmen.

HUSEIN IBN AHMED.

Sultan of the Fadhli, usually resident at Shūghrah, but lately transferred at his own request to Aden, on the revolt of his tribesmen. An old man over 80, deposed in 1877 by the Bombay Government for political misconduct, and confined in the fort of Ahmednagar; but allowed to return to Aden in 1886, and reinstated about 1910, when his son and successor had died after giving much trouble to Aden. His grandson, 'ABDULLAH ED-DĪN IBN AHMED, ruling in Abiyān, who is always ready to supplant him, was reported recently to be in seditious correspondence with the Turks; but Sultan Husein cast him into prison. The cadets of this house, ruling in Abiyān, always try to feather their nests and take independent action. Sultan Husein visited 'Ali Sa'īd Pasha late in 1915 and was made much of at Lahej. He was ordered to stop Aden supplies, but did not do so effectively. Aden called on him to explain himself, and put an embargo on his port of Shūghrah. (See also p. 264.)

KA'AITI, FAMILY OF.

The ruling house of Shiheir and Makalla. The old "Jemadar" 'Awad, who assumed the title Sultan in 1902, died in 1911, and was succeeded by his eldest son, GHĀLIB (now SIR GHĀLIB IBN 'AWAD, K.C.I.E.). He is about 55 and resides at Makalla; visited Delhi 1911. Has one son, SĀLIH IBN GHĀLIB, about 35, who visited Europe in 1907 and Delhi in 1911. Sultan Ghālib is in touch with India, owing fealty to the Nizam of Haidarabad, in whose Arab bodyguard his ancestor served. He is wealthy and influential, but without much tribal influence. Anglophil and in frequent relations with Aden, which has lately supplied him with arms and munitions for use against the Kathīri. His possessions extend from the coast into the Hadhramaut, where he owns the towns of Hajarein, Haurah, Qatan, and Shibām; but the middle and lower Hadhramaut is hostile to him, the Kathīri Sultans of Seyyūn and Terīm being his peculiar enemies. His younger brother, 'OMAR IBN 'AWAD, aged about 50, now rules at Shiheir; he used to live at Haidarabad; a clever enlightened man, who visited Delhi in 1911.

? MANSŪR IBN GHĀLIB IBN MUHSIN 'ABD EL-KATHĪRI.

Paramount Chief of the Kathīri and Sultan of Seyyūn in Hadhramaut. Received his investiture from the Ottoman Sultan, and has the latter's name mentioned in the prayer at Kathīri mosques. Not on good terms with the Ka'aiti (q. v.). Heir: son, MOHASSIM.
(The above is according to information not certainly correct or up to date.)

MOHAMMED 'ALI ABU 'AWAD.

Chief '*Aqil* of the Ahl es-Sa'īdi; resides at Nūbat es-Suwah, and receives tribute from the Yazīd as well as from his own tribesmen.

MOHAMMED ATYUK.

Qādhi of Beihān ed-Daulah, which comes under the Beida Sultanate. A strong personality, but without much influence over the tribes.

MOHAMMED IBN MOHAMMED 'ABDULLAH.

'*Aqil* of the Kaur and Paramount Chief of the 'Audillah tribe, which will listen to him. But in his mountain fastness he is almost impossible to reach or constrain.

MOHAMMED SĀLIH EL-AKHRAM.

Chief of the Quteibi; suspicious and aloof since our punitive expedition of 1903, but disposed to be friendly. Has not got his tribe in hand, and is on bad terms with the 'Alawi; but formally reconciled in 1912 by the late Sultan of Lahej. Refused to join the Turks, but was pressed thereto by his nephew, Muqbil 'Abdullah (q.v.), who went to Lahej to see 'Ali Sa'īd Pasha.

MOHAMMED TAHAR.

Of Jebel Jihāf, and reported its "spiritual master". Owner of many villages. Has been useful to our Political Agent at Dhāla. Reliable.

MUHSIN 'ASKAR.

Joint chief of the Mausata section of the Upper Yāfa', with his brother 'Ali (q.v.).

MUHSIN IBN FĀRID.

Chief of the Ahl Ma'an (Upper 'Aulaqi) who resides in the Yeshbum valley. Age about 45. Made a treaty with us, December 1913, and accepted a subsidy. Has shown himself friendly, but is little known. Had not joined or helped the Turks up to spring 1916.

MUHSIN IBN SĀLIH.

Sultan of Izzān, part of the 'Abd el-Wahīd Sultanate. A man of wild, ungovernable character, who is unpopular with the tribes; a robber and bad governor. Blackmailed the Austrian Expedition in 1898, and is said to have tried to raise money in the early nineties by pledging his Sultanate, in Yemen to the Turks and in Jibuti to the French. Visited Aden, 1909, and is subsidized. Allied with the Ka'aiti. Now about 46 years of age. (See also p. 247.)

MUQBIL NĀJI'.

Sheikh of the Zindāni family on Jebel Jihāf. A trimmer who has intrigued alternately with the Turks and Aden.

MUQBIL 'ABDULLAH.

Nephew of the Quteibi chief (Moh. Sālih el-Akhram, q.v.); influential with the tribe and his uncle. Visited 'Ali Sa'īd Pasha at Lahej in January 1916, but did not commit the Quteibi to the Turkish side.

NÁSIR ABU THÁLIB.
Sultan of the Ahl Nasi'īn, under Nisāb ; of the ancient Abu Thālib dynasty.

NÁSIR IBN SÁLIH.
Sultan of Habbān, part of the 'Abd el-Wahīd Sultanate. Unpopular with the tribes, especially the Lakmūsh and Ahl Iswad. Hereditary foe of the Ahl Ma'an. Not to be depended on, and opposed to any European penetration of his Sultanate.

NÁSIR IBN SHÁ'IF IBN SEIF.
Emir of Dhāla, Chief of the Amīri and son of the Emir who attended the Delhi Durbar during the Bombay Commission, 1902. About 36 years of age, good-natured, thriftless, avaricious, weak, easily influenced, and of no marked ability. Reported to have joined the Turks since their descent to Lahej. His younger brother, 'ABD EL-HAMĪD, is acting at Dhāla. A third brother, SEIF, about 21, is a man of more energy and character than either of his elders. He has been to College, was at Delhi 1911, and is described as likely to make a good ruler. (See also p. 250.)

'OMAR IBN QAHTÁN.
A Chief of the Dhubi, a powerful tribe of Upper Yāfa' ; about 50 years of age. Joint signatory of the Aden treaty, 1904. Straightforward. Deposed by the tribe, 1913, for making a fresh treaty with Aden, but later reinstated (?).

QASĪM IBN HAMĪD EL-GHĀBIR.
Titular Sultan of the 'Audillah tribe, resident at Loder (Laudar) on the Sa'īdi plain. A man of small influence with the 'Audillah (v. Moh. ibn Moh. 'Abdullah), but the only ready channel by which they can be approached. Strongly pro-British. (See also p. 250 f.)

SABT BALAKSAH, SHEIKH.
An Agent (wakīl) of Idrīsi at Aden. Mustafa el-Idrīsi (q. v.) stayed with him in March 1915, while negotiating with the Resident. (See Moh. Yahya Ba Sāhi.)

SÁLIH EL-BEDĀWI EL-HADHRAMAUTI.
Agent of Seyyid 'Ali el-Morghani (q.v.), and has often visited Arabia on behalf of the latter. He is reported an authority on Arab politics and trustworthy. To be heard of from Seyyid Hāmid Ibag 'Alawi el-Barak, merchant in Aden.

SÁLIH IBN 'ABDULLAH.
Of Bālhāf. Long recognized by Aden as Sultan of the 'Abd el-Wahīd Federation with a small subsidy, but had not much influence ; lost his position after an attempt to trade away his Sultanate to the Ka'aiti. Now living at Makalla. Anglophil hitherto.

SĀLIH IBN 'ABDULLAH.

Sultan of the Upper 'Aulaqi ; about 54 years of age. Energetic, and has more influence over his tribes than most Sultans. Signed the Aden Treaty, 1904, by proxy. Keeps a standing force of about 1,000 men, and can call up about 9,000 more at a pinch. Refused to join the Turks.

SĀLIH IBN QAHTĀN.

Of the Dhubi, brother of 'Omar ibn Qahtān (q.v.) and a thorn in his side. Has succeeded him since 1913 (?). Formerly Sultan of the Muflahis of Upper Yāfa', and paramount over the Rub'atein.

SĀLIH IBN AHMED IBN TĀLIB.

Sultan of the Wahīdis of Bir 'Ali. Age about 63 ; a pleasant, intelligent man. Enemy of the Ka'aiti. Made a treaty with us, 1888, and accepted a subsidy.

SĀLIH IBN 'AWAD.

Sheikh of Haurah ; age about 50. Made a treaty with us, 1902, and accepted a subsidy. Was subsequently deposed, but reinstated, 1904. Illiterate and friendly.

SALĪM HUSEIN.

Chief of the Dhāmbari, nominally under the Haushabi Sultan. Lives at Nakhlein fort, which was battered by our punitive expedition in 1903. Has joined the Turks.

SALĪM IBN 'AMR.

Chief of the Sheibi, a tribe connected with Upper Yāfa', impinging on Ottoman territory towards the Bana. Ill reputed among the tribesmen for his treachery. Attacked a British post on Yāfa' territory in 1903 and was hammered.

SHAHĪR IBN SEIF.

Chief of the Mansūri section of the Subeihi since 1901. Age about 22. During his minority SĀLIH IBN AHMED ruled for him (till 1913). Resides at Mashārij and used to be subsidized, but joined the Turks as soon as they moved south. The only chief with any general influence over the Subeihi. (See p. 269 f. for lesser Subeihi sheikhs and notables.)

SHAMMAKH IBN GHANNAM.

Sheikh of the Bal Hārith clan of the Beihan. A man in middle life, who visited Aden in 1904 and confirmed the treaty made by Ahmed ibn Muhsin (q. v.).

YAHYA IBN SĀLIH.

Sheikh of Deiri of the Muflahi clan of Amīri ; in the Radfān hills. Friendly with the Emir of Dhāla and well disposed to us.

REGION V

GULF COAST

OMAN, Sultanate of

THIS is, in fact, rather the Sultanate of MUSCAT than of Oman, since the populations of both the interior and the west and north of Oman, i. e. the great proportion of the inhabitants, do not at present acknowledge the Sultan's authority and live in practical independence of him under their own chiefs. The Sultan's jurisdiction covers, however, all the coast-line from Kharīfōt to Khōr Kalba.

The reigning family of the Āl Bu Sa'īd owes its elevation to AHMED IBN SA'ĪD of the Azd tribe, formerly a trader and then Governor of Sohār for Seif ibn Sultān, the last Ya'rabi Imam of Muscat. He mustered the inland tribesmen in 1741, and expelled the Persian allies of his predecessor from the country. His lineal descendant in the fifth generation is the present Sultan. Other inland chiefs, however, and in particular the Sheikhs of Rostāq, have never acquiesced willingly in the claim of the Sultans of Muscat to exercise overlordship over them, and they have more than once come near expelling them from their capital. As lately as January 1915 disaster was only averted by the intervention of our Indian troops. In fact, no Sultan for some generations has been able to establish or maintain his authority without our help. The title of the Sultan is, nowadays, properly *Seyyid*, not *Imām*, the Ibadhi sectaries, who predominate in the population of Oman, according the latter title to their ruler not of his right, but only if he be peculiarly competent in religious learning. At the present time the principal Ibadhi Sheikh has put up an Imam in the person of Sālim ibn Rashīd el-Kharūsi of Tanūf (q. v.), in opposition to the Seyyid of Muscat.

Our treaty relations with Muscat began in 1798, and the Sultan has been under a binding agreement with the Indian Government since 1891. It was in 1856 that Lord Canning mediated in the disputed succession occasioned by Sultan Sa'īd's death after a reign of forty-eight years; and, confirming Tūrki in possession of Muscat, assigned to the other claimant, his brother Majīd, Zanzibar and other African possessions, which the late Sa'īd had conquered. Majīd entered into full possession four years later.

The Sultan of Muscat receives a large annual subsidy, as well as a guarantee of protection, at the hands of the Indian Government, on condition of his observing the terms of the agreement of 1891, the most important of which are that he shall alienate no part of his territory except to the British, that he shall direct his policy in conformity with ours, and that he shall accept no help, pecuniary or other, from any other foreign power.

OMAN, SULTANATE OF, *continued*.
TEIMUR IBN FEISĀL.

Reigning Sultan. Born in 1886; eldest son of his predecessor; succeeded on October 4, 1913, and was recognized by the British and French Governments on November 15. He is not on very good terms with his uncle, Moh. Ibn Tūrki, who had expected to succeed his brother. He found his realm in a bad state, owing to recent friction over the "arms traffic" which had strained relations with Great Britain; also to decline of trade, to the rebellion under 'Abdullah es-Sālimi and Sālim ibn Rashīd el-Kharūsi (q.v.), and to the weakness of his predecessor's rule. Friction ensued with the British Resident over the import of cartridges for the Beni Bu 'Ali at Sūr; but, after the banishment of 'Ali Mūsa Khān, the Baluch trader, this matter was smoothed over.

The subsequent enforcement, however, of our restrictions on the arms traffic, under which munitions could be imported and exported through no other port than Muscat, and there only through a controlled warehouse, caused an acute crisis with the chiefs of the interior, who desired both arms and the profits to be made by the trade in them. A serious rebellion, fomented by an Ibadhi Sheikh, 'Abdullah es-Sālimi (q.v.), broke out in May 1913, and raised nearly all Jebel Akhdhar against the Sultan. Nizwa fell in June, and Izki and 'Awābi a little later. The forts of Bidbid and Semā'il followed in August; but meanwhile Indian troops had been landed and had occupied Beit el-Felej, near Matrah. In April 1915 we bombarded Barkah and Quryāt, where the Beni Battāsh were giving trouble, and so checked the rebels that a truce was concluded. But in autumn the tribes began to gather again and Indian reinforcements were sent to Beit el-Felej. These foiled an attempt by 3,000 tribesmen on Muscat in January 1915; but the rebel party still dominates the interior. In July the Sultan went to Quryāt and received the surrender of Heil and Daghmar in August.

Sultan Teimur is a well-meaning, but apparently not very strong ruler. He has a young heir, born in 1910.

Other members of the House of some importance are:

MOHAMMED IBN FEISĀL.

Second son of the late, and brother of the reigning, Sultan of Oman; he takes little part in the government, but is reputed the cleverest of his family.

NĀDIR IBN FEISĀL.

Third son of the late Sultan of Oman. A man of character, who takes considerable part in the administration under his brother, and represents him in his absence (e.g. in July 1915).

OMAN, SULTANATE OF, continued.

Has the revenues of Sīb and Barkah, and owns two ships. Only solvent member of his family. Rumour has it that his relations with the Sultan are not cordial.

HĀMID IBN FEISĀL.

Fourth son of the late Sultan of Oman ; his father's favourite, and regarded with some disfavour by his brothers, who have kept him in the background during the new reign. But in 1915 he was entrusted with the command against the Beni Battāsh, and decorated by the Sultan on their surrender.

SĀLIM IBN FEISĀL.

Youngest son of the late Sultan. Made Vali of Gwādar by his brother in November 1915. Quarrelled with the Hindu Community, which demanded his recall. Sultan promised it and recalled him in October (?).

MOHAMMED IBN TŪRKI.

Brother of the late, and uncle of the present, Sultan of Oman. Aggrieved at the succession of his nephew.

DHI'ĀB IBN FAHHĀD IBN TŪRKI.

Nephew of the late, and first-cousin of the present Sultan. Educated in England, and considered likely to play a considerable part in the future. Married a sister of the Sultan on Sept. 6, 1915.

SULTANS (SEYYIDS) OF MUSCAT (since the beginning of the nineteenth century)

SA'ĪD IBN SULTAN IBN AHMED IBN SA'ĪD, *acc.* (as sole Regent) 1804

THUWEINI, *acc.* 1856.	TŪRKI, *acc.* 1871 (after usurpation of Azzān ibn Keis, 1868).	Majīd (recognized Sultan of Zanzibar in 1860).	Barghāsh (succeeded as Sultan of Zanzibar, 1870).	Eleven other sons.
SALIM, *acc.* 1866.				

daughter (=Mohammed ibn Feisāl, 1910).	daughter (=Nādir ibn Feisāl, 1910).

FEISĀL, *acc.* 1888.	Mohammed. sons.	Fahhād Dhi'āb

TEIMUR, *acc.* 1913.	Mohammed.	Nādir.	Hāmid.	Sālim.
Sa'īd.				

TRUCIAL CHIEFS.

The Sheikhs of the six largest settlements on the " Pirate Coast ", i. e. the coast from 'Odeid to Khōr Kalba, which faces WNW. just within the entrance of the Gulf, and runs out in the Ras el-Jebel Peninsula to Ras Musandam. Geographically part of Oman, this coast and peninsula are politically independent. The six Sheikhs are, theoretically, independent also of one another ; but the Sheikh of SHĀRJAH claims suzerainty over Ras el-Kheimah and the whole apex of the peninsula down to Khōr Kalba on the Oman coast, and also a certain authority over all the other five sheikhs. This claim, however, is not recognized by them or by us.

These settlements have been separately under treaty with us since 1820, when, after the conquest of Nejd by Egypt, the Wahabite influence declined in the district, and we took steps to check the piratical practices for which it was notorious. In 1853 the Chiefs were compelled to sign jointly a treaty of perpetual peace under our protection, and in 1892 to engage (like the Sultan of Oman) to admit relations with no other foreign power, or alienate territory except to us. Their subjects now live mainly by pearl-fishing.

From west to east the settlements and their chiefs are :

1. ABU DHABI.
Chief : HAMDĀN IBN ZEID EL-KHALĪFAH.

Succeeded his brother Tahnūn in 1912. A firm ruler who keeps good order, but has dabbled in the arms traffic under plea of the necessity of securing himself against Ibn Sa'ūd, after the latter had conquered Hasa. In 1913 he negotiated a truce between the Sultan of Oman and the rebellious chiefs. His territory extends north-west to 'Odeid.

2. DIBAI.
Chief : SA'ĪD IBN MAKHTŪM.

Succeeded in 1912 his cousin, Buti ibn Suheil, with whose family and the Bu Felāsah clan he lives in continual feud. Had to be warned by the Indian Government in August 1913, after a boat of H.M.S. *Sphinx* had been fired upon from the town. He is one of the wealthiest of the Chiefs, Dibai having become the distributing centre for the district, and at one time a focus of the arms traffic.

3. SHĀRJAH.
Head-quarters of the British Residential Agent for the whole district.

Chief : KHĀLID IBN AHMED.

Succeeded his cousin, Sagar ibn Khālid, in 1914. Chief of the Jawāsim, and claimant to the whole Ras el-Jebel peninsula. Probably a stronger ruler than his predecessor, who was a smuggler of arms ; but too soon to judge.

4. 'AJMĀN.
Chief: HĀMID IBN 'ABD EL-'AZĪZ.
Succeeded his murdered father in 1910, and is at feud with Mohammed ibn Rashīd, the murderer, and his family. Dependent to some extent on Dibai. An uncouth boor who has given us trouble about the arms traffic.

5. UMM EL-QAIWEIN.
Chief: RASHĪD IBN AHMED.
At feud with his expelled half-brother, Nāsir, who claims the chiefdom. A troublesome client of ours, who had to be coerced by a British squadron in March 1914. The piratical tradition is strongest here.

6. RAS EL-KHEIMAH.
Chief: SĀLIM IBN SULTĀN.
Appointed, 1910, by his nephew, Sagar, then Sheikh of Shārjah; but not accepted by all the district, e.g. not by the islanders of Jezīrat el-Hamra, nor immediately recognized as independent by the Indian Government. Since Sagar's death, however (1914), he has established himself firmly.

Further, it should be noted that 'ABD ER-RAHĪM, the Sheikh of HAMRĪYAH, near Zōra, nominally a vassal of Shārjah, but really independent since 1875, will probably be recognized as a seventh Trucial Chief by the Indian Government, if his conduct continues satisfactory (he commands Zōra where it is proposed to erect a wireless installation; in February 1916 he definitely revolted against Shārjah, but was coerced into submission by H.M.S. *Philomel*).

Other settlements likely also in the future to be so recognized are:
FUJEIRAH. Chief: NĀSIR IBN SHĀHIN ET-TAWĀR.
KHŌR FAKKĀN.
Both on the east coast of the Ras el-Jebel peninsula.

EL-QATAR (PENINSULA), RULER OF.

This district, ruled from Dōhah, has been independent since the retirement of the Wahabites of Riyādh, about 1870; but Dōhah was occupied by a Turkish military post up to 1914, when the troops, driven out of Hasa by Ibn Sa'ūd in 1913, were cut off there, together with the remnant of the original garrison, by a British force. The Ottoman claim to El-Qatar, put forward since 1871, was never admitted by the Indian Government. We had an agreement with the Sheikh of the same kind as with the Trucial Chiefs up to 1882, when we allowed it to lapse; but we now exercise an informal protectorate over El-Qatar.

'ABDULLAH IBN JASĪM ETH-THĀNI.
Ruler of El-Qatar; second son of Sheikh Jasīm; succeeded his father in July 1913; formerly Governor of Dōhab, and right-hand man of his father. Maintains good relations with the British, and is

friendly with Ibn Sa'ūd, as was his father, who acted more than once as the latter's agent in overtures to Indian Government. His elder brother, KHALĪFAH, who supplanted him at Dōhah in 1912 and resides in the Rumeilah quarter, is hostile to him, and so are his cousins, sons of Sh. Ahmed eth-Thāni. Sheikh 'Abdullah has been friendly to us since the outbreak of war, but is not a very energetic ruler. On the outbreak of war with Turkey he acknowledged our Resident's announcement without comment. He conducted the negotiations with the Turkish garrison in August 1915, and was presented with the fort by H.M. Government after the surrender. A good deal of arms smuggling goes on at Dōhah.

BAHREIN, Ruler of.

The Sheikhs of the Khalīfah family of the 'Utūb tribe, which seized Bahrein in 1782, have been in direct relations with us since 1805, and under treaty since 1820. But it was not till 1880 that the present ruler entered into a binding pact of the same kind as that afterwards accepted by the Sultan of Muscat (q.v.). A British Resident is stationed at Manāmah, on the main island of the group. The present ruler owed his accession to our influence, and is supported by us against other claimants of the Khalīfah family. He resides on Muharraq Island off Manāmah for four summer months, and at Manāmah the rest of the year.

'ĪSA IBN 'ALI EL-KHALĪFAH, C.I.E., C.S.I.

Succeeded in 1867, and is now an old man. Has always needed a firm hand to keep him up to his obligations, and has betrayed more than once a tendency to intrigue with the Ottoman power at the head of the Gulf. Is jealous of his independence, and slow to accept suggestions by the Resident, until these are pressed upon him with insistence ; but is an intelligent man who knows how far to go, and has, on the whole, administered his charge well, meeting with wisdom and energy the economic crisis in the pearl-fishing trade caused by the present war, which reduced his customs receipts 80 per cent. Later the plague caused much distress (spring 1915) and led to about 5,000 deaths. It ended in June. Sheikh 'Īsa has three sons :

1. HĀMID, the heir apparent, a moderate man. Lives at a country house behind Manāmah, near the palm-gardens.
2. MOHAMMED, who made the pilgrimage to Mecca in 1912.
3. 'ABDULLAH.

KHĀLID IBN 'ALI EL-KHALĪFAH.

Brother of the ruling Sheikh, and virtually independent holder of the islands of Sitrah and Nebi Sālih, together with the coastal villages on the E. side of Brahrein I., to the south of Khor el-Kabb, and, inland, the two Rifā's (east and west). The revenues of these places he enjoys absolutely. Lives in summer on Sitrah I., where he has a fortified house at Khārijīyah.

KHALĪFAH IBN HAMĀD IBN MOHAMMED EL-KHALĪFAH.

An influential malcontent of the ruling house, who has intrigued with the Ottoman Government. At the end of 1911 he went to Constantinople to complain and solicit the Porte's interference in a suit between him and Sheikh 'Isa, *re* property sequestered by the latter. Returned to Basra in 1912, and got the Vali to write to Sheikh 'Isa. The latter insisted on replying direct, despite the protest of our Resident that this course violated the Treaty of 1880.

KOWEIT, SULTAN OF.

The Khalīfahs now ruling in Koweit are said to have been originally sheikhs of a small settlement at Umm Qasr, near Bandar Zobeir, on the Khōr 'Abdullah. Expelled thence by the Turks in the earlier part of the eighteenth century, they built a fort (*Kūt* or *Kōt*) on the south shore of the Qrein (Grain) Inlet, which originated the name of Koweit (diminutive of *Kūt*).

In 1871, when Midhat Pasha, Vali of Baghdad, initiated a policy of Ottoman expansion in Arabia, and occupied Hasa, the Sheikh of Koweit was induced to declare himself an Ottoman subject, and accept the style of a Kaimmakam. But in 1899, when the project of a transcontinental railway from Constantinople via Baghdad had taken shape, and the question of its Gulf terminus had been raised, the Indian Government began to pay more particular attention to Koweit, and secured its own predominance by a treaty. Various attempts by the Turks to coerce Koweit directly or indirectly (through Ibn Rashīd) were frustrated by us, and in 1907 we entered into a specific agreement with the late Sultan, Mubārak, under which we acquired a perpetual lease of the Bandar Shuweikh foreshore on the Qrein Inlet, and the right of pre-empting all and any of his territory which he should propose to alienate. In return we engaged to protect him against any aggression from without. A Political Resident had already (1904) been stationed at Koweit. Mubārak seems to have recognized Turkish authority when a Commission arrived early in 1914 to try to establish a *modus vivendi* for the Turks in East Arabia; but at the outbreak of the present war he formally repudiated all connexion with the Ottoman Government, which withdrew its detachment from Umm Qasr. The Sultan of Koweit claims as his own the coast and islands from the head of the Khōr 'Abdullah southward to Musallamīyah Bay. His inland boundary is undefined, but roughly may be said to follow the line dividing the Summān steppe from the Dahanah desert.

SULTANS OF THE KHALIFAH FAMILY OF KOWEIT

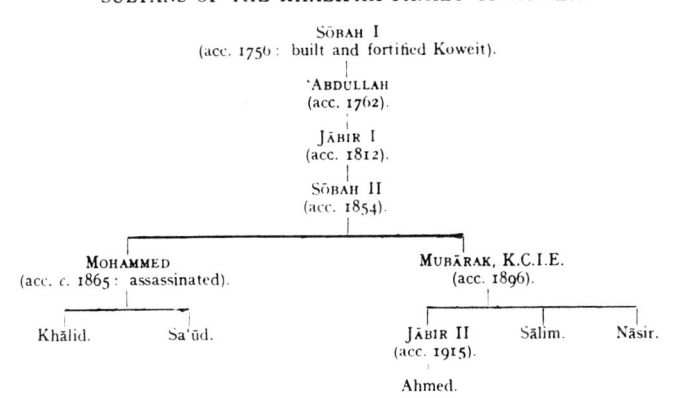

SŌBAH I
(acc. 1756: built and fortified Koweit).
|
'ABDULLAH
(acc. 1762).
|
JĀBIR I
(acc. 1812).
|
SŌBAH II
(acc. 1854).
|
———————————————————————
| |
MOHAMMED MUBĀRAK, K.C.I.E.
(acc. c. 1865: assassinated). (acc. 1896).
| |
———————— ————————————————
| | | | |
Khālid. Sa'ūd. JĀBIR II Sālim. Nāsir.
(acc. 1915).
|
Ahmed.

JĀBIR IBN MUBĀRAK IBN SOBAH EL-KHALĪFAH.

Succeeded, on November 28, 1915, his father, a strong ruler, who did much to improve his position and advance Koweit, and was long friendly to, and in treaty relations with us. Sultan Jābir has formally asked for a continuance of our protection and, at the end of December 1915, received Sir P. Cox and assured him of loyalty. He began his reign well by renouncing his claim to one-third of proceeds of sales of lands, reducing the import duty on dates by one-half, and releasing all prisoners. His house has some authority with the 'Ajmān Arabs, but is often at feud with them, and in December 1915 gave them notice (at Ibn Sa'ūd's request) to leave Koweit territory. On this the tribe seems to have gone north to join Ibn Rashīd. It can call, also, on some smaller tribal groups (e.g. of Hawāzin, Muteir and Beni Khālid), which range near the capital; but its desert power is not considerable.

Koweit is at virtually perpetual feud with the Muntefiq tribe (q.v.), and especially with that part of it which follows 'Ajeimi ibn Sa'dūn (q.v.). With these used to go the Dhafīr tribe, and sometimes the 'Alwi section of the Muteir tribe (see Feisāl ed-Derwīsh), but both these appear now to be friendly with Koweit. Sultan Jābir's father also was engaged intermittently in hostilities with Ibn Rashīd (q.v.), from whose attack a British landing-party saved him in 1905. With the Ibn Sa'ūds (q.v.) his relations were fairly consistently good. He protected 'Abd el-'Azīz, the present ruler of

Nejd and his father, 'Abd er-Rahmān, in exile before 1902, and welcomed the former's attack on Hasa in 1913. Though somewhat affronted by the subsequent agreement (1914), under which Ibn Sa'ūd accepted the title of Ottoman Vali of Nejd, its futility and the representations of our Resident prevented a breach. He was always on very friendly terms with Sheikh Khaz'al of Mohammarah, but had little communication with his distant relative, Sheikh 'Isa of Bahrein (q.v.). The present Sultan is not on terms with Ibn Rashīd, who would have attacked him directly after his accession, had the Dhafīr agreed to co-operate. Sultan Jābir has a son, AHMED, who was in command of an expeditionary force against the 'Ajmān in July 1915, and brothers :

1. SĀLIM.

Long estranged from his father, and resident at Fantās, on the coast S. of Koweit ; reconciled in 1912 through the good offices of the Sheikh of Mohammarah. Of dissolute character. Leader of the force sent by Sultan Mubārak to co-operate with Ibn Sa'ūd against the 'Ajmān in July 1915.

2. NĀSIR.

'ABD EL-'AZĪZ IBN SĀLIM IBN BEDR.

Secretary and confidential adviser of the late Sultan of Koweit.

'ABDULLAH IBN HUMEID ES-SĀLIMI, Sheikh.

A Chief of Ibadhi tribesmen, who was principal agent in raising the rebellion of 1913 against the Sultan of Oman, setting up his son-in-law, Sālim ibn Rashīd el-Kharūsi (q.v.), as Imam.

'ABDULLAH IBN RASHĪD EL HĀSHIMI.

Qādhi of the Imam of Tanūf ; his counsellor and medium in communications with our Political Resident at Muscat in June 1915. Met our Resident at Sīb on Sept. 15, but showed much bigotry, and appears to have been influenced by Turco-German propaganda.

'ABD EL-LATĪF MANDĪL, Sheikh.

A Dosiri chief at Bahrein, to whom Ibn Sa'ūd farmed the customs of 'Oqair and Qatīf early in 1916. Described in a Bahrein report, Sept. 15, 1916, as in Hasa " reorganizing the taxes, customs, &c." at the Sa'ūd's request and raising a certain amount of discontent.

'ABD EN-NĀBI KAL EWĀZ.

Leading Persian merchant in Bahrein. Has come into collision with our Residency on account of his issuing *teskerehs* to Persians going to Lingeh and other Persian ports, which implied that Bahrein was Persian territory.

AHMED (HAMAD) IBN IBRĀHĪM.
Sheikh of Rostāq ; succeeded his elder brother Sa'īd, murdered by his cousins, Ibrāhīm and Mohammed, in March 1912. Contumacious towards his cousin, the Sultan of Oman, and too strong for the latter to coerce. Supported 'Īsa ibn Sālih, and surrendered the forts of Rostāq and Hazam to the Imam in July 1916.

'ALI IBN 'ABDULLAH.
Confidential adviser and vizier of Sheikh 'Īsa of Bahrein since 1910.

'ALI IBN 'ABDULLAH IBN SĀLIM EL-'ALAWI.
Emir of Ja'lān. Succeeded his father early in 1913. On friendly terms with the British Agency at Muscat, and visited the Resident in April 1913 with his cousins, MOHAMMED IBN NĀSIR and HAMDĀN.

'ALI IBN SĀLIH EL-HĀRITHI.
Brother of 'Īsa ibn Sālih el-Hārithi (q. v.), and at issue with his brother. Much inferior to 'Īsa in ability.

GOGUYER, Firm of.
French mercantile house in Muscat whose head was at one time a very active anti-British agent and organizer of the arms traffic. He lent money to the Sultan (e.g. in 1907), in spite of the latter's agreement to accept loans only from the British Resident.

HAMYĀR IBN NĀSIR.
One of the " Imam's " two chief lieutenants in the Oman rising of 1913. Was with the force defeated by British troops near Muscat in January 1915. Later addressed a letter to the Ja'lān chiefs in order to seduce them from the Sultan, saying " the government is ours and we are the leader of it ".

HITHLEIN, Family.
The ruling house of the 'Ajmān ; of the Nāja' clan of the Ma'īdh.

THEIDĀN.
Formerly Paramount Chief but now superseded by Sultān (q. v.). He raised the revolt against Ibn Sa'ūd in 1915, and finally fled north to Koweit and submitted to Sultan Mubārak at the end of the year. When the 'Ajmān were expelled in the following February, at Ibn Sa'ūd's request, Theidān went to 'Ajeimi ibn Sa'dūn and offered his men to the Turks. Later joined Ibn Rashīd at Safwān with only a hundred men, and raided Koweit territory, returning afterwards to 'Ajeimi, but with a still more diminished following.

SULTĀN.
A young man of about 20. Nephew (or cousin ?) of the above and now Paramount Chief in his place. After following Theidān's fortunes till May 1916, he broke away with the Nāja' and Sifrān clans and settled at Safwān, where most of the other 'Ajmān have joined him. Has made overtures to us and visited Basra in August 1916.

HUMEID EL-FULEITI, SEYYID.
Of Wādi Ma'āwal in Oman. A man of intelligence and education, with commercial and political relations in Socotra and Aden. Visited our Resident at Muscat in 1915 to see if some agreement could be come to between the Sultan and the Imam. Later ranged himself more definitely with the Imam, who was in Wādi Ma'āwal in July 1916.

'ĪSA IBN AHMED.
Head of the Dosiri (Dawāsir) tribesmen in Bahrein ; used to intrigue with the Turks in Hasa, but in 1912 rallied to the British.

'ĪSA IBN SĀLIH EL-HĀRITHI, SHEIKH.
Important chief, who, after threatening the Sultan of Muscat in 1912 for stopping the arms traffic, joined the " Imam's " rebellion in 1913, after the fall of Izki. His father led a great revolt against the late Sultan of Muscat in 1895. 'Īsa had been a friend of the late Sultan of Oman, and treated with his successor, visiting Muscat with his brother 'Ali in December 1913, after a conference with other rebel chiefs at Sīb. A truce was then patched up. Later, 'Īsa became one of the two chief lieutenants of the " Imam ", and attacked Muscat in January 1915. He suffered heavy losses, which he retired to repair. He met our Resident at Sīb on Sept. 15 but the conference came to nothing. In October he was preparing to attack Sūr. He is a man of austere life and strong character, and the principal figure in the rebellion.

JASĪM, SHEIKH.
Principal *Qādhi* of Bahrein. A level-headed straightforward man who denounced the preaching of *jihād* in the Sunni mosques at Bahrein on the outbreak of war with Turkey, and reported the matter to Sheikh 'Īsa and to our Agent.

KUMEIYIDH IBN MUNEIKHIR.
Chief of the Sifrān clan of the 'Ajmān, who followed Theidān ibn Hithlein north in 1915 and ultimately joined 'Ajeimi ibn Sa'dūn. His clan left him and went to Safwān.

QASIM IBN SEYYID IMĀM KADRI, SEYYID.

An Indian. Superintendent of the Arms Warehouse at Muscat, appointed 1912. Charged with the legitimate sale of arms and prevention of smuggling. Also owns and works lime-kilns near the town.

MANSŪR IBN JUMA PASHA.

Of Qatīf. Influential with the Ottoman authorities before the evacuation, and at feud with the Beni Khālid (q.v.).

NABHĀN, SHEIKH.

"Tamīmah" of the Beni Riyām of Oman ; one of the leaders of the "Imam's" rebellion against the Sultan of Muscat in 1913.

NASIB IBN MOHAMMED, KHĀN SĀHIB.

Of Muscat ; naval contractor. Blackmailed by the Beni Battāsh, in 1915, on account of his palm-gardens at Hajar.

NĀSIR IBN HUMEID, SHEIKH.

Chief of the Nidābi tribe of Oman, and Sheikh of Bahlah since 1885, when he murdered his two brothers. A *persona grata* to the Sultan and sent to him by the "Imam" on a peace mission in March 1916 ; but he was not supported by the Imam, who changed his mind, in spite of heavy bribes offered by the Sultan, in the form of ammunition and rice. In June 1916 he deserted the Sultan, turned his Vali out of Bahlah, and himself fled to 'Arāqi in W. Oman.

NĀSIR IBN SULEIMĀN SIYABI.

Of Semā'il. One of the leaders of the rebellion against the Sultan of Muscat. Author of a letter in February 1915, stating that there would be no surrender on the part of the Imam.

SĀLIM IBN 'ABDULLAH EL-KHEIMRI.

Superintendent of the Customs at Muscat, appointed in 1913 to succeed 'Abd el-Kerīm. Proved very troublesome to British merchants in 1914 by unnecessarily detaining consignments, and was reprimanded by the Sultan. In July 1915 dismissed at one blow all the Indian clerks, but had to recall them, finding the department could not be administered otherwise. The Muscat merchants have refused supplies to the Sultan so long as Sālim remains at his post.

SĀLIM IBN RASHĪD EL-KHARŪSI.

"Imam" of Tanūf. Son-in-law of the principal Ibadhi Sheikh, 'Abdullah ibn Humeid, and by him set up as "Imam of the Moslems" in May 1913, to head a rebellion against the Sultan of Oman, which continued throughout 1914, and is not yet (1916) quite at an end. He has the support of practically all the Hināwi tribes and some of the Ghāfiri also.

SULTĀN MOHAMMED IBN NAIMI.

Sheikh, who rebelled against the Sultan of Muscat in 1910, and defeated his force near Sohār ; made peace on condition of receiving a subsidy (jointly with the Sheikh of Abu Dhabi) in October.

REGION VI

CENTRAL ARABIA

EMIRATE OF NEJD [IBN SA'ŪDS].

THE principality was founded about 1745 by Mohammed ibn Sa'ūd, Sheikh of Dar'īyah in Wādi Hanīfah, said to be of the Hasanah tribe of the Anazah, and of honourable lineage. He was the earliest important convert made by Mohammed ibn 'Abd el-Wahhāb, the ascetic revivalist of Hareimlah (Ayaina), and it was with his sword that Wahabism was propagated throughout the Nejdean oases.

His son, 'Abd el-'Azīz, and his grandson, Sa'ūd, pushed religious conquest afield, to Kerbela on the one hand, to the Red Sea on the other, and almost to Damascus in the north; and when Sa'ūd died in 1814, he was acknowledged by almost all Arabia except Yemen and the districts south of the Great Desert.

Sa'ūd's successor, 'Abdullah, however, lost to the Egyptian forces of Ibrāhīm Pasha all that his ancestors had gained. In 1818 Dar'īyah was destroyed, and the Emir taken prisoner to Cairo. From that date till 1849 the Emirate remained more or less dependent on Egypt; but thenceforward, under Feisāl, it recovered freedom of action in its new capital, Riyādh. In the meantime, however, a rival Emirate had arisen under 'Abdullah ibn Rashīd in Hā'il, which soon grew strong enough to detach Jebel Shammar altogether from the Nejdean domain, and to dispute the possession of Qasīm. By 1872, moreover, the Ibn Sa'ūds' dominion on the Gulf coast, which had been reasserted by 'Abdullah, son of Feisāl, was lost, and the Emir could claim jurisdiction only over the southern group of oases with an undefined environment of steppe and desert.

This first long struggle between the rival Emirates, lasting nearly fifty years, was decided in favour of Hā'il. Riyādh was taken in 1886 by Mohammed ibn Rashīd, and again in 1891; and for ten years following Nejd remained in vassalage to Jebel Shammar, Riyādh suffering much at the hands of the Rashīdites. In 1902, however, the present Emir returned from Koweit, drove out the Rashīdites, and established himself. He rebuilt Riyādh, and has since recovered both Qasīm and Hasa, which last region he had avowedly been coveting since 1906, as the only territory, once belonging to Nejd, which could restore the finances of the Emirate. He is, therefore, master now of a much larger territory than the Emir of Hā'il, and is one of the two most powerful independent potentates in Arabia.

The basis of the Nejdean Emir's power is both religious and secular He is the recognized champion of Wahabism, and he commands the population of the most thickly inhabited settled districts in Central Arabia,

EMIRATE OF NEJD, *continued.*

as well as certain nomad and half-settled tribes (see *infra*). Since 1842 Nejd has remained free both of direct Ottoman interference and of the active influence of the Emir of Mecca. Its rulers have made various overtures to the Indian Government. An agreement was reached in 1866 about the Trucial Coast and Oman, and the immunity of British subjects generally from molestation ; but it lapsed about 1882 and was not renewed till lately. After various proposals, a Political Officer was allotted to Nejd in 1914. Captain Shakespear, however, who undertook the duty, was killed in March 1915, in the course of a fight between forces of the two Emirs near Mejma', and no successor has been appointed. At one time (1905) Ibn Sa'ūd recognized the suzerainty of the Ottoman Sultan, and in 1914 he accepted the title Vali of Nejd. But he has never taken this title seriously, and he entered into binding treaty obligations with the Indian Government in the autumn of 1915, disowning all relations with the Turks.

'ABD EL-'AZĪZ IBN 'ABD ER-RAHMĀN.

Succeeded as Emir of Riyādh and all Nejd in 1902 ; previously a refugee among the north-eastern tribes and, with his father, at Koweit, whence he set out with a small force of only about forty men, after the murder of his uncle, the vassal Emir, by Ibn Rashīd's order. He collected adherents in N. Nejd (Sedeir and 'Āridh), driving out the Rashīdite officials, and was welcomed in Riyādh. In 1903 he occupied Qasīm, and in 1904 defeated Ibn Rashīd and a Turkish contingent near Boreidah. In 1905 he was driven back to Nejd by Ahmed Feizi Pasha's force, but in 1906 recovered Qasīm and expelled all the Turks. In 1910 he had to meet an act of aggression on the part of the Sherif of Mecca, who sent a force into Qasīm and seized his brother, Sa'd ; but he quickly got the upper hand and induced the Sherif's army to withdraw without effecting anything. By 1912 he had formed a large tribal confederacy including the Muteir, Sebei', Sahul, and Ahl Murrah, and after testing it in a raid upon the Ateibah, who had harboured certain malcontent relatives of his own, known as the " Aulād Sa'ūd " (expelled from Harīq), he descended in 1913 on Hasa, took Hofūf on May 5 almost without resistance, and Qatīf ten days later. The Turkish Governor and his 500 soldiers were sent down to 'Oqair, whence they proceeded to El-Qatar. Once in possession of Hasa, Ibn Sa'ūd made overtures to us, and our Political Agents at Bahrein and Koweit went to 'Oqair to meet him in December. Early in the following year the Porte recognized the *fait accompli* by sending a Commission to meet Ibn Sa'ūd near Koweit, and styling him Vali of Nejd. But he continued to invite closer relations with the Indian Government, and cordially received Shakespear when sent up to him as Political Officer at the end of the year.

EMIRATE OF NEJD, *continued*.

In the tribal fighting, which followed the outbreak of the European War, Ibn Sa'ūd consistently opposed Ibn Rashīd and his pro-Turk federation ; but was not able to subdue Jebel Shammar, and fought no better than a drawn battle with Ibn Rashīd at Mejma' in Sedeir in March 1915. Since then his relations with his rival have not greatly improved, in spite of a formal peace concluded in the summer at the instance of the Sherif's son, 'Abdullah, who arrived with a large escort to collect the Sherif's dues, agreed upon under the pact of 1910. In the summer of 1915 he had serious trouble in N. Hasa with the powerful 'Ajmān tribe. He experienced reverses at the outset, lost his brother, Sa'd, and was himself wounded in a skirmish; but in the end he got the 'Ajmān under, inflicted very serious punishment, and prevailed on the Sultan of Koweit to withdraw his protection from them. Subsequently he had to deal similarly with the Ahl Murrah, who had been incited by his rebellious kinsman, Suleimān (see Aulād Sa'ūd).

The Emir is a man of about 40 years of age, six feet high and broad in proportion, of kindly face and simple manners ; intelligent, energetic, and warlike. He has been described as, in appearance, a typical Arab chief. He shows great philoprogenitiveness, marrying one wife after another, and giving each away, either at once or after her first child is weaned, to other sheikhs or followers. He adheres to the pro-British and anti-Turk traditions of his house, and at the end of 1915 signed a definite treaty with Sir P. Cox, acting on behalf of the Indian Government, of the same kind as those in force with Gulf potentates. Under this we engage to protect him against aggression (" by the subjects of any foreign power "), while he, for his part, must follow our policy in Arabia and in regard to Turks. He was friendly with the late Sultan Mubārak of Koweit (though he was not very honestly dealt with by that astute prince), and remains so with Sultan Jābir, and he is sympathetic to Idrīsi ; and he keeps on terms of courtesy, and even friendship at present, with the Emir of Mecca (though each depreciates the other to us). As for Ibn Rashīd, war alternates with armed neutrality ; and relations have not been improved by the defection of several Shammar Sheikhs to the Sa'ūd flag.

Ibn Rashīd, in an Agreement signed on June 10, 1915, recognized the following tribes as in Ibn Sa'ūd's sphere of influence : Muteir, Ateibah, Harb, B. 'Abdullah, 'Ajmān, Ahl Murrah, Manāsīr, B. Hājir (Hajar), Sebei', Sahul, Qahtān, and Dawāsir. But this must not be taken to imply that Ibn Sa'ūd really controls all these tribes ; it means merely that Ibn Rashīd disclaims influence over them. The Ateibah and Harb, for example, acknowledge no authority but that of the Emir of Mecca.

EMIRATE OF NEJD, *continued*.
'ABD ER-RAHMÂN IBN FEISÂL.
Youngest son of the famous Emir who received Palgrave and Pelly, and father of the ruling Emir. Attempted to establish himself as Emir in 1891, and imprisoned Ibn Rashīd's governor, but was driven out of Riyâdh and escaped first to Hasa, then to Koweit. He stayed at Koweit till 1902, when he returned to Nejd to live under his son. Acted as the Emir's representative in a conference with the Vali of Basra and the Sultan of Koweit in 1905. Is styled "Imam", and has the direction of religious affairs in Riyâdh, though his son, the Emir, usually leads the prayer. An old man, born about 1850, tall, keen-eyed, dignified, white-bearded, of pleasant manners, who was very cordial to Captains Leachman and Shakespear, and helped Raunkiaer. He is a firm believer in Great Britain, and has a wide acquaintance with Arab politics.

TÛRKI IBN 'ABD EL-'AZĪZ.
Eldest son of the ruling Emir, about 20 years of age. Appointed by his father to lead a considerable raid from Qasīm into Jebel Shammar in spring 1916. Reached Jebel Selmah and obtained much booty of live-stock. Ibn Rashīd was absent in the north at the time.

AULĀD SA'ŪD (or 'ARĀ'IF).
Grandsons of the Emir Sa'ūd ibn Feisāl, who was an elder brother of 'Abd er-Rahmān. They claim the Emirate for the elder branch of Feisāl's descendants, and, in 1910, attempted to raise Kharj, Hariq, and Hautah against 'Abd el-'Aziz. They were unsuccessful, and fled to Hasa and to the Ateibah. Later, when Ibn Sa'ūd harried the Ateibah and occupied Hasa (1913), some of the rebels took refuge with the Sherif and some with Sheikh 'Īsa of Bahrein. Two of the latter, Suleimān and Fahhād, left Bahrein in 1915 ostensibly for Oman, but they seem to have landed at Abu Dhabi and gone to 'Odeid, whence they intended to raid into Hasa. But Suleimān was defeated near 'Oqair, and returned to Abu Dhabi in November 1915. Expelled thence, he joined the Ahl Murrah, and thence fled to El-Qatar. Fahhād was killed.

SA'UD FAMILY

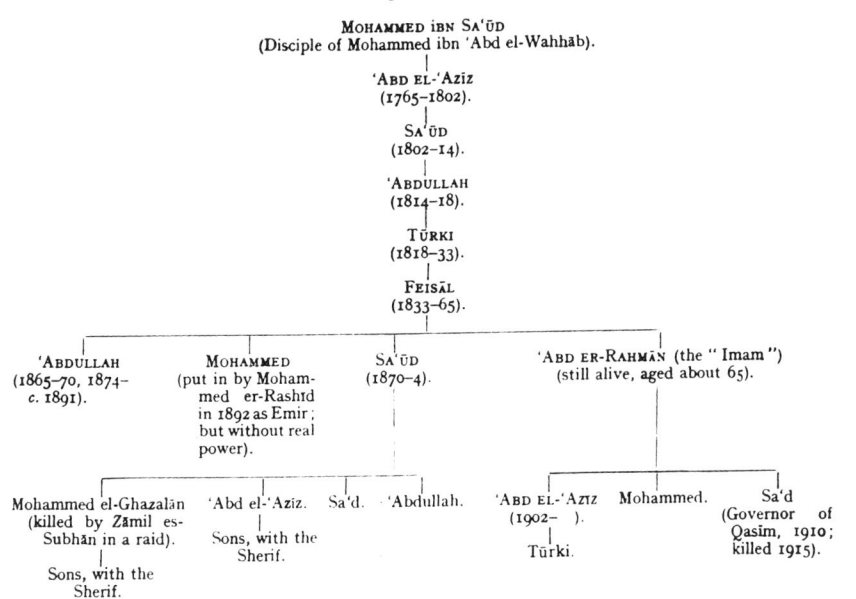

MOHAMMED IBN SA'ŪD
(Disciple of Mohammed ibn 'Abd el-Wahhāb).
|
'ABD EL-'AZĪZ
(1765–1802).
|
SA'ŪD
(1802–14).
|
'ABDULLAH
(1814–18).
|
TURKI
(1818–33).
|
FEISĀL
(1833–65).

| 'ABDULLAH (1865–70, 1874– c. 1891). | MOHAMMED (put in by Mohammed er-Rashīd in 1892 as Emir; but without real power). | SA'ŪD (1870–4). | 'ABD ER-RAHMĀN (the " Imam ") (still alive, aged about 65). |

| Mohammed el-Ghazalān (killed by Zāmil es-Subhān in a raid). | 'Abd el-'Azīz. | Sa'd. | 'Abdullah. | 'ABD EL-'AZĪZ (1902–). | Mohammed. | Sa'd (Governor of Qasim, 1910; killed 1915). |
| Sons, with the Sherif. | Sons, with the Sherif. | | | Tūrki. | | |

EMIRATE OF JEBEL SHAMMAR [IBN RASHĪDS].

This Principality was founded by an 'Abdah Shammar Sheikh, 'Abdullah ibn Rashīd, who in 1835 was made Governor of Hā'il by the Emir Feisāl of Riyādh. Previously (since the last years of the eighteenth century) all Jebel Shammar had been under Nejd, and most recently under Egyptian overlordship. 'Abdullah did not, however, throw off his dependence at once, but greatly increased his power during Feisāl's detention for five years in Cairo, and dying in 1847, left his successor, Telāl, virtually free of Nejd. The latter's successor, Mohammed, the strongest native ruler seen in Arabia in the nineteenth century, consolidated his principality, and not only maintained complete independence but formed the greatest confederacy of tribes ever collected, and in 1892 conquered all the dominions of Nejd, and ruled as sole Emir of Central Arabia till his death in 1897. How Nejd recovered independence five years later has been told under 'Abd el-'Azīz ibn 'Abd er-Rahmān.

Since that time Jauf also has been lost to Nūri esh-Sha'lān (q.v.), and, despite active Turkish support in 1904–5, no territory has been permanently added. The Emirate, therefore, is confined to Jebel Shammar, i.e. the steppe and hill country round the capital, Hā'il, with the Southern and Eastern Nefūd, and Teima.

The basis of Rashīd power is tribal. The great Bedouin clans of the

Southern Shammar support it ; but, like most powers which have any duration in Arabia, it rests in the first instance on a paid force of professional soldiers, the camelry known as the *rajājil*, who number about 500 men.

The Ibn Rashīds maintain closer relations with the Ottoman Government than do any other independent Arabian princes; and the House has also been consistently friendly with the Sherifate of Mecca. Besides the Emir of Nejd, its most constant foes are the Sultan of Koweit, Nūri esh-Sha'lān of the Ruweilah Anazah, and Hamūd ibn Suweit of the Dhafīr tribe. Nor is it on cordial terms with Ajeimi ibn Sa'dūn of the Muntefiq.

The Rashīd House is accounted infamous, even in such a land of violence as Arabia, for its record of domestic murders. Another noble Shammar family, the SUBHĀNS, is very intimately connected with it, and shares its notoriety. Besides having supplied viziers to the Rashīds for nearly a century, it has so often intermarried with the latter that its members are now of almost as genuine princely blood. One Subhān woman, Mudhi (q.v.), for example, has been married successively to three Rashīds (two Emirs) and one Subhān. Therefore the two families will be considered together, and a genealogical table will be appended of each. It will be observed that Sa'ūd, the ruling Emir, appears in both genealogies.

SA'ŪD IBN 'ABD EL-'AZĪZ.

Emir of Hā'il and Jebel Shammar since 1908. Son of 'Abd el-'Azīz, who reigned from 1897 to 1906, when he was killed in battle against the combined forces of the Muteir and Ibn Sa'ūd of Riyādh. 'Abd el-'Azīz was succeeded by his son Mit'ab, who before he had reigned a year was murdered by a cousin, Sultān ibn Hamūd er-Rashīd. Sultān was then killed by his brother, Sa'ūd ibn Hamūd, but the latter in his turn was murdered in 1908, at the instigation of Hamūd ibn Subhān, who brought back his nephew, Sa'ūd ibn 'Abd el-'Azīz, from Mecca, where he had been sent for safety, and set him up as Emir.

Sa'ūd's mother, Mudhi bint Subhān (q.v.), was first married to the Emir Mohammed er-Rashīd, who died in 1897. On his death she married 'Abd el-'Azīz, his successor and nephew. The Emir Sa'ūd, therefore, cannot be more than twenty-one. He has, however, his full complement of wives, who have borne him at least two sons. His uncle, Hamūd, died in 1907, leaving a distant cousin, Zāmil es-Subhān, to succeed him in his rôle of monitor and vizier. Zāmil was murdered in 1914 under circumstances of peculiar atrocity, and his place in the counsels of the Emir was taken by another of the Subhān house, Sa'ūd ibn Sālih (q.v.), reported murdered in his turn in early autumn, 1916.

EMIRATE OF JEBEL SHAMMAR, continued.

The Emir Sa'ūd is said to be an irresponsible boy of boorish manners and violent and ungovernable passions, verging on madness. He has a reputation for cruelty, and, even in Arabia, is accounted shifty and faithless. An envoy, sent to him from Basra, described him as a "jungle youth". A Shammari, formerly of his following, but now Governor under Ibn Sa'ūd, of Jalājil in Nejd, said to Shakespear in 1914, that Sa'ūd showed no sign of being a man beyond having got a son. He has failed to recapture the oasis of Jauf from Nūri esh-Sha'lān (q. v.), but has maintained his position against Ibn Sa'ūd, and the traditional relations of his house with the Ottoman Government. He has representatives in Damascus, Constantinople, Baghdad, and Nejef. His friendship with the Ottoman Sultan has been rewarded by large presents of arms, by a considerable sum of money sent up with Eshref Bey early in 1915, and by the title of Pasha. Between Jebel Shammar and Koweit there is a veiled hostility; but in 1914 Sa'ūd was on good terms with the Muntefiq. Early in 1916 he moved north to Leinah, and his movements and the help given by him to those buying camels for the Turks at £T.10 each, caused us to warn him that his food-caravans would not be allowed, in future, to buy in the Euphrates Valley markets, till his attitude was more satisfactory. He continued, however, to threaten the Shatt el-'Arab and Koweit, and camped near Safwān in June. He decamped at our threat of taking action, but went north and tried to harry Dhāri et-Tuwālah of the Aslam Shammar, but was driven off. He declared himself an Ottoman vassal, ready to co-operate with the Turks if they should push south, but ready to keep the peace meanwhile, if allowed to buy in the Euphrates markets. He showed much animosity towards the Sheikh of Zobeir. In August he was reported to have returned to Hā'il, and later he appears to have given active assistance to the Turks in Hejaz, both by providing camels and by sending raiding parties against the Emir of Mecca's adherents.

Since the loss of Jauf, his only outlying possession of importance is Teima. In 1914 Qasīm had ceased to recognize his authority, and the towns of Boreidah and Aneizah pay tribute to Ibn Sa'ūd. In 1915 Ibn Rashīd tried to regain Qasīm without success, and in 1916 that province was used as a base by Tūrki ibn Sa'ūd for raiding his country. Between Teima and Hā'il, the Bishr tribes pay him a small tribute; but the Huteim have made the passage of caravans dangerous, carrying their raiding expeditions almost to the gates of Hā'il. On the NE. the pasturing grounds of the Shammar tribes and the caravan tracks to Nejef are constantly raided by the Dhafīr.

EMIRATE OF JEBEL SHAMMAR, *continued*.

The Emir draws his fighting men both from the Shammar tribes, who are devotedly loyal, and from the villagers of the small oases round Hā'il. One authority states that he can muster, mount, and arm 20,000 (?) men; but Doughty put Mohammed er-Rashīd's force in his annual raids at only about 800, which was the number the Emir Sa'ūd was said to have with him in 1914 in his campaign against Nūri esh-Sha'lān. Doughty reckoned that Mohammed could, at the most, mount and arm 3,300 men, of which some 600 were drawn from tribes which are no longer under the control of his successor. Doughty's estimate is probably under the mark, but it can only be by very exceptional stress that Ibn Rashīd can muster anything like 10,000 armed men.

The Emir Sa'ūd is, virtually, the last of his blood-stained race, except his own infants. The only members of the family, therefore, to be considered are rather Subhāns than Rashīds.

DHĀRI IBN FAHD IBN 'UBEID ER-RASHĪD.

Fled from Hā'il, 1908, when the Emir Sa'ūd was murdered. Tried to seize the Emirate, killing three male Rashīds (grandsons of Hamūd?) who stood between him and the succession; but failed. Still, however, maintains his pretensions. Left wife, son and daughter in Hā'il, and fled to Riyādh and became right-hand man of Ibn Sa'ūd. Tuberculous and was treated at Bombay for four months and afterwards by the American doctor, von Vlach of Bahrein. Now cured. Of much repute among Arabs and trusted by Ibn Sa'ūd; said to be of capacity and judgement. His younger brother, FEISAL, aged 25, is also with Ibn Sa'ūd and in his confidence. Both brothers were seen by Shakespear at Koweit after their flight.

FĀTIMAH.

Widow of Subhān, vizier of the Emir Mohammed, and grandmother of the present Emir, Sa'ūd, whose mother is her daughter Mudhi. An old woman of strong character and considerable political influence. In 1914 she held the keys of the Treasury during the Emir's absence. No decision could be taken without her consent, and though, nominally, the administration of Hā'il was in the hands of Ibrāhīm es-Subhān (murdered in May 1914), she was *de facto* governor. Said to have great authority over the Emir. She rules the women of the Palace with a rod of iron.

NŪRAH BINT 'ABD EL-'AZĪZ.

Half-sister of the Emir Sa'ūd. She was married first to Hamūd es-Subhān, who brought back his nephew, the young

Emir Sa'ūd, from Mecca, and set him upon the throne in 1908. By him she has three sons, 'Ali, Mohammed, and Mit'ab. The two eldest boys, aged about 13 and 14, are treated with great respect in Hā'il as the grandsons of the Emir 'Abd el-'Aziz. Hamūd died in 1909, and Nūrah married her brother-in-law, Sa'ūd ibn Sālih es-Subhān, the murderer of Zāmil and Ibrāhīm. By him she has a son, born in 1913. If it is true that Sa'ūd has been murdered, she is once more a widow. She is a pretty woman, but without political influence.

MUDHI BINT SUBHĀN.

Daughter of Subhān, vizier to the Emir Mohammed, and of Fātimah. She was married first to the Emir Mohammed. On his death in 1897, she married the Emir 'Abd el-'Aziz, to whom she bore a son, Sa'ūd, the present Emir. She became the wife of Sultān er-Rashīd, who was murdered by his brother Sa'ūd, and subsequently, of Zāmil es-Subhān, murdered in 1914. By the latter she had a child. She is still a beautiful and gracious woman, but she has no political influence, being completely dominated by her mother Fātimah (q. v.).

SA'ŪD IBN SĀLIH ES-SUBHĀN.

Brother-in-law of the Emir Sa'ūd, and vizier; of considerable wealth. Married to Nūrah, half-sister of the Emir (q. v.). He instigated the murder of Zāmil es-Subhān and his brother Ibrāhīm in 1914, having bought over the *rajājil*. The Emir's jealousy had been excited by reports of invidious comparisons drawn by the Shammar between himself and Zāmil, to whom, in the first instance, he had owed his throne. He therefore acquiesced in the murder, riding on ahead while it was being perpetrated, and he accepted Sa'ūd as vizier in the room of his victim. [Reported killed in September 1916.]

'ABBĀS EL-FALEIJI.

Of Boreidah in Qasīm ; the richest local merchant.

'ABD EL-'AZĪZ HAMŪD.

One of the Emir of Hā'il's *rajājil*, and his agent in Damascus. 'Abd el-'Azīz is familiar with Constantinople, where he has been sent on the Emir's business. He was there during the Balkan War.

'ABD EL-'AZĪZ IBN SA'ĪD.

Governor of Jalājil in Sedeir for Ibn Sa'ūd. A Shammari tribesman. About 32 years of age ; tall and of fine presence. Formerly governor for Ibn Sa'ūd in Hasa, and before that one of Ibn Rashīd's men in Hā'il. Spoke disparagingly of the Emir Sa'ūd to Shakespear.

RASHID FAMILY

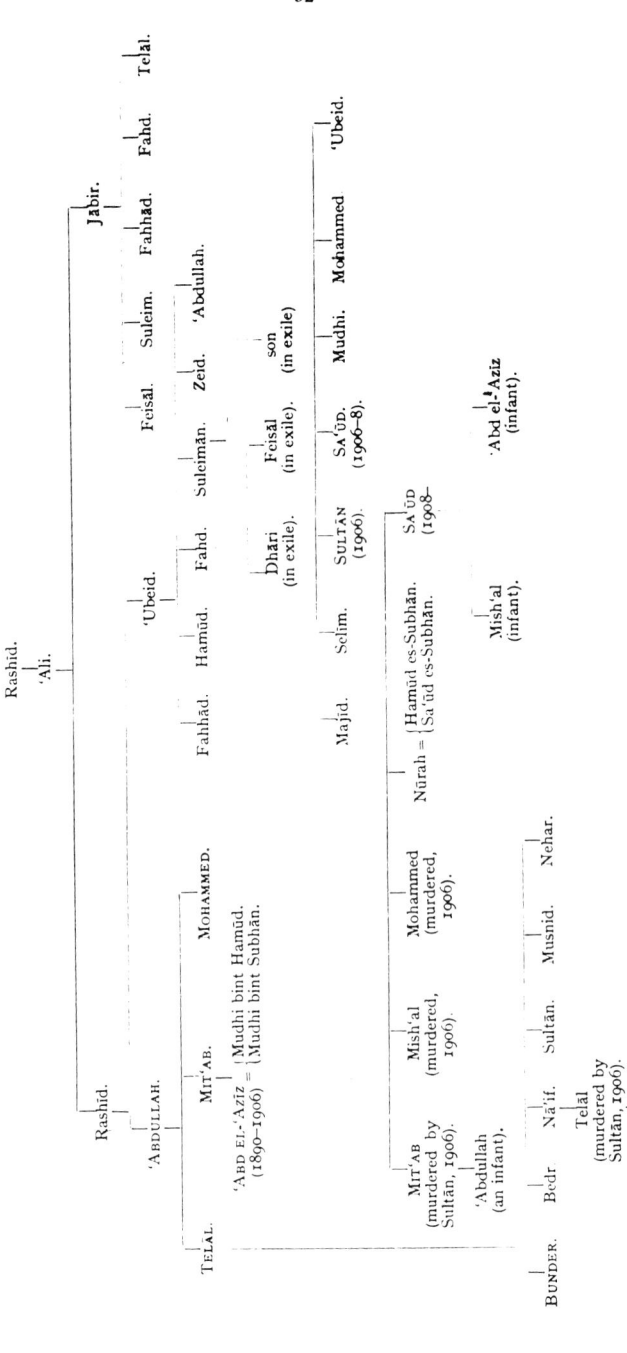

Rashid.
|
'Ali.
|
┌──────────┬──────────┬──────────┐
Rashid.   'Ubeid.   Jabir.
| | |
'ABDULLAH.   (see below) (see below)
|
┌─────────┬─────────┐
TELAL.   MIT'AB.   MOHAMMED.
| |
| 'ABD EL-'AZIZ = {Mudhi bint Hamūd.
| (1890–1906)   {Mudhi bint Subhān.
|
┌──────────┬──────────┬──────────┐
MIT'AB   Mish'al   Mohammed
(murdered (murdered, (murdered,
by Sultān, 1906).   1906).
1906).
|
'Abdullah
(an infant).

TELAL
|
┌────┬─────┬──────┬──────┬──────┐
Na'if. Sultān. Musnid. Nehar.
Bedr   Telal
        (murdered by
        Sultān, 1906).

BUNDER.
|
'Abdullah   Mohammed
(aet. 16)   (aet. 13).

'Ubeid branch:
┌─────┬──────┬──────┐
Fahhād. Hamūd. Fahd.
                  |
              Dhāri
              (in exile)

Hamūd:
┌──────┬──────┐
Majid. Selim. Nūrah = {Hamūd es-Subhān.
                       {Sa'ūd es-Subhān.
                       |
                    Mish'al
                    (infant).

From Dhāri line:
SULTĀN (1906).
SA'ŪD (1908–)
SA'ŪD (1906–8).
|
'Abd el-'Aziz
(infant).

Jabir branch:
┌─────────┬─────────┬─────┬─────────┬────────┬────────┐
Suleimān. Feisal. Suleim. Fahhād. Fahd.   Telal.
          |
      ┌───────┬────────┬──────────┐
      Feisal Zeid.   'Abdullah.
      (in exile)
      son
      (in exile)
      |
   Mudhi. Mohammed 'Ubeid.

SUBHAN FAMILY

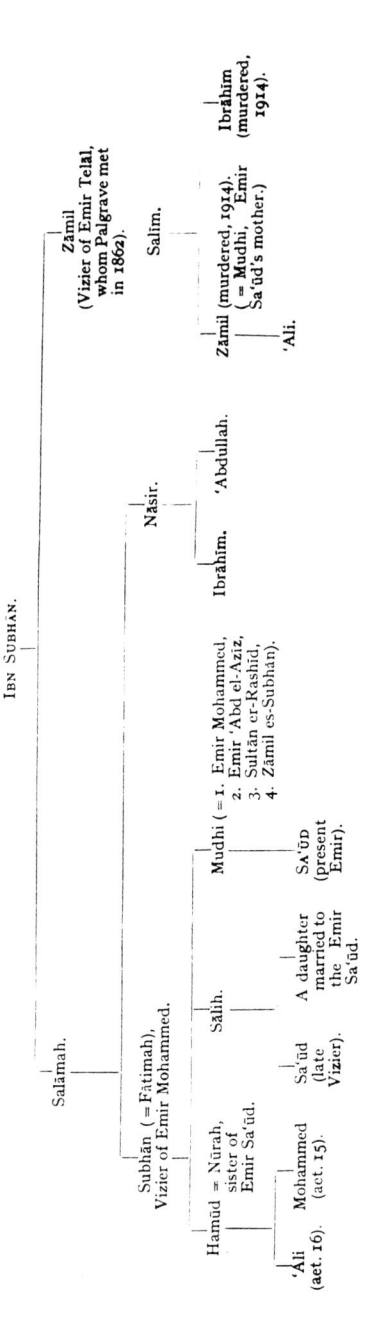

```
                                    Ibn Subhan.
            ┌──────────────────────────┼─────────────────────────────┐
       Salāmah.                                                    Zāmil
            │                                              (Vizier of Emir Telāl,
    Subhān (= Fātimah),                                    whom Palgrave met
    Vizier of Emir Mohammed.                                      in 1862).
            │                                                        │
  ┌─────────┼──────────┬─────────────────────┐                ┌──────┴──────┐
  │                    │                     │              Nāsir.         Salim.
Hamūd = Nūrah,       Sālih.        Mudhi (= 1. Emir Mohammed,  │              │
sister of                           2. Emir 'Abd el-Aziz,   ┌──┴────────┐  Zāmil (murdered, 1914).
Emir Sa'ūd.                         3. Sultān er-Rashid,  Ibrāhim. 'Abdullah. (= Mudhi, Emir
  │                                  4. Zāmil es-Subhān).                    Sa'ūd's mother.)
  │                                                                           │
  │                    │                     │                               'Ali.
  │                   Sa'ūd             Sa'ūd                                 │
  │                   (late           (present                              Ibrāhim
  │                  Vizier).          Emir).                             (murdered,
  │                                                                         1914).
  │                                  A daughter
  │                                  married to
  │                                  the Emir
  │                                  Sa'ūd.
┌─┴──────────┐
'Ali      Mohammed
(aet. 16).  (aet. 15).
```

'ABDULLAH IBN 'ASKAR.
Governor of Mejma', capital of Sedeir, for Ibn Sa'ūd. Hospitably entertained Shakespear in March 1913 in a fine house, having known him previously in Koweit. So again in 1914. Has a son, 'Abd el-'Azīz. His brother was killed at the capture of Qatīf in 1913. The 'Askar house was formerly attached to Ibn Rashīd, and Mejma' resisted the present Emir of Riyādh for some four years, submitting finally on condition of retaining an autonomy under its 'Askar Emirs similar to that enjoyed by Aneizah in Qasīm. It remains disaffected to Ibn Sa'ūd and a focus of Rashīdite influence.

'ABDULLAH IBN EL-JALĀL.
One of the *rajājil* of the Emir of Hā'il, and a man of some importance. In 1914 he was entrusted with the fetching from Medā'in Sālih of a large consignment of arms, which was sent down from Damascus in February by the Hejaz Railway. He had requisitioned 1,000 camels for this purpose (50 rifles is a camel load), but had succeeded in obtaining only 400. (N.B.—These are Arab figures, and are probably exaggerated.)

'ABDULLAH EL-KHALĪFAH.
Of Boreidah. A fat and greasy Arab who once kept a shop in Cairo. Becoming bankrupt, he worked his way as a fireman to New York, and there drove a hackney. Saved about £1,000, and returned to Boreidah. Has since made more money, e. g. at Bombay in 1913, and is now rich and of much consideration.

'ABDULLAH IBN SALMĀN.
Of Zilfi. Formerly governor for Ibn Sa'ūd; now superseded by 'Ali ibn Badah (q. v.), but still the man of most local influence.

'ABDULLAH IBN SA'ĪD, Dr.
Of Aneizah in Qasīm. The best-known native physician in Central Arabia. Trained in Beirut and Constantinople. Attended Ibn Sa'ūd in his 'Ajmān campaign in summer 1915 and was wounded. Had 400 wounded to deal with. Went to Bombay in December to procure medicines and instruments.

'ABDULLAH IBN ZĀMIL.
Of Aneizah in Qasīm; brother of the ruling Emir of the town.

AHMED ETH-THANAYYĀN.
Of Riyādh. Born of a Circassian mother. Was educated in Constantinople, and speaks French well. A relative of the Emir, who joined in receiving Leachman. Descended from Ibn Thanayyān,

grandson of the Emir 'Abd el-'Azīz I. This man ruled Nejd during Emir Feisāl's captivity, and, on the latter's return in 1849, tried to exclude him, but was betrayed by Ibn Suweilim.

'ALI IBN BADAH.

Governor of Zilfi (both towns, Shamālīyah and Jumbra). About 18 years of age; pleasant manners. Appointed by Ibn Sa'ūd in 1912, after the murder of his uncle. Lives in Zilfi Shamālīyah. Received Shakespear in 1914 very hospitably.

DHĀRI IBN BARGHĀSH ET-TUWĀLAH.

Paramount Chief of the Aslam section of the Shammar, which ranges near 'Irāq, the chief being usually in the vicinity of Cha'bdah. It is at enmity with the 'Abdah and Ibn Rashīd, and friendly with the Sinjārah and Tūmān sections. At present Dhāri is allied with us. About 30 years of age, good looking with straightforward determined mien; not given to superfluous compliments. A friend of Nawwāf ibn Nūri esh-Sha'lān (q. v.). He has fought Ibn Rashīd on more than one occasion.

FAHHĀD IBN MA'MIR.

(Former ?) Emir of Boreidah, appointed by Ibn Sa'ūd. A weak man of disagreeable appearance and manners, who gave Raunkiaer trouble in 1912, and was only tolerably civil to Shakespear in 1914. Under the influence of negro slaves. The Ma'mir family is of old standing in Nejd, having been sheikhs in Wādi Hanīfah before the establishment of the Sa'ūd Emirate.

FEISĀL IBN SULTĀN ED-DERWĪSH.

The most powerful Muteir sheikh. Chief of the 'Alwi sub-tribe. Fat, but energetic and warlike. Fought Ibn Rashīd in the spring of 1915, and afterwards tried to come to terms with Ibn Sa'ūd. Had relations with Shakespear at Koweit. Of considerable reputation in the desert as a raider and, perhaps, the same Feisāl, who exacted dues from Raunkiaer's caravan on its way from Koweit to Zilfi in 1912.

IBN HAYA.

A family of some importance at Aneizah. One of the brothers was killed by the former Emir of Aneizah, 'Abd el-'Azīz ibn Suleim; two of the others, Sālih Haya and Hamād, together with a nephew, Ibrāhīm, were living in dudgeon at Hā'il in 1914. Ibn Sa'ūd had offered them blood money which they refused, saying that they must have a life. They intended to join a raiding expedition, which was to be sent out from Hā'il against Aneizah in the autumn of 1914, but it was generally believed that when they had taken their revenge for the slain, they would declare in favour of Ibn Sa'ūd.

MAHD IBN SA'ŪD.

Emir of Shaqrah (Woshm); received Leachman in 1912 and Shakespear in 1914 hospitably. Not bigoted. Now subservient to Riyādh, but formerly hostile (Shaqrah resisted the Emir for 45 days). A young man of pleasant manners and enlightened views. No relation of the Emirs of Riyādh.

MAS'ŪD ES-SUWEILIM.

Of Riyādh. Representative of a wealthy noble house, descended directly from the first Mohammed ibn Sa'ūd. An ancestor, Ibn Suweilim, delivered up the usurper, Ibn Thanayyān, to Emir Feisāl in 1849. Mas'ūd, who had been Ibn Sa'ūd's envoy to our Resident at Koweit in 1906, met and entertained Shakespear at Riyādh in 1914. Early in 1915 he was sent again to Koweit to ask help from Sultan Mubārak against the rebellious 'Ajmān, and was successful. He returned by Bahrein.

SA'D IBN 'ABD EL-MUHSIN ES-SEDEIRI.

Governor of Ghāt in Sedeir; nearly related to Ibn Sa'ūd on the mother's side. Man of about 45, thin and wizened. Barely civil to Raunkiaer in 1912, but received Shakespear well in 1914. Was at the capture of Hofūf (Hasa) by Ibn Sa'ūd in 1913.

SA'ID EL-MOHAMMED.

Head eunuch of the palace at Hā'il, a position he has occupied since the days of the Emir Mohammed. A coal-black negro of villainous aspect. He is the agent of Fātimah, the grandmother of the Emir Sa'ūd, and has considerable power. He enjoys great consideration in the town.

SĀLIH IBN ZĀMIL.

Emir of Aneizah in Qasīm, elected by the townsmen. An oldish man, not bigoted. Of pleasant manners and real influence. Very cordial to Shakespear in 1914. Son of the famous Emir who received Doughty in 1878, consistently upheld the liberties of Aneizah against Mohammed er-Rashīd, and was the most redoubtable warrior in Arabia.

TURKĪYAH.

A Circassian slave girl, one of the four sent by the Sultan 'Abd el-Hāmid to Mohammed er-Rashīd. She was married by Mohammed before his death to one of his *rajājil*, 'Ubeid el-Gharāmil, brother to the standard-bearer of the Hajj, and was given a house in Hā'il as a marriage portion. She is a woman of quick intelligence, with some influence in the palace, especially among the *harīm*, by whom her knowledge of Constantinople and the outer world is much appreciated.

REGION VII

SYRIAN DESERT AND SINAI

ABU JĀBIR.
A FAMILY of Christians of Nazarene origin, now settled at Salt, and owning lands on the Hajj Railway north of Jīzah, at Yadūdah. There the two brothers, ABU SĀLIH FREH and ABU SA'ID FERHĀN, have built a substantial stone house. They are men of intelligence and great physical vigour, well known and much respected in the desert on account of the unlimited hospitality which they extend to the tribes. They are anxious to improve the cultivation of their lands, and complain bitterly of the hindrances which the Ottoman Government puts in their way, and the complete lack of protection which it affords. At Juweidah, three or four miles from Yadūdah, another of the family, SELĪM ABU JĀBIR, has a farm, while farther south, at Urum Kundum, the BISHARRA family, related by marriage to the Abu Jābir, have a large farm. A notable group of sturdy cultivators, holding their own against the tribes. One of the Bisharra sons, Hanna, was educated in Switzerland, and has taken an agricultural degree. Another Christian, Nimrūd Hasan, has a small farm at Tneib, SE. of Urum Kundum. Tneib is about the limit of possible cultivation, owing to the lack of rain farther east.

'AJEIMI IBN SA'DŪN.
Most influential Chief among the Muntefiq. Succeeded his father (put to death at Aleppo) in 1911. Not so powerful with the various sections of this much subdivided tribal group as his father. At first anti-Turk, and had designs on Basra. Was forestalled by our advance in 1915, and turned against us; but lost much prestige by inaction at the battle of Sheiba. Since then has been hostile but ineffective. Has operated against the Sultan of Koweit. A man of bad reputation among Arabs.

'ALI IBN SULEIMĀN ESH-SHARQI.
One of the Paramount Sheikhs of the Duleim. He is on excellent terms with the Government; but moments of tension are apt to occur when his people raid the Euphrates caravan road. The Duleim were put down with a strong hand by Nāzim Pasha in 1910-11. Jemāl, Nāzim's successor as Vali of 'Irāq, struck up a friendship, however, with 'Ali Suleimān, and gave him a general invitation to visit him in Constantinople. 'Ali Suleimān owns cultivated lands and a house at Rumādi. He is a man of mediocre wits, but has

inherited a considerable position from his father, who was a notable strong man in the desert. The Duleim maintain friendly relations with the 'Amārāt.

FAHD BEY IBN 'ABD EL-MUHSIN EL-HADHDHĀL.

Paramount Chief of the 'Amārāt. A man over 60, not very intelligent; a pan-Arabist, who hates the Turks for personal reasons, having been imprisoned by them at Mosul more than once. He owns profitable palm-gardens at Ghazāzah near Kerbela, and has planted lands on the Euphrates at Bagdad. He is much respected in the desert, but is now old and timid, pre-occupied by anxieties about his settled property, the value of which, he fears, may be diminished by the opening of the Hindīyah Escape. It is essential for him to remain on good terms with whoever controls the water of the Euphrates. Rules about 3,000 tents. (See also p. 107.)

FAWWĀZ IBN TELĀL.

Eldest son of Telāl ibn Fā'iz abu Meshkūr, and almost as influential as his father with the Beni Sakhr. Accepted office under the Turks as Kaimmakam of Jīzah, but is believed to be pan-Arab. A secretive man of about 35; moderately intelligent, energetic, and untrustworthy. (See also p. 113 f.)

GHĀLIB IBN MIT'AB EL-QANJ.

Chief of the Serdīyah, who are an offshoot of the B. Sakhr, but independent and usually at feud with the latter, and always with the Ruweilah. Ghālib is on good terms with the Turkish authorities, and was favoured by Sāmi Pasha in 1911. He has many friends in Damascus, and is said by them to be a sound Arab Unionist. He commands about 150 tents. His importance, however, is not measured by these. His grandfather, famous for his giant strength, made a name in the desert which still counts for much. The grandson, however, is less active and formidable, and inclines perforce to the Turks in self-defence. (See also p. 114.)

HĀKIM (PRON. HĀCHIM) IBN MUHEID.

Chief of the Dhana Kuheil section of the Fed'ān. Next to Nūri esh-Sha'lān of the Ruweilah, perhaps the most powerful of the Anazah Chiefs, and certainly abler than he. Age about 40. Intelligent, very open-minded, fond of money, and vain; anti-Turk and pan-Arab. Loves politics and his own free-will. Rules about 2,000 tents. (See also p. 107.)

HAMĀD ES-SŪFI.

Of the Terābīn tribe of N. Sinai and lives at Beersheba. Chief of the Najamāt sub-tribe of the Terābīn and also of the small Haiwāt tribe. Active in helping Turkish propaganda in autumn 1914, and claims to have been made a Pasha. He has a stone house, and is local Mayor (Ra'is el-Belediyah), but possesses only about 20 camels; age about 70. His son, Jadira, age about 30, has no great influence outside his own tribe. Hamād's father was killed by the Abu Sittah, another Terābīn sub-tribe, and Hamād has a blood-feud with them. His authority is not widely recognized outside his own sub-tribe, and the Haiwāt. Afraid of the Turks, and in December 1915 was said to have become disaffected towards them, and to have refused to put his men into Turkish uniform.

HAMŪD IBN SUWEIT.

Paramount Chief of the Dhafīr tribe. About 40 years of age, intelligent and reputed a good tribal administrator and politician. An old foe of Ibn Rashīd, who refused the latter's invitation to join in a campaign during the winter 1915–16 against the rulers of Koweit and Riyādh. Recently (early 1916) he has mobilized his tribesmen together with the Bedūr (a half-settled tribe of some 30,000 souls who live between Khidhr and Sūq esh-Shuyūkh) in the desert, west of Sūq esh-Shuyūkh, to counteract any movement of Ibn Rashīd or 'Ajeimi of the Muntefiq against us in Mesopotamia. He has been attacked by the Shammar and the 'Ajmān; but, though worsted, has been able to defeat 'Ajeimi. Ibn Sa'ūd himself recommended our enlisting him on our side. He controls about 2,500 tents. (See also p. 137.)

HUSEIN IBN HUMEITAH.

Chief of the Sa'ūdīn sub-tribe of the Huweitāt, between Ma'ān and Akaba. Reported a brave honest man, who can obtain a large number of camels, at need, from the main body of the Huweitāt.

MOHAMMED IBN TŪRKI IBN MIJLĀD.

Chief of the Dahāmishah sub-tribe of the 'Amārāt and has some authority over the whole tribe. Said to control 1,200 tents.

MOHAMMED PASHA JERŪDI.

Hereditary Chief of the oasis of Jerūd; he has a house in Damascus where he spends the winter, and is very well known. He is of Anazah stock, a man verging on 70, fat and infirm. He breeds horses, and maintains good relations with the tribes. Has been a source of considerable trouble to the Ottoman Government, but is nevertheless useful as an intermediary with the tribes. It is owing to his position in the desert that he has enjoyed more clemency than he deserves. Wealthy and avaricious.

MOHAMMED, SHEIKH OF TADMOR.

A fine looking man who has been in Europe, and maintains constant relations with H. M. Consulate at Damascus. A settled Arab who controls the Ottoman Mudir of Tadmor, and makes money out of the traffic on the road from Hīt to Damascus, but has no tribal influence.

NAWWĀF IBN NŪRI ESH-SHA'LĀN.

Son of the paramount chief of the Ruweilah, and governor of Jauf since it was taken from Ibn Rashīd. A man of considerable intelligence and some education; regarded by the pan-Arab party in Damascus as a staunch adherent and a valuable ally, but subsidized by the Turks (£T. 4,000 ?). Sheltered refugees from Syria in the winter of 1915-16. His reputation bids fair to eclipse that of his father. In his absence, his little son, SULTĀN, received Shakespear at Jauf in 1914. (See also p. 106.)

NŪRI BEY ESH-SHA'LĀN.

Paramount Chief of the Ruweilah. Perhaps the most powerful individual chief among the Bedouins. Reported to have been ordered in August 1914 not to go to the desert, but to collect camels for the Turks; seems to have supplied a considerable number, but was not paid, and, in 1915, refused to renew the supply. A man between 50 and 60; fond of politics and intrigue, but rather obtuse. He has three or four sons, of whom one is often at Mecca with the Sherif. Joined pan-Arab movement, but continued for some time to draw a large subsidy from the Turks (£T.5,000 ?). Nurses a bitter grudge against the Ottoman Government by reason of his having been invited to Damascus by Sāmi Pasha in 1911, and held there imprisoned. Captured the oasis of Jauf from Ibn Rashīd in 1910, and fears the extension of the Hejaz Railway down W. Sirhān, a project under discussion in 1913. In June 1916, was reported to be in league with the Sherif of Mecca, and later (August) was further reported (incorrectly) to have gone to Mecca and taken command of reinforcements and guns for the force blockading Medina. The Sherif claims him as a firm friend. He is said to rule over 5,000 to 6,000 tents (like all Arab figures the number is probably exaggerated). (See also p. 106.)

RASHĪD IBN SUMEIR.

The principal chief of the Wuld 'Ali as a whole, and chief of six of its sub-tribes ('Ateifāt, Mesālikh, Hammāmīd, Hajjāj, Tulūh, and Saqra—in all about 1,500 tents). His family has long held the chieftainship (e. g. in Burckhardt's time).

SELĪM ABU IRBE'A.

Chief of the Thulam tribe of Sinai, ranging from Gaza to the

Dead Sea. An intelligent, well-mannered Arab of real influence with his tribe, and paramount over its sub-tribes, which total some 2,000 souls, with, perhaps, 2,000 camels.

TELĀL IBN FĀ'IZ ABU MESHKŪR.

Paramount Chief of the Beni Sakhr. Claims to be able to call out 10,000 men (?). The pan-Arab party in Damascus claims him as an adherent. The Beni Sakhr are responsible for the Hajj line from Jīzah to Kerak. Their southern pastures run down as far as the Jebel Tubeiq. They summer round Mādeba and in the Ghōr. The Chief's father, Fā'iz, is still alive, but plays less part than the son in desert politics. The Fā'iz group owns about 500 tents, the whole of the B. Sakhr tribe having about 1,500. Telāl refused to provide camels for the Turkish attack on the Canal in January 1915.

THE BEDOUIN TRIBES

This section is designed to give an account of those tribal constituents of present-day Arabian society which are essentially nomadic—those, in short, to which Arabs themselves concede the name Bedu. The Bedouin (*Bedāwi*) type of society is the product of desert and steppe conditions, and cannot survive long under others. A tribe, which has left such conditions to settle in an oasis or other permanently arable land, does not necessarily cease to be a tribe, but it does cease to be a nomad or Bedouin tribe. The settled and half-settled tribes are therefore treated separately.

In the present section, Bedouin constituents of Arabian society which have passed wholly or in part northwards out of the peninsula are included. Not having changed the essential conditions of their life, but still ranging deserts and steppes, they have remained Bedu. It would be unsatisfactory, therefore, not to take account here of the nomad tribes of the Syrian Hamād and the Mesopotamian Jezīrah. They are regarded by the peninsular Bedouins as forming one great social block with themselves, and some, e.g. certain constituents of the great Anazah group, still pass at regular seasons southward into the peninsula, while others have their own home ranges in the peninsula itself. Moreover, many, like the Ruweilah, Dhafīr, and Huweitāt, move habitually from one side to the other of the border-line, and some, e.g. the Mesopotamian Shammar, though they stay to the north of it, are integral parts of larger tribal units still at home in the south.

For convenience, we adopt a geographical division of Bedouin tribes into Northern, Central (Western and Eastern), and Southern.

At the outset, a tree of tribal descent from the Arch-Patriarch, Abraham, will show what Arabs consider to be the true Bedouin stock. To know this pedigree is of practical value to any one who has to deal with Arab nomads, owing to the value which they themselves attach to genealogy, the social distinctions which they base upon it, and the estimation in which they hold those expert in its intricacies. Whoever doubts this, is forgetting the Old Testament and its insistence on descent.

ABRAHAM

Ishmael (Nizârite or Ma'addite Tribes, Ahl esh-Shimâl).

- Mudhar.
  - Hudheil.
  - Kinânah
    - Qoreish.
- Kelb.
- Billi.
- 'Udhra.
- B. Khâlid.
- Uteibah.
- Harb.
- Tamîm.
- Dhabbah.
- Qeis.
  - Ghatafân.
    - 'Abs.
    - Dhubyân
      - Fazîrah
  - Suleim.
  - Hawâzin.
    - 'Uqeil.
      - Muntefiq.
    - Qusheir.
    - Kilâb.
      - B. Hilâl.
    - 'Adwân.
  - 'Abd el-Qeis.
  - Namir.
- Wâ'il.
  - Taghlib.
  - Bekr.
    - Beni Hanîfah.
- Asad.
- Anazah.

Qahtân (Yemenite Tribes, Ahl Qiblī).

- Kahlân.
  - Azd.
    - Ghassân.
    - Khuzâ'ah.
    - Aus.
    - Khazraj (Ansâr).
    - Balhârith.
    - Bajîlah.
  - Tayy.
  - Hamdân.
  - Madh-hij.
  - 'Amilah.
  - Judhâm.
  - Lakhm.
  - Kindah.
  - Qudhâ'ah.
    - Bahra.
    - Tanûkh.
  - Juheinah.
- Himyar.

Rabî'ah.

A. Northern Tribes

1. *The Anazah.*

The great group of the ANAZAH ('*Anazah*), numerically probably the largest group of nomad Arab tribes, occupies the triangle of the Syrian Desert, the Hamād, which has its base on the Nefūd, about lat. 30°, and its apex near Aleppo, about lat. 36°. On the east bank of the Euphrates the pasture lands N. of Deir ez-Zōr and along the Khābūr are also Anazah country : while a smaller group of kindred tribes is seated round Teima, between the Hejaz railway and the SW. borders of the Nefūd. Ibn Sa'ūd is said to come of the same stock (Hasanah).

The Anazah belong to the people of the North, Ahl esh-Shimāl. Historians give their descent from 'Anazah, son of Asad, who sprang from Rabī'ah, one of the two great branches of Nizār. The modern Anazah tribesman will always claim descent from Wā'il, who belonged to a younger branch of the Asad group, and relate that it is his son 'Anz or 'Anaz who is the eponymous founder of the tribe. They are not, however, united under one head, but are divided into several large sections which maintain towards one another an attitude generally friendly, though it does not exclude marauding expeditions and private feuds among the smaller Sheikhs. The hereditary foes of the Anazah are the Shammar ; indeed, the history of nomad Arabia is dominated for the last 150 years by the rivalry between these two.

The original seat of the Shammar seems to have been to the N. of the Wādi er-Rummah, on the pilgrim road from Basra to Medina, or even farther south towards Yemen. One of those mysterious impulses which, from the beginning of historic times, have set the inhabitants of the peninsula migrating northwards—influences which may spring from an almost imperceptible change in climatic conditions coupled with slow increase of population in a land incapable of supporting more than very small numbers—began to disturb the Anazah in the second half of the eighteenth century. They followed on the heels of the Shammar into the Syrian Desert. The Fed'ān and the Hasanah pushed the Shammar before them across the Euphrates, and established themselves in the northern steppes, which are less arid, enjoying a greater rainfall, than the wastes of central Arabia. The 'Amārāt, Sibā', and Wuld 'Ali seem to have come next, and towards the end of the eighteenth century the Ruweilah.

Their herds have flourished and increased in a climate more beneficent than that which they had left. The most famous stocks of horses are found among the northern Anazah, and the greatest numbers of camels. Bedu of the purest blood and tradition, they have remained entirely beyond the control of the Ottoman Government ; and except for a few palm-gardens on the Lower Euphrates, a little cultivation on the Khābūr, and a village near Damascus, their Sheikhs have given no pledge to established order by the acquisition of settled lands, nor is any part of the Syrian Desert ploughed or harvested. Their geographical position gives them command over some of the main trade-routes of Turkish Arabia. The Hamād is a bridge rather than a barrier between Syria and Mesopotamia. Until 1911, the camel post from Damascus to Baghdad passed over it once a fortnight, and regularly during the winter and spring the agents of the Damascene sheep merchants cross it, paying dues to the Anazah for safe conduct, while the camel herds of the latter supply the markets both of Syria and of Egypt ; indeed, it is not too much to say that the greater part of the camel trade is in their hands. Moreover, the road down the Euphrates from Aleppo to Baghdad is largely at their mercy, as well as the first half of a frequented carriage road from Deir, *via* the Sinjar, to Mosul. The Anazah are thus the first of the great independent tribes with whom administrators of the settled lands must come into contact, and upon their goodwill depends freedom of intercourse between Syria and Mesopotamia. Last century they played a large part in Syrian politics, and have still a zest for the game. Their own dependence on the Syrian markets must always make it a matter of the first importance to them to maintain friendly terms with those who control the province commercially ; but it must be remembered that commercial control of Syria is not, and never has been, in the hands of the Turks.

The western side of the Syrian Desert is occupied by the RUWEILAH (Ruwalla). With their powerful confederates the Wuld 'Ali and the Muhallaf, who are in the closest relations with them, and also their allies, the Hasanah, they number about 7,000 tents. They wander over the desert from Homs and Hamāh in the north, where the Hasanah have their summer pasturages and are beginning to settle down as cultivators, to Qasr el-Azraq, south of Jebel Durūz (where the Ruweilah dīra touches that of their foes, the Beni Sakhr) and down the Wādi Sirhān to the oasis of Jauf el-'Amr, which the Ruweilah took from Ibn Rashīd some five years ago. In summer they occupy the pasture grounds S. of Damascus and push as far west as the Jaulān. To the east the limits of the Ruweilah do not extend far beyond Jebel 'Amūd and the sources of the Wādi Haurān.

The loose confederation of tribes, of which the WULD 'ALI are composed, holds the steppe east and south-east of Damascus and along the first part of the old post-road to Baghdad. Ibn Sumeir owns the village of 'Ain Dhikr at Tell el-Faras, some 12 hours from Damascus, with the cultivation round it. A detached group round Teima, the FUQARA and the B. WAHAB, are also to be reckoned among the subtribes of the Wuld 'Ali, but they have no political connexion with them, and fall under the authority of Ibn Rashīd whenever he is strong enough to exercise it. The Fuqara are a small poor tribe, with few camels, which depends for its livelihood partly on the payment it receives from the Ottoman Government for protecting the Hejaz railway from Dār el-Hamra to Medā'in Sālih, and partly on a little cultivated land which it possesses in the rocky Harrah of Kheibar. The Billi and the Huweitāt, with their close allies the B. 'Atīyah, are their enemies. The AIDA, who are the Sheikhly clan of the southern Wuld 'Ali, have charge of a section of the Hejaz railway south of Medā'in Sālih.

In summer the Ruweilah draw into the Wādi Sirhān or go with the Wuld 'Ali towards the fertile Matkh plain, watered by the Barrada; but the volcanic Harrahs east of Jebel Durūz are inhabited by tribes hostile to the Anazah, the Serdīyah, a branch of the Beni Sakhr, and the Jebelīyah, composed of Ghiyādh, Beni Hasan, Masā'īd, and others, all allied with the Druzes. With these and with the Druzes themselves the Anazah have always been at enmity.

The paramount chief of the RUWEILAH is of the house of Sha'lān and the sub-tribe of Mur'idh. The present representative is Nūri esh-Sha'lān. His own sub-tribe, the Sha'lān, together with the Nuseir, who come directly under him, consists of about 1,000 tents, but over all the Ruweilah he is unquestioned autocrat, and his authority is recognized by the Wuld 'Ali and the Muhallaf. He is probably the most powerful of all purely nomad chiefs, and, since his capture of Jauf, has shown himself a successful rival of the Shammar. His son, Nawwāf, a convinced adherent of the pan-Arab party, is his representative at Jauf. Though more colourless than his father, he is better educated and is considered by the Arab Unionist party in Damascus, among whom he is well known, to be the most advanced political thinker in the desert. He has the inherited interest in the Turkish question which those of his house can scarcely escape, since it touches their own future so closely. Nūri himself bears a bitter grudge against the Ottoman Government, by reason of his having been invited to Damascus by Sāmi Pasha in 1911, and there held a prisoner for almost a year. The grievance was aggravated by the fact that he had previously offered his assistance to Sāmi Pasha for the subjugation of the Druzes. He dreads any extension of Turkish authority towards the desert, and strongly opposed a scheme set on foot in 1913 to carry a branch of the Hejaz railway from Jīzah to Qasr el-Azraq, and thence down the W. Sirhān to Kāf. In 1914 he refused to collect camels for the Ottoman Government, who were in need of transport animals for the Egyptian campaign, thereby greatly enhancing their difficulties. He removed his people into their eastern pasturages, where the Turks had no hold over them, and he is said to have acted similarly a year later and, in 1916, to have joined the Sherif of Mecca.

E. of the Ruweilah and the Wuld 'Ali, the Syrian Desert up to the Euphrates is held by the 'AMĀRĀT and by the two great subdivisions of the BISHR, the FED'ĀN and the SIBĀ' (Sba), who claim descent from various mythical heroes of whom Wā'il was the progenitor. The 'Amārāt country is the SE. corner of the Syrian Desert bordering on the Euphrates from Kerbela to above Hīt. The tribesmen touch the N. edge of the Nefūd and go down SE. into Shammar territory if pasturage is lacking elsewhere, maintaining a truce with the Sheikhs of that dīra. The early spring finds them in a wide depression, the Qa'rah (Ga'rah), two days' journey

W. of Hīt, while in summer they come back to the Euphrates or cluster about the springs in the Haurān valley, round Māt.

The FED'ĀN range from Aleppo to Deir on both sides of the Euphrates and up the Khābūr valley almost to the Sinjar. The SIBĀ', famous breeders of camels, are seated on the middle sections of the Palmyra road. They go up towards Homs and Hamāh on the west, to Resāfah on the east, and north almost to Aleppo. If pasture is lacking on the Syrian side of the desert, they seek it in the Fed'ān country and in winter their Sheikhs come down, with those of the 'Amārāt and the Fed'ān, to Māt and the Wādi Sirhān. The 'Amārāt also cross the Euphrates on occasion, and camp with the Fed'ān along the Khābūr. The Wuld Suleimān, who roam between Teima and the Nefūd, are of Fed'ān lineage and a part of Bishr, but they stand politically outside the confederacy ; for, like their allies and neighbours the Fuqara, they pay tribute to Ibn Rashīd. They have not many camels, but own a few patches of palm-growing lands in the Kheibar Harrah, which are cultivated, on their behalf, by the Huteim.

The paramount chief of the 'AMĀRĀT is of the house of Hadhdhāl, Fahd Bey being the present sheikh. His tents number about 3,000. He is wealthy, and owns palm-gardens at Ghazāzah near Kerbela, at Baghdādīyah above Hīt, and elsewhere on the Euphrates. Although his wisdom and skill in tribal diplomacy is much vaunted, he is now an old man and not so active as Nūri of the Ruweilah ; nor does he concern himself with external politics. He has suffered imprisonment at the hand of the Turks, and cordially dislikes them, but his closest link with affairs outside the desert is his landed property on the Euphrates. He fears that if the Hindīyah escape, a part of Sir W. Willcocks's scheme of Mesopotamian irrigation, were to be put into execution, his gardens at Ghazāzah might be partly submerged, and he was inclined to blame the English for their share in that project. He could only with difficulty be reassured on this head, and shown that the better distribution of the water would be of benefit to himself in common with all other landowners.

A more striking personality is Hākim (Hāchim) ibn Muheid, who, with Hākim ibn Qeishīsh, rules over the FED'ĀN, some 3,500 tents in all. Ibn Muheid is possibly second only to Nūri esh-Sha'lān in the Anazah federation. He is a man of about 40, vain, money-loving, and strongly pan-Arab. His position on the middle reaches of the Euphrates enables him to close the riverain road to traffic whenever he pleases. Until the Baghdad railway is completed, this road is the customary, and by far the shortest, means of communication between Aleppo and Baghdad, and is now connected with Constantinople by a railway, broken only by a short interruption on the Taurus. The SIBĀ' are less numerous, some 1,800 tents all told ; their ruling families are the Beni Murshid and the Beni Hudeib (Hadeib).

Upon all the Anazah the Ottoman Government levies, so far as it is able, a sheep-tax and a camel-tax. The great sheikhs receive

Ottoman subsidies, paid with something less than regularity. The sums are not large. A man like Nūri may be given about £20 a month, paid to his agent in Damascus, who uses the money for the purchase of necessary supplies which he sends out to his chief in the desert. The Ruweilah, who raise no crops, are entirely dependent on Damascus for provisions.

The paramount Anazah sheikhs, Ibn Sha'lān, Ibn Hadhdhāl, Ibn Sumeir, and Ibn Muheid, could each of them put into the field from 1,500 to 2,000 men, armed and mounted on camels, with a small proportion of horses. The Sibā' sheikhs could muster another 1,000. The united Anazah forces would therefore number about 9,000 men, if it were conceivable that they could ever be gathered together at the same time—an exceedingly improbable contingency in regions where there are no adequate means of communication, and none but a loose tribal organization. Nor are the conditions of pasturage and water-supply, prevailing in the Hamād, suitable to large concentrations of men and animals. The total number of camels among the Ruweilah, 'Amārāt, Fed'ān, and Sibā' must be greater than in any other part of Arabia. They cannot, all told, be reckoned at much less than an average of 50 to a tent. The Wuld 'Ali are not so well supplied, but they may own about 20 to a tent. At this estimate the camel-herds of the northern Anazah would touch a very large figure—some 600,000 animals.

ANAZAH
DHANA MUSLIM

Tribe.	Sub-Tribe.	Clan.
RUWEILAH. 3,500 tents Sh. Nūri esh-Shaʻlān	*Murʻidh*, 500 tents Nūri esh-Shaʻlān el-Murʻidh	*Nāʻif* Nūri's tribe *Zeid* 'Arsān Abu Jizlah *Mijwal* *Meshūr* *Muʻabhil*
	Nuseir, 500 tents Ibn Nuseir	
	Nāsir, 300 tents Munāhi ibn Nāsir	*Radhān*
	Durʻān, 300 tents Sālim ibn Maslat	
	Furjah, 500 tents 'Asaf el-Fureij	*Khudhʻān Filitta* Ghāzi el-Fuleita
	Dughmān 'Arsān ibn Dughmi	
	Manāyiʻ Māniʻ el-Khidhr	
	Kaʻkaʻ, 800 tents Hayyān el-Kaʻkaʻ ibn Ghoshm	
	Kawākibah, 400 tents Māniʻ el-Kuweikib	*Woklān*
	Mshitta, 150 tents Ibn Musheit	
MUHALLAF. 1,500 tents Ibn Maʻjil Ibn Majīd Ibn Jandal	*Ashjaʻ*, 450 tents Qasīm ibn Maʻjil	*Mahayub* *Balaʻis*
	ʻAbdillah, 400 tents Mughāthi ibn Majīd	
	Suwalma, 400 tents Fayyādh ibn Jandal	
	Budūr, 2–300 tents Ibn Maʻjil	
WULD ʻALI. 1,800 tents Rashīd ibn Sumeir has about 1,000 tents Mohammed et-Tayyār Saʻūd ibn Milhem Shahāb el-Faqīr	*ʻAteifāt*, 200 tents Ibn Sumeir	
	Mesālikh, 300 tents Ibn Sumeir	
	Hammāmid, 300 tents Ibn Sumeir	
	Hajjāj, 300 tents Ibn Sumeir	
	Tulūh, 150 tents Ibn Sumeir	
	Saqra Ibn Sumeir	
	Mashādiqah, 500 tents Mohammed ibn Sālih et-Tayyār	*Tayyār* *Mureikhāt* *Wuleikah*
	Hasanah, 600 tents [1] Saʻūd ibn Milhem	
	Fuqara, 300 tents [1] Shahāb el-Faqīr	*Sālih* *Kuleib* *Khamākah* *Hamdān* *Mughassib* *Zuwārah* *Hujr* *ʻAināt* *Suqūrah*
	Southern Wuld ʻAli El-Aida [1]	*Aida* *Tuwalla* *Thuweibah* *Jebārah*

DHANA WĀ'IL

Tribe.	Sub-Tribe.	Clan.
'AMĀRĀT. 1. Jibāl. 3,000 tents Fahd Bey ibn Hadhdhāl	*Hablān*, 500 tents Fahd ibn Dugheim el-Hadhdhāl (nephew of Fahd Bey) *Suqūr*, 500 tents 'Āmish ibn Dhal'ān	
2. Dahāmishah. 1,200 tents Mohammed ibn Tūrki ibn Mijlād	*Suweilimāt* Jaza' ibn Mish'ān ibn Bekr *Zebīnāh* Jaza' ibn Rakkan ibn Mijlad *Salātīn* Maslat ibn Quneifidh *'Ali* Hais ibn Mijlad *Dubei'ān* Dhāri ibn Dhubyān *Jumeishāt* Shilash el-Ureiyidh *Muheināt* Mohammed abu Rūs *Ayyāsh* Dhāri *Jaleid* Hamīd ibn Quweit *Fuweizah* Haza ibn Muthib *Surumah* Burjās *Juwāsim* Bedr ibn Jasīm *Qa'bān* Mu'aidi ibn Fāhis *Suleilāt* Ibdi Huleihil Sayyah	

DHANA 'UBEID

Tribe.	Sub-Tribe.	Clan.
FED'ĀN. 3,500 tents (Dhana Kuheil), 2,000 tents Hākim ibn Muheid ibn Nawwāf Hākim ibn Qeishīsh	*Wuld* Mohammed and Mudhim ibn Tūrki *Rūs* Jedu' el-Kira *Ajajra* Zeid ibn Hureimis *Shumeilāt* Ibn Lubeidān *Sāri* Feihān ibn Qā'id *Hanātiyah* Qudeim ibn Jubeil	
(Dhana Majīd), 1,500 tents Hākim ibn Qeishīsh	*Kharasa* 'Askar abu Sunūn *Ghabīn* Sālih ibn Ghabīn *Jida'* 'Eibān ibn 'Arnān *Amāmarāt* Suleimān el-Awāmir *Mikathera* Haza' ibn Bugheiz *Auwād* Rudein ibn 'Ali *Wuld Suleimān*, 400 tents Mash'ān el-'Awājah	*'Awājah* Mash'ān el-'Awājah Ji'āferah Murta'id

SIBÀ'

Tribe.	Sub-Tribe.	Clan.

1,800 tents	*Qumussa*, 800 tents
	Githwān ibn Murshid
		Ressālin
		  Hamād ibn Aida
		Khumsān
		  Sagr ibn Museirib
		'Anūrah
		  Shinān ibn Sheteiwi
		Rahammah
		  Mohammed ibn Sa'īd

	'Ubida, 1,000 tents
	Burjās ibn Hudeib
		Musika
		  Mubārak ibn Qiladān
		Muwā'iqah
		  Fādhil ibn Muweini'
		Duwwām
		  'Uqeil el-Fiqīqi

SELQA

Tribe.	Sub-Tribe.	

800 tents
Sājir er-Rafadi
	Shimlān
	Madhyān
	  'Uqeil ibn Madhyān
	Metarafah
	  Buneyyah ibn Wuteif	

2. *The Duleim.*

The DULEIM are of mixed blood. According to their own tradition they came out of Nejd into the Syrian desert. They say that Thāmir, *jidd* of the Duleim, and his brother Jabbār, *jidd* of the Jubūr, guided by a man of the Sulubba, occupied the wells of Muheiwir in the Wādi Haurān.

They wander over the desert on either side of the Euphrates from Fellūjah almost to Ānah, sharing the Eastern Shāmīyah, the Syrian desert, with the 'Amārāt, with whom they are in close alliance. They have cultivated ground in the Euphrates valley, and rear large flocks of sheep which supply the Damascus market. Every winter the dealers come out across the Hamād, and, staying each with his own Sheikh, purchase the season's lambs, and drive them home across the grassy steppe in the spring. The Duleim are not camel-breeders; their supply is little more than sufficient for their own needs. The Shammar of the Jezīrah are their enemies, and there is constant feud between them and the Shiah tribes of 'Irāq, such as the Beni Hasan, who pasture their sheep in the desert round Kerbela. They are noted thieves, and have always given trouble on the Euphrates highroad, where they hold up every unprotected caravan. In 1910 Nāzim Pasha repressed them with a stern hand, and during his brief administration at Baghdad, travellers and merchants journeyed in security. 'Ali Suleimān, the paramount Sheikh of the Duleim, was on terms of friendship with Jemāl Pasha, who succeeded Nāzim, and he has continued to court the favour of the Ottoman Government. He owns a house and palm gardens at Rumādi, and can, therefore, be coerced into good behaviour. He is not a man of much intelligence, and prefers, to any active share in politics, a quiet life and the peaceful enjoyment of the position left him by his father, Suleimān esh-Sharqi, who was a commanding figure in the 'Irāq. Ibn Qu'ād camps mostly on the east bank of the Euphrates.

DULEIM

Tribe.	Sheikhs.	Sub-Tribes.
3,000 tents.	'Ali Suleimān esh-Sharqi.	Mahāmidah.
	Ibn Qu'ād.	Abu 'Īsa.
		Qureit.
		Abu Alwān.
		Abu Fahd.
		Abu Redmi.
		Abu 'Ubeyyah.
		Abu Nemis.

3. The Jebelīyah (or Zobeid).

The JEBELĪYAH are a loose confederation of independent tribes acknowledging no common Sheikh, but united by common interests and conditions. They are known either as the Jebelīyah or by the older name of ZOBEID (Zubeid). They inhabit the volcanic districts to east and south of the Jebel Haurān and the Leja between the Haurān hills and Damascus. They own a little cultivated land, mainly in the Ruhbah, and flocks of sheep, but few camels. They are, as a whole, poor and of bad reputation ; like all tribes on the frontier of the desert they rob and pillage their neighbours, the settled inhabitants, but they usually escape unpunished ; for the Sultan's writ fails a few miles out of Damascus, and the stony camping grounds of the Jebelīyah are difficult of approach.

The GHIYĀDH used to plunder the desert post when it travelled fortnightly across the desert to Baghdad. Since its cessation, in 1912, they have occupied the outlying Turkish station, the *qishlah* east of Dhumeir, which was abandoned by the gendarmerie. The Jebelīyah are close allies of the Druzes, of whom they stand in awe. They pasture the Druze flocks in the low-lying Safah during the winter, and in summer come up into the foothills of the Jebel Haurān. They are usually on bad terms with the Anazah, and steal the sheep and camels of the Wuld 'Ali and Hasanah whenever an opportunity offers ; and they are always at feud with the Beni Sakhr, who are the foes of the Druze.

The MASĀ'ĪD are said to be the most numerous of the Jebelīyah tribes ; the Ghiyādh are next in importance.

The 'ĪSA, though they range Jebel Durūz and are classed vulgarly as Zobeid, are of Sakhr stock and acknowledge the kinship. The tribes of Jebel Durūz and the Leja are only a part of the Zobeid. Another large group is found east of the Tigris and is Shiah. The Aqeidāt, Duleim, and Jubūr all claim Zobeid origin. All Zobeid tribes claim a common Qahtān ancestor and therefore are Ahl Qibli.

JEBELĪYAH (Zobeid)

Masā'īd.
500–600 tents. E. part of J. Durūz.
Ibn Ayyash en-Na'air and Ibn Lāfi.

Ghiyādh.
500–600 tents. In the Ruhbah and Safah.

Adhamāt. 500 tents. J. Durūz.
Sherāfāt. 500 tents. ,,
Hadiyah. 400 tents. ,,
Sulūt. 400–500 tents. In the Leja.
Hasan. 400 tents. Ibn Mutla', Ibn Khudeir. Jebel Durūz.
'Īsa. 400–500 tents. Rat'ān ibn Mad-hi. Jebel Durūz.

4. *Beni Sakhr.*

The BENI SAKHR, usually known as Ahl esh-Shimāl, ' People of the North ', are of the northern Arabian stock, and reckon their descent from Mudhar, either through 'Abs or through Tamīm. Legend gives varied accounts of their origin, one being that the eponymous founder of the tribe was a certain Sakhr who came from the east ; another that their ancestor was a child abandoned in the desert ; he was adopted by a Bedouin called Dahāmsh, who gave him his daughter in marriage, and was nicknamed Toweiq (Tuweiq) on account of a small ring which he wore round his neck ; for this reason the whole tribe is sometimes known as the Tauqah: It is also occasionally named, after the foster-father of its founder, the Dahāmshah. All traditions agree, however, that the Beni Sakhr spring from a common ancestor whose tomb is venerated at Bir Bā'ir. This cenotaph, built in an ancient caravan-station on the road from Damascus to Teima, which fell into disuse in the early Abbasid period, is covered with small votive offerings, and the great Sheikhs of the tribe, when they move down to summer quarters here, would not venture to enter the Wādi Bā'ir without sacrificing a camel in honour of the *jidd*.

The sub-tribes of the Sukhūr are all descendants of Toweiq, the genealogical tree being as follows :

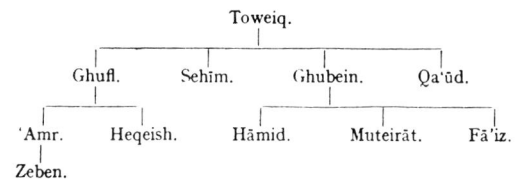

```
                         Toweiq.
         ┌───────────┬───────────┬───────────┐
        Ghufl.     Sehīm.    Ghubein.     Qa'ūd.
         │                       │
   ┌─────┴─────┐           ┌─────┴─────┐
 'Amr.      Heqeish.     Hāmid.    Muteirāt.   Fā'iz.
   │
 Zeben.
```

The territory of the Beni Sakhr stretches from the Jebel Durūz in the north to the depression of Jafar, near Ma'ān, in the south ; it is bounded on the east by the Wādi Sirhān, and on the west by the Jordan. It is a rolling country, sparsely covered with grass, and intersected by deep valleys which are rich in vegetation. In the spring the Sukhūr go down as far south as the Jebel Tubeiq, when they are on good terms with the Huweitāt ; but relations between the two tribes are usually somewhat strained, and more than one pitched battle has been fought in the rocky Tubeiq hills. In the summer the wells of Bā'ir give abundant water, and the deep valley is never bare of pasturage ; but the greater part of the tribe withdraws to the country round Mādeba and the northern Belqa, though the gradual extension of cultivation along the line of the Hejaz Railway has restricted their pasture grounds. Some of the Fā'iz sub-tribe hold cultivated lands round Jīzah, and Fawwāz, eldest son of the paramount Sheikh Telāl ibn Fā'iz, has built himself a house on the ruins of the Roman fortress of Qastal.

The completion of the Hejaz Railway has undoubtedly strengthened the hold of the Ottoman Government upon the independent tribes who range along its northern sections. The Sukhūr, for example, do not enjoy the full measure of their former autonomy; for though they are unassailable when they retire into the desert, retribution falls upon them when the summer droughts force them back into the pastures west of the railway, and their cornfields at Jīzah, Duleilah, Netel, and elsewhere along the line enable the Turks to put a further turn on the screw. Fawwāz has become an Ottoman official, being Kaimmakam of Jīzah; but he is too close to Damascus to have escaped the political movement which has its centre in the capital of Syria, and Arab Unionists speak of him as a firm adherent of the Nationalist party. He is about 35, fairly intelligent, energetic, secretive, and untrustworthy. The Sukhūr are responsible for the Hejaz Railway, as they used to be responsible for the Pilgrim Road; they guard the line from Jīzah to Kerak, and receive a yearly subsidy in return for their services.

Jaussen[1] reckons the united strength of the tribe at from 700 to 800 tents, including in this estimate the three principal tribal divisions, the AGHBEIN, the GHUFL (with the two big sub-tribes, the ZEBEN and the HEQEISH), and the KHADHĪR. To these, however, must be added the KHURSHĀN and the JUBŪR, originally constituents of the KA'ABNAH, a tribe once powerful, but now almost non-existent as a tribal unit. The Khurshān, formerly known as the Hammād, under their Sheikh Hadīthah, are politically inseparable from the Beni Sakhr, though a wholly different tribe-mark bears witness to their different origin. They are a warlike people, breeders of horses and camels; their pasture grounds are near the Jebel Haurān. The Jubūr are sheep owners, and only half-nomadic.

The SALEITAH, with a total of about 100 tents, are clients of the Sukhūr and live among them. The JAHAWASHAH, though they are reckoned as a clan of the Fā'iz, are not of Beni Sakhr stock. They are a fraction of the USEIDAH, who, after a bloody quarrel, abandoned the Belqa, and took refuge with the Fā'iz. They do not intermarry with the Sukhūr, though in all other respects they form part of the tribe. On the other hand, the small but valiant tribe of the SERDĪYAH, an offshoot of the Sukhūr, are politically independent of the latter, and not infrequently at feud with them. They inhabit the eastern edge of the volcanic country to the east of the Jebel Haurān, and owe their position in the desert to the reputation of their late paramount Sheikh, Mit'ab el-Qanj, said to have been the strongest of living men. His son Ghālib, the present Sheikh, is about 30, not so noted a raider as Mit'ab, less ambitious than his father, and of mediocre intelligence. He is in close touch with Damascus, and counted by the younger Nationalist politicians as a friend and ally; but he is not sufficiently powerful to dispense with any protection which he can obtain from the Ottoman Government, and in 1911 he successfully invoked the aid of Sāmi Pasha against his hereditary foes, the Ruweilah.

The Beni Sakhr are almost always at war with the Anazah con-

[1] *Coutumes des Arabes au Pays de Moab*, p. 400.

federation on their east frontier; with the Huweitāt their relations are doubtful, with a general tendency to hostility, and the same applies to their north-western neighbours, the 'Adwān. The Druzes to the north are their sworn enemies, and the Zobeid confederation (the Jebelīyah), who roam the slopes of the Jebel Haurān, usually throw in their lot with the Druzes against the Sukhūr, though they are on fairly good terms with the Serdīyah. The cultivators from Mādeba and Salt, mainly Christians, who own most of the ploughed lands on the Hejaz Railway, are obliged to maintain friendly relations with the Beni Sakhr, since the Ottoman Government offers them little or no protection. They keep open house for the tribesmen, who profit largely by their hospitality, and hold them in commensurate esteem. Such families as the Ibn Jābir and the Bisharra are much respected, and enjoy a considerable influence in the desert. The cultivated land does not extend far beyond the railway, east of which the soil is too thin and the rainfall too scanty for successful corn-growing.

The latest information is, that after the outbreak of war between Great Britain and Turkey in the winter of 1914, when the attack on the Canal was developing, the Beni Sakhr, fearing that the Ottoman Government would seize their camels for transport purposes, withdrew across the Sirhān. Having been for the past year at peace with the Ruweilah, they took refuge in their country. They were last heard of between 'Amūd and Māt, in the Wadyān district, and had even pushed as far east as the 'Amārāt pastures.

The Sukhūr are not among the great camel-owning tribes, but their herds can scarcely amount to less than some 12,000 to 15,000 head.

5. *The Humeidah.*

The dīra of the HUMEIDAH lies round Dhibān. It is bounded on the south-west by Khirbat es-Sarfa and the Wādi Beni Hammād; on the west by the Dead Sea; on the north by the Zerqa valley, Mareijimah and Duleilah, and on the east by Umm Shureif, 'Arā'ir, and the Wādi Mojib. It extends, therefore, from 7 miles north of Kerak to 4 miles south of Mādeba, a distance of about 28 miles, and is about 17 miles from west to east. The tribe, which had an evil reputation for unruliness and violence, has, since the occupation of Kerak by the Ottoman Government some twenty years ago, been reduced to complete submission and almost ruined by exactions. It pays £T3,000 in taxes. The Mudir of Wālah was specially appointed to take charge of the Humeidah. They number about 700 tents, and claim descent from a common ancestor called Fādhil, who came into the Dead Sea region with Sakhr, the *jidd* of the Sukhūr. For this reason they recognize a distant kinship between themselves and the Beni Sakhr. They are sheep-breeders, and grow crops in the fertile Kūrah district. Some of the Beni Tarīf are to be found at

BENI SAKHR

Tribe.	Sub-Tribe.	Clan.	Military Value.		
			Horsemen.	Camelriders.	Armed men.
BENI SAKHR. Telāl ibn Fā'iz (Not recognized by all the clans as paramount.)	Aghbein	Fā'iz Telāl	90	150	
		Hāmid Ibn Quftān	95	20	
		Jahawashah 'Ajāj	7		180
		Dahāmshah	4		40
		Muteirāt Fanhūr	20		70
700–800 tents	Ghufl Zeben Falāh	'Athmān Shaubash			
		'Abd el-Qādir Hamd ibn Qam-'ān	110	200	
	Heqeish	Zeidān Fahad ez-Zeidān Beshīr			
		'Aqīlah ibn 'Eitān Sālim Fahhād ibn Ma-'eishah Mōr	80	250	
	Khadhir Qablān ibn Dakhthāni	Clans and numbers not known			
(Ka'abnah) 120 tents	Khurshān, 120 tents Hadīthah el-Khureishah		60		300
320 tents	Jubūr, 320 tents Sālim ibn Izheir Fureij	Fureij A'qamah Dīkah Ghayālin			
1,140–1,240 tents			466	620	590
	Serdīyah, 150 tents Ghālib ibn Mit-'ab el-Qanj		40		250
SALEITAH. 100 tents	Rusheid Ghathuyān Abu er-Rujeilah Jau'id	Radhāya (at Lejjūn and Umm er-Rusās)			

Kerak, and there are about 30 houses of Humeidah at Buseirah, east of Tāfilah, under Sheikh Sālim ibn Masyūghah.

HUMEIDAH

Tribe.	Sub-Tribe.	Clan.
ABU RUHEIHAH. 170 tents	Suweilim, at El-Kūrah (Dhibān)	Wansah Su'ādah Hawāwshah Sarārhah Hawātimah
BENI TARĪF. 300 tents	Mansūr, at Zeqeibah, W. of Shihān	Ruwāhanah Dhurab'ah Heisah Shihānbah Falāhāt Shuqūr Hamādin
ABU BUREIZ. 230 tents	Mohammed, at Mekāwir, NW. of Dhibān	Diyārnah Jawafi'i Qubeilāt Faqaha Rubūtah Hurūt Tawālibah Qa'aidah Muteilah Hāshim

B. TRIBES OF THE CENTRAL WEST

1. *The Huweitāt.*

The HUWEITĀT are a stout and warlike tribe whose country extends from near Teima in the south to Kerak in the north, and on the east to the Nefūd and the Wādi Sirhān. On the west it is scattered down the Gulf of Akaba and Midian coast, and through Sinai into Egypt. Huweitāt are nomads in the desert north-east of Cairo, and settled as cultivators round Tanta. The Huweitāt of Akaba, Sinai, and Egypt have no political link with the Sheikhs whose head-quarters are at or near Ma'ān; but they recognize certain claims of kinship, and if a Huweiti of the Tawāyah or Beni Jāzi got into difficulties with the Ottoman Government, he would seek refuge, if he could escape, in Sinai or in Egypt. The Huweitāt have, however, an exceptionally bad name for treachery. They are divided among themselves, and do not respect their own blood-ties. One clan will set upon a caravan under the convoy of a *rafīq* of another clan, shoot the *rafīq*, and rob and murder the merchants.

On the Syrian side the leading sub-tribe is the BENI JĀZI, and 'Arār ibn Jāzi is nominally the paramount Sheikh; but he is not recognized by the ABU TAYY, and the two groups are frequently at feud. The Tayy are an off-shoot of the Jāzi, and owe their position to the restless energy of their Sheikhs. The late chief, 'Audah, was one of the most famous raiders of his time, and did not hesitate to carry his expeditions across the Hamād to the Euphrates, where he raided Ibn Hadhdhāl of the

'Amārāt. On one occasion, when he was out against the Sibā', he pushed almost as far north as Aleppo.

The Huweitāt are on close terms of friendship with the Beni 'Atīyah, and are at liberty to camp through all the 'Atīyah country. The Sheikh Ahmed ibn Tuqeiqah occupies the Red Sea coast between Muweilah and Dhaba, with his head-quarters at Dhaba. They are at war with the Shammar, except the clan of the Rammāl, which is connected by marriage with the Tayy; and they are usually on bad terms with the Wuld Suleimān and the Fuqara. With the Sukhūr relations are always delicate, and the two tribes often break into sharp conflict. In 1914 the jealousy between Ibn Jāzi and Abu Tayy led to continuous raids between the sub-tribes. Ibn Jāzi took refuge with the Sukhūr, and the Tayy with the Ruweilah. But the outbreak of war between Great Britain and Turkey filled the tribes with a common fear that their camels might be requisitioned by the Ottoman Government for transport purposes; the Huweitāt made up their differences, and together with the Sukhūr retired east into the Anazah dīra, where the Government could not reach them. They are charged with the protection of the Hejaz Railway from Kerak to Ma'ān, and receive a yearly subsidy. Since Sāmi Pasha's expedition into the desert in 1910, they have regarded Ottoman authority with a certain amount of respect. 'Audah's cousin, Mohammed abu Tayy, was imprisoned for several months in Damascus, and upon his release was made responsible for the payment of the sheep- and camel-tax of his tribe—a lucrative position which he would be unwilling to forfeit.

In the spring, the Tayy pasture over the north and east of the Jebel Tubeiq; the Jāzi camp to the south and south-west. In the summer the tribe draws in to Ma'ān, where it owns a little cultivation, and to Jafar, a depression east of Ma'ān. Ma'ān is the northern limit of the sandstone desert. Here the grassy downs of the Beni Sakhr country give place to forbidding leagues of rock weathered into fantastic shapes and diversified by sand-hills. Wells are few; nevertheless, in the sandstone bottoms there is a sufficiency of small shrubs and succulent weeds after the scanty rain.

The Huweitāt are not among the great camel-owners; probably the whole of the Syrian branch has not more than 5,000 to 8,000 animals.

The Huweitāt claim to be Ashrāf, i. e. descendants of the prophet through his daughter Fātimah; but it has been conjectured that they have a history which is ethnologically of far greater interest. They may be the descendants of the Nabataeans, who held the caravan road to Yemen—the old spice road—and had their capital at Petra, a few hours west of Ma'ān.

Tribe.	Sub-Tribe.	Sheikh.
HUWEITĀT. 400 tents.	Beni Jāzi, 100 tents.	'Arār ibn Jāzi.
'Arār ibn Jāzi.	Dhiyābāt, 15 tents.	Sālim ibn Dhi'āb.
	Tawāyah, 150 tents.	
	Demāni, 40 tents.	Sālim ibn 'Aleyān.
	Rukeibāt, 80 tents.	Sālim abu Rukeib.
HUWEITĀT OF AKABA.	'Amrān.	
Hasan ibn Jād.	'Alawīn.	Hasan ibn Jād.
HUWEITĀT OF SINAI.	(Sarei'īn.	
1,200 camels.	(Ghanamīn.	Sa'd abu Nār.
	Dubūr.	Suweilim abu Dhuhūr.

2. Beni 'Atīyah.

The BENI 'ATĪYAH are an old tribe closely akin to the Anazah. They claim descent from Ma'z, who is said to have been brother of 'Anz, the ancestor of the Anazah. A part of the tribe in the Hisma plain, east of Akaba, is known as the Ma'zi. Some authorities state that the 'Atīyah tribe was the origin of the Huweitāt, the Heiwāt, the Terabīn, Ma'zi, and Tiyāhah. Whether or no this be the true explanation of the relation between the 'Atīyah and the Huweitāt, it is certain that their connexion is exceedingly close. The two tribes camp in each other's country, and aid each other against common enemies.

The 'Atīyah occupy the northern half of the 'Aweiridh Harrah, and are separated from the Mawāhib Harrah by the hollow plain of the Jau, through which there is a road from Wejh to Tebūk. The Jau is reckoned to be the dividing line between the Ahl esh-Shamāl and the Ahl Qibli, the northern and the southern Arabs. The 'Atīyah are held responsible for the Hejaz line from Ma'ān to Dār el-Hamra. The coast from Sheikh 'Antar up to the Gulf of Akaba is in their hands (or those of the Huweitāt, their allies), as well as the high barren hills between the Harrah and the sea. Their rugged mountain district is unsuitable for camel-breeding. Of the sub-tribes, the SIDENYĪN and the KHUTHEIRAH inhabit the 'Aweiridh Harrah, the Sidenyīn being at the northern end with the SUBŪT to the west of them. The 'UQEILĀT (Ageylat) used to be carriers of goods between Ma'ān and Tebūk, but the railway must have taken some of their trade.

The 'Atīyah are stout in arms. Their foes are the Shammar and the allies of Shammar, the Fuqara and Wuld Suleimān. With the Fuqara, the 'Atīyah maintain an inextinguishable feud. They raid the Harb and the central clans of the Huteim.

Tribe.	Sub-Tribe.
BENI 'ATĪYAH.	Robilāt.
Mohammed ibn 'Atīyah.	'Uqeilāt.
	Sidenyīn.
	Khutheirah.
	Subūt.

3, 4, 5. *The Billi, Mawāhib, and Juheinah.*

The plain of the Jau running through the 'Aweiridh Harrah is counted the frontier between the Ahl esh-Shimāl and the Ahl Qibli. To the north lie the B. Atīyah; to the south the Mawāhib, who, though they are of Anazah descent, being a tribe of the Sibā', are Billi by adoption. The Billi and their southern neighbours, the Juheinah, are both of the Himyar stock, and therefore rightly described as Ahl Qibli. The MAWĀHIB (Moahib) inhabit the southern part of the 'Aweiridh, a rugged mass of volcanic rock upon a platform of sandstone. They are sheep-breeders, and are reduced to small numbers, though they were once powerful enough to drive the Beni Sakhr from the 'Aweiridh. Scattered clans are to be found among their kinsmen, the Sibā', and with the Beni Sakhr in the Belqa. There is besides an ancient colony of Mawāhib husbandmen, keepers of cattle, in the Hasa. Their dīra marches with the Hejaz line from a little above El-Akhdhar to Medā'in Sālih; in the west they go down to the country of the Sehāmah, a clan of the Billi, and in summer the Sehāmah come up with their flocks into the harrah.

The BILLI (Bali) and the JUHEINAH (Jeheina), both probably settled from very ancient times in the Tihāmah or coast region, extend from Na'mān Island to south of Yambo'. Both are charged with the protection of sections of the Hejaz Railway, and both are part cultivators and part Bedouins. The Billi are rice-carriers to the Arabs for the Wejh merchants and Turkish subjects, as are also the Juheinah, though neither are subject to much control. They are at feud with the Fuqara and the Wuld Suleimān, and the Juheinah are always at enmity with the Harb.

Tribe.	Sub-Tribe.	Clan.
BILLI. 8,000 souls.		
Suleimān Afnān		
Rufādah of Wejh.		
I. KHUZĀM.	*Wabsah*, 2,000 souls.	Āl Zartah.
	Faraj el-Qireyid.	Āl Iqasah.
		Sibut.
	Fu'ādhla, 360 souls.	
	Mahfuz el-Fadhli.	
	Quweyyīn, 300 souls.	
	Mohammed ibn Quwyān.	
	Jothul, 400 souls.	
	Sālim el-Jithli.	
	Sara'btah, 300 souls.	
	Salim es-Sireibti.	
	Āl Buweināt, 300 souls.	
	'Audah el-Buweini.	
	Āl Asabsīn, 1,000 souls.	
	Suleimān ibn Rufādah.	
II. MUKHALAD.	*Āl Maqlah*, 1,000 souls.	Judeyyīn.
	Fiheimān ibn Rufādah.	Dhawi Masūd.
		Āl 'Uweidhah.
		'Abeid.
		Dhawi Mayūf.
		Sawāmah.
		Āl Suleimān.
	Āl Sehāmah, 1,000 souls.	Āl Sālim.
	Dhubeyyān ibn Ruweihil.	Āl Zābin.
		Āl Hurūf.
	Āl Wohashah, 300 souls.	Ma'riyīn.
		Dhawi Sa'īd.
		Āl Ni'eirāt.
	Rumūth, 2,000 souls.	Rushūd.
	Mūsa Hathar.	Ziwānah.
		Quweyyīn.
		Āl Athamein.
	Minqarah, 200 souls.	
	Suleimān ibn Salmān.	

(The above scheme is imperfect, especially in the enumeration of clans. For larger units it may be regarded as fairly complete.)

Tribe.	Sub-Tribe.	Clan.
MAWĀHIB. 400 souls.	Serāhīn.	
	Dihibian.	
	Rahyat.	
	Manāsir.	

Tribe.	Sub-Tribe.	Clan.
JUHEINAH. 18,300 souls.		
I. BENI MĀLIK. Mohammed 'Ali ibn Bedeiwi, of Yambo'.	Erwa, 2,500 souls. Mu'azzi ibn Mufarrih el-Huweikin.	Shalakba, Mesād, Āl Jirājirah, Sawalha, Buweinat, Jammāli, Shawafi, Akhadra.
	Beni Kelb, 600 souls. 'Awad ibn Mu'azzi.	Khidarah, Sukkān, Za'i 'Areifān.
	Zeidah, 200 souls. Mufdi ibn Hamid.	'Akab, Ghaladin, Meseyyer.
	Qodhah, 200 souls. Dākhilullah el-Qādhi.	Dhawi Mesed, Murrah, Reyaha.
	Hashakla, 100 souls. Salim el-Hashkali.	
	Al Hudbān, 100 souls.	Āl Yedeyāt, Āl Abu Sirr.
	Al Mu'albah, 600 souls. Weled 'A'idh ibn 'Awad.	Khleimi (in mountains).
	Raghabān, 100 souls. Sa'id ibn Suleyah.	
	Masha'la, 200 souls. Awamra, 300 souls. Salim ibn 'Abdallah.	Mubārik, Wasla, Rayāt. Alāt, Tawalin.
	Sayadah, 150 souls.	Dhawi Misfer, Kheshamān, Hamūd.
	Al Huseināt, 200 souls.	Dhawi Thābit, Telāl; Dhawi Nasir, Dhawi Hasan.
	Rifa'i (Arfu'a), 500 souls.	Mashahiza, Hasauna, Halahla, Āl Shuweishāt, Aghrika, Henwa, Nawahya, Dhawi Rashdān, Dhawi Salmi, Ruj, Āl Zuweida, Wahbān.
	Encināt, 200 souls. Burghāsh ibn Mohammed.	
	Al Dibesah, 200 souls. Mureibid.	
	Al Kitinah, 300 souls. Sanafa, 100 souls. 'Ābid ibn Salim.	Dhawi Meshbah.
	Mankufa, 200 souls.	'Anūf.
	The following are villagers (Āl Hadhar):	
	1. ASHRĀF. Jābir el-Ayashi.	
	Ayashiyah, 300 souls. Jābir el-Ayashi.	Dhawi 'Ali, Dhawi Mohammed, Dhawi Sanād, Dhawi Dheifullah, Dhawi Kanan, Dhawi 'Abd el-Kerim.
	Jibsān, 150 souls. Ibn Jaudah Hamdān.	
	Āl Nighram, 100 souls. Raji ibn Beneyah.	
	Shalabin, 150 souls. Faraj el-Fidāni.	
	Horibāt, 100 souls. Mohammed ibn 'Abdullah.	
	Thaqafa, 300 souls.	Dhawi 'Amr, Dhawi Suleimān, Ma'tqa, Fqaha, Harashin, Yadeyāb, Sanadra.
	2. NON-ASHRĀF. Mohammed ibn Jibārah es-Sarāsiri.	
	Sarāsirah, 300 souls. Mohammed ibn Jibarah.	Dhawi Misfir, Dhawi Ghanim, Dhawi 'Atiyah, Dhawi Fuseil, Dhawi 'Awad, Dhawi Muhsin, Dhawi Sa'd, Shahabin.

Tribe.	Sub-Tribe.	Clan.
BENI MĀLIK (contd.)	Shatariyah, 200 souls. Ahmed ibn Hamād. Masā'wiyah, 400 souls. Hasan ibn Fāris.	
	The following are Beduins under Mohammed 'Ali ibn Bedeiwi:	
	Seyyādilah, 300 souls. Hamid Abu Deij.	Dhawi 'Ali, Yata'ma, Dhakah, Hanetshah, Zuweidah, Mahameid (Ashrāf), Asaweidah, Beit el-Faqih, Rawāshidah.
	Dhawi Hajar, 300 souls. Mohammed 'Ali ibn Bedeiwi	Dhawi Bedeiwi, Dhawi 'Abdullah, Dhawi 'Abd el-Moneim, Dhawi 'Obeidullah, Dhawi Husein, Dhawi Nāsir, Darābīyah, Dhawi 'Abd el-Kerim, Kaneira, Dhawi Mohammed, Dhawi Tūrki, Dhawi 'Abd el-Mālik.
	Dhawi Hazza, 250 souls. Sherif 'Abdullah ibn Thurai.	Hawāshimah, Matahiah, Dhawi Gheitk, Dhawi 'Abdullah, Dhawi Sanād, Dhawi Koleib.
II. BENI MŪSA. Sa'd ibn Ghaneim of Umlejh.	Āl Simirah, 1,000 souls. 'Abdullah ibn Feyyādh.	Maradsah, Dhurma'n, Āl Awinān, Dhawi Salim, Dhawi 'Atiyah, Shariqah, Masawinah.
	Hibeidh, 500 souls.	Masaheir, Dawakhah, Tibisah, Nawalāt, Āl Himid, Āl Soba't.
	Sinā'n, 600 souls. 'Audah Dhamīn.	Ru'ūs el-Bil, Jina'ah, Barayerah, Raharishah, Dhawi Rashud, Dhawi Rufeyah.
	Fuaceidah, 600 souls.	Linah, Dhawi Mu'īn, Nawaflah, Dhawi Shawiyah, 'Urūdh, Ridanah, Raheifah, Zurra, Thibeitāt, Marzeiq.
	'Alawīn, 600 souls.	Jowadāt, Mitarah, Fawazīyah, Dhawi 'Omar, Hala'bīn, 'Ateifāt, Ridfān.
	Āl Himidah, 600 souls. Rashīd ibn Salāmah.	Sa'dīn, Shadawīn, Jabarīn, Rishadah, Nizān, Āl Ghireibāt, Āl Feheidāt, Āl Aweishah.
	Ela'āt, 200 souls. Muslim el-Bereiri. Ghaneim, 100 souls. Mohammed ibn Sālih. Mahasna, 100 souls. Sa'īd ibn Ayab. Mehadi, 50 souls. Dhāri ibn Muslim. Zorfān, 250 souls. Sa'd ibn Fahd.	Tiheilāt, Dhawi Mohammed, Maseibah, Dhawi Hamdān. Alafein, Enteyitah. Mimasah, Aweishah, Shibeirīn.
	Āl Ruqbān, 30 souls. 'Ā'idh ibn Eid er-Ruqbah. Āl Mereiwanyim, 60 souls. Misid Seidi. Dhawi Itqān, 300 souls. Faraj el-Kabeidi. Dhawi Dahthūm, 100 souls. Mufdi ibn Aqeil. Matar, 200 souls. 'Ā'idh ibn Hammād.	Mirāshid, Āl Komalat, Dhawi Misfir, Dhawi Lati, Āl Katabein, Dhawi Amār, Āl Mileihat.

Tribe.	Sub-Tribe.	Clan.
BENI MŪSA (contd.):	Baraghthah, 300 souls.	
	Bureighith el-Marwāni.	
	Heleitah, 60 souls.	
	Jābir el-Heleiti.	
	Al Ghinamah, 500 souls.	Barākīn, Āl Misahah, Āl Hirarah, 'Awadāt, Āl Siqarah, Shafiyah, Dhawi Hamūd.
	Muflih ibn 'Atīyah.	
	Nazzah, 300 souls.	Dhameikhah, Atamīn, Malafīyah, Āl Wadhareyyah, Zameid, Āl Fuzūr.
	Al Muhaya, 300 souls.	Nejeimāt, Hujūr, Qaseirah, Mashahnah.
	'Ā'idh abu Jidda.	
	Matafein, 150 souls.	Zawahrah, Nihahāt.
	Sālih ibn Nuweiji.	
	Natafein, 150 souls.	
	Khuneifidh el-Natifi.	
	Dhobyān, 1,500 souls.	Muslih, Āl Moheimat, Shabah, Āl Khiyatah, Āl Ghirbān, Āl Mudajnāt, Al Sihābah, Āl 'Ateifāt, Āl Najada', Āl Tilyān.
	Beni Ibrāhīm, 300 souls.	Dhawi Hureibi, Āl Seilah, Beit el-Faqīh, Āl Halātik, Āl Qayitah, Āl Siqāt, Āl Bathaliyah.
	'Abd er-Rahmān ibn 'Awad	
	Āl Muwal, 300 souls.	Shuharah, Dhawi Ahmed, Dhawi 'Ā'idhah, Safarīn, Āl 'Alawīnah, Āl Zuheirāt, Dhawi Zāhir, Dhawi Rizk, Āl Kireishāt, Dhawi Zimeyid, Dhawi Husein.
	Mutlaq ibn Matlūq.	

6. *The Harb.*

The HARB are Ahl esh-Shimāl. They are a powerful and warlike tribe of the Hejaz and of Nejd, occupying the coast of the Red Sea from Yambo' to near Qunfudah (with a break from near Jiddah to south of Līth), the mountain country between Medina and Mecca, and the desert to the north-east up to Jebel Abānāt. Inland, their country extends just across the Wādi er-Rummah. On the south they push down to the Sha'īb el-'Useibiyāt and the Qishb Harrah, i. e. the vicinity of the caravan road from Boreidah to Mecca, if the Ateibah are in their southern pastures; but this country is really the dīra of the latter.

In the days of the Emir Mohammed of Hā'il, the eastern Harb paid tribute to the Rashīd; but they are now independent. The clans in the Hejaz come under the influence of the Sherif, though they pay him tribute only when it suits them. They are responsible for the safety of the southernmost section of the Hejaz Railway, but their connexion with the pilgrim traffic is chiefly of a less respectable kind; for they rob caravans on the Mecca road, kill and plunder stragglers, and extort money at every opportunity. The arrangement and constitution of the Harb are less certainly ascertained than those of any other of the greater Arabian tribes. The majority of the best authorities (e. g. among the older ones, Burton and Doughty) recognize only two main sections, BENI SALIM and MASRŪH, and include under the latter the BENI 'AMR

('AMŪR), the 'AUF, and the ZOBEID, of all which are ranked by some other authorities as independent sections. While, therefore, the BENI SĀLIM, with its principal sub-sections, can be set out systematically with fair assurance, the scheme of all the rest, as given below, must be understood to be provisional, and, in any case, not complete as regards sub-sections. Of these latter only those are given about whose existence and connexion with larger sections two or three good authorities agree.

The Hejaz Harb include all the BENI SĀLIM and also the 'AUF and ZOBEID sub-sections of the MASRŪH. These are cultivators, fishermen, and carriers for the greater part, but contain also many nomads, e. g. the bulk of the SUBH sub-section of the BENI SĀLIM and several 'AUF clans, notorious for their predatory instincts and life. The ZOBEID, as a whole, are settled along the coast from near Yambo' down to Serūm, their centre being at Rābugh, and there is also an Asiri section south of Līth. The Harb of NW. Nejd are mainly the BENI 'AMR whose principal sheikhs live outside Hejaz. They own, however, most of the date gardens east of Medina; one of the sub-sections, the Beni 'Ali (a turbulent lot of Shiahs), cultivates those nearest to Qubbah in the 'Awali plains.

HARB, about 200,000 souls

Section.	Sub-Tribe.	Clan.
I. BENI SĀLIM (or *Beni Meimūn*).	*Ahamda.*	*Hadari.*
	Khalīl ibn Sa'd.	
	Khalaf ibn Sa'd.	
	Hasan Nāsir ibn Dhi'āb.	
	Hawāzim.	
	Mohammed el-Jarf.	
	Subh.	
	'Abd el-Muhsin Subhi.	
	Mahāmid (Beni Mohammed).	
	Mihmad ibn Miyala.	
	Rahalah.	
	'Awad Salīmi.	
	Temām (Tamīm)	
	'Useidi (or *Sa'adīn*).	*Ruweithah.*
	Ahmed el-'Useidi.	Hāmid ibn Nāfi'.
	Mohammed el-'Useidi.	
	Muzeināt.	
	Burjīs el-Mizeini.	
	Dhuwāhir.	
	Mansūr ibn 'Abbās.	
	Nāsir ibn 'Abbās.	
	Huwāfah.	
	Sa'd el-Huweifi.	
II. MASRŪH.	1. *Beni 'Amr.*	*'Abidah.*
	Sheikh Sa'd ibn 'Arubeij of Modhiq.	Ibrāhīm.
		Humrān
		Sa'd ibn 'Arubeij.
		Beni Jābir.
		Mohammed ibn Hamid.
		Jahm (Shiah).
		Sa'd ibn 'Arubeij.
		Bishr.
		Sa'd ibn 'Arubeij.
		Beni 'Arubeij.
		Sa'd ibn 'Arubeij.

HARB—continued

Section.	Sub-Tribe.	Clan.
MASRŪH (contd.).	Beni 'Amr (contd.).	Bedarin.
		Mufadhdhal el-Bedrāni (?).
		Bilādiyah.
		Tūrki el-Bilādi.
		Shawahlah.
		'Abd el-'Aziz Tayyar.
		Beidān.
		Nahidh ibn Mūjid (?).
		Jarājirah.
		'Utūr.
	2. 'Auf.	Sahliyah.
	Sheikh Furn of Suweir-	Munawwar ibn Mūjid.
	qīyah.	Mohammed ibn Mūjid.
		Mohammed ibn Kasam.
		Sawad.
		Kanādirah.
		Beni 'Ali (Shiah).
		'Ali ibn 'Abdullah.
		Firidah.
		Sifrān.
		Mutlaq el-Hiseyīn.
		Lehābah.
		Mohammed ibn Hamād.
		Sihāf.
		Husein ibn Fuzān.
		U'sum.
		'Abd el-Muhsin ibn Assīm.
	3. Zobeid.	Juhadhlah.
	Husein ibn Mubeirik of	Mohammed, ibn 'Ārif
	Rābugh.	'Areifān.
		Jidān.
		Mohammed abu Sheneif.
		Jarājirah.
		Hamid ibn Dukheil.
		Mughāribah.
		'Obeidullah ibn Suheifi.
		Sa'āyadah.
		Ibn 'Asm.

7. *The Ateibah.*

The ATEIBAH ('Uteibah) are the most powerful tribe in Central Arabia, strong in arms and great camel-breeders. Among all the nomads they are second in importance only to the Anazah. They occupy the eastern side of the Hejaz with the volcanic harrahs between the Hajj road and the Central Arabian Steppes. Their pasturages run east to Qasīm and Woshm, and south to the dīras of the Qahtān, of the Buqūm and Shalāwah, and of the Sebei'. This country abounds in wells; it has a regular if small rainfall in winter, and is not wholly dry in early autumn, when it receives the end of the monsoon rains. It supports large herds of sheep and camels, and in places the grass grows so richly that the Bedouins gather a hay-crop; everywhere there is a low growth of acacias, and game is plentiful. The clans in the Hejaz, such as the Helissah, Meraukhah, Kurzān, Sebbahah, Marāshidah, and Semarrah, are small in numbers and breed sheep only. There is a little cultivation in the harrahs, no more than palm-groves and small Ateibah villages.

The two chief sections of the tribe are the RŪQAH and the BERQAH. The Rūqah are chiefly in the Hejaz, the Berqah in the eastern desert. But there are also three less important sections, ranging in the west and south of the Ateibah country. The tribe has no one Paramount Chief. Its sub-sections are not well known, and the scheme below must be regarded as provisional and, probably, incomplete. The whole tribe acknowledges now the authority of the Emir of Mecca ; but Ibn Sa'ūd of Riyādh puts in from time to time a claim to the allegiance of the Berqah section, which used to acknowledge him, more or less. He has not forgiven them for harbouring the rebel Aulād Sa'ūd in 1911 and, unless restrained by agreement with or fear of, the Emir of Mecca, he is always apt to raid them, as he did in 1911 and 1912. They, for their part, sometimes raid into his province of Woshm, and interfere with Qasīm. The control of them and the right of taxing them form the chief bone of contention between Riyādh and Mecca. The whole tribe is now well armed, and it supplied about 18,000 men to the Meccan army in 1916 ; the difficulty of making these and Harb tribesmen work together proved serious.

The Ateibah are foes of the Harb, than whom they are more powerful ; they are generally on good terms with the two small tribes on their southern frontier, the Buqūm and Shalāwah, and at feud with the Qahtān.

THE ATEIBAH

Section.	Sub-Tribe.	Section.	Sub-Tribe.
1. *Rūqah* (Ri-	*Hufwa*	*Berqah* (contd.):	*Thiyābah*
wāqah)	Jalā'an		Munir ibn Hunud
Feihān ibn	*Marāshida*		*Al Misīn*
Muheyya	Abu Hisheib		Es-Silayah
	Dhawi Breish		*Fizrā'an*
	Mu'eisil		Feihān ibn Munir
	Dharabha		*Naweirah*
	Ibn Asan		Ja'id ibn Naweir
	Mazahma		*Dhawi 'Omar*
	Sheri'ah el-Fu'ādi		Dheifullah
	Dhawi 'Atīyah		*Beni Khawātir*
	Thu'eil el-Kharrās		'Atīq
	Silāsah		*Al Jaramīn*
	Hamud ibn Wejh el-		Ja'id ibn Mu'āyid
	Qeia		*Dhawi Sinā'n*
	Qureish		Sa'id ibn Badhān
	Ahmed abu Sukr		*Fuqaha*
	Mahadlah		Mu'āyir
	Nejm ibn Shuleiwikh		*Warqān*
	Sihārah		Suleyyib ibn Halzhaq
	Ibn Zeid		*Hawā'ma*
	Maghāyirah		Nafil
	Ibn Beyyīn		*Dhawi Suleimān*
	Huteim		Fitina ibn Dhayan
	Ghā'ib el-Khiwi		*Farā'na*
	Hufa'ah		Mithāyib ibn Jināyih
	Sa'id ibn Tauyid		*Al Sighāyin*
	Al Himrān		Maddad
	Abu Sinūn		*Al Qumeishāt*
2. *Berqah*	*Dawāsir*		Mishari
Ibn Himeyid	Filhān		*Al Jabārin*
	Jidān		Khilāyif ibn Hadaf
	Ghazi ibn Ghureibah		

ATEIBAH—continued

Section.	Sub-Tribe.	Section.	Sub-Tribe.
Berqah (contd.) :	Hiddāf	'Abūd (contd.) :	Al Ashashamah
	Khilāyif ibn Hadaf		Ibn Hamid
	Mahāmid		Dihasah
	Mu'āyid abu Kilāb		Mohammed ibn Mahdi
	Dhafārin		Hitamah
	Ibn Zahrān		Ibrāhīm ibn Ghad
	Hijizah	4. Dara'īn	Muheyya
	Ba'dah ibn Iteiq	Hamūd ibn	Jarāfin
	K'hanāfirah	Darān	Ibn Musāfir
	'Abdullah ibn Fihrān		Dhawi Khalifah
	Al Khimād		Ibn Samhān
	Falih el-Mizmil		Dhawi 'Abdullah
	Al Hawāranah		Arhab
	Milhāyib ibn Mihyi	5. Nafārin	Jidah
	Mafaleit	Sultān ibn	Hamūd
	Mitib ibn Soyib	Sanhut	Nikhashah
3. 'Abūd	Jibarah		Ibn Hathlul
	Sultān ibn 'Abūd		Nifa
	Al Khalad		Ibn Hijnah
	Sāri		
	Dawanīyah		
	Abu Raqabah		

8. *Minor Tribes of Southern Hejaz.*

Several small independent tribes share the south part of Hejaz with the two greater tribes, Harb and Ateibah, of which the first lies along the coast, the second inland from Tā'if. They are all, in part, settled or half-settled, and almost all acknowledge the authority of the Sherif.

(*a*) The HUDHEIL (Hatheil) are divided into two main sections, a northerly and a southerly. The first ranges east and south of Mecca, and especially along the road between that city and Tā'if, the second beyond Tā'if. No. I is said to have seven clans: Mutārafah (Wādi Fātimah), Mas'ūd (Ri' es-Seil), Sowahar (Rī' es-Seil), B. 'Amr, Met'ān (from Mecca to Jiddah), Lahiyān (east of Mecca), Janābir (El-Kōr). No. II has eight clans: Garhīyah, Marzūqīyah, Sarwāni, Kabkabi, B. Fahm, Nadwīyah, Dadīyah, and 'Abdīyah.

(*b*) BENI FAHAM, a small tribe living in Wādi Waghar, to the east of the Juhadlah and between them and the Beni Thaqīf. They are entirely nomadic and are noted for their skill in tracking. They are friendly with the Beni Thaqīf and Juhadlah, and are still faithful to Sherif 'Ali, the deposed Emir of Mecca. The Chief Sheikh is Ismā'īl ibn Dahyān. They number about 1,000 men. Related to the Qoreish.

(*c*) The JUHADLAH (*Juhādlah*) are an entirely nomad tribe with no defined limits, but such boundaries as they have may be said to start just south of Serūm (Serom), the southern limit of the Harb, and run thence almost to Līth, covering all the coast and taking a wide sweep inland to the east of Jebel Abu Shauk and Jebel Sa'dīyah. Their neighbours on the south are the Āl Mahdi and Dhawi Barakāt, and, to the north-east of Līth, the Beni Faham.

They also mingle with the Dhawi Surur and Shenabrah to the south of Mecca, and are generally to be found along the road from Mecca to Jebel 'Arafāt and east to Shedād and Jebel Mohram. From Serūm to Līth, however, is their original district, the chief centre being round Sa'dīyah. They number about 4,000 men, and although good fighters are not quarrelsome. Their country is a poor one, and affords scanty pasturage to their herds of camels, in which they are fairly rich. In times of drought they go south to Wādi Dokhah in the Dhawi Barakāt country. They do not cultivate, but buy all their grain from Tā'if or Līth, in return for the *semn* which they sell. They all carry spears and knives and, those who can afford them, rifles.

For purposes of internal administration the tribe is divided into two parts, the one under Mohammed ibn Sa'īd, the other under Mohammed ibn Hanesh. The former is faithful to the Sherif of Mecca. Sheikh Mohammed ibn Hanash, who rules over the Āl Munīf or Munīfīyah, dislikes the Sherif, owing to his habit of commandeering camels whenever his followers go to Mecca, and therefore keeps chiefly to Sa'dīyah and the coast. He has made overtures to Idrīsi, but is too far off and too weak to do more than sympathize with him. He was neutral during the Turco-Sherifian expedition in 1910, and removed his tribe into the inaccessible mountains.

The two chief Sheikhs are on good terms with each other and the sub-tribes freely intermingle. They are friendly towards the Dhawi Hasan and Beni Faham, but inimical to the Harb. The Ateibah, though distant, raid them when they stray too far east. The Hudheil and they are of one origin and are on terms of the closest friendship.

The Juhadlah are hospitable to strangers, but they have little religion and seldom go on the pilgrimage. In person they are taller than most Arabs, wear their hair short, and are dressed in a red 'tob' (*thūb*) which reaches from the waist to the knee, the end being thrown over the left shoulder.

(i) Chief Sheikh, Mohammed ibn Sa'īd.

Sub-Tribes: 'Alyānīyah, Sheinīyah, Hershīyah, Jamshīyah, Tha'bānīyah, Hasnānīyah, Jirshīyah.

(ii) Chief Sheikh, Mohammed ibn Hanash.

(1) Āl Munīf, of which the chief subdivisions are:

Āl es-Sihim	Mohammed es-Sultān
Āl Madāthir	Husein ibn Huneish
Beni Bur	Mas'ūd ibn Mohammed
Āl Yām	Mohammed ibn Muhsin
Āl Zahein	Mizhar ibn Sihmān

(2) Hijrīyah, of which the chief subdivision is:
Āl Faham   Haidar ibn Huneish

(*d*) The ĀL MAHDI are a small semi-nomad tribe near Līth, who make their living chiefly as fishermen. They are a poor and down-trodden people, thoroughly awed by their powerful neighbours the Dhawi Hasan. They do not number more than 200 souls.

Chief Sheikh, Mohammed ibn Qasīm.

Chief Clans.

| Mujeishah | Ahmed ibn Mas'ūdah |
| Āl Hasan | Ibn Ahmed er-Rideini |

(*e*) The BENI MĀLIK of the Hejaz are a small tribe, numbering not more than 2,000 men, who live in the mountains inland of Līth. The adjoining tribes are the Beni Sa'd on the north, the Shalāwah nomads on the east, the Zahrān on the south, and the Juhadlah on the west. The Beni Mālik are not a fighting tribe, but they are hospitable and industrious, and cultivate figs and grapes in the wādis as well as wheat, barley, and dhura. During the pilgrimage season most of them go to Mecca and Jiddah and act as porters. They thus come more into contact with the outside world than most tribes and are more civilized. They are devoted to the Sherif and pay him taxes.

Nāsir ibn Rawwāf is their chief Sheikh.

They live at peace with their neighbours, except the Shalāwah, who occasionally raid them. Most of their villages are clustered in Wādi Lūz and Wādi Rummān.

(*f*) The SHENABRAH are a small nomad tribe to the south of Mecca, numbering not more than 150 men. They are one of the twenty-one Ashrāf clans (see pp. 157 ff.), and, being nearly related to the 'Abādilah, used to support the Sherif of Mecca, but are now reported disaffected. Sherif Judallah is their head. The Shenabrah are brave and lawless, and are generally at loggerheads with the Dhawi Surur.

(*g*) The DHAWI SURUR (*Surūr*) number about 200 men, and wander over the country to the south of Mecca, being entirely nomadic. They are one of the twenty-one Ashrāf clans (see pp. 157 ff.), and are connected with the Dhawi Zeid. They are opposed to the Shenabrah. Sherif Dukhān is their chief Sheikh. Clans are Aulād el-Hasan and Āl 'Azīz. They all obey the Sherif.

(*h*) The BENI THAQĪF, a tribe descended from Himyar in the highlands to the south of Tā'if. They are bounded on the north by the northern section of Juhadlah, on the south by the Beni Nasri, east by the Shalāwah, and west by the Beni Faham. They are almost entirely settled and agricultural, and grow cereals, grapes, and other fruits for the Tā'if market. For water they depend partly on the summer rains, but chiefly on well water. Nāsir ibn Ghuzeil is their chief Sheikh, a firm adherent of the Sherif of Mecca. He commands about 2,000 fighting men. In times of crisis they combine with the Beni Mālik, Beni Sa'd and Beni Nasri. They are always at feud with the Beni Faham and are not cordial to the Juhadlah. They possess very few camels. A certain proportion of the tribe lives permanently in Tā'if. The chief sub-tribes are Sufyān, Mu'adhdher, and Rabī'ah.

(*i*) The BENI SA'D, a tribe which traces its descent to Himyar. It is bounded on the north by the Nasri, on the south by the Beni Mālik, east by the Shalāwah, and west by the Beni Faham and southern Juhadlah.

Their country is more fertile than that of their northern neighbours, wells being plentiful, and they raise cereals and fruits. There are no nomads amongst them. They favour the Emir of Mecca and can provide him with about 1,000 men.

Hamsa ibn Mohammed is their chief Sheikh.

There is enmity between them and the Shalāwah, and with the Juhadlah they are by no means friendly. They combine with the Beni Thaqīf, Beni Mālik, and Nasri, in times of danger.

9. *Tribes of the NE. Asir Borderland.*

Certain tribes which inhabit the region between Northern Asir and Southern Nejd (so far as this is not occupied by the Ateibah) must be mentioned, although it is very doubtful if any of them can be regarded as predominantly nomadic. It is certain, in any case, that a large proportion of their members are partly settled, either in the upper valleys of the inland Asiri wādis or in the Nejd oases; and it is probable that enough of them are now permanent cultivators to deprive the tribes of the Bedouin character they once had. Comparatively little, however, is known about them.

The most numerous and important tribe is the SEBEI', whose homeland is the ill-known region of Wādi Sebei', which lies between N. Asir and Woshm and appears to include the lower basins of two of the great Asiri wādis, Turabah and Ranyah. Not only, however, are settled Sebei' found also in towns and villages of almost all the Nejd districts, but nomad members wander even east of these into Summān, and over many parts of Eastern Toweiq. The nomad element of the tribe numbers at least 1,000 tents, and is divided in allegiance, the Sebei' of Wādi Turabah being tributary to the Sherif, while the rest (the larger part) acknowledge Ibn Sa'ūd. The whole tribe is either Wahabite or Hanbali Sunnite.

The names of some seventeen sub-tribes are known, but almost all in connexion with settled Sebei' (see p. 332).

Connected with the Sebei' and possibly constituting a sub-tribe only are the SAHUL (or *Sahūl*), of which nomad members range S. Nejd and into Hasa. If identical with the SHALĀWAH, their homeland is Wādi Sebei'. But it is practically certain that they are now more settled than nomadic, and have become only less a permanent element of the Nejd population than the Fadhūl. They have probably not above 300 tents, and in religious colour and political allegiance follow the Sebei'.

The BUQŪM are intimately connected with the two foregoing tribes, but are both more predominantly nomadic and less scattered abroad. They are found in the basins of all the inland Asiri wādis, including Wādi Bīshah, and appear to be accepted equally by the Ateibah on the north and the Qahtān on the south, and to divide their allegiance in the same manner as the Sebei'. They are said to have about 500 tents.

C. TRIBES OF THE CENTRAL SOUTH

1. *The Qahtān.*

The QAHTĀN are almost the only very ancient Arabian people which still maintains its importance as a tribal unit. They are, according to Arab tradition, the mother-stock of the Ahl Qibli, and it is not improbable that for a very long period of time they may have occupied their present district near the southern limits of the habitable desert. No travellers have penetrated into their country and little is known about them. Strange, and seemingly quite baseless, accounts of their customs are repeated among the northern tribes ; for, like all distant and unknown peoples, they are a peg on which to hang marvels. Their country lies to the west of Hautah and is divided into three districts, Hasāt, Areiji, and Tathlīth, the last being near Asir. The Shahrān and the Sebei' lie to the west, the Dawāsir to the south and south-west, the Buqūm and Shalāwah to the north. Somewhere north of Bīshah is the Bilād Qahtān, with a group of villages known as the Qahtānīyah (Tarīd, 'Azīm, and Kir'ān are among their number), and the Beni Wahab villages inhabited by a small tribe of that name.

The Qahtān acknowledge the authority of Ibn Sa'ūd and join him in his raiding expeditions. So far as they are Moslems at all, they are Hanbali Sunnites or Wahabites. They come up to Shaqrah in the Woshm for dates, and when they are camping in the southern parts of their country they buy dates from the Dawāsir villagers, but they themselves have no lands in the valley and are not cultivators. They are very rich in camels, which are sold to the Qasīm buyers when the herds come north, towards Nejd. The settled section of the Qahtān, which includes six autonomous tribes and owns the paramount authority of Mohammed ibn Duleim, is dealt with later (p. 187).

2. *The Dawāsir.*

The nomadic DAWĀSIR are Wahabite and more or less under Ibn Sa'ūd. Half-settled, they have villages in the Wādi Dawāsir which they inhabit during the summer. They breed camels, though not in such large quantities as the Qahtān. The Qasīm dealers do not come as far south as the Dawāsir, but the latter bring their camels into the Hasa and dispose of them there to the Qusmān.

The Dawāsir have overflowed into the easterly provinces of southern Nejd, and now form a considerable settled element in Aflāj, where they are the chief owners of land, worked by men of the *fellāh* tribe of Beni Khadhīr. To a less extent they are found also in Harīq and 'Āridh, where they contribute a proportion of the village and even the town population. Small parties of their nomads wander between Nejd and Hasa and trouble the routes. A considerable body is settled in Bahrein. Indeed, so small a proportion of the Dawāsir is in any sense Bedouin that the tribe hardly comes within our purview here, and it is not worth while to enumerate its imperfectly known sub-sections.

D. TRIBES OF THE CENTRAL EAST

1. *The Shammar.*

The SHAMMAR are northern Arabs. They do not spring from a single ancestor, but account for themselves by saying that they are a mixture of Taghlib, 'Abs, and Hawāzin, the first a constituent of Rabī'ah, the two last of Mudhar. The Ja'far, to which the ruling family of the Rashīd belongs, is a sub-tribe of 'Abdah, and the 'Abdah claim descent from the 'Abidah, a part of the settled Qahtān: they could, therefore, be Yemenites. Beyond these vague traditions, the Shammar are ignorant of their own history before they established themselves in Jebel Shammar, 'the two mountains of Tayy' frequently mentioned in pre-Mohammedan literature, where they displaced (and probably partly incorporated) the ancient Tayy nation, a branch of the Qahtān. About the middle of the seventeenth century they began to stretch their frontiers into the Syrian desert, where they encountered, and, after a brief struggle, defeated, the Mawāli, then the most powerful tribe in the northern steppe, driving them into the north-east borders of Syria.

Early in the nineteenth century the Anazah forced the Shammar northwards across the Euphrates, and split the tribe into two parts, interposing themselves between these two in the Syrian desert. Thus the Shammar of Jebel Shammar and those of the Jezīrah (Mesopotamia) came to be geographically and politically distinct. The southern group follows Ibn Rashīd, the northern Ibn Jerba. But ethnologically they are one; the same sub-tribes are found in either group, and though they do not offer united resistance to their common enemy, the Anazah, they are always on terms of friendship with one another. Any small sheikh of the Jezīrah may bring down his tents and flocks to J. Shammar for a year's pasturage, if he be so minded.

The SOUTHERN SHAMMAR must be considered, not only as a powerful nomad tribe, but also as the masters of the oases in J. Shammar. The settled population of the latter is mostly of the Beni Tamīm, an ancient branch of Mudhar which once inhabited all north-east Arabia, but now has relinquished the nomadic life (see p. 136). The Shammar, for their part, are nomads, though they come down to the oases during the summer drought. The Emir of J. Shammar plays a double part. He is Paramount Chief of his own tribal confederation; but also he is ruler of a settled country, of which Hā'il is the capital, a prince with a fixed habitation, exercising authority over other Bedouins whose connexion with him is not tribal but political. The Shammar tribal frontiers remain more or less unchanged, but the sphere of the Emir's influence varies with the vicissitudes of his dynastic fortunes.

The Shammar tribe ranges the south-east Nefūd and the country to the north almost up to Nejef. To the east its limits have been somewhat restricted by the Dhafīr, who are always at feud with it and encroach upon its dīra. Since the old eastern pilgrim road, the Darb Zobeidah, is seldom safe from Dhafīr raids, it has been abandoned by the Emir's caravans in favour of a more westerly track past the fortified wells of Hayyānīyah; but the proper Shammar pasture grounds extend up to it and across it. To the north, the loss of Jauf el-'Amr has shut the Shammar into the Nefūd. They do not wander far beyond Jebel 'Irnān on the west, nor southwards beyond Mustajiddah; while the summer camping-ground of Beidha Nethīl is occupied sometimes by Shammar, but mostly by the Anazah of the Teima district.

The political influence of Hā'il has decreased notably since the death of the Emir Mohammed, in 1897. At the height of his power he ruled over Riyādh and the Qasīm, and levied tribute from the northern Harb, the Huteim, Fuqara, Wuld Suleimān, and Beni Wahab. The Southern Shammar tribes, great breeders of sheep and camels, number something under 4,000 tents. The villages of J. Shammar contain probably not much over 20,000 souls. Both tribesmen and villagers are devotedly loyal to the Emir. The subject tribes from whom he might be able, on occasion, to raise fighting men, number at most 1,200 tents. Teima, which is subject to him, must have a population of from 1,500 to 2,000.

At a rough estimate Ibn Rashīd could probably raise from 500 to 800 fighting men from the villages, and 2,000 from the Shammar tribes. He might obtain another 500 or 600 from the tribes between Jebel Shammar and Teima, though their support would always be doubtful. The tribesmen would bring their own camels, but they would depend on the Emir for food and ammunition. The villagers he would have to mount and arm as well as feed. His own camel herds, seriously reduced in numbers since the days of the Emir Mohammed, may now amount to about 1,000 camels, including those which are not yet fit for service. The Shammar tribes are not as rich in camels as the Anazah, but they must average some 20–30 camels to a tent, which would bring the numbers up to 80,000 or rather more, including breeding camels and calves.

The relations between the Shammar and the Muteir are usually hostile. With the Dhafīr the Shammar are always at feud, but the Muntefiq were recently on good terms with Ibn Rashīd. The Huteim are out of hand and raid Shammar territories when the Emir is occupied with distant expeditions against the Ruweilah or the Dhafīr. On the western borders the Huweitāt are the foes of all Shammar, except the sub-tribe of Rammāl, with whom one of the Huweiti Paramount Sheikhs is connected by marriage. The Beni 'Atīyah are hereditary enemies, and the Juheinah and Billi raid both the Wuld Suleimān and the Shammar.

Arab tribal federations or states, however, are held together only by an autocratic ruler, and their strength increases or diminishes in exact ratio to his weight and capacity. The Southern Shammar had their day under the Emir Mohammed. Since his death they have been handicapped by the violence and folly of their leaders. But, nevertheless, their numbers, their great tradition, and the support of the Ottoman Government make them still one of the chief factors in Central Arabian politics.

The NORTHERN SHAMMAR of the Jezirah are variously estimated. Probably a total of 2,000 tents is not far from the true figure; but they have been put as high as 10,000 tents. Their pasture-grounds are between the Tigris and the Euphrates, though occasionally they cross the Tigris in the region of the Lesser Zāb. They come down to Baghdad and even south of Baghdad as far as Zobār. To the west they extend to Deir ez-Zōr, which is a head-quarters of the tribe; thence north up the Khābūr and to near Nisībīn they wander over the fertile desert which is watered by the Jaghjagh and its affluents. They are at feud with their Anazah neighbours, both Fed'ān and 'Amārāt, and usually on bad terms with the Kurdish tribes to the north and north-east. Traditional rebels against Ottoman authority, they slip between the fingers of the Mutesarrif of Deir and the Vali of Mosul, paying taxes to neither. They exact dues from the caravans on the Tigris road and not infrequently hold up the traffic along this important link between Asia Minor and Baghdad, forcing travellers, and sometimes even the Government post, to take the longer route by Irbil and Kerkūk. The keleks on the river are subject to their exactions also. In 1911, the cup of their iniquities having overflowed, Nāzim Pasha, then Vali of the 'Irāq, sent an expedition against them under his Chief of Staff, Hasan Riza Bey (murdered during the siege of Scutari in the following year). He conducted matters very skilfully. The Shammar came in without resistance, camel- and sheep-dues, many years in arrear, were collected at a great camp formed at Hatrah, and the rights of the tribe over the Mosul road were defined. But the fall of Nāzim immediately afterwards, and the resignation of Hasan Riza, took the heart out of this agreement.

The Shammar of the Jezīrah are all under the Sheikhly family of the Jerbān, who sprang into political importance about 1830 with Sheikh Sufūq ibn Jerba, a bitter enemy of the Turks. His eldest son, Ferhān, was a lover of peace and kept on good terms with the Government; but the contest was continued by Ferhān's brothers, of whom the youngest, Fāris, took refuge in J. Shammar with Ibn Rashīd. He returned to the Jezīrah in the seventies, and from that time shared the position of Paramount Sheikh, with Ferhān. He took the camping-grounds on the Khābūr, while Ferhān held those round Mosul with his head-quarters at Hatrah and on the brackish springs of the Wādi Tharthar. In 1911 'Āsi, the eldest of Ferhān's sixteen sons, was appointed by Hasan Riza Bey Paramount Sheikh, and made responsible to the Government for all Mesopotamian Shammar. He is a man advanced in years, peaceable and upright. He keeps to the Mosul district, while two of his cousins, 'Abd el-Muhsin and Mohammed, sons of 'Abd el-Kerīm, roam the Khābūr country. The sons of Fāris are young and not of much account. The eldest now living, Mish'al, is nephew, through his mother, of Noweidis et-Timyāt of the TŪMĀN (Shammar of the Jebel). Some of the many sons of Ferhān own cultivated land on the southern reaches of the Tigris, and one, Humeidi, has almost dropped nomad habits and passes much of his time in a house which he has built in Baghdad.

Between 'Amārah and Baghdad there is a group of small tribes, the TAUQAH (Toga), who call themselves Shammar, though they are of mixed blood. They are half-nomadic, going out into the desert west of the Euphrates in spring with their sheep and donkeys, and coming back into their Jezīrah villages in the summer. The chief of these tribes are the MAS'ŪD (Mes'ūd), between Museyyib and Kerbela, the ZAGĀRIT, round Kerbela, and the ZAUBA' (Zoba), five hours west of Baghdad. They are Shiah, and, like all settled Arabs, fairly numerous.

SHAMMAR OF NEJD

Tribe.	Sub-Tribe.	Clan.

'ABDAH. 1,500 tents
Ibn Jebrīn
Ibn 'Ajīl
Ibn 'Ali
	Mufadhdhal
	  Mitni ibn Jebrīn
	Fadhl
	  'Aqab ibn 'Ajīl (maternal uncle of Emir 'Abd el-'Azīz)
	Ja'far
	  Wādi ibn 'Ali
	Weibār
	  Ibn Shureim
	Jeniddah
	  Hāmid el-Hihi
	'Amūd
	  Slash ibn Feisāl
	Deghairāt (small)
		Bureik
		  Ibn Bureik

ASLAM. 1,200 tents
Dhāri et-Tuwālah
	Juheish
	Mas'ūd
	  'Adhib ibn El-Gheisim
	Firidah (Fruddah)
	  'Amash el-Ferīd
	Wureik
	  'Aqab ibn Wureik
	Rumāh
	  Mutlaq er-Rumāhi
	Tūmān
	  Noweidis et-Timyāt
	  Munāhi ibn 'Ayyāsh
	Wahab
	  Toweirib ibn Munabbih
	Raba' (or Ruba'ah)
	  Samad er-Raba'i
	Husein
	Qwei (small)
	Dhawīyah (small)
		Hadbah (Hidbah)
		  Mutlaq ibn 'Aish
		Wudhāh (Widhāh)

SINJĀRAH. 1,000 tents	Zumeil
	  Qasīm ibn Rakhīs
	Salmān
	  Fallāj ibn 'Ardān
	Ghufeilah
	  'Ayada ibn Zuweimil
	Ghi'thah (or Ghīthah)
	Suweid
	  Ibn Duweihi
	Rammāl
	  Ghadhbān ibn Rammāl (daughter married to 'Audah Abu Tayy of the Huweitāt, with whom he is friends)
	Shilqān
	  Ibn Duheilān
		Namsān (Nimsān)
		Jirdhān

SHAMMAR OF JEZĪRAH

Tribe.	Sub-Tribe.	Clan.
SHAMMAR. 2,000 tents	Khārisah (Khrussah)	
'Āsi ibn Ferhān	'Āsi ibn Ferhān	
'Abd el-Muhsin ibn 'Abd el-Kerīm	'Abdah	Bureik
Mohammed ibn 'Abd el-Kerīm	Menāwir ibn Suqi	
	Sinjārah	
	'Abd el-Muhsin Mohammed (Sinjārah) Thābit	
	Mit'ab el-Hadab el-Qu'eit	
	('Abdah) 'Amūd	
	(Tūmān) Sā'ih	
	Jed'ān ibn Hasan	
	Ferhān es-Sudeid	
	('Abdah) Fedāghah	'Aleyyān
	Bander ibn 'Ayādah	

SHAMMAR OF 'IRĀQ

Tribe.	Sub-Tribe.	Clan.
TAUQAH.	Mas'ūd	
	Zagārit	
	Zauba'	
	Dhāhi el-Mohammed	

2. Beni Tamīm.

The BENI TAMĪM are a famous stock of the northern people, who played an important part in Arabian history before the age of the prophet, when they extended from the Syrian desert to Yemāmah. They maintain their ancient seat, for they still form a large proportion of the settled population of Nejd and Jebel Shammar; the oases of Qasīm are almost exclusively inhabited by them and by the Beni Khālid. But they are no longer an independent tribe; they acknowledge the authority of Ibn Sa'ūd or of Ibn Rashīd. At a very early date, probably before the Mohammedan invasion, they began to come up into Mesopotamia, where they are still to be found near Tārmīyah (some 1,500 families). All these are shepherds, and while the Tamīm of Nejd are strict Wahabites, their kinsmen of Mesopotamia are Shiahs.

3. The Dhafīr (or Dhufīr).

The DHAFĪR form an important tribe whose district extends south of the Shatt el-'Arab and Euphrates from near Zobeir to Samāwah. From Samāwah a line drawn almost due south to the vicinity of Hafar in the Bātin would mark their frontier, and the depression of the Bātin forms the SE. side of the triangle which encloses their territory. Their neighbours are the Muntefiq Confederation to the NE., the Shammar to the W., the Muteir and 'Ajmān to the E., while to the south they are in touch with the Sebei', one of the tribes which acknowledge the authority of Ibn Sa'ūd. The Samīd section, and more particularly the Juwāsim (or Jawāsim, orig. Qawāsim), are accustomed to cross the Euphrates in the summer and pasture their flocks in the 'Irāq.

The Dhafīr are foes of the Muteir and are almost always on bad terms with the Shammar, whom they raid when they are in their spring pasturages east of the Nefūd. They harry the Darb Zobeidah and hold up the Emir's caravans from Hā'il to Nejef; indeed the Darb Zobeidah has become so unsafe that the western pilgrimage road is now almost always chosen by caravans in preference to it. For the past year, however, the Paramount Sheikh, Hamūd ibn Suweit, has been at peace with Ibn Rashīd, though he is said to have rejected the latter's proposal that he should join him in aiding 'Ajeimi ibn Sa'dūn and the Turks against the British. The Shammar sub-tribe of the 'Ajil are still hostile to the Dhafīr. With the Anazah they are always at feud, and though the Anazah sheikhs seldom approach within four or five days' journey of their country, the Dhafīr carry their raids as far north as Shifāthah, and west into the Anazah pastures. They are on good terms with some of the Muntefiq group, of whom the Budūr camp habitually under their protection in the spring, when the latter go out with their sheep into the desert. But with the Sa'dūn themselves their relations have been anything but cordial, and since 1915 Hamūd has definitely sided against 'Ajeimi; but he has not succeeded in carrying his whole tribe with him, and the Husein and Dhar'ān sections, as well as other smaller sheikhs of the Samīd, have followed 'Ajeimi's lead against us.

The Dhafīr are composed of two main sub-tribes, the Butūn and the Samīd, of which the Butūn is the more numerous. It is not a homogeneous tribal unit, but has been formed from sections of other tribes which have been welded together. The various constituents have preserved the memory of their origin; the Suweit and the Beni Husein are Ashrāf of the Hejaz; the Sa'īd, 'Areif, and Beni Khālid, with the Kathīr, who are an offshoot of the Beni Khālid, are Qahtān; the 'Adwān are Ahl esh-Shimāl, descended from Rabī'ah or Mudhar; the Misāmīr and the small Tulūh clans are Anazah; the Rasimi are Shammar; the Mu'āleim are Beni Tamīm, and the Juwāsim are from the neighbouring Sebei'. The important Dhar'ān section are 'Abīd, that is to say, they spring from the slaves of some nomad group.

The Dhafīr are wholly nomadic and do not engage in any trade. Their country is sufficiently supplied with wells, and they own large flocks of sheep, besides being breeders of camels. In religion they are Sunnis of the Maliki sect. They are well armed with modern rifles, and may number some 3,000 fighting men. They maintain good relations with the Sultan of Koweit, and come into Koweit for needful provisions and utensils. Sections of the tribe near the Koweit territory have occasionally paid the Sultan tribute; while in the days of Mohammed er-Rashīd, the western sections of the Dhafīr yielded tribute to the Shammar. The paramount Sheikh, Hamūd ibn Suweit, is a man of about 45, intelligent, and reckoned a fairly good politician and tribal administrator. His son, Barghāsh, is a boy of 17.

DHAFĪR

Tribe.	Sub-Tribe.	
BUTŪN.	Suweit.	Hamūd ibn Suweit. 2,000 tents
Hamūd ibn Suweit.	Sultān	
	Miz'ar	
	Haulah	
	Battah	Hamūd ibn Suweit
	Ma'ālib	
	Tulūh	
	'Afnān	Haza ibn Aqrab
	Dhuweihi	'Ali edh-Dhuweihi
	Rasimi	Shuwei
	Sa'īd	Mutni ibn Khallāf
	Husein	Khallāf ibn Jā'id
	Beni Khālid	Zeil ibn Mandīl
	'Adwān	Mandīl ibn Kāmil
	Awāzim	Ibn Hadbah
	Kathīr	Jali ibn Jureid
SAMĪD.	Dhar'ān	Lizām abu Dharā'
Lizām abu Dharā'. 1,500	Mu'āleim	Et-Tumeish el-Boreisi
tents.	Misāmīr	'Ajīl ibn Huzein
	'Areif	Fad'us el-Aslib
	'Askar	Munawwakh ibn Quheisān
	Juwāsim (Jawāsim)	Haleis ibn 'Ufeisān

4. The Muteir and the Barrīyah.

The MUTEIR, closely akin to their western neighbours, the Harb and the Ateibah, are people of the north, claiming descent through Mudhar from Ma'add. Their territory touches the Persian Gulf round Koweit, and runs down the Bātin till it reaches Ibn Sa'ūd's district near Zilfi. The Beni Khālid and the 'Ajmān lie to the south. A turbulent tribe, some 1,500 tents strong, the Muteir stand in close relations with the Sultan of Koweit; but with Ibn Rashīd they are perpetually at feud, and no year passes without raiding expeditions from one dīra to the other. It was a Muteiri who in 1908 killed the Emir 'Abd el-'Azīz, father of the present Emir of Hā'il, at Raudhat el-Mahanna, near Boreidah. The Muteir harry the outlying settlements of Qasīm, and not infrequently interrupt the caravan traffic to the Gulf. Their principal Sheikh, Feisāl ed-Derwīsh, pastures in the Koweit area, and is lord over some 800 tents. All the Muteir belong to the confederation of Ibn Sa'ūd, and contribute fighting men to his raiding expeditions. They are camel-breeders and entirely nomadic; they possess no cultivated ground.

The BARRĪYAH are an independent tribe, but so closely allied with the Muteir that they are often held to be of the same stock. In all political relations they are at one with the Muteir, and, like them, they come under the authority of Ibn Sa'ūd. Their pasturages are in Qasīm. The last report concerning them is that they opposed 'Abdullah, the second son of the Sherif, when he raided Sedeir at the end of 1914 in order to collect overdue taxes from the eastern Ateibah, and that after some fighting they were defeated.

MUTEIR AND BARRĪYAH

Tribe.	Sub-Tribe.
MUTEIR. 1,500 tents.	*Alwi.*
Feisāl ibn Sultān ed-Derwīsh.	Feisāl ibn Sultān.
Ghaza ibn Shuqeir.	*Jiblān.*
	Sahūd ibn Lāmi.
	Rakhmān.
	Muhsin ibn Zureibān.
	Sahabah.
	Ghaneim ibn Shiblān.
	Malā'ibah.
	Khilf el-Fighm.
BARRĪYAH. 1,200 tents.	*Abayāt.*
Nā'if ibn Masīs.	Munāhi ibn 'Ashwān.
	Deyāhīn.
	Shabāb el-Qureifah.
	Barzān.
	'Aqab Abu Shuweibāt.
	Tha'lah.
	Jermān el-Humeidān.
	'Abdillah.
	Ibn Saqīyān.
	Wāsil.
	Ibn Thamnah.

5. *Beni Khālid.*

The BENI KHĀLID are an ancient tribe of irreproachable lineage, greatly fallen in estate. Stranded witnesses to its former wide range are to be found in a Khālid element of the settled population of Qasīm (especially at Aneizah), of Zilfi in Sedeir, of Malham in 'Āridh, and elsewhere in Nejd. The main remnant, however, is the Bedouin tribe of the name which ranges north of the 'Ajmān on the Gulf shore between the Wādi Maqta' on the north and the middle of the Bayādh district on the south. Inland they wander into the Summān plateau. Scattered communities have settled in various outside localities, e.g. Oman, Musallamīyah Island, Qatīf, the Hasa Oasis, Bahrein, and Koweit, where the tribesmen have become pearl-fishers, &c. The nomads own considerable date-groves.

Up to 1830 the Beni Khālid ruled the Hasa ; but they had long been at war with the Wahabites, to whom, being themselves Maliki Sunnites, they are unsympathetic, and they finally succumbed to the Emir Tūrki of Riyādh. Latterly, after recognizing Turkish suzerainty, more or less, for forty odd years, they have come again under Riyādh. They are great breeders of horses and cattle, and cultivate more than most Bedouins. Their tents are noted for their great size ; and in dress (they wear the fine Hasa *abbas*), deportment, physiognomy, and coloration these nomads are more like oasis-dwellers than Bedouins. They number about 14,000 souls, and claim to send out 4,000 fighting-men.

They are in alliance with the 'Ajmān and share dīras with that tribe, but maintain feuds with the Muteir and the Ahl Murrah. A small isolated section ranges north of Koweit with the Dhafīr. The tribe is well armed and more trustworthy than the 'Ajmān. Its Paramount Chief is the Sheikh of a settled clan, Āl Khālid, of the 'AMĀ'IR sub-tribe, who lives on the island of Musallamīyah.

BENI KHALID

Sub-Tribe.	Clan.	
'Amā'ir .	Dawāwdah	'Amā'ir has other settled clans.
	Il-Hasan	
Subeih .	Havyah	Subeih has other settled clans.
	Makhāsim	
	Zaban	
Nahad .	. . . .	Mainly nomad.
Miqdām	. . . .	Mainly nomad.
Muhāshir	. . . .	Mainly nomad.
Jabūr .	. . . .	Half-settled.
Humeid .	. . . .	Small and decayed.

6. The 'Ajmān.

The 'AJMĀN, who range south of the Beni Khālid, trace their descent to Qahtān through Nafura of Nejrān ; but this pedigree is not accepted by Arab genealogists in general.

They are, however, an important Bedouin tribe, which is the strongest nomad unit on the Gulf Coast, although its claim to turn out 10,000 fighting-men is excessive. It is singularly at one within itself, its different sub-tribes and clans not having distinct dīras, or falling into sectional groups. 'Ajmi tribesmen of all sections may be found in any camp in any part of the range of the tribe. They also appear to have unusual instinct for federation with their weaker neighbours, thus securing more elbow-room. Under ordinary conditions both the Beni Khālid and the Beni Hajar are its allies, and the 'Ajmān have free range in their dīras. The whole tribe is well provided with breach-loading firearms, and being Sunnite of the Hanbali School, it is sympathetic to Wahabism, and has some of its dour spirit.

Its proper summer range is the Gulf lowlands from Taff down to 'Oqair, enveloping the Hasa oasis on north and east. Inland it ranges back over the Summān plateau, where its herdsmen wander in winter as far west as the confines of Sedeir ; and at the same season 'Ajmān push even into Kharj. On the littoral they straggle sometimes into El-Qatar, and habitually wander north up to Koweit, relying on their agreement with the Beni Khālid, whose proper dīra they thus invade. They are to be found, therefore, at one season or another, over an area of not less than 20,000 square miles.

Very few 'Ajmi tribesmen have ever adopted settled life, though they own some date-groves in Hasa. Their wealth lies in horses, camels, and the smaller cattle. In particular they are horse-breeders. They may total between 4,000 and 5,000 tents.

During the Ottoman occupation of Hasa and Qatīf, the 'Ajmān were consistently recalcitrant, in spite of subsidies doled out to their sheikhs, and the screw which could be put upon the tribe when, according to its custom, it camped near Hofūf, and wished to dispose of live stock, &c., in the local markets. They maintained the while relations of old standing with the Emirs of Riyādh, and welcomed 'Abd el-'Azīz ibn Sa'ūd when he invaded Hasa in 1913. But when his became the established government, the 'Ajmān liked him and his taxes little better than the Turks, and he had to organize drastic punishment of their raiding in the summer of 1915, finally driving great part of them north into Shammar country. Their traditional foe is the Ahl Murrah tribe, and of late they have added Ibn Rashīd and the Shammar. With the Sultan of Koweit and the Paramount Sheikh of El-Qatar they have generally, though not invariably, kept on terms.

The Paramount Chieftainship is in the Ibn Hithlein family of the MA'ĪDH sub-tribe (Nāja' clan). On the murder of Mohammed ibn Hazm ibn Hithlein in 1910, the chieftainship was put in commission; Sheikh Fahd, the elder brother of the late chief, had most support for the sole succession, but he appears to have given way later to Sheikh Theīdān, who submitted to Riyādh at the end of 1915. The Nāja' clan is said to be in close alliance with the SIFRĀN sub-tribe, which, though not numerous, contains the most formidable of all the 'Ajmi fighting-men. According to Lorimer (*Gazetteer of the Persian Gulf*), the Jiblān section of the Muteir (q. v.) joined forces with the 'Ajmān before 1908.

'AJMĀN

Sub-Tribe.	Fighting Strength.
Ma'īdh	2,700
Suleimān	1,270
Mahfūdh	1,200
Hitlan	1,150
'Arjah	650
Shāmir	600
Hādi	500
Dhā'in	400
Sifrān	300
Hammād ibn Rāshid	300
Rusheid	200
Misra	200
Miflih	100
Saleifi	100
Salīm	100
Sureih	100
Heiraf	100
Hayyān	100
Shawāwlah	80
Khuweitir	50
Total	? 10,200

7. *Beni Hajar.*

The BENI HAJAR (or Hājir, often pronounced by Bedouins Hāyir) are nomads of bad reputation, ranging Hasa and part of El-Qatar, south of the 'Ajmān, with whom they have an agreement allowing them to use the 'Ajmi dīra, if provided with authorized *rafīqs*. They were always troublesome to the Turks, and are so now to both Ibn Sa'ūd and the Sheikh of El-Qatar.

They are pastoral and breeders, but are said also to make excursions into piracy. They allow their women great liberty. Their extreme range is from 'Odeid to the 'Ajmān limit in Hasa; but by consent they wander as far north as Koweit. They have no one Paramount Chief.

Their total strength is about 6,000 souls, and they claim to have 1,500 fighting-men. The two sub-tribes are at feud.

BENI HAJAR

Sub-Tribe.	Clan.	
Makhadhabah (mainly in El-Qatar).	Dibisah.	
	Faheid.	
	Hamrah.	
	Haseyyin.	
	Jarārhah.	
	Khayyārin.	
	Madhāfirah.	
	Māna'.	
	Mazāhimah.	
	Qumzah.	
	Sa'ayyid.	
	Shabā'in.	(Sheikh is Chief of whole sub-tribe.)
	Shahwān	
	Shara'ān.	
	Sharāhīn.	
	Sultān.	
	Tawwa.	
	Zabar.	
	Zakhānin.	
Ahl Mohammed (mainly in Hasa).	'Amirah.	
	Filahah.	
	Kidādāt.	
	Kilabah.	
	Misārir.	
	Qarūf.	
	Sha'āmil.	(Sheikh is Chief of whole sub-tribe.)
	Simāhin.	
	Tāya'.	

8. The Ahl Murrah.

The AHL MURRAH (Ahl Morra), a savage and ill-known tribe, wholly nomadic, range to the south of Hasa, into the Jāfūrah Desert, and down to the wild oasis of Jabrīn which lies beyond on the confines of the great South Desert. On the north they come up to near 'Oqair, while inland they lie south of the Hofūf-Riyādh routes (which they harry) as far as the borders of Kharj. In most of this inhospitable tract they wander alone, and neither the Turks nor the Ibn Sa'ūds (whose feudatories they nominally are) have ever been able to follow them far enough to subdue them. In 1915–16 they gave the Emir of Riyādh a great deal of trouble. Their savagery and treachery are due mainly to the wild character of their dīra, but perhaps their evil reputation is due also in some degree to the small knowledge of them possessed by the outside world.

They have, however, physical and linguistic peculiarities, which make it possible that they are survivors of the pre-Arab population of the Peninsula, like the inhabitants of Ras Musandam and the southern Mahrah. They are virtually pagans, but profess, on occasion, Islam of the Hanbali School, which is akin to Wahabism. They are as ill-armed as they are ill-provided with any domestic apparatus or clothing in advance of the Stone Age; but they are brave fighters, who have twice in recent years made short work of Turkish punitive detachments. They own many camels.

They are said to number about 7,000 souls, and to turn out 2,000 fighting men. Their Paramount Chief is the Sheikh of the Fuheidah clan of the SHABĪB (or Bishr) sub-tribe, which is notorious for outrages committed on travellers, fishermen, and Turks. The whole tribe is unashamedly predatory, recognizing no code but its own. It maintains perpetual feud with the 'Ajmān and the Beni Khālid.

AHL MURRAH

Sub-Tribe.	Clan.
Shabīb (or Bishr).	'Adhbah.
	Baheih.
	Bureid.
	Dāwi.
	Fuheidah.
	Ghafrān.
	Hādi.
	Hasan.
	Juheish.
	Shabīb.
	Zukeimah.
	Zibdān.
'Ali ibn Murrah.	Ghiyāthin.
	Jarāba'ah.
	Nābit.
Jābir.	Ghadhbān.
	Ahl Ibn-Na'ām.

9. *The Manāsīr.*

The MANĀSĪR are a small independent tribe in the ill-known Dhafrah district, bordering on the domain of the Sheikh of Abu Dhabi, to whom, if to any one, they owe a vague allegiance, having for a generation or so been free of tribute to Ibn Sa'ūd. They are the last predominantly nomadic tribe towards the south, the Great Desert and the Jāfūrah Desert enclosing their dīra S. and W., and the mainly settled and friendly Beni Yās of the Trucial Coast lying E. North lies the dīra of the Ahl Murrah, with whom the Manāsīr seem to be on better terms than any one else is. In winter the whole tribe moves into or near El-Qatar. In summer part of it may be found as far south as the Bireimi Oasis in NW. Oman. Mainly pastoral, the Manāsīr possess arable land and summer settlements in Dhafrah (Līwah district), and are much in advance of the Ahl Murrah in civilization.

Both in religious tenets and political connexions they pertain to Oman. There seems to be no Paramount Mansūri Chief. The tribe does not number above 1,500 souls.

MANĀSĪR

Sub-Tribe.	Clan.
Mundhir.	Ka'abarah.
	Māni'.
	Murāshīd.
	Metāwa'ah.
	Medāhimah.
Rahamah.	Khail.
	Tareif (or Janūb).
	Tarārifah.
	Wabrān.
Sha'ar.	Ghuweinam.
	Rasheyyid.
	Thuweibit.

SUPPLEMENT

NON-BEDOUIN NOMADS

1. *The Sherārāt.*

The SHERĀRĀT are not reckoned among the Arabs as Bedu, that is to say, they do not spring from either of the great nomad families, Qahtān or Nizār. They are said to be of one stock with the Huteim who, like the Sherārāt, are not *asīl*, of known race, and the true Bedouins will not intermarry with them.[1] Nor is there any definite area over which they exercise acknowledged rights of possession; they have not their own dīra, but camp with other tribes. Their tents are scattered from Jebel Durūz in the north to Teima in the south, and east from Kerak to Jebel Shammar. They are to be found among the Sukhūr, the Huweitāt, the Ruweilah, and the Shammar, either in the encampments of the big Sheikhs, or by preference *khalāwi*, i.e. solitary, in the wilderness. In summer small numbers of Sherārāt gather round the fast-drying waterholes and the permanent wells, when the big tribes have moved off with their herds towards the Hejaz Railway and the Jordan valley, or out into the depths of the Hamād. At Ḥausa in the Jebel Tubeiq, and at Imleih and 'Obeid on the edges of the Nefūd, they find enough water for their slender needs, and the hard surface of the desert is covered with the circular marks of their threshing-floors where in August they harvest the wild *semh*.

The Sherārāt honour an ancestor called Suleim, who is buried in the Wādi Mōjib, but they seldom visit his tomb. They have a cult for 'Āqil Walad 'Azzām, whose tomb is in the Jebel Tubeiq. They regard the Jebel Tubeiq as their own special dīra, while the Sukhūr and the Huweitāt are intruders.

In Ibn Rashīd's country the Sherārāt will pay tribute to him; in Moab they pay tribute to the Ottoman Government. Wherever they may be, they must buy the goodwill of the Paramount Sheikh of that region. They are skilled hunters, and their camels are said to be the best in Western Arabia, especially as freight-carriers. Although their small tents are almost destitute of furniture and their coffee-hearths are bare, many of the Sherārāt are well-to-do. A man clothed in rags may be the owner of 20 camels, and a Sherāri sheikh is a rich man in the desert. But a hunter wandering solitary for a year or more, with his tiny tent, his wife, his single camel and little flock of goats, living mainly on such animals as he can trap, content with black cakes of *semh* seed in place of bread, and chewing the green weeds of early spring like one of his own goats, has brought the amenities of existence to the irreducible minimum. The men take service with the cultivators of the Jīzah district, and often settle down among them; but their former trade of supplying the Hajj camels with grass from the Nefūd has vanished with the opening of the railway.

---

[1] They are sometimes reckoned, however, as descendants of the Beni Hilāl.

2. *The Huteim.*

Closely related to the Sherārāt are the HUTEIM (Heteym), and they are even more widely scattered. They are to be found on the Persian Gulf, in Yemen, on the Red Sea, and in Egypt ; but their main range is in Central Arabia, from near Medina, north-east to Jebel Shammar. The name Huteim is used carelessly by the Arabs as a synonym for any base-born, half-settled tribe. The Huteim are rich and numerous ; those of the Kheibar and Medina districts pay taxes to the Government, while those of Jebel Shammar used to be taxed by Ibn Rashīd, but are now out of hand and raid his villages when he is away with his fighting-men. The Huteim breed excellent riding-camels, and own large flocks of sheep and goats. Their women are renowned for beauty, but would not be taken in marriage by any Bedouin of good stock. The men are reputed to be timid and of no value as fighters.

3. *The Sulubba.*

The SULUBBA (Solubba) are an interesting tribe about whose origin nothing certain is known. Probably they are the dispersed remnants of some old stock ; but legend has been busy with their ancestry, and has given them as forbears the Indian dancers of Hārūn er-Rashīd's court at Baghdad. They are sprinkled over the whole of nomad Arabia, but the various groups under their separate sheikhs keep to their own regions, where they ply their trades as smiths, tinkers, carpenters, and cattle-surgeons among the Bedouins and the oasis-dwellers. Their skill in hunting has passed into fable with the Arabs ; and in fact they are so expert that they live well, even in the most barren wilderness, from the fruits of the chase. They are well-to-do, earning an ample livelihood by their craftsmanship, and they travel without fear throughout all the desert, where no thief would rob them and no raider harry them. Their knowledge of the country is unsurpassed. They have no camels ; their beasts of burden are donkeys, the best breed being a large white ass almost as powerful as a mule. They rear herds of sheep and goats in the Hamād, and their tents are well stocked with every kind of nomad gear. A northern Sulubbi will wear in winter a warm robe of gazelle-skins. The Bedouins accuse them of eating carrion and beasts that have died of themselves, as well as vermin ; and there would seem to be truth in the first charge as far as the Suleib (Soleyb) and Ghaneimi are concerned, and in the second if it is limited to locusts and hedgehogs (the locust, however, is a delicacy much prized not only by the Sulubba, but by all nomads). It is impossible to estimate the numbers of the tribe, since they never assemble in any one place.

4. *The Sunnā'.*

The SUNNĀ' are the smiths' caste, sometimes settled in the villages and sometimes wandering with the tribes (*Sunnā'* is plural of *Sani'* = artizan, smith). They are braziers, farriers, tinners, blacksmiths, and

A T

workers in wood and stone among the tribes and in the oases. Thus they are both villagers and nomads. They may marry with the Huteim but with no Bedouins. They are probably a different race from the Arabs, and are distinguished from them by their features.

5. *The Nawār.*

The NAWĀR are gipsies found in Arabia as in other parts of the universe, but not in great numbers. Their habits and activities are the same there as elsewhere.

6. *The Hawāzin.*

The HAWĀZIN (Hawāzim or 'Awāzim) are a nomad tribe which is not admitted to marriage and fellowship by true Arabs. As a considerable tribal unit it is found only in and about the principality of Koweit, ranging from the outskirts of the town itself (where some 250 Hawāzin families are settled), down the coast nearly to Musallamīyah, and for some distance inland. They must be the 'Koweit nomads' who, Raunkiaer says, graze their herds south of the town in winter and resort in summer northwards to the districts round Zobeir, and also control the wells of Tawīl. There are also, however, Hawāzin elsewhere, who have the same sort of status, but are members of Huteim or Harb (e.g. in Jauf el-'Amr, Teima, Sedeir, &c.); and there is a distinct Harb clan of the name at Wādi el-Kheif near Jebel Fiqra (see HARB). The Koweit Hawāzin are partly pastoral, partly follow marine occupations—pearl-diving and fishing. They are great breeders of camels, often taking service (e.g. at Qatīf) under alien masters for stud-labour. They are subjects of Koweit, and form the bulk of the Sultan's fighting forces: it is due also to their activities that he is able to claim Būbiyān Island, to which some of their herdsmen resort. They are allied with the 'Ajmān, and number some 4,000 souls. It appears that they are comparatively new-comers into Koweit territory, and their tradition is that they were formerly with the Harb in East Hejaz. The one thing certain is that they are regarded by Bedouins as of the same standing as Huteim or Sulubba, and credited with secret non-Islamic beliefs. In fact, however, they are Maliki Sunnites.

NON-BEDOUIN NOMADS

Tribe.	Sub-Tribe.	Clan.
SHERĀRĀT. 800 tents	Fuleihān	
Ibn Hâwi	Ibn Hâwi	
Ibn Wardah	Huleisah	
	Ibn Duweiji	
	'Azzām	
	Ibn Wardah	
	Dhubein	
	Ibn Shushān	
	Khayyāli	
	Suweifli	
HUTEIM.	Beni Rashīd, 1,000 tents	Nuwāmisah
	Duleim ibn Barak	Ibn Nuwās
	Sālim ibn Simra	Ibn Barak
	Nr. Hā'il	Ibn Jelladān
		Ibn Dammūk
		Ibn Simri or Thiyabbah
		Mothābarah
		Feradissa
		Heizān
		Khiyārāt
		Qabīd
		Suweidir
		Fehjāt
		Bedaunah
	Jerābis. Nr. Wejh	
SULUBBA.	Seidān. In Nejd	
	Ghaneimi. In Nejd	
	Suleib	
	Ibn Mālik. In 'Irāq and the Hamād	
HAWĀZIN.		
No Paramount Sheikh of their own tribe, that authority having passed to the Sultan of Koweit.	Kū'ah	Hadhālīn
		Bureikāt
		Shaqufah
	Ghiyādh	
		Malā'ibah
		Musāhimah
		Musā'idah
		Adhyeibāt
		Jawāsirah
		Muhālibah
		Muweijīyah
		Aghrubah
		Karāshah
		Sawābir
SUNNA'. Smiths		
NAWAR. Gipsies		

7. The 'Uqeil.

The 'UQEIL (Ageyl) are the guides and conductors of caravans in Arabia. They are not a tribe but an organization partaking of the nature of a club or society or a masonic lodge. They have no connexion with the ancient 'Uqeil tribe of the Ahl esh-Shimāl, from whom the Muntefiq

T 2

claim descent; this seems to have disappeared and left no trace. The modern 'Uqeil are all Nejd Arabs, townsfolk or nomads of any tribe from Hasa, 'Āridh, Qasīm or Jebel Shammar; but men of Sedeir and the Wādi Dawāsir are not admitted; nor are members admitted from any of the big tribes, such as the Harb and Ateibah, who are engaged in interminable blood feuds, the object being to keep the 'Uqeil society neutral. Settled Beni Tamīm and Beni Khālid of Nejd and Qasīm are most suitable for its purposes. The head-quarters of the society are at Baghdad, and its president, who is always a native of Boreidah, lives at Baghdad and there enrolls the members.

The 'Uqeil are of two kinds: JEMĀMĪL, camel-men forming the fraternity of caravan leaders, and DHOGORTI, poor men, pedlars and mercenaries, who help to compose an irregular cavalry under the Ottoman flag and serve as escort to the Hajj and as guards to the *kellas*, (stations or halting-places), on the Hajj road. These last do not belong to the society. The true 'Uqeil are recognized throughout Arabia as professional guides whose presence vouches for a caravan of merchants or travellers and removes it from all suspicion of hostile intentions. It is the 'Uqeil who conduct the camel-trade of the desert, being employed by the dealers of Damascus to purchase from the tribes in Arabia, in the Syrian desert, and in Mesopotamia.

Such an institution as this society, with universal freedom of passage, is essential to the conduct of business in Arabia, where no tribesman, unless he be engaged on a raiding expedition, dare venture outside his own tribal territory for fear of hereditary feuds and enmities which imperil his existence. Thanks to their recognition as carriers by all Arab tribes, the 'Uqeil can be of great service to a European traveller, as they are in a position to conduct him anywhere in more or less security, provided he agrees to go by their route and at their pace. It is very dangerous for such a traveller to assume the character of an 'Uqeil: but Arabs, who wish to shield the caravan in which the traveller is from molestation, will sometimes impose it on him (this was done to Shakespear near Wādi el-'Arabah in 1914). His best course, then, is, on the approach of any stranger, to feign illness and remain rolled up, face and all.

SEDENTARY TRIBES OF THE NORTH-WEST

(A) BELQA

The Belqa is a district east of Jordan and the Dead Sea, which extends roughly from Zerqa, north-east of 'Ammān (Ammon), to the Wādi Zerqa, south of the ancient Christian village of Mādeba, and eastward nearly to Qasr el-Azraq. The Jebel Haurān and the Jebel 'Ajlūn bound it on the north. The BENI SAKHR are the predominant tribe in its southern reaches, the RUWEILAH penetrate into the eastern pasturages near Azraq, the 'ADWĀN are paramount over the Jordan valley (the Ghōr), the Beq'a (i.e. the hills between the Ghōr and the Heshbān), and the lands round Heshbān. The smaller tribes of the Belqa acknowledge the authority of the principal 'Adwān Sheikh, Sultān ibn 'Ali Dhi'āb, whose head-quarters are at Heshbān; and it will therefore be convenient to treat the whole of the BELQAWĪYAH, including the 'Adwān, under one head.

They are a half-settled people, scattered pretty thickly over a comparatively small area; for though the Belqa is not in extent considerable, it is a country rich in pasturage, with plentiful rains in winter, and supports a much larger population than any corresponding area of the Hamād. At a moderate reckoning there must be at least 4,500 tents within its confines, in addition to the big villages of Salt, 'Ammān, and Mādeba, which hold permanently settled inhabitants.[1] It contains much cultivated land and still more which would repay husbandry. The valleys leading down to Jordan are full of timber, oak, terebinth, and smaller trees, and even the uplands might be well wooded, but for the depredations of the goats and charcoal-burners. Round Salt the hillsides are terraced for vineyards, and the gardens of the sturdy Christian and Moslem population are planted with fruit-trees. The pasture grounds of Heshbān are famous, and Mādeba, which is still largely Christian, is set in cornfields. At 'Ammān an industrious Circassian colony has filled the valley with gardens and poplar groves, constructed roads along which they can drive their two-wheeled carts, and covered the slopes of the hills with corn. Innumerable ruin-fields, remains of villages of the Christian period before the Mohammedan invasion, testify to the fertility of the soil, and its capacity for carrying a larger population. In the winter the warm Jordan valley is favourable for early crops, and forms an ideal refuge for flocks and herds.

Unhappily the edges of the desert suffer notoriously from the shortcomings of the Turkish administration. Since 1895 the Ottoman Government has occupied Kerak and Ma'ān, placing a mutesarrif at the former and a kaimmakam at the latter; there are mudirs at Wālah, Tafīlah,

[1] The villagers themselves are grouped into tribal confederations.

and Shōbak, a kaimmakam at Salt, and mudirs at Mādeba and 'Āmmān. With the opening of the railway to Ma'ān in 1905 communications have been facilitated and small military posts are established along the line. The results have been disappointing. The Belqawīyah, like all the border tribes, have lost touch with the desert law, though they have not acquired any other code in its place. They maintain a tribal organization and a vast network of tribal feuds in which the Ottoman Government seldom interferes, even on behalf of settlers, Circassian, Christian, or Moslem. The whole country is turbulent, crime abounds and justice is almost non-existent. The villagers protect themselves as best they can, partly by force of arms, but mostly by paying tribute to the Arab Sheikhs in the form of unstinted hospitality and liberal propitiation by gifts in kind. The Circassians, a race detested by the Arabs, incur more hostility from the tribes than other townsfolk, but are also better able to hold their own, being born fighters and well armed. Though the disputes often lead to bloodshed, they are usually small affairs, petty robberies taking the place of raids among the border tribes. But in the summer, when great numbers of the Beni Sakhr come up to the northern pasturages, and the Anazah draw in from the east, the Belqa is the scene of continuous disturbance, ranging from pitched battles to the satisfaction of individual blood-feuds, and no established authority intervenes.

Yet it is just in such frontier lands as these that any strong administration would seize its chance, and herein lies the political importance of tribes like the Belqawīyah. They are cultivators, after the inefficient manner of the Arabs, and like all the half-settled people their numbers are surprisingly large in comparison with those of purely nomadic tribes. They have few camels, and those which they possess are bought from the Bedouins, not bred by themselves; but they rear large flocks of sheep and goats, and live richly on their milk during the spring. The fact that they own cultivated ground should give the Government a firm hold over them; they are immobilized thereby, nor do their pastoral conditions give them the means of rapid transport. Their numbers would make them a solid barrier between their wandering kinsmen, who can slip through the fingers of the law at any moment leaving no pledge behind, and the permanently settled lands. Moreover, their geographical position makes them the first problem to be dealt with, a problem on which the security of wide and fertile regions, now lying to a great extent derelict, must depend.

A group of the 'ADWĀN, some 700 tents, is seated in Mesopotamia at Qorinshār, west of the Khābūr. Numerically the largest of the Belqa tribes are the BENI HASAN, who are sometimes counted among the Jebelīyah since they are an offshoot from one of that group, the Ghiyādh. They go up into the slopes of the Druze hills, and sometimes wander into the volcanic country to the east. The SHAWĀBKAH, as their name indicates, come from Shōbak and are a new tribe; but the 'Adwān are an old confederation tracing their descent through Qeis to Mudhar, a respectable lineage. The 'AJĀRMAH venerate an ancestor, Sōbah, who, they relate, came from lands farther east. His son, 'Ajram, is the eponymous founder of the tribe.

No doubt all the Belqawīyah are, like the 'Adwān, Ahl esh-Shamāl, and though their own stories of their parentage are mere legend and usually devoid of any historic basis, it is reasonable to conjecture that they must have taken part in the gradual sweep northwards of the Hejaz tribes after the Mohammedan conquest. They displaced and even wholly obliterated the powerful Yemenite nation of the Beni Ghassān, which held the marches for the Roman Empire along the Haurān harrahs and in the Belqa, just as the Ghassānids had stepped into the place of the Nabataeans and tribes of the Safah, whose Aramaic dialects, attested by countless graffiti, link them with the civilization of Eastern Arabia and the frontiers of Mesopotamia. It is conceivable that the legendary origin of the 'Ajārmah from an Eastern ancestor may have some real foundation in history, and that they may be connected with strata of culture long since submerged by later migrations, which go back to the last centuries before the Christian era.

The SIRHĀN, now a small tribe scattered over the Belqa, the Jordan valley, and the Southern Haurān hills, are reckoned to be of the best Northern Arab blood, though they have fallen to low estate. They owned the whole of the Wādi Sirhān, which is named after them, and were ejected from it by the Anazah. They are now sheep-breeders, like the rest of the Ghawāmah, and reduced to small numbers.

BELQAWĪYAH

Tribe.	Sub-Tribe.	Clan.
'ADWĀN. 400 tents Sultān ibn 'Ali Dhi'āb, Heshbān	Sālih, 140 tents Sultān ibn 'Ali Dhi'āb, at Heshbān Nimr, 60 tents Fahd ibn Qablān, nephew of Sultān ibn 'Ali at Zabūd near Heshbān 'Assāf, 70 tents Qablān, east of Salt Kā'id, 90 tents Fā'iz ibn abu 'Arabi, in the Beq'a Thawābīyah, 40 tents Rumeilah, in the Ghōr Juhrān el-'Abid Suleimān Hamdān, at Masūh Cultivators, vassals of Sultān ibn 'Ali, paying him tribute and giving military service	
'ABBĀD, 600 tents Nahār el-Bukheit, Wādi Sīr	Manāsīr Nahār el-Bukheit, near 'Arāqīl Amīr Ifqaha, 70 tents Fellāh esh-Shaddād at Jeri'ah Nu'eimāt, 200 tents Sālim, NW. of Salt Duweikāt, 120 tents Duweik, at Bahāth, W. of Wādi Sīr	

BELQAWĪYAH (continued)

Tribe.	Sub-Tribe.	Clan.
'AJĀRMAH. 300 tents Nā'if ibn Shahawān, near Heshbān and down to the Ghōr.	*Muteiri'īn*, 70 tents 　'Aqil el-'Aqil, at Suwānīyah and Mushaqqar *Isifah*, 40 tents 　Sa'īd esh-Shahawān, at El-'Āl, near Heshbān *Sawā'ir*, 30 tents 　Fanash, at Sāmek *'Ifeishāt*, 25–30 tents 　'Abd el-'Azīz, at Nā'ūr, near Heshbān *Harāfīs*, 30 tents 　Ihris, plain of Mahālah *Sheneiqīyīn*, 20 tents 　Rāshid el-Hasan, at Heshbān *Sahuwān*, 60 tents 　Ibn Mustafa	*Halāhalah* *Manā'isah*
BENI HASAN, 860 tents 'Awwād ibn Kallāb, Zerqa	*Izīra*, 50 tents 　'Awwād esh-Shahhādah, at Rumṁānah and Kamsa, S. of Zerqa *Khawāldah*, 150 tents 　'Ali, at 'Aluq *Khalā'ilah*, 40 tents 　'Ali Suleimān, S. of Zerqa *Ghaziyālah*, 120 tents 　Falāh ibn Rusheid, at Sarrūt, S. of Zerqa *Beni 'Aleim*, 100 tents 　Hammād el-Hārhashi, at Qafqafa, N. of Zerqa *'Amūsh*, 300 tents 　'Awwād ibn Kallāb *Rusheidāt*, 100 tents 　Ahmed abu Rusheidah, at Mutawwi	
GHAWĀMAH (Arabs of the Ghōr) Independent tribes	*Mashālkha*, 60 tents 　'Ali Sa'd, at Abu 'Ubeidah in the Ghōr *Balāwanah*, 40–60 tents 　'Ali Sa'ūd, at Rajeb, N. of Zerqa *Ghazāwīyah*, 100 tents 　Mohammed el-Mijwal, at Sheikh Abīl *Sukhūr el-Ghōr*, 90–100 tents 　Rajah abu el-Leben, at Zār el-Bāsha *Bashātwah*, 150 tents 　Hasan, at Majama' *Saqr*, 260–300 tents 　'Ursān ibn Mulāk, at Beisān *Duleikah*, 350 tents 　Fadhīl el-'Īsa, at Zuheir el-Qiddis *Masā'id*, 80 tents 　Dhāmin el-Mas'ūdah, Wādi Fārah, W. of Jordan *Riyāhanah*, 100 tents 　Fahd, at Jericho *Beni Khālid*, 300 tents 　'Othmān el-Qādhi, at Zawīyah, W. of Sheikh Sa'd *Sirhān*, 200 tents 　Sālim Abu Rāfi', from the Ghōr to the Jebel Haurān	
SHAWĀBKAH 'Abdullah el-Metā'ibah, W. of Heshbān	*Metā'ibah*, 100 tents 　'Abdullah *Munā'ihah* *Dhawāt* *Harā'id*	

BELQAWĪYAH (continued)

Tribe.	Sub-Tribe.	Clan.

SHAWĀBKAH (contd.).	Hawāzin, 700 tents
	  'Ali Abu Wandi, at Mā'īn
	Nijādah
	  'Ali Abu Wandi
	Humeimāt
	  'Ali Abu Wandi	

SHAWĀKRAH, 50–60 tents Bāshir el-Farūj, at Kufeir Abu Ghina	Shakhātrah Khalbalāt 'Abīd At Kufeir Abu Sarbūt	

YAZĀ'IDA. 70 tents
Bāshir el-Turmān, at Judeid. Allies of Ghanamāt
	Sharūqiyīn
	  Bāshir el-Turmān
	Qureiniyīn
	  Mohammed el-Khawātra	

GHANAMĀT. 90 tents Sālim abu Manāwir el-Husein, at Mount Nebo	Masāndah, 3 tents Harāwi, 4 tents Sha'ra, 2 tents Wakhyān, 40 tents 'Atawīn, 2 tents And other small clans.	
MARĀSHDAH Sa'd Raqād, 16 tents at Kufeir near Mādeba. Some of the tribe are near 'Ammān	Butnān Siyūf Dahām Ghaleilāt 'Abīd Shakhatrah, 5 tents 'Eid	

ARABS OF 'AMMĀN
Independent tribes
	Dhiyīb, 65 tents
	  Shebāka, N. of 'Ammān
	Sawārbah
	Jawāmis, 60 tents
	  Muheimir, at Markah NE. of 'Ammān
	Da'ja, 100 tents
	  Muheimir, at Markah
	Aghsalāt, 30 tents
	  Suleimān el-Qureir, at Umm Quseir
	Ahnītīn
	  Rashīd, at Abu 'Alinda
	Ibn Hadīd, 50 tents
	  Ishtiwi ibn Hadīd, at Umm el-Heirān
	Debībah, 20 tents
	  Marj Debībah at Itbuqa	

ARABS OF MĀDEBA
Independent tribes
	'Azeizāt, 47 tents
	  Ya'qūb
	Ma'āyah, 34 tents
	  'Udetallah
	Karādshah, 37 tents
	  Salāmah ibn 'Azārah	

(B) KERAK AND SHŌBAK

THE Arabs of the Kerak-Shōbak district were long the bane of all travellers and entirely beyond official control. They are noted robbers, cruel, faithless, and intractable. Since the establishment of a Turkish Mutesarrif at Kerak and a Kaimmakam at Shōbak, they have been reduced to some sort of order; but in the autumn of 1910 the Majālīyah of Kerak revolted, tore up the Hejaz Railway in several places, killed the employés, held up the trains, and stripped the passengers. They were severely repressed by Sāmi Pasha, who called all the Bedouins as far as Ma'ān to account, including the Huweitāt. His energetic action has not yet faded entirely from memory.

All the tribes of this group are cultivators and sheep-breeders. Those who have houses in Kerak or Shōbak send out their flocks into the desert in spring. The Shōbak Arabs exact tribute from the Kerak people. The list here given is taken from Jaussen, who explains that the word *house*, used as a unit in his computation, implies the patriarchal family, including the married sons with their wives and families.

TRIBES OF KERAK AND SHŌBAK

Tribe.	Sub-Tribe.	Clan.
ARABS OF KERAK. Sālih el-Mujalli	Majālīyah, 140 houses Sālih	'Ashīrat Yūsuf Sālih
		'Ashīrat Suleimān Khalīl
		'Ashīrat Ghabūn Khalīl ibn Dā'ūd
		'Ashīrat Dā'ūd 'Awwād
	Ma'ā'itah, 240 houses Yūsuf Saher	'Ashīrat Rashā'idah Sāhir
		'Ashīrat Zaqā'ilah Yūsuf
		'Ashīrat Beyā'idah Ja'far
		'Ashīrat Jalāmdah
		'Ashīrat Laghawāt
	Sarā'irah, 160 houses Yahya	'Ashīrat 'Ai Yahya
		'Ashīrat Aqā'ilah Sālim ibn 'Isa
		'Ashīrat Dā'ūd Salīm ibn 'Ayyād
	Tarāwinah, 200 houses Husein ibn Mohammed	'Ashīrat Tarāwinah Husein ibn Mohammed
		'Ashīrat Qatā'unei Yūsuf
		'Ashīrat Nawā'isah Mushawwah
	Dhumūr, 160 houses Mahmūd ibn Tāha	'Ashīrat Dhumūr Mahmūd ibn Tāha

TRIBES OF KERAK AND SHŌBAK (continued)

Tribe.	Sub-Tribe.	Clan.

ARABS OF KERAK (contd.)	Dhumūr (contd.)	'Ashīrat 'Uqūl
		  Ahmed
		'Ashīrat Sa'ūb
		  Hattāb
		'Ashīrat Mubeidhīn
		  Yūsuf ibn Fālih
		'Ashīrat Suheimāt
		  Suleimān

	Qedha, 40 houses
	  Muqbil ibn 'Īsa
	Bashā'ishah, 20 houses
	  Husein
	Habā'ishah, 130 houses
	  Derwīsh
		'Ashīrat Habāshah
		  Derwīsh
		'Ashīrat Arūd
		  Buseibas
		'Ashīrat Rehā'ifah
		  'Abd el-Mu'tī
		'Ashīrat 'Asāsfah
		  Hammād
		'Ashīrat Ramādhin
		  Mohammed
		'Ashīrat Zuneibāt
		  Fāris
		'Ashīrat Kefāwīn
		  Hāmid

	'Amr, 50 houses
	  Ghāfil ibn Tubeiti
	'Arab el-Batūs, 50 houses in Wādi Khanzirah
	  Musallim el-Mājūdi
	'Arab el-'Irāq
	  3 hours from Kerak
	  Mohammed ibn Hasan
	'Arab el-Brārshi, 200 houses
	  At Kafr Rabba, S. of Kerak
	Hadāyāt, 120 houses, E. of Dhāt Ras
	  Sālim	

CHRISTIAN TRIBES.
houses
	200 Halasa
	  'Īsa el-Qaus
	Zereiqāt
	  Mezzi Jirjis
	Madānāt
	  Suleimān ibn 'Īsa
	Hejāzīn
	  Yūsuf
	Beqā'īn
	  Suleimān
	'Akasha
	  Selmān en-Nesrāwīn
	Mara'āya or Sunna
	  Butrus
	Haddādīn
	  Khalīl ibn Ibrāhīm	

MOSLEMS OUTSIDE KERAK	Mahmūdiyīn, 100 tents
	  Khallāf ibn Sa'īd
	  In the Ruweih; they go up to Kerak	

TRIBES OF KERAK AND SHŌBAK (*continued*)

Tribe.	Sub-Tribe.	Clan.
MOSLEMS OUTSIDE KERAK (*contd.*)	*Manā'in.* N. of Shōbak and E. of the Jebāl	*'Āqir*, 100 tents 'Ali *Rudeisi*, 60 tents Sālim
	Sa'ūdiyin, 60 tents Between Shōbak and the Jebāl	
ARABS OF SHŌBAK	*Rashā'idah* Za'l ibn Saqr SSW. of Shōbak *Ghawāflah*, 40–50 tents Salmān ibn Hasan, in esh-Shera', S. of Petra *'Amārin* Sālim	
ARABS OF TAFĪLAH	*'Awarān*, 600 houses Dhi'āb	

SEDENTARY TRIBES OF THE WEST

(A) ASHRĀF

THE ASHRĀF (Sherifial clansmen) in general are the descendants of Hasan, who was son of 'Ali and Fātimah, and through the latter grandson of the Prophet. There are said to be twenty-one clans of this descent scattered over Arabia, of which fifteen live wholly or in part in Hejaz or North-west Asir, and chiefly in and near Mecca. For the most part numerically small, they derive importance from the consideration which their individual members enjoy throughout Arabia. Theoretically, the Emirs (Grand Sherifs) of Mecca might be chosen from any clan of the Ashrāf; but, in fact, they have belonged to one or another branch of the descendants of Abu Numej (who was of the Qatadah stock) for so many generations, that nowadays succession to this office is, in practice, as much confined by prescription to only two or three clans, as the Sultanate of Turkey is to the House of 'Othmān.

The mutual affinities, the interconnexion, and the present condition of the Ashrāf clans, are not well known; and many of them are mere names to us.

(a) *Abādilah* is the ruling clan at present, being that to which the Emir (Grand Sherif) and his house belong. It is descended from Sherif 'Abdullah, grandson of Mohammed Abu Numej (1631). It was raised to power by Mohammed 'Ali of Egypt in 1827 during his occupation of Hejaz, in place of the Dhawi Zeid, who had held the throne since the latter part of the eighteenth century and also at an earlier epoch. In the earlier eighteenth century the Emirate had been with the Dhawi Barakāt. The 'Abādilah clan of Hejaz is entirely settled, the bulk of it living outside Mecca south of the Jiddah road. Many of its members hold office under the Emir. There is another branch in Asir (see p. 159) and scattered families are found in other parts of Arabia.

(b) *Dhawi Zeid*. The Dhawi Zeid clan, which descends from Zeid, great-great-grandson of Mohammed Abu Numej, is settled in Mecca. The houses of 'Abd el-Mutallib and Ghālib are of the Dhawi Zeid clan, and there is rivalry and bad feeling between it and the 'Abādilah.

The only leading members of the clan who live at Mecca are Sherif Zeid, son of Feisāl, a young man of about twenty, and the Sherifah Azza, daughter(?) of Sherif 'Aun er-Rafīq. The latter appears to be a woman of considerable character, with a keen interest in politics and some power over the Harb. She is unmarried and about sixty years old. The Dhawi Zeid own a large amount of property in Mecca and Jiddah and possess many slaves.

(c) *Shenabrah*. The Shenabrah descend from an eponymous Sherif, Shanbar, not of a ruling house. They are nomadic, and are dealt with on p. 129.

(d) *Dhawi Surur*. The Dhawi Surur are descendants of Sherif Surur, who ruled as Emir in the latter part of the eighteenth century. They are nomadic, and are treated on p. 129.

(e) *Dhawi Barakāt*. The Dhawi Barakāt, descendants of Barakāt, third son of Mohammed Abu Numej, are no longer in Hejaz proper, where they held the supreme power up to the latter part of the eighteenth century and, at a slightly later period, were robbers in Wādi Fātimah. They are said by Burckhardt to have been exhausted by family wars of succession. They are now found in North-western Asir organized as a tribe (see p. 167).

(f) *Dhawi Hasan*. Descendants of Hasan, second son of Mohammed Abu Numej, are also no longer in Hejaz, but in North-western Asir organized as a tribe (see p. 174).

Other Ashrāf clans of Hejaz, e.g. *Hirāz, Dhawi 'Abd el-Kerīm, Hurith, Menema, Dhawi Jizān, Dhawi Judallah, Manādil, Dhawi Ibrāhīm*, and *Dhawi 'Amr*, are, apparently, not of actual political importance. For the *Ja'āfirah* of Asir see p. 177.

Ashrāf are numerous and powerful in Yemen, in the districts of Māreb and Harib, and in Wadyān Dawāsir; but, as is natural, they are most conspicuous and best known in Hejaz.

(B) ASIR

1. *Abādilah.*

One of the twenty-one clans of Ashrāf.

1. By far the more important section is that settled in Mecca, on which see previous section.

2. There is a small colony of them which has been settled for many generations in the Beni Qutābah country of the Rijāl el-M'a. Their influence is local and unimportant. Sherif 'Abd ibn 'Abdullah is their leading representative.

3. Another small colony has lived for many years with the Dhawi Barakāt, about four hours east of Shakkat el-Yemenīyah. They are allied with the Dhawi Barakāt and friendly with the Zobeid. Their chief Sheikh is Sherif Tālib ibn Qasīm.

2. *Beni 'Abs.*

The BENI 'ABS inhabit the country between Wādi Habl on the north and Wādis 'Ain and Wārith on the south. Their territory extends from the sea to the first foot-hills some 25 miles inland, and is bounded on the north by the Beni Hasan, on the east by Beni Aslam and on the south by the Wa'zāt. They are from the people of the north and trace their descent from 'Adnān through 'Abs the son of Ghatafān, the son of Qeis, the son of Mudhar. They say that they originally came from the Hejaz, and after moving south at some unknown period to Beit el-Faqīh, they again passed north about 500 years ago till they came to their present territory. There is still a small remnant of the tribe, whose present Sheikh is Sheikh Bekhīt, near Beit el-Faqīh, immediately to the north of the powerful tribe of Zaranik (Dharāniq). The northern 'Abs can put into the field about 3,000 good fighting men well armed with Mausers and Martinis, and are enthusiastic adherents of Idrīsi. In 1915 Yahya 'Ali ibn Thawāb, their paramount Sheikh, was joint Commander of Idrīsi's second army opposed to the Turkish forces near Loheia. With Hādi ibn Ahmed el-Heij the chief of the Wa'zāt and the main local supporter of the Turks, the 'Abs have a long-standing feud. Between them and the Beni Aslam there is an enmity which leads to frequent fighting when the rest of the world is at peace, but which is laid aside when the interests of their common lord, Idrīsi, demand. With the Beni Zeid, who are the allies of the Beni Aslam, their relations are the same. They stand to the Beni Hasan as protectors and friends and range freely over their country up to Wādi Heirān. They are partly nomad and partly settled and trading, and though less in number than the Wa'zāt they are richer. They sow enough grain for their needs and trade with the tribesmen from the hills, taking from them skins and coffee, and selling to them articles of clothing and the like which in times of peace they bring from Loheia and Hodeidah. Their two chief villages are Sūq el-Himāri and Sūq 'Abs, where every Friday and Sunday respectively are held markets to which the neighbouring tribesmen come. Sheikh Yahya ibn 'Ali Thawāb is responsible that peace is kept at Sūq el-Himāri. The Sheikhs of the Qutābah and Bitarīyah see to the security of Sūq 'Abs.

Chief Sheikhs: Yahya 'Ali ibn Ahmed Hādi Thawāb and Hasan 'Ali Thawāb his brother.

3,000 fighting men.

Sub-Tribes.	Sheikh.	Place.
METWALA	'Ali Hasan Quwah	W. of Sūq Himāri.
MANAZIR GUEIRA	Hādi Ahmed Geilān Dawiyah	N. of Sūq Himāri.
QAFRA	'Urciq Ahmed	E. of Sūq Himāri.
RANF	Suweid 'Ali	S. of Sūq Himāri.
SHAFAR	'Ali Saghīr	Between Sūq Himāri and Sūq 'Abs.
KHARAZAH	Harib Ayya	To the E. in the hills up to W. Ghadir the Beni Aslam boundary.
QUTĀBAH	Ahmed 'Ali	Sūq 'Abs and W. to the sea.
BITARĪYAH	'Īsa	With Qutābah.
MUDANI'I	Hādi Ahmed ibn 'Abdu	Isolated colony in the mountains near Rufā'ah, 4 hours E. of Sūq 'Abs.

3. *'Alqam el-Hūl (Haul).*

The 'ALQAM EL-HŪL occupy a narrow strip of country beginning about 2 miles north of Ibha and running out to the west for about 20 miles. The Rabī'ah wa Rufeidah adjoin them on the north, the Beni Mālik on the east, the Beni Mugheid on the south, and the Rijāl el-M'a on the west.

They are divided into two sections, 'Alqam es-Sahil near Ibha and 'Alqam el-'Alein to the west. Each of these numbers about 2,000 men. The chief Sheikh of the 'Alqam es-Sahil is Ahmed ibn Hamīd, a prosperous man of about 45, who is a member of the 'Town Council' at Ibha. The 'Āl Yūsuf are noted for the beauty of their women, many of whom are married to Turks. The 'Alqam el-'Alein are not on good terms with the 'Alqam es-Sahil, and their Sheikh Abu Matīr, a man of 65, is said to have pro-Idrīsi tendencies. The tribe is, however, thoroughly under the control of the Turks and pays its taxes regularly. It is generally on bad terms with the Beni Mālik and Beni Mugheid, although there can be no actual fighting, and is friendly with the Rabī'ah wa Rufeidah, the Beni Qeis and the Beni Zeidīn sections of the Rijāl el-M'a. It has a good reputation for bravery. It traces its descent to Qahtān.

(a) *'Alqam es-Sahil.* Settled. 2,000 men.

Paramount Chief: Ahmed ibn Hāmid.
Chief Muftis: 'Abdullah ibn Hujahri and Ibn 'Abbās.
Chief villages:—

'Ain Ibn Musāfi	Murei Abu Zu.
Hamārah	Mushabbab ibn Ta'yīn.
Umm Makmar	Nāsir ibn Mushabbab.

Umm Shatt	'Ā'idh ibn 'Ā'idh ibn Mushabbab.
Āl Umm Ghaidah	'Ali ibn Mushabab.
Wādi el-Beih	'Ali ibn Jurāwi.
Āl Yūsuf	Hinbis.
Qarādah	'Abdullah ibn 'Uqrān.
Dein Sunum	Sa'īd Shaghlah.
Mahsān	Mohammed Abu Hanash.
Āl Wādi Mutah	Yahya Tāhir es-Stambūli.

(b) *'Alqam el-'Alein.* 2,000 men.
Beni Ma'āzin.
Chief Sheikh : Abu Matīr.

Chief villages :—

Jau Umm Nejeim	Mohammed ibn Muhsin.
Jebel Kotheiri	Mufarrih ibn 'Ā'idh.
Juhān	Ibn Duseiri.
Ghiana	Sha'bān.
Umm Mujādhah	Ahmed ibn Fa'ai.
Sūda Āl Thawābi	Mohammed ibn Zeid.
Āl Umm Gaseir	Ibn Daumān.

4. *Beni 'Amr.*

The BENI 'AMR are a small settled tribe in the highland country through which the Ibha–Tā'if road passes. Their northern boundary adjoins the Bulqarn and on all other sides they are surrounded by the Beni Shihir, the nomadic Neid being to their east and the settled Ka'b to their south and west. Their country is well watered and productive, wooded except where the ground has been cleared for cultivation. The chief Sheikh is Sa'īd ibn 'Othmān, who lives at Shij, and is said to be a good tribal chief. The Beni 'Amr number about 2,000 men and are hospitable and a fine fighting tribe. They have always been violently anti-Turk and about ten years ago, under Sa'īd ibn 'Othmān, defeated a strong Turkish column led by Mohammed Amīn Pasha which was sent to subdue them. They pay allegiance to Idrīsi but not to the extent of allowing him to levy taxes. They are allied with the Bulqarn and have an old feud with the Ka'b, Beni Kerīm, and Neid sections of the Beni Shihir.

The tribe traces its descent to the Rijāl el-Hajar.

Paramount Sheikh : Sa'īd ibn 'Othmān of Shij. 2,000 men.
Clans :—

Āl Suleimān	Mukhāsir ibn Mohammed.
Udheidāt	'Abd ibn Talhah.
Beni Rāfi'	Dhuleim ibn Bukheikh.
Āl esh-Sheikh	Sa'īd ibn Rahmah.
Ahl Jebel el-Mutla	Dalīr ibn Mohammed.

5. Bahr Ibn Sekeinah.

The BAHR IBN SEKEINAH live along the Muhā'il-Birk road from about 9 miles south-west of Muhā'il to within 18 miles of Birk, a distance of approximately 29 miles. They are bounded on the north by the Āl Mūsa, on the east first by the Beni Thuwwah and then by the Rijāl el-M'a, on the south by the Rijāl el-M'a, and on the west by the Beni Hilāl.

They number 1,000 men of whom 600 are settled and the rest, the Latīm and the Makhlūtah, nomad. They share with the Beni Hilāl the reputation of being one of the most unregenerate and irresponsible tribes of Asir, and the nomads are still Moslems merely in name, though the influence of Idrīsi during the past few years has done something to reform them. They have never acknowledged the sway of the Turk nor have the latter been able to subdue them. Their country in the highlands of Asir is thickly forested, abounding in running streams, but only a little has been cleared for cultivation.

Their paramount Sheikh is Seyyid Mustafa, a man of 35 years of age, and one of the most prominent figures in Asir. He belongs to a family of Seyyids and not to the tribe itself. In 1912 Idrīsi placed him in supreme command of the forces opposing the Turks and the Sherif of Mecca. When the fighting was over the Rijāl el-M'a, who will suffer no outsider, complained to Idrīsi against his being put over them and even went so far as to try to murder him. He has his own tribesmen thoroughly under control and is looked up to as a stern but just ruler. He is responsible for collecting tribute for Idrīsi and, reserving for himself a quarter of all he receives, has grown rich and lives in some state in Jannah.

The most serious engagement in the war of 1912 took place at 'Ayādi in his country, resulting in a check for Idrīsi.

The Bahr Ibn Sekeinah claim kinship with the Rijāl el-M'a and are usually on good terms with them. They reckon the Beni Thuwwah amongst their friends but are always at feud with the Beni Hilāl and Āl Mūsa.

Chief Sheikh : Seyyid Mustafa.

Villages : 600 men.
Bahr   Mohammed esh-Shar.
Jannah   Mohammed ibn Ahmed.
Mayādi   Ibn Kheir.
Khamīs el-Bahr   Mohammed ibn Abdullah.

Nomads : 400 men.
Latīm   Abu Zoa.
Makhlūtah   Mohammed Abu Hanash.
Aulād Islām

6. Balahmar.

The BALAHMAR live in the rich highland country to the north of

Ibha, their southern boundary coming to within ten miles of that town. The tribes which adjoin them are on the north the Balasmar, on the east the Shahrān, on the south the Beni Mālik, and on the west the Rabī'ah wa Rufeidah. The tribe is a strong one and numbers about 7,000 men, of whom 4,000 are settled, the rest nomad. Their country is well watered and produces fruits as well as cereals. The paramount Sheikh of the settled portion is 'Abdullah ibn Milhem, a young man of 25, who is liked by the tribe both for his justice and the open house which he keeps. He is a warm supporter of Idrīsi and collects taxes for him.

'Ali ibn 'Abshān, or 'Ali Ghālib Bey as the Turks call him, is the nominal head of all the nomads, but for the last few years he has only had the Āl 'Asla under his control. In his younger days he went to Constantinople and received a military training for five years. On his return to Asir with the rank of Bimbashi he was appointed by the Turks chief tax-collector for the whole district. When Idrīsi revolted he stood by the Government but was not supported by the Balahmar who, with the exception of the Āl 'Asla, all went over to Idrīsi. For the last few years he has lived entirely at Ibha, fearing to go back to his country. He had a house in the village of Malaha in the Beni Mālik district which was razed to the ground a few years ago by Seyyid Mustafa of the Bahr Ibn Sekeinah, the chief general of Idrīsi in Asir. His son 'Ali was one of the first to be chosen to sit in the Ottoman parliament, but on his return from Constantinople was captured between Qunfudah and Ibha by Idrīsi's men and died in captivity at Sabia about six years ago. 'Ali ibn 'Abshān himself is now about 55 years of age and is said to be brave and capable.

The Balahmar say that they are descended from the Rijāl el-Hajar; but they are probably from some other stock, since they are fairer than other Arabs and most of them have red hair which they wear short, and light eyelashes. The villagers have a reputation for cowardice, but the nomads are stout fighters. The whole tribe, however, has an evil name for treachery and theft and are known amongst other tribes as ' Kilāb en-Na'al ', intimating that, as a dog in the night, they will steal the shoes from their sleeping guests.

The Balahmar are friends with the Balasmar, Rabī'ah wa Rufeidah, and Beni Mālik, but are enemies of the Shahrān.

(a) Settled. 4,000 men. Paramount Sheikh : 'Abdullah ibn Milhem.
Chief villages are :—

Beihan	Mushabbab ibn Yūsuf.
Āl A'mer	Mohammed ibn Musheit.
Sabah	Sheikh Himri.
Shijr	Hamūd ibn Mohammed.
Mowein	Sheikh Abu Hanki.
Āl Husein	Sheikh Abu Sha'rab
Āl Meshad	'Othmān ibn Rifā'ah.

Āl Mohammed es-Sahīl	'Amr ibn 'Ali.
Āl Qasīm	Sa'ūd ibn Sa'd.
Wādi Ibl	Mahmūd ibn Mohammed.
Āl Umm Sha'īr	Sultān ibn Ahmed.
Misfarah	Sheikh Abu Hakam.

(b) Nomads. 3,000 men. Paramount Sheikh : 'Ali ibn 'Abshān.
Chief divisions are :—

Āl 'Asla	Himri.
Bahāshah	'Abdullah Ferthān.
Beni Tha'labah	Safar ibn Dūh.

7. Bal'aryān.

The BAL'ARYĀN or 'Sons of nakedness' have received their name from the poor and savage conditions under which they live. They appear to be mostly of African extraction and, save for a few miserable villages, they are nomads. Their exact boundaries have not been ascertained, but it is known that they have the Ghāmid on the north, the Bulqarn et-Tihāmah on their east, the Beni Shihir on their south, and the Zobeid on their west.

They are divided into four sections, the Bal'aryān, the Beni 'Isa, Beni Suleim and Beni Suheim, and are said to number 6,000 men. In normal times they quarrel amongst themselves, but unite when danger from outside threatens.

They reckon all their neighbours as foes, but have been known to help the Shamrān against the Ghāmid. The Beni 'Isa pay a nominal allegiance to Idrīsi, which means that they help him in war if there is a prospect of loot, and in peace refuse to pay him taxes. The other sub-tribes are completely independent and refuse to recognize the authority of any one. There are many of these tribesmen scattered all over the country as far as Muhā'il and Birk, plying the trade of butchers. Although respected for their bravery, they are despised by all true Arabs for their mixed blood, and their lack of religion which almost amounts to paganism.

Sub-tribes :—

Bal'aryān, 2,500 men, mostly nomad.
Beni 'Isa, 1,200 men, mostly settled.
Beni Suleim, 2,000 men, mostly nomad.
Beni Suheim, 600 men, mostly nomad.

8. Balasmar.

The BALASMAR are a strong tribe, reported to number some 9,000 men, and situated due east of Muhā'il from which they are divided by the Reish. The adjoining tribes are the Beni Shihir on the north, the Shahrān on the east, the Balahmar on the south, and the Reish on the west. They are said to be descended from the Rijāl el-Hajar, and are of the same stock as the Beni Shihir. They dwell on the fertile slopes of the hills and up to the long ascent known as the Aqabah Sajein to the top of the main ridge of Asir, and are known accordingly as people of the mountains or people of the Tihāmah. Much coffee is grown on the hill terraces, and wheat and other cereals round the villages.

Jebel Hada is the chief centre of the tribe and the most productive. The Ibha-Tā'if road runs through their territory for about seven miles between Madfa'ah and Tanūmah.

The paramount Sheikh of the whole tribe is 'Ali ibn Mohammed, a man of 50, tall and powerful, with a scar over the right eyebrow. He lives at Madfa'ah and is a firm adherent of Idrīsi, as are the rest of the tribe. Idrīsi takes taxes from them. In former days Turkish influence reached them, but since Idrīsi's rise to power they have been left alone.

The Balasmar are friendly with the Balahmar and the Beni Shihir; with the Reish and Shahrān they are at enmity. Their reputation for hospitality and prowess in war is good.

'Ali ibn Rā'ih is the mufti of the tribe, a dark-skinned man of about 55 with a long flowing beard. He is said to have Turkish leanings, and is on bad terms with 'Ali ibn Mohammed, but he is sound in his judgements and generous, and is liked by the tribe.

Paramount Sheikh : 'Ali ibn Mohammed, of Madfa'ah.   9,000 men.

(a) *Ahl el-Jibāl.* 4,000 men.

Chief villages are :—

Sadwān	'Ali ibn Hasan.
Hudhwah	Yahya ibn 'Allāmah.
Āl Ikhrein	Mohammed ibn Sādiq.
Madfa'ah	'Ali ibn Mohammed.
La'bān	'Ali ibn Sa'īd.

(b) *Ahl et-Tihāmah.* 5,000 men.

Chief villages are :—

Ahl Jebel Haddah	'Abd er-Rahmān.
Umm Zerībah	Mohammed ibn Salīm.
Khamīs Makhādah	Zabān Abu Sudr.
Umm Hajju	Ghurmallah.
Ahl Sūq el-Ithnein	'Ali ibn Shehāb.
Hadar	Barakāt ibn Husein.

9. *Ahl Barak.*

The four tribes of HUMEIDAH, ĀL MŪSA IBN 'ALI, ĀL ISBA'I, and ĀL JEBĀLI are known collectively in Asir as the AHL BARAK, and it will therefore be convenient to class them together, although they do not form a confederation or trace their descent to the same ancestors.

The district of Barak begins about 15 miles north of Muhā'il, and covers an area of about 20 miles from north to south and 30 miles from east to west. It is a fertile country with plentiful rains and is largely cultivated, simsim being the principal crop. It is bounded on the north and east by the Beni Shihir, on the south by the Reish, Āl Dureib, and Rabī'at et-Tahāhīn, and on the west by the Rabī'ah Mujātirah. The most important tribe is the Humeidah, numbering 7,000 men, of whom 4,000 are nomads. They occupy the western part of the district, and the Muhā'il–Qunfudah road from Dhahab to Ghār el-Hindi is in their territory. They quarrel with the Āl Isba'i and are divided amongst themselves, the villagers favouring the Turks, the nomads Idrīsi. Mohammed ibn Hayāzah is their Sheikh, and the paramount Sheikh of the whole district by the nomination of Idrīsi. He is a man of about 45, and has the reputation of using his position with wisdom and moderation.

The Āl Mūsa ibn 'Ali occupy the south-eastern portion of the district along the first stages of the Barak-Tanūmah road, and number about 3,000 men. They are entirely sedentary and agricultural, and disagree with the Āl Jebāli. They are friendly with the Reish and the pro-Idrīsi section of the Āl Mūsa.

The Āl Isba'i are between the Āl Mūsa ibn 'Ali and the Humeidah and north of the Āl Jebāli.

Both the Āl Isba'i and Āl Jebāli are entirely settled in villages.

Taken as a whole the tribes support Idrīsi, with the exception of the settled Humeidah, and pay him taxes. They are peaceful and pleasure-loving, and by no means fond of war. At the same time they are not above harrying small Turkish convoys. The road from Muhā'il to Qunfudah, however, is so beset with unfriendly tribes that the Turks seldom pass over it except in numbers sufficiently large to repel any ordinary attack.

Humeidah. Chief Sheikh : Mohammed ibn Hayāzah. 7,000 men. Chief villages, 3,000 men.

A'jamah	Zāhir Akhu Talah.
Rabu' el-A'jamah	Mohammed ibn Zāhir.
Jidhreimah	Ahmed ibn Hayāzah.
Basham	Mohammed ibn Hasan.
Khabt Āl Hajri	Abu Dōsah.

Nomads, Chief Sheikh : Fa'i ibn Hasan. 4,000 men.

Umm Mahshakah   Fa'i ibn Hasan.
Mishghalah.
Marabah.
Āl-Jemīl.
Āl Sa'īdah.
Āl 'Ablah.
Āl Mohammed.

Al Mūsa ibn 'Ali. Chief Sheikh : Mohammed Abu Tarash. 3,000 men.

Chief villages :—
Jureihah   Abu Dōsah.
Bashamah

Al Isba'i. Chief Sheikh : Hayāzah ibn Hasan. 1,500 men.
Chief villages :—
Sahil	Zabān.
Khamīs Sahil	Milbis.
Umm Ma'āsh	Ibn Umm 'Arīyah.
Sa'dah	Sa'īd Mohammed ibn Nebyah (well-known merchant).

Al Jebāli. Chief Sheikh : Hawāsh. 800 men.
Chief villages :—
Mifah.
Uthrub.

10. *Dhawi Barakāt.*

The DHAWI BARAKĀT are one of the tribes of Ashrāf related to the Qoreish. They occupy a barren stretch of the sea-coast from Shakkat esh-Shāmīyah to about 25 miles south and extend inland for about 14 miles. The Wādi Dōkhah runs through their country and provides water for their annual crop of dukhn and dhura. They number only 400 men, but make up for their paucity of numbers by their reckless daring.

Coastal dhows give their shores a wide berth, for they live chiefly on what they can make by piracy, and in their swift vessels take toll of all who come their way. Their chief is Sherif Hasan Abu Mandīl, a man about 45 years old, who recognizes the authority of neither the Sherif, the Turks, nor Idrīsi. His right-hand man and the one most noted in raiding is Sherif Mohammed ibn Sa'īdah.

They maintain a perpetual feud with their piratical rivals the Dhawi Hasan, but are on friendly terms with the Zahrān, their eastern neighbours, and with the Zobeid to their south. There is a small colony of 'Abādilah Ashrāf in their country, which is allied to them.

An offshoot of the tribe lives at Manādil in the Belā'ir country.

Paramount Sheikh : Sherif Hasan Abu Mandīl. 400 men.
Clans :—
Manādil	Sherif Zein ibn Qasīm.
Hawātimah	Sherif Hāshim ibn 'Ubeid.
Ruwājihah	Sherif Dahshān ibn Khudherr.

Section of Manādil in Belā'ir country. 300 men.
Chief Sheikh : Abu Tālib.
'Abīd el-Manādil   Sheikh Jāmūs.

11. *Belā'ir.*

The BELĀ'IR are a strong and truculent tribe inhabiting the country from between Khabt el-'Umr and Jumā'ah Rabī'ah to Habil and Jōz Belā'ir, on the Qunfudah-Barak road. They are bounded on the north and north-east by the Zobeid, east by the Rabī'ah Mujātirah, south-east by the Rabī'at et-Tahāhīn, south by the Aulād el-'Alaunah, and west by the Marāhibah section of the Beni Zeid.

They are divided into two main divisions, the Nawâshirah, 3,000 men, and the 'Umr, 4,000, the former partly settled, the latter entirely nomad, and ranging the country to the south of their borders. Their situation astride the two main roads from Qunfudah to Muhâ'il is an excellent one for raiding, and they take full advantage of it. They hate the Turks, who can only pass through their country in force. The chief Sheikh is 'Ali ibn Medîni, a man of 50, who was formerly paramount Sheikh of the whole tribe. He was bought over by the Sherif of Mecca in 1912, and his desertion of Idrîsi lost him the support of all the 'Umr and of the Nawâshirah with the exceptions of the Firshah and Sa'dah clans, and the inhabitants of the village of Jôz Belâ'ir. The tribe is still split in two, and Sheikh Ibn Kheirah of the Nawâshirah has gathered most of the power into his hands, and is reckoned amongst the Idrîsi adherents.

Their country includes both plain and hills, and is rich enough to give pasture for large herds of camels, goats, and cattle, and to grow cereals in the rainy season. They are allied with the Zobeid, but are generally at loggerheads with their other neighbours. The most extreme section and the one most feared by travellers is a colony of about 300 of the Dhawi Barakât called the Ashrâf Manâdil, living at Manâdil, just to the west of Jôz Belâ'ir on the main road to Qunfudah. They have lived there for many years and have severed all connexion with their parent tribe, but they have retained the tribal reputation for lawlessness. Their chief is Sherif Abu Tâlib, who pays allegiance to 'Ali ibn Medîni. The colony, however, keeps to itself and does not intermarry with the Belâ'ir nor does it adopt the local custom of allowing its women to go unveiled. The Belâ'ir Arabs are lax in their marriage customs, but they do not marry outside their own tribe. Although truculent and quarrelsome, they have a reputation for clean fighting, and are hospitable to those with whom they are not at feud.

Paramount Sheikhs : 'Ali ibn Medîni of Jôz Belâ'ir ; Ibn Kheirah.

(a) *Nawâshirah.* 3,000 men.

Chief Sheikh : Ibn Kheirah.

Clans :—

Shawâridah	Abu Tommah.
Firshah	Sa'd.
Mujâ'adah	'Ali ibn Ma'addi.
Heil el-Mujâ'adah	Mohammed Munjar.
Habil	Mohammed ibn Hâdi.
Sa'dah	Mohammed ibn 'Abdu.

(b) *'Umr.* 4,000 men.

Mohammed ibn Ahmed.

Clan :—

She'i el-'Umr	Mohammed ibn Musâfir.

12. Bulqarn.

The BULQARN are divided into the Bulqarn es-Serrah and the Bulqarn et-Tihāmah, and stretch in a south-westerly direction from near Bīshah across the tangled mass of mountains which form the backbone of the Asir range, and down towards the seaward slopes. They are bounded on the north by the Shamrān and Khath'am, on the east by the Shahrān and nomads of Beni Shihir, on the south by the Beni 'Amr and Beni Shihir, and on the west by the Bal'aryān and Ghāmid.

The Bulqarn es-Serrah are two-thirds settled and one-third nomad, the Sheikh over all being Mash'ad ibn Bahrān, who lives at 'Alāyah, a large village about eight hours west of Qal'at Bīshah. He is a rich landowner, and also possesses date-groves in Bīshah. The country appears to be fertile and well wooded, and supports large herds of camels, goats, and cattle. The nomads draw in to the cultivation during its season, and when it has been harvested take flour to Bīshah, which they exchange for dates. There is a general truce with the Shahrān amongst all the tribes during the date season at Bīshah, which lasts about four months. At other times the Bulqarn are at feud with the Shahrān, Beni Shihir, Ghāmid, and Shamrān. They are friendly to the Khath'am and Beni 'Amr.

The Bulqarn el-Yemen occupy the lowland district of 'Urdīyah and are wholly given up to farming. Their chief Sheikh is Mujarri ibn Sa'īd.

The two sections of the tribe are friendly, and help each other in war. They are not remarkable for their courage, but can render a good account of themselves. In politics they all favour Idrīsi and pay him taxes. They are hospitable in character, and passage through their country is generally safe.

A. *Bulqarn esh-Shām or es-Serrah.* 6,000 men.
    Chief Sheikh : Mash'ad ibn Bahrān of 'Alāyah.
    1. Settled. 4,000 men. Villages are :—

        Āl Sihil   'Abdullah ibn Nāsir.
        Āl Barqūq   Hanash ibn Jarāwish.
        Sahwah   'Abdullah ibn 'Abd.
        Nakhlah   Merzūq ibn Mohammed.
        Wajrān   'Abdullah ibn Salim.

    2. Nomad. 2,000 men.

        Āl 'Itfāfah   Ibrāhīm ibn Masad.
        Āl Hirīr   Mūsa ibn Ya'qūb.
        Āl Dahshān   Mohammed ibn Hasan.

B. *Bulqarn el-Yemen or et-Tihāmah.* 1,000 men.

        'Urdīyah   Mujarri ibn Sa'īd.
        Āl Mabnah   Ma'addi ibn Suweih.
        Āl Dhirwah   Safar ibn Mohammed.
        Āl Atīm   'Abd el-'Azīz ibn Kheir.
        Beni Suheim   Mohammed ibn Nāsir.

Clans :—
>Āl esh-Sha'eir.
>Āl Shahbah.
>Beni Tala'.
>Āl el-Mudeifir.
>Āl Mizhim.

13. *Āl ed-Dureib.*

The ĀL ED-DUREIB are a small tribe numbering some 800 men, to the north-west of Muhā'il. They occupy about ten miles of the Sikkat el-Helāwīyah from Muhā'il to Qunfudah between the villages of Turqush and Ma'mal Ikhleif, and stretch up along the Barak road for about five miles north of Musabbah, which is in their territory. They are bounded on the north by the Āl Mūsa, west by the Reish, south-east by the Āl Mūsa, south by the Beni Hilāl, and west by the Rabī'at et-Tahāhīn. They are a good fighting race, but are not naturally quarrelsome or bellicose. Idrīsi, however, frequently incites them to cut Turkish communications. Their country is fertile, and they possess many flocks and herds. The Āl Mūsa and Rabī'at et-Tahāhīn are friendly to them, the Āl Jebāli, Reish, and Beni Hilāl as a rule inimical. They have the reputation of being hospitable beyond the ordinary, and travellers can journey without fear in their country.

There is a small offshoot of their nomad sub-section, the Āl Ikhleif, situated in the Rabī'ah Mujātirah country near Ghār el-Hindi, who have cut themselves adrift from the main tribe.

Mohammed ibn 'Amr Akhu 'Abdīyah, a man of 35, is the chief Sheikh. He has been to Mecca several times, and frequently goes to Sabia. During his absence the tribe is governed by his sister 'Abdīyah, who married a Turkish officer, now dead, named 'Ali Bey Rida.

Chief Sheikh : Mohammed ibn 'Amr Akhu 'Abdīyah. 800 men.

Villages :—

Turqush	Mohammed ibn el-'Allāmah.
Musabbah	Mohammed ibn Hedeyyah.
Juzān	Rājih.
Wādi Musabbah	Mushātir.
Wādi el-Ushir	Ma'addi.
Rāhah	Mohammed ibn Bārūd.
'Ain ed-Dureib	Mohammed ibn Kheir.

Nomads :—
>Āl Ikhleif.

14. *Ghāmid.*

The GHĀMID own a wide stretch of territory in the highlands of southern Hejaz and northern Asir, roughly from latitude 19° 30' to 20° 15' and longitude 41° 30' to 42°. The tribes which adjoin them are, on the north the Shalāwah, east Shamrān, south Bulqarn and Bal'aryān, and west

Zobeid and Zahrān. It is difficult to estimate their numbers, reports varying from Burckhardt's estimate of 5,000 to 10,000 fighting men, to a native estimate of 60,000 men. The first is probably as wrong as the last, but there seems no doubt that they are considerably more numerous than any of their neighbours.

The inland road from Ibha to Tā'if runs through the midst of their country, which is well watered and fertile. The tribe is divided into two portions, the nomad and settled, who are always at odds with one another. The nomads are Āl Seyah, a tall race of fine fighters who live to the north of the settled portion and roam far afield to the Shalāwah country round Turabah, to Ranyah, Tathlīth, and Wādi Dawāsir. They are rich in horses, camels, and goats, and recognize no authority. Their chief is Mohammed ibn 'Abd er-Rahmān, a man of about 45, and a noted warrior. He is entirely independent of outside influences.

The chief of the settled Arabs is 'Azīz ibn Musheit, a young man of 25 years of age, who follows the Sherif of Mecca and frequently visits him. He is at enmity with Mohammed ibn 'Abd er-Rahmān. A large number of his men go yearly to Mecca, Jiddah, and Tā'if, and act as porters during the pilgrim season. They remain there for about four months, and return with supplies for the rest of the year. Many invest their savings in rifles, which they buy at one of the two chief markets, Ru'eis near Jiddah or Nuzūlah Beni Mālik. They also buy rifles from the Rijāl el-M'a. Although not noted for their fighting skill they yet are frequently at war, their chief foes being the Zahrān, and after them the Bal'aryān, Bulqarn, Shamrān, and Shahrān. Even the Āl Seyah, who are the better fighters, combine with them when trouble with the Zahrān arises. Their friends are the Zobeid and Beni Mālik of Hejaz.

Their women occupy a much more important position than in most tribes, and take an equal share in all harder forms of manual labour, and even have a say in the tribal councils. The tribe is still nicknamed the Khādimīn ed-Derwīshah, after a woman who died about fifty years ago, having ruled them for nearly 40 years. The women also weave camel's-hair garments and blankets. Owing to the annual migration to the Hajj, the tribe is more civilized than most and has a good reputation for hospitality.

In May 1915, some of their Sheikhs, whose names are not known, wrote to Idrīsi proposing to join him. Idrīsi advised them to keep quiet until a more favourable moment arrived, but sent a Qādhi to collect money from them. At the beginning of 1916 he was still in communication with them.

A man of importance in the tribe is Sālih ibn 'Ajalah. He is the richest merchant, and controls most of the trade between Mecca and the Ghāmid. The export of tobacco, of which a considerable amount is grown, is entirely in his hands.

Another man of influence is Mohammed ibn 'Ali of the Beni Kebīr. He was chosen as one of the representatives of Asir in the Ottoman parliament ten years ago, and went to Constantinople for one session. Not liking the life, he resigned his seat, but still keeps up his Turkish connexions.

Paramount chief : 'Azīz ibn Musheit.

(a) Settled.

Beni Dhubyān	Mohammed ibn Ati.
Beni Kebīr	Ismā'īl ibn Mohammed.
Beni Kebīr	Mohammed ibn Ibrāhīm.
Bal Jurashi	Hizām ibn Ismā'īl.
Humrān	Sa'īd ibn Mohammed.
Āl edh-Dhafīr	Sālih ibn Yāsīn.
Āl Ramādah	Sa'īd ibn Habīb.
Āl Za'lah	Dhi'āb ībn Nāsir.
Beni Sandal	'Abd er-Rahmān el-Merzūq.
Āl Bahdān	Mubārak ibn Muwalla.
Āl Bāh	Dhāfir ibn Sa'īd.
Ahl Wādi Shibriqah	Salīm ibn Mohammed.
Āl Ferza'ah	Hizām ibn Husein.
Beni Munaḫabah	Fā'iz ibn Mohammed.
Beni 'Omar	Mubārak ibn Muwalla (different from above).
Ahl Wādi Batat	Mohammed ibn Mukhāsir.
Beni Lām	Sa'īd ibn 'Abdullah.
Āl Laḥdah	Mohammed ibn Dhubyān.
Beni Muntazar	Haneish ibn 'Ablah.
Beni Talaq	Mohammed ibn Sa'īd.
Beni Khutheim	
Beni Jābūs	'Atīyat Allah.
Beni 'Abdillah	Mohammed ibn Ferhat.
Beni Mintisher	'Ali Jamah.
Beni Balsham	
Beni Nāshir	
Balhirsh	Mohammed ibn 'Atīyah.

(b) Nomad.

Āl Seyah	Mohammed ibn 'Abd er-Rahmān.

15. *Ahl Hali.*

The AHL HALI consist of four tribes which may conveniently be considered together, since, although of different origin, they are politically one, sharing the same country, uniting against common enemies, and being ruled over by one chief. Their country embraces the coastal village of Hali and the district round of the same name. The boundary starts from the coast about five miles north of Hali, runs north-east along the Beni Ya'lah territory, and thence follows a line parallel to the Hali-Jumā'ah Rabī'ah road and about four miles to the west, up to Kidwah, which is 18 miles NNE. from Hali and close to the boundary of the 'Umr section of the

Belā'ir. Thence it goes south-east for about ten miles along the Rabī'at et-Tahāhīn and Beni Dhi'b territory to Kiyād, which is 21 miles NE. of Hali. Here it reaches the Beni Hilāl and follows their line towards the coast, which it touches about 12 miles south of Hali.

The four tribes are the 'Ābid el-Emīr, Ghawānimah, Aulād el-'Alaunah, and Kinānah, who are all settled with the exception of the Salālimah clan of the 'Ābid el-Emīr and the Fellāhah clan of the Aulād el-'Alaunah, both small and unimportant units.

The largest tribe is the Aulād el-'Alaunah, who number 3,000 men and are strung out along the Jumā'ah Rabī'ah road from Kidwah to Minjīyah.

Next in importance are the Ghawānimah (1,500) from Radha to Khā'i along the Muhā'il road; then the Kinānah from the Beni Hilāl to Minjīyah, and finally the 'Ābid el-Emīr (600 men) on the Beni Dhi'b frontier.

The paramount Sheikh over all is Ibn 'Aji, a man of about 55, who in the past was a friend of the Turks, but seceded to Idrīsi when the latter began to grow powerful. The Turks used to occupy Hali, but they were driven out sixteen years ago, and have been unable to regain a footing. The confederation is a rich one, having sufficient water for its agricultural needs and possessing large herds of cattle.

They are noted warriors, and maintain feuds with all their neighbours. The Rijāl el-M'a are the only tribe which they regard with friendly eyes. Their relations towards each other are at times strained, but they unite for common defence and when Idrīsi calls them out.

The 'Ābid el-Emīr were originally slaves of Sudanese stock, but have long since gained their emancipation and now rank on an equality with the Arabs. A number of them go every year on the pilgrimage to Mecca, where they have an evil reputation for robbery and theft.

The Kinānah are an ancient and famous tribe, who probably came into being about A. D. 100, and are descended from the Mudhar branch of Nizār. The Qoreish are a branch of them. They were at first settled near Mecca, and took a prominent part against Mohammed the Prophet, by whom they were subdued. When Africa was invaded part of the tribe went to the Sudan, where they are still found in Kordofan, while others went to Egypt and from there pushed as far west as Morocco. The Arabian remnant had meantime taken up their residence near Hali, where they were reported to be by Ibn Batūtah in 1353.

Some severe fighting took place in the Hali country during the campaign with the Sherif of Mecca and the Turks in 1910, in which the Ahl Hali, who were fighting for Idrīsi, gave a good account of themselves.

Paramount Sheikh : Ibn 'Aji of Aulād el-'Alaunah.

(a) *'Ābid el-Emīr.* 600 men. Ibn Saghīr.

Villages :—
Kiyād   Ibn Zemīm.
Sabt el-Kiyād   Hasan ibn Ahmed.
Bedouins :—
Salālimah.

(b) *Ghawānimah.* 1,500 men. Khalīl el-Ghānim.
Villages :—
Khā'i
Kidwat el-Ghawānimah
Radha
Ibn Shabīb.
Hasan Ghebeish.
Mohammed ibn 'Ajil.

(c) *Aulād el-'Alaunah.* 3,000 men. Hasan Shijeifi.
Villages :—
Minjīyah
Beishi
Ferīq
Fiqāhah
Mashā'ikh
Salāmah
'Ajam Je'eirah
'Ali Shumeih.
Ghabeish.
Hasan Suh.
Medīni.
'Ali Sheikh.
'Ali Serūwi.
Ahmari.
Bedouin :—
Fellāhah.

(d) *Kinānah.* Subdivided into :—
1. Shawārah. 1,000 men. Mohammed ibn 'Abd.
Villages :—
Kidwat el-'Ābid
Beidein
Sheikh 'Ali
Makhshūsh
Sūq el-Ithnein Makhshūsh
Qadab
Merzūq.
Abu 'Alam.
Mubārak ibn Hasan.
Shāmi ibn 'Abbās.
Ahmed ibn 'Abbās.
Ibn Zaghlūl.

2. Beni Yahya. 400 men. Sheikh : Abu Radīyah.
Villages :—
Sulb
Ma'āshīyah
Āl Khirshān
Melhah.
Mohammed ibn Hādi.
'Ali Dellāq.
Sa'īd 'Abdullah ibn Khirshah.

16. *Dhawi Hasan.*

The DHAWI HASAN occupy the coast-line from just north of Līth down to Shakkat esh-Shāmīyah, a distance of about 45 miles, and inland to the beginning of the mountains, which are here only a few miles from the sea. They are of Sherifial stock and connected with the Qoreish, but they do not reflect credit on the tribe, for they pay small attention to religion and concentrate all their energies on piracy, being the most notorious band of freebooters and sea-robbers along the whole coast. The Turks have a garrison about two hours inland from their main post at Līth, and exercise a certain restraint over them ; but the Dhawi Hasan hate both the Turks and the Sherif, and what little deference they show to any one is paid to Idrīsi, who is sufficiently far away to be attractive.

Sherif Mustur represents the Sherif at Lith, and collects a certain amount of taxes.

The chief of the tribe is Sherif Mohammed ibn Hasan ibn el-'Aud, whose name is known with dread by every sailor along the coast. Almost equally feared are his followers, Sherif Ismā'īl Abu Khurfān, Sherif Rājib ibn Dajhid, and Murzut ibn Bakhīt, a Sudanese slave who won his freedom by his skill in raiding. They are friendly with the Zahrān and Juhadlah, their eastern and northern neighbours, but have a long-standing feud with the Dhawi Barakāt, who lie to their south.

The Dhawi Hasan possess many slaves, and the cruelty with which they are treated is notorious in the Hejaz. Blacks captured at sea are invariably enslaved and hamstrung to minimize their chance of escape.

Chief Sheikh : Sherif Mohammed ibn Hasan ibn el-'Aud. 3,000 men.

Āl Āsaf	Sherif Hasan ibn Husein
Khumjān	Sherif Mahjūb ibn Barakāt
Āl Hasan ibn Ahmed	Sherif Haza' ibn Fuzān
Āl Jisās	Sherif Bureik ibn Ahmed

17. *Beni Hasan.*

The BENI HASAN inhabit the country between Wādis Heirān and Habil from the sea to about 20 miles inland, and are bounded on the north by the Beni Marwān, on the south by the Beni 'Abs, and on the east by the Beni Zeid. They are firm friends of the Beni 'Abs, who protect them and range over their country, and they keep on good terms both with the Beni Zeid, whom they fear, and with the Beni Marwān. In number about 2,000 souls, they can put 500 fighting men into the field. Manjūr is their chief village, about 20 miles ESE. of Mīdi; Hasan es-Sa'īd and Mūsa Hasan are their chief Sheikhs.

18. *Beni Hilāl.*

The BENI HILĀL occupy a broad expanse of country stretching from the Sikkat esh-Sherāf between Hali and Muhā'il to Birk on the sea-shore.

Their exact boundary starts at Sabt es-Sawālah, about 23 miles from Hali, and runs just north of the Sikkat esh-Sherāf and Wādi Dofa' up to within 4 miles of Muhā'il, a total distance of about 34 miles. On the north they are bounded by the Rabī'at et-Tahāhīn and Āl ed-Dureib. From Sirr the boundary goes south-west to Birk, marching first with the Āl Mūsa, and finally, near the coast, with the Munjahah. The coast is theirs for about 18 miles north of Birk, and then the boundary goes inland and so up to Sabt es-Sawālah along the Hali border. The country is densely wooded, and provides pasturage for large herds of camels and goats. The tribe is divided into the Ahl Birk, the Āl Ikhtarsh (who live in the direction of Muhā'il, and are subdivided into the Āl Misjar and Āl Umm Jam'ah), and the Arabs of the western parts whose subdivisions have not been ascertained. The Āl Ikhtarsh are said to number 5,000 men, and the remainder, including the Ahl Birk, 7,000.

The Ahl Birk and the Arabs inhabiting the villages along the sea coast, such as Nakhl el-Birk, Nahūd, and Sobākhah, form the only respectable portion of the tribe. They cultivate a little, grow date-trees in some of the villages, and supplement this by collecting salt near Birk, which they sell to the neighbouring tribes. Mohammed ibn 'Abdu is the chief Sheikh, a man of 35 years of age and a staunch adherent of Idrīsi. He is nominal chief over the whole tribe, and does in fact have considerable influence over it. But to keep it entirely in check is almost an impossibility, for it has the well-earned reputation of being one of the wildest and most intractable tribes of the Asir.

Almost pagan, the Hilāl lead an entirely nomadic life, subsisting on meat and milk and buying what little they need from outside. They have closed the Sikkat esh-Sherāf to the Turks, who are obliged to travel by the more northern roads, the Sikkat el-Helāwīyah or the Barak road, and even ordinary travellers do not dare to pass through their country except in large armed parties. As far as they may be said to have any politics, they are pro-Idrīsi, but they are much too out of hand to be of value as allies. They are at daggers drawn with all the neighbouring tribes with the exception of the Rijāl el-M'a, whose hand they fear.

'Ali ibn 'Abdu, the Sheikh of Birk, was recently reported to be in the pay of the Turks, and to be smuggling mails up to Ibha, but the well-known attitude of the tribe renders this improbable. In 1910 the Sherif tried to suborn him with the offer of £3,000. 'Ali ibn 'Abdu's only reply was to send him a Mauser cartridge.

Mohammed ibn Hasan, chief of the Āl Ikhtarsh, is a notorious highwayman, and has a most unsavoury reputation for treachery and cunning.

1. *Ahl Birk.* Chief Sheikh: Mohammed ibn 'Abdu, of Birk.
    Other prominent Sheikhs:

    'Ali ibn 'Abdu (Sheikh of Birk).
    'Ali ibn Muqdi (merchant).
    Sha'bān
    Mohammed ibn Fayy.

2. *Western Arabs.*
3. *Āl Ikhtarsh.*   Mohammed ibn Hasan.
    Āl Misjar.
    Āl Umm Jam'ah.

19. *Ja'dah.*

A small Sunni tribe between the Beni Marwān and Masārihah just south of Wādi Ta'shar, about 10 miles north of Mīdi. Their chief Sheikhs are Mohammed Ahmed and Sheikh Maqbūl, both of whom have been fighting for Idrīsi.

20. Ja'āfirah.

One of the 21 tribes of Ashrāf. They are settled in and round Jōz el-Ja'āfirah to the north of Jeizān. Sherif Mohammed 'Ali is their chief Sheikh. He is said to be secretly disaffected to Idrīsi but openly is on good terms with him. The tribe numbers about 600 men.

21. Khamīsīn.

A tribe, rather smaller than the Beni 'Abs, inhabiting the hills east of Haradh. They are allies of their western neighbours, the Beni Marwān, and adherents of Idrīsi. Their chief village is Sūq el-Mughāsil, where a market is held every Sunday.

22. Khath'am.

The KHATH'AM are a small settled tribe on the Ibha–Tā'if road, with the Shamrān to their north and west and the Bulqarn to their east and south. They do not muster more than 1,500 men, and are partly nomadic. The chief village of the settled portion is Lasfar, where lives their chief Sheikh, Juheish ibn 'Aqad, an old man of 60. The nomads are camel owners, and are almost all engaged in the carrying trade to Bīshah and Namas. They excel in fighting, and are allied with the Bulqarn and Shamrān.

Their chief menace comes from the Ghāmid, and the Khath'am, Bulqarn, Beni 'Amr, and Shamrān all unite against that powerful tribe when it threatens any one of them. In politics they favour Idrīsi. The tribe traces its descent back to the Rijāl el-Hajar.

Paramount Sheikh : Juheish ibn 'Aqad, of Lasfar.

(a) Settled sections :—
    Āl Murrah   Thawāb ibn Nāsir.
    Āl Serdān   Mohammed ibn 'Alam.
(b) Nomad sections :—
    Mazāriqah   Juheish ibn 'Aqad.
    Āl Selmān   Shuweib ibn Mohammed.

23. Beni Mālik.

The BENI MĀLIK live to the north of Ibha, their southern boundary being only 2 miles away. The adjoining tribes are, on the north the Balahmar, east the Shahrān, south the Beni Mugheid, and west the 'Alqam el-Hūl and Rabī'ah wa Rufeidah.

They are of Qahtān stock, and with the Beni Mugheid, Rufeidat el-Yemen, and 'Alqam el-Hūl form what is strictly speaking Asir. The tribe numbers about 5,000 men of whom 2,000 are nomads.

The villagers are under Sheikh 'Ali ibn Ma'addi, and are divided into the three chief clans of Āl el-Mujemmil, Beni Rizām, and Beni Rabī'ah. They are Turkish in sympathy with the exception of the Beni Rizām, whose Sheikh, Tāhir Abu Hashar, was imprisoned for a year at Ibha for attempting a revolt. They all pay taxes, and are peaceful and unwarlike people, looked down on by all the neighbouring tribes, who have named them in derision " Jauba " or donkeys.

The nomads are good fighters, and pay only a nominal allegiance to the Turks. They come into the villages during the harvest, and for the rest of the year wander to the east round Janfur (Jinfur), an isolated village of theirs in the Shahrān country, or go down to the 'Alqam el-Hūl or Rabī'ah wa Rufeidah. They are at enmity with the Beni Tha'labah section of the Balahmar.

The country is fertile, and largely supplies Ibha with fruits.

'Ali ibn Ma'addi, the chief Sheikh, is an old man of 60, and is a member of the Ibha town council. He is reported to be mean and avaricious.

Sa'd ibn Dhuh, the chief of the nomads, is a brave old warrior of over 70, and is anti-Turk. He is supported by his seven sons.

(a) Settled. 3,000 men.
    Chief Sheikh : 'Ali ibn Ma'addi.
    his sons {Ahmed ibn 'Ali.
                Mansūr ibn Ma'addi.
    Chief religious Sheikh : Mufti ibn Khudra.

1. *Āl el-Mujemmil*   Mūsa ibn Mushāfi.
   Chief villages :—
     Āl Atana   Sheikh Humeidi.
     Serūr   Sheikh Malaf.
     Shab   Abu Shamil ibn Ghatīyah.
     Āl Umm Ruwi   Mohammed Abu Qahas.

2. *Beni Rizām*   Tāhir Abu Hashar.
   Chief village :—
     Āl Umm Ruweidi   Abu Aftān.

3. *Benī Rabī'ah*
   Chief villages :—
     Āl Ya'lah   Walad Abu Dhibah.
     El-Mahālah el-'Alīyah   Mohammed ibn Shuweil.
     El-Mahālah es-Siflah   Ahmed 'Ali Dhibah.
     'Aij   Yahya ibn 'Audah.
     Wādi 'Atf   Mohammed ibn Jerān.
     Āl Tabīb   'Abdullah ibn Na'sah.
     Nejlah   Mohammed ibn Na'sah, his brother.
     Āl Ghalīdh   Walad ibn Dufrān.
     Āl Lasān   Mohammed ibn Ahmed.
     Āl Felāt   Nāsir ibn Muzallifah.
     Āl Jerja   Sheikh Qadan.
     Āl Lashrān   Yahya ibn Lashrān.
     Dārah   Ahmed ibn Muftih.

4. *Other villages.*

Muslit	Ibn eth-Thibeit.
Meiza'a	'Ali ibn Sūdān.
Feyah	'Ali ibn Shahr.
Melāhah	Misfar ibn Humrah.
Seyyad	'Ali Ghareifah.

(b) Nomads. 2,000 men.
Chief Sheikh: Sa'd ibn Dhuh.
Clans :—

Āl Habashi	Sa'd ibn Dhuh.
Āl Rumei'ān	Sheikh Sofar.
Beni Minbah	Sheikh Sālikhah.
	Sheikh Mujerri of Janfur.

24. *Beni Marwān.*

A Sunni tribe numbering about 1,000 fighting men and inhabiting the country from Wādi Heirān on the south almost to Wādi Ta'ashar on the north. They are bounded on the north by the Masārihah, on the east by the Ahl Haradh and Khamīsīn, and on the south by the Beni Hasan. The port of Mīdi is in their country, and their chief village is Sūq el-Kairān. Formerly they were partisans of Idrīsi, but they rebelled against him when he accepted help from the Italians. They are evidently still disloyal, for Idrīsi is reported to have sent a punitive expedition against Ibn Bakri, their chief Sheikh, in November 1915. Sheikh Tāhir 'Ali is the Sheikh of Mīdi.

25. *Masārihah.*

A Sunni tribe supporting Idrīsi, who occupy the country from Wādi Ta'shar almost up to Abu 'Arīsh and Jeizān on the north and east to the first foothills. They are bounded on the north by the Reish, on the south by the Ja'dah and Beni Marwān, and on the east by the Beni Mohammed. Their chief village is Samtah, and they are said to muster 1,000 fighting men. The chief Sheikhs are Ahmed Masāwah, 'Othmān Siwādi, Abu Halīm, and Yahya Mihah.

26. *Beni Mohammed.*

A tribe east of the Masārihah in the hills south-east of Jeizān. They support Idrīsi.

27. *Beni Mugheid.*

The BENI MUGHEID are a fine fighting tribe dwelling in the steep hill country which leads up to Ibha from the south and in and around Ibha itself. The adjoining tribes are, on the north the 'Alqam el-Hūl and Beni Mālik, on the east the Shahrān, on the south the Sha'af Rashah and Āl Yinfa'ah sections of the Shahrān and the Rabī'at el-Yemen, and on the west the Rijāl el-M'a.

Their southern limit is the Wādi Shahlah, which flows into the Wādi Dhilah (or Dhil'a) at Heidat et-Tihāmīyah. The tribe numbers about 7,000 men, of whom more than 5,000 are firm adherents of the Turks, and as their fortresses are practically impregnable in Arab warfare, they are a valuable asset to the Ottoman Government.

The tribe is divided into seven divisions, the Āl Yazīd, Āl Nājih, Āl el-Wāzi, Āl Umm Sherāf, Āl Umm Jerei'āt, Āl Umm Wādi Malah, and Āl Weimān. Their country is fertile, with running streams, and produces coffee and fruits.

The Āl Yazīd are the ruling clan, and are subdivided into the families of Ibn Mufarrih, Āl Abu Sārah, and Aulād el-Emīr Mohammed ibn 'Ā'idh, who ruled supreme over all Asir before the days of the Turks and Idrīsi.

Idrīsi's rise to power has split up many a tribe in Asir which was formerly united, and the Āl Yazīd have not escaped the general feeling of discord. The head of the Aulād el-Emīr Mohammed ibn 'Ā'idh is Hasan ibn 'Ali, a young man of 26, who has already distinguished himself in battle. He was at one time with Idrīsi, but in 1910 was bribed by the Sherif of Mecca and seceded to the Turks, who made him Vali of Asir, which strictly speaking only includes the tribes of Beni Mālik, 'Alqam, Rufeidat el-Yemen, and Beni Mugheid, who are all descended from Qahtān, but it is used loosely to include all the tribes from Wadā'ah to Zahrān. In practice Hasan only rules those tribes which recognize Turkish authority. The Turks, as is their custom with local chiefs whom they wish to keep in good humour, have made him a Bey. His own house is divided against him, for while his cousins Nāsir and Mohammed ibn 'Abd er-Rahmān support him and occupy positions under the Turks, the rest of his family, including his brother 'Ali, a young man of 20, have Idrīsi sympathies and refuse to countenance the Government. The family lives at Reidah and Harmalah, about 15 miles to the south-west of Ibha, Hasan ibn 'Ali himself occupying the strong fortress of Qasr 'Ali ibn Mohammed.

The Aulād ibn Mufarrih live at Sijah, three miles north of Reidah, and are descendants of Sheikh Mufarrih, who ruled over Asir until he was ousted by the house of 'Ā'idh. On this account there has always been ill-feeling between the two families, which has developed into open hatred in the present generation owing to the murder of Ahmed ibn Mufarrih, father of 'Abdullah ibn Mufarrih, by the father of Hasan ibn 'Ali, some years ago.

The Aulād ibn Mufarrih rebelled against the Turks when Idrīsi arose, and under 'Abdullah ibn Mughethil defeated a force sent against them. 'Abdullah ibn Mufarrih is their chief, a man of 45, who holds the title of Bey from the Turks, and, on account of his large estate and his landed property in Ibha, is outwardly on good terms with them, but secretly in communication with Idrīsi.

Of the Āl Abu Sārah, whose head-quarters are at Dhohyah, just to the north of Sijah, 'Ali ibn Lāhik and his son Husein were formerly with the Turks, but have seceded and allied themselves with the 'Aulād ibn Mufarrih. Mohammed Abu Dūsah has long been a noted opponent of the Turks.

The Āl Nājih are just to the west of Ibha and are divided in their sympathy. Their Sheikh, Yahya ibn Salīm, was taken captive and imprisoned by Idrīsi five years ago for refusing to pay taxes to him.

The Āl el-Wāzi live near the 'Alqam el-Hūl boundary, and are especially noted for their bravery, which has earned their nickname of Tūrk el-'Arab. They are all pro-Turk.

The Āl Umm Sherāf are all settled along the Āl Sirhān (Shahrān) boundary and are entirely out of hand, being at open enmity with the Turks and all their neighbours, as well as their own tribe. Their country is the focus of all the thieves and highwaymen of the district, and they continually hold up the roads and rob innocent travellers. They also go up to the Wādi Tayyah in the Rabī'ah wa Rufeidah district, and help the Āl Hārith in their war against society. The most notorious amongst them are 'Abdullah ibn Mifdhil, Nāsir and Mūsa ibn Sherein, and Gharām ibn Rābih.

The Āl Umm Jereī'āt and Āl Umm Wādi Malah are both settled in and round Ibha, and are with the Government.

The Āl Weimān, a small section of 400 men who live near the Rabī'ah border to the south, are under the influence of Idrīsi.

The Beni Mugheid are not a quarrelsome race, and live at peace with all their neighbours, except the Rijāl el-M'a, with whom they have a hereditary feud. They take a considerable part in the local government, occupying many of the smaller posts, such as clerkships and the like, and a few have been chosen to represent Asir in the Ottoman Parliament. Amongst these are Ahmed ibn Umm Shibah of the Āl Umm Mufarrih, a man of 50, fat, dark, and of average height. He is an eloquent speaker, a keen politician, and very pro-Turk, with a strong hatred of the Sa'dah. When at Ibha he sits on the town council. He is a rich landowner, but is unpopular on account of his meanness.

'Ali ibn Khanfur is another deputy, and belongs to the Āl Umm Wādi Malah. He belongs to a middle-class family, his people being traders in hides in a small way. He used to be Bashkātib of accounts in Ibha, having worked his way up from a small clerkship. He is a small man of about 40, whose face is pitted with small-pox. He is very intelligent, and used to be religious, but has latterly taken to drink. He is not liked by the tribe.

Mohammed ibn 'Azīz, of the Āl Umm Manādhir, is another man of importance. He married a sister of Husein Eff. Walad Muzeiqah Julas, a deputy for Asir and the Finance Minister (Sandūq Amīni), and is accustomed to act for the latter during his absence abroad. He is also responsible for assessing the taxes in all the Turkish districts. A man of 25 years of age, small and dark, he is clever and has a good reputation.

His brother, Mansūr ibn 'Azīz, was sent to Constantinople three years ago to represent certain grievances of the people of Ibha, and succeeded in securing the dismissal of several Turkish officials.

Mohammed ibn Musallat, who is Sheikh of the Āl Umm Wādi Malah, is also president of the town council at Ibha. A man of 30 years of age he is not liked by the tribe, but is capable and has a fine fighting record. He is also a rich landowner.

(a) *Āl Yazīd*. (Mugheid el-Khōtah). 300 men.

    1. 'Aulād el-Emīr Mohammed ibn 'Ā'idh.
        Hasan ibn 'Ali, paramount chief.
        'Abdullah ibn 'Ali, his brother.
        Nāsir ibn 'Abd er-Rahmān ibn 'Ā'idh }
        Mohammed ibn 'Abd er-Rahmān ibn 'Ā'idh } brothers.
        'Ā'idh ibn 'Abd er-Rahmān ibn 'Ā'idh } are cousins
        'Abdullah ibn 'Abd er-Rahmān ibn 'Ā'idh } of the above.
        Sa'd ibn Nāsir.

    2. 'Aulād Ibn Mufarrih.
        'Abdullah ibn Mufarrih.
        Sa'd ibn Mufarrih.
        'Abd er-Rahmān ibn Mufarrih.
        'Abdullah ibn Mughethil.

    3. Āl Abu Sārah.
        'Ali ibn Lāhik.
        Husein ibn 'Ali, his son.
        Lāhik ibn Hisn.
        Husein ibn Merzim.
        Mohammed Abu Dūsah.
        'Abd er-Rahmān ibn el-Qādhi Mufti.
        Ahmed ibn el-Qādhi.

(b) *Al Nājih*. 1,500 men.

    Chief Sheikh: Yahya ibn Salīm.
    Chief villages are:—

'Ithrabān	Mohammed ibn Sālim.
'Alāyah	Ahmed ibn Mirei.
'Azīzah	'Ā'idh el-Felwalli.
Āl Jerr el-Wādi	Mohammed Dalih.
Jōz	Ahmed ibn 'Ali.
Imsiqah	Mohammed ibn Delbūh.
Āl Umm Hanak	Mohammed ibn Sa'īd.
Āl Umm Shi'bah	Umm Saghīr.
Umm Misrāb	Mishar ibn 'Ali.
Āl Tamām	Mohammed et-Tamām.
Āl Sakrān	Mohammed ibn 'Ā'idh.
Āl el-Jabei'i	Mohammed ibn Sultān.

(c) *Al el-Wāzi.* 1,800 men.
Paramount Sheikh: Mohammed ibn 'Awad.
Chief villages are:—
Badlah	Mohammed ibn 'Abdullah.
Umm Shahrah	Ahmed ibn 'Ali.
Shebārijah	Ahmed edh-Dhi'b.
Āl Zeidi	'Ali Hejāzi.
Āl Umm Zenwah	Mushāfi ibn Sa'īd.

Bedouin:—
Umm Naghālah	'Ali ibn Salāmah.

(d) *Al Umm Sherāf.* 600 men.
Chief Sheikh: Ahmed ibn Shiblān.
Chief villages are:—
Husn el-Ā'la	'Abdullah ibn Nāzih.
Husn el-Asfal	Mohammed ibn Nāzih.
Āl Bel Fellāh	Sā'd ibn Mufarrih.
'Umārāt	'Abdullah Abu Lahbah.
Āl Umm Nesīm	'Abdullah ibn 'Ali esh-Shā'ir.
Beni Jura'i	'Ali ibn Jurfileish.
Khadbah Beni Jura'i	Ahmed el-Juthradi.
Mugheid el-Wata	'Abdullah ibn Nimshah.

(e) *Al Umm Jerei'āt.* 1,000 men.
Chief Sheikh: 'Abdullah ibn Nimshah.
Chief villages:—
Rudāf	Mohammed ibn Mūsa.
Busrah	Sebeih.
Musheyy	Nāsir ibn 'Areidān.
Merjat	Mohammed ibn Hādi.
Heilah	Mohammed el-'Asmi.
'Arīn	Sa'īd ibn 'Abdullah Humrān.
Ja'ad	Mohammed ibn 'Abūt.
Jitāt Ferhān	Ibn Serūr.

(f) *Al Umm Wādi Malah of Ibha.* 1,500 men.
Chief Sheikh: Mohammed ibn Musallat.
Chief villages:—
Miftāhah	'Ā'idh ibn Darāsh.
Qara	Mubārak Mirwa.
Manādhir	Mohammed ibn Feza'.
Na'mān ('Ābid el-'Ā'idh)	Sa'īd ibn Faraj.
Rabu	'Ali Dibah.
Makhlūtah	Merzūq ibn Delmakh.
Khūshi	Nāsir ibn Meri.
Umm Nusāb	Humeid ibn Nimshah.
Muqābil	Shei Abu Na'mah.

(g) *Al Weimān.* 400 men.
    Mohammed ibn Musā'idi.
    Chief villages :—
        Dafan   Abu Shenlah.
        Wādi Kheishah   Abu Hanash.
    Nomads :—
        Āl Weilah   Mohammed ibn Mushārı.

    Āl Yazīd esh-Sha'af.   150 men living in Shahrān country.
    Yahya ibn Hādir.

    Clans are :—
        Āl M'alaf   Sa'd ibn Tāli.
        Āl Hamām   Mohammed Abu Hamāmah.
        Āl Ba'wal   Sheikh Sūdāʜ.

28. *Munjahah.*

The MUNJAHAH occupy the sea-coast and a few miles inland from just south of Birk almost to Shuqaiq, and are bounded on the north by the Beni Hilāl, east by the Rijāl el-M'a, and south by the tribes of Mikhlāf el-Yemen. They muster about 6,000 men, of whom five-sixths are nomads. The villagers live in the small ports of Wasm, Wahlah, and Khasa'ah. They have a little cultivation and a few date-trees, and eke out their existence by acting as porters in their own villages and at Birk. These places, though small, are important as being the chief inlets for arms and ammunition, a trade which is chiefly in the hands of the Rijāl el-M'a. Idrīsi stations his port officers at them, but the Rijāl el-M'a, who treat with him as equals rather than subjects, refuse to recognize his right to tax them, and he does not press the point. The Munjahah, however, all pay him taxes, Sheikh Hasan Fasīkh being deputed to collect them.

The nomads are fairly well off in sheep and camels. They are fishermen and sell dried fish in the interior. They also export dom nuts to Musawwa'.

Their reputation is very evil, and even their guests sleep with their rifles by their sides. Their solemn oath has no meaning for them, and they are notorious for their treachery. Before Idrīsi reduced them to order they were slave-dealers and kidnappers, highwaymen and sea pirates, and used to raid right up to Muhā'il and Barak.

They do not dare now to commit more than an occasional robbery or murder, for the Idrīsi's police are always stationed in their country and punish severely any attempt to return to the old way of living.

They are disliked by all the surrounding tribes, but in ordinary times they wander out of their country to the Bahr Ibn Sekeinah and Beni Hilāl. They do not go south of Shuqaiq at all, having no wish to come into closer contact with Idrīsi than is necessary.

Their chief Sheikh, 'Ali ibn Fayy, is a man 45 years old, and helps Idrīsi to maintain law and order. His house is in Wasm, where he owns considerable property. He has seen much fighting, and always leads his tribe in battle.

Chief Sheikh : 'Ali ibn Fayy. 6,000 men.

(a) Settled. 1,000 men.

Chief villages are :—

Qahmah	'Ā'idh ibn 'Īsa.
Wasm	Mohammed ibn Fayy.
Rehasa'ah	Mohammed ibn Tāli'.
Raqabah	'Omar ibn Mohammed.
Wahlah	Mohammed ibn Gharāmah.

(b) Nomad : *Mohammed ibn Zeid.* 5,000 men.

Chief clans are :—

Āl Umm Khareis   Mohammed ibn Zeid.
Āl 'Abdīyah.
Āl Zeid.
Āl Umm Hadish.
Āl Sarīyah.
Āl esh-Shihbi.
Weled Islām.

29. *Al Mūsa.*

The ĀL MŪSA own the town of Muhā'il and the country round within a radius of from 5 to 10 miles. They are mostly settled, but the clans of Umm Jirbān and Beni Yazīd are nomad. The tribe is a mixed one, the nomads and a few of the townsmen being of pure Arab blood, the rest being blacks, originally of some African strain. No doubt they were at one time slaves, but they have long since earned their emancipation by their courage, and are now on an equality with the Arab portion of the tribe, although no intermarriage takes place. The tribe is fairly rich in flocks and herds, and although their country, which stands comparatively low, cannot rival the fertility of the highlands, it nevertheless produces good crops in the rainy seasons.

The enmity between the Turks and Idrīsi has disorganized the tribe, and divided it into two opposing factions. Sheikh Suleimān ibn 'Ali, who is by right of inheritance the paramount chief, has thrown in his lot with the Turks, and has behind him the Umm Jirbān and about half the villagers.

The remainder have broken loose under the leadership of Dhakīr ibn Sha'r, and many of them have retired to live at Jannah in the Bahr Ibn Sekeinah country, refusing to stay at Muhā'il so long as there is a Turkish post there. From Jannah they carry on a guerilla warfare, closing the roads and cutting off Turkish convoys whenever they can.

The tribe is bounded on the north by the Āl ed-Dureib and Reish, on the east by the Reish and Beni Thuwwah, on the south by the Beni Thuwwah and Bahr Ibn Sekeinah, and on the west by the Beni Hilāl. Against the Beni Hilāl and Beni Thuwwah the whole tribe has had a feud for many generations. Their other neighbours, who are all pro-Idrīsi, look askance at those who sympathize with the enemy, but maintain friendly relations with Dhakīr ibn Sha'r and his followers.

There are two nomad Arab offshoots of the tribe called Beni Shi'b (or Dhi'b) and Sawālihah, who occupy a small portion of the Sikkat el-Helāwīyah near Kyād, about 20 miles from Hali. They are of no political importance, and being separated from the rest of the tribe by the wild Beni Hilāl country do not maintain very close relations with it.

Chief Sheikh : Suleimān ibn 'Ali.

(a) *Clans of Muhā'il.* 2,500 men.

Umm Shehāri	Suleimān ibn 'Ali.
Āl 'Ajil	Dhakīr ibn Sha'r.
Āl Amir	Ibrāhīm ibn Jābir.
Āl Sha'r	Mohammed ibn Fars.
Āl Z'ebah	Mohammed Abu Zoa.
Āl Sherīfah	'Ali Saghīr.
Qurūn	Zein.
Āl Umm Khālid	Suleimān ibn 'Ali.

(b) *Quarters of Muhā'il.*

Rabu'	Ahmed Jatān.
Sabt Āl Makhluta	Abu Rasein.
Sabt Āl Mūsa	Mohammed abu Rādi.
Jebel Shasa'.	

(c) *Settled clans round Muhā'il.* 400 men.

Umm Hamālah	'Abdullah Abu 'Allāmah.
Umm Hajaf	El-Qādhimi.
Umm 'Allamah	Ibn Wuda'ah.
Umm Ma'āsh	Mohammed ibn Zeqa.
Umm Dhira'	Mohammed Abu Thommah.
Āl Fahimah	Mohammed ibn Hādi.
Aulād el-Mashāyikh	Sa'īd Benān.

(d) *Nomads round Muhā'il.* 400 men.
Chief Sheikh : Ahmed ibn Sha'r.

| Umm Jirbān | Mohammed ibn Ma'addi. |
| Beni Yazīd | Ahmed ibn Sha'r. |

(e) *Nomads near Hali.* 500 men.
Beni Shi'b (or Dhi'b).
Sawālihah.

30. Naj'u.

The NAJ'U are an entirely nomadic tribe, numbering about 6,000 men, inhabiting the portion of the district of Mikhlāf el-Yemen between Sabia and Darb. They possess small herds of camels and goats but, although numerous, are of little political importance, since they are poor fighters and there is little cohesion amongst their clans. They earn their living chiefly by selling milk and semn in Sabia. Sheikh Mohammed ibn Musa'i is their chief. The tribe pays taxes regularly to Idrīsi.

Chief subdivisions are the Beni Mohammed (not connected with the Beni Mohammed farther south), the Hajowi or Haju, and Beni Mufarrih.

31. *Beni Nashar.*

A small tribe in the mountains east of the Wa'zāt and to the south of the Beni Aslam. Their chief village is Sūq Beni Nashar, where a market is held every Wednesday. They do not number more than 1,000 souls, but afford what help they can to the Beni 'Abs and Idrīsi against the Wa'zāt. Sheikh Yahya Saghīr is the principal Sheikh, others being 'Ali el-Qahm (who was originally with Hādi ibn Ahmed el-Heij of the Wa'zāt, but submitted to Idrīsi two years ago) and Ahmed Janāh.

32. *Qahtān.*

The Qahtān of Asir are the Rufeidat el-Yemen, Beni Bishr, Senhān el-Hibāb, 'Abidah, Wadā'ah and Shereif. They are known in Asir generically as the Qahtān, and Sheikh Mohammed ibn Dhuleim of the Shereif is Emir over them all by appointment of Idrisi, as was his father by appointment of the Turks; but they are in fact six separate tribes, each living within its own boundaries, having its own particular ambitions, its special likes and dislikes, its peculiar customs, and forming by itself a completely independent unit. Part of the Rufeidat el-Yemen are under Turkish influence.

It is only in times of great crisis, as when the Shahrān rose in a body against them about a hundred years ago, that they answer to the call of their common blood, or nowadays when the Idrīsi calls on them to rally to his standard under their tribal leader. In normal times some are at enmity with others, and although Sheikh Mohammed ibn Dhuleim may be called in to settle tribal disputes and is responsible to Idrīsi for their good order, he has nothing to do with their tribal administration. They are in fact a loose confederation, who will only combine for defence in face of a danger which threatens to extinguish all, and for offence at the bidding of Idrīsi.

On this account they are dealt with one by one, but are grouped together under the heading of Qahtān for convenience of reference.

They are far too removed from the northern Qahtān to keep in touch with them, and never go near their country. Sometimes, in times of drought, a few of the former come down south and are always well received, but the connexion ends at that.

The southern Qahtān tribes are for the most part, and with the exception of certain nomad sub-tribes, well conducted and prosperous, and interested in trade or agriculture. The different sections vary considerably in military skill, and few of them appear to have inherited the characteristics which have earned for their northern relations such an unsavoury reputation.

33. 'Abidah.

The 'ABIDAH (or *Abidah*) appear to be the bravest as well as the most prosperous and enterprising section of the Qahtān. Their boundary in the south, where they have their villages, is well defined, but to the north their nomads wander over a vast stretch of country, and for almost 150 miles their western boundary adjoins that of the Shahrān. To the east lies Tathlīth and the Yām tribes, to the south the Beni Bishr, and to the south-west the Rufeidat el-Yemen.

The 'Abidah will follow Mohammed ibn Dhuleim in battle, but they do not like the Shereif in normal times, and look to their own chief Sheikh, Sa'd ibn Suleim, in tribal matters. The latter is a man of about 40, and lives at Khamīs 'Abidah, the principal village and market-place of the tribe. He is a rich man, and owns a large estate, and is much liked by his tribesmen, both for his justice and fairness and because he always is in the forefront of every fight. His sister married one of the sons of 'Abd el-'Azīz Musheit, chief of the Shahrān, about 20 years ago, and a truce was made between the two tribes. Shortly afterwards he had the misfortune to kill another of 'Abd el-'Azīz's sons in a petty tribal dispute, and war again broke out and continued until Idrīsi pacified the country. There is still a bitter hatred between the two, which shows itself in periodical outbreaks. So deep is the enmity that in the case of a murder of an 'Abidah man by a Shahrān no question of blood money is entertained, and the murdered man's relations do not rest until they have killed a Shahrān tribesman in return. Sheikh Sa'd ibn Suleim was formerly with the Turks, but he joined Idrīsi in his first revolt and has been one of his most faithful followers ever since. Idrīsi has a representative at Khamīs 'Abidah, who collects taxes from all the tribe.

The 'Abidah engage largely in trading, and buy up much of the coffee which comes from the district round Jebel Razah through Wada', subsequently selling it throughout Asir. Some of them live permanently in Rijāl, Ibha, and Namas, and others are engaged in the Jiddah trade. They are a very industrious race, always on the look-out for making money, and their villages are numerous and well built. They also specialize as masons and ply their trade throughout Asir. They do not agree with the Shereif or Beni Bishr in peace time, but are friendly with the Rufeidat el-Yemen and Senhān el-Hibāb.

Unlike a great many tribes the 'Abidah are entirely united, and the nomads are guided in their policy by the villagers. They are rich in dark-haired camels and black sheep, and take great pride in their pedigree horses. They will sell their poorer animals in the market, but they take great care of their finer beasts, feeding them on milk and only parting with them on special occasions, such as when they make a present to the Idrīsi. The Āl Hamdān and Hurjān, who number about 3,000 men and 2,000 men respectively, are the two largest sections of the nomads. They come down to Khamīs 'Abidah for the harvest, and afterwards go up to Bīshah with the other nomads for the date season. They also wander out to Tathlīth, where they meet other Qahtān Arabs and those of the Yām tribes, and where are to be found succulent grasses on which to fatten their herds. Their country abounds in gum, which they collect and sell in Khamīs 'Abidah.

In war they fight on camel- or horse-back, and carry rifles, lances, and long curved *jenābih*. For a long time the Āl Rusheid and Āl Ghamar of the Shahrān used to pay them money in order to escape being raided, but Sheikh 'Abd el-Azīz ibn Musheit refused to countenance this.

They are always at odds with the northern nomads of the Shahrān, and sometimes cut across and raid the Bīshah-Ibha road round Bir Umm Sarar.

The 'Abidah do not seem to have inherited the bad qualities of the northern Qahtān. The whole tribe has a reputation for hospitality, and the nomads, though wild and rough, are not reckoned treacherous.

Paramount Sheikh : Sa'd ibn Suleim.

(*a*) Settled. 6,000 men. Clans are :—

Āl Ejreish	Nāsir ibn Qidim.
Āl Bassam	Sha'eil.
Āl es-Sadr (Saqr)	'Abd el-'Azīz ibn Jalāl.
Āl Umm 'Ammir	Sa'īd ibn el-Ghamas.
Āl ez-Zuheir	Mohammed Abu Lughud.
Beni Talaq	Sa'd Abu Hadīyah.
Wahābah	Abu Raqabah.
Āl Ferdān	Mohammed ibn Sihmān.
Āl 'Abis	'Ā'idh ibn Khamzah.
Turib	Mubārak ibn Mohammed.
'Arīn	Mohammed ibn Rashīd.

(*b*) Nomads. 7,000 men. Clans are :—

Āl Hamdān	Ibn Mujit.
Hurjān	Sa'īd ibn Dhi'b.
Fahar	El-Wuteid.
Āl Kera'an	Mubārak Silih.
Jerābih	Sa'd Abu Hakam.
Jahatein	Mohammed ibn Khazmah.
Sifālah	Mohammed Abu Hakam.

34. *Beni Bishr.*

The BENI BISHR stretch from the down country of the central plateau to the mountainous slopes leading down to the district of Mikhlāf el-Yemen, their nearest point to Sabia being about 30 miles away. Their country is barren in the east, but productive and well forested near the sea. The adjoining tribes are the 'Abidah on the north, Yām, Shereif, and Senhān el-Hibāb on the east, Beni Jum'ah on the south, and the Naj'u and Rufeidat el-Yemen on the west. The tribe numbers about 1,000 settled men and 3,000 nomads. 'Abd el-Hādi is the chief Sheikh, but his influence over the nomads is only nominal. He deserted the Turks some years ago, and all the tribes pay taxes to Idrīsi now. The settled portion is hospitable and prosperous, but the nomads are wild and intractable, almost without religion, and with no marriage laws. They roam chiefly about the Tihāmah, and are rich in a breed of large black sheep. The tribe is friendly with the 'Abidah and Rufeidat el-Yemen and generally at odds with the Naj'u, Senhān, and Yām.

Chief Sheikh : 'Abd el-Hādi. 4,000 men.

(a) Settled. 1,000 men. Chief villages are :—

Usrān	Mohammed ibn 'Abd.
Shaqb	Meidh.
'Abidīyah	Selmān.
Āl Umm 'Ā'idh	Shei ibn Mohammed.
Mufarrij	Mohammed ibn Hādi.
Āl Ferhat	Sa'd ibn Hasan.

(b) Nomads. 3,000 men. Āl 'Urfān is the chief division, clans being :—

Āl Heyal.	Āl Ferhān.
Tihmān.	Āl Ar'ab.
Āl Umm Mohammed.	

35. *Rufeidat el-Yemen.*

The RUFEIDAT EL-YEMEN is a large tribe, numbering some 15,000 men, to the south-east of Ibha, extending up the main mountain ridge and on to the plateau to beyond the source of the Wādi Shahrān.

The tribe is divided into four main divisions, the Āl el-Jihāl, Bishat ibn Salīm, Beni Qeis, and Sha'af Yarīmah wa Khutab.

The chief Sheikh over all the tribe is Husein ibn Heif, a man of 40, who lives at Mudhīq, where he is a large and prosperous landowner. His father was a mudir under the Turks, and died in the Ghāmid country fighting for them ; but Husein ibn Heif joined Idrīsi when he first revolted, and fought for him in 1910. His tribe shares his dislike of the Turks, and respects and obeys him.

The Āl el-Jihāl have for generations been separated from the rest of the tribe, and lived a few miles to the west with the Sha'af Rashhah and Āl Sirhān sections of the Shahrān. They have not, however, intermarried with the latter, and are obedient to Husein ibn Heif, although they do not join in any of the quarrels which constantly occur between their own tribe and their hereditary enemies the Shahrān. They are strongly in favour of Idrīsi and have fought for him on several occasions.

The chief of the Bīshat Ibn Salīm is Mohammed ibn 'Ali walad 'Ali ibn Murā'i, a shifty and cowardly man of about 45, who supports the Turks and is paid by them. This section pays taxes to the Government.

The Beni Qeis lie to the east of the Bishat Ibn Salīm, and also pay taxes to the Turks. Their Sheikh, Mohammed Abu Salām, is now an old man of 75 and deaf. He has always had the reputation of siding with the strongest party.

The nomad portion of this section, the Āl Shuwāt, are independent of him and the Turks.

The Sha'af Yarīmah wa Khutab who live to the south are likewise free, and the allegiance which they pay to Idrīsi is only nominal. They are a wild and suspicious people, and though they have no objection to entertaining guests, they will not suffer them to sleep in their tents.

The country of the Rufeidat el-Yemen is for the most part fertile and densely wooded on the slopes of the hills, and the tribe is a prosperous one. They are not noted for their martial ardour, though the Āl el-Jihāl and the nomads can fight well. They are nicknamed by the other tribes the "Muhanyatein el-Murrah", owing to their habit of staining their women with henna.

All that portion of the tribe which is against the Turks recognize the overlordship of Sheikh Mohammed ibn Dhuleim of the Shereif. The sister of Husein ibn Heif is married to Sheikh Mohammed, and the two chiefs are close friends.

Paramount Sheikh : Husein ibn Heif.   15,000 men.

(a) *Āl el-Jihāl.*   4,000 men.   Mohammed ibn Shuweil.

All settled.   Chief clan is :—

Beni Jabrah	Mohammed ibn Umm Bishr.

Chief villages are :—

Dhibat Āl el-Jihāl	Sa'd ibn Shuweil.
Mahjar	Mohammed ibn 'Aun.
Qelt	Efeir.
Jarr	Muhfar.
Umm Rahwah	Mohammed Hibābah.
Jara	Ibn Dheifah.
Mahshūsh	Abu Ghazwān.
Āl Ramadhān	Mohammed ibn 'Ā'idh.

(b) *Bīshat Ibn Salīm.*   Chief Sheikh : Mohammed ibn 'Ali Walad 'Ali ibn Murai'i.   Settled.   5,000 men.

Chief clans are :—

Beni Thābit	Muri ibn Dehsān.
Beni Wahhāb	Mohammed ibn 'Aun.

Chief villages are :—

Dha'i	Sa'īd ibn 'Ali.
Bōthah	Mansūr ibn 'Ali.
Āl Hideilah	Husein ibn Dirri.
Āl Umm Hayyah	Abu Zirbān.
Āl Hetrush	Mohammed ibn Dosri.
Āl Hayyah	Mohammed ibn Shelti.
Waqashah	Mohammed ibn Rashīd.
Āl Mushabbab	Mohammed ibn Safar.
Shi'b	'Ali ibn Dhubbi.

(c) *Beni Qeis.* Chief Sheikh : Mohammed Abu Salām. 3,000 men.
　　1. *Settled.* 2,400 men. Chief clan is :—
　　　　Beni Tamīm　　　　　Husein ibn 'Abūd.
　　　　Chief villages :—
　　　　Al Mudhīq　　　　　Mohammed ibn Heif.
　　　　Al Abu Midrih　　　Mohammed ibn Hādi.
　　　　Al Mudīr　　　　　 'Abdullah ibn Shahil.
　　　　Fara'ain　　　　　 'Ā'idh ibn Mishif.
　　　　Al Jafei　　　　　　Harfash.
　　　　Al Farawān　　　　'Abd ibn Sa'd.
　　　　Jarāhah　　　　　　'Abūd Hareish.
　　　　Al Lūt　　　　　　 Husein ibn 'Omar.
　　　　Al Meisarah　　　　Safar ibn Mohammed.
　　2. *Bedouins.* Al Shuwāt. Chief Sheikh : Mohammed ibn Hashāsh. 600 men.
(d) *Sha'af Yarīmah wa Khutab.* Chief Sheikh : Jeleid.
　　1. *Settled.* Beni Burrah. 1,000 men.
　　2. *Al Jelīhah Nomads.* 1,000 men.
　　　　Beni Meleik.
　　　　Al Hilami.

36. *Senhān el-Hibāb.*

The SENHĀN EL-HIBĀB inhabit the Asir plateau, and are bounded on the north by the Shereif and Yām, east by the Wadā'ah, and west by the Beni Bishr.

The tribe numbers about 4,000 men, of whom three-quarters are nomads. The villagers have a good reputation with travellers, but the nomads are wild and savage, frequently cutting the roads and sparing neither man, woman, nor child when on the raid. The nomads do not cultivate, but they are rich in a dark breed of camels, and collect gum which they sell chiefly in Khamīs 'Abidah. They wear long black garments.

They are a warlike tribe, and are well led by Sheikh Ferdān ibn Dhuleim, a man of about 35, who lives in Rāhat es-Senhān. The villagers pay taxes to Idrīsi, but the nomads will not do more than help him in war. Their friends are the 'Abidah and Beni Bishr ; their foes the Shereif, Wadā'ah, and Yām. When Idrīsi calls on them to fight they unite under Mohammed ibn Dhuleim of the Shereif, but in normal times they pay him only a nominal allegiance.

　　Chief Sheikh : Ferdān ibn Dhuleim. 4,000 men.
(a) Settled. 1,000 men. Chief villages are :—
　　　　Rāhat es-Senhān.
　　　　Hadhb.
　　　　Khadd.
　　　　Al Ferwān.
　　　　'Irq.

(b) Nomads. 3,000 men. Chief Sheikh : Jilūd. Chief divisions are :—
 Āl Zerbah.
 Āl Ghāzi.
 Āl esh-Sherīf.
 Āl Selmān.
 Āl Shōqān.

37. *Shereif.*

The SHEREIF inhabit the down country to the west of the Yām tribes, and are bounded on the north by the Beni Bishr and Yām, on the east by the Yām, on the south by the Senhān el-Hibāb, and on the west by the Beni Bishr.

Their country is flat and treeless, and most of their cultivation is from well water. They are traders rather than agriculturists, and are well conducted and unwarlike. Their number does not exceed 800 men, of whom a quarter are nomads. They are chiefly known on account of their leader, Sheikh Mohammed ibn Dhuleim. His father, Dhuleim ibn Sha'r, who died about 16 years ago, was a famous man in Asir, and for many years was the Mudir of all Qahtān tribes. His head-quarters were at Harajah in Shereif, where there was also a Turkish garrison. Mohammed ibn Dhuleim succeeded him at a monthly salary of £25, but seceded to Idrīsi when the latter raised his standard of revolt. The Turks thereupon sent an expedition against him and burnt his fortress in Harajah, but were ultimately forced to retire and have not penetrated to his country since. Idrīsi made him one of his Muqdamis or generals, and he was in command of the Qahtān tribes in the fighting against the Turks and the Sherif of Mecca in 1910. Afterwards he and Seyyid 'Arār ibn Nāsir led Idrīsi's army against the Imam's forces under Mohammed Abu Nuweibah, in the Sahar country, about three years ago. He is still a young man about 35 years of age, rich according to the standards of the country, and with an excellent reputation both as a leader in war and a tribal administrator.

Chief Sheikh : Mohammed ibn Dhuleim. 800 men.
(a) Settled. 600 men.
 Chief villages are :—

Āl Dhuleim	Nāsir ibn Dhuleim.
Āl 'Ajlah	Mohammed ibn Jabbān.
Harajah	'Awad ibn Mihmas.
Hamra	Sa'īd ibn Benāyah.
Beidha	Mas'ūd.

(b) Nomads. 200 men.
 Āl Seri   Dhuleim ibn Shayy.

38. *Wadā'ah.*

The WADĀ'AH are a small mercantile tribe numbering about 600 men, living in the district of the same name near the Yām tribes of Nejrān. They are bounded on the north and east by the Yām, and on the west by the Senhān el-Hibāb. Their country is not naturally productive, but they have a large number of wells, and grow grapes which they convert into raisins and sell as far as Ibha and Rijāl. They also import coffee from Jebel Razah and Khaulān esh-Shām, and sell it in Asīr or to the merchants of Rufeidat el-Yemen. They are generally on bad terms with the Yām tribes, but are not a quarrelsome or pugnacious tribe. Idrīsi has his police and tax-gatherers amongst them as he has amongst the other Qahtān tribes.

'Ali Rukwān, their chief Sheikh, goes on pilgrimage nearly every year, and acts as Emīr el-Hajj for all the southern Qahtān tribes.

Chief Sheikh : 'Ali ibn Rukwān. 600 men. Chief villages :—
Dhahrān.
Safwān.
Beida.
'Irj Wadā'ah.

39. Rabī'ah Mujātirah.

The RABĪ'AH MUJĀTIRAH are a wild nomad tribe numbering about 5,000 men. The Barak–Qunfudah road runs through the middle of their territory for about 20 miles between the villages of Ghār el-Hindi and Jumā'ah Rabī'ah. They are bounded on the north by the Beni Shihir, on the east by the Humeidah, on the south by the Rabī'at et-Tahāhīn, and on the west by the Belā'ir. They are said to be fairer of face than most Arabs, with blue eyes, and to wear their hair well down over the shoulders. They are almost pagan, and at odds with all the world except the Rabī'at et-Tahāhīn, who are as savage as themselves. Idrīsi sometimes succeeds in levying taxes on them, but his influence is only nominal. Passage through their country is dangerous both to the Turks and ordinary wayfarers. They are rich in camels and cattle.

A small clan of the Āl Ikhleif section of the Āl ed-Dureib lives in the north-east corner of their territory with their consent.

40. Rabī'at et-Tahāhīn.

The RABĪ'AT ET-TAHĀHĪN hold the country on either side of the Sikkat el-Helāwīyah (Muhā'il–Qunfudah road), between the villages of Ma'mal Āl Ikhleif and Markh, a distance of about 30 miles.

They are bounded on the west by the Belā'ir, on the north by the Belā'ir, Rabī'ah Mujātirah and Humeidah, on the east by the Āl Jebāli and Āl ed-Dureib, and on the south by the Beni Hilāl and the Hali tribes. Their country is mountainous and well wooded, and they are rich in camels, goats, and cattle. About 2,000 in number of fighting men, they are entirely nomad, despise all forms of husbandry, and are a terror to travellers on the road. They are allied with the Rabī'ah Mujātirah and Āl ed-Dureib, and generally on fair terms with the Hali tribes. With the Beni Hilāl, Belā'ir, Humeidah, and Āl Jebāli, they keep up incessant feuds.

The Turks have never been able to do anything with them, but Idrīsi is able to tax them to a certain extent, and what outside sympathies they have are for him.

41. *Rabī'ah wa Rufeidah.*

The RABĪ'AH WA RUFEIDAH stretch from a few miles NNW. of Ibha to within about 15 miles of Muhā'il, their country being about 35 miles from north to south, and 20 miles from east to west on the average, though it tapers to a point in the north. The tribes which adjoin them are: on the north the Reish, on the east the Balahmar and Beni Mālik, on the south the 'Alqam el-Hūl, and on the west the Rijāl el-M'a and Beni Thuwwah. The tribe is divided into four main divisions, the Rabī'at esh-Shām, Āl 'Asimah, Rufeidat esh-Shām, and Āl Hārith. The Rabī'at esh-Shām and Rufeidat esh-Shām have no relationship or connexion with the Rabī'at el-Yemen and Rufeidat el-Yemen as might be supposed.

The Rabī'at esh-Shām occupy the southern portion of the territory, being entirely settled in villages along the Ibha–Athālif road.

They have no Chief Sheikh, having expelled 'Ā'idh ibn Hasan, their former Sheikh, on account of his desertion to the Turks.

The Āl 'Asimah are partly settled and partly nomad, chiefly along the Beni Thuwwah boundary.

Their Chief Sheikh, 'Ali ibn Hamūd, fought for Idrīsi in 1910, was captured by the Turks, and after a year's imprisonment was released and reinstated.

The Āl Hārith, who are both settled and nomad, live in the Wādi Tayyah, along which is the main road from Ibha to Muhā'il, and for years have given a great deal of trouble to the Government. The Wādi Tayyah is the head-quarters of all the bad characters in the neighbouring country, and a caravan has to be very strong to pass through without paying toll. The Āl Hārith are notoriously treacherous, and their hand is against the whole world, including their own tribe. They engage in the camel-carrying trade to a certain extent between Muhā'il and the Rijāl el-M'a, but they seldom venture near Ibha, nor can the Turks levy taxes from them, as they sometimes do from the rest of the tribe. Their Sheikh, Mohammed ibn Shāhir, has a very bad reputation.

The tribe as a whole favours Idrīsi, chiefly because it is discontented with the Government. It is, however, notoriously fickle and unreliable, and goes with the side which pays it best. It maintains a hereditary feud with the Rijāl el-M'a. It is descended from Qahtān.

(a) *Rabī'at esh-Shām.* Settled, 1,500 men.

    Chief clan is Beni Ghanmi. Sheikh: El-Fejīh.

    Chief villages are :—

Teihān	'Amr ibn 'Abdullah.
Umm Sherāf	'Abdullah ibn 'Abdillah.
Umm Sauli	Ahmed ibn Ghanmi.

Wādi Zebnah   Mohammed ibn 'Abdu.
Bahah Rabī'ah   Mohammed ibn Sultān.
Umm Mesjawi   'Abdullah ibn Misfir.
Rahbān   'Abdullah ibn Fejīh.
Sheikh Misfir ibn Ma'sir is Mufti.

(b) *Āl 'Asimah.* 2,000 men.
Chief Sheikh : 'Ali ibn Hamūd.
(i) Settled, 1,000 men. Chief villages are :—
Umm Rahwah   Ibn Māni'.
Jau ibn Sheibān   Ibn Haza'.
(ii) Nomad, 1,000 men. Chief clans are :—
Āl Umm Haneish Tihāmah   Māni' ibn Hanash.
Āl Jeheishah   Abu Karāthah,
Āl 'Aqabah   Musaffir.
Sahar Āl 'Asim   Jābir.

(c) *Rufeidat esh-Shām.*
Chief Sheikh : 'Abdullah ibn Muzerqah, 600 men.
Chief villages are :—
Wādi Tabab   Sa'īd ibn Sultān.
Āl Umm Jeish   Sha'r ibn Muzerqah.
Āl Bāsha   Zuheir.
Āl Mahmūd   Sa'īd ibn Mohammed.
Āl Jemāl   Mahshi.
Āl Umm Hadan   Ibn Suleim.
Āl Bayād   Ibn 'Abūt.
Āl Shadād   Yahya ibn Sultān.
Sharāmah   Mohammed ibn Hasan.
Āl Umm Jalūli   Yahya ibn 'Audah.
Āl Bundar   Simm ibn Sā'il.
Āl Umm Ghāl   Ahmed ibn Sā'il.
Talhah   Mohammed ibn 'Awad.

(d) *Āl Hārith.* 1,000 men.
Chief Sheikh : Mohammed ibn Shāhir.
(i) Settled. Chief villages are :—
Umm Jīzah   'Amr ibn Jelfa'ah.
Umm Zahra'ah   'Ali ibn Shāhir.
Umm Muqza'ah   Lāhiq ez-Zeidāni.
A'farah.
Lasāfah.
(ii) Nomad. Chief clans are :—
Āl Dhi'b   Ahmed ibn Dhāfir.
Āl Nahyah   Hidha'ah.
Āl 'Aqabah   Mughra'ah.

42. Rabī'at el-Yemen.

The RABĪ'AT EL-YEMEN are a nomadic tribe keeping chiefly to Wādi Dhil'a (Dhulah) and Wādi Shahlah, and sometimes going down to Shuqaiq or up to the Beni Mugheid country. The adjoining tribes are the Beni Mugheid on the north and north-east, the Shahrān on the south-east, the Beni Shi'bah and other nomads of Mikhlāf el-Yemen on the south, and the Rijāl el-M'a on the west. They are rich in camels, donkeys, and flocks, and make a good living by selling *semn* in Ibha. They are well armed with the type of French rifle which they call "Abu Bukrah", and carry shields, as well as long curved knives (*jenābih*.) They are noted for their bravery, and deem it a disgrace to die in their beds.

Though wild and rough and with such a contempt for marriage that as a rule they have to be known by the names of their mothers, they are nevertheless hospitable, and clean in their fighting, and have the reputation of never going back on their word once given. In person they are very tall and fairer than most Arabs, with blue eyes. They say they are descended from the Ashrāf el-Huseinīyah, but their enemies name the Sulubba (Sulābah), or wandering gipsy tinkers, as their forefathers. They pay but little attention to religion, and on the first day of Ramadan choose thirty young men, whom they dress in white and compel to fast for one day at some appointed place, on behalf of the whole tribe. Having done this they have a feast, and taunt the neighbouring nomads for their inability to rise to such heights of self-sacrifice.

They are a united and conservative tribe, condemning those who smoke, and in their contempt for foreign luxuries eating only milk and meat. They live in straw-plaited tents.

Their friends are the Beni Mugheid: their enemies, the Rijāl el-M'a, Shahrān, Beni Shi'bah, and Naj'u. The Turks have never been able to keep them in order, and their attitude to Idrīsi depends entirely on his power to make them obey. 'Ali ibn Jabbār is their chief Sheikh, a man of 45 and a noted warrior. He is said to have the tribe well in hand: he pays a nominal allegiance to Idrīsi, but will not allow him to collect taxes.

(*Aulād Āl Umm Husein*).

Chief Sheikh : 'Ali ibn Jabbār.

All nomads. 5,000 men. Clans are :—

Āl Bawāh	Mohammed ibn Sa'd Buqjān.
Umm Farahnah	Mufarrih ibn Museibakh.
'Ali Fellāh	Mufarrih Mashāf.
Āl Shūkah	Mufarrih ibn Gharāmah.
Āl Museibakh	Mūsa ibn Ghazāmah.
Darājin	Mohammed ibn Jarawash.
Mugheidīyīn	Mufarrih ibn Mohammed.
Umm Sherīfīyīn	Hasan Abu Zahrah.
Āl Mughīdhah	Sa'd ibn Mīhi.

Al Mas'ūd	Yahya Abu Hayyah.
Al Mushni	Mohammed ibn Juwei'id.
Al 'Arafīn	Sa'd ibn 'Abdullah.
Al Sālim	Hasan ibn Mas'ūd.

43. *Reish.*

The REISH are to the north and north-east of Muhā'il, and are bounded on the north by the Āl Mūsa ibn 'Ali and the Umm Shahari section of the Beni Shihir, on the east by the Balasmar, on the south by the Beni Thuwwah and Āl Mūsa, and on the west by the Āl ed-Dureib. Their southern boundary comes to within 5 miles of Muhā'il.

They are divided into two sections of Reish and Āl Meshwal, and number about 2,500 men. But although fairly numerous, they are cowardly and unwarlike, and are classed in contempt with the Beni Mālik, by the fighting tribes round. They all favour Idrīsi and pay him taxes. They tried to make a stand in 1912 against the Sherif of Mecca, but were badly worsted and their country laid waste. They are entirely sedentary and engaged in farming. The country is fairly level, thickly wooded, and productive, with running streams in places. Their enemies are Balasmar, Beni Shihir, and Balahmar; their allies, the Barak tribes, the Āl Mūsa, Beni Thuwwah, and the Beni Qutābah and Beni Dhālim of the Rijāl el-M'a. An isolated colony own the village of Mandar in the Balasmar country, and hold aloof from any hostilities which take place between the two tribes. Their Sheikh, Mohammed ibn Muzhar, has no cause to love the Turks, who killed his son in 1910.

Chief Sheikh: Mohammed ibn Muzhar. 1,500 men.

Chief villages:—
Mandar	Ibn Dhiheib.
Qurn el-M'a	Rājih.
Umm Quddūs	Sa'īd Abu 'Allāmah.
Muneidhir	'Amr ibn Hādim.
Hadhān	Mohammed ibn Tāli'.
Āl Umm Sha'tha'.	

Al Meshwal. 1,000 men. Chief Sheikh: 'Ali ibn Tāli'.

Chief villages:—
Umm Hajju	Mohammed Abu 'Allāmah.
Madba'	Sahfān.
Sakkan er-Reish	Ibn Salāmah.

44. *Rijāl el-M'a.*

The RIJĀL EL-M'A, though not so numerous as some of the Asir tribes—it can at most put 17,000 men in the field—is nevertheless one of the most renowned for its courage and dash in war, its internal unity, and its pride of independence. Its country lies between Ibha and the sea, and is roughly a stretch of 50 miles from NW. to SE., and 25 miles from NE. to SW. Its neighbours are the Bahr ibn Sekeinah and Beni Thuwwah on the north, Rabī'ah wa Rufeidah, 'Alqam, Beni Mugheid, and Rabī'at el-Yemen on the east, Ben Shi'bah on the south, and Munjahah and Beni Hilāl on the west.

The tribe is divided into seven subdivisions: the Beni Qutābah, Beni Dhālim, Beni Jūnah, Jeis ibn Mas'ūdi, Beni Zeidīn, Shahāb, and Umm Bina.

The chief Sheikh of the whole tribe is Ibrāhīm ibn Muta'āli of Julla, a man much respected for his prowess in war and his wisdom in tribal matters. He is now over 70 years of age, and for some time most of the administration has devolved on his son, Ahmed ibn Muta'āli. The latter is a tall man of about 30, with a fair skin, who first made his name as a fighter when the Rijāl el-M'a overran Mikhlāf el-Yemen just before the rise of the Idrīsi. He fought the Sherif in 1910 at Muhā'il and in the Balahmar country, but withdrew his forces at a critical moment owing to the appointment of Seyyid Mustafa, of the Bahr ibn Sekeinah, as general of the whole Asir army. So greatly did the Rijāl el-M'a resent having an outsider placed over them, that soon after one of their minor Sheikhs, Seyyid Yahya walad esh-Sheiri, with the full approval of the tribe, attempted to murder him. Idrīsi gave way on the matter, but the mischief had been done, and the Rijāl el-M'a took no further part in the campaign.

Of the sub-tribes, the Beni Qutābah live in the fertile valley of Wādi 'Us, which rises near Suda, and joining the Wādi Ahābesh near Athālif eventually flows into the Wādi Dhofa' by Muhā'il. The Beni Qutābah stretch from near its source to beyond Athālif in a succession of villages surrounded by cultivation. The slopes of the hills and the valleys, except where cleared, are here, as elsewhere in the Rijāl el-M'a country, deeply forested. The Beni Qutābah, though dwelling in villages, are of a wandering temperament, and are the chief camel carriers on all the trade routes of Asir, going to Sabia, Qunfudah, Birk, and sometimes as far as Bīshah and Mecca. There is a small colony of 'Abādilah Ashrāf, who live with them and wield a certain amount of influence.

The Sheikh of Athālif, Ibrāhīm el-Hufdhi, is a man of some notoriety. His father was made a Kaimmakam by the Turks, and granted a pension of £15 a month, which was paid to his family until the tribe revolted. Ibrāhīm el-Hufdhi went to Constantinople in 1914 to assert his loyalty to the Turks and ask that the pension should continue to be paid to him. His influence in the tribe is not great.

The Beni Dhālim lie to the south of the Wādi 'Us and are entirely settled. They are the largest section, numbering 4,000 men, and also by far the richest. They have most of the trade of Asir in their hands, and bring petroleum, sugar, tea, clothing, &c., from Aden and Musawwa', which they sell chiefly in the large village of Rijāl. They have been the foremost pioneers in the importation of fire-arms from Jibuti, which has increased so largely during the last few years and which the Turks have found it impossible to check. Rijāl is the focus of all local products and skins; gum and semn are brought from as far as the Shahrān country, bought by the Beni Dhālim merchants, and exported to Aden. The village next in importance is Sha'bein, the chief rifle market.

The Rijāl el-M'a never marry outside their own country, but as they have grown rich, they have bought much land in the neighbouring districts of 'Alqam el-Hūl and Rabī'at el-Yemen. Amongst the most wealthy of them is a family of Seyyids, known as the Sa'dat en-Na'āmiyah, who have lived amongst them for many generations, and whose head, Seyyid Husein en-Na'āmi, is the most important leader in war after Ahmed el-Muta'āli and Ahmed el-Hayyāni.

The Beni Jūnah are partly settled in villages and partly nomad, and inhabit the country towards the Munjahah. They, too, engage in trade to a certain extent, and one of their Sheikhs, Ayuh, was the first man to start the gun-running venture. The village of Jabūt was the chief centre, and received its name from Jibuti. They are also occupied with home industries, and both men and women are employed in making straw woven articles, such as matting, baskets, and hats, which they call 'toffush', and which are largely worn by the women of Asir.

The most important man of the Beni Dhālim and one of the best known in Asir is Zein el-'Ābidīn, chief Mufti of Asir, and greatly trusted by Idrīsi. Educated at Zebīd, he had already become a force in Asir before the rise of Idrīsi, by reason of his learning and the justice of his decisions. He now has powers of life and death, and is the chief judge of appeals from the judgements of the tribal Qādhis and Muftis wherever the power of Idrīsi runs. He is also frequently called in to arbitrate in the more important tribal disputes, and as the Rijāl el-M'a have implicit confidence in him and are willing to back it by force of arms, his influence is very great. He is now a man of about 40 years of age, and has houses in Sabia and Rijāl.

The Jeis ibn Mas'ūdi live near the 'Alqam el-Hūl border and are the aristocrats of the tribe. The paramount family belongs to them, and they consider it beneath their dignity to engage in trade of any sort. They live for fighting alone, and have as high a reputation for courage as any tribe in the country. Their integrity, too, is unchallenged, and in most of the tribal disputes in neighbouring friendly tribes they are called in to arbitrate.

In the south are the Beni Zeidīn along the Beni Mugheid and Beni Shi'bah boundaries. They, too, are noted fighters. They grow much coffee on the slopes of the hills and their nomad clans are rich in flocks. Their chief Sheikh is Ahmed el-Hayyāni, who lives at Hiswa. He is a man of about 45, and after Ahmed ibn Muta'āli he is the most important man in the tribe. An enemy of the Turks since childhood, he eagerly supported Idrīsi, and is said to have almost as much influence with him as Mohammed Yahya Ba Sāhi. He is a great friend of Seyyid Mustafa, and keeps on good, though at times jealous, terms with Ahmed ibn Muta'āli.

The Shahāb and Umm Bina share the country in the Wādi Ahābesh to the north.

They are entirely agricultural and pastoral, and seldom leave their borders except to fight.

The Rijāl el-M'a are foes with the Beni Hilāl, Beni Mugheid, Rabī'ah wa Rufeidah, Āl Mūsa, and Munjahah. With the Beni Thuwwah, 'Alqam, and Beni Shi'bah they are allies. They were once good friends of the Bahr Ibn Sekeinah, but relations have been strained since the Seyyid Mustafa episode. Before Idrīsi arose, they were under the domination of the Turks, but since his revolt they have entirely thrown off their yoke. During the last few years, the road to Muhā'il from Ibha, via Athālif, has been closed to the Turks, and frequent dashes are made to the main Muhā'il–Ibha road when news is received that a Turkish convoy is passing through.

They support Idrīsi as equals, rather than as subjects, and will neither consent to pay him taxes nor suffer his officers to rule them.

They have a code of justice amongst themselves which is fairly rough and ready, but is rigidly enforced. Murder is severely punished, sometimes by death, sometimes by the payment of blood-money; theft, after two warnings and when proved by witnesses on oath, by the loss of a hand. There is a fixed dowry, both for rich and poor of ₤120, and plurality of wives is the exception. There is a strong feeling against divorce without adequate reason. A man is considered justified in taking a second wife, if the first fails to bear him children, but such a failure is not a sufficient excuse for a divorce.

Paramount Sheikh: Ibrāhīm ibn Muta'āli and his son, Ahmed ibn Muta'āli. 17,000 men.

1. *Beni Qutābah.* Chief Sheikh: Ahmed ibn Mufraj. 2,500 men in Wādi 'Ūs.

    Chief villages :—

Beit Shāji'	Mohammed ibn Shāji'.
Āl Umm Shābi	Mohammed ibn Musallat.
Āl Umm Mas'am	'Ali ibn 'Amr.
Āl 'Amr	Amr ibn 'Ali.
Ghanmah	Ahmed ibn 'Amr.
Umm Jizā'	Mohammed Abu Rubāh.
Umm Dhaharah	Mohammed el-'Askari.
Beni 'Ābidīn	Ibrāhīm Abu Rubāh.
Sha'bein	Sherīf 'Abdillah.
Athālif	Ibrāhīm el-Hufdhi.
Ashrāf	Sherīf 'Abd ibn 'Abdullah.

2. **Beni Dhālim el-Hāshir.** 4,000 men.
   In Rijāl. Mohammed ibn Ahmed èl-Jahwashi.

   Chief villages :—

Umm Qadahah	Ibrāhīm ibn Fa'i.
Āl 'Othmān	Fa'i ibn Ibrāhīm.
Umm Nusūb	Fa'i Judeimi.
Manādhir	Mohammed ibn Sālim.
Umm Barāyah	Ibn Zuleil.
'Asalah	Seyyid Husein en-Na'āmi.
Sa'dat Na'āmiyah	Seyyid Hasan en-Na'āmi.
Ghamārah	Ibrāhīm Rijni.
Āl Ja'eidah	Qāsim Ja'eidi.
Āl Umm Selāmi	Mohammed ibn Zeid.
'Amja	'Abd er-Rahmān ibn Ghala.
Umm Shurafa	Walad Abu 'Ā'idh.
Shasa'	Abu Merjūk.
Umm Jerf	Mohammed ibn Sultān Abu Hāmid.
Na'jah	Ahmed el-Hufdhi.
Āl Mahūb	Zeid ibn Gharāmah.

3. **Beni Jūnah.** Chief Sheikh : 'Ali Midkom. 2,000 men.

   (a) Settled. 1,000 men. Chief villages :—

Betīlah	Ayyūb.
Kisān	Mohammed ibn Nasīlah.
Khamīs Kisān	Ibrāhīm ibn 'Abdullah.
Jabūt	Ya'qūb.
Āl Umm Ruweyyi	Ibn Jabrān.

   (b) Nomads. 1,000 men. Clans are :—

Āl Mahlīyah	Gharām ibn Heif.
Sawājah	Mohammed Abu Hanash.
Naj'u	Abu Ghabeish.

4. **Jeis ibn Mas'ūdi.** 1,500 men. Ibrāhīm ibn Muta'āli.

   (a) Settled. 1,000 men. Chief villages are :—

Umm Jallah	Hasan ibn Muta'āli.
Āl Umm Mukhīli	Mohammed ibn Māni'.
Wādi el-Mirār	Ahmed Makbūt.
Wasānib	Murā'i ibn Mukhāli.
Jebel Jeis	Mohammed ibn Mukhāli.

   (b) Nomads. 500 men. Clans are :—

Umm Jarawīyah	'Amr ibn Mohammed.
Umm Muqlabah	Hādi Abu Hadīyah.
Āl Hanash	Abu Sultān.
Beni Shibli	Abu Mashūf.

5. *Beni Zeidīn.* 3,000 men. Chief Sheikh : Ahmed el-Hayyāni.

(a) Settled. 1,000 men. Chief villages are :—

Salab	Hanash ibn Mas'adi.
Hiswa	Thawābi.
Āl Zahwān	Ibn Khatmah.
Wādi Hiswa	Abu Zenādah.
Maqtal es-Sa'īd	Mohammed ibn Musaffir.
Wādi Hamāmah	'Izz ed-Dīn.
Umm Raddah	Mohammed Tamrān.

(b) Nomads. 2,000 men. Clans are :—

Āl Dākir	Ahmed ibn Gharāmah.
Āl Wājih	'Ali ibn Heidhah.
Āl Umm Haddi	Ahmed ibn Mohammed.
Āl Umm Zāri	Mohammed ibn Sultān.

6. *Shahāb.* 1,500 men. Chief Shiekh : Mohammed ibn Mūsa.

(a) Settled. 5,000 men. Chief villages :—

Natan	'Abdullah Abu Miskah.
Wādi Nimr	Mohammed ibn Qasīm.
Wādi Natrān	Mohammed edh-Dhi'b.
Sheri	Khilāf.

(b) Nomads. 1,000 men. Clans are :—

Āl 'Ashar	Abu Hādi.
Āl Abu Sha'rah	Mohammed ibn Ma'addi.
Umm Nujū'ah	Mohammed ibn Hasan.
Āl Ifdheilah	Talhān.

7. *Umm Bina.* Chief Sheikh : Mohammed ibn Hanash. 2,500 men.

(a) Settled. Chief villages are :—

Sahar Umm Bina	Mohammed ibn Māni'.
Sherī'ah	Abu 'Allāmah.
Jebel Jadrān	Mohammed ibn Hasan.
Ja'ja	Abu Sahmān.

(b) Nomads. Clans are :—

Āl Beheijān	Musaffir.
Beni Isarah	Abu Ramzah.
Āl Umm Fādhil	Mohammed abu Husein.

45. *Ahl Sabia (Sabīyah).*

The term Ahl Sabia is vaguely used in Asir to include both the people of Sabia itself and the villages round within a considerable radius. They are in no sense a tribe, but as mention of them is sometimes made in reports, and they are closely connected with Idrīsi, whose head-quarters are at Sabia, a brief description is given here. Before Idrīsi's rise to power these villages were a succession of small independent units, each a law to itself and generally at odds with its neighbour. The Turks never attempted a proper administration of the country, and violence was rife to such a degree that only large armed parties could travel with safety. Only when the hillsmen descended on them was there any degree of cohesion, and in the last attack of the Rijāl el-M'a, which took place about thirteen years ago, the villagers all combined to save their homes.

The first task of Idrīsi was to conciliate the different warring elements and to promote peace, and to-day the district is thoroughly under control and law abiding.

The largest element of the population is of Sudanese blood, partly unemancipated slaves, but chiefly those who have gained their freedom. With these are the Muwallads, Sudanese with an Arab strain, and over them the Arabs of pure blood and the Sa'dah and Ashrāf. Sabia itself, of course, contains merchants from other Mohammedan countries, the strongest element coming from the Hadhramaut. Mohammed Yahya Ba Sāhi, the chief adviser of Idrīsi, and the Emir of all Mikhlāf el-Yemen, which of course includes Sabia, is from that country.

The Idrīsi's standing army of about 500 men is entirely recruited from amongst the Sudanese round Sabia, and they can muster about 10,000 men when the general rally is sounded.

The following is a list of the chief villages and their approximate number of fighting men.

Sabia. Chief sections are :—

Ashrāf el-Khawāji	Sherīf Idam	300
Sa'dah	Seyyid El-Hasan	400
Āl 'Arār	Seyyid 'Abd er-Rahmān ibn 'Arār	400
Huseinīyah	Sheikh 'Othmān	300
Ma'āsir	Ahmed 'Ali	400

Villages round Sabia :—

Adeyyah	Mohammed ibn Nāsir	200
Muhalla	Husein Abu Shu'ūbi	1,500
Dahna	Seyyid El-Husein	600
Melhah	Seyyid Husein el-Mekki	800
Qadab		200
Shahādah		100
Wādi Musliyah		600
Wādi 'Iseirah		200
Wādi Beish		400
Ta'shar		50
Jebel Feifa		500
Umm el-Khishab (Khashab)		400
Salāmah		1,000
Dhamād		600

Khulab	100
Hammah	120
Jebel el-Milh	50
Wādi Beidh	200
Jebel en-Nadhir	300
Madhāyah	200

46. *Shahrān.*

The SHAHRĀN cover a greater stretch of country than any other tribe in Asir, and are the largest numerically. The country round Bīshah is theirs and they follow the Wādi Shahrān to its source and thence to within 20 miles of Sabia, a distance from north to south of more than 200 miles. Their boundary from east to west of the Wādi Shahrān is undefined and constantly changing, as one or the other of the neighbouring nomad tribes gains the upper hand. Farther south it is fixed and varies from 5 to 50 miles in breadth. Their neighbours on the north are the wandering Shalāwah and Sebei', on the east the 'Abidah and Rufeidat el-Yemen, on the south the Naj'u, and on the west, starting near the sea and working north, the Beni Shi'bah, Beni Mugheid (where these come to within four miles of Ibha), Beni Mālik, Balahmar, Balasmar, Beni Shihir, Bulqarn, and Shamrān. The Shahrān, like the Beni Shihir, Shamrān, and other tribes of Asir, trace their descent to the Rijāl el-Hajar. The tribe is divided into nine main divisions, the Āl Musheit, Āl Rusheid, Āl Ghamar, Nahās, Qa'ūd, Beni Bijad, Beni Wahhāb, Sha'af Rashhah, and Āl Yinfa'ah.

The Āl Musheit are numerically the smallest, but politically the most important sub-tribe, since they contain the ruling tribal family. In former days its influence over the whole tribe was unquestioned, but since Idrīsi's rise to fame some sections have joined him, while others have remained faithful to the Turks, and discord has crept in and weakened its power. It is still, however, very powerful, and in purely tribal matters has the ultimate word over the majority. The paramount chief is 'Abd el-'Azīz ibn Musheit, now an old man of 60, who lives in considerable state at Dhahbān, and also owns a house in Khamīs Musheit, the largest and most important trading centre in Asir. Sheikh 'Abd el-'Azīz is a rich man, since he levies his own taxes in this town, taking a piastre for every donkey sold, 2 piastres for each camel, and 5 piastres for a skin of semn, &c. The Turks do not interfere with him in this, but content themselves with taking "'ushūr" from the local cultivators. He is, however, expected to entertain freely members of the outlying sub-tribes who visit him, and always keeps an open house. In his old age he has taken to drink, and leaves all the active management of the tribe to his son, Sa'īd ibn 'Abd. The latter like his father supported the Turks, but he is also said to be in correspondence with Idrīsi. He is now about 32 years old, and is popular with the tribe and, as a leader, famous in war. The only other man of importance in the family is Sheikh 'Abd el-'Azīz's nephew, Sa'd ibn Husein, who has been won over by Idrīsi with the promise of the chief Sheikhship if he can oust his uncle and cousin.

His appointment, however, would not be popular with the tribe, for he is reputed to be mean and overbearing. His two brothers, 'Abd ibn Ibrāhīm and Husein ibn 'Abd, are with him but have not much influence.

The Āl Rusheid live round Khamīs Musheit and towards Ibha and number about 4,000 men. 'Ali ibn 'Iteij is their chief Sheikh, a fighter of repute.

They all support the Turks but they refuse to pay them taxes, nor do they join the local gendarmerie. They are a prosperous community and their nomads are rich in a breed of large white sheep. They also own many horses. They have not a good reputation in war.

The Āl Ghamar are braver than the Āl Rusheid and quarrel with them. They live along the Beni Mālik boundary, and muster about 1,000 men, of whom 600 are nomads. Mohammed ibn 'Urūr, their chief Sheikh, dislikes Sheikh 'Abd el-'Azīz and supports Idrīsi. His followers, however, keep very much to their own country and do not meddle in politics.

The Nahās are a purely nomad section and are rich in horses and sheep. They live out to the east along the 'Abidah boundary, and are of all the Shahrān the most famous in war. They do all their fighting on horseback, principally against the 'Abidah. The Qa'ūd and the Āl Rusheid pay them "khāwah" at the rate of 12 piastres for every well as a bribe against being plundered. They have no cultivation and live by selling semn and their animals in Khamīs Musheit. Their young men are not permitted to wear rings until they have killed a man, and once blooded they cut a notch on the stock of their rifles for each of their victims. Utterly out of hand, they never approach Ibha, and recognize neither the Turks nor Idrīsi nor their own paramount Sheikh. 'Ā'idh ibn Jabbār is their chief, a man of 50, who has led them into battle for years.

The Qa'ūd are entirely settled in Wādi Tindāhah, which flows into the Wādi Shahrān, and is the most fertile of all the Shahrān country. They are peaceable and unwarlike, and obedient to Sheikh 'Abd el-'Azīz.

The Beni Bijad are a large sub-tribe numbering 10,000 men, of whom 7,000 are nomads. The settled portion lives along the Ibha–Bīshah road between Āl Batāt and Shafān, and is entirely agricultural. The nomads are warlike and fight both on horseback and on foot. Their cavalry carry lances as well as rifles. They are on bad terms with the Beni Wahhāb and fight the 'Abidah, Balahmar, and Balasmar. Like most nomads they go up to Bīshah for the date season. Sa'īd ibn Hashbal is chief over all the sub-tribe. He was formerly with the Turks, but now sides with Idrīsi, and only pays a nominal allegiance to Sheikh 'Abd el-'Azīz. He collects tithes from his followers, with whom he is popular, and is a rich man.

The Beni Wahhāb are the largest sub-tribe, numbering 15,000 men, of whom 13,000 are nomads. They live in the Wādi Shahrān up to Bīshah. Of all Arabs they have the most evil reputation. They are robbers and highwaymen, treacherous, even to their guests, have little religion and no marriage laws, and kill women and children in their raids, a custom which is execrated by all other fighting tribes. They are also unclean in their feeding and eat rats and jerboas. The man with the strongest hand rules them, and the present Sheikh, Nāsir ibn Heif, and Heif ibn Nāsir, his son, won their position by forcibly ejecting the former Sheikh, Ibn Hashāl, who has now degenerated into a petty and uninfluential highwayman.

They are against every tribe and every Government and are paid by other weaker tribes to refrain from raiding. The villagers of Bīshah and the clans who live near, such as the Rimāthān, Uqlub, and Beni Sulul, are, however, slightly more civilized. Only during the date season at Bīshah, which lasts about four months, there is a general truce and Arabs from all over the country foregather. Sheikh 'Abd el-'Azīz owns large and valuable date groves, and both the Sherif of Mecca and Idrīsi have agents there. These two agents belong to the Beni Wahhāb, Sheikh Yahya ibn Fā'iz acting for the Sherif, and Nāsir ibn Kurkmān for Idrīsi, for the purpose of collecting "Zakāt". The former is the more influential. The Beni Wahhāb go out to Tathlīth at certain seasons of the year, where there is excellent grazing for their many flocks and herds.

The Sha'af Rashhah and Āl Yinfa'ah occupy the Tihāmah to the south of Ibha, from which they are separated by the Beni Mugheid. The Sha'af Rashhah, who are to the north of the Āl Yinfa'ah, are entirely settled and peaceful. The Āl Yinfa'ah live in the district of Temnīyah (Thimnīyah), which is the most fertile of all Asir, and approach to within 20 miles of Sabia. They are numerous and wealthy and have a good reputation for hospitality and courage. 'Abdullah ibn Hamād is the chief Sheikh of both sections, a tall man of about 55, with a long white beard. He was formerly on the side of the Turks but broke with them and with Sheikh 'Abd el-'Azīz about 8 years ago, when his son was murdered by the Beni Wahhāb, while a guest of Sheikh 'Abd el-'Azīz. Since then he has joined Idrīsi, and being a man of great influence has brought his tribe with him. Idrīsi now collects taxes from them and keeps about 100 police at Temnīyah. The enemies of these two sub-tribes are the Rufeidat el-Yemen and Rabī'ah: their friends, the Arabs of Mikhlāf el-Yemen. The nomads of Āl Yinfa'ah are horse owners and sell their stock in the Sabia market.

(a) *Al Musheit.*

'Abd el-'Azīz ibn Musheit, paramount Sheikh: Sa'īd ibn 'Abd, his son.

Sa'd ibn Husein
'Abd ibn Ibrāhīm } 3 brothers who are nephews of 'Abd el-'Azīz ibn Musheit.
Husein ibn 'Abd

(b) *Al Rusheid.* Chief Sheikh: 'Ali ibn 'Iteij.

1. Settled. 4,000 men.

Chief villages are:—

Hirīr	'Ali ibn Sa'īd.
Waqabah	'Abdullah ibn Sihmān.
Na'mān	Hasan ibn Zubein.

Dhahbān	Sherīf Abu Nūrah.
Sofq	Mohammed ibn Mubārak es-Sofār.
Rōnah	Ibn 'Ukah.
Āl Jassāb	Ibn Nimshah.
Darb	Sa'īd ibn Benāyah.
Khamīs Musheit	Behir.
Jambar	Abu Mikha'.
Soma'dah	Salīm ibn Zumei'.
'Itwid	Sa'īd Abu Milhah.

2. Nomad. 500 men. Chief clans :—

Āl Shubeil	Nāsir ibn Shubeil.
Āl Ghanum	Mohammed ibn Hāzim.
Āl Tazzah	Sa'īd ibn Ghuzeil.

(c) *Āl Ghamar.* Chief Sheikh : Mohammed ibn 'Urūr.

1. Settled. 400 men.

Tayyib el-Ism	Sa'īd ibn 'Urūr.

2. Nomad. 600 men. Chief clans :—

Aulād Muhur	Ibn Shatf.
Āl Shahra	Ibn Rabu'i.
Āl et-Tayyār	Ibn Ghudheif.
Āl Sa'dūn	Ibn Tūrki.
Beni Zerābah	Jeheish.

(d) *Nahās.* All Bedouin. 1,000 men. Chief Sheikh : 'Ā'idh ibn Jabbār.
Clans :—

Āl Khazqa	'Uweir ibn Hizām.
Āl Hazra	Dhi'b Ladqam.
Āl el-Heiza'ah	Dhi'b ibn Jidhei'.
Āl 'Alīyah	Samghān.

(e) *Qa'ūd.* Settled. 3,000 men. Chief Sheikh : 'Abdullah ibn Sana.
Chief villages are :—

Tindāhah	Mohammed ibn Sana.
Āl edh-Dhi'b	Ibn Rafī'ah.
Āl 'Ujeir	'Abdullah el-Wuteid.
Gheithān	Mi'tiq ibn Mohammed.
Āl Zalāl	Mohammed ibn Sana.
Āl Mustanīr	Mohammed ibn Durei'.
Sadr	Dhi'b ibn Jer'ān.
Āl Zayān	Wad'ān.
Hauta	'Ali ibn Dakhīl.

(f) *Beni Bijad.* Chief Sheikh : Sa'īd ibn Hashbal.

1. Settled. 3,000 men. Chief villages are :—

Rashda'	Mohammed ibn es-Sa'ān.
Āl Batāt	Hereish.

Āl Bithor	Ibn Hanash.
Āl Umm Zeitil	Nejeir.
Ghireirah	Safeir.
Shajrah	Abu Milhi.
Madhah	Ibn Fudghram.
Shafān	Mohammed ibn Sa'īd.

2. Nomads. 7,000 men.
Beni Munebbih el-Hakam.
Sheikh Sa'īd ibn Hakam.

(g) *Beni Wahhāb.* 15,000 men.
Chief Sheikhs : Nāsir ibn Heif, Heif ibn Nāsir.
 1. Settled. 2,000 men. Chief villages :—

Khadhra	Ibn Huweilah.
Museiriq	Zuweiki.

(Bīshat en-Nakhl), Chief Sheikhs : Yahya ibn Fā'iz, Nāsir ibn Kurkmān.

Raushīn (Roshīn)	Nāsir ibn Kurkmān.
Nimrān	Ibn Barrāsh.
Āl Bashūk	Abu Jerīdah.
Zereib	Abu Khazmah.
Āl Khālit	Heif.
Wādi el-Leimūn	Zereik ibn Mustūr.
Āl Shukbān	Yahya ibn Lazar.

 2. Nomads. 13,000 men. Chief clans are :—
Āl Buljārib.
Āl Mustur.
Sifālah.
Mo'āwiyah Husein ibn Zāhir.
Rimāthān ⎫
Uqlub. Sh. Madāf ibn ⎬ Nomads of Bīshah.
 'Atīyān ⎭
Beni Sulul ⎱ Nomads. Sh. Amīr ibn es-Sayyiri
 Jerādīn ⎰ of Bīshah.
Mahlaf Yahya ibn Fā'iz.

(h) *Sha'af Rashhah.* 4,000 men. Settled. 'Abdullah ibn Hamūd.
Chief villages are :—

Idādā	'Ali ibn Murai'i.
Āl Umm Teir	'Awad el-Mujaddad.
Āl Ferza'	'Abdullah abu Hamām.
Āl Sirhān	'Ali ibn Thābit.
Dhibat Āl Sirhān	Ahmed ibn 'Uksha.
Musji (Masqi ?)	'Ali ibn 'Awad.
Āl Umm Jizā'	Walad ez-Zihri.

(1) *Al Yinfa'ah.* Settled. 6,000 men.
Chief Sheikh : 'Abdullah ibn Hamūdh of Tammah.

1. Chief villages :—

Al 'Othmān   Zeidāni.
Al 'Ali   Mohammed ibn Tāli'.
Umm Jariyah   Abu Sihim.
Al Ba'wal   Shuweil el-A'raj.

2. *Al Yinfa'ah of Tihāmah.* Nomad. 8,000 men. Chief clans are :

Jahārah   Mashāf.
Al Ihlāmi   Baqjān.
Reith   Abu Dūsah.
Beni Majūr   Ibn Ghālah.
Al A'rābi   Mufarrih.

3. *Al Yinfa'ah of Jahar* } Nomads in Mikhlāf el-Yemen.
4. *Al Yinfa'ah of Hajawi* }

47. Beni Shi'bah.

The BENI SHI'BAH live chiefly round 'Itwad ('Itwid) and up the Wādi Dhila' (Dhilah) to the Rabī'at el-Yemen boundary, but their nomads have no fixed boundaries and wander all over Mikhlāf el-Yemen, north of Sabia. Their Sheikhs and chief families are Arabs and trace their descent to Qahtān, but the majority of the tribe are Sudanese, who have been emancipated for many generations. They are excellent fighters, amenable to discipline, and are generally known as the 'Asākir', or soldiers.

They all support Idrīsi and pay him taxes.

The Beni Shi'bah do not engage in trade, the villagers being agriculturists and the nomads possessing large herds of camels, cattle, and sheep. They also own horses and nearly always fight as cavalry. They are friendly with the Munjahah, Rijāl el-M'a, and the Mikhlāf tribes, but are hereditary enemies of the Rabī'at el-Yemen and generally on bad terms with the Beni Mugheid, whose country they avoid.

Chief Sheikh : Ibrāhīm abu Mu'ammed. 3,500 men.

Chief villages : 1,000 men.

Darb Beni Shi'bah   Ismā'īl Abu Mohammed.
Qasabah   Mohammed Abu Dōshah.
'Askar   Deilabi.
'Abīd   Balāl ibn Hasan.
Al Abu Dōshah   El-Hufdhi.

Nomads. 2,500 men.

Al Hadra   Mohammed ibn Mushrāi.
Al Hassān.

48. Beni Shihir.

The BENI SHIHIR are one of the most populous tribes of Asir. They are a tall and well-made race, and their women are noted for their beauty. They inhabit the country from the Tihāmah 25 miles east of Qunfudah up the main mountain range and across the watershed almost to Wādi Shahrān.

The tribes which adjoin them are, on the north, starting from the Tihāmah, the Bal'aryān, Bulqarn, and Beni 'Amr, on the east the Shahrān, on the south the Balasmar, the Reish, the Āl Mūsa ibn 'Ali, the Humeidah, and the Rabī'ah Mujātirah. On the west, where their boundary has narrowed to about 15 miles, are the Zobeid. Their territory is funnel-shaped, widening out as it goes inland, till it reaches the Shahrān in the east, with whose boundary it marches for over 60 miles.

The settled portion of the tribe have shown little sympathy with Idrīsi, and are almost entirely pro-Sherif and Turk. They are divided into three main sections, the north, south, and Tihāmah, ruled over by different Sheikhs, who are usually on bad terms with each other, but unite against common enemies.

The largest section and the most important politically is the Beni Shihir esh-Shām, who live chiefly along the Ibha-Tā'if road, between 'Asābīli and 'Uqrum. The leading family and one of the noblest of Asir, is that of Ibn Qurūm, closely connected with Mecca, both by sympathy and relationship, Sherif Mohammed ibn 'Abd el-Mu'īn ibn 'Aun, the grandfather of the present Sherif, having married into the family.

The present head of the family is Sa'īd ibn Fā'iz, an old man now, with two sons, both born of a Circassian mother, Faraj Bey ibn Sa'īd, who has been one of the Hejaz representatives in the Ottoman Parliament, and Fā'iz ibn Sa'īd. They all visit Constantinople and Mecca regularly, have a house in Ibha, and have furnished their house at 'Asābīli in semi-European style, and having also adopted the western habit of smoking and drinking, are looked at with dislike and suspicion by other tribes. They are, however, large landowners and rich men and are a decided asset on the side of the Turk and Sherif. In the event of a split between the two, they would probably join the latter.

Faraj Bey ibn Sa'īd is a tall man of about 38, with a fair skin, which he gets from his mother. He was formerly Kaimmakam of Qunfudah, Muhā'il, and Hali district, where his cruelty when in his cups made him greatly feared. He speaks Turkish and French and has a Circassian wife in Constantinople. He is a notorious libertine and drunkard, but is a force to be reckoned with.

His brother, Fā'iz ibn Sa'īd, a young man of 25, is much more steady and takes greater interest in tribal matters.

About a third of the Beni Shihir esh-Shām are nomads, whose main subdivision is that of the Neid. They have little to do with the settled parts, and do not acknowledge Sa'īd ibn Fā'iz, the Sherif, or the Turks.

Most of their life is spent in bickering with the Shahrān, but what political leanings they have, are in favour of Idrīsi.

The Beni Shihir el-Yemen occupy the rich district of Namas and are under 'Ali Bey ibn Dhāfir, who, like the Qurūm family, is strongly pro-Turk. He is, however, a man of much stricter morals, and is respected by the tribes. His mother is a Circassian. This section is entirely settled in permanent villages, and provides a large proportion of the local Turkish gendarmerie. There are said to be a few Idrīsi sympathizers, but they dare not openly express their views.

The Beni Shihir of the Tihāmah are neither as numerous nor as powerful as those of the uplands, but their country is fertile and they are more prosperous than most of their neighbours. Their Chief Sheikh is Abu Mismār, who is said to favour Idrīsi secretly.

The nomads under Sheikh Khadān ibn Mohammed, are all on the Idrīsi side. They live chiefly in 'Aqabah Sajein and 'Aqabah Sihān, between the Namas district and the Tihāmah, but go down to lower ground for the harvest.

The Beni Shihir are a good fighting tribe, and on account of their political tendencies are almost hemmed in by foes, the Balasmar being the only tribe with whom they have a pact. The Zobeid and they have a feud of many years' standing.

They are well armed and receive rifles from the Turks at Ibha. They are descended from the Rijāl el-Hajar.

(a) *Beni Shihir esh-Shām.* 20,000 men.

  Sa'īd ibn Fā'iz Walad Fā'iz ibn Qurūm of 'Asābili and his sons Faraj Bey ibn Sa'īd (member of Ottoman Parliament), and Fā'iz Bey ibn Sa'īd.

  1. Settled. 13,000 men. Chief sections are:—

Ka'b	'Abdullah ibn Sārah.
Beni Kerīm	Nāji ibn Sa'īd.
Āl Abu Jubeis	Fādhil ibn Jubeis.

  Chief villages are:—

Idwah	Sa'īd ibn Mubārak.
Rabu' es-Sarw	Hāzimah ibn Mohammed.
Halabah	Hizmi.
Sadr	Mohammed ibn Safar.
Kafāf	Rushwān ibn Mohammed.
Akhādhirah	'Abd el-Khāliq.
Kalāthimah	'Abd el-Khalīj.

  2. Nomads. 7,000 men.
  Neid.

(b) *Beni Shihir el-Yemen.* Settled. 15,000 men.

  'Ali Bey ibn Dhāfir Walad Dhāfir ibn Jāri of Namas.

  Chief sections are:—

Beni Bukr	Sa'īd ibn Jāri.
Beni Mashhūr	Dhāfir ibn Mohammed.
Āl Shi'b	Mahbūb ibn Merzūq.

Chief villages are :—

Dhahārah	Sa'īd ibn Qurūm.
'Aqabat el-Lambūsh	Lāfi ibn Mohammed.
Wādi Laghr	Shibeili ibn Mohammed.
Tanūmah	Mohammed ibn El-'Arīf.
Sabt Ibn El-'Arīf	Dhāfir ibn El-'Arīf.

(c) *Beni Shihir et-Tihāmah.*

1. Settled. 8,000 men. Chief Sheikh : Abu Mismār.

Chief sections :—

Al Limāsh	Haidar ibn er-Rawwāf.
Al Khāt	Ruhūmah.
Majāridah	Mohammed Abu'l Qasīm.
Beni Teim Tihāmah	Mohammed ibn Tummah.
Al Dūshah	Abu Mismar.
Al Thureibān	Ibn Ma'ariyah.
Al Thirbān	Abu Muhsin.
Umm Shahari	Mohammed ibn Dheheil.

Chief villages :—

Sadr	Mohammed Abu'l Qasīm.
Jebel Yithrib	Abu Saja'.

2. Nomads. 5,000 men.

Chief Sheikh : Khadān ibn Mohammed.

Al 'Omar	Khadān ibn Mohammed.
Beni Ethla	'Abdullah Dhaffār.
Al Husein	Nāsir ibn Sa'īd.
Ahl 'Aqabah Sajein	Qurūm ibn Dhāfir.
Al Umm Jeheini	Mohammed ibn Shātir.
'Umārah	Sheikh Shubeili.

49. *Ahl esh-Shuqaiq.*

The AHL ESH-SHUQAIQ are a small community inhabiting the small port of Shuqaiq in Mikhlāf el-Yemen. They are chiefly merchants in the hide and semn trade with Musawwa', which they often visit. 'Ali ibn Mubhi is the chief Sheikh, a nominee of Idrīsi. The most important man, however, is Ibn 'Abbās, who was formerly Sheikh, but was imprisoned by Idrīsi for three years for conspiracy. He is now out on guarantee, and, being the biggest merchant and richest landowner in Shuqaiq, is to be reckoned with.

The Ahl esh-Shuqaiq, like all the inhabitants of Mikhlāf el-Yemen, with the exception of the 'Abs, are descended from the Qahtān.

Chief Sheikh : 'Ali ibn Mubhi. 1,000 men.

Chief villages :—

Khasām	Ahmed 'Ali.
Ramlah	'Ali ibn Hawi.
Khabātiyah	Mohammed ibn Husein.
Hesu	Sherīf Hamūd.

50. Shamrān.

The SHAMRĀN occupy a part of the high upland country through which runs the Ibha–Tā'if road and extend down the slopes of the hills to the Tihāmah.

They are bounded on the west and north by the Ghāmid, on the east by the Shahrān, and on the south by the Khath'am and Bulqarn. They are divided into the Shamrān esh-Shām, Shamrān et-Tihāmah, and the nomads, each section numbering about 2,000 men. The northern Shamrān and the nomads are under the Sheikhship of Hasan ibn Matar, a young man of 30, who has a good reputation for wisdom in tribal matters, and has made a name for himself in war. Their chief centre is Balūs, the largest of a number of villages near the Khath'am border, set in a rich and well-wooded valley.

The nomads, the Suhāb and Āl Mubārak, wander down into the Tihāmah in the winter, or stay round Balūs, and in the summer go up with the Bulqarn and other nomads to the Shahrān country round Bīshah for the date season.

They own many sheep and goats, but few camels.

The most important section of the Shamrān et-Tihāmah is the 'Ubus, under Sheikh Is-hāq ibn Muzellaf, whose chief village is Marwa'. They have permanent villages in which they live during winter, but in summer most of them lead a nomadic life, living in straw-woven tents. The whole tribe unites in war, their chief enemies being the Ghāmid. They are also usually at odds with their weaker neighbour the Khath'am. Their reputation as a fighting race is good, and they share with the Bulqarn the custom of purifying themselves and wearing their finest clothes before going into battle. In normal times, they are a hospitable and light-hearted race, every ready to find an excuse for relaxation. Marriage festivals are celebrated on a much larger scale than is usual in Asir. Their outside political leanings are strongly in favour of Idrīsi, as against the Sherif of Mecca and the Turks.

The tribe is descended from the Rijāl el-Hajar.

(a) *Shamrān esh-Shām.* Settled round Balūs. 2,000 men.
  Chief Sheikh : Hasan ibn Matar.
  Āl Mahshakah   Mashari ibn 'Ali.
  Beni Matar   Mushabbab ibn Sa'īd.

(b) *Bedouins.* 2,000 men, also under Hasan ibn Matar.
  Suhāb   Nāsir ibn Fuzān.
  Āl Mubārak   Sa'ūd ibn Mishrik.

(c) *Shamrān el-Yemen* (or *et-Tihāmah*). 2,000 settled.
  'Ubus   Is-hāq ibn Muzellaf.

51. Beni Thuwwah.

The BENI THUWWAH lie to the south of Muhā'il and are astride the main Ibha–Muhā'il road between Butūh and the Wādi Sha'b el-'Asla, a distance of 10 miles, and the Ibha–Athālif–Muhā'il road between Jebel Hawīlah and Hu'ūs Beni Thuwwah, a distance of 15 miles. The territory between these roads is theirs, and their boundary on the north approaches within 5 miles of Muhā'il.

Their neighbours on the north are the Āl Mūsa and Reish, on the east the Balasmar, on the south the Āl Nahyah and Āl Hārith of the Rabī'ah wa Rufeidah, and on the west the Bahr Ibn Sekeinah.

The tribe numbers some 2,000 men, of whom two-thirds are settled, the remainder nomad.

They are a bold and fearless tribe who live chiefly by raiding, and unprotected parties, either of the Turks or ordinary travellers, are never safe while in their country. They have never submitted to Ottoman authority, and, since the rise of Idrīsi, have quite got out of hand. Their chief Sheikh, Sheikh Sarwi, is one of the most noted highwaymen of Asir, and has given endless trouble to the Government. They are generally at feud with the Āl Mūsa, Rabī'ah wa Rufeidah and Balasmar, and allied with the Rijāl el-M'a and Balahmar. Their relations with Bahr Ibn Sekeinah are neutral.

Chief Sheikh : Sarwi. 2,000 men.

(a) Chief villages. 1,300 men.

Ida	Shuflut.
Umm Butūh	'Ali ibn Yahya.
Bedlah	Ibrāhīm ibn Musa'ad.
Qarein	Mushātir.
Āl Umm Ba'eirah	Mohammed ibn Tāli'.
Wādi el-Hāfir	Ibn Hadhīyah.
Āl Ghanīyah	Sha'bān.

(b) Nomads. 700 men.

Bodu Āl Ghanīyah	Abu Jahīlah.
Āl Qabeis	Ahmed ibn 'Adwān.
Āl Fidheilah	Ahmed Abu Hanash.

52. Beni Ya'lah.

The BENI YA'LAH are a small settled tribe, numbering 500 men, situated along the coast a few miles north of Hali. They are bounded on the north by the Marāhibah section of the Beni Zeid, on the east by the Aulād el-'Alaunah section of the Ahl Hali, and on the south by the Shawārah section of the Ahl Hali.

They are divided amongst themselves, Sheikh Bahrān of Shija'fah favouring Idrīsi, and the remainder, under Sheikh Beit-'ali Abu 'Atanah, paying allegiance to the Turks.

The Belā'ir and Hali both raid them, and they depend chiefly on the Turks for their existence as a tribal unit, since they are as unwarlike as their only allies, the Beni Zeid.

Chief Sheikh : Beit-'ali Abu 'Atanah. 500 men.

Villages :—

Ya'bah	Mohammed ibn Sālim.
Sabt Beni Ya'lah	A'ji.
Arja'	Mohammed ibn 'Abdu.
Shija'fah	Bahrān.
Kidwa	Er-Ridwīli.
Melāhah	Musaffir.
Nikhl	Abu Radīyah.

53. *Zahrān.*

The ZAHRĀN is one of the largest tribes of Asir and is bounded on the north by the Beni Mālik and Shalāwah, on the east by the Ghāmid, on the south and south-west by the Zobeid, and on the west by the Dhawi Barakāt for a few miles and then the Dhawi Hasan. Their western boundary approaches in places to within 15 miles of the coast, and inland they go up the main mountain range and beyond the Ibha–Tā'if road.

Their country is a fertile one and is thickly populated, the whole tribe being said to number 30,000 men.

It is divided into two main divisions, the settled and the nomad, of equal size.

Rāshid ibn Jum'ān is paramount sheikh of the villagers and belongs to the main sub-tribe, the Beni Sadr ; Sa'īd ibn Aseidān rules over the nomads. The former got his title by inheritance, the latter by his prowess in war ; but they are both good men, and have their tribesmen well in hand. When he was a young man, Rāshid ibn Jum'ān sided with the Turks and was made a Bey, but twelve years ago he raised a successful revolt and has barred the country to the Turks ever since. The nomads were always against them and against the villagers for the same reason, but since the revolt the two chief sheikhs have been good friends. Rāshid ibn Jum'ān is now a large fat man of 55. He lives at Dūs and is married to Nafalah of the Aulād el-Emīr Mohammed ibn 'Ā'idh family of the Beni Mugheid.

The Zahrān are purely a fighting race and never leave their country, except to raid. They cultivate and become rich thereby, but they despise all other forms of manual labour.

The Ghāmid are their great and hereditary enemies. They declared for Idrīsi when he first raised his standard in Asir, and fought for him in 1912 against the Turks and Sherif of Mecca. In May 1915 they wrote to Idrīsi, proposing to join him, but Idrīsi, doubtless realizing that they could do little good while hedged in between the Turks at Ibha and the Sherif, advised them to adopt a passive attitude for the present. He, however, sent a Qādhi to them to obtain monetary help, and early in 1916 reported that he was still in friendly communication with them.

The Zahrān, like several other tribes of Asir, trace their descent to Rijāl el-Hajar.

(a) Settled.

Paramount Sheikh : Rāshid ibn Jum'ān. 15,000 men.

Dūs	Mohammed Abu Sandalah.
Āl Bassām	Nāsir ibn 'Aqīl.
Āl Dashwān	Bekr ibn Tūrki.
Āl Forza	Munīr ibn Hassān.
Āl Mustanīr	Mohammed ibn Sa'dah.
Beni Sadr	Munīr ibn Mohammed.

(b) Bedouin.

Paramount Sheikh : Sa'īd ibn Aseidān. 15,000 men.

Āl Wādi el-Ahmar.
Beni Su'eif.
Bel Khasmar.
Beni 'Omar.
Kinānah.
Shubeikah.
Beni Hasan.
Beni Sālim.

54. *Beni Zeid (Northern).*

The northern BENI ZEID focus round Qunfudah and are entirely under Turkish influence.

To the north they inhabit the villages along the Qunfudah–Līth road for some 14 miles, till they reach the boundary of the Āl Difra section of the Zobeid. To the east they stretch along the Barak road for 12 miles, almost to 'Umr of the Nawāshirah section of Belā'ir, and then, keeping always about 10 miles from the coast, their boundary runs south for 20 miles, marching first with the confines of the Majā'adah section of the Belā'ir and then with the 'Umr Bedawi till it reaches the Beni Ya'lah, when it turns due west to the coast.

They are partly settled and partly nomad, the former numbering about 4,000 men, the latter 3,000.

The villagers are by no means wealthy, but there is a sufficiency of rain to enable them to cultivate in the summer and their wells provide water to grow vegetables in the dry season. The two nomad sections are the Rabī'ah Weina and the Marāhibah : the former strung out along the Qunfudah–Barak road, the latter roaming the country to the south of Qunfudah, along the coast and inland. They are rich in camels, and are the chief carriers to Hali, Muhā'il and Barak. Most of them carry antiquated rifles, swords, and a curved knife about 3 feet long, called a

Janbiyān. They also supply Qunfudah with milk, and are looked down on by the more independent tribes, both for this practice and for their lack of prowess in war.

Hasan ibn Khidhr is the principal Sheikh of the whole tribe, a man of about 30, who has proved a faithful servant of the Turks. He held firm when Idrīsi threatened Qunfudah in 1912, and was given 2,000 rifles by the Turks for defence. The Beni Zeid doubtless owe a great deal to the Turks, for they are on terms of enmity with their neighbours the Belā'ir and 'Umr, and are raided by such distant tribes as the Beni 'Isa, Dhawi Barakāt, and Dhawi Hasan, who slip through the Zobeid country and back again before they can be brought to book. The Zobeid themselves regard them with tolerance, and the Beni Ya'lah are their allies.

Chief Sheikh : Hasan ibn Khidhr.

(a) Settled. 4,000

Chief villages are :—

Jā'	Hasan ibn Khidhr.
Zayālah	Midhish.
Ahl Dār el-Wādi	Medīni.
Sa'dah	Jemāl el-Leil.
'Abīd el-Sa'dah	Jauhar.
Mashā'ikh	Mohammed ibn Misfir.
Rahmān	Abu 'Ajīl.

(b) Nomads.

Rabī'ah Weina	Mohammed Khenein.	1,000.
Marāhibah	Mohammed Abu Jabbār.	2,000.

55. Beni Zeid (Southern).

A small tribe numbering about 1,500 souls inhabiting the mountains immediately to the east of Beni Hasan. The paramount Sheikh of the tribe and of one of its subsections, the Beni 'Aqal, is Mohammed 'Ali Sebāk. They are on friendly terms with the Beni Hasan, who stand in fear of them, and close allies with the Beni Aslam. They are old enemies of the Beni 'Abs, but sink their differences when fighting for Idrīsi, as they are doing now.

56. Zobeid.

The Zobeid are a detached section of the Harb (see p. 124), and indeed are locally called Harb as often as by their real name. When on the pilgrimage, they generally visit their northern brethren, and are received with honour, and similarly extend a warm welcome to any Harbi who may be in their country. They are hospitable and well conducted, and appear to possess the bravery of their race without its traditional lawlessness.

Their boundary starts about 7 miles north of Qunfudah and, after running along the coast for rather more than 20 miles, turns inland and follows the Dhawi Barakāt boundary, till it reaches the Zahrān. From there it runs parallel to the coast and about 30 miles inland along the confines of the Zahrān, Ghāmid, Bal'aryān, and Beni Shihir till it reaches a point due east of Qunfudah and then follows the boundaries of the Belā'ir and Beni Zeid to the sea.

The Zobeid are settled in permanent villages and are rich in cattle. Their land near the sea is barren except in the wādis, but increases in richness and fertility as soon as the mountains are reached.

They are said to number 15,000 men, and their paramount Sheikh is Mu'ādi ibn Khair. The whole tribe is strongly in favour of Idrīsi, and pay him taxes. They are equally strong in their feelings against the Turks, who in spite of their proximity have not ventured to interfere with them for years. Their chief enemies are the Beni Shihir, but they dislike and despise the Beni Zeid. With the Dhawi Barakāt, the Ghāmid, and Zahrān, they are friends. The Zobeid go in for gun-running to a certain extent, buying their rifles from Ru'eis near Jiddah, or from Birk, and selling them chiefly to the Zahrān.

Paramount Sheikh : Mu'ādi ibn Khair. 15,000 men.

Clans :—

Al Khair	Hasan ibn Mohammed.
Bein Zibdah	'Ali ibn Halīm.
Al es-Sa'īdah	Mubārak ibn Bekhīt.
Al Imlāhi	Mīhi ibn Mohammed.
Beni Etma	Yahya ibn Sālim.
Al Sula'bah	Ahmed el-Hayyāni.
Al Difra	Hanash ibn Qarāwish.
Al Mashāf	Museibikh ibn Mufarrih.
Al Jamīl	Hādi ibn er-Rabh.
Jadreimah	Mizhar ibn Sihmān.
'Ajelein	Ahmed el-Humrāni.

C. YEMEN

1. Āl 'Absi ('Absīyah).

THE Āl 'Absi extend from the coast S. of Hodeidah to the fort of J. Bura', about 30 miles from W. to E. and 15 miles N. to S. The E. half of their country is fertilized by W. Sihām, and the southern part by W. Ghadīr. Their numbers are estimated at 5,000 to 6,000 men, divided into the following sections: Rabasah (round Hodeidah), Munāfirah (E. of these), Hawwah (round Mandar, on the coast, 10 miles S. of Hodeidah), B. Sālih (under J. Bura'), Ahl el-Khalīfah, Ahl esh-Sha'rah (E. of Marwah), Dār ed-Dōm and Ahl Assabt el-Haradah (near J. Bura').

The principal sheikh is Suleimān Hasan of Mahad. There are important settlements of Seyyids at Marwah and at Mansūrīyah. Principal villages:

'Asal (Sheikh Yahya Harisah). Mandar ('Ali Wahhābān).
Mahad (Suleimān Hasan). Khalīfah (Moh. 'Atīyah).
Mukeimīnīyah (Yusūf 'Ali). Shar'a (Moh. Suleimān).

2. Amarīyīn.

A small Zeidi tribe, living round Jebel Qara, on the boundaries of the Hāshid country, about 20 miles NW. of Shehārah. They own 15 or 20 small villages, of which the largest is Beit Jashīsh. Their chief Sheikh is Sheikh Daghshar, a man of about 55, who has considerable influence in the country round. He is a great friend of the Imam and has frequently tried to make peace between him and the Idrīsi.

3. Aflāh.

A small and unimportant tribe allied to the Khairān, to the east of the Beni Aslam in Hajūr. Half Zeidi.

4. Beni Ahlās.

A small tribe, numbering about 2,400 souls, of the Dā'ūdīyah sect, settled to the east of the Beni Murrah and Beni Muqātil, with whom they are allied. They are good fighters and support the Turks, chiefly by reason of their hatred of the Imam and his Zeidi followers. Coffee and *kat* are grown in their country. Their chief Sheikh is Nāsir Husein el-Ahlāsi, an old man of about 65, who visited Constantinople just before the deposition of Sultan Abd el-Hamīd.

Chief villages: Seihān, Marābah, Rabitah, and Masna'ah.

5. *Ahl 'Ammar.*

A large and peaceful Zeidi tribe about 20 miles NE. of Qa'tabah, living round Shekāb 'Ammar, and cultivating cereals and *kat* in Wādi Bana. They are descended from Ma'az ibn Jebel Qurishi, who originally lived at Medina, and being sent by the Prophet to the Yemen as governor, settled in Wādi Bana, where his descendants still are. Paramount Sheikh: Tāhir Husein el-Farah, of the clan Beit el-Farah.

They come under the Kaimmakam of Qa'tabah, and are allied with the 'Ūd and the Ahl Shā'ir.

The chief clans are Beit el-Farah (Sheikh Tāhir Husein) and Beit et-Tayyib (Sheikh Hizām es-Sāwi).

6. *Āl 'Ammar.*

A large Zeidi tribe descended from Beni Tamīm, owning land round Sa'dah, and leading a nomadic life in the mountains to the E. In the south they go down the W. Amashīyah to the country of the Hāshid, with whom they are on good terms. They are excellent fighters and firm adherents of the Imam, whose representative at Sa'dah is Seyyid Mohammed abu Nuweibah, and generally at feud with the Āl Damaj.

Chief Sheikhs: Seyyid 'Abdullah el-Ma'an, Hādi abu Shihah, and 'Ā'idh ibn 'Ali.

Settled. Chief clans: Beni Merj (Hasan Kumalli), B. Surūr (Sālih 'Atīf), 'Abādilah ('Abdullah el-'Abdalli), B. 'Abdān ('Ali 'Abdān).

Nomads. Chief clan: B. Ruham.

7. *'Anazah.*

Two sections. Sunni, Agricultural.

(*a*) Between the Wa'zāt and the Najrah, in the mountains. Chief Sheikhs are Ibn Mas'ūd and Husein ibn 'Ali. Neutral towards the Wa'zāt. Favour the Imam.

(*b*) S. of J. Reima and W. of the Anīs, with whom they are not friendly. They hate the Imam and also the Turks, by whom they have been greatly persecuted. Their chief Sheikh is 'Ali ibn Yahya, a man of 45, who has made overtures to the Idrīsi.

8. *Anīs.*

The boundaries of the Anīs stretch from a short distance west of Dhamār due north nearly to Wa'lān, keeping always a short distance to the west of the Dhamār–San'ā road. To the west they extend along the B. Matar confines almost to Mefhaq and then, skirting Menākhah and cutting the W. Sihām, go down a few miles south of Jebel Reima, and then across almost to Dhamār.

The paramount Sheikh is 'Ali Miqdād, who lives at Jebel esh-Sharq. He is a man of about 50, and used to be a firm adherent of the Imam. He fought for him in 1911 and captured the Turkish Kaimmakam of Dhur'ān,

Zakari Bey. In August 1916, however, he was reported to have quarrelled with the Iman and closed the road against him. The Imam accused him of collecting revenues for himself, and dispatched the Dhamār Arabs against him, with what result is not known. The tribe numbers from 8,000 to 10,000 men, but not more than 3,000 can take the field owing to lack of rifles. Their country is fertile, wheat, oats, barley, and dhura being the principal crops. They are on good terms with their northern neighbours the Beni Matar. They dislike the Arabs of Jebel Reima, and also the Khaulān, whom they fought 12 years ago. With the Beni Muqātil, who are of the Dā'ūdīyah sect and opposed to the Imam, they have a long-standing feud. There is a well-known Seyyid at Dhur'ān, their chief town, by name Seyyid 'Ali ibn Ismā'īl. He was exiled to Rhodes by Ahmed Pasha Feizi, but was pardoned and is now the Imam's representative with the Anīs.

Paramount Sheikh, 'Ali el-Miqdād.

Representative of the Imam : Seyyid 'Ali ibn Ismā'īl.

Other Sheikhs are :

Mohammed el-Hadrāni	of Hadrān.
Mohammed es-Siblāni	of Jebel esh-Sharq.
Sālih Haidra	of Sihām.
Fiki 'Ali el-Ani	of Hudra.
Mohammed Shaqdam	of Jebel Burhān.
Sa'īd el-Bā'i'	of Qā' el-Haqal.
Ahmed Sālih Shaqdam	of Wādi Qūma.
Sālih el-Barashi	of 'Udhein.
Mohammed 'Abdullah	of Nuweid.
'Ali Hātim	of Beni Hātim.
'Ali Sālih	of Beni Jaradah.
'Abdrabbih es-Senhāmi	of Mikhlāf ibn Hātim and half Fersh.
'Omar 'Atif	of half Fersh.
Sa'īd esh-Shubai	of Shubai.

9. *Beni Aslam.*

A large Shafei tribe with some 3,000 good fighting men, inhabiting the mountains to the east of the Beni 'Abs, with whom they have a feud which is only relaxed when the Idrīsi calls on the services of both. N. are the Khamāsīn ; S. the Beni Nashar ; E. the allied Zeidi tribes of Beni Ghill, Beni Zāfir, and Beni 'Azīz. They are separated from the Beni 'Abs by Wādi Ghadīr.

Chief village : Sūq Harīqah.

Paramount Sheikh : 'Ali Bedāwi of Sūq Harīqah.

Other Sheikhs: Husein Burt and his brother ' El-Effendi' of Ghadīr, and Ahmed Sultān of Sūq Harīqah.

10. *Beni 'Awwam.*

A small Zeidi tribe south-west of the Beni Husein and Wādi La'ah, and about 50 miles due east of Loheia in the mountains. Their chief Sheikhs are 'Ali Da'ām and Husein ibn Hasan. They come under the suzerainty of the Turks, but are said to be discontented with them and with the Imam.

11. Beni ʻAzīz.

A small Zeidi tribe of Hajar el-Yemen, living at Hubūr Meili just to the south of the Beni Zāfir and Beni Ghill with whom they are allies. Formerly under the Turkish Markaz of Qufl, but came under the Imam by the treaty of 1911. Good fighters. Noted for their fruits, coffee, and *kat*.

12. Bekīl.

See *Hāshid wa Bekīl*.

13. Buraʻ.

Zeidi tribe living in Jebel Buraʻ, SSW. of ʻUbāl. Chief Sheikh is Husein ibn ʻAbd er-Rahmān el-Buraʻ, who is on unfriendly terms with the Imam, and hates the Turks under whose immediate jurisdiction he is. He is a friend of Nāsir ibn Mabkhūt of the Hāshid. The tribe is allied to the Hufāsh, Sāri, and Mahweit. They are a peace-loving people, numbering about 2,000 men. Yahya ʻAbad is the Sheikh appointed by the Turks over Jebel Buraʻ, Hajeilah, and ʻUbāl. He is about 65 years of age and lives at Hajeilah, which, with ʻUbāl, can muster about 400 men. The chief villages are Manwab, Kamah, Fayish, and Rukab.

14. Āl Damaj.

A small tribe to the E. of the Āl ʻAmmar, with whom it is generally at feud. Little is known of it except that it is Zeidi and under the Imam. The chief Sheikh is Saʻd ibn Saʻd. The chief Seyyids are ʻAli ed-Damaji and Husein Merzaʻ. The chief clans are Āl Wādi (Sheikh ʻAbdullah), Āl ʻUtuf and Āl ʻAwadah (Sheikh Qahtān Damaji).

15. Garābih.

A small tribe of about 1,000 men settled in Wādi Sardūd, whose chief village is Dhāhi (Sheikh, Yahya ʻIzzān). They number 400 fighting men, and their chief Sheikh is Hasan Ahmed es-Sulh. They are under the jurisdiction of the Kaimmakam of Bājil. Their fighting reputation is good : they are hostile to the Beni Suleil and the Quhrah, their northern and southern neighbours.

16. Beni Ghill.

A small Zeidi tribe of Hajūr el-Yemen living in Mikhlāf el-Yemene, between the tribes of Beni Zāfir on the north and Beni ʻAzīz on the south, with whom they are allied. Formerly under the Turkish Markaz of Qufl, but since the treaty of 1911 under the Imam : good fighters. Noted for their fruits, coffee, and *kat*.

17. *Hajjah.*

Small Zeidi tribe in and round the town of Hajjah (Hadda). There is a Kaimmakam in Hajjah, so they come under the direct jurisdiction of the Turks, whom they dislike, and against whom they fought in 1911. Since the Imam made peace with the Turks their relations with him have been strained. Paramount Sheikh is 'Ali ibn Hizām. The tribe is descended from Beni Tamīm.

18. *Hamdān.*

There are two sections of the Hamdān, both claiming descent from Qahtān.

(*a*) Hamdān esh-Shām, a very large Zeidi tribe, almost entirely Bedouin, and roaming over the country a day and a half to the north-east of Sa'dah. They are bounded on the north by the Yām tribes of Nejrān, east by the Bekīl, west by Bedouin tribes, and south by Bekīl nomads. At present they are on bad terms with the Imam. They are quite independent, and will fight for any one who pays them. Chief Sheikh is Sherīf Sālih ibn 'Ali. They are of the same stock as the Hamdān el-Yemen, but too far off to be in touch.

(*b*) Hamdān el-Yemen.

Living to the W. and N. of San'ā, chiefly in Wādi Dhahir. They are of the same origin as the Hamdān esh-Shām. Owing to close proximity to San'ā, they do not show their real feelings, but are said to dislike the Turks and the Imam, and to have a secret understanding with Nāsir ibn Mabkhūt of the Hāshid. Their chief Sheikh, 'Ali Shawi', is in the pay of the Turks with the rank of mudir.

Chief clans: B. Dhurhān (Sherif 'Ali Hamūd), B. Beshir (Sheikh 'Alāwi), B. 'Afar, B. Dhayyān, B. Hārith, B. Meimūn (Sālih ibn Meimūn), B. Jabrān.

Chief villages: Mehājir ('Ali Matlaq), Luqamah ('Ali Yahya el-Hamdāni), Tubar ('Ali et-Tubri), Qebīl (Ahmed Salāmah).

19. *Hashābirah.*

A small Sunni tribe living a few miles south of the Turkish post of Zeidīyah, east of the Kamarān Islands, and coming under the jurisdiction of 'Abdullah Pasha el-Bōni. To their south is the Quhrah tribe. They number between 250 and 300 fighting men, and their chief Sheikhs are Ismā'īl 'Ali and 'Abdullah Mashhur. Their chief villages are Qariyah, Dār el-Bahri, and Mahāl.

20. *Beni Hasheish.*

A Zeidi tribe immediately to the north-east of San'ā, living in Wādi Sirr, Wādi Sawān, and down to Jebel Nuqūm. They cultivate grapes extensively and also engage in trading. They muster some 1,500 men, but, living so near San'ā, possess few rifles. In sympathy they are pro-Imam. Their chief Sheikh is Muhsin el-Jamrah.

21. *Hāshid wa Bekīl.*

It is not clearly established whether the Hāshid wa Bekīl are all of the same descent and therefore one tribe, or a confederation of two tribes of differing origin. The available evidence seems to show that the Hāshid trace their descent back to Himyar and the Bekīl to Qahtān. Whatever the truth, there is no doubt that their names are commonly linked together by natives in Yemen, that they are on terms of close friendship and have been so for many generations, and that together they form one of the most powerful tribal bodies in Southern Arabia. The home country of the Bekīl is to the east in Marashi and Barat, but, as will be seen from the description given below, there are also tribal units living in the midst of the Hāshid country and even so far south and west as Hajjah, Wādi Shīrs, and Mahweit. The Hāshid occupy the country from a few miles north of 'Amrān almost to Sa'dah, and to the west they extend almost to Hajūr. To the east they are settled in Bilād el-Kharf and round Dhibin, but their nomads wander far afield to the north and towards Barat and Jauf.

For many generations the fortunes of the Hāshid wa Bekīl have been intimately connected with those of the Imams of Yemen; and this must always be so, both on account of their common creed and because some of the chief strongholds of the Imam, such as Shehārah, Qāfilat 'Udhr, and Madān, are set in the midst of the Hāshid country. The Imams have drawn largely on the confederation for their fighting material, and in return have rewarded its chief men by governorships in different parts of the country. Thus, before the Ottoman conquest, the chief family of the Himrān tribe of Hāshid ruled all the country from Najrah to Wādi La'ah and Kaukebān, and the head of the Wada' governed Mikhādir just south of Jiblah. The leading Bekīl Sheikhs were equally powerful; and the family of Ausat held the overlordship of Ibb, Suhul, 'Udein, Nadrah, and Ta'izz, while the family of Shā'if were Emirs of Hajjah and Zufeir.

The conquest of the Yemen by Mukhtār Pasha in 1872 and the consequent restriction of the power of these Sheikhs left them with a strong hatred of the Turks and a lasting desire to regain their lost territories; and the many Yemenite revolts against Ottoman authority during the last forty years have always seen them taking a leading part. They bitterly resented the declaration of peace in 1911, and the Imam's treachery towards Idrīsi; and his proposition that they should pay taxes to the Turks caused Nāsir ibn Mabkhūt, the chief of the Himrān and paramount Sheikh of the Hāshid, to withdraw his tribes and enter into relations with Idrīsi. A truce was arranged in the following year; but there is still bad feeling between the two which is not likely to cease until the Imam declares definitely against the Turks. The defection of so powerful a body of supporters has of course reacted in favour of Idrīsi, who during the last few years has been steadily working to make the feeling permanent. He has, however, to contend against a sentiment of loyalty to the Imam, which has been handed down for many generations, and his lack of ready cash has prevented him from doing more than keep relations between the latter and the confederation strained. He has been in constant touch with its chief Sheikhs for the last few years, and has said that money is the only thing required to bring them on his side.

The outstanding figure of the Hāshid wa Bekīl confederation is Sheikh Nāsir ibn Mabkhūt. This Sheikh, a man of forcible and ruthless character, has gained almost complete ascendency over the Hāshid tribesmen and largely influences the Bekīl chiefs. He is cruel and unscrupulous, and will join whichever side pays him most. His power is such that, given adequate material help, he can in all probability force the Imam to what terms he likes.

No attempt has been made to estimate numbers in the account which follows, but the confederation is said to have put over 50,000 men in the field against the Turks in 1911.

A. HĀSHID

The boundaries of the Hāshid have already been described. The tribe is largely an agricultural and pastoral one, but certain sections, especially the Himrān, are engaged in trade.

The most important sub-tribes are the Himrān, Dhu 'Udhrah, and Dhu Fāri', and most of the tribal policy seems to be guided by Sheikhs Sālih ibn Muslih, Sālih Ma'id, Mas'ūd el-Barak, and Dirhem ibn Yahya, under the direction of Sheikh Nāsir ibn Mabkhūt. The only sections which have stood out against them and solidly supported the Imam are the Ahnum, Āl Ahim, Suleimah, and the southernmost tribes, the Beni Sur' and Arhab.

The country of the Hāshid is by no means uniformly fertile, and, in consequence, there are many nomad sections. Theoretically taxes are payable to the Imam, but of late years they have mostly found their way into the coffers of Nāsir ibn Mabkhūt. The Seyyids are very powerful in the Hāshid country, Hūth being their most important centre in the Yemen after San'ā and Sa'dah. They stand with the Imam, or against him, according to the favours they receive from him. His meanness and parsimony seem to have sent the majority into Nāsir ibn Mabkhūt's camp.

The tribes which follow are placed in the order of what is believed to be their numerical and political importance, irrespective of their geographical position.

i. HIMRĀN

Chief Sheikhs:

Nāsir ibn Mabkhūt.

Tall, powerfully built, fair-skinned with a small white beard. About sixty. Ambitious and unscrupulous. Rules chiefly by fear. Is rich through taxes levied on his people. His two chief sons are Hamūd (age about 35) and Nāsir (age about 25). His chief strongholds are at Hamri, Habūr, and Dhōfir.

Sālih ibn Muslih.

Nephew of Nāsir ibn Mabkhūt and his most important lieutenant. Age about 40. Is rich and generous, and well liked by the people. Lives at Hamri.

Range :

(*a*) The majority live in villages between Khamir and Hūth.

(*b*) There are several small sections in Wādi La'ah and Hajjah.

The Himrān traders travel over most of the Yemen. There are many of them in San'ā and Hodeidah.

Sub-Tribes :

(*a*) Settled between Khamir and Hūth :

Dhu 'Ali, Dhu Mufurrih, Dhu Quteish, Beni Ma'mar, Dhu 'Ainash, Beni Shatir, 'Useimāt, Beni 'Amr, Dhu Hibah, Beni Jadā'an.

(*b*) Nomads, extending chiefly to the west :

Beni Qeis, Dhu Mana', Beni Shāwiyah.

(*c*) Settled in Wadi La'ah and Hajjah :

Beni Sirah, Deyaba', Āl 'Amr.

ii. DHU 'UDHRAH

Chief Sheikhs :

Sālih ibn Ma'id el-Moghrabi.

Living in Khartūm. A firm friend of Nāsir ibn Mabkhūt and a well-known warrior. Age about forty.

Mas'ūd el-Barak.

A rich man of about sixty. Is anti-Imam, but reported to be a coward.

'Ali ibn Sālih.

Supporter of Nāsir ibn Mabkhūt.

Range :

(*a*) Due north of Hūth to Qāfilat 'Udhr, and to the east and west of the latter place.

Chief villages : Qāfilat 'Udhr, Butanah, Khartūm, Sadān, Haddad.

(*b*) A small section in Sherāf near Hajūr.

The Dhu 'Udhrah are traders, farmers, and shepherds. Their country is fertile and gives good crops. Those in Sherāf favour the Imam ; the rest are discontented with him, with the exception of the Beni Jukhdim.

Sub-Tribes :

(*a*) Settled in the neighbourhood of Qāfilat 'Udhr :

Beni Jukhdim, Beni Shosah, Beni Barak, Dhu Hatum, Beni Hilāl, Dhu Sukeibat, Dhu Tamīm, Beni 'Arif, Beni Hadayān, Beni 'Anzah.

(b) Nomads round Qāfilat 'Udhr :
Beni Hizein, Beni Jarad, Āl Wādi, Dhu Hātim, Beni Miqdad, Beni Bukr, Beni 'Aishan, Beni Sa'd, Hawāzim, Āl Mahsūr.
(c) Settled in Sherāf :
Beni Hafaj, Beni Shammam, Beni 'Akm.

iii. DHU FĀRI'

Chief Sheikhs :
Dirhem ibn Yahya Fāri'.
One of the chief Sheikhs of Hāshid, and a friend of Nāsir ibn Mabkhūt.
Ahmed ibn Yahya Fāri'.
Brother of above. Was subsidized by the Turks in 1911, and refused to rebel with his brother against the Imam. The latter attacked him and drove him out. He now lives chiefly in San'ā. Is in the confidence of the Imam and was chosen by him to take letters to the Sherif of Mecca in the autumn of 1915. He has little influence in the tribe.
'Ali ibn Yahya Fāri'.
Brother of the above. Sides with Dirhem.
Hizam ibn Qasīm.
An important Sheikh in the tribe.

Range :
From Wādi 'Amashīyah through Qā' el-Harf to Dhibin. Chief villages are Madhakah, Moghrabi, Khaiwān, 'Unqān.
The majority of the tribe are nomadic and rich in camels, cattle, and sheep.

Sub-Tribes :
Suweidah, Āl Kethīrān, Beni Ibrāhīm, Beit en-Nefeish.

iv. SUFYĀN

Chief Sheikhs : Munāsar el-'Useimi.
'Ali ibn Seilah.
'Abdullah el-Gharbi.
The above support Nāsir ibn Mabkhūt.

Range :
From Wādi 'Amashīyah to Qāfilat 'Udhr and west to Wādi Ahnum. Chief villages are Hajeirah and Mahāsir.

Sub-Tribes :
(a) Settled :
Beni Hilāl, Dhu 'Akam, 'Useimāt, Beni Ghanim, Damaj, Beni Nūf. Dhu 'Ibri, Beni Jurmān, Beni Khazan, Beni Turab.
(b) Nomads :
'Awāmir, Beni Dhobyān, Āl Thawābah, Beni Fuwāz, Beni Shuheid, 'Ateibāt.

v. Ahnum

Chief Sheikhs :
Qasīm Shebīb.
Supporter of the Imam and opposed to Nāsir ibn Mabkhūt.
Seyyid Ahmed el-Madani.
Representative of the Imam.

Range :
Wādi Ahnum and Bilād el-Hajar. Chief villages are Madān, Sūq el-Hajar, Jashīsh, Jelīlah, and Sameikah.

The Ahnum are a rich trading and agricultural community, and less quarrelsome than most of the other tribes of the confederation.

Sub-Tribes :
(a) Settled :
Beni Dub, Dhu Sukeibāt, Beni Kindah, Āl Hāyim, Āl Mesh-hadi.
(b) Nomads :
Beni Mohammed, Beni Harrāsh, Beni Sālih, Dhu Shahi, Beni Murdān, Beni Qureitah, Beni Sa'd, Beni Weil, Beni Hatum, Āl Khubeishah.

vi. Beni 'Arjalah

Chief Sheikhs :
Ahmed el-Na'māni.
Sālih 'Arjalah.
Qasīm 'Arjalah.
The above are allied with Nāsir ibn Mabkhūt.

Range :
West of Shehārah. The country is fertile, and they are chiefly settled.

Sub-Tribes :
(a) Settled :
Beni Hamzah, 'Aneizah, Beni Saqaf, Beni Dinar, Āl Manāsīr, Beni Ahmed, Beni Khureimah, Qawāsim, Sherāfah.
(b) Nomads :
Beni Shuqarah and Beni Sha'lān.

vii. Suleimah

Chief Sheikh and representative of the Imam :
Seyyid Lutf Sari.

Range :
Between Khamir and Habūr. Entirely settled and agricultural. Supporters of the Imam.

Sub-Tribes :
Beni Tamīm, 'Ajeilah, Āl Shadad.

viii. ĀL AHIM

Chief Sheikhs:
Abu Nā'ib.
Seyyid Ahmed Dabwān.
'Ali Sahil.
All firm adherents of the Imam.

Range:
West of Ahnum and north of Hajūr. Mostly settled.

ix. KHIYAR

Chief Sheikhs:
'Ali ibn 'Ā'idh Shuweit.
An important man. Follower of Nāsir ibn Mabkhūt.
Sālih ibn 'Ali.

Range:
Round Sūq el-Ghill, their chief market-place, due south of Khamir.

Sub-Tribes:
Beni Qeis, Wad'ah.

x. JARAF

Chief Sheikhs:
Seyyid 'Ali and Husein 'Asheish.
Hereditary Sheikhs living at Sinnatein. Rich men. Partisans of Nāsir ibn Mabkhūt.

Range:
Khamir to Ghail, inhabiting the same country as the Khiyar. Cultivators and traders.

Sub-Tribes:
Beni Surein, Beni 'Aishah, Beni Mālik, Beni Ghathimah, Beni Muhsin, Dhu Zeid, Beni Sinān.

xi. AHL EL-WĀDI

Chief Sheikh:
Dabwān ibn 'Anz.
A well-known warrior. Age about 35. Supports Nāsir ibn Mabkhūt. Lives at Debbah.

Range:
Khish Khash and Jebel Ghurbān to Khamir.
Chief villages are Debbah, Rahābah, and Qa'dah.

Sub-Tribes:
(a) Settled:
Beni el-Faqīh, Dhu Husein, Beni Harrāsh, Beni Nāji'.
(b) Nomads:
Beni Madhkūr.

xii. KHARIF
Chief Sheikh:
Qā'id ibn 'Ali.
Partisan of Nāsir ibn Mabkhūt.

Range:
South of Khamir. All settled.

Sub-Tribe:
Āl 'Amrān.

xiii. BENI SUR'
Chief Sheikhs:
Sakhr ibn Khālid.
Ahmed Wahhās.
Supporters of the Imam.

Range:
East and north-east of 'Amrān in the district of Qā' el-Būn.

Sub-Tribes:
Beni 'Atīf, Beni Zuheir, Beni 'Ajlān, Beni Deheish, Beni Hujrah, Beni Suleimān, Beni Mukram, Āl 'Ardan, Beni Harbah, Sharakwah.

xiv. ARHAB
Chief Sheikhs:
Muhsin el-Qaramāni.
Thābit ibn Yahya Dugheish.
Seyyid 'Ali el-Arhabi
Seyyid 'Ali ibn el-Mutawakkil } Representatives of the Imam.

Range:
All settled in the district of Qā' el-Būn. Pro-Imam.
Chief villages are Hijrah, 'Uri, Mahak, Duneidān, Sa'i.

Sub-Tribes:
Beni Bu'sān, Beni Adham, Beni 'Afar, Beni Mezwād, Beni Laqamah, Beni Jalīd, Beni Dugheish, Beni Dhofār, Beni Hideyyah, Beni Harash, Beni Qafan.

B. BEKĪL

The Bekīl are mainly settled in the oases of Barat, Ruhub, and Khabb, which lie some days to the NE. of the Hāshid territory, and they are engaged chiefly in the raising of horses and sheep. The most powerful tribe both in numbers and in military prowess is that of the Dhu Mohammed, whose Sheikhs have nearly all followed the fortunes of Nāsir ibn Mabkhūt. The Bekīl tribesmen do not find their home country sufficient for all their needs, and many have emigrated to Jauf and different parts of the Hāshid country. Thus whole tribes are found in the latter, such as the Beni Mālik near Shehārah and the Beni Jabr round

Sudah, while there are still in Hajjah, Wādi Shīrs, and Mahweit survivors from the old days when the Bekīl Sheikhs were all-powerful in those districts. The Bekīl and Hāshid Sheikhs are on terms of close friendship with the Dhu Husein of Jauf, so much so that the latter are sometimes spoken of as a part of the Bekīl. But there is no doubt that the Dhu Husein are descended from the Ashrāf (Sherifs), and they are therefore dealt with separately. The chief Sheikhs of Bekīl are 'Abdullah ibn Ghazeilān, Yahya ibn Yahya esh-Shā'if, Nāji' ibn Yahya, and Abu Harbah. No personal details are known about them except that they rose with Nāsir ibn Mabkhūt in 1911 against the Imam and have followed his fortunes ever since. The influence of the Seyyids of Hūth is almost as strong amongst the Bekīl as amongst the Hāshid. The Emir Seyyid Ibrāhīm Muhsin er-Rusās of Hūth is their chief Hākim Sherā'i, and he has agents all over their country collecting tithes.

The chief Bekīl tribes are as follows :

i. DHU MOHAMMED

Chief Sheikhs :

'Abdullah ibn Ghazeilān, of Dhu Ghazeilān.
Yahya ibn Yahya esh-Shā'if, of Shā'if.
Nāji' ibn Yahya, of Āl Ausat.
Abu Harbah.

Range :

(*a*) The majority in Barat. Chief villages : Sūq el-'Anan and Rajuzah.
(*b*) Small sections in Wādi Shīrs, Mahweit, and Hajjah. Traders, shepherds, and horse-breeders.

Sub-Tribes :

(*a*) Settled in Barat.
Dhu Ghazeilān, Shā'if, Āl Ausat, Āl 'Anan, Āl Abu Ras, Dhu Nafeishān, Āl Na'mān, Āl 'Arif, Dhu Hadeyān, Beni Hejlān.
(*b*) Nomads in Barat.
Sheradrah, Beni Hātim.
(*c*) Settled in Hajjah.
Dhu Ghazeilān.
(*d*) Settled in Wādi Shīrs.
Āl Tufeyān. (Muhsin and 'Ali Tufeyān.)
(*e*) Settled in Mahweit.
Beni Hebeish. (Naqīb Ahmed ibn Hebeish.)

ii. ĀL QA'AITI

Chief Sheikh :

Yahya el-Qa'aiti.

Range:
　Khabb.

Sub-Tribes:
　Nomads: Ghufârah and Rimânah.

iii. NIHIM

Chief Sheikhs:
　Mohammed ibn Misân.
　Sâlih el-'Awaj.

Range:
　Round Jebel Lôz in Barat.

iv. BENI JABR

Chief Sheikhs:
　Sa'd ibn Ahmed et-Tarâf.
　'Abdullah et-Tarâf.

Range:
　Mostly settled near Sudah in the Hâshid country.

Sub-Tribes:
　Beit en-Nini, Beni Nini.

v. BENI MÂLIK

Chief Sheikhs:
　Ibn 'Ajmân.
　Mohammed el-Kamarâni.

Range:
　Settled south of Beni 'Arjalah in Hâshid country. Chief villages are Rahâbah, Harfah, Sayat, Heifah.

Sub-Tribes:
(a) Settled:
Beni Sinân, Beit el-Haddi, Dâ'ûdah, Beni 'Askâr, Beni Iswid, Beni Thaqâfah, Beni Kenânah.
(b) Nomads:
Beni Dâ'ûd, Beni Fadl, Beni Misbah.

22. *Beni Hubeish.*

A Zeidi tribe about 40 miles west of San'â. Revolted with the Kam'âlah and other Zeidi tribes under Emîr esh-Shibi against the Turks in 1914.

23. *Beni Hibah.*

A small Zeidi tribe under the Imam to the east of the Beni Aslam in Hajûr.

A.　　　　　　　　G g

24. *Hufāsh.*

A tribe between Jebel Melhān and Bājil. They are Zeidis and belong to the Imam, though they come immediately under the authority of the Turks, whom they hate. They are allies of their northern neighbours the Sāri and Mahweit, and also with the Bura' of Jebel Bura'. Chief Sheikh is 'Ali ibn Yahya.

25. *Beni Husein.*

A small Zeidi tribe just to the NW. of Hisn Jemīmah and west of the Beni 'Udhāqah and Jebel Meswar. Pro-Imam. Sheikh, Ahmed Husein. Formerly under Seyyid Ahmed ibn Mohammed el-Kaukebāni, Emir of Kaukebān and the surrounding country. Seyyid Ahmed was defeated by Mukhtār Pasha and died in captivity at Sàn'ā. His family, Beit Sherāf ed-Dīn, fled to Hūth. There is a small Turkish garrison at Hisn Jemīmah.

26. *Dhu Husein.*

The Dhu Husein are a powerful tribe of Sherifial descent inhabiting the fertile oasis of Jauf. Although somewhat isolated by reason of the distance which separates them from the main centres, they have always kept in close political and commercial touch, and have played an important part in the history of the Yemen. Their relations have always been intimate with the Hāshid wa Bekīl, so much so that they are sometimes spoken of as forming an integral part of that confederation. The troubles between the latter and the Imam have had their effect on the Dhu Husein and drawn them into two opposing camps, of which the larger seems to have remained faithful to its old allegiance.

There are several Sheikhs who appear to rank equally in importance. Of these, Sherīf Ahmed ibn Husein has always supported the Imam, and gave him valuable help against the Turks in 1911. Sherīf Muhsin ibn 'Abdullah is also a trusted friend, and was sent by the Imam to Aden on a political mission in August 1914. Previously he had commanded an army against the Idrīsi.

The chief opponent of the Imam and a close friend of Nāsir ibn Mabkhūt is Husein ibn Thawābah.

The tribe is noted for its fighting qualities, and its Sheikhs are better educated than is commonly the case in Yemen ; their capital, Matamah, being a well-known centre of learning. The Dhu Husein go in largely for horse-breeding, and own perhaps the best pedigree stock in Southern Arabia.

The chief sub-tribes are :

Āl Thawābah (Sheikh Husein ibn Thawābah) ; Beni Furyān (Sheikh Suleimān ibn Ahmed); Dhu Ghailān ; Āl Wajhah (Sheikh Nāsir el-Akhram); Dhu 'Akam ; Beni 'Aseyyān ; Beni Hāshim.

27. Beni Ismā'īl.

A small Shafei tribe in the mountains round Menākhah, numbering about 2,500 souls, and neutral during its siege in 1911. They are now under Turkish domination. They are brave and well armed. Their country is fertile, producing coffee and cereals. The chief Sheikh is 'Ali Muhsin Yahya. The chief clans are: Āl Jaradi, Āl Jebāli, Beni 'Atīyah, Beni Bishr, and Beni Rajab. The chief villages are Masāribah, Jalbein, Jurn Ja'dal, and Jurn 'Arah.

28. Jāmi'.

A Shafei tribe just north of Loheia and east as far as Zāhirah, which is their chief village. In 1911 they fought the Turks on behalf of Idrīsi, but they are now close allies of Ibn el-Heij of the Wa'zāt. The chief Sheikh is Mohammed Zeid, who comes from the Ashrāf of Sabia, and is Mudir of Zāhirah. He is under his cousin Sherif Hamūd, the Kaimmakam of Loheia, who lives at Mutāridh, and governs the Beni Jami' and Wa'zāt.

29. Jemīmah.

A small Zeidi tribe living round Jebel Jemīmah, about 15 miles east of Qufl in Hajūr. They are outside Turkish jurisdiction, and are ruled by the Imam's nominee Seyyid Ahmed ibn Qasīm. Their chief Sheikh is 'Ali ibn Nāsir.

30. Beni Jumā'ah.

A powerful and independent Zeidi tribe, partly nomad but chiefly settled, living in the country north-east of Abu 'Arīsh almost to Jebel Razah. Eight years ago the important Sheikh, Seyyid ed-Dahyāni, at that time Emir of Sa'dah and district, quarrelled with the Imam and fled to the Beni Jumā'ah for protection. Since then he has lived with them and established a firm place for himself amongst them. He is a great friend of Idrīsi, whom the Beni Jumā'ah also support.

31. Kam'ālah.

A Zeidi tribe about 40 miles west of San'ā, which revolted with the Beni Hubeish and others against the Turks in 1914 under Emīr esh-Shibi.

32. Khaulān.

There are two branches of this tribe.

(1) Khaulān et-Tawāl. A Zeidi tribe to the east and south of San'ā, inhabiting the country on either side of Wādi Meswar. They are settled and agricultural, and number 7,000 to 8,000 fighting men. Kibs, 3 hours due east of San'ā, is their chief town, and the head-quarters of the influential Seyyid family of Kibs. Seyyid Ahmed Mab'ūth el-Kibsi and his brothers Seyyid Husein and Seyyid Mohammed ibn Ismā'īl are the heads

of the family. The Khaulān have always fought for the Imam. The representative of the Imam, who is responsible for the collection of tithes, is Seyyid 'Abbās. The Khaulān dislike the Anīs, and fought them 12 years ago owing to the expulsion of a Khaulāni from Anīs. They trace their descent to Ghassān. Sālih ibn Mohammed et-Tawāl is the most important Sheikh of this tribe.

The chief clans are : Beni Jābir ('Abdullah ibn Sa'īd el-Jabri), Beni Kibs (Seyyid Hasan ibn Mohammed el-Kibsi), Yemanyatein ('Abdullah es-Sufi), Beni Dhobyān ('Ali Mahdi Shudeiq), Sihmān ('Ali ibn Yahya el-Qādhi), Beni Sihām (Muhsin ibn Muhsin en-Nini), Sa'b (Sālih ibn Mohammed Talwah).

The chief villages are : Hisn Dhobyatein, Dhobeinah, Qada', Beit Nini, Qarwah, Marbūk, Tanam, Shafīq.

(2) Khaulān esh-Shām. A strong fighting Zeidi tribe in the fertile country between Jebel Murran and Jebel Razah due west of Sa'dah. They are related to the southern Khaulān, but are too far off to be in touch with them. They have a good fighting reputation, and are allied with the Beni Murran, the Āl 'Ammar, and the Sahār in opposition to the pro-Idrīsi tribes of Jebel Razah. The Imam has a fortress at their chief village, Saqein, from which his representative and one of his chief military leaders, Seyyid Qasīm Seifi, governs the tribes of the district. Here lives also the Paramount Chief, Sheikh Jum'ān ibn Safīq. The country is said to contain gold, and is rich in wheat and coffee, of which last a large quantity is exported into Asir through Dahrān.

Chief divisions : Beni Quteim (Sheikh el-Jā'fari), Āl Thureim (Sheikh el-Hajj), Beni Kumamah (Sheikh Abu Qutābah), Beni Jumā'ah (Sheikh Jum'ān ibn Safīq), Kadubah, Marwah (Seyyid 'Abd el-Bāri), Mansūrīyah (Ahmed Yahya Bahr), Quti' (Mohammed Hamūd), Ghanamīyah, Āl Fudhah and Beni Qobah (Sheikh 'Abd el-'Aziz ibn Fudhah), Beni Hāshim (Sheikh 'Abdullah 'Adham), 'Anazah (Sheikh Dabwān). Seyyid Ahmed Yahya Bahr is of great influence in the Tihāmah and looked on by the Suleil, Qahrah, 'Absi, and Zaranik as their religious leader.

Chief villages : Saqein, Tawīlah, and Shi'bah.

33. *Kheirān.*

A small and unimportant tribe, allied to the Aflāh, to the east of the Beni Aslam, in Hajūr. Half Zeidi.

34. *Beni Khotab.*

A small Zeidi tribe settled about three hours' journey S. of Menākhah. They number about 2,300 souls, and are under the Turks. Chief Sheikh : Husein el-Mudmāni. Chief villages : Hasabar, B. 'Atab, Juda, Beit Madar, Mujwarat el-Kirham.

35. *Kokha.*

A tribe near Mocha, which fired on a ship's cutter of H.M.S. *Lama* and killed two men late in 1915. The Sheikh was made prisoner, but disavowed complicity, and after being taken to Aden was released. Commerce between Aden and Kokha was forbidden. The Sheikh is a figurehead, and powerless, but inimical to the Turks.

36. *Mahweit.*

A Zeidi tribe just south of Jebel Milhān. They are directly administered by the Turks, but are in favour of the Imam, and are allies of their southern neighbours the Hufash, Sāri, and Bura' of Jebel Bura'.

37. *Makārimah.*

A small remnant, numbering about 2,600 men, of the house of Makrami, the ruling family of Yām, still left in the district of Harāz. For 12 years the Makramis held the Emirate of Heima, Harāz, Menākhah and district by gift from the Imam Muhsin, but they were expelled by Mukhtār Pasha in 1872. Their followers who remained behind have little political importance now, and are chiefly engaged in trade. Like the rest of their tribe they are of Ismā'īlīyah sect. In 1911 they fought for the Turks against the Imam. They occupy the villages of Mughāribah, Safīyah, Beit el-Hūd, Khiyam, Beit el-Ghail, Beit el-Akhbari, and Qushamīn. Their chief Sheikh is Qā'id el-Luf, who lives at Mughāribah. They are continually at feud with the Shafei, Zeidi, and Dā'ūdīyah tribes of the vicinity.

38. *Manāri.*

The mercantile tribe of the district between Loheia and Hodeidah, peace-loving and settled. Their chief village is Munīrah ; Seyyid Mohammed en-Niha is their principal Sheikh. They come under 'Abdullah Pasha el-Bōni and possibly are a section of the Beni Suleil.

39. *Beni Marhab.*

A small Zeidi tribe immediately to the west of Zufeir, who come under the Kaimmakam of Hajjah, and are of no political importance.

40. *Masār.*

A Zeidi tribe in the mountains round Menākhah, who were neutral during its siege in 1911. They inhabit the Mazar block of hills which bears WNW. of the town and ends west of it. The chief Sheikh of Masār and the villages round it is Ahmed el-Jans, a man of about 55 and a large landowner.

41. *Beni Matar.*

A strong Zeidi tribe in the fertile country between Wa'lān and Mefhaq, just north of the Anīs, with whom they are on good terms.

They are hostile to the Imam, who assassinated their chief Sheikh, Ibn Rumāh, whilst a guest of his at San'ā in 1905. At present Mohammed ibn Hasan Rumāh is their head, appointed Mudir by the Turks. 'Ali ibn 'Ali es-Salāmi of Hijrat ibn Madi is another important chief.

42. *Mekhādir.*

A small Zeidi tribe half an hour south of Jiblah. For many years they were ruled by representatives of the Wada' section of the Hāshid, until Mukhtār Pasha subdued Yemen and banished Ahmed ibn Muqbil el-Wada'i to his own country.

43. *Mesrūh.*

A small Zeidi tribe under the Imam, just to the south of the Khamsīn, in the mountains about 30 miles east of Mīdi.

44. *Metwah.*

A tribe in the mountains round Menākhah, which was neutral during its siege in 1911. Of the Dā'ūdīyah sect.

45. *Ahl Milhān.*

These live in a mountain district N. of Wādi Sardūd and E. of the Suleil country. It is a small district but very fertile, with a population estimated at 10,000. The principal Sheikh is Ibrāhīm Hasan es-Sujaf of Khuslah. The clans are: Ma'zibah, Habbāt, Beni Useifri, Hamdān, Beni 'Ali, Jubah, Yamamīyah, Beni Wahhāb, Āl 'Asabah, Āl Khuslah, Surub, and Āl Mahras.

46. *Beni Mohammed.*

A small tribe east of Kamarān. South of the Beni Qeis and between Zeidīyah and the hills. Sheikh 'Ali Saghīr. 250 fighting men.

47. *Muqātil.*

A warlike tribe in the hilly country between Menākhah and Mefhaq, Hīsn 'Awwād being their chief fortress. During the siege of Menākhah in 1911 their country was overrun by the Imam's troops, and they fought against him in self-defence. They bear no love to the Turks, but on that occasion were glad to receive arms and food from the Kaimmakam of Menākhah in return for their help. They are of the Dā'ūdīyah sect and are markedly hostile to their Zeidi co-religionists, such as the Anīs. They muster between 2,400 and 2,700 fighting men, and are allied with the Beni Murrah and Beni Ahlās.

48. *Beni Murrah.*

A small tribe of the Dā'ūdīyah sect, inhabiting with the Muqātil and Beni Ahlās, their allies, the country between Menākhah and Mefhaq. They have no love for the Turks, and equally little for the Imam and his followers, whom they fought in 1911. They number about 2,500 souls, and their mountainous country produces coffee and *kat*. The chief Sheikh is Hibah Murrah, a rich old man. The chief villages are: Luqumat el-Qādhi, Hamīdi, Luqumat el-Miq'ab, Hisn Ibn ez-Ziyād, and Zayah.

49. *Beni Murran*.

The Beni Murran inhabit the rich coffee country round Jebel Murran which lies a few miles W. of Sa'dah. Their chief village is at Tawīlah on the slopes of Jebel Murran. The tribe, reported strong, supports the Imam, and fought for him against Idrīsi in 1911. Hizam ibn Qā'id et-Tawāfi is Paramount Chief, and the Imam's representative is Seyyid Qasīm ibn Yahya. The chief divisions are Beni Sa'd, Beni Dheiba'i, Hawāzim, Hijrah, and Hadahidah.

50. *Qafalīyah*.

A small Zeidi tribe attached to the Imam, north-east of the Beni Aslam in Hajūr.

51. *Beni Qeis*.

The Beni Qeis occupy Wādi Maur and Wādi La'ah from their confluence near Reighah for a day's march E. The country is well watered with springs and running streams. Their hill camels take over caravans coming from the plains and carry up the traffic through the difficult passes leading to Sūq Shīrs and Hajjah. The principal Sheikh is 'Abdullah Pasha el-Bōni of Reighah, whose father was Kaimmakam and very influential. But the Beni Qeis now incline towards Idrīsi. They are about 2,000 men. The principal villages are Raighah, Tōr, and Musallam.

52. *Quhrah*.

An important tribe on the first stages of the Hodeidah–San'ā road from the sea, for about 50 miles E., as far as Hajeilah. Their neighbours are: on the N. the Jarābihah; E. the tribes of Jebel Harāz and Jebel Bura'; and S. the 'Abs. Between the coast and Bājil, 25 miles, the country is mostly desert, and the inhabitants live in temporary huts in the Khabt: but E. of Bājil there is cultivation. The Quhrah own many camels, and transport from Hodeidah to Hajeilah is mainly in their hands. They can put from 3,000 to 4,000 men in the field, and they gave valuable help to the Turks in 1911 when these occupied the Zahab heights. They are generally at feud with the Beni Suleil.

The chief Sheikh is Mu'āfa Sherāf. Others are Hasan 'Abdullah and Ibrāhīm 'Ali. The chief villages are: Bājil (Sheikh 'Ayad ibn 'Ali Humeidah), Buhāh, 'Ubāl, and Hajeilah (Seyyid Husein 'Ali).

53. Rada'ah.

A Zeidi tribe living round the town of the same name ESE. of Dhamār. They are descended from Qahtān, and are chiefly cultivators and traders. Their chief Sheikh is Hamūd ibn Mohammed, who comes under the Turkish mutesarrif of Rada'ah.

54. Rahāminah.

A small tribe south-west of Zebīd between Zebīd and Wādi Suweirah.

55. Ahl Razah.

A Zeidi tribe living round Jebel Razah to the west of the Khaulān esh-Shām and Sa'dah. They are supporters of Idrīsi, and their country was the scene of the first fighting between Idrīsi and the Imam in 1912. Their chief fortress is Hisn en-Nazīr, situated on the slopes of Jebel Razah. The country is fertile, and coffee is largely grown, while there is said to be gold in the mountains. They claim descent from Khazraj, and acknowledge as chiefs Sheikh Ahmed ibn Sālih and Seyyid 'Ali ibn Huseini. The chief clan is the Dhu Hātim (Sheikh Sa'd 'Abdullah). Seyyid Yahya 'Arār ibn Nāsir, one of Idrīsi's chief muqdamis, administers the country of both the Ahl Razah and the Beni Jumā'ah.

56. Ahl Reimah.

The Ahl Reimah occupy the fertile Reimah massif, always spoken of by Arabs as the finest district in Yemen. Coffee, fruits of all sorts, and cereals are produced. The district is bounded N. by J. Bura' and Wādi Sihām ; E. by Salfīyah and J. 'Utmah ; S. by Wādi Reimah, and W. by the 'Abs and Zaranik districts. The Sheikh is Murshid ibn Mohammed el-Jābi, who is Turkish Kaimmakam. The Mudir is Seyyid Mahmūd. There are said to be seventy Sheikhs and seventy districts in J. Reimah, and a total strength of over 50,000 men. The principal clans are : Beni Waghid, Jad, Sa'īd, Walid, Mukhtār, Tuleibi, Mas'ab, Ghuzi, Nomah, Yafuz, Ahl Dalamlam, Beni Harāzi, Ahmed, Khudam, Ahl Jābi, and Beni en-Nahāri. The last defeated a Turkish expedition sent to collect taxes in 1914 and captured the Kaimmakam of Menākhah. Their chief Sheikh is Seyyid 'Abdullah en-Nahāri. His brother, the late Sheikh, Yahya, was defeated by the Turks, and died a captive. This clan is generally on bad terms with the Anīs.

Principal villages : Jābi (head-quarters of the district and of Sheikh Murshid), Raubat en-Nahāri (Sūq of Sheikh Murshid), Kusmah, 'Alujah (Sūq of Sheikh Mahmūd), and Hadīyah.

57. Beni Sa'fān.

A tribe in the mountains WNW. of Menākhah, and separated from it by the Mazar section of the Dā'ūdīyah sect. They helped the Turks in

1911, and 'Abdullah Beshīr, their Sheikh, by his friendly co-operation, enabled the Turks to turn the Imam's flank and relieve Menākhah. He is about 65, an experienced fighter. The tribe is a large one, numbering nearly 10,000 souls. It is generally on bad terms with the neighbouring Shafei, Zeidi, and Ismā'īlīyah tribes.

The chief clans are : Beni 'Ali Yahya and Beni Hārūn. The chief villages are : Metwah, Za'lah, Ashkar, Jari, Sharaji, Mujwan, and Hijri.

58. *Sahār*.

The Sahār are a fairly numerous tribe, of which the settled portion lives in and round the town of Sa'dah and is engaged in agriculture and trading. Owing to internal disunion and an absence of tribal feeling it does not possess the political importance which its numbers should warrant. The villagers are all under the authority of the Imam, but the nomads are almost completely independent and are accustomed to range far afield to the North and East in the direction of Nejrān and Barat. The tribe keeps on good terms as a rule with its neighbours, the Hāshid and the Arabs of Khaulān esh-Shām.

'Ali Ma'wad is the chief Sheikh of the settled portion. Seyyid Ahmed and Qasīm el-Hāshimi are the representatives of the Imam.

Settled :

Chief clans : Beni Hāzim (Sheikh Tabrān Muqbil), Beni Sa'd (Sheikh Taheir), Beni Hamdān and Āl Nuqeim (Sheikh Hamdān el-Jirbi), Beni Dhufeir (Sheikh 'Abdullah Dahmi), Beni Sineidar (Sheikh Ahmed Sineidar), Beni Hurān and Beni 'Umarah (Seyyid Qasīm), Beni Jurmān (Ahmed el-Hāshimi), Beni Jumā'ah (Sheikh Dahmash).

Nomads :

Chief clans : Āl Sinān and 'Amālaqah (Sheikh Sālih Qādir), Beni 'Ajlah and Beni Hureimah (Sheikh Ibn el-'As), Beni Shāmi and Beni Beddar (Sheikh 'Ali el-Wada'i), Beni 'Awad and Beni Haddād (Sheikh Mansūr el-Haddād).

59. *Sāri*.

A tribe just north of the Hufāsh and south of the Ahl Jebel Milhān, whose chief Sheikh is Sālih ibn Muslih. They are Zeidis and under the Imam, but their country is administered by the Turks, whom they hate. Allied with their northern neighbours, the Mahweit, also with the Hufāsh and Bura'.

60. *Senhān*.

A small Zeidi tribe stretching from just south of San'ā to Mehāqarah and the northern edge of the Bilād er-Ruhus. On the east they are bounded by the Khaulān. They are entirely devoted to cultivation, and number about 700 men. Seyyid Mohammed Sibsib of Mehāqarah is the chief Sheikh. The tribe is loyal to the Imam, who has his representative the Qādhi, Lutf ez-Zubeir, living there.

The chief villages are: Na'd, Jūzah, Qulfān, Hazyaz, Lubād, Safīyah, Mahāqarah, and Sha'asān.

61. *Serbih.*

Their stronghold is Da'ān, 3 hours north of 'Amrān. Their chief is Sheikh Rājih, who was granted the grade of Mirmirān before the Constitution and was made Pasha to secure his loyalty, but he remained staunch to the Imam and fought against the Turks in 1911. Peace was signed at Da'ān between 'Izzet Pasha and the Imam in 1911.

62. *Ahl Sha'ir.*

A large and peaceful tribe inhabiting the district round Jebel Sha'ir in southern Yemen. They cultivate *kat* and cereals in the fertile valley of Wādi Bana. Their paramount Sheikh is Sālih ibn Yahya Hizām, of the Beni Hizām, who comes under the Kaimmakam of Qa'tabah. Sheikh Hajj el-Kabs, of the Beni Kabs, and Yahya el-Qeishi are also important men in the tribe.

63. *Shamar.*

A small Zeidi tribe attached to the Imam, north-east of the Beni Aslam, in Hajūr.

64. *Shemsān.*

A small Zeidi tribe numbering about 1,000 souls, east of the Beni Ghill in Hajūr. They pay outward allegiance to the Imam, but are said to favour the Idrīsi. Their chief is Seyyid Yahya ibn el-Hādi.

65. *Beni Suleil.*

The Beni Suleil occupy a large area from the coast opposite Kamarān to the foot of the hills below Jebel Milhān. On the north they have the Bu'ajah, Za'līyah, and Beni Qeis, on the east the Beni Qeis, and on the south the Hashābiri, who are perhaps really only one of their sections.

The main road, which runs north and south through the Tihāmah near the foot of the hills, passes through their country, as well as that of those other tribes mentioned above, and they and the Beni Qeis control the caravan trade going up to the Wādi Maur. Estimates of their numbers vary from 1,500 to 10,000 fighting men. The western part of their territory is desert, but they have a good deal of cultivable land under the foot-hills in the east.

The tribe supports the Turks, and their two chief men, 'Abdullah el-Bōni and 'Abdullah Kauzi, have each received the title of Pasha and been appointed Kaimmakam of Zeidīyah and Mudir of Kenāwuz respectively. They are friendly with the Wa'zāt but independent of them. Towards the Quhrah they are always hostile.

Their chief villages are: Zeidīyah (Sheikh 'Ali Nukar), Kenāwuz, Ibn 'Abbās, and Salīf on the coast. There are important salt-works at the last-named, and a jetty where sea-going ships come alongside.

66. Ahl el-'Ūd.

A large and peaceful tribe living about 13 miles north-west of Qa'tabah, and coming under the Turkish Kaimmakam of that place. They live round Jebel Madra, and cultivate *kat* and cereals in Wādi Bana. Hizām es-Sayādi is their chief Sheikh.

67. Udhāqah.

A Zeidi tribe who claim descent from 'Anazah and 'Adnān, and live round Jebel Meswar to the west of 'Amrān, where there is a strong fortress at present occupied by the Turks. Their Emir is Seyyid Mohammed ibn el-Hādi, a servant of the Imam.

68. Wa'zāt.

The Wa'zāt occupy the country to the north of Loheia, which has been the scene of the recent fighting between the Turks and the Idrīsi. To the north, Wādi 'Ain and Wādi Wārith form the boundary between them and the pro-Idrīsi tribe of Beni 'Abs; to the east are the Beni Nashar; to the south their boundary is the Wādi Maur, including Mu'taridh and Ghanamah, but not Zāhirah, which belongs to the Beni Jāmi'. Their chief villages are Mu'lūq, near Jebel 'Izzān in the district of Jarb, and Deiramshuma, a fortified Turkish post about an hour south of Wādi 'Ain. The paramount Sheikh is Hādi ibn Ahmed el-Heij, a staunch supporter of the Turks who, always anxious to encourage the Sunni opponents of the Idrīsi, have made him Pasha and Mudir of the district. He comes second to the Sherif Hamūd, one of the Ashrāf of Sabia who have seceded from the Idrīsi, and who as Kaimmakam of Loheia governs the Wa'zāt and their allies, the Beni Jāmi'. Ibn el-Heij has long been opposed to the Idrīsi, and three years ago the Idrīsi captured his brother 'Abdullah and still holds him prisoner. With the Beni 'Abs the Wa'zāt have an ancient feud. During the Turko-Italian War, Ibn el-Heij wavered in his allegiance and took money from the Italians, but in the past two years he has been most active on the Turkish side. In September 1915 he raided the Beni 'Abs and was wounded. Idrīsi retaliated by cutting off his supplies, and Ibn el-Heij, finding himself short of food and his followers beginning to desert, appealed to the Imam for help. The latter sent the discouraging reply that he would send troops if they were fed.

The Wa'zāt are reported to number between 1,500 to 3,000 fighting men. Sheikh 'Ali Ibrāhīm is the most important Sheikh after Hādi ibn Ahmed el-Heij.

69. Ya'bir.

A tribe of the Ismā'īlīyah sect in the district of Harāz, which sided with the Turks against the Imam in 1911.

70. *Yām.*

The Yām tribes form a powerful confederation. They stretch from the northern boundary of the Bekīl in Barat up the Wādi Nejrān and Wādi Habūnah far to the north in the direction of Tathlīth and Wādi Dawāsir.

Joseph Halévy, the only European who has visited their country, found it in 1870 a fertile and productive region inhabited by a well-to-do population. In religion they are Ismā'īliyah and are known to the rest of Yemen as the Mu'tazilah or isolated sect; but as Wādi Nejrān was the last refuge of Christianity, and has remained far removed from external influence, it is possible that traces of the ancient worship still exist. Halévy was not long enough in the country to verify this, but the tolerance and even favour which he found extended to the Jews in Mikhlāf were hardly in the spirit of strict Mohammedanism. The religious chiefs are probably more orthodox than the bulk of the inhabitants, since they are in communication, not only with the chief Ashrāf of Yemen, but with the Āghā Khān, their spiritual head.

The ruling family is that of Makrami, descended from their famous ancestor who, in the middle of the eighteenth century, preached his reforming Gospel from Nejrān to Hasa. About the middle of the nineteenth century they developed ideas of expansion, and obtained from the Imam Muhsin in 1860 the Emirate of Heima, Harāz, and Menākhah. Their tenure, however, was short-lived, as in 1872 they were defeated and banished to their own country by Mukhtār Pasha. There is still a small remnant of the tribe, calling themselves the Makārimah, in the Harāz district, who fought for the Turks in 1911 but are chiefly traders and have little political importance.

The present Emir of Nejrān is Ismā'īl el-Makrami, who owes no allegiance. His tribesmen, however, are willing as a rule to serve as mercenaries with either the Imam or the Turks, if well paid. They have a reputation for ruthless bravery. Idrīsi has been in negotiation with them at various times during the present war, hoping with their help to force the Imam's hand against the Turks; but up to the present without result.

71. *Beni Zāfir.*

A small tribe of Hajūr el-Yemen living in Mikhlāf esh-Shems, which is noted for its fruits, coffee, and *kat*. Formerly they were counted as in the Turkish Markaz of Qufl, but after the treaty of 1911 between the Turks and Imam they came under the jurisdiction of the latter. They are Zeidis, good fighters, and allied with the neighbouring Zeidi tribes of Beni Ghill and Beni 'Azīz.

72. *Za'līyah.*

A small tribe immediately to the south of Loheia and the Wādi Maur down to the Beni Suleil. They are independent of the Wa'zāt, their northern neighbours, and come under 'Abdullah Pasha el-Bōni. Sheikh Hādi 'Ali, living at Dār el-Muhannab, is their chief Sheikh. They number 400 men.

73. *Zaranik (Dharāniq)*.

A powerful and warlike tribe divided into two sections, the Zaranik esh-Shām and Zaranik el-Yemen, and occupying the country between the sea and the hills from a few miles north of Beit el-Faqīh almost to Zebīd. The Zaranik have for long been a thorn in the side of the Turks, and especially during the Turco-Italian War. Repeated expeditions have failed to subdue them, but latterly there have been reports that part of the highland section, under Sheikh 'Ali ibn Hamūd, have succumbed to Turkish bribes. Mohammed Yahya el-Hibah Fashīk, the chief of the lowland section and paramount over the whole tribe, living at Huseinīyah, nine miles north of Zebīd, has, however, continued to hold out stoutly. In November 1915 he made common cause with Idrīsi in taking active measures against the Turks, and has succeeded in effectually cutting all communications in the Tihāmah from north to south. At the beginning of 1916 he was attacked by an irregular force from Mocha, increased by 300 Arabs under the leadership of Abela Effendi, the brother of Elias 'Osman, Kaimmakam of Mocha, but unsuccessfully. In May 1916 he again took the offensive and looted the Turkish serai in Beit el-Faqīh. The two most important Sheikhs after Sheikh Fashīk, and closely allied with him, are Shāmi and Munāsar Saghīr of Kokar, chief of the Highland section. Other Sheikhs, of whom nothing is known save their names, are 'Abdullah Munāsar of Huseinīyah, Nāsir Jurmush, Ismā'īl Ahmed, Sheikh of Qaramshah, 'Abdullah Duneidinah of Zebīd, Ahmed Risqallah of the Āl 'Ali, Hasan Rīsh of Jīz, Samūd of Āl Mūsa, Hasan Mubārak of Umm Faza', and Ibrāhīm Dhumbi of Direihimi.

74. *Zufeir*.

Small Zeidi tribe 5 miles north of the Hajjah, with whom they are allied. They come under the Kaimmakam of Hajjah, but are said to dislike the Turks and to have lost confidence in the Imam.

SEDENTARY TRIBES OF THE SOUTH ADEN PROTECTORATE

1. *'Abdāli*.

THE Ottoman attack on Aden in July 1915 resulted in the occupation of the 'Abdāli country by the Turks, the fall and sack of Lahej, its capital, the death of the ruling Sultan, and the retreat of most of his subjects to the Aden lines.

Previous to that event the 'Abdāli tribe occupied the country immediately round Aden. Its boundaries extended about 35 miles inland to the Haushabi tribe on the North, to the Fadhli Sultanate on the East, and the Subeihi tribe on the West. Formerly it held the Aden peninsula until an outrage perpetrated on a shipwrecked crew and the absence of any satisfaction led to the British bombardment and occupation of Aden in 1839.

The Sultan of Lahej, who is the head of the 'Abdāli, still receives a yearly subsidy from the British Government for its occupation of the town of Sheikh 'Othmān, and leases to it a large area of land in the neck of the isthmus. The present Sultan, 'Abd el-Kerīm ibn Fadl ibn 'Ali, is a man of 35, of sedentary habits, who has up to the present shown no marked ability. He is fairly well educated according to Arab standards, but knows no English. He is very popular with the tribe. He succeeded his cousin H. H. Sultan Sir 'Ali ibn Ahmed ibn 'Ali, K.C.I.E., on July 13, 1915, when the latter was accidentally shot during the Ottoman occupation of Lahej.

The tribe owes its importance more to its wealth than to its military prowess. It is entirely settled and agricultural with the exception of the Ahl Bān, who are chiefly pastoral but have arable land westwards in Abiyān near the Fadhli Sultanate. The population is estimated at 14,500.

The late Sultan of Lahej controlled the first stage of the main caravan road from Aden to Yemen up the Wādi Tiban and maintained armed and fortified posts at Zeidah, Sha'qah (Shaka), and 'Anad. He also had a customs post for the Aden traffic at Dār el-Amīr. He was then able to put into the field about 2,000 men, who were of doubtful fighting value but strong enough to repel any tribal attacks, knowing that British troops would come to their aid in the event of serious trouble.

'ABDĀLI

Tribe.	Sub-Tribe.	Clan.
'ABDĀLI.	Ahl Bān.	Mūsabein.
Sultan 'Abd el-Kerīm ibn Fadl ibn 'Ali.	'Udheibi.	Mansūri.
		Sh. Sālih Mansūr.
		'Ali Mansūr.
		Mohammed Mansūr.

2. 'Abd el-Wahīd Sultanate.

The 'Abd el-Wahīd confederation lies immediately to the East of the Upper and Lower 'Aulaqi Sultanates, with whose tribesmen it is at constant feud.

Tribally it is divided into the Sultanates of Bālhāf, Habbān, and Izzān.

The Sultan of Bālhāf, who lives in the town of that name on the sea-coast, is Sālih ibn 'Abdullah, who used to be officially recognized at Aden as the head of the 'Abd el-Wahīd confederation, and who received a small subsidy from Government. He is well-conducted, anglophile, but without much influence over his turbulent tribesmen. The latter have an hereditary feud with the Ba Kāzim, but lack their resolute grit and hardihood. Passage from one country to the other is dangerous, and supplies from Aden ordinarily come by sea.

The Sultan of Habbān, the chief mercantile town of the district, is Nāsir ibn Sālih. He is untrustworthy, and strongly opposed to any European penetration of his dominion. He is unpopular with his tribesmen, and frequently has trouble with the Lakmūsh and Ahl Iswad, two small but turbulent vassal tribes who lie between him and his hereditary enemies, the Ahl Ma'an of Upper 'Aulaqi.

The chief of the Izzān Sultanate, which lies 25 miles to the East of Habbān, is Muhsin ibn Sālih. He is a man of about 45, unpopular with his tribes, a robber, and a bad governor. He was expelled by the tribesmen in the early nineties, and after taking refuge with the Ahl Ma'an, went to Aden, Jibuti, and Hodeidah. Having tried in vain to raise money by pledging his Sultanate in turn to the French and the Turks, he returned via San'ā and managed to reinstate himself. In 1898 he again came into disfavour by endeavouring to blackmail the Austrian Expedition. He is now recognized by the Aden authorities as paramount, and receives a subsidy of Rs. 720 per annum. He is also supreme at Bālhāf, but shares the dues with Sālih ibn 'Abdullah.

Officially recognized Sultan, Muhsin ibn Sālih of Izzān.

> Subsidiary Sultans :
> Nāsir ibn Sālih of Habbān
> Tribes :
> Ahl Iswad.
> Lakmūsh.
> Sālih ibn 'Abdullah of Bālhāf.

3. Ahl Karab.

The Ahl Karab is a nomad tribe ranging the desolate tracts north of Upper 'Aulaqi and penetrating as far west as Beihān el-Jezāb and the Mūsabein country. They are a tribe of marauders and robbers, and though nominally vassals of the Upper 'Aulaqi Sultan, are always at war with the Ahl Hammām.

Their chief is Hāmid ibn Nāsir abu Kateyān, who lives at Shabwah, a town of about 3,000 inhabitants, some 55 miles north-east of Nisāb, built on the ruins of an ancient Himyarite city. They muster 400 men.

4. *Ahl es-Sa'īdi.*

The Ahl es-Sa'īdi are a small confederation bounded on the North by the 'Audillah, on the East by the Oleh, on the South by the Oleh, and on the West by the Yāfa'.

They are chiefly to be found near Dakhlah and the Sa'īdi plain, and are the original owners of the soil under the tenure of the Sultan of Upper 'Aulaqi, whose influence extends as far as Qarn Murshid. A landtax is due to him from them, and is always withheld until he comes down to fetch it with a large force. This happens about every five years.

The chief 'Āqil is Mohammed 'Ali abu 'Awad, who resides at Nūbat es-Suwa, and also holds supreme authority over the Yazīd, who pay taxes to him. The confederation numbers about 300 men, and are the nucleus of the following sub-tribes:

(1) AHL DIYĀN. Living at El-'Ain and Hamra. Their 'Āqil, Nasr Hamīd, lives at El-'Ain and receives a small tax from them, but at Thuwarein they pay a far larger tax or *'ushr* to Mohammed ibn 'Ali, a chief of the Ahl es-Sa'īdi, whose grandfather was formerly 'Āqil on condition of receiving *'ushr* from the Ahl Diyān, which was levied on land which they tilled, belonging to the Ahl es-Sa'īdi. The 'Āqilship passed from that family, but the *'ushr* is still paid. The Ahl Diyān muster about 200 men and are an offshoot of the sub-tribe at Khaura, but may now be considered as a component part of the Ahl es-Sa'īdi Confederacy.

(2) AHL YAZĪD. Living at Dakhlah. They muster about fifty men.

There are three more actual subdivisions of the Ahl es-Sa'īdi, but they barely muster between them 100 men and are scattered throughout the neighbouring villages in a most confusing manner.

There is a settlement within their territory called Hafa, which is peopled by Sādah (or *Seyyids*), whose origin is from Waht ('Abdāli country), where is the shrine of a well-known saint, 'Amr abu 'Ali, who, it is stated, formed a friendship with 'Amr abu Sa'īd (now enshrined at Mijdah) and was granted by him a small tax on the land round Dakhlah, which these Sādah collect. It is payable in kind, as are all these ecclesiastical contributions, and is about 5 per cent. on the year's crop. There is a shrine at Hafa (Fātimah bint Ahmed), and its attendants form the balance of the population.

5. *'Aqrabi.*

A small and peaceably disposed tribe, numbering about 700 souls, ranging north of Aden lagoon and west of Bir Ahmed, the tribal capital. Here is the residence of the local Sultan, the tall mud tower of which can be plainly seen from Aden harbour. The inhabitants are agricultural and pastoral. Their chief is Sheikh Fadhl ibn 'Abdullah Ba Haidarah, who succeeded his father in 1905. He is now about 31 years old, and is said to be fairly intelligent. His uncle, 'Ali Ba Haidarah, a shrewd old man of nearly 70, unsuccessfully pressed his claim to the Sheikhship in 1905, but later worked in harmony with the present chief.

In the present war pressure from their powerful northern neighbours, the Subeihi, and from the Turks has brought them in temporarily on the side of the latter.

Their Sultan is said to be a prisoner in Turkish hands.

6. *'Alawi.*

A small tribe of 1,200 souls whose chief village is at Suleiq, about 55 miles north of Aden. They live just south of the Quteibi tribe. Sheikh 'Ali ibn Nāshir ibn Shā'if, who lives at Kasha', is the present chief. He has the tribe well in hand in spite of the chronic disputes with the Quteibi. A middle-aged man of no particular influence, he was at first loyal and amenable to advice, but for some years his hatred and jealousy of the Quteibi, combined with excessive indulgence in *kat*, led him into trouble. The animosity between him and the Quteibi finally cooled down and a permanent settlement was effected between them in 1913 by the late 'Abdāli Sultan, Sir Ahmed Fadhl. He succeeded to the Chiefship in 1898 and signed an agreement for the safety of the trade routes in July 1914, under which his stipend was raised from Rs. 600 to 1,200 per annum.

Early in January 1916 he and his tribe were reported to have submitted with the Quteibi to the Turks and to be marching against the Fadhli Sultan.

7. *Amīri.*

The Amīri is a pastoral and agricultural tribe numbering 5,000 souls and occupying the country round and south-east of Dhāla, their capital.

The original Emirs of Dhāla were Muwallads or half-caste slaves of the Imams of San'ā. When the power of the latter was broken up, the Dhāla district was in the hands of certain Seyyids, from whom it was seized by the forefathers of the present chief. There has been a long line of Emirs, and since the occupation of Aden by the British these chiefs have been in receipt of a subsidy, except during the period from 1873 to 1878 when the Ottoman Government made a strong aggressive effort to place the district under their own control.

By allegiance or conquest several additions have been made to what may be called the district of Dhāla proper. These consist of Kharāfah, Jebel Harīr, the valley of the Suheibīyah as far south as Kaflah, the Dhubayyat hill (only nominal), Sufyān, and Zobeid.

The population of the Amīri territory is of a mixed nature. Firstly there are the descendants of the original Amīrs, constituting a large clan, although, as at present, not always united; secondly, such Sheiri Sheikhs as are content to acknowledge the authority of the Emir; thirdly, the various settlers who have from time to time become possessed of land which they cultivate; fourthly, the ever-present Seyyids or descendants of the Prophet; and, lastly, a colony of Jews.

The Emir is Nāsir ibn Shā'if ibn Seif, who lives at Dhāla. He became Emir in 1911 and is the son of Shā'if ibn Seif 'Abd el-Hādi who attended the Delhi Durbar during the Boundary Commission of 1902. He is a man of 36, good-natured but weak and avaricious and of little ability. He has two brothers, 'Abd el-Hamīd and Seif, the latter of whom is said to possess a considerable amount of energy and character. The ruling house is unpopular with the tribesmen.

When the Turks appeared in 1915 they took from him some fifteen hostages and deprived him of his position. Towards the end of the year they summoned him to Lahej and made a settlement by which they released the hostages, keeping his son in their stead, and reinstated him with the gift of 50 rifles and a subsidy. It is doubtless owing to this that the neighbouring tribes of Quteibi and 'Alawi were coerced into joining them. Sheikh Qāsim of Zobeid, who accompanied him to Lahej, received a gift of 10 rifles.

Emir, Nāsir ibn Shā'if ibn Seif, 'Abd el-Hamīd ibn Shā'if ibn Seif, Seif ibn Shā'if ibn Seif.

Sub-Tribes.	Sheikhs.
Sheiri	(1) Ahmed Muthanna of Āl Beishi. Friend of Emir. Former tribal influence has passed to Sheikh of Melāhah. Has custom house at Khoreibah.
	(2) Sāmih Sālim.
Deiri Muflahi	Yahya ibn Sālih in Radfān hills. Influential and well disposed.
	Seyyid 'Abd el-Razzāq ibn 'Abd er-Rahmān of Jebel Harīr. Loyal and influential in tribal disputes.
	Seyyid Mohammed Tahar. Spiritual master of J. Jihāf. Old but loyal and revered by people.
	'Ali ibn 'Ali ez-Zindāni of Sarīr. Loyal but uninfluential.
	Seyyid 'Ali Ridthwyn es-Safāni of Jebel Dhubayyat. Influential in tribal affairs.
	Seyyid Fadl ibn 'Alawi of Radfān hills. Popular. A hypocrite but useful.
	Ghālib ibn Ahmed Hidiyān, Naqīb of Jebel Kifa, south of Jebel Jihāf. On bad terms with Emir. Loyal to us.
	Muqbil Nāji', of Zindāni family on Jebel Jihāf. Was pro-Turk, but made overtures to Aden in 1914.
Azraqi	Hasan ibn Ahmed. Loyal to us. Declares himself independent of the Emir, to whom his adherence is very important.
Mihrābi	
Ahl Ahmed	

8. 'Audillah.

The 'Audillah is a predatory tribe mustering 5,000 fighting men (including '*asākir*) and inhabiting the Kaur, the main ridge of the Aden Hinterland. It is bounded on the north by the Beida Sultanate, on the south by the Oleh confederation of Dathīnah, on the east by the 'Aulaqi, and on the west by Yāfa'. The tribesmen are mainly pastoral, but cultivate sufficient barely for their needs. They hold a weekly market at Laudar, near the south foot of the Kaur, which the neighbouring tribes attend under a mutual understanding of neutrality. Here lives their Sultan, Qasīm ibn Hamīd el-Ghābir, a man who is powerless to curb their freebooting tendencies, but who provides the only ready channel by which the tribe can be approached. He made overtures for treaty relations in 1902, but was not at the time considered of sufficient importance for these to be encouraged. In 1912 he renewed his request, and as it was confirmed that the Turks had been making advances to him, a protectorate treaty was concluded in September 1914. The tribe have remained loyal during the present war. The only man who exercises any influence is Mohammed ibn Mohammed 'Abdullah, 'Āqil of the Kaur, a powerful chief whom, owing to the natural strength of his fortress, it is almost impossible to reach or constrain.

The chief tribe is the Ahl Demān.

'*Audillah Confederation*, 3,000.

Sultan, Qasīm ibn Hamīd el-Ghābir.

'Āqil, Mohammed ibn Mohammed 'Abdullah.

'AUDILLAH

Tribe.	Nos.	Clan.	Remarks.
AHL DEMĀN 'Aqil,'Ali'Amr (living at Demān)	1,800	Ahl Lamaki	Lower reaches of Wādi Ruqub (agricultural).
		Ahl Lukfa	Mountains NE. of Demān. Bedouins.
		Ahl Kafai	S. of Demān. Part agricultural, part Bedouin.
		Ahl Seyyari	NE. of Demān. Bedouin.
		Ahl Nāhcin er-Rahab	Half-way between Sauma'ah and Demān. Bedouin.
		Ahl Buker er-Reidah	S. of Ahl Nāhcin.
		Ahl Wahesh	NE. of Ahl Buker.
		Ahl Yczīd	N. of Ahl Wahesh.
		Ahl es-Seil	E. of Sauma'ah.
AHL BUKER EL-HĀDHĪN	300		NE. of Mijdah. Bedouin.
AHL BU TAHIF	200		Between Ahl esh-Shā'ah and Ahl Buker el-Hādhīn.
AHL HADHĪN	200		E. of Ahl Buker el-Hādhīn. Bedouin.
AHL 'ALI MOHAMMED	200		Summit and N. of Kaur along road to Sauma'ah. Bedouin.
AHL ESH-SHĀ'AH	100		N. of Mijdah. Agricultural.
MISHERI	100		NE. of 'Ali Mohammed. Bedouin.
BIRKĀN	100		E. of 'Ali Mohammed. Bedouin.
AHL GHAI MELAN			W. Tilhāk.
AHL MARZŪQ (MERZOQ)			
AHL ELHĪN			

With '*asākir*, and a few scattered clans not mentioned above, the total strength is said to be 5,000.

9. *Upper and Lower 'Aulaqi*.

The 'Aulaqi country is inhabited by a large tribal confederation, divided for political purposes into the Sultanates of Upper and Lower

'Aulaqi, but maintaining close inter-tribal relations and uniting in the event of any aggression from outside.

It extends from the edge of the Ruba' el-Khāli to the Aden Gulf, and is bounded on the east by the 'Abd el-Wahīd Sultanate and on the west by the Sultanates of Beida, 'Audillah, Oleh, Yāfa', and Fadhli. The inhabitants are mainly pastoral and semi-nomadic, but there are large tracts of arable land, while the main wādis all have their settled population.

The history of the confederation is as follows : From the Prophet's epoch (or still earlier), the Nisāb Sultanate was in the hands of the Umm-Rusās dynasty of Beida, while the whole of Wādi Yeshbum (then called Wādi Kahai) was under the Sultanate of 'Abd el-Wahīd, whose capital was then at Habbān. Wādi Yeshbum seems to have then been inhabited chiefly by *raya*, who paid taxes to the 'Abd el-Wahīd dynasty.

The Ba Kāzim were then confined to Heid Herīf (a part of the Utheili system) while Ahwar and district was in the hands of a tribe called the Ahl Zeidi.

Soon after the Prophet's death considerable political dissension seems to have occurred in the land of Jauf, where dwelt the remnants of the ancient and powerful Minaean dynasty, which flourished before the Sabean kingdom, owing to the death of the paramount chief, named Ma'an. The house of Ma'an was much persecuted and fled the country, together with two branches of a former ruling chief named Sālih, whose descent was as follows :

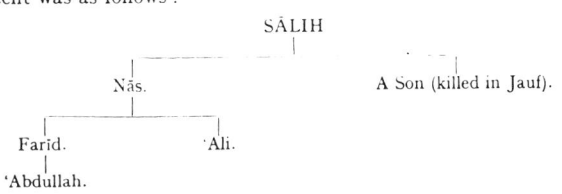

```
                    SĀLIH
          _____|_____
          |                     |
         Nās.              A Son (killed in Jauf).
     _____|_____
     |         |
   Farīd.     'Ali.
     |
  'Abdullah.
```

These three clans, the Ahl 'Abdullah, Ahl 'Ali, and the Ahl Ma'an, wandered across the outskirts of the Great Desert until they came upon Wādi Yeshbum, where they settled side by side with the *raya* of 'Abd el-Wahīd on the spot where now stand Wāsitah and Sa'īd. They had, of course, to become *raya* themselves, as they were aliens under the protection of another Sultanate, and for many years they paid tribute to the Sultan of Habbān.

In the course of time, however, they increased enormously in numbers, and the Ahl Ma'an left the Wādi and adopted a pastoral and semi-nomadic life in the mountains, leaving the two branches of Manāsīr Bu Sālih still settled in the Yeshbum Valley. About the middle of the sixteenth century these latter became very discontented with their lot owing to excessive taxation, and in A.D. 1590 they persuaded the Ahl Ma'an to join them in an attack on the Umm Rusās dynasty at Nisāb, with a view to the annexation of the whole of that district. The Ahl Bunyar, who now inhabit the plateau of Dahr but then occupied the Nisāb district as well, fought desperately for their Sultan, but could not stand before the rush of the Ahl Ma'an, who were fighting for their very existence as a tribe. The then representative of the Umm-Rusās dynasty at Nisāb fled for his life, and the Ahl Bunyar were chased up Wādi Khaura with great slaughter. The Ahl 'Abdullah received the Sultanate, and from them the present Sultan is descended.

Many of the Ahl Ma'an settled in this new Sultanate, as will be shown later on when considering the distribution of the various sub-tribes. The remainder returned to their pastoral life near Wādi Yeshbum, the Ahl 'Ali going back to their settlements in the wādi.

The Ba Kāzim now realized that this alien race was becoming a formidable power, and having also views of expansion, sent a deputation to the Ahl 'Ali asking for their assistance in wresting Ahwar from the Zeidi, offering them the Sultanate of that district.

A famous diplomat and ascetic, Sheikh Abeid, whose name is still revered in both Upper and Lower 'Aulaqi, arranged the treaty between the two parties. It was agreed that the Ba Kāzim should have three-quarters of the arable land at Ahwar and the Ahl 'Ali the other quarter, the latter receiving the Sultanate. In the attack on Ahwar the Zeidi were completely defeated. Some tendered their submission, and are there to this day as mere tributary raya, and the rest fled towards the north-west, and no trace of them remains, although it is said that a small colony of them are settled at Jauf.

The Ba Kāzim then spread all over the country now known as Lower 'Aulaqi, but never seem to have submitted to the suzerainty of their nominal Sultan, whose dynasty they regarded as aliens whom they themselves had pitchforked into power.

After the Ahl 'Ali had left Yeshbum, one of the two divisions of the Ahl Ma'an abandoned their pastoral life and settled in the wādi. This was the Ahl 'Ali Bu Hamid, the other division, the Ahl Mohammed Bu Hamid, still following their nomadic life in the mountains.

The Upper 'Aulaqi Sultan is Sālih ibn 'Abdullah, who lives at Medak, a short distance from Nisāb. He is a man of about 55, energetic and with considerable influence over the tribes. He was a signatory by proxy of the Aden Treaty in 1904, and has maintained his anglophile attitude during the present war by refusing to join the Turks in their attack on Aden. His descent is as follows:

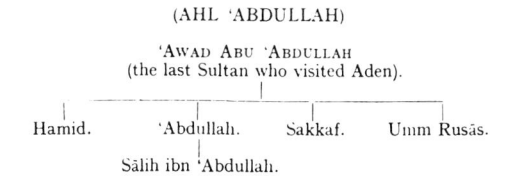

(AHL 'ABDULLAH)

'Awad Abu 'Abdullah
(the last Sultan who visited Aden).

| Hamid. | 'Abdullah. | Sakkaf. | Umm Rusās. |

Sālih ibn 'Abdullah.

His tribesmen are inclined to be predatory, and although he does not give his official sanction to their raids, he nevertheless connives at them and generally receives some of the plunder in an unostentatious manner. At the same time he keeps a firm control over his subjects, and only permits measures to be taken against turbulent and aggressive tribes whom it is necessary to punish. The 'Audillah are always blockading the roads through his country, and the Ahl Demān have an evil reputation for acts of violence and oppression perpetrated on petty traders. The Elhīn and the Ahl Diyān are similar offenders. The ethics of such measures are, of course, doubtful, but it can at least be said that many tribes and sub-tribes abstain from predatory acts, deterred by the fear of bringing wholesale ruin and disaster on themselves and their fellow tribesmen.

The two chief tribes are the AHL MA'AN and the AHL MEHĀJIR. The Ahl Ma'an, with the exception of a large detached section, the Ba Thubān near Wādi Khaura, east of Nisāb, inhabit the fertile valley of Yeshbum and its surrounding hills. They are noted for their bravery and fighting qualities, and can muster about 5,000 fighting men. Their ruling family is the Fārid; its present representative, Muhsin ibn Fārid. He is a man of about 45, and has always been anglophile. He signed the Aden Treaty in 1903, and was granted a stipend of Rs. 1,440 per annum. He succeeded his elder brother Erwes, who was deposed by the tribes in about 1895 for intriguing with the then Sultan of Habbān, Muhsin ibn Sālih, and committing them to the sack of Habbān, a venture which they refused to undertake. His family is as follows:

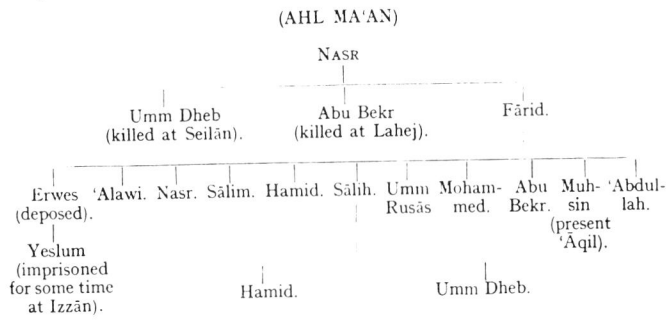

(AHL MA'AN)

NASR
|
Umm Dheb — Abu Bekr — Fārid.
(killed at Seilān). (killed at Lahej).

Erwes. 'Alawi. Nasr. Sālim. Hamid. Sālih. Umm Moham- Abu Muh- 'Abdul-
(deposed).   Rusās med. Bekr. sin   lah.
| (present
Yeslum   'Āqil).
(imprisoned
for some time   Hamid.   Umm Dheb.
at Izzān).

The Ahl Mehājir have no paramount chief. They can raise about 4,000 fighting men, but their strength is not concentrated like that of the Ahl Ma'an. They lead a more nomadic life, and range the country from the northern boundary of the 'Audillah and the Kaur el-'Aud to the desert stretches north of the Nisāb and the wild country of the Ahl Karab and the Mūsabein, who pay a nominal allegiance to the Sultan of Upper 'Aulaqi, but are ever swift to raid his tribesmen when an opportunity occurs.

The most northern section of the Mehājir, the Ahl Hammām, are themselves inclined to be predatory, and scour the Hammām Desert on the look-out for caravans. When the depredations become too frequent and obtrusive, the Sultan of Nisāb marches his troops into their country and quickly restores order, dealing out condign punishment on any raiding parties met with. The Hammām 'Āqil, Husein abu Ahmed, has not much control over his people and cannot check marauding.

In addition to his own tribesmen, the Sultan exercises suzerainty over the following :

1. The BAL HĀRITH, who pay immediate allegiance to the Sherif of Beihān, who in turn is under Nisāb influence and pays a private, semi-voluntary tribute.

2. The MŪSABEIN, merely nominal.

3. The AHL KARAB, also nominal.

4. The AHL SA'ĪDI, who pay him land tax under pressure. A further description of the above will be found under their names.

5. The AHL NASIYĪN, who derive their origin from the almost extinct race of Beni Hilāl, a few surviving representatives of which may be found at Heid Hādhinah. They number 700 men, and their territory stretches from Hajar to Heid Jehūr and towards the south-east. Its limit occurs at Jaul (or Jāl) Heirūr, and may be said to lie along the Wādi Markhah within the limits named. The Sultan is Nasr abu Thālib, who belongs to the Abu Thālib dynasty, an offshoot of the Nisāb dynasty. His sway is, of course, subject to the jurisdiction of Nisāb.

6. Three clans who are termed 'ASĀKIR. They do not come directly under the Sultan, but are bound by treaty with the Ahl Ma'an to give their services in battle in case of a war.

(a) Ahl Ba Zal, leading a pastoral life in the Kaur el-'Aud near the source of Wādi Marbūn.

(b) Ahl Wahar, living at Heid Keneb and Hisn Makūsrah, agricultural.

(c) Ahl Reid, who occupy a district north-east of Arq (the frontier village of Lower 'Aulaqi). They lead a pastoral life along the banks of the Wādi Reid, which joins the Wādi Rafal just above Arq, under the name of Wādi Maleik.

7. AHL BA FEYYĀD, a powerful tribe, who are not related to the Ahl Ma'an, but are bound to them by a mutual offensive and defensive alliance. They muster 600 men and live along Wādi Yeshbum, between Safāl and the gorge of Nakabah. Origin not known.

8. AHL BA HADAH, another treaty tribe of the Ahl Ma'an, who number 300 men and extend from below the Nakabah gorge to within a short distance of Habbān.

9. KHALĪFAH, a treaty tribe living on the western slopes of Heid Hādhinah, a range to the west of the Hammām Desert, and mustering about 1,000 men.

The fighting strength of the Sultan, including his 'Asākir or standing army, is as follows :

Troops at Medak, Nisāb, Wādi Dhura, Wādi Abadan (or Abdān), Wasat, and Beihān	1,100
Ahl Ma'an and Treaty Tribes	4,900
Ahl Mehājir and Nasayīn	4,400
	10,400

In case of a great emergency the Sultan would, as suzerain, secure the services of the desert tribes lying east and north-east of the Hammām as far as human life can be supported in the desert. The Beihān tribes would join as a matter of policy, for they are too close to escape being crushed by the fall of the 'Aulaqi dynasty. The people of Jauf would certainly throw in their lot with the 'Aulaqi, for it has always been the policy of the Nisāb Sultans to keep in touch with the parent tribeship, and Jaufi chiefs are often entertained at Nisāb. The Khalīfah of Hādhinah would also come forward, as a serious reverse to Upper 'Aulaqi would cut them off from all their trade routes to Nisāb, Yeshbum, and Habbān.

Lower 'Aulaqi would follow the lead of the Ahl Ma'an, as between Umm Rusās abu Fārid and 'Ali abu Muhsin, the paramount chief of the Ba Kāzim, there is firm friendship and also a defensive treaty. Only in the case of aggression against the 'Abdāli Sultan would the Ba Kāzim keep out, there being a close alliance between 'Ali abu Muhsin and the 'Abdāli Sultan.

If the position of Dathīnah is considered, it will be seen that the Oleh confederacy must join in or be annihilated, and besides, their sympathies are with the 'Aulaqi.

Under such circumstances the forces may be estimated as follows ·

Upper 'Aulaqi	10,400
Lower 'Aulaqi	4,800
Jauf and tribes between them and Beihān	12,000
Beihān	6,000
Desert tribes, Ahl Karab, &c.	8,000
Khalīfah of Hādhinah	1,000
Oleh of Dathīnah	3,200
	45,400

The Ahl Bunyar, who number about 4,000, are excluded, as they would follow the Beida Sultan, and some tribes, whose forces are not known, are also omitted.

The supply of breech-loading rifles amongst those tribes has increased enormously during the last few years, and they have some good mounted troops. Their military spirit is undeniable, their history for the last century being full of martial episodes.

The Ba Kāzim with its numerous subdivisions compose the entire tribal population of Lower 'Aulaqi, and can put into the field about 5,000 men. They are a hardy and turbulent race, always engaged in petty feuds amongst themselves, or raids on their immediate neighbours, the 'Abd el-Wahīd, Fadhli, and Oleh. They have a bad reputation with the other tribes on account of their fondness for drink and their slackness in religious observances, but are redeemed by their genuineness and bravery.

They have no paramount chief, such influence as the tribe will permit being exercised by the brother chiefs of the Ahl 'Ali section at Ghidabah, Fadhl, and 'Ali Muhsin.

The late Sultan of Lower 'Aulaqi, Bu Bekr ibn Nāsir, lived at Ahwar, about five miles from the coast, and had very little influence over the Ba Kāzim tribesmen. His successor has not yet been appointed.

UPPER 'AULAQI

Ahl Ma'an

Ahl 'Ali abu Hamid. Wādi Yeshbum from Wāsitah to Safāl, 2,200.

Tribe.	Nos.	Clan.	Remarks.
Ahl Bu Bekr	1,000	Ahl Yeshbum Erwes	Ruling house of Ahl Ma'an. Present representative Muhsin ibn Fārid. They inhabit Sa'īd and Wāsitah.
		Ahl Bu Bekr	Pastoral and nomadic, Kaur Edth and Wādi Khaiwān.
		Ahl Sālim	Inhabit Qarn Mabr and Heid Shūq (see vicinity of Yeshbum Sūq). Settled and agricultural.
		Ahl 'Abdullah	In Heid Rafal, where they are pastoral and nomadic; also in lower reaches of W.Sha'bah, near its junction with W. Yeshbum. Here they have a little land.
Ahl Atik	500	Ahl Ajūz	At Arashān and Mehlāl along W. Shabdh. Settled and agricultural; small proportion pastoral and semi-nomadic.
		Ahl Merwān	At Arashān, settled and agricultural there, but at least half of them are pastoral. A few reside at Mehlāl.
		Ahl Mehrān	In upper reaches of W. Sha'b. Pastoral.
		Ahl Ga'ar	In Hisn Sha'b, close to junction of W. Sha'b and W. Sha'bah. Settled and agricultural. A few follow pastoral life farther up the wādi.
Ahl Madhaji	400	Ahl Masās	Upper reaches of Wādi Hasbasah. Pastoral. A few inhabit Jehdil and Hejil.
		Ahl Lijam	Jehdil and Modāl. Settled and agricultural.

A.   K k

UPPER 'AULAQI (continued)

Tribe.	Nos.	Clan.	Remarks.
		Ahl Hanash	At Hejil. Settled and agricultural.
		Ahl esh-Shawāhi	At Edat Shems. Settled and agricultural.
AHL BA RAS	300	Ahl Hādi	At Kaulah. Settled and agricultural.
		Ahl 'Awad	At Shreij. Settled and agricultural.
		Ahl Sālim	Small settlements under Heid Tahm at entrance to Rajalān Pass, chiefly pastoral, in wet weather become nomadic, ranging about the Ba Ras limits in order to make use of numerous grazing grounds which then afford luxuriant pasture throughout the tribeship.

AHL MOHAMMED BU HAMID, 1,650

AHL SULEIMAN	800		Divided into several *afkhādh*, but names not known. Live far up the Rajalān Pass towards Hādhinah. Bedouin.
AHL MATOSALAH	300		All Bedouin, no husūn.
		Ahl Jedah	Kaur el-'Aud.
		Ahl Ba Sheir	Kaur el-'Aud.
		Ahl Ba Rajelah	Kaur el-'Aud.
		Ahl Mudun	Pastoral and agricultural. Some large tracts of arable land in the upper reaches of Wādi Khumar.
AHL HĀMED	150		Live at Hisn es-Surr and vicinity of W. es-Surr. No *afkhādh*. Settled and agricultural.
AHL BA THOBĀN	200		Occupy country SE. of Jaul el-Heirūr on the Nasin border and extend S. to near junction of W. Hajar and W. Subhān.
AHL MAKRAHAH			Stretch S. and SW. of the Ahl Ba Thobān.

AHL MEHĀJIR

(Mehājir is an abstract title given to this group of tribes.)

AHL HAMMĀM	1,200		The Hammām is the most powerful of the Ahl Mehājir, and their 'Āqil, Husein Abu Ahmed, is one of the mainstays of the Ansab Sultan. Territory extends westwards to Heid Qabr and Hisn er-Ruqbah and NW. as far as junction of W. Markhah and W. Hammām. Their limits are somewhat vague as they are entirely nomadic and pastoral.
		Ahl Shemlān.	Occupy the country E. of Heid Mejah.

UPPER AULAQI (continued)

Tribe.	Nos.	Clan.	Remarks.
		Ahl Diyāb	Extend from NE. of Heid Mejah into the desert.
		Ahl Husein	E. of Hisn er-Ruqbah, and in time of drought graze and water their camels in Wādi Abadan. Other *afkhādh* names not known.
AHL MERĀZIQ	900		Northern limit an imaginary line drawn from Ansab eastwards through Qarn Lemah. S. limit border of Ahl Nitosalah in Jaul ed-Dahrah. They may be practically said to inhabit the mountain system that runs along the E. borders of Jaul el-Mutti and Jaul ed-Dahrah, both these plains being uninhabitable except in very wet weather, when they afford fair pasturage. They are pastoral.
AHL ER-RABĪZ	600		Bounded on N. by Ahl Dakar; on S. their limits reach to Hisn Jabrah; on the E. Wādi Hanak forms their frontier line. A powerful tribe, but much diminished by small-pox. Above number represents fighting strength in 1910. Partly pastoral, partly settled and agricultural.
AHL DAYA'	700		Inhabit the Khaura district. Settled and agricultural.
AHL DAKAR	100		Inhabit the vicinity of Abadan, bounded on the N. by the Ahl Mabīth and on the E. by Wādi Hanak.
AHL LAQĪT	150		Inhabit the mountains of Laqīt, which extend from W. Sa'd to W. Jibah. Bedouin and pastoral.
AHL MABĪTH	70		Live between Ahl Dakar and Ansab. Entirely pastoral.

LOWER 'AULAQI
Ba Kāzim, 4,789.

AHL SHAMMA	300		Settled and agricultural.
		Ahl er-Rashid }	At Kubth, but moving towards Lebākhah.
		Ahl ez-Zenu }	
		Ahl Hawāfil	Jidhābah.
		Ahl Konah	Kubth.
		Ahl 'Ali	Kubth and Mehfid.
		Ahl Sālih bu Nasr	Kubth.
		Ahl Husein	Kubth.
		Ahl Mohammed bu Nasr	Jidhābah.

LOWER 'AULAQI (*continued*)

Tribe.	Nos.	Clan.	Remarks.
AHL KARLAH	400		All settled and agricultural.
		Ahl Gawil	At Arakein.
		Ahl Dahas	At Lebākhah.
		Ahl Ba Hal	At Lebākhah.
		Ahl Mansūr bu Sālim	At Lebākhah.
		Ahl Ba Weden	Arakein (these are Sādah).
		Ahl Shauf	Arakein and vicinity.
		Ahl Hādi	Lebākhah.
		Ahl Humeid	Lebākhah.
AHL MANSŪR	450		Chiefly Bedouin, but a few husūn.
		Ahl Muhlik	Low down in Wādi Rafal.
		Ahl Makrum	In Wādi Kafah below Heid (Leimūn).
		Ahl Heidarah	Upper reaches of Wādi Meriyah.
		Ahl Mas'ūd	Below Ahl Haidarah in Wādi Mera.
		Ahl Lehwik	Upper reaches of Wādi Faki.
		Ahl Khalīl	Below Ahl Lehwik in Wādi Faki.
		Ahl Nubah	In Wādi Kafah above Ahl Makrum.
		Ahl Nasr	Between Ahls Nubah and Makrum.
AHL BA KRAD	130		Bedouin and pastoral.
		Ahl Sa'd	Slopes of Heid Salr (a little land and one hisn).
		Ahl Hādi	Wādi Legīb (flows into Wādi Kafah from Heid Herīf).
		Ahl Yeslum	On eastern border of the Dathīnah.
		Ahl el-Lefiyah	S. of above.
		Ahl Gabr	Kaur el-Utheili.
		Ahl Ligrab	Heid Raham.
AHL MANA	25		Partly agricultural and partly Bedouin.
		Ahl Lisāmah	Land on left bank of Wādi Meriyah near Kaurat el-'Āliyah.
		Ahl Daur	Kaurat el-'Āliyah.
		Ahl Sa'd	Kaurat Ahl Mana.
		Ahl 'Awad	Half-way down Wādi Faki.
		Ahl Sālih	Kaurat es-Sifālah.
AHL SA'ĪD	20		Partly agricultural and partly Bedouin.
		Ahl Makasa	At Bir esh-Shukab, where they have land and husūn.
		Ahl Salamin	
		Ahl Sālim bu Qamar	Near Seilat en-Nettakh (pastoral).
AHL BA SELĀHAH	24	*Ahl el-Awar*	All follow a pastoral life on Heid Hamr, a system E. of Heid Raham.
		Ahl Haidarah	
		Ahl el-Hindi	
		Ahl Lidwa	
		Ahl Ba Bedu	
		Ahl Dedwah	
		Ahl 'Aqab	
		Ahl Bil Ed	
AHL LAHAK	500		Partly Bedouin and partly agricultural.

LOWER 'AULAQI (*continued*)

Tribe.	Nos.	Clan	Remarks.
		Ahl Heitham	All in the district of Ludi, a well-watered country S. of Lebākhah. Extent uncertain, but its S. line probably approaches the barrier range which runs parallel with the coast.
		Ahl Tamūs	
		Ahl Mareith	
		Ahl 'Ali Bu Sa'id	
		Ahl Sabrah	
		Ahl Jedah	
		Ahl Zomah	
		Ahl Kahtar	
		Ahl Husein	
		Ahl Mokah	
		Ahl 'Uyūn en-Nabah	
		Ahl Dhi'b el-Aswad	
AHL LESHAR	100		Live half-way down Wādi Leikah and are also scattered among the mountain ranges towards Dathīnah. Bedouin.
AHL AHTALAH	900		Partly Bedouin and partly agricultural.
		Ahl Yeslam	At Ahwar and lower reaches of Leikah.
		Ahl Haidarah	In Wādi Gahr (or Jahr), near junction with Leikah.
		Ahl el-'Afu	At Ahwar.
		Ahl Luthfah	Wādi Tisabah (comprises Dathīnah systems and joins Wādi Gahr).
		Ahl Baseniyah	Upper reaches of Wādi Gahr.
		Ahl el-Asad	Below Ahl Haidarah in Wādi Gahr.
		Ahl Ambur	East of Ahl Luthfah.
		Ahl Umerthi	At Ahwar and Hisn 'Ariyat 'Ali (or bu 'Ali).
		Ahl 'Ali	Left bank of Wādi Leikah.
AHL AJAM (Ajara) (Dār)	150		Between Ahl Mansūr and Ahl Ahtalah. Bedouin.
AHL HAMID (Dār)	300		
AHL HAIDARAH (Dār)	250		
AHL MANAS (Dār)	220		Southern slopes of Heid Raham.
AHL BU BUL (Dār)	180		Between Heid el-Aswad and Bir Subbāhiyah.
AHL BAHAN (Dār)	200		East of Ahwar.
AHL YAHĀWI	150		Settled and agricultural.
		Ahl Gabr	At Misāni S. of Ahwar.
		Ahl Soban	At Hanad.
AHL BEDU (Dār)	230		At Hanad.
AHL HAMID (Dār)	160		At Hanad.
AHL UMM BUSHTI (Dār)	100		SE. of Ahwar on right bank of the Wādi.

10. Bal Hārith.

See Beihān.

11. Beida.

The Beida is a plateau Sultanate north of the Kaur, impinging on the Yemen along its western boundary and reaching northwards to Beihān ed-Daulah. To the east is the Upper 'Aulaqi Confederation and on the south the 'Audillah.

Formerly its power was more wide-reaching, and in the Prophet's time, or even earlier, all the land round Nisāb was in the hands of the Umm Rusās dynasty of Beida and his chief tribe, the Ahl Bunyar. This they held until the year 1590, when they were forced back up the Wādi Khaura and to the Dahr plateau by the Ahl Ma'an and other tribesmen who now form the Upper 'Aulaqi Confederation.

The Sultan resides at Beihān Umm Rusās, and can muster about 1,000 men of his own retainers and 'asākir. An unsuccessful attempt was made some years ago to enter into relations with him. He still stands out from treaty relations with us and is in correspondence with the Imam.

The principal tribe is the Ahl Bunyar, occupying Soma (or Sauma'ah) and the Dahr plateau. Their chief is 'Abd en-Nebi Husein, who lives in the fortress of Dhimrah, which guards the thriving trading town of Soma from attack. He is a man of about 50 years and carries his influence beyond his borders to the 'Audillah and Upper 'Aulaqi tribes. He commands some 4,000 men. Farther north come the tribe of the Beni Yūb, who used to exact customs dues on the Beihān Jezāb and Yeshbum caravan road until prevented by the Ahl Hammām. They range along Wādi Markhah and up to Rahwat er-Ribbah. The Ahl Azan, the third chief tribe, are chiefly pastoral, with the exception of the Ahl 'Omar, who are a trading and agricultural community.

Tribe.	'Aqil.	Sub-Tribes.
AHL BUNYAR. 4,000 men	'Abd en-Nebi Husein.	
BENI YŪB		
AZANI. 1,500 men		Ahl Sa'īd.
		Ahl 'Omar.
		Ahl 'Obeid.
		Ahl Yahya.
		Ahl Wahish.
		Ahl Sei.
		Ahl Kesiyīn.
		Ahl Mohammedin.

12. Beihān.

Beihān is the name given to the district adjoining Wādi Beihān from the point where it leaves the mountain system of Beida down to the region where it loses itself in the Great Desert. Commencing from the upper reaches, the land on both sides of the wādi is in the hands of the Beida Sultanate. Farther down are the limits of the Mūsabein, chief town Hajarah. Below them the Sultan of Nisāb has some land, and farther down are the tribal limits of the Bal Hārith, in which are the towns of Durb, Hakaba, and Seilān ; the two latter belong to the Ashrāf of Beihān, and Durb belongs to a large and influential family of Sādah. The above towns have also a large population of *raya*, or trading classes, all of whom pay taxes to the Sultan of Upper 'Aulaqī. The Ashrāf and Sādah also pay a private semi-voluntary tribute (Jibār) to him, and he exercises considerable influence in the district. The position of these Ashrāf requires some explanation ; they are descended as follows :

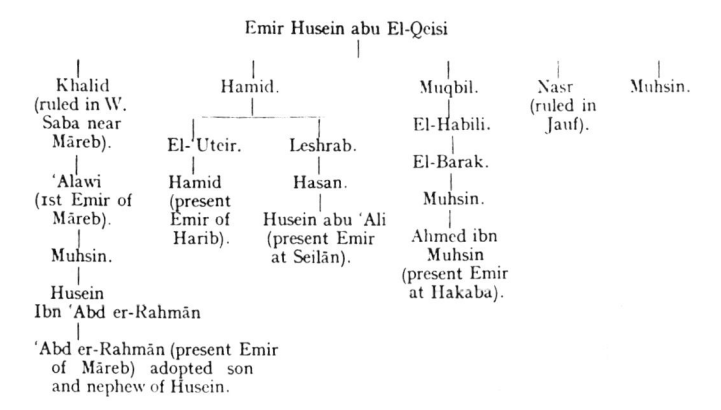

Emir Husein abu El-Qeisi

- Khalid (ruled in W. Saba near Māreb).
  - 'Alawi (1st Emir of Māreb).
    - Muhsin.
      - Husein Ibn 'Abd er-Rahmān
        - 'Abd er-Rahmān (present Emir of Māreb) adopted son and nephew of Husein.
- Hamid.
  - El-'Uteir.
    - Hamid (present Emir of Harib).
  - Leshrab.
    - Hasan.
      - Husein abu 'Ali (present Emir at Seilān).
- Muqbil.
  - El-Habili.
    - El-Barak.
      - Muhsin.
        - Ahmed ibn Muhsin (present Emir at Hakaba).
- Nasr (ruled in Jauf).
- Muhsin.

The chief Emir at Beihān is Ahmed ibn Muhsin of Hakaba, who also resides at Beihān el-Jezāb. He is an old man of about 67, crafty, but less powerful than he pretends. He is comparatively wealthy, entertains lavishly, and is very popular with the Bal Hārith, among whom he lives for a great part of the year as a Bedouin, in the lower reaches of Wādi Beihān. He acts as an abitrator and dispenses justice. As regards his outside relations, he is on bad terms with the Sherif of Māreb. He has always been anglophile and signed the Aden Treaty in 1903. More recently he has expressed anxiety to extend the British sphere of influence northwards over Beida, Māreb, and Jauf. The Sheikh of the Bal Hārith is Shammakh ibn Ghannam, a middle-aged man who visited Aden in 1904 and confirmed the treaty concluded with Ahmed ibn Muhsin in the preceding year.

Neither he nor any of the Ashrāf have any influence with the Mūsabein. The Bal Hārith, Sādah, and Ashrāf number together 2,000 men. The Mūsabein are said to muster more than 4,000 men. The sand dunes which surround Beihān on three sides prevent anything in the nature of a cavalry dash for raiding purposes, but marauding parties (especially from the Hammām), frequently slip through on saddle-camels and play havoc with the Mūsabein. The Bal Hārith and their Sādah and Ashrāf are, however, never molested.

13. Dhāmbari.

A small tribe north of Aden, about 40 miles east of the Haushabi, whose Sultan claims suzerainty over them, a claim which they only admit when it suits them. They have always given trouble, and in 1903 a British column meted out punishment to them for raiding the mail, and destroyed their fortress at Nakhlein. The chief Sheikh is Sālim Husein. They are reported to have recently joined the Turks.

14. Fadhli.

The Fadhli are a large and warlike tribe, numbering about 8,000 fighting men, who are probably well-armed owing to their large seaboard and resources. They are pastoral and agricultural, and extend from Maqātīn (the Lower 'Aulaqi boundary) to the Fadhli border and British frontier line at 'Imād, where the tribeship is a mere coastal strip and uninhabited. To the north is the Oleh confederation, over whom the Sultan claims a suzerainty, which is not admitted. In actual practice his power does not extend inland of the maritime ranges. The Sultan is Husein ibn Ahmed, resident at Shūghrah (Shuqrah). He is an old man of 90, and in 1877 was deported to India and confined in the fort of Ahmednagar for 9 years, having been implicated in the murder of his brother Heidīyah, who was then Sultan. Heidīyah was succeeded by Sultan Husein's son, Ahmed ibn Husein. The latter died in 1907, after giving much trouble to the authorities, and Husein was proclaimed Sultan. He is unpopular with his subjects, and his grandson 'Abdullah Dīn ibn Ahmed has greater influence and is anxious to supplant him. He has a son aged 31 named 'Abdullah ibn Husein, who acted for him during his absence in Delhi at the Durbar in 1911, and again in 1913 when he visited Jerusalem. Sultan Husein visited Aden late in 1915, afterwards returning to Shūghrah. In January of this year he was summoned to Lahej and received by 'Ali Sa'īd Pasha with much honour. After remaining there for some time he returned to Shūghrah and reopened correspondence with Aden, claiming to have been compelled by *force majeure* to visit Lahej. His subsidy has been withheld and an embargo been placed on Shūghrah. He has been ordered to Aden to state his case, but it is not expected that he will comply until the situation is clearer.

The Fadhli Sultan is in a favourable position, owing to the convergence of several caravan routes from the northern and eastern districts, to collect onerous transit dues and hamper traffic generally. The cadets of his house in Abiyān, which owes its fertility to W. Bana and other streams between the Fadhli and Aden, have always been independent of him, and bleed the unfortunate traders a second time before they can pass.

The chief tribe is the Merqūshi (Markashi), who live round J. 'Uris and the neighbouring hills.

FADHLI

Sultan.	Tribes.	
Husein ibn Ahmed of Shūghrah.	Merqūshi (Markashi).	Round J. 'Uris.
	Ahl Haidarah Mansūr.	In Abiyān.

15. Haushabi.

The Haushabi are a powerful tribe extending from Dareijah to Nūbat Dakīm, and controlling the Yemen caravan road along the Wādi Tiban, north of the 'Abdāli territory. They claim suzerainty over the Dhāmbari, which that tribe admits only when it suits them. They are agricultural and pastoral and number about 6,000 souls.

The capital is Musemir, a town 60 miles north of Aden, situated on a small plateau overlooking the left bank of the Wādi Tiban. The Sultan 'Ali ibn Mani threw in his lot with the Turks when they appeared in 1915, and accompanied them south in their attack on Aden. He is said to be under the influence of Mohammed Nāsir Muqbil of Māwiyah. He had always shown signs of weakness and irresolution, and although his conduct improved just before the war broke out he had the misfortune to be in the hands of ill-disposed and irresponsible advisers, of whom the chief is Fadl ibn 'Ali Humādi.

16. Hajariyah.

The Sheikh of this district is Ahmed Na'mān, formerly a tax-farmer and made a Kaimmakam by the Turks. He maintains a Zeidist levy of 500 men, and raised a larger force to help the Turkish expedition against Aden. Sub-Sheikhs under his influence attacked us at Sheikh Sa'īd late in 1914. Early in 1915 he attacked Sh. Mohammed Hasan, the chief of a religious fraternity at Jebel Habashi, near Ta'izz, for refusal to pay tithe. More lately he has been reported to have been killed and succeeded by his son Mohammed, who was formerly A.D.C. to the Commandant of Ta'izz, and is said to be energetic and anti-British.

17. Quteibi.

A small tribe, about 50 miles north of Aden, whose head-quarters are at Dhi Hajarah. The Sultan of the Amīri, who rules immediately to the north, claims suzerainty over them, but cannot enforce it, nor do they admit the claim.

The tribe rebelled in 1903 and a British expedition was sent against them. Their Sheikh, Mohammed Sālih el-Akhram, nursed a grievance about this for some years, but was eventually won over. He has not much influence over a restless and quarrelsome tribe. He was at odds with the 'Alawi until 1912, when the 'Abdāli Sultan effected a reconciliation. The real power lies with his nephew Sheikh Muqbil 'Abdullah, who has always been an unreliable factor. Sheikh Mohammed Sālih endeavoured to remain neutral when the Turks advanced in 1915, and as late as November in that year wrote to the Resident at Aden, saying that the Turks were exercising pressure on him, and that he was afraid of invasion. He was still holding out in March 1916, but his nephew had been to Lahej to treat and temporize with the Turks.

18. *Māwīyah*.

The Sheikh of Māwīyah, Qa'tabah, and Shurmān is Mohammed Nāsir Muqbil, a powerful chief on the Yemen boundary, whose influence extends from Qa'tabah to Sheikh Sa'īd on the west, and south-east to the Haushabi country. He was originally a tax-farmer, whom the Turks made Kaimmakam of Shurmān and Kama Ira. He opposed us in 1901 and, after an initial success against the Haushabi, was defeated by a British column which blew up his fortified tower at Dareijah. On our protest to the Ottoman Government he was officially degraded as scapegoat, but was promoted later.

In February 1915 he signed an agreement with the Resident at Aden, agreeing in return for a subsidy to expel the Turks and recalcitrant chiefs from the Liwa of Ta'izz. Subsequently he joined the Turkish advance, bringing with him his permanent levy of 500 Feidis and some fighting men from the neighbouring tribes. Latterly he has been reported as being at Lahej with the Haushabi.

19. *Mūsabein*.

A wild semi-nomad tribe between the country of the Sherif of Beihān, who has no influence over them, and the Bal Hārith tribe. Their headquarters are at Hajarah and they range east to the Ahl Karab country. They are nominally vassals of the Upper 'Aulaqi tribe, but are on bad terms with the Ahl Hammām, who frequently send small raiding parties against them through the difficult sand dune country which surrounds them. They are said to have 4,000 men.

20. *Oleh*.

The Oleh are a powerful confederation of tribes, descended from a chief of that name, in a district known as Dathīnah, which, however, only occupies the centre of the confederation. Its limits are rather vague. The boundaries of the confederation are, on the north Upper 'Aulaqi, on the south the Marqūshi (Markashi) section of the Fadhli Confederation, on the east Lower 'Aulaqi, and on the west and north-west the 'Audillah, with whom they have an hereditary feud.

They number about 3,000 fighting men of good material, but undisciplined and lacking cohesion. They have no paramount chief, but Sheikh 'Ali ibn 'Alawi of the Elhīn, who claims descent from the common ancestor, Oleh, influences tribal policy to a certain extent. He has the right to adjust disputes between any tribes of the confederation.

There are three main family divisions of the Oleh, their family names being at the present time merely abstract titles denoting the branch from which each tribe was originally descended. They are the Ahl Ba Leil, the Ahl Armān, and the Ahl Sa'īd. The Ahl Ba Leil are the most numerous division, mustering nearly 1,500 fighting men. They occupy the south-eastern portion of the confederation and have a bad name for raiding caravans, although such acts are by no means common. Their 'Āqil is 'Awad ibn Haidrah of the Ahl Hanash. They are all nomadic and pastoral, but own a few fortified villages and possess a little arable land.

The Ahl Armān number 700 men and are mountaineers, pastoral and semi-nomadic. The Ahl Sa'īd dwell in the plain of 'Amūdīyah and are the richest and most civilized portion of the confederation. They are agricultural, settled and trading.

OLEH CONFEDERATION

Ahl Ba Leil. 'Āqil, 'Awad ibn Haidarah of the Ahl Hanash.

Tribe.	Nos.	Sub-Tribe.	Remarks.
AHL HANASH	300		S. of Heid el-Hamra, nearly to Heid Lamas.
AHL JADĪNAH	300		SW. of Ahl Hasanah, between them and Ba Kāzim frontier.
AHL BA KUN-NĀSHI	150		S. of Hanashi borders. Eastward of Heid Lamas.
AHL MARŪMI	150		Between Heid and Hamra on N. Hanashi border.
AHL AWENI	70		Due S. of Jadinah, Ba Kāzim on the E., Hanashi on the W., Ba Kunnāshi on the S.
AHL MEHWARI	100		Range the N. and NE. slopes of Jebel 'Arīs.
AHL MAHĀTHIL	100		E. of Surr between Ardh en-Nahein and Hanashi.
AHL SHUWEINI	300		Entirely isolated. Many years ago friction between them and the Ahl Hanashi; they migrated westwards. Now in mountains NW. of Mis-hāl; graze their flocks along the great plain occupied towards NE. by the Ahl es-Sa'idi. Yāfa' frontier on W.

AHL ARMĀN

ELHĪN 'Ali ibn 'Alawi			Most important tribe of Confederation; descended in direct line from common ancestor Oleh. Occupy large range of country between Wādis Khaura and Dhura (or Durra). Bounded on N. by Upper 'Aulaqi frontier and on S. by 'Audillah.
		Ahl edh-Dheib	Near source of W. Dhura and westwards.
		Ahl el-Merda	N. of the Ahl edh-Dheib.

OLEH CONFEDERATION (continued)

Tribe.	Nos.	Sub-Tribe.	Remarks.
		Ahl es-Sakri	W. of the Ahl el-Merda and Ahl edh-Dheib. Western limit W. Khaurān.
AHL FATHAN	200		Northern limit Hisn Gabrah, southern the big 'Aqabah.
		Ahl el-Kahal	E. of Ahl edh-Dheib. The Fathani 'Āqil belongs to this *fakhdh*; lives at Hisn el-'Atfah on the mountain route to Dathīnah. Owing to position of his "hisn" and enclosed nature of the route he is in a position to tax caravans relentlessly.
		Ahl Hāmid Bu Mansūr	E. of Heid Wajr.
AHL 'ARWĀL	200		S. and SW. of Ahl Fathan Southern limit just to SW. of Hisn Hanīb.
		Ahl el-Melh	Near Hisn Dhelamah.
		Ahl Suleimān	N. of the above.
		Ahl Hejlān	Between the above and the Elhin border.
		Ahl el-Faqir	At Hisn Hanīb.
		Ahl el-Hauti	East of above.
AHL HĀTIM	100		SW. of the 'Arwāli on the crest and S. slopes of Heid Maran.
		Ahl el-Makshum	Range the summit of Heid Maran.
		Ahl en-Nesr	Lower slopes of above and in Heid Thūwwah.

AHL SA'ID

Tribe.	Nos.	Sub-Tribe.	Remarks.
MEYĀSIR	400		Plain of 'Amūdīyah.
'Āqil, UmmHeithami Abu Fadhl		Ahl Faraj	At Jiblah and El-Qarn.
		Ahl Sālih	At 'Aqbābah and NE. to Hisn Maran.
		Ahl Mamrad	At Mamrad.
		Ahl Shemlah	Under the E. and SE. spurs of Heid Khamah.
HASANAH	600		Plain of 'Amūdīyah.
'Āqil, Mijāli Abu Misudah		Ahl Nasr	At Quleitah.
		Ahl Ba Kām	At Dobah and Qaus.
		Ahl 'Uleid	On Heid Wajr.
		Ahl Sheid	At Jiblah, Waznah and N. of Quleitah.

The Meyāsir and Hasanah live side by side on the broad plain of 'Amūdīyah and are the plain-dwellers of the Confederation. There is no distinct border between the two, but an imaginary line joining the SE. spurs of Heid Gamrah and Heid Sumr will show the Meyāsir limit; then comes a stretch of neutral ground and then the Hasan border, beyond whom to the SE. lie the Jadīnah, and on the W. and NW. the Ba Kāzim frontier.

21. *Subeihi.*

The Subeihi are a large tribe, numbering nearly 20,000 souls and inhabiting the country bordering on the sea from Ras Imrān Bāb el-Mandeb to within a few miles of Aden. They are bounded on the north by the Maktāri, Sharjabi, Athwāri, and other tribes under Turkish suzerainty.

Of all the tribes in the vicinity of Aden the Subeihi approach most nearly to the typical Bedouin in character. True "Children of the Dawn", as their name by some is said to imply, they by preference select that hour for their attacks on wayfarers. They are divided into a large number of petty clans, and there is no paramount chief. Except for some arable land near Umm Rija, they pay little attention to agriculture, nor do they engage in commerce to any extent. Many members of the tribe, however, earn a livelihood by becoming "muqaddams", or leaders, of caravans from other districts which pass through the Subeihi country *en route* for Aden. On account of their frugal diet, which consists of little else than "jowari", they are very spare in frame, but possess great powers of endurance and have a high reputation for courage, unfortunately blemished by their character for treachery. In consequence of their poverty, few of them own camels, none horses, but the camels in the district are considered equal in speed to the latter animal, in consequence of the great attention which is paid to their breeding.

They were placed under the sovereignty of the 'Abdāli in 1881, but overthrew his control and resumed their old position of independent relations with the Residency in 1886. Agreements were made with the Dubeini, Mansūri, Makhdūmi, and Rujei subdivisions of the tribe, whereby, in consideration of a monthly allowance, the traffic passing through their districts was freed from transit dues and protection granted to travellers.

They were one of the first tribes to join the Turks in 1915 and took part in the attack on Lahej.

Sub-Tribe.	*Clan.*	*Sheikh.*
Mansūri		Shahīr ibn Seif. About 22 years old. Elected in 1901 on death of his father, Seif ibn 'Abdullah Ba Khadra. His relative, Sālih ibn Ahmed, ruled for him till 1913. Resides at Mashārij. Drew a stipend of Rs.600 a year. Is of family formerly paramount over whole tribe. Respected by tribesmen.
Bruhīmi		'Ali ibn Ahmed Umm Tomi. Aged 49. Was stipendiary.
Bureimi		'Alawi ibn 'Ali. Aged 42 years. Lives at Mujābah. Non-stipendiary.
Dubeini		Muqbil Hasan. Stipendiary. Lives at Tāfih on the Aden–Mafālis caravan route.
,,	Jereiwi	Derwīsh Battāsh. Aged 43 years. Ambitious to be Sheikh over all Dubeinis. Sometimes useful.
,,		Seif Diban. Muqaddam for caravans.
,,	Mashāki	Haza Qasīm. Young, intelligent, formerly well disposed.
'Atīfi	'Aweida	'Ali Ba Sālih Ba Rājih. Aged 42 years. Lives at Khatabīyah or Kadthi. Stipendiary. Weak and unable to control his unruly following, who are a clan of nomadic robbers.

SUBEIHI (*continued*)

Sub-Tribe.	Clan.	Sheikh.
Jurabi	Masfari	Seyyid Mohammed Ya'qūb. 52 years old. Lives at Gharaqah. Has some influence. Generally on good terms with Aden, but his avarice led him astray. Non-stipendiary.
,,		Ahmed Sa'īd. Mansab of Weli Sanāwi shrine on the Subeihi Humeidi boundary. Aged about 51 years. Is revered for his sanctity. Lives in Hābil es-Sabt or Sanāwi. Was useful to Boundary Commission and afterwards visited Aden ; intelligent. News reporter for district to Aden.
Mutarrifi		'Abdallah Ba 'Imād. Aged about 58 years. Lives at Mulehīyah. Has some influence with his sub-tribe, which is nomadic.
Wahāsha	Ma'mei	Ahmed Umm Basūs. Joint Sheikh. Aged about 57 years. Lives at Umm Shreijau. Relations with Aden were satisfactory on the whole. Frequently visited Aden. Non-stipendiary.
,,	,,	Seyyid Ja'far, joint Sheikh with above. Aged 52 years. Rendered some service in obtaining recovery of mail bags looted by 'Atīfis in January 1906. Means well but weak.
,,	Juleidi	'Imād ibn Ahmed. Aged about 48 years. Resides at Shawar. A man of stubborn disposition and intriguer. Non-stipendiary.
Makhdūmi		Murshid Ba Nāsir. Aged about 55 years. Stipendiary. Lives at Wādi Marasa. Influential and regarded by his sub-tribe and Mansūri as a prudent and pious leader.
Humeidi		'Ali Ba Sālim. Aged about 63 years. Lives at Jebel Asharwān near Haushabi border. Influential with sub-tribe, which is mainly nomadic. Non-stipendiary.

22. *Upper Yāfa'*.

The Confederation of Upper Yāfa' is situated to the NE. of Aden, and is bounded by the Lower Yāfa' Sultanate on the south, the Beida and 'Audillah on the east, and the Amīri and Dhāmbari on the west.

The inhabitants are warlike and hardy mountaineers, always ready for active service, which they seek in different parts of the world. As a confederation they lose power owing to the lack of cohesion and a uniform policy and the personal ambition of the different Sultans.

Like many other tribes in the south of Arabia, they were formerly subject to the Imams of San'ā. The tribe is called after their ancestor " 'Afīf ".

Although known as "Upper Yāfa'" in English, the confederation is called in Arabic Yāfa' es-Sufla, or " Lower Yāfa' ".

The rightful Sultan of Upper Yāfa' is 'Omar Qahtān, who succeeded his father in 1913, but was expelled by the tribe for coming to Aden to make a treaty with us, as they were jealous of his selection. He belongs to the Dhubi section, though originally of the house of Sheikh 'Ali Harharah. He was opposed by his brother, Sālih ibn 'Omar, and, despite English influence, failed to get himself reinstated. The Government accordingly refused to recognize him as Sultan and gave him a year within which to bring about his rehabilitation. They, however, continued to pay the stipend received by his father, Qahtān, who was a man of little influence and in his later days an exile from his capital. His brother Sālih ibn 'Omar, who is a man of much stronger character, was recognized in 1911 by the Maflahis as their Sultan and receives tribute from Rub'atein.

There are four chief tribes : the Mausata, Maflahi, Sheibi, and Dhubi. The Sheikh of the Mausata is Muhsin 'Askar. He is a man about 75 years old and comes of a family of intriguers, but wields undoubted influence. He signed the treaty with the Bombay Government in 1904 as joint signatory with his brother 'Ali 'Askar. The latter died in 1907 and was succeeded by his son Nāji' 'Ali 'Askar, but most of the power has remained with his uncle Muhsin 'Askar.

The Sheibi are the most northerly tribe of the Confederation and impinge on Ottoman territory towards the Bana. Their Sultan is 'Ali Mauna es-Sakladi.

The Sheikh of the Dhubi is Sālim Sālih ibn 'Atif Jābir. He is a stipendiary and his predecessor was the first Upper Yāfa' Sheikh to conclude a treaty with us (1903).

Two other stipendiaries of this section are the brother Sheikhs Mohammed and 'Omar ibn Muthanna ibn 'Atif Jābir. The latter has little influence and has not justified his selection as stipendiary. He is grasping and a master of intrigue. Rub'atein is an appanage of the Dhubi tribe. The three principal Sheikhs are Yahya ibn 'Askar, Sālih ibn Ahmed, and Yahya Nāsir. Before the war they were all fearful of Turkish intrigue and desired closer relations with the British Government.

Another important tribe is that of the Maflahi, whose chief is 'Abd er-Rahmān ibn Qasīm. He is a stipendiary and has always been a well-wisher of the English. His residence is at Jurba.

The conduct of the Upper Yāfa' Sheikhs has not been entirely satisfactory lately. Some of the non-stipendiary Sheikhs have long resented their exclusion from the list of recipients of doles and have turned to the Imam of San'ā. The descent of the Turkish forces opened an avenue for securing loot and monetary consideration from Sa'īd Pasha. The stipendiaries have been outwardly loyal, but there is evidence to show that some sort of secret understanding exists between them and the transborder Arabs. A section of the Mausata have actually gone over to the enemy, and the rest will follow where they think that their interest leads them.

UPPER YĀFA' CONFEDERATION

Tribe.	Chief.	Clan.
MAUSATA	'Ali 'Askar (Nāji)	
	Muhsin 'Askar	
SHEIBI	'Ali Mauna es-Sakladi	
DHUBI	Sālim Sālih ibn 'Atif Jābir	
	Mohammed ibn Muthanna	
	'Omar ibn Muthanna	Khalaki

23. Lower Yāfaʻ.

The district of Lower Yāfaʻ is inhabited by the Beni Qāsid tribe. Their late Sultan, ʻAbdullah ibn Muhsin, who died early in 1916, was a man of eccentric habits and disliked both the British and the Fadhli. The newly elected Sultan is as yet an unknown quantity, but is said to be Turkophobe. His tribes are out of hand and several have addressed themselves to Aden asking to know the policy of the Government. They have long been at variance with the Fadhli and a short time ago were in danger of having their supplies cut off from Shūghrah. Saʻīd Pasha, however, intervened and succeeded in arranging a three months' truce between them.

HADHRAMAUT

1. *Akābarah.*

A SMALL nomad tribe, descended from Himyar, along the sea-coast west of Makalla and between Makalla and the Beni Hasan. They number 500 fighting men.

2. *'Amūdi.*

A nomad tribe which was formerly powerful and owned the Wādi Dō'an almost up to Meshed. They were almost annihilated about 15 years ago by the Sultan of Makalla. The survivors, numbering only about 150 men under Sheikh Sālih ibn 'Abdullah, are still suffered to live in the Wādi Dō'an.

3. *Awābthah*

An independent nomad tribe of Himyar, living in Wādi 'Ain, south-east of Haurah. Their chief Sheikh is 'Abdullah ibn Ahmed and they number about 2,000 men. They are allied with the Seibān and with them maintain a continued warfare with the Hamumi. The chief families of Ashrāf are the Ahl Ba Wazīr and Beni Sheibān.

Paramount Sheikh, 'Abdullah ibn Ahmed.

Sub-Tribes.
BANIS.	'Abdullah ibn Ahmed.
BAZAR.	Ibn Kurdūsah.

4. *'Awāmir.*

A strong nomad tribe to the north of Terīm. They pay a nominal allegiance to the Sultan of Seyyūn and Terīm and unite with the Kathīri against aggression from outside.

5. *Dein.*

A tribe, chiefly nomad but partly agricultural, in the country north-west of the Nu'a and between them and the Āl Hamīm. They trace their descent from Kindah. They are entirely independent, but maintain friendly relations with the Nu'a and Āl Hamīm. Sālim Bamar is their chief Sheikh with a following of about 2,000 fighting men.

Paramount Sheikh, Sālim Bamar.

Sub-Tribes.
BAMSADUS.	Sālim Bamar.
BA HENHEN.	'Abdullah ibn Ahmed.
BA SUWEIDAN.	'Abdullah ibn Mubārak.
YĀS.	Ahmed ibn Yislam.
BA KARSHUM.	

6. Al Hamīm.

A powerful and warlike Bedouin tribe, north-west of the Nu'a and Dein, living in the country round Shura and Wādi 'Irmah and ranging the country north to the Empty Quarter. They possess many horses and were of great assistance to the Nu'a in their fighting against Ghālib ibn 'Awad el-Ka'aiti, Sultan of Makalla. They can muster from 8,000 to 10,000 men under Thābit ibn 'Omar, their Paramount Chief.

7. Hamumi.

A strong and warlike nomad tribe descended from Himyar in the country north of Makalla. They are entirely independent, can put nearly 10,000 men in the field and are always at war with the Sultan of Makalla, the Awābthah, and the Seibān. Their chief Sheikh is Sheikh Halreish. The principal sub-tribes are Beit Jerzat, Beit 'Ali, and Beit Sa'īd.

8. Beni Hasan.

A small nomad tribe descended from Himyar, and numbering 200 men, in the country along the coast between the Mohammedīn and the Akābara west of Makalla.

9. Jābiri (pl. Jawābir).

A strong nomad tribe, south of Seyyūn, having a defensive alliance with the Kathīri and paying a nominal allegiance to the Sultan of Seyyūn and Terīm.

10. Jada.

The Jada are an independent Bedouin tribe, tracing their descent from Kindah, and living in the Wādi 'Amd to the south-east of Haurah. They number 3,000 men.

Chief Sheikh, Ibn Shemlān.

Clans.
Beni Shemlān.   Ibn Shemlān.
Beni Humeid.
Beni Madhi.

11. Kathīri.

The Kathīri tribe is one of the most warlike and powerful tribes in the Hadhramaut and is the chief menace to the ever-increasing power of the Sultan of Makalla. They are partly settled and partly nomad, and occupy the country between Terīm and Seyyūn, their chief towns, almost up to the Sultan of Makalla's frontier city of Shibām. The feud between the two arose in the early seventies of last century and has ever since dominated the politics of the Hadhramaut. At that time the Kathīri Sultan of Seyyūn borrowed three lakhs of rupees from the head of the Ka'aiti family, and afterwards repudiated the debt. Recourse was had to the Political Resident of Aden, and after arbitration had proved abortive, Shiheir and Makalla, then in the possession of the Kathīri

Sultan, were bombarded by a British ship and handed over to the Ka'aiti. Since then there has been an increasing feud which has at times led to actual warfare.

The present Kathīri Sultan is Mansūr Kathīri, a man who has been unable to enforce his will on his independent tribesmen; the latter are said to number 10,000 to 15,000 fighting men, and with their allies the 'Awāmir, Tamīmi, and Jābiri, who can put into the field another 5,000 warriors, they form a very powerful confederation. Like all tribal confederations, however, jealousies and an innate independence prevent them from making full use of their power.

12. *Manāhil.*

A warlike and independent nomad tribe, roaming the country to the north of the Hamumi, numbering between 5,000 and 6,000 men. They are allied to the Hamumi in opposition both to the Seibān and the Sultan of Makalla.

13. *Mohammedīn.*

A small nomad tribe, numbering 300 men, between the Nu'a on the west and the Beni Hasan on the east. They trace their descent to Himyar. Sa'īd ibn Suleimān is their Sheikh, living at Haseisah, the main tribal centre.

14. *Nahad.*

The Nahad are a Bedouin tribe, descended from Kindah, numbering from 3,000 to 4,000 men and occupying the country due north of Haurah. They are on friendly terms with the Sultan of Makalla's representative at Haurah, but are bitter enemies of the powerful tribe of Sa'ar to their north. Their Paramount Chief is Sheikh ibn Minīf.

15. *Nu'a.*

The Nu'a are a Bedouin tribe, descended from Himyar, with headquarters round the valley of Wādi Hajar. They are bounded on the west by the tribes of the 'Abd el-Wahīd Sultanate, on the north-west by the Dein and Āl Hamīm tribes, on the north by the Numan, and on the east by the Seibān and Mohammedīn.

Between Bir 'Ali and Haseisah they come down to the sea. They cultivate dhura and wheat in Wādi Hajar and raise dates, but their chief wealth is in camels, of which they are said to possess about 6,000, and in sheep and goats. The Sultan of Makalla cast covetous eyes on their possessions and for 12 years strove to wrest the Wādi Hajar from them. He met with no success, and two years ago relinquished his attempts and made peace. The Nu'a can put from 5,000 to 6,000 men in the field, all armed with rifles. Their chief Sheikh is Ahmed ibn Qādim, who lives at Lubnah, a man of about 45, strong and well liked by his tribes. He keeps on good terms with the Sultan of Bālhāf and with the Dein, and is allied with Thābit ibn 'Omar, the chief of the Āl Hamīm, who helped him in his war against the Sultan of Makalla. The Ashrāf are strong in the district, and Sherīf el-Beit of Kanīni is much sought after as an arbitrator in quarrels between the different clans.

Paramount Sheikh, Ahmed ibn Qādim.

Sub-Tribes.	
BAQARWĀN.	Ahmed Abeidan.
BA DIYĀN.	Sa'īd ibn 'Ali.
BA FAQASH.	
BADBAS.	'Ali ibn Mohammed.
BURSHEID.	Ahmed ibn Qādim.
BASAM.	Sa'īd ibn 'Ali.
BA HAMISH.	Mohammed ibn Sālim.
BA HAKIM.	'Abdullah ibn Sa'īd.
LIMUS.	'Omar ibn Ahmed.

16. *Numan.*

A nomadic tribe, numbering about 1,000 men, descended from Himyar, who roam the country north of the Nu'a and Wādi Hajar. Their chief Sheikh is Sālih ibn Selīm ibn Qutam.

17. *Sa'ar.*

The Sa'ar are probably the most numerous tribe in the Hadhramaut; but though completely independent and lawless, they are too far removed to play a very important part in its politics. They roam the country north of the Nahad and Haurah right up to the edge of the Empty Quarter and are said to number 20,000 men. An old feud exists between them and the Nahad. Their chief is Ibn Jarbu. They claim descent from Kindah.

18. *Scibān.*

A Himyarite tribe of nomads inhabiting the desolate plateau to the west of the upper reaches of the Wādi el-'Aisār. They are bounded on the north by the 'Amūdi, on the south by the Akābarah and Beni Hasan, and on the east by the Hamumi.

'Omar ibn Ahmed is their chief Sheikh, but they come also under the suzerainty of the Sultan of Makalla. They are friendly with the Nu'a and the small tribes on their south. With the Hamumi they have a long-standing feud which leads to continual fighting. They put about 2,000 men in the field. Abd er-Rahmān esh-Shatri has great influence over them.

Paramount Sheikh, 'Omar ibn Ahmed.

Sub-Tribes.	
BASARAH.	'Omar ibn Ahmed.
BASARĪYAH.	'Omar ibn Ahmed.
BA QUR.	Mohammed ibn Suleimān.
SAMŪH.	Mohammed ibn 'Ali.

19. *Tamīmi.*

A nomad tribe to the east of Terīm and the Kathīri, with whom they are allied for purposes of defence.

20. Yáfa'.

The Yáfa' tribe, whose real home is in the Sultanates of Upper and Lower Yáfa' to the north-east of Aden, are represented in the Hadhramaut by the influential and wealthy family of Ka'aiti. Some six generations ago the Seyyids of the Abu Bekr family, at that time the most powerful in the Hadhramaut, were seriously threatened by the Bedouin tribes, and in their extremity invited the assistance of the Yáfa' Sultan. The Ka'aiti were sent to the rescue, and having repulsed the enemy, established themselves in the country, where they have been ever since. Their power has steadily grown and was notably increased in 1874 by the expulsion of the Kathíri Sultan from Makalla and Shiheir and the presentation of these two towns to them by the British Government in settlement of a debt which had been repudiated by the Kathíri. They now own Makalla, Shiheir, Shibám, Haurah, and Hajarein, and exercise a suzerainty, which at times is only nominal, over the tribes of 'Amúdi, Seibán, and Nahad.

Their wealth comes chiefly from the Straits Settlements, whither many Hadhramis migrate, leaving their own sterile country to seek their fortunes abroad. Their connexion with Haiderabad is also very close, the Nizam maintaining a Hadhrami bodyguard, which is always commanded by one of the Ka'aiti family.

The present head of the house, styled Sultan of Makalla, is Ghálib ibn 'Awad el-Ka'aiti, a man of fifty, who is anglophile and maintains close relations with Aden. He keeps a permanent bodyguard of 1,000 men, but frequently has recourse to hiring mercenaries both to maintain himself against his implacable enemies the Kathíri and their allies, and the Hamumi, and also in furtherance of his ambition to add fresh territories to his dominions and become the ruling force in the Hadhramaut.

He has three brothers, 'OMAR, HUSEIN, and MANASSAR, all of whom he has quarrelled with and expelled from the country.

OMAN

1. *'Abābid* (sing. *'Abbādi*).

A TRIBE of the Oman Sultanate, numbering 250 souls, Hināwi in politics and Ibadhi in religion; settled at Felej Shirāh in Wādi Fara', in Western Hajar.

2. *'Abādilah* (sing. *'Abdūli*).

A tribe of Trucial Oman, numbering 1,200 souls. Hanbali in religion and Ghāfiri in politics; settled at Shārjah town, Ghāllah in Shameilīyah, Khaleibīyah, near Wādi Hām, and on Sheikh Shu'aib Island.

3. *'Abriyīn* (sing. *'Abri*).

A tribe of Nizāri descent in the Oman Sultanate, belonging to the Ghāfiri political faction; in religion they are mostly Ibadhis, but a small minority are Sunnis. They are found in Dhāhirah at 'Arāqi; in Western Hajar at 'Awābi, at 'Aqair in Wādi Shāfān, at Zāmmah and Hāt in Wādi Beni 'Auf, at Beit el-Qarn in Wādi Fara', at Tabāqah in Wādi Beni Ghāfir, and at 'Amq, Fashah, Maqamma, and Mabu in Wādi Sahtan; in Oman Proper at Bahlah, Farq, Ghamr, and Hamra: their number is estimated at 6,500 souls. They cultivate dates and corn, and are generally a well-behaved and peaceable tribe. They are the real masters of 'Awābi, but Bahlah is their tribal capital and Hamra their largest separate village.

4. *Beni 'Adi* (sing. *'Adwāni*).

A tribe of the Oman Sultanate, numbering about 5,000 souls. Hināwi in politics, settled chiefly in Western Hajar at the villages of Sawālih, Murbah, Qasra, Ghashab, and Wabil in Wādi Fara', but also found on the coast at Quryāt and at Ghuweisah in the sub-vilayet of Saham.

Those at Ghashab belong to a section called Beni Bekr.

5. *'Ajam, or Persians* (sing. *'Ajmi*).

A tribe of the Oman Sultanate, numbering about 10,000 souls, mostly now arabized Shiahs; settled at Muscat town and in Bātinah at Masna'ah, Suweiq, Sūr esh-Shiyādi, Ghuweisah, Liwa, and Sohār; also in Ru'ūs el-Jibāl at Bakhah.

6. *Āl 'Ali* (sing. *'Alīyi*).

A tribe of Trucial Oman, numbering 6,750 souls, including 140 families of Bedouins; Ghāfiri in politics and professedly Hanbali, though virtually Wahabite in religion. The settled portion are at Umm el-Qaiwein, Shārjah, and Ras el-Kheimah; the Bedouins between Umm el-Qaiwein and Jezīrat el-Hamra and inland to Felej Āl-'Ali. They claim connexion with the Muteir of Nejd. There is a branch 3,500 strong in the Shībkūh district across the Gulf.

7. Beni 'Ali (sing. 'Alawi).

A tribe of the Oman Sultanate, numbering 4,500 souls, Hināwi in politics and Ibadhi in religion, settled in Western Hajar at Wuqbah, Heil beni 'Ali, Yanqul, Murri, and Felej Sedeiriyīn, and in Bātinah at Saham town. Their tribal capital is Yanqul. They are a leading Hināwi tribe who have generally supported the present ruling family of Muscat. They grow grain and dates.

8. Beni Bu 'Ali (sing. 'Alawi).

The principal Ghāfiri tribe of the Ja'lān and Sharqīyah districts in the Sultanate of Oman. They are partly nomadic and partly settled : the Bedouin portion inhabit Ja'lān and possess considerable herds of camels and goats, while the settled portion cultivate dates and corn in the Beled Beni Bu 'Ali oasis, and are found also at Sūr and at Ras er-Ruweis, Suweih, Khōr Beni Bu 'Ali, Jumeilah, and Lashkharah, on the SE. coast of Oman, where they are mostly mariners and fishermen. A few occur at Khabbah in Wādi Khabbah.

Some authorities connect the Beni Bu 'Ali with the Āl 'Ali of Trucial Oman and the Shībkūh district of Persia.

They number in all about 7,000 souls, of whom 1,000 are Bedouins. They became Wahabites at the time of the Nejdi invasions of Oman about a century ago, and as late as 1845 were strict if not fanatical in the observance of Wahabite principles. They have since relaxed somewhat and now smoke tobacco, but they continue to be exact in the forms and times of prayer and are accounted the most religious tribe in the Oman Sultanate. They belong to a Wahabite sect known as Azraqah.

They are on the average men of middle size with short features and quick deep-set eyes ; gloomy and determined in expression and character ; warlike and independent, with a high reputation for courage and dash.

Their favourite weapon was originally a thin, straight, two-edged sword, sharp as a razor and attached by a leather thong to a shield 14 inches in diameter, in addition to which they carried matchlocks ; their armament is now more modern, but they still have few breech-loaders (1905).

They are the only tribe of the Sultanate who have met a British force on land. On November 9, 1820, they defeated a force of British Indian Sepoys at Beled Beni Bu 'Ali, and on March 2, 1821, suffered severe retribution near the same place. On the latter occasion the tribe lost heavily in killed and wounded, the town and fort were destroyed, and a large number of prisoners were taken, including the principal Sheikh, Mohammed bin 'Ali ; but the date groves were spared—an act of clemency that was much appreciated and is still remembered. The prisoners, after being kept for two years at Bombay, were repatriated and received grants of money from the Indian Government to enable them to rebuild their houses and restore irrigation. Since this episode the tribe have uniformly shown themselves well-disposed to the British and have treated hospitably more than one British traveller, but they have never fully regained their position in tribal politics.

They have a chronic feud with their neighbours the Beni Bu Hasan. The following are the chief sections, &c., of the tribe :

Section.	Sub-section.	Fighting strength (1905)
Fahūd	Fahūd	50
	Muwāridah	60
	Ruwātilah	50
Ja'āfarah	Ghanābīs	200
	Beni Ibrāhīm	120
	Āl Abu Muqbil	200
	Aulād Sakhīlah	40
	Salābikhah	50
Razīq (Beni)	Āl Hamūdah	200
	Aulād Hasan	100
	Aulād 'Abd el-Jalīl	40
	Aulād Khanjar	40
Sinadah	Majāghamah	60
	Mazāmilah	100 ⎫ In addition about 1,000
	Aulād Seif	50 ⎭ Bedouins.

9. *Āl Bu 'Amīm* (sing. *'Amīmi*).

A small tribe of Trucial Oman, numbering 120 souls. Settled in Abu Dhabi town, now merged in the Beni Yās, originally belonging to the Beni Tamīm.

10. *Beni 'Arābah* (sing. *'Arābi*).

A tribe of the Oman Sultanate, numbering 1,000 souls, of unascertained politics and religion, found chiefly in Wādi Tāyīn at Sibal, Qurr, Hammām, and Shāt. They are said to have been a large tribe once, but cholera killed off a great number. They have been at feud with the Siyābiyīn for many years, but relations are less strained now. The singular form 'Arābi is avoided because it means a hill donkey.

11. *Beni 'Auf* (sing. *'Aufi*).

A tribe of the Oman Sultanate, numbering in all 1,000 souls : Ghāfiri in politics ; Ibadhi in religion. They are found in Oman Proper at Farq in Wādi Kalbu ; in Western Hajar at Qasmītein and Teikha in Wādi Beni 'Auf, at Fara', Misfāh, and Nāzīyah in Wādi Fara', and at 'Awābi in Wādi Beni Kharūs.

12. *'Awāmir* (sing. *'Amiri*).

A large tribe of the Oman Sultanate, numbering probably 10,000 souls ; of Nizāri descent, but now Hināwi in politics and Ibadhi in religion ; about 6,500 are settled and 3,500 are Bedouins.

To take the settled portion first : In Oman Proper they possess the villages of 'Aqīl, Qal'at el-'Awāmir, Felej, Hameidah, Qurīyatein, Qārūt, Khurmah, Shāfa', Seiyāhi, and Sūq el-Qadīm, and are found at Nizwa ; they occur also at Muscat town, Beit el-Felej, and Ruwi in the Muscat district ; at Ghāllah and Sād in Wādi Bōshar ; at Heil Āl 'Umeir, Sīb, and Ma'bīlah in Bātinah ; at Khōdh in Wādi Semā'il and at Khubār and Luwīz in Daghmar. Their sections are Aulād Ahmed, Aulād 'Ali ibn Hamad, Aulād 'Ali ibn Khalf, Aulād Amīr, Harāmilah, Ja'āfarah, Aulād el-Jā'id, Khanājirah, Mohammed, Aulād Mūsa, Rakhbah, Aulād Rāshid, Aulād Saba, Aulād Seif, Aulād Salīm, Aulād Sand, Sarāhīn, Sarāhīn el-Muweilah, and Aulād Shīrāz ; at Sīb a section called Aulād Maheyyi is found.

The Bedouin portion range the borders of the Ruba' el-Khāli from Trucial Oman in the north, which they occasionally visit in small numbers, to the district of Dhofār on the southern coast of Arabia. A term 'Afār frequently used in connexion with the 'Awāmir appears to denote a portion of the tribe inhabiting a territory, called 'Afār, between Mahōt and Dhofār ; it includes representatives of many sections. The 'Afār are popularly supposed to feed upon carrion : they deny this, but they wear skins and admit that they are not infrequently reduced to devouring them.

The 'Awāmir are reputed brave and warlike but crafty, treacherous, and predatory ; they are said to plunder indiscriminately all whom they meet, not excepting members of their own tribe with whom they happen to be unacquainted.

They speak a peculiar dialect of Arabic, which varies to such an extent that the westernmost Bedouin sections are hardly understood by their settled brethren in Oman Proper.

The 'Awāmir are at feud with the Jannabah and the Darū'.

13. *'Awānāt* (sing. *'Awāni*).

A tribe of Trucial Oman, now practically extinct ; about 50 are found at Khatt and Jezīrat el-Hamra. Some even deny that these 50 are genuine 'Awānāt.

14. *Āl* (or *'Ayāl*) *'Azīz* (sing. *'Azīzi*).

A small tribe, numbering 700 souls, settled in Dhank town in Dhāhirah ; in politics Ghāfiri, in religion Ibadhi and Sunni. They are usually reckoned as Na'īm, but their true origin is not known.

15. *Beni 'Azzān* (sing. *'Azzāni*).

A very small tribe, numbering 20 souls, settled in Nakhl in Western Hajar ; in politics Ghāfiri, in religion Ibadhi.

16. *Badā'ah* (sing. *Bada'i*).

A small tribe, numbering 120 souls, settled in Bidit in Wādi Mabrah in Western Hajar ; in politics Ghāfiri, in religion Ibadhi.

17. *Al Badar* (sing. *Badari*).

A tribe of the Oman Sultanate, numbering 1,200 souls. Hinâwi in politics, and Ibaḍhi in religion; settled at Barkah and Billah in Bâtinah.

18. *Bahārinah* (sing. *Bahrāni*).

Bahrāni does not mean "native of Bahrein". It is the name of the race, or class, to which nearly all the Shiahs of the Bahrein Islands, of the Hasa and Qatīf oases, and the Qatar promontory belong. The Sunni inhabitant of Bahrein describes himself as Ahl el-Bahrein. As employed along the western coast of the Persian Gulf the term Bahrāni is practically a synonym for a Shiah whose mother tongue is Arabic.

Altogether the Bahārinah number not less than 100,000 souls, of whom only 850 are in Oman, viz. 250 in Sohār town in the Oman Sultanate and 600 in the towns of Abu Dhabi and Dibai in Trucial Oman. They are all Shiahs, unwarlike in character and engaged in peaceful pursuits; the richer living by trade and the poorer by husbandry, pearl-diving, and various handicrafts.

The local tradition is that they are descended from Arab tribes who were converted to Shiism 300 years ago, but some European writers are inclined to regard them as aborigines conquered by the Arabs.

19. *Beni Bahri* (sing. *Bahri*).

A small tribe of 500 souls, settled in Western Hajar at 'Aliya and 'Awābi in Wādi Beni Kharūs and at Hibra in Wādi Ma'āwal; in politics Ghāfiri, in religion Ibadhi.

20. *Balūchi*, or *Balūsh* (sing. *Balūshi*).

In Baluchistan the word *Balōch* is strictly used to designate certain respectable middle-class tribes of the country only; but in the Gulf of Persia and Oman it is used in a wider sense to include all immigrants from Baluchistan and persons whose mother tongue is the Baluchi language.

In the Oman Sultanate there are 20,000 Baluchis excluding Jadgāls, who in Baluchistan are reckoned as Balōchis but here are designated under their proper name from other Balūsh. In Trucial Oman they number 1,400.

In religion they are seldom Shiahs, even abroad, and they settle more readily among Arab than Persian communities. They were originally introduced as mercenaries, and are still largely in military service. The rest incline to sea-faring occupations, and some have amalgamated with the Arabs inland.

Their distribution is as below:

In the Sultanate.

Muscat District	Muscat town, Matrah, Sidāb, Qābil 'Ali ibn Zamān, Mizra' el-'Alawi.
Bātinah	Sīb, Barkah, Sūr el-Balūsh, Saham, Sūr Heyyān, Masna'ah, Wudām, Suweiq, Shilu, Sallān, Majīs, Sohār, Haseifīn, Liwa, Shinās, Haseifīn Sūr el-Balūsh.
Western Hajar	Buweirid in Wādi Fara'.
Eastern Hajar	Quryāt.
Dhāhirah	'Arāqi and Aflāj Beni Qitab.
Ja'lān	Dīdu.

In Trucial Oman at :—

Dibai town.
Ghāllah.
Ras el-Kheimah.

21. *Beni Battāsh* (sing. *Battāshi*).

A tribe of the Oman Sultanate numbering 7,000 souls of Yemeni descent, Hināwi in politics and Ibadhi in religion; settled in Wādi Tāyīn, where they occupy a large number of villages including Heil el-Ghāf, and found also in Wādis Maih, Hilu, and Beni Battāsh, at Daghmar and Quryāt, and at one or two other places on the coast of the Muscat district. They bear a good character and are peaceable, concerning themselves chiefly with trade and the cultivation of dates. It is said that they used to breed horses for the Indian market on grazing grounds near Quryāt, but they have long ceased to do so.

They are sometimes at feud with the Siyābiyīn.

Their sections are the following :

Section.	Fighting strength.	Location.	Remarks.
Beni Dhakar	150	Wādi Beni Battāsh	
Aulād Fāris	200	Wādi Beni Battāsh	
Beni Ghasein	80	Madeirah in Wādi Tāyīn	Shepherds
Aulād Hazam	60	Madeirah in Wādi Tāyīn	Shepherds
Juma'ah	50	Mazāra' in Wādi Tāyīn	Carriers and date-growers
Ma'āshirah	550	Yiti, Bandar Kheirān, and Kheisat esh-Sheikh on the Muscat coast; Mizra' el-'Alawi, Mizra' el-Hadri, and Rija' in Wādi Maih. Hiwar and Felej el-Hilam in Wādi el-Hilu	
Aulād Mālik	120	'Aqair, &c., in Wādi Beni Battāsh	Carriers and date-growers
Aulād Salt	120	'Aqair, &c., in Wādi Beni Battāsh	Carriers and date-growers
Beni 'Umr	650	Hida, 'Uqdah, 'Ajma, Malahlah Gheiyān, Sidafi, and Rikākīyah in Wādi Tāyīn.	
Aulād Ward	30	Lashkhar in Wādi Tāyīn	Date-growers

22. Bawārih (sing. Bārihi).

A tribe of the Oman Sultanate numbering 120 souls; Hināwi in politics and Sunni in religion; settled at 'Adeibah in the Muscat district.

23. Bayāsirah (sing. Bayāsar).

A community or tribe of inferior social status, found everywhere in Oman, but specially at Nakhl, Bahlah, and Nizwa, and in the coast towns of Muscat, Matrah, Saham, and Sohār; they also occur at various places in Wādi Semā'il and at Misinnah and Mali in Wādi Beni Ghāfir. Their origin is doubtful; some authorities state that they are of Hadhramaut origin, but most of them appear to be the children of Oman Arabs by slave mothers. They are not united either in religion or politics. They are peaceable and industrious and some have accumulated wealth, but the Arabs do not entrust them with command, and they are accustomed to remove their sandals before kissing the hand of a Sheikh.

They number perhaps 10,000 souls, and are connected among others with the following tribes:

Beni Hasan, 400 houses.
Beni Ruwāhah, 70 houses.
Beni Battāsh, 30 houses.
Habūs, 20 houses.

A few have emigrated to Dhofār proper and are settled in cultivation at Hamrān.

Their sections are:

Aulād Barakein.
Aulād 'Abdu.
Aulād Subāh.
Āl Khaseib.
Aulād Hamad.
Aulād 'Ubeidān.

24. Bidāh (sing. Bidāhi).

A small tribe of 100 souls of Yemeni origin; settled at Dūt in Wādi Dhank in Dhāhirah and at Bidit in Wādi Mabrah in Western Hajar; in politics Ghāfiri. Their religious sect is not ascertained; they are sometimes at feud with the Miyāyīhah Ibadhis.

25. Bidūwāt (sing. Bidwi).

A tribe of the Oman Sultanate numbering 1,000 souls; Hināwi in politics and Sunni in religion; settled at Fuleij Bin Qafeyyir in Western Hajar and at Khadhrawein in Bātinah. A few Bedouins among them.

26. Āl Bōshar (sing. Bōshari).

A tribe of the Oman Sultanate numbering 300 souls; settled in Wādi Semā'il; Hināwi in politics and Ibadhi in religion.

27. Yāl Breik (sing. Breiki).

A tribe of the Oman Sultanate numbering 1,500 souls; Hināwi in politics, in religion partly Sunni and partly Ibadhi; settled in Bātinah at Masna'ah, Shirs, Qasbiyāt Yāl Breik, Dīl Yāl Breik, Umm el-Ja'ārīf, and Saham town.

28. Daheilāt (sing. Ad-heili).

A tribe of Trucial Oman numbering 200 souls; settled in Abu Dhabi town, by some regarded as a section of the Āl Bu Maheir.

29. Dahāminah (sing. Dahmāni).

A tribe of Trucial Oman numbering 150 souls. Sunni in religion, Ghāfiri in politics; settled in Wādi el-Qōr at Raha, Fashrah, and Nuslah, and close by at Manei'i.

30. Dalālīl (sing. Dallal).

An inferior caste who trade in cattle; they really belong to various tribes, and their name is simply taken from their occupation. They number 800 souls, and are settled in Western Hajar at Mahādhar and Hawājiri in Wādi Fara'. In politics they are Ghāfiri.

31. Darāmikah (sing. Darmaki).

A tribe of the Oman Sultanate numbering 600 souls; Ibadhi in religion and Hināwi in politics; settled in Oman Proper at Saddi and Izki and in Bātinah at Mureir es-Saghīrah.

32. Darū' (sing. Dara'i).

A tribe of the Oman Sultanate belonging to the Ghāfiri faction: originally they were all nomads of the Ruba' el-Khāli, but some are now settled at Tana'am and other places in Dhāhirah and a few at Barkah in Bātinah. Estimates of their numbers differ very widely: those in Dhāhirah may amount to 3,000 souls, of whom about one-third are settled.

The Bedouin portion now frequent the neighbourhood of Jebel Hamra. They are a wild and predatory race, and hardly a rising of the eastern tribes occurs in which they are not involved. They rear large numbers of camels, which they graze on the confines of the great desert.

The Bedouin Darū' are said to be Ibadhis; the settled portion are Sunnis.

The Darū' are divided into the following sections: Badiwei, Batūn, Farādīs, Hāl Bu Hādi, Janīn, Hāl Khamīs, Yāl Khamīs, Mahābinah, Mahāridah, Majāli, Makhādir, Marāziqah, Hāl Mohammed, Mutāwihah, 'Ayāl Nafāfi, 'Ayāl Salīm, Shamātah, 'Ayāl Sultān, Thuweil, and Zuweyyah.

33. *Dawakah* (sing. *Daweiki*).

A tribe of the Oman Sultanate numbering 300 souls; Hināwi in politics and Ibadhi in religion; settled in Bātinah at Barkah. There is a small Bedouin portion ranging round Fuleij in Sharqīyah.

They are clients of the Hirth.

34. *Beni Dāwud* (sing. *Dāwudi*).

A small tribe of 200 souls found in Eastern Hajar in the hills between Sūr and Kalhāt; Ghāfiri in politics, in religion Ibadhi.

35. *Dhabābihah* (sing. *Adhbeibi*).

A tribe of Trucial Oman numbering 200 souls; settled in Wādi Sfuni and its tributary Wādi Neidein. Their descent is unknown and they are said to be aborigines.

36. *Dhahūl* (sing. *Dhahli*).

A small tribe of 700 souls, settled in Western Hajar at 'Awābi and Tau esh-Sheikh in Wādi Beni Kharūs and in Bātinah at Liwa town; Ghāfiri in politics, in religion Ibadhi.

37. *Dhahūriyīn*.

A tribe of the Ru'ūs el-Jibāl district in the Oman Sultanate, numbering about 1,750 souls, settled in the villages of Film (60 houses), Habalein (25 houses), Mansal (6 houses), and Maqāqah (100 houses), in Ghubbat Ghazīrah; Midah (1 house), Qānah (40 houses), Sham (25 houses), and Sībi (7 houses), in Khōr esh-Shām; Beled (20 houses) in Ghubbat Shābūs; Muntaf (15 houses) and Shīsah (15 houses) in Ghubbat Shīsah. There are about 200 of them in Lārak Island also, closely connected with the people of Kumzār.

The Dhahūriyīn are practically a part of the Shihūh tribe, by whom they are surrounded, but they claim connexion with the Dhawāhir of Bireimi and do not admit that they are in any way subordinate to the Shihūh. They are Ghāfiri in politics; in religion they are Hanbali, except those at Film and Mansal, who are Shafei.

In the cold weather they live by fishing; in spring, leaving only caretakers behind, they migrate bodily to Khōr Fakkān, Dibah, and Khasab, where they attach themselves to some of the permanent residents and bivouac in the date plantations.

38. *Fawāris* (or *Āl Fāris*) (sing. *Fārisi*).

In Oman this name is used to designate arabicized Persian immigrants and their descendants. They number 5,000 souls; Sunni in religion; settled in Bātinah at Suweiharah, Sohār, Sallān, Sharu, and Fanjah.

39. *Fazāra‘* (sing. *Fazāra‘i*).

A tribe of the Oman Sultanate numbering 400 souls; Hināwi in politics and Ibadhi in religion; settled in Bātinah at Makhailīf and Khōr el-Hamām.

40. *Beni Fileit* (sing. *Fileiti*).

A small tribe of 400 souls settled at Wāsit in Wādi Ma‘āwal in Western Hajar; Ghāfiri in politics, in religion Ibadhi.

41. *Futeisāt* (sing. *Futeisi*).

A small tribe of 450 souls settled at Furfārah in the Liwa sub-vilayet of Bātinah; Ghāfiri in politics, in religion Ibadhi.

42. *Ghafeilāt* (sing. *Ghāfili*).

A tribe of the Oman Sultanate numbering 250 souls; Hināwi in politics, Ibadhi in religion; settled in Bātinah at Bu ‘Abāli.

43. *Ghafalah* (sing. *Ghafeili*).

A Bedouin tribe of Trucial Oman numbering 500 souls; Hanbali in religion and Ghāfiri in politics; well disposed to the Sheikh of Abu Dhabi. They own 700 camels and inhabit the plain country inland of Ras el-Kheimah and Umm el-Qaiwein, not extending into the hills. Their favourite haunt is the Jiri plain and near it.

44. *Ghafalah* (sing. *Ghafli*).

A small tribe of 500 souls settled at Liwa town in Bātinah; Ghāfiri in politics, in religion Sunni.

45. *Beni Ghaith* (sing. *Ghaithi*).

A tribe of the Oman Sultanate numbering 1,500 souls; Hināwi in politics, Ibadhi in religion; settled in Western Hajar at Halāhil, Rābi, Heil Ibn Suweidān, Gharrāq, and Sihlat, and in Bātinah at Waqībah and Fitnah.

46. *Ghawārib* (sing. *Ghāribi*).

A tribe of the Oman Sultanate numbering 350 souls; Hināwi in politics, Ibadhi in religion; settled in Bātinah at Bu ‘Abāli and Barkah.

47. *Habūs* (sing. *Habsi*).

A tribe of the Oman Sultanate, numbering probably 7,000 souls, of whom 100 are Bedouins; Hināwi in politics, Ibadhi in religion; settled in Western Sharqīyah in Baldān el-Habūs, in Wādi ‘Andām at Wāfi and Muteili‘, in Oman Proper at Manah in Wādi Mi‘aidin.

They are a wild, uncivilized tribe, less wealthy and important than their neighbours the Hirth, with whom they have an alliance, or the Hajriyīn. They own camels, but are chiefly engaged in growing dates. The small Warūd tribe is tributary to them.

Mudheibi is their political capital and Rōdhah in Wādi Samad their largest settlement, both in Baldan el-Habūs.

Their principal divisions are:

Section.	Fighting strength.	Section.	Fighting strength.
'Ayāl 'Abdu	100	Nājiyah	100
'Asīrah	100	Beni Bu Sa'īd	60
Yāl Dhanein	200	Sawālim	140
Ghanānimah	200	Yāl Shabīb	80
Ghasāsimah	100	Shamātarah	80
Aulād Haban	100	Beni Thāni	100
Jawābir	200	This last section is Bedouin, owning 60 camels, 30 donkeys, 50 cattle, and 2,000 sheep and goats.	
'Ayāl Mahrah	160		
Maqādamah	30		

48. Hadādabah (sing. Haddābi).

A tribe of the Oman Sultanate numbering 2,500 souls; Ibadhi in religion and Hināwi in politics; settled at Shirs in Bātinah and Sharu and Fanjah in Wādi Semā'il in Eastern Hajar. Those at Fanjah are sometimes at feud with the 'Abriyīn.

49. Beni Hadhram or Hadharmi (sing. Hadhrimi).

A small and scattered tribe of 500 souls settled in Western Hajar at Hadash in Wādi Mistāl, Nakhl in Wādi Mā'āwal, and Kafarah in Wādi Semā'il; in Oman Proper at 'Izz and Nizwa; in Muscat at Matrah. They are Ghāfiri in politics, and in religion probably Ibadhi.

50. Aulād Hadīd (sing. Hadādi).

A small tribe of the Oman Sultanate numbering 200 souls; Ibadhi in religion and Hināwi in politics; settled at Sīb and Laghshībah in Bātinah.

51. Hādiyīn (sing. Hādi).

A tribe of the Oman Sultanate numbering 1,400 souls; Ibadhi in religion; Hināwi in politics; settled in Eastern Hajar in Wādi 'Andām and in the Muscat district at Khafeiji in Wādi Maih and Quram in Wādi 'Adai.

52. Hajriyīn (sing. Hajari).

A tribe of the Oman Sultanate numbering 7,500 souls; Ibadhi in religion, Hināwi in politics and Yemeni in descent. They inhabit the whole Badīyah division of the Sharqīyah district, are found also at Mudheibi and deal with the port of Sūr. They are rapacious and turbulent and have not a good name for honesty, nevertheless they are one of the wealthiest and most enterprising communities in this part of the country. They are engaged in cultivation and trade and own a number of boats; some of them visit Bombay and Zanzibar. Their tribal capital is Wāsil in Badīyah, but at present they have no *tamīmah*. It was the Hajriyīn who in 1813 attacked Mutlaq, the Wahabite leader, slew him and expelled his force from the country ; Sa'd, the son of Mutlaq, in revenge completely broke their power, and they have never entirely recovered their former position.

The subdivisions of the tribe are as follows :

Section.	Fighting strength.	Location.
Bahārinah	200	Wāsil, Heili, and Hātūh
Bahārinah Habābasah	80	Wāsil, Dabīk, and Qā'
Aulād Bu Heid	300	Rāk and Mintirib
Mahādinah and Mahāddah	400	Yāhis, Shāraq, and Shāhik
Mahāsinah	400	Ghabbi and Mintirib

53. *Halālamah* (sing. *Hallāmi*).

A tribe of Trucial Oman, only 75 souls ; Maliki in religion ; settled in Abu Dhabi town, and attached to the Beni Yās.

54. *Āl Hamad* (sing. *Hamadi*).

A tribe of the Oman Sultanate, 500 souls, with some Bedouins amongst them ; Ibadhi in religion, Hināwi in politics ; settled at Barkah in Bātinah. The Bedouins range in Sharqīyah.

55. *Beni Hamīd*.

A few at Heir in Shameilīyah.

56. *Beni Hamīm* (sing. *Hamīmi*).

A tribe of the Oman Sultanate, numbering 200 souls ; Ibadhi in religion, Hināwi in politics ; settled at Nizwa and Bahlah in Oman Proper and at Rostāq in Western Hajar.

57. *Beni Hammād* (sing. *Hammādi*).

A tribe of the Oman Sultanate, numbering 900 souls ; Sunni in religion and Hināwi in politics ; settled at Wudām in Bātinah.

58. *Hanādhilah* (sing. *Handhali*).

A tribe of the Oman Sultanate, numbering 1,000 souls, settled in Eastern Hajar at Ghubrat et-Tām in Wādi Tāyīn ; at Samā'īyah, Khabbah, and Waljah in Wādi Khabbah : Ghāfiri in politics, in religion Ibadhi.

59. *Harāsīs*.

These are few in number and only visitors to Murbāt in Dhofār. Their proper habitat, religion, &c., are unknown.

60. *Beni Harrās* (sing. *Harrāsi*).

A considerable tribe of the Oman Sultanate numbering 4,000 souls, settled in Western Hajar at Jammah (500 houses), Buweirid (25 houses), Mansūr (40 houses) in Wādi Fara' ; at Hillat Beni Harrās (100 houses) in Wādi Semā'il ; at Nakhl (65 houses) and Hibra (40 houses) in Wādi Ma'āwal ; at 'Awābi in Wādi Beni Kharūs and at Fīq in Wādi Mistāl. They also occur at Teimsa (40 houses) in Oman Proper. The ruling family is called Aulād Thineyyān, the tribal capital is Jammah. In politics they are Ghāfiri, in religion Ibadhi.

61. *Beni Hasan* (sing. *Hasani*).

A tribe of the Oman Sultanate numbering 2,000 souls ; Ibadhi in religion, Hināwi in politics ; found in the Muscat district at Qantab, Matrah, Dārseit, Sāru, Khuweir, and Ghubrah, all on the coast ; at Jāl, Bōshar Ibn 'Amrān, Sād, Felej, Ghāllah, and Fuleij esh-Shām, all in Wādi Bōshar ; at Quram in Wādi 'Adai and at Mizra' el-'Alawi in Wādi Maih.

One of the sections is called 'Amārīyah.

62. *Beni Bu Hasan* (sing. *Hasani*).

A tribe of the Oman Sultanate numbering 5,000 souls or, with some subordinate tribes mentioned below, 7,000 souls ; Hināwi in politics and Ibadhi in religion with the exception of the Ahl Jebel section, which is Azraqah Wahabite in religion. Their principal settlement is Beled Beni Bu Hasan in Ja'lān, where they number about 4,000 souls ; about 500 are settled at Barkah and Hadhīb in Bātinah, and a few at Jināh near Sūr and at Fita in Eastern Hajar. The subordinate tribes are mostly Bedouin, ranging near 'Aqībah and in Jebel Mashā'ikh in Ja'lān and, except for one tribe, the Hāl 'Umr, they are all robbers.

The settled portion grow dates and grain, and are well provided with camels. In language and appearance they do not differ from their Bedouin neighbours. They are nearly all armed with rifles of various kinds and are constantly fighting with the Beni Bu Hasan and the Beni Bu 'Ali. Their divisions are :

Sections.	Fighting strength.	Sections.	Fighting strength.
Darū'	30 settled	Masārīr	200 settled
Farārijah	40 ,,	Rawājih	100 Bedouins
Huwājir	60 ,,	Shikālah	100 settled
Beni Jābir	70 ,,	Suwābi'	100 ,,
Hāl Bu Matāni	200 ,,		

Client tribes. All Bedouins except the Hāl 'Umr.

Ahl Jebel, 60 households ; Azraqah Wahabite ; robbers.
Mashā'ikh el-Beled, 40 households ; Ibadhi ; robbers.
Mashā'ikh el-Jebel, 250 households ; Ibadhi ; robbers.
Beni Sarhān, 40 households, Ibadhi ; robbers.
Hāl 'Umr, 100 households ; own 2,000 date-palms.

63. *Hasrīt* (sing. *Hasrīti*).

A very small and poor tribe, practically all Bedouins, numbering 150 souls and distributed along the SE. coast of Oman and Dhofār ; Ghāfiri in politics, in religion Ibadhi.

64. *Beni Hawāl* (sing. *Hawāli*).

A very small tribe of the Oman Sultanate numbering 100 souls, settled in Heil and Muta'ārishah in Wādi el-Hilti : Ghāfiri in politics, in religion Ibadhi.

65. *Hawāshim* (sing. *Hāshimi*).

A tribe of 1,000 souls in the Oman Sultanate settled in Western Hajar at Felej el-Wusta, Shabeikah and Dāris in Wādi Fara' ; and in Oman Proper at Adam and Manah : Ghāfiri in politics, in religion Ibadhi.

66. *Hawāsinah* (sing. *Hausini*).

A large and important tribe of the Oman Sultanate numbering 17,500 settled and also some Bedouins ; Hināwi in politics, partly Sunni and partly Ibadhi in religion. They occupy the whole of the Wādi el-Hawāsinah, excluding the tributary Wādi Beni 'Umr ; nearly all of Wādis Sārrāmi and Shāfān in Western Hajar ; also most of the town of Khābūrah in Bātinah ; they are also found at Qasbiyat el-Hawāsinah in the sub-vilayet of Saham. Their capital is Ghaizein in Wādi el-Hawāsinah. They are generally at feud with the Beni 'Umr who adjoin them on the west.

Wādi el-Hawāsinah is deep and narrow. The villages are built upon the hill-sides and the date-trees grow on artificial terraces to which spring water is conducted in channels : there are no wells. The houses are of stone and mud ; the crops besides dates are wheat, barley, bajri, maize, millet, lucerne, beans, sweet potatoes, and fodder grasses ; the Hawāsinah keep camels, cattle, sheep, goats, and donkeys. The fruits grown are limes, mangoes, grapes, olives, plums, pomegranates, figs, quinces, and almonds. Trade is carried on with Khābūrah and Suweiq.

The divisions of the tribe are :
Hawāmid.
Najāja'ah.
Aulād Rasheid.
Beni Sa'īd.
Sawālim.
Beni Sinān.

67. *Beni Haya* (sing. *Hayā'i*).

A small tribe of 500 souls in the Oman Sultanate settled in Dhāhirah at Dhank town and in Bātinah at Sīb and Laghshībah. Ghāfiri in politics, in religion Ibadhi.

68. *Hikmān* (sing. *Hikmāni*).

A tribe found on the SE. coast of Oman ; the Barr el-Hikmān or mainland between Masīrah island and Ghubbat el-Hashīsh is named after them. Mahōt is their principal settlement, but they also occur along the coast for 40 miles to the SW. of Ghubbat el-Hashīsh and at Murbāt in Dhofār, at Barkah and Wādi Manūmah in Bātinah.

Their number may be 800 souls. Seventy years ago they were an independent tribe, Ghāfiri in politics and Sunni in religion, regarded as cognate with the Jannabah; but since that time they have partially lost their tribal individuality, those of Barr el-Hikmān having attached themselves to the Beni Bu 'Ali, while others have become Hināwis under the Sheikh of Abu Dhabi, to whom they pay annual visits, receiving from him presents.

69. *Beni Hilāl* (sing. *Hilāli*).

A small tribe of the Oman Sultanate, numbering 400 souls; settled in Oman Proper at Bahlah and Nizwa; Ghāfiri in politics, in religion Ibadhi.

70. *Beni Hina* (sing. *Hinā'i*).

A tribe of the Oman Sultanate, numbering 9,000 souls; of Yemeni descent, Hināwi in politics and Ibadhi in religion. The Hināwi faction, formed in Oman at the beginning of the eighteenth century, derived its names from the Beni Hina, whose chief sheikh at that time, Khalf el-Quseir, was the first leader of the faction.

The Beni Hina dwell chiefly in Hajar and in Oman Proper. Their capital is Nizwa in Oman Proper, where they have 300 houses. Their settlements are given below, the number of houses being stated in brackets.

In Hajar. Qurein (100), Habbās (80), Heili (200), Qadīmah (40), Jammah (50), Naghzah (50), Hārithīyah (20), and Khōdh (120), all in Wādi Semā'il; Hajrat esh-Sheikh (50), Hārat el-Jabah (80), Saqairīyah (30), and Shabeikah (40), all in Wādi Fara'; Haweil (45) and Hōqain (200), in Wādi Beni Ghāfir; Khān (40), in Wādi el-Jizi.

In Oman Proper. Nizwa (300), Bilād Seit (40), and Ghāfāt (50). In Bātinah: Liwa town (160). In Dhāhirah: Heil (100) and Dham (80).

There is a small section called Hawāqinah at Nizwa, and the Jabūr, though treated here as a separate tribe, is perhaps a branch.

The Beni Hina are brave and warlike, and were in 1905 at feud with the Jannabah, Darū', and Beni Kalbān.

71. *Hinādis* (sing. *Hindāsi*).

A small tribe of the Oman Sultanate, numbering 150 souls; Ibadhi in religion and Hināwi in politics; settled at 'Adeibah in the Muscat district and at Ghalīl in Bātinah.

72. *Hirth* (sing. *Hārithi*).

An important tribe of the Oman Sultanate, numbering 9,000 souls, excluding five client tribes who can muster 1,130 fighting-men as detailed below. They are said to be of Nizāri descent, but now belong to the Hināwi faction; in religion they are Ibadhis.

The central division of Sharqīyah, called Baldān el-Hirth, with its villages and towns belongs entirely to the Hirth ; their principal places are Ibra and Mudheirib, the former being the tribal capital. They are also found at Mudheibi, Nizwa, Samad, and Sīb. The bulk of them thus are located between the Hajriyīn on the East and the Habūs on the West. Though they retain some of the characteristics of Bedouins they are chiefly occupied in agriculture and date-growing. A few of them are wealthy traders owning merchant vessels, and some who emigrated to Zanzibar have become men of substance and position there.

The Hirth do not deal with Sūr ; their ports are Matrah and Muscat. They are a warlike tribe, and now armed with rifles of various kinds. Their principal sections (in 1905) were :

Section.	Fighting strength.	Section.	Fighting strength.
'Asirāh	150	Maqādihah	150
Barāwanah	250	Marāhibah	100
Ghayūth	150	Mashāhibah	150
Aulād Hadām	200	Matāwabah	150
Aulād Hadri	150	Rashāshidah	200
Aulād Harfah	150	Saqūr	100
Khanājirah	300	Samrah	300
Ma'āmir	280	Hāl Sinā'u	300
Maghārah	100		

The five client tribes, all Ibadhis and largely Bedouins, were (in 1905) :

Tribe.	Fighting strength.	Habitat.
Dawakah	100	Barkah, Shakhākhīt, and Bu Mahār in Bātinah
Muwālik	500	Wādi Beni Khālid
Nuwāfil	80	Bu 'Abāli, Sha'ībah and Majiz en-Nawāfil in Bātinah
Āl Bu Rasheid	170	'Abbāsah and Khadhra in Bātinah
Shabūl	280	Heyyadh, Sohār town, and Wādi Bōshar

73. *Hishm* or *Beni Hāshim* (sing. *Hāshimi*).

A tribe of the Ja'lān and the Eastern Hajar districts of the Oman Sultanate ; they are Nizāri by descent, Ghāfiri in politics, in religion partly Ibadhi and partly Sunni. They are supposed to number about 8,000, of whom about 6,500 are settled at Kāmil (200 houses), Dīdu (50 houses), Humeidha (15 houses), and Buweirid (55 houses) in Ja'lān ; at Tahwa (60 houses), near Jebel Khadhar ; at Zilaft (50 houses), 'Adhfein (200 houses), Halfah (95 houses), Badh'ah (150 houses), Sīq (180 houses), and Sibt (160 houses), in the lower course of Wādi Beni Khālid ; a few are found at Khabbah in Wādi Khabbah, and at Sūr in Bilād es-Sūr they have perhaps 80 houses. There are also about 1,500 Bedouins belonging to the tribe, who own some 500 camels, 250 donkeys, 700 cattle, and 8,000 sheep and goats.

They command the road from Sūr to Ja'lān above Rafsah, and can close it at pleasure. The whole of the Wādi Beni Khālid is under their control, for the other tribes inhabiting it are always disunited and pay dues, it is said, to the Hishm.

The Hishm always supported Seyyid Tūrki when Sultan of Oman (1871–88) and were even with him at the capture of Matrah from 'Azzān in 1871. They took part with his son and successor, Seyyid Feisāl, in the crisis at Muscat in 1895, under the leadership of 'Abdullah ibn Sālim of the Beni Bu 'Ali.

Sections, &c., as obtaining in 1905 :

Sections.	Fighting strength.	Habitat.	Religion.
Hirzah	150	Kāmil	Sunni
Hishāshimah	200	Kāmil	,,
Kuwāshim	200	Humeidha	,,
Marāhibah	300	Dīdu, Sīq	,,
Aulād Nāsir	200	Buweirid	,,
Beni Rāshid	300	Badh'ah, Sīq	Ibadhi
Beni Seif	300	Halfah	,,
Sarāhimah	200	'Adhfein, Sibt	,,
Thuwāni	50	Zilaft	,,
Tuwā'i	200	Sibt	,,
Beni 'Umr	400	Kāmil, Sīq	,,
Zaheimiyīn	200	Wādi Khabbah	,,
Zeiyūd	150	Dīdu, Kāmil	Sunni

74. *Hūwalah* (sing. *Hōli*).

A tribe numbering 17,000 outside Oman, but represented in Oman by 1,500 souls, in religion partly Maliki, some Shafei settled in Shārjah town. They have altogether lost their fighting qualities and are given up to money-making.

75. *Huyūd* (sing. *Heidi*).

A tribe of the Oman Sultanate numbering 200 souls ; Ibadhi in religion and Hināwi in politics ; settled at Dhiyān in Bātinah.

76. *Āl Bu 'Isa*.

A small Bedouin tribe of Ja'lān who occasionally visit Masīrah island for nefarious purposes, ostensibly as fishermen but really as wreckers.

77. *Beni 'Isa* (sing. *'Isā'i*).

A tribe of the Oman Sultanate numbering 2,000 souls ; Ibadhi in religion, originally Ghāfiri but now (1905) Hināwi in politics ; settled in Western Hajar at Hībi in Wādi Sarrāmi,

Ghadheifah } in Wādi 'Āhin.
Ghareifah }

Khabt }
'Ablah } in Wādi el-Hilti.
'Abeilah }

78. *Ja'far*.

These are about 100 in number and found in Murbāt, Dhofār. Nothing is known about them.

79. *Beni Jābir* (sing. *Jābiri*).

An important and in every way superior tribe of the Oman Sultanate, also the strongest numerically. They are smarter in dress, more intelligent and better educated than most other tribes. They claim descent from the tribe of Dhubyān, famous in Arab poetry, and are at bitter enmity with the Beni Ruwāhah, who descend from the rival tribe of Abs.

The total number of the tribe is 25,000 souls, and they are found chiefly in Hajar. Their principal seat is the group of the three valleys of Hilam, Tīwi, and Shāb, known collectively as Wādi Beni Jābir I (to be distinguished from the Wādi Beni Jābir II, the western tributary of Wādi Semā'il). Hilam and Tau are equally regarded as their tribal capital. They are widely dispersed, but keep in touch and act as a body, and have often been used to close the passes leading to Muscat against the Sultan's enemies in Sharqīyah.

Further details of their distribution are given below against each section of the tribe.

In politics they are Ghāfiri, in religion Ibadhi.

Subdivisions, &c., as obtaining in 1905.

Section.	Fighters.	Habitat.
Aulād Burhān	400	Seijah in Wādi Beni Jābir II (tributary of Wādi Semā'il)
Dafāfi	50	Hājir in Wādi Semā'il
Beni Fahd	200	Firjāt in Wādi Beni Jābir II
Beni Falīt	240	Qaiqa in Wādi Beni Jābir II
Beni Ghadānah	240	Bimah } on the coast of E. Hajar Fins }
Ghazāl	150	Daghmar } on the coast of E. Hajar Dhibāb }
Beni Hadhrami	400	Seima in Oman Proper. Wādi Semā'il

(There is some confusion between this section and the distinct tribe of the Beni Hadhram)

Aulād Hameid	180	Muqazzih in Oman Proper
Beni Harb	240	Majāzah in Wādi 'Andām
Beni Ibrāhīm	240	Wādi Semā'il
Aulād Khamīs	160	Wādi Semā'il
Aulād Lurhān	300	Wādi Semā'il
Ma'āmarah	400	'Amq and Felej el-Qabā'il in the Sohār sub-vilayet
Beni Mazrū'	240	Hil in Wādi Beni Jābir II

(Some regard the Mazārī' of Wādi Fara' as of this section)

Beni Muqīm	600	Ghail esh-Shāb, Jahl and Jeilah in Wādi Shāb ; Tīwi, Seima, Mībām, and 'Amq in Wādi Tīwi
Aulād Nāsir	320	Wādi Hilam
Beni Qurwāsh	160	Wādi Semā'il
Aulād Rāshid	480	Wādis Hilam, Tīwi, and Tau
Aulād Rāshid ibn 'Āmir	240	Wādi Semā'il
Beni Sa'd	240	Wādi Semā'il
Āl Saba'	70	Samā'iyah and Khabbah in Wādi Khabbah
Aulād Saheim	140	Bir and Misfāh in Wādi Beni Jābir II
Aulād Sa'īd	160	Hōb in Wādi Beni Jābir II
Aulād Salīm	240	Jeilah in Wādi Beni Jābir II
Salūt	640	Hilam in Wādi Hilam and most villages of Wādi Tīwi ; Ghāllah in Wādi Bōshar
Sha'ībiyīn or Shu'aibiyīn	350	Kabda and Kalhāt and Halfah in Wādi Beni Khālid

(Those of Kalhāt went over in 1907 to the Hināwis and have allied themselves to the Beni Bu Hasan)

Shajbiyīn	200	Wādi Semā'il
Aulād Wādi	80	Bidbid and elsewhere in Wādi Semā'il

80. *Jabūr* (sing. *Jabūri*).

A tribe of the Oman Sultanate, perhaps a section of the Beni Hina, numbering 700 souls ; Ibadhi in religion and Hināwi in politics ; settled at Mutahaddamāt in Wādi 'Adai and at Hifri in Wādi Beni Kharūs.

81. *Jadgāl*, or *Zidjāl* (sing. *Zidjāli*).

A tribe of Persian Mekrān, now reckoned there as Baluchis, and said to have come from Sind. In Oman they number 10,000 souls ; Sunni in religion. They occupy an entire suburban quarter of Muscat town and are found at Matrah, and generally wherever a Baluchi settlement exists. They have been introduced into Oman at various times as mercenary soldiers.

82. *Jahādhim* (sing. *Jahdhami*).

A tribe of the Oman Sultanate, numbering 500 souls ; Ibadhi in religion, Hināwi in politics ; settled at Samad in Sharqīyah.

83. *Jahāwar* (sing. *Jauhari*).

A tribe of the Oman Sultanate, numbering 4,000 souls, settled in Western Hajar at Heilein and Mabrah in Wādi Mabrah ; at Litheibāt, 'Aqair, Heyyadh, Khabt, 'Ablah and 'Abeilah in Wādi-el-Hilti. Ghāfiri in politics, in religion Ibadhi.

84. *Jelājilah* (sing. *Jaleijali*).

A tribe of Trucial Oman, numbering only 50 souls ; settled in Furfār, Heil, and Indūk. Divided in allegiance between the Sheikh of Shārjah and his rival, the rebel Sheikh of Fujeirah.

85. *Jannabah* (sing. *Janneibi*).

A large tribe of the Oman Sultanate, Yemeni by extraction, but now belonging to the Ghāfiri faction, and Sunnis in religion. They number in all about 12,000, of whom 3,000 are nomads. Their tribal capital is Sūr, but they possess also Masīrah Island, and interspersed with the Hikmān and Āl Wahībah occupy in a desultory fashion the SE. coast of Oman from Ras Jibsh, where they have a village, to the borders of Dhofār ; some of them visit Murbāt in Dhofār ; the cave dwellings on Ras Sājar and the small hamlet of Safqōt at the west end of Dhofār are said to be occupied by them. A few reside among the Hikmān of Mahōt, and detached colonies are found at Bahlah, Khadhra Ibn Daffā', and 'Izz in Oman Proper and at Wādi Manūmah in Bātinah.

It is necessary to distinguish the settled portion, resident chiefly at Sūr, from the migratory, pastoral, and fishing sections farther south. The former, known in common with some of the Beni Bu 'Ali as "Sūris", own and navigate a large number of sea-going vessels which run to Bombay, Zanzibar, and the Red Sea ; they are also merchants having large depots at Sūr, and the Hajriyīn of the interior carry on all their foreign trade through them.

The pastoral portion are dark-skinned, thin and under-sized, but not ill-looking ; they wear their hair long and confine it round the head with a leather thong. They are disliked by their neighbours, and appear to have little or no religion. In the cool season they come down to the coast with their herds of camels and goats, which are said to be very large, retreating again to caves on the hills on the approach of the SW. monsoon. It has been noticed that those who fish are of a lighter complexion than the rest, and that their cranial and facial type is peculiar to themselves.

As a tribe the Jannabah bear an evil reputation. Those of Sūr indulged in slave-dealing and even piracy as long as these courses were open to them, while those of the SE. coast are wreckers and robbers to a man. They have a perpetual feud with the Āl Wahībah, the enmity between them being more deadly than between any other tribes in Oman.

Their subdivisions and fighting strength are given below :

Section.	Fighting strength.		Habitat.
'Arāmah	400 (under-estimated)		Sūr.
Fawāris	600	,,	Sūr, in Ja'lān and Masīrah Island.
Ghayyālīn	450	,,	Sūr and Masīrah Island.
Maja'alah	300	,,	Nomad.
Makhānah	500	,,	Sūr and Masīrah Island.

86. *Yāl Jarād* (sing. *Jarādi*).

A tribe of the Oman Sultanate, numbering 2,000 souls ; Ibadhi in religion, Hināwi in politics ; settled at Bu 'Abāli, Masna'ah, and Marāghah in Bātinah. A few are Bedouin.

87. *Jissās* (sing. *Jissāsi*).

A small tribe of the Oman Sultanate, numbering 350 souls, settled at Kubārah in Dhāhirah and at Bahlah in Oman Proper : Ghāfiri in politics. Those settled at Kubārah are subordinate to the Ya'āqīb of 'Ibri.

88. *Beni Ka'ab* (sing. *Ka'abi*).

A tribe of about 7,250 souls in the interior of the Oman promontory, having their head-quarters at Mahadhah, in the neighbourhood of which most of them are found. There are some about the head of Wādi el-Qōr and also in the Sultanate of Hadaf in Wādi Hatta, and at Haseifīn, Sūr el-'Abri, and Tareif in the Liwa sub-vilayet of Sohār. They number 1,250 in the Oman Sultanate and 6,000 in Trucial Oman. In politics they are Ghāfiri, in religion Sunni.

Their principal sections, &c., are :

Section.	Habitat.	Number.
Drisah	Wādi Shīya	150 nomads
Makātīm	Mahadhah and Kahal	600 settled
Misā'īd	Wādi Bu Jila'ah	350 ,,
Miyādilah	Wādi el-Hayūl and Shibakah in W. Qahfi	500 ,,
Miyā'isah	Jaweif and Sharam in Wādi Khadhra	150 ,,
Mizāhamiyīn	Mahadhah	50 ,,
Naweijiyīn	Khatwah in Wādi Bu Sa'd, Khabbein, Zāhar and Subeithah in Wādi 'Abeilah affluent of Wādi el-Jizi	1,400 ,,
Salālāt	Mahadhah	300 ,,
Sawālim	Nawei'i	300 ,,
Shweihiyīn	Wādi Shweihah and Shibakah in Wādi Qahfi	1,000 mostly nomad

(A subsection of Shweihiyīn known as Hibnāt are found in Shibakah)

Ahl Yidhwah	Mahadhah, Kahal, and Sharam in Wādi Khadhra	600 settled
Zaheirāt	Mahadhah and Nawei'i	300 settled

89. *Beni Kaheil* (sing. *Kaheili*).

A small tribe of the Oman Sultanate, numbering 300 souls; Ibadhi in religion and Ghāfiri in politics; settled at Majīs in the sub-vilayet of Sohār.

90. *Beni Keleib* (sing. *Keleibi*).

A tribe of the Oman Sultanate, numbering 1,400 souls, settled in Western Hajar at Kitnah, Rābi, Heil Ibn Suweidān, Khaweirij, and Wāsit in Wādi el-Jizi and its tributaries: Ghāfiri in politics, in religion Sunni. They are divided into three sections:

Hadādinah (sing. Haddāni) at Rābi.
Rasheidāt (sing. Rasheidi) at Heil Ibn Suweidān.
Shawāmis (sing. Shāmsi) at Kitnah, Wāsit, and Khaweirij.

91. *Beni Kelbān* (sing. *Kelbāni*).

A tribe of the Oman Sultanate, numbering about 8,000 souls, inhabiting both slopes of Western Hajar. On the Dhāhirah side they are found at Maqnīyāt (740 houses), which is their tribal capital, at Sammah (60 houses), at Khadal (100 houses) on an affluent of Wādi Dhank, and at Miskin (200 houses), Najeid (40 houses), and 'Āridh (300 houses) in Wādi el-Kebīr, and at 'Ibri. On the Bātinah side their villages are Zūla (20 houses) in Wādi Beni Ghāfir, Deiqarah (25 houses), Hiyāl (70 houses), Minzifah (25 houses), and Raqayyid (25 houses), in Wādi Mabrah, and Rattah (90 houses) in Wādi Sarrāmi. There are also 30 houses of theirs at Bahlah in Oman Proper. There are no Bedouins among them. In politics they are Ghāfiri, in religion Ibadhi. In 1883 they sided with the Sultan of Oman.

Their subdivisions are:

Aulād 'Ameirah, 300 households in Maqnīyāt and Miskin.
Ghabābīn, 200 households in Maqnīyāt.

Jarāwinah, 720 houses in Maqnīyāt, 'Āridh, and Khadal.
Aulād Sinān, 200 households in Maqnīyāt.
Aulād Subeih, 150 households in Maqnīyāt and Miskin.
Beni Tiyūm, 20 households in Zūla, in Wādi Beni Ghāfir.

There is also a section or subsection called Quyūdh found at Raqayyid.

92. *Āl Bu Kelbi* (sing. *Kelbāni*).

A tribe of Trucial Oman, numbering only 70 souls, perhaps forming a subsection of the Āl Bu Khareibān section of the Na'īm. They are settled in 'Ajmān town.

93. *Aulād Kāsib* (sing. *Kāsibi*).

A small tribe of the Oman Sultanate, numbering 400 souls, all Bedouins, found round Sūr in Eastern Hajar : Ghāfiri in politics, in religion Ibadhi. Formerly they were a section of the Jannabah, now they are incorporated in the Beni Bu 'Ali.

94. *Āl Kathīr* (sing. *Kathīri*).

The principal tribe in Dhofār proper, where all the villages except Tāqa belong to them ; they are represented in the Samhān hills also by several sections who act as a partial counterpoise there to the uncivilized Qaras. A few emigrants of the tribe are settled at Dōhah in the Muscat district near Muscat town.

The tribe numbers 4,500, of whom 2,500 are settled and 2,000 nomad.

The settled Kathīr are agriculturists, and grow bajri, maize, millet, cotton, and a little wheat and sugar-cane. They also grow coco-nuts for home consumption only ; no dates ; tobacco in small quantity—not enough for home consumption even ; water and musk melons, papai, and a few plantains and mulberries. In the way of vegetables they have bindis and chilis (red pepper). Ploughs are not used ; the ground is worked with spade or hoe. Fish abound, and acres of small fish called '*a'īd*, resembling the sardine, may be seen drying near villages.

They wear their hair long, tied by a fillet round their heads ; Seyyids, however, and the poorest classes have their heads shaved. For clothing they ordinarily have only one garment, a dark blue sheet, 9 ft. by 4½ ft., which forms a kilt by day and a sheet by night.

The subdivisions of the settled portion are :
    Beit 'Ali ibn Badr, 150 families.
    Beit 'Amr ibn Mohammed, 40 families.
    Āl Fādhil, 120 families.
    Bu Ghawwās, 150 families.
    Beit el-Marāhīn or Marhūn, 50 families.
    Āl Mohammed ibn Hamad, 150 families.
    Shanāfirah, 225 families.

This section is loyal to the Sultan of Oman; they are said to have been 'Awāmir originally, but are now reckoned Āl Kathīr.

The Bedouin sections are:

Beit Bekhīt ibn Sālim, Beit el-Hamar, Beit Jadād, and Beit Masan. They own cattle and camels and collect frankincense like the Qaras. They arrange their hair in a top-knot instead of binding it with a fillet. Their dialect differs from that of other Bedouins of Oman and has not been investigated yet.

The Āl Kathīr are a Hināwi tribe, and claim to have emigrated from Hadhramaut three centuries ago, conquering Dhofār proper and establishing a capital at Dahārīz. In religion they are Ibadhis. They are at constant feud with the Qaras, whom in their arms, clothing, and habits they resemble.

95. *Ahl Ras el-Kheimah.*

A tribe of Trucial Oman, numbering 2,000 souls, all resident in the town of Ras el-Kheimah. They are a mongrel race formed by the fusion of various Arab tribes.

96. *Beni Khālid* (sing. *Khālidi*).

An Arab tribe of Eastern Arabia, who formerly had a very large range. They are still predominantly Bedouin, but here only the portion in Oman is dealt with, and that portion is settled in the Oman Sultanate at 'Abbāsah, Hajeirah, Khōr el-Milh, and Manātif in Bātinah. Here they number 5,500 souls, Sunni in religion and Hināwi in politics.

97. *Āl Khameyyis* (sing. *Khameisi*).

A small Bedouin tribe, numbering 400 souls, found in Oman Proper; Ghāfiri in politics, in religion Ibadhi.

98. *Khamārah.*

A tribe of Trucial Oman, numbering 375 souls, all resident in Abu Dhabi town. They are Maliki in religion. They came originally from Khamīr in Persia, and claim connexion with the 'Utūb.

99. *Yāl Khamīs* (sing. *Khamīsi*).

A tribe of the Oman Sultanate, numbering 200 souls; Ibadhi in religion and Hināwi in politics; settled at Khabbah and Sha'ībah in Bātinah.

100. *Beni Khammārah* (sing. *Khammāri*).

A tribe of the Oman Sultanate, numbering 400 souls; Ibadhi in religion and Hināwi in politics, settled at Sūr Heyyān in Bātinah.

101. *Beni Kharūs* (sing. *Kharūsi*).

A tribe of the Oman Sultanate, numbering 4,500 souls, of whom 1,500 are Bedouins. They inhabit the northern slopes of the Western

Hajar and are settled at Misfāh (45 houses), 'Aliya (80 houses), Taqab (12 houses), Istāl (80 houses) Saneiba' (80 houses), Shau (10 houses), Hijār (90 houses), Tau esh-Sheikh (20 houses), 'Awābi (70 houses), and Felej Beni Khazeir (20 houses), all in Wādi Beni Kharūs; at Nakhl in Wādi Ma'āwal they have 40 houses. Hijār is their tribal capital. The Bedouin section of 1,500 souls is named Yāl Khameyyis. They possess 150 camels, 300 donkeys, 150 cattle, and 2,000 sheep and goats. The Beni Kharūs are Ghāfiri in politics and Ibadhi in religion.

102. *Khazeimāt* (sing. *Khazeimi*).

A tribe of the Oman Sultanate, numbering 500 souls; Ibadhi in religion and Hināwi in politics; settled at Haseifīn Sūr el-Khazeimāt.

103. *Khazeir* (sing. *Khazeiri*).

A tribe of the Oman Sultanate, numbering 450 souls; settled at Nakhl in Western Hajar; Ghāfiri in politics, in religion Ibadhi.

104. *Beni Khazam* (sing. *Khazami*).

A tribe of the Oman Sultanate, numbering 400 souls; Ibadhi in religion and Hināwi in politics; settled at Sīya, 'Arqi, and Habūbīyah in Wādi Sarein in the Muscat district.

105. *Khōjah*, known to Arabs as *Lawātiyah*.

The head-quarters of the Khōjah sect in the Persian Gulf are at Matrah, where they number about 1,050 souls; but they are found also at Khābūrah (125 souls), Sohār town, Suweiq (30), Barkah and Masna'ah in Bātinah; at Quryāt (1 family), and at Gwādar (300 souls); some also at Dibai, Ras el-Kheimah and Shārjah towns. In Matrah the entire community lives in a large fort or enclosed quarter upon the sea beach for security and privacy. They marry for the most part only among themselves. About 10 families now adhere to Āgha Khān of Bombay, the rest have been converted to Thein 'Ashari Shiism, but preserve to some extent their old social usages and customs. The majority are petty merchants and shop-keepers; a few of them share in the trade between India and Oman, importing rice from Calcutta, piece goods, oil, and drugs from Bombay, and exporting dates and dried fish. In the ports they are mostly British subjects. A few have acquired land.

106. *Aulād Kuleib* (sing. *Kuleibi*).

A tribe of the Oman Sultanate, numbering 100 souls; Ibadhi in religion and Hināwi in politics; settled at 'Adeibah in the Muscat district.

107. *Kunūd* (sing. *Kindi*).

A scattered Ghāfiri tribe of Oman, Ibadhi in religion, numbering 1,500 souls, all settled. They are found at Nizwa in Oman Proper, where they have 40 houses, and which may be regarded as their tribal capital;

at Nakhl (50 houses) in Wādi Maʻāwal; at Saheilah (100 houses), Mileyyinah (15 houses), Heil esh-Shiya (10 houses), Heil er-Rafsah (60 houses), and Thiqbah (20 houses) in Wādi el-Jizi and its tributaries; at Heil, Ghāllah (20 houses), and Furfār in the Shameilīyan tract, and finally in independent Oman at Bireimi village and in Mahadhah.

108. *Beni Lamak* (sing. *Lamki*).

A tribe of the Oman Sultanate, numbering 300 souls; Ibadhi in religion and Hināwi in politics; settled at Lamki in Wādi Beni Ghāfir.

Qasra
Umm Himār } in Wādi Faraʻ.

109. *Maʻāwal* (sing. *Maʻwali*).

A tribe of the Oman Sultanate, numbering 8,000 souls; Ibadhi in religion and Hināwi in politics; settled in Wādi Maʻāwal in Western Hajar, where they own the villages of Āfi (1,000 houses), ʻAreiq (40), Musilmāt (300), and part of Hibra (80); also at Khabbah (150) and Barkah (20) in Bātinah. There is also a Bedouin section, by name Yāl Bin Rashīd. Āfi is the tribal capital. The Jalandite rulers of Oman, who flourished at the time of the conversion of the country to Islam, or somewhat earlier, are supposed to have belonged to this tribe.

The trade of Wādi Maʻāwal is with Barkah. Wheat, barley, lucerne, and beans are grown, and there are about 100,000 date-palms.

110. *Āl Bu Maheir* (sing. *Maheiri*).

A considerable tribe in Trucial Oman, found in all the coast towns. They have 400 houses in Dibai, 200 in Shārjah, 120 at Ras el-Kheimah, 100 at Abu Dhabi, 100 at Batīn, 80 at ʻAjmān, 60 at Khān, and 30 at Umm el-Qaiwein. By some the Daheilāt of Abu Dhabi town are regarded as a section of the Āl Bu Maheir, who in their turn are reckoned, in Abu Dhabi, as a section of the great Beni Yās tribe.

In all they number about 5,500 souls, of whom only about 100, in the Abu Dhabi principality, are Bedouin in their habits.

They are said to be of Mahrah stock and to have come originally from Hadhramaut.

In religion and politics they follow the Sheikh of the principality in which they happen to live.

111. *Mahārah* (sing. *Mahri*).

A tribe of Trucial Oman, numbering 1,250 souls, all resident in Ras el-Kheimah town, of which they form one of the main elements.

112. *Mahārib* (sing. *Mahāribi*).

A tribe of the Oman Sultanate, numbering 300 souls; Ibadhi in religion and Hināwi in politics; settled in Eastern Hajar, at ʻAmqāt in Wādi Semāʼil, and at Farfārah in Wādi Dhabaʻūn.

113. *Mahārīq* (sing. *Mahrūqi*).

A tribe of the Oman Sultanate, numbering 2,200; settled at Adam and Bahlah in Oman Proper and at Sanā'u in Sharqīyah; Ghāfiri in politics, in religion Ibadhi.

The Beni Wāl form one of their sub-tribes.

114. *Mahārizah* (sing. *Maheirizi*).

A tribe of Trucial Oman, numbering 250 souls, sharing with the Sharqiyīn two villages in Wādi Hām, viz. Masāfi and Tayyibah, where they keep some live-stock and grow dates.

115. *Mahras*.

A few in Murbāt in Dhofār. Nothing known about them.

116. *Aulād Mahriz* (sing. *Mahrizi*).

A tribe of the Oman Sultanate, numbering 800 souls. Ibadhi in religion; settled at Ba'ad in Wādi Tāyīn.

117. *Majālibah* (sing. *Majlabi*).

A tribe of the Oman Sultanate, numbering 150 souls; Ibadhi in religion and Hināwi in politics; settled in Eastern Hajar at Hillat el-Majālibah in Wādi Semā'il.

118. *Manādharah* (sing. *Mandhari*).

A tribe of the Oman Sultanate, numbering 1,850 souls; Ibadhi in religion and Hināwi in politics; settled in Western Hajar at Hawājiri, Hallah, and Mizāhīt in Wādi Fara'; in Oman Proper at Izki and Saddi; in Dhāhirah at Saleif; in Muscat at Matrah.

119. *Manāsīr* (sing. *Mansūri*).

A Bedouin tribe of Trucial Oman, with head-quarters in Dhafrah; their range is from Qatar on the NW. to the Bireimi oasis on the E., and they are found all over Dhafrah, but especially in Dhafrah proper and Līwah; also in Khatam. A few frequent the neighbourhood of Abu Dhabi town and visit the Bireimi oasis, and some are settled in the coast towns of Khān and Jumeirah. In all they number about 1,400 souls, of whom only 100 are settled. Most of them winter in Qatar or its neighbourhood and summer in Līwah, where they have temporary villages of huts made of date-sticks and leaves, and possess as joint tribal property some date-groves. When their sojourn in Līwah is over for the year they close up their dwellings and stop up their wells with sand. Their principal grazing ground is in Dhafrah proper, but in the summer they leave their camels in Beinūnah with those of the Beni Yās. They are Hināwi in politics and Maliki in religion.

They were formerly subject to the Wahabite Government, and in

1865 were understood to pay a contribution worth 2,000 dollars a year, chiefly in kind, into the Wahabite treasury; now they are independent of all control, but maintain some intercourse with the town of Abu Dhabi and its Sheikh.

For the Bedouin Manāsīr, see above, p. 143.

120. *Manāwarah* (sing. *Maneiwari*).

A tribe of the Oman Sultanate, or possibly a branch of the Beni Bu Hasan, numbering 200 souls; Ibadhi in religion and Hināwi in politics. Settled at Hadhīb in Bātinah.

121. *Maqābīl* (sing. *Maqbāli*).

A tribe of the Oman Sultanate, numbering 5,000 souls, settled for the most part in Western Hajar. Their villages are Khān (40 houses), Heil 'Adha (20 houses) and Hansi (20 houses) in Wādi el-Jizi and its tributaries; Muta'ārishah (60 houses), Heil (40 houses), Litheibāt (25 houses), and 'Aqair (20 houses) in Wādi el-Hilti; Murri (60 houses), Mahbab (60 houses), Nizūk (20 houses), Madīnah (25 houses), and Salam (30 houses) in Wādi Beni Ghāfir. They have outlying settlements at Bāt (180 houses) in Wādi Sharsah, in Dhāhirah, and at 'Aweināt (50 houses), Himbār (90 houses), and Tareif (200 houses) in Sohār in Bātinah. Heil in Wādi el-Hilti may be regarded as their tribal capital.

The Maqābīl belong to the Ghāfiri faction. In 1905 they gave trouble to the Sultan of Oman, and were expelled by his troops from a fort in Wādi el-Hilti.

The Beni Kheil in Muta'ārishah and the Samāh in Bātinah are sections of the Maqābīl.

122. *Maqānnah* (sing. *Maqaini*).

A tribe of the Oman Sultanate, numbering 400 souls; Ibadhi in religion, Hināwi in politics. Settled at Wudām in Bātinah.

123. *Marar* (sing. *Marri*).

A tribe found chiefly in the coast towns of Trucial Oman, but also in the interior; they have 200 houses at Shārjah in the Leyyah quarter, 40 at Abu Dhabi, and 30 at Dibai; besides these there are about 70 families of Bedouin Marar who inhabit Līwah in Dhafrah.

They claim to be a section of the Āl Murrah, but their pretensions in this respect do not appear to be well founded.

Most of them are pearl-divers by occupation. In politics they are Hināwi. In religion they are Maliki Sunnis.

124. *Marāzīq* (sing. *Marzūqi*).

A tribe of the Oman Sultanate, numbering 300 souls; Sunni in religion and Hināwi in politics. Settled at Sūr Heyyān in East Bātinah and at Hamām in Saham. They are supposed to be the same tribe as the Marāzīq of the Shībkūh district of the Persian coast, though the latter are Wahabites.

125. *Masākirah* (sing. *Maskari*).

A Ghāfiri tribe of the Oman Sultanate, Ibadhi in religion, numbering in all 6,000 souls, of whom 1,600 are Bedouins. They inhabit the 'Alāyah or northern quarter of Ibra, sharing that town with the Hirth, and also occupy Yahmadi and other villages of the Baldān el-Masākirah division of Sharqīyah. Some live at Bilād es-Sūr. They have at times been at feud with the Hirth, but in 1877 were suspected of aiding the Hārithi rebel, Sālih, pecuniarily.

The Bedouin Masākirah are divided into three sections, viz. :

Faleihāt, 300 souls, owning 30 camels, 25 donkeys, 40 cattle, 200 sheep and goats.

Nahad, 500 souls, owning 50 camels, 40 donkeys, 30 cattle, 600 sheep and goats.

Masā'īd or Masā'idah, 800 souls, owning 300 camels, 200 donkeys, 100 cattle, and 800 sheep and goats.

The principal Sheikhs are at Ibra and Yahmadi.

126. *Masālihah* (sing. *Maslahi*).

A small tribe of the Oman Sultanate, numbering 150 souls, settled at Qaryah in Oman Proper and in Wādi Beni Khālid in Eastern Hajar; Ghāfiri in politics, in religion Ibadhi.

127. *Mashāfirah* (sing. *Masheifari*).

A tribe of the Oman Sultanate, numbering 700 souls; Ibadhi in religion and Hināwi in politics; settled at Rumeis and Barkah in Bātinah and at Qābil in Sharqīyah, where some are Bedouins.

128. *Mashārifah* (sing. *Masharrafi*).

A tribe of the Oman Sultanate, numbering 1,000 souls. Ibadhi in religion, Hināwi in politics; settled in and about the Wādi Fara' at Lamīm, Teima, Ghassah, Fuleij (or Faleij), Rafsah, and Mislaq in Eastern Hajar. They are entirely dominated by the Beni Bu Hasan.

129. *Mashā'ikh*.

A few in Murbāt in Dhofār. Nothing known about them except that they are a sacred class.

130. *Matārīsh* (sing. *Matrūshi*).

A tribe of Oman, numbering 1,700 souls, of whom 1,000 are settled in Trucial Oman at Shārjah town and 700 in the Sultanate at Harādi and Mureir el-Kebīrah in Bātinah; Ghāfiri in politics, in religion Sunni.

131. *Mazārī'* (sing. *Mazrū'i* or *Mizra'i*).

A tribe of Oman, numbering about 6,400 souls, of whom 5,000 are in the Sultanate and 1,400 in Trucial Oman. In the Sultanate they are found at 'Alāyat el-Mazārī' and Wusheil in Western Hajar and at 'Aqr in Bātinah. In Trucial Oman they are found in Abu Dhabi and Dibai towns, in the village of Khān near Shārjah town, in Wādis Hām and Sfuni in the Ras el-Kheimah district, and in Wādi Sfei in the district of Shameilīyah.

They are as a rule Ghāfiri in politics and Hanbali in religion.

In Abu Dhabi territory they are regarded as a section of the Beni Yās.

132. *Mishāqisah* (sing. *Mashqasi*).

A tribe of the Oman Sultanate, numbering 600 souls, settled at Heil, Mizāhīt, and Wusheil in Wādi Fara'; Ghāfiri in politics.

133. *Miyāyihah* (sing. *Miyāhi*).

This tribe of the Oman Sultanate is also called Beni Ghāfir, but the alternative name is apt to lead to confusion between the Miyāyihah tribe and the Ghāfiri political faction to which the tribe belongs and to which it gave its name. It has not now, and never had, as a tribe, any dominant position in the Ghāfiri political faction: that the faction was named after it was due not to the strength of the tribe but to the personal energy and talents of its Sheikh, Mohammed ibn Nāsir, who commanded the faction in the earliest struggle against the Hināwi. The Tamīmah of the Miyāyihah is no longer head of the Ghāfiri faction.

The Miyāyihah number about 7,000 souls, all settled. Their villages are Dhab'a (25 houses), Kahaf (30 houses), Dhaweihir (20 houses), Tayyib (25 houses), Rijlah (20 houses), Qarti (40 houses), Ruweibi (15 houses), Difa' (30 houses), Marji (50 houses), Khafdi (30 houses), Tabāqah (20 houses), Dihās (20 houses), 'Amār (25 houses), and Zawājir (35 houses), all in Wādi Beni Ghāfir; Khadhra (40 houses) in Wādi Sahtan; Rostāq (400 houses), Mizāhīt (65 houses), and Hazam (40 houses), in Wādi Fara'; Darīz (200 houses), in Wādi el-Kebīr; Beit el-'Ainein (20 houses), in Wādi Saneisal; Wahrah (100 houses), in Wādi Sharsah; Bahlah (30 houses), in Oman Proper.

They are Ghāfiri in politics and Ibadhi in religion, except only those at Darīz, who are Sunni. Though not a very large tribe they were in 1881 simultaneously at feud with eight tribes, and have a reputation for skill and courage in war.

A complete list of their subdivisions is not available. The few sections known are:

>Beni Salmān, at Marji and Mizāhīt.
>Salāmiyīn, at Dihās.
>Maqārishah, at Bahlah.
>Khanābishah, at Nizūk (20 houses) and Madīnah (25 houses) in Wādi el-Hōqain, a tributary of Wādi Beni Ghāfir.

134. *Muwālik* (sing. *Māliki*).

A tribe of the Oman Sultanate numbering 2,000 souls; Ibadhi in religion, Hināwi in politics; settled at Barkah, Shakhākhīt, and Rumeis Bu Mahār in Bātinah, and at Dawwah in Wādi Beni Khālid in Eastern Hajar. They are dependent on the Hirth.

135. *Muwālikh* (sing. *Mālikhi*).

A tribe of the Oman Sultanate numbering 700 souls; ? Ibadhi in religion, Hināwi in politics; settled at Hadd.

Their sections are:
Beni 'Āmir.
Beni Ghazal.
Beni Mahari.

136. *Beni Na'ab* or *Nu'abah* (sing. *Na'abi*).

A small but distinct tribe of the Oman Sultanate, numbering perhaps 1,500 souls; Hināwi in politics, religion unrecorded. Settled at Lājāl, which belongs to them, and at Manah in Oman Proper; at Sīya and elsewhere at Wādi Sarein; in Wādi Mi'aidin; at Mazāra' in Wādi Tāyīn in the hills on the right bank of the Tāyīn in the Wādi Dheiqah section they are shepherds and form a warlike section of the Beni Battāsh. They are possibly of non-Arab descent but are considered Arab now.

137. *Beni Na'mān* (sing. *Na'māni*).

A tribe of the Oman Sultanate, numbering 100 souls; Ibadhi in religion, Hināwi in politics; settled at Sanā'u in Sharqīyah. They took part in the attack on Muscat in 1895.

138. *Nabāhinah* (sing. *Nabhāni*).

A tribe of the Oman Sultanate which, at the end of the sixteenth century, furnished the rulers of Oman. They number only 600, and are settled at Sharqatein in Wādi Semā'il; at Hammām el-Ā'li and Sunub in Wādi Bōshar; and at Nakhl. They are Ghāfiri in politics, in religion Ibadhi.

139. *Na'īm* (sing. *Na'aimi*).

An important tribe of Oman with independent branches in Bahrein and Qatar. Only the main tribe is dealt with here. They number in all 13,000 souls, of whom 10,500 are settled and 2,500 Bedouins. In the Sultanate 4,500 are settled at Dhank town (660 houses), Sanqar (45 houses), Saneinah (200 houses); in Trucial Oman 3,500 at Heirah (250 houses), Hamrīyah (250 houses), 'Ajmān (25 houses), Dheid (30 houses), Haqālah (10 houses), and Shārjah town (100 houses); in independent Oman at Qābil (180 houses), Hafīt (150 houses), Su'arah (100 houses), and Bireimi village (100 houses).

The Bedouins range over the entire central portion of the Oman promontory at its base. The district of Jau, in which the Bireimi oasis is situated, may be regarded as their head-quarters, but they predominate in Dhāhirah on the east, and on the west extend to Khatam, which they share with the Beni Yās and the Dhawāhir. In the winter some of them pasture their animals on the watershed between the Bereimi oasis and Sohār, and are an important factor in tribal politics at the head of Wādi Hatta. On the north their principal grazing ground is the plain of Jiri, which is shared by their Khawātir section with the Ghafalah tribe. In the direction of Shārjah the tract known as Gharīf was once in their possession, but they were displaced by the Beni Ka'ab, who, in their turn, have had to cede it to the Beni Qitab.

Roughly speaking there are ordinarily 1,200 Na'īm Bedouins in Trucial Oman, 900 in the Sultanate, and 400 in independent Oman.

Subdivisions :

The Na'īm, whether settled or nomadic, belong to one of two main divisions—the Āl Bu Khareibān, who are said to be descendants of Khazraj, and the Āl Bu Shāmis, who are said to be descendants of 'Aus. The following are some of the better known sections of these two main divisions.

Āl Bu Khareiban sub-tribe :

'Aryān at Hafīt, 140 souls.
Āl Bu Adhnein or Dhanein at 'Ajmān and elsewhere, 700 souls.
Hamīrat at 'Ajmān and elsewhere, 180 souls.
Khawātir at Hafīt and the Jiri plain, 500 souls.
Qarātisah at Bireimi and Su'arah.
Āl Bu Kelbi of 'Ajmān town (perhaps a section).

The Āl Bu Shāmis sub-tribe:

'Ayāl 'Azīz at Dhank town, 700 souls; believed not to be really Na'īm (see above, p. 281).
Darāwishah at Heirah, Hamrīyah, Shārjah town, and Ras el-Kheimah town, 1,500 souls.
('Ayāl) Hiyah or Ahiya in Dhank town, 150 souls.
Kilābinah at Hafīt and Sanqar.
Shawāmis at Bizeili, Saneinah, and Dhank, 1,400 souls.
Wahā'ishah at Dhank town, 250 souls.

The Na'īm are Ghāfiri in politics, and, with few exceptions, Hanbali in religion.

140. *Naqbiyīn* (sing. *Naqbi*).

A tribe of Trucial Oman, numbering 1,800 souls; Hanbali in religion and Ghāfiri in politics ; settled in Shārjah principality on the east side of the Oman promontory at Khōr Fakkān, Ghāllah, Lūlayyah, Zubārah, Dībah, Fahlein, Khatt, and Diftah. They are generally hostile to their neighbours the Sharqiyīn. They are all engaged in agriculture.

141. *Al Bin Nāsir* (sing. *Nāsiri*).

A tribe of Trucial Oman, numbering 120 souls; Sunni in religion; all settled in Abu Dhabi town. They live by pearl-diving and fishing and petty trade apparently.

142. *Nawāfil* (sing. *Naufili*).

A tribe of the Oman Sultanate, numbering 300 souls. Ibadhi in religion, Hināwi in politics; settled in Bātinah at Bu 'Abāli, Sha'ībah, Majiz en-Nawāfil, and Masna'ah. They are dependent on the Hirth and a few are Bedouins.

143. *Nidābiyīn* (sing. *Nidābi*).

A settled tribe of the Oman Sultanate, numbering 3,500 souls; Ghāfiri in politics, in religion Ibadhi. Their villages are Lizugh, Mizra' Bu Ba'arah, Fankh, Da'sar, Sinsilah in Wādi el-'Aqq; Mizra' and Mizra' el-Heitani in Wādi Seijāni; Mahbūb, Hassās, and Sarūr in Wādi Semā'il; Jarda in Eastern Hajar.

Though not a large tribe their position in Wādi el-'Aqq and Wādi Seijāni commands the principal route from Sharqīyah to Matrah and Muscat towns, and their services have frequently been retained by the Sultans of Oman to bar the progress of insurgents from Sharqīyah to the capital.

144. *Nidheiriyīn* (sing. *Nidheiri*).

A small tribe of the Oman Sultanate, numbering 300 souls, settled at Dawwah in Wādi Beni Khālid in Eastern Hajar; Ghāfiri in politics, in religion Ibadhi.

145. *Beit el-Qalam.*

A few at Murbāt in Dhofār. Nothing known about them.

146. *Qara.*

A wild tribe in the Samhān hills in Dhofār, ranging from Sadah on the east to Rakhyūt on the west, and inland as far as the country is habitable, which is not a great distance. They number about 5,000 souls, all nomadic except a few hundred settled at Kharīfōt (30 houses), Murbāt (10 houses), Rakhyūt (65 houses), Sadah (20 houses), and Tāqa (20 houses). They call themselves Hakli, speak a language which has been described as a dialect of Mahri, and are commonly stated to be a branch of the Mahrah tribe. They differ greatly in appearance and character from the typical Arab, who regards them as heathens. They are classed as Sunnis of the Ghāfiri faction, but it is doubtful whether they are Arabs at all. They keep camels, cattle, sheep, and goats, and subsist chiefly by collecting frankincense and other gums. They also do a little cultivation and a little business in hides and *ghi*. In winter they live in caverns which, if large enough, they share with their animals.

One cavern at Dirbāt is 150′ × 50′ × 30′. A few have guns, the rest use iron swords, daggers, and even pointed throwing sticks. They carry a shield which serves also as a hat or water bucket or stool as desired. They quarrel and fight amongst themselves, and are a restless irresponsible lot, but are not a resolute or really dangerous tribe. They may annoy their neighbours by damaging their crops at night, but they never attack settled villages.

Their principal divisions are :

Beit 'Ak'āk, at Rakhyūt, 150 fighting men.
Barā'amah, in Samhān hills, behind Salālah, 160 fighting men.
Beit Hardān, in the hills near Rakhyūt, 70 fighting men.
Beit 'Īsa, at Rakhyūt, 80 fighting men.
Beit Jabūb, in the hills, 160 fighting men.
Beit Qatan, in the hills, 150 fighting men.
Beit Ka'bōb, in the hills.
Beit Kishōb, in the hills, 170 fighting men.
Kathōb or Ma'ashani at Tāqa, and in the hills about Wādi Dirbāt, 700 fighting men.
Beit Sa'īd, in the hills behind Hāsiki, 300 fighting men.
Shamāsah at Rakhyūt, 90 fighting men.
Beit Tabōk, in the hills, 170 fighting men.
Beni (or Ahl) 'Umr, at Murbāt and in the hills near by, 1,200 fighting men.

This section is friendly to the Sultan of Oman, and has a subsection, Beit Makhayyir.

147. *Il Bu Qarein* (sing. *Qareini*).

A tribe of the Oman Sultanate, numbering 400 souls ; Ibadhi in religion, Hināwi in politics ; settled at Dhiyān and Hajeirah in Bātinah. Some at Hajeirah are Bedouins.

148. *Qateit* (sing. *Qateiti*).

A tribe of the Oman Sultanate, very few in number ; Sunni in religion, Hināwi in politics. Settled in Khābūrah town.

149. *Qawā'id* (sing. *Qā'idi*).

A Bedouin tribe of Trucial Oman, numbering 250 souls. They range round about Shōkah in Wādi Hām ; some of them cultivate a little, and are semi-settled at Shōkali. They are believed by some to be an off-shoot of the Mazārī', but this is doubtful.

150. *Qawāsim* or *Jawāsim* (sing. *Qāsimi* or *Jāsimi*).

This is the family or small tribe to which the ruling sheikh of Shārjah belongs ; it claims descent from the prophet Mohammed. Outside Trucial Oman the subjects of Shārjah are sometimes spoken of as Jawāsim, and a tribe which has submitted to the sheikh is said to have become " Jāsimi" ; to this fact is probably due the indiscriminate application in old British records of the term " Joasmee " to all the piratical inhabitants of what is now Trucial Oman. The Trucial flag of 1820 unfortunately came to be known, and is still known, as the Jāsimi flag, and the Beni Yās of Abu Dhabi have consequently always shown a disinclination to fly it.

The genuine Qawāsim in Trucial Oman in 1905 only numbered 18 adult males. Other Qawāsim to the number of 650 occur at Duvvān in the Lingeh district of the Persian coast.

A tribe of Qawāsim, supposed to be identical with the genuine Qawāsim by some, while others hold it to be a section of the Nidābiyīn, is settled in the Oman Sultanate at Miltiqa in Wādi Semā'il, Nafa'ah in Wādi Mansah, Felej el-Hijāri in Wādi Riseil, Mizra' el-'Alawi in Wādi Maih, and at Bandar Jissah on the Muscat coast.

This tribe numbers 1,100 souls.

151. *Beni Qitab* (sing. *Qitbi*).

A tribe of Oman, having a considerable range over the promontory and in Dhāhirah. They number about 4,800, of whom 2,500 are settled in the cluster of villages known as Aflāj Beni Qitab, in Dhāhirah, and 200 at Dheid, in the Shārjah principality. The remaining 2,100 are Bedouins, whose territory is bounded by the northern end of the Dheid plain, the towns of Shārjah and Dibai, the Bireimi Oasis, and the western slopes of the promontory. The Bedouins muster 600 fighting-men in their seven sections, as follows:—Farāriyah, 100; Hawāfir, 80 ; Khasāwinah, 120 ; Ma'āliyah, 40 ; Masā'īd, 180 ; Midlāqarah, 30 ; Shibānāt, 50.

The Sheikh of Abu Dhabi has recently admitted the Beni Qitab to be clients of the Sheikh of Umm el-Qaiwein. In politics they are Ghāfiri, and in religion Sunni.

152. *Radeināt* (sing. *Radeini*).

A tribe of the Oman Sultanate, numbering 250 souls ; Sunni in religion, Hināwi in politics ; settled at 'Abbāsah in Bātinah.

153. *Rahbiyīn* (sing. *Rahbi*).

A tribe of the Oman Sultanate, numbering 5,000 souls ; Ghāfiri in politics, Ibadhi in religion ; settled in the upper part of Wādi Tāyīn and in Wādi Mansah and its tributaries. Wāsit, between Wādis Tāyīn and Mansah, is the seat of the principal Sheikh.

The Suwābiq at Beyyadh is one of their sections, and the Aulād or Beni Mahriz at Ba'ad and Mizbur is perhaps another.

154. *Ramāh* (sing. *Ramhi*).

A tribe of the Oman Sultanate, numbering 1,500 souls. Ghāfiri in politics, Ibadhi in religion ; settled in Western Hajar, at 'Ain er-Ramāh, and not found anywhere else. They are goldsmiths.

155. *Beni Raqād* (sing. *Raqādi*).

A small tribe of the Oman Sultanate, numbering 250 souls ; originally Yemeni, now Ghāfiri in politics and Ibadhi in religion ; settled at Misfāh, Lansab, and Ghāllah in the Muscat district and at Badī'ah in Wādi Tāyīn in Eastern Hajar.

156. *Āl Bu Rasheid* (sing. *Rasheidi*).

A tribe of the Oman Sultanate, numbering 600 souls; Ibadhi in religion, Hināwi in politics ; settled at 'Abbāsah and Khadhra in Bātinah. They are partly Bedouin and dependent on the Hirth.

157. *Beni Rāshid* or *Rawāshid*.

A tribe of the Oman Sultanate, numbering 3,500 souls ; Ibadhi in religion, Hināwi in politics ; settled in Bātinah at Khishdah in Sohār ; in Dhāhirah at 'Arāqi and Darīz in Wādi el-Kebīr ; in Oman Proper at Adam, Bahlah, Khadhra Bin Daffā' in Sharqīyah, and Nizwa at Sanā'u.

158. *Beni Rāsib* (sing. *Rāsibi*).

A tribe of the Oman Sultanate, numbering 1,500 souls ; Ghāfiri in politics and bigoted Wahabite in religion ; settled at Wāfi in Ja'lān and at feud with the Beni Bu Hasan. Their sections are Aulād Fāris, Marāziqah, and Aulād Rabī'.

159. *Beni Riyām* (sing. *Riyāmi*).

A somewhat peculiar tribe of the Oman Sultanate, numbering 11,000 souls ; Ghāfiri in politics, Ibadhi in religion ; settled at Izki (450 houses), Kamah (20 houses), Manah (140 houses), Birkat el-Mōz (250 houses), Karsha (20 houses), Muti (300 houses), Nizwa (500 houses), Tanūf (40 houses), and Zikeit (15 houses), all in Oman Proper ; also at Shareijah (100 houses), and Seiq (60 houses) in Jebel Akhdhar ; also at Misfāh (100 houses) in Wādi Beni Kharūs, and at Hijār (50 houses) and Qorah (40 houses) in Wādi Mistāl.

They are said to be of Yemeni descent and among the earliest Arab settlers in Oman. They are well to do and peaceable, but those of the hills are disliked as being irascible, slothful, immoral, and inhospitable ; the prejudice against them may be partly due to their disregard of Mohammedan principles in drinking a wine made by themselves from home-grown grapes. They are described as haggard and prematurely old, and lacking the usual vivacity and strength of mountaineers. The women go unveiled, and are sometimes of a clear ruddy complexion. Their sections are Jawāmīd at Seiq and Shareiqiyīn at Misfāh.

160. *Riyāyisah* (sing. *Rīsi*).

A tribe of the Oman Sultanate, numbering 1,000 souls; Sunni in religion, Hināwi in politics; settled at Haseifīn Sūr er-Riyāyisah in Bātinah, at Tawi in Western Hajar, and in Shinās town.

161. *Beni Ruwāhah* (sing. *Ruwāhi*).

An important tribe of the Oman Sultanate, numbering 18,500 souls; Ibadhi in religion and Hināwi in politics, though said to be of Nizāri descent. Their principal seat is the upper part of Wādi Semā'il, called Wādi Beni Ruwāhah, which they monopolize, having 900 houses there; but they also inhabit the lower villages of 'Adhdah (50 houses), Rissah (20), Rufei'ah (80), Qarwāshīyah (50), Naghzah (50), Suharah (100), Hijrat Aulād Sa'ad (50), Jammār (75), Hijrat el-Bakriyīn (100), Ibrāhīmīyah (40), Beit Weled el-Khalīli (100), Subārah (50), Daqdaqain (20), and Tasāwīr (25). In Wādi Bōshar they are found at Fuleij esh-Shām (15), in Wādi Dima at Hājir (100), and in Oman Proper at Izki, Khadhra Bin Daffā' (60), Nizwa (4), and Saddi (10). In Wādi Mistāl they occur at Ghubrah Beni Ruwāhah (40) and Heil (40). The greater part of Wādi 'Andām belongs to them and the whole of Wādi Mahram.

They are a troublesome tribe; they were against the Sultan of Oman from 1871 to 1888 consistently, and are supposed to be still very hostile; but they can be bought, as they were in 1905, when the Sultan made use of them.

Half a mile below the village of Wabāl, in Wādi Beni Ruwāhah, is a wall with towers and a gate through which the highway leads. This is called Darwazah (door), and its object is to close the route up the valley. It is permanently held by a garrison of the Beni Ruwāhah.

The tribe apparently owns few camels but many cattle, donkeys, sheep, and goats, and thousands of date-palms. They also go in for trade, market-gardening, cultivation, and transport.

The principal subdivisions of the Beni Ruwāhah are:

Section.	Houses.	Habitat.
Aulād 'Ali	200	Wādi Mahram
Aulād 'Aqīd	95	Wādi 'Andām
'Awāmir	200	Rissah and Rufei'ah in Wādi Semā'il, also Wādi 'Andām
Aulād 'Āyish	200	Wādi Mahram, &c.
Bahālil		Naghzah in Wādi Semā'il
Aulād Bin Bahīs	30	Sabārah in Wādi Semā'il
Bakriyīn	160	Hijrat el-Bakriyīn, Ibrāhīmīyah, and Sabārah in Wādi Semā'il
Aulād Barkat	80	Wādi Mahram
Aulād Hamad	100	Wādi Mahram
Beni Hamīm	100	Wādi Mahram
Aulād Harmal	150	Wādi 'Andām
Aulād Hasan	180	Wādi 'Andām
Beni Hāshim	60	Mihall in Wādi Semā'il, &c.
Aulād Husein	50	Wādi 'Andām
Aulād Ibrāhīm	60	Wādi Semā'il
Aulād Khalf	70	Wasād in Wādi Semā'il
Aulād Khalīl	200	Suharah and Beit Weled el-Khalīli in Wādi Semā'il
Aulād Khamīs	60	Biyāq in Wādi Semā'il, &c.
Aulād Mas'ūd	80	Biyāq in Wādi Semā'il and Himamt, &c.
Beni Na'mān	50	Wādi 'Andām
Aulād Nāsir Mohammed	20	Wabāl in Wādi Semā'il
Qurūn	70	Suharah in Wādi Semā'il
Aulād Rāshid	200	Himamt, &c.
Aulād Sa'd	100	Hijrat Aulād Sa'd in Wādi Semā'il
Aulād Salīm	120	Wādi Mahram
Aulād Suleimān ibn 'Umr	10	Hibāt in Wādi 'Andām
Aulād Wakīl	140	Dighāl in Wādi Semā'il, &c.

The Beni Ruwāhah occur also in Oman Proper and in some other places.

162. *Beni Sa'd* (sing. *Sa'di*).

A tribe of the Oman Sultanate, numbering 1,500 souls; Ibadhi in religion, Hināwi in politics; settled in Bātinah at Liwa town, Diwānij, and Asrār Beni Sa'd.

163. *Yāl Sa'd* (sing. *Sa'di*).

A large tribe of the Oman Sultanate, numbering 13,000 souls; Hināwi in politics, Ibadhi in religion. They occupy a block of territory 25 miles in length towards the east end of Bātinah, but a number of coastal villages in their tract are in other hands. Their traditional boundary on the east is the lower reach of the Wādi Beni Kharūs; on the west the farthest point they occupy is Khadhra. Their principal settlements are at Masna'ah (50 houses), Tau esh-Shawi (20), Tarīf (60), Muladdah (400), Raqqās (100), Ghareifah (500), Sūr el-Qarat (200), Tharmad (250), Bat-hah Suweiq (600), Khadhra (230), and Sūr Heyyān (50). They are also found at Khabbah and Hadhīb, the town of that name 5 m. E. of Khābūrah.

Among Arabs they are reputed unwarlike, mean-spirited, and inhospitable. They are wealthy, owning hundreds of thousands of date-palms and a considerable area under grain; also many trading and fishing boats.

They pay nothing to the present Sultan, and have always been inclined to side with the 'Azzān branch of his family. On the whole, however, they give no trouble so long as they are left alone.

The principal divisions are:

Section.	Fighting strength.	Location.
Yāl Heyyiz	700	Muladdah, Bat-hah Suweiq, and Khadhra
Yāl Hilāl	550	Masna'ah, Sūr el-Qarat, and Tharmad
Khaneijarah	400	Masna'ah, Sūr el-Qarat, and Tharmad
Khuweitar	300	Tarīf, Muladdah, and Raqqās
Maghābishah	400	Masna'ah, Tau esh-Shawi, Raqqās, and Khadhra
Shuweikāt	300	Khabbah and Hadhib

Mention is made of another tribe of Yāl Sa'd in the Oman Sultanate, numbering 150 souls; Ibadhi in religion but Ghāfiri in politics; settled at Dāris in Wādi Fara'. It is not stated whether they are connected with the Hināwi Yāl Sa'd.

164. *Yāl Sa'd* (sing. *Yāl Sa'di*).

A small tribe of the Oman Sultanate, numbering 150 souls, settled at Dāris in Wādi Fara'; Ghāfiri in politics, in religion Ibadhi.

165. *Sa'ādiyīn* (sing. *Sa'di*).

A tribe of the Oman Sultanate; Ibadhi in religion, and Ghāfiri, but subject to neighbouring Hināwi tribes, in politics; numbering 700 souls; settled at Muqal in Wādi Beni Khālid.

166. *Āl Bu Sa'īd* (sing. *Sa'īdi*).

This is the tribe of the Sultans of Oman; in politics Hināwi, in religion Ibadhi, with a few Sunnis among them. They number 6,000 souls, and are widely diffused. Their settlements are at Muscat town (8 houses), where they mostly belong to the Sultan's family; at Sawāqim (20 houses) in Wādi Mijlās; Heil el-Ghāf in Wādi Tāyīn; Dhiyān (65), Qasbiyat Āl Bu Sa'īd (20) in Bātinah; at Hibra (80) in Wādi Ma'āwal; at Fath Āl Bu Sa'īd (50) in Wādi Bōshar; at Hārat el-Jabah (20) and Beit el-Qarn (5) in Wādi Fara'; at Jammār (75) in Wādi Semā'il; at Samad (50), Khadhar (25), and Sherī'at Āl Bu Sa'īd (10) in Wādi Samad; at Adam (150), Birkat el-Mōz (20), Felej (20), Mahyūl (10), Manah (200), Nizwa (250), and Raddah (20) in Oman Proper.

167. *Sā'idah* (sing. *Sā'idi*).

A small tribe of the Oman Sultanate; Ghāfiri in politics, Sunni in religion; numbering 250 souls; settled at Dūt in Wādi Dhank.

168. *Saleimiyīn* (sing. *Saleimi*).

A tribe of the Oman Sultanate, numbering 800 souls; Ibadhi in religion and Ghāfiri in politics; settled at Rumānīyah in Wādi Fara', Western Hajar.

169. *Yāl 'Abd es-Salām* (sing. *Salāmi*).

A tribe of the Oman Sultanate, numbering 1,500 souls; Ibadhi in religion, Ghāfiri in politics; settled in Dīl Yāl 'Abd es-Salām in Saham in Bātinah.

170. *Salāmiyīn* (sing. *Salāmi*).

A tribe of the Oman Sultanate, numbering 3,000 souls; Ibadhi in religion, Ghāfiri in politics; settled at Nakhl and Rumānīyah in Wādi Fara', Western Hajar.

171. *Salātınah* (sing. *Saltāni*).

A tribe of the Oman Sultanate, numbering 100 souls; Hināwi in politics and probably Sunni in religion; settled at Furfār es-Salātinah in Liwa in Bātinah.

172. *Sareiriyīn* (sing. *Sareiri*).

A tribe of the Oman Sultanate, numbering 100 souls; Hināwi in politics and Ibadhi in religion; settled at Nakhl in Western Hajar. Some of them are potters.

173. *Beni Sārikh* (sing. *Sārikhi*).

A tribe of the Oman Sultanate, numbering 300 souls; Hināwi in politics, formerly Ghāfiri; settled at 'Ain Beni Sārikh in Dhāhirah.

174. *Yāl Shabīb* (sing. *Shabībi*).

A tribe of the Oman Sultanate, numbering 250 souls; Ibadhi in religion, Hināwi in politics; settled at Masna'ah in Bātinah and Lizq in Sharqīyah.

175. *Shabūl* (sing. *Shabli*).

A tribe of the Oman Sultanate, numbering 1,000 souls; Ibadhi in religion and Hināwi in politics; settled at Sohār town in Bātinah; at Heyyadh, Heil 'Adha, Hansi, and Furfār in Western Hajar, and at Jifār in Wādi Bōshar. They are dependent on the Hirth.

176. *Beni Shaheim* (sing. *Shaheimi*).

A tribe of the Oman Sultanate, numbering 4,000 souls; Ibadhi in religion, Ghāfiri in politics; settled in Eastern Hajar in all the villages of Wādi Dima except Hājir.

177. *Shahā'irah* (sing. *Ashhari* or *Shahyāri*).

A tribe of Trucial Oman, numbering 125 souls; Ghāfiri in politics; settled at 'Asimah in Wādi Hām. They are considered to be aborigines.

178. *Beni Shahūm* (sing. *Shahmi*).

A tribe of the Oman Sultanate, numbering 900 souls ; Ibadhi in religion, Ghāfiri in politics. Settled in Western Hajar, at Sa'abah, and Bilād esh-Shahūm in Wādi Beni Ghāfir.

179. *Beni Shakeil* (sing. *Shakeili*).

A tribe of the Oman Sultanate ; Ghāfiri in politics, Ibadhi in religion ; numbering 4,000 souls. Settled in Western Hajar at Umm Himār, Mīdān, Meihah, Sani, Maqham, Qariyah, and Heil Ghāfah ; in Dhāhirah at 'Āridh ; in Oman Proper at Bahlah, Bisya, and Seifam. Their tribal capital is Seifam.

180. *Shakhārīyīn* (sing. *Shakhāri*).

A small tribe of the Oman Sultanate ; Ghāfiri in politics and Ibadhi in religion. Settled at Felej esh-Shakhārīyīn in Wādi 'Āhin in Western Hajar. They number 250 souls, and are allies of the Maqābīl.

181. *Shakūr* (sing. *Shakūri*).

A tribe of the Oman Sultanate ; Ghāfiri in politics and Ibadhi in religion ; numbering 500 souls ; settled in Dhank town in Dhāhirah.

182. *Beni Shameili* (sing. *Shameili*).

A tribe of Trucial Oman, numbering 1,000 souls, originally Jews ; settled at Shimil in Sīr, except for a few who are nomads among the Shihūh in Ru'ūs el-Jibāl. They are now closely connected with the Shihūh, and may almost be regarded as a section of that tribe. At Shimil, which they entirely possess, they have 4,000 date-palms and some livestock, including 50 camels.

183. *Shamūs* (sing. *Shamsi*).

A tribe of the Oman Sultanate, numbering 100 souls. Ibadhi in religion, Hināwi in politics ; settled at Khōr el-Hamām in Saham.

184. *Shāqōsh*.

These form a section of the Beni Ma'in of Qishm, and there are only a few of them. They are Ghāfiri in politics, and reside at 'Ajmān town where they have 12 houses. They are pearl-divers and fishermen.

185. *Sharā'inah* (sing. *Sharā'ini*).

A tribe of the Oman Sultanate, numbering 800 souls ; Ghāfiri in politics and Ibadhi in religion ; settled in Western Hajar at Beit el-Qarn in Wādi Fara' and 'Ain esh-Sharā'inah in Wādi Beni Ghāfir. They are allies of the Beni Kelbān.

186. *Sharqiyīn* (sing. *Sharqi*).

A tribe of Trucial Oman, numbering 7,000 souls, residing entirely within the jurisdiction of the Sheikh of Shārjah, found chiefly in the Shameilīyah tract and in Wādi Hām, but also in smaller numbers in the Jiri plain and in the Ras el-Kheimah district. Their principal settlements are at Bidyah (300 houses), Fujeirah (150), Gharfah (100), Marbah (100), Qareyyah (100), Qidfa' (100), and Ghāllah (70).

About half of those residing in the Shameilīyah tract have succeeded (1905), under the leadership of the Sheikh of Fujeirah, in casting off the yoke of Shārjah. Their independence has not, however, been recognized by the British Government.

The occupations of the Sharqiyīn are various. They cultivate, fish, dive for pearls, trade with Muscat and Sīb, grow dates and keep live-stock according to the facilities of the place where they reside. Their sections are Hafeitāt, Yamāmahah, Hamūdiyīn. Some claim the Jalājilah, Mahārizah, and Zahūm as sections of the Sharqiyīn, but this is not certain.

187. *Shawāfi'* (sing. *Shāfa'i*).

A tribe of the Oman Sultanate, numbering 400 souls; Ghāfiri in politics and Ibadhi in religion; settled at 'Aweināt in Sohār in Bātinah.

188. *Shawāmis* (sing. *Shāmisi*).

A tribe of the Oman Sultanate, numbering 100 souls; Hināwi in politics; settled at Habbās in Wādi Semā'il. There is a Shawāmis section of the Na'īm and also of the Beni Keleib.

189. *Shihūh* (sing. *Shihhi*).

A peculiar tribe who inhabit the Oman promontory from Bei'ah northwards on the eastern coast, and from Khōr Khuweir northwards on the western coast. The whole of the Ru'ūs el-Jibāl district is in their occupation, except a few villages belonging to the Dhahūriyīn. They also occupy Sha'am, Ghalīlah, and Khōr Khuweir in the Shārjah principality and the village of Heil in Sīr, and are found, too, at Saham town in Bātinah. Their number is roughly estimated at 21,500 souls, of whom 14,500 are on the coast and 7,000 in the interior. Those of the interior are described as Bedouin, but some of them have houses built of loose stone. The Shihūh are almost entirely included in the dominions of the Sultan of Oman. Only about 2,000 of those on the coast and a few of those in the interior are resident in Trucial Oman.

There is little intercourse between the coastal Shihūh and their brethren of the interior, many of whom never come down to the coast. The former are chiefly engaged in diving and wading for pearls and in fishing, though they keep goats and grow dates where they can: their food is chiefly fish which they catch, rice which they import, and dates which they grow and import. The latter are engaged in tending large flocks of goats and in agriculture. With irrigation from natural reservoirs in the hills they grow almost all the grain they want for home consumption. They live on the produce of their cultivation and their goats, and have nothing to do with the sea.

In religion the Shihūh, both settled and nomad, are mostly Shafeis, but from and including Sha'am and Bei'ah southwards on either side of the promontory they are now Hanbalis. As a tribe they are still imperfect Moslems; those in the hills have no mosques and are extremely superstitious, still offering sacrifices to the mountain Jinns. From the time of the Wahabite movement, however, they have given up worshipping at Mazārs or tombs of holy men.

There are two languages spoken amongst them. The more general is the Shihhi dialect of Arabic; the other is an Iranian dialect chiefly spoken at Kumzār, and on Lārak Island by the Kumāzirah subdivision of the Beni Shateir and their Dhahūriyīn relations. From this fact it is inferred that the Shihūh are a composite tribe, originally Arab, but now containing some Persian elements.

There are two main divisions of the tribe:

1. Beni Hadīyah.
2. Beni Shateir.

The coastal Shihūh regard only these two main divisions and classify themselves in detail by villages and not by sub-sections. In the interior the classification is by sub-sections.

The following is the classification by sections among the nomad Shihūh of the interior:

1. *Beni Hadiyah.*

Section.	Families.	Location.
Beni Mohammed 'Abeid	100	The hills above Khasab
Beni 'Ali. Two clans of equal strength: (1) Ahl 'Aqabah; (2) Beni Yideid	200	Hills above Līmah
Beni Ibrāhīm	70	Hills near Ras el-Kheimah
Khanāzirah	100	Seih above Khasab
Beni Ham Mazyūd	? 100	Hills east of Khasab

2. *Beni Shateir.*

Beni el-Asamm	70	Musellih near Līmah
Ahl Heil	70	Maskin el-Heil near Bei'ah
Beni Hamūd	35	Khabbah or Heir above Līmah
Beni Kanar	70	Kaneif and Sahwah
Khanābilah	90	Raudhah, Salhad, Maqaleili
Mahābīb	60	Various places in hills
Maqādihah	60	Saqattah near Dibah
Ahl Muqām	100	Khabbah Sōt near Dibah
Beni Murrah	35	Sal'alah and Ghīshah
Qayyāshah	100	Beighūt
Sā'ad	100	Hills above Ghalīlah
Ahl Salhad	180	Salhad and Khabbah Sōt

190. *Shiyābinah* (sing. *Sheibāni*).

A small Bedouin tribe of the Oman Sultanate, numbering 150 souls; Ghāfiri in politics and Ibadhi in religion; ranging round Adam in Oman Proper.

191. *Shiyādi* (sing. *Shīdi*).

A tribe of the Oman Sultanate, numbering 300 souls; Sunni in religion, Hināwi in politics; settled at Sār esh-Shiyādi, Ghuweisah, and Abu Dhurūs in Saham in Bātinah.

192. *Shurūj* or *Sharūq* (sing. *Sharji*).

A tribe of the Oman Sultanate, numbering 650 souls; Ibadhi in religion, Hināwi in politics; settled at Samad town and Mukhtari' in Wādi 'Andām in Sharqīyah.

193. *Shweihiyīn*.

A tribe of Trucial Oman, numbering 2,050 souls; Hanbali in religion; settled in Dibai and Shārjah towns. The bulk of them are in Shārjah, where they have 400 houses.

194. *Beni Sinān* (sing. *Sināni*).

A tribe of the Oman Sultanate, numbering 1,500 souls; Ghāfiri in politics and Sunni in religion; settled at Quryāt and Sūr (Saneisalah) in the Eastern Hajar.

195. *Siyābiyīn* (sing. *Siyābi*).

A tribe of the Oman Sultanate, numbering 5,500 souls; Ghāfiri in politics and Ibadhi in religion; somewhat widely distributed, found chiefly in the Hajar and Muscat districts. Their tribal capital is Nafa'ah (300 houses) in Wādi Mansah; other principal settlements are Sib edh-Dhafar, Ghail ed-Dakk, Ghubrah, Dan, Bidbid, Mizra', Qurtā', Milayyinah, and 'Amqāt, all in Wādi Semā'il; Rissah and Seijāni in Wādi Seijāni; Felej Shirāh and Misfāh in Wādi Fara'; Khabbah in Wādi Khabbah; Ghubrat et-Tām in Wādi Tāyīn; Sa'āl, Ghāllah, and both Misfāhs in Wādi Bōshar. Mareirāt, Jafnein, and Riseil in Wādi Riseil; Sīb and Barkah; in Bātinah and at Matrah. Those at Rissah belong to a section called Mubāsili.

Some of the Siyābiyīn are rich, but the tribe generally are not held in much repute. They are inclined to be friendly with the Beni Jābir and at enmity with the Nidābiyīn, Beni Battāsh, Beni 'Arābah, and Hadādabah. There are no genuine Bedouins among them.

196. *Beni Subh* (sing. *Subhi*).

A tribe of the Oman Sultanate, numbering 500 souls; Ghāfiri in politics and Ibadhi in religion; settled at Abyadh in Wādi Beni Kharūs in Western Hajar, and also in Oman Proper (not stated where).

197. *Sūdān* (sing. *Suweidi*).

A tribe of Trucial Oman, El-Qatar, and Bahrein; they are closely connected with the Kunūd, and their descent from Aswad el-Kindi—supposed to have been an immigrant from Yemen in the time of Mohammed—is generally admitted.

They number in all about 5,500 souls, of whom nearly 5,000 reside in the ports of Trucial Oman. They have 375 houses at Abu Dhabi town, 30 at Batīn, 250 at Dibai town, 300 at Shārjah town, 20 on Bu Mūsa Island in the Sheikhdom of Shārjah, 12 at 'Ajmān, 80 at Dōhah in Qatar, 10 at Hadd in Bahrein, and 49 on Sirri Island.

There is little to differentiate the Sūdān of Trucial Oman from the other tribes among whom they dwell; but those of Qatar are distinguished from most of their Sunni neighbours by being Hanābilah and not Muwālik.

Their two principal divisions are the Āl Ramdha and the Āl Sālmīn. They now live by dealing in and diving for pearls and other seafaring occupations.

198. *Suwālih* (sing. *Salhi*).

A tribe of the Oman Sultanate, numbering 600 souls; Sunni in religion and Hināwi in politics; settled at Suweiq in Bātinah.

199. *Suwāwifah* (sing. *Suwāfi*).

A tribe of the Oman Sultanate, numbering 1,500 souls; Hināwi in politics, except for those at Khabbah, who are Ghāfiri. They are settled in Eastern Hajar at Khabbah and Quryāt; in Sharqīyah at Sanā'u; in Dhāhirah at Saleif in Wādi el-'Ain.

200. *Teiwānīyah* (sing. *Teiwāni*).

A tribe of the Oman Sultanate, numbering 300 souls; Ibadhi in religion and Hināwi in politics. Settled at Muscat town and in Oman Proper at Nizwa.

201. *Tatimmaha* (sing. *Tamtami*).

A tribe of the Oman Sultanate, numbering 300 souls; Ibadhi in religion and Hināwi in politics. Settled at Misfāh and 'Awābi in Wādi Bōshar.

202. *Taneij* (sing. *Taneiji*).

A tribe of Trucial Oman, numbering 4,000 souls, Hanbali in religion and Ghāfiri in politics; 2,500 are settled at Rams (400 houses), Dheid (70), and Hamrīyah (30), and 1,500 are Bedouins ranging round Dheid.

Rams belongs exclusively to the Taneij. Their houses are mostly of mud and stone. The chief occupations of the settled portion of the tribe are fishing and pearl-diving. They have some date plantations two miles inland at Dhāyah.

203. *Thameirāt* (sing. *Thāmiri*).

A tribe of Trucial Oman, numbering 120, residing in Abu Dhabi town. They are reckoned among the Beni Yās.

204. *Al 'Umeir* (sing. *'Umeiri*).

A tribe of the Oman Sultanate, numbering 1,000 souls; Ghāfiri in politics and Ibadhi in religion; settled in Oman Proper at Izki, Birkat el-Mōz, and Mahyūl; also in Bātinah at Heil el-'Umeir, and Sīb.

205. *Beni 'Umr* (sing. *Ma'amari*).

A tribe of the Oman Sultanate, numbering 11,000 souls; Ghāfiri in politics and in religion partly Ibadhi and partly Sunni; settled in Western Hajar and Bātinah, with very few, if any, Bedouins attached to them. In Western Hajar they occupy the whole of the Wādi Beni 'Umr, a tributary of the Wādi el-Hāwāsinah, viz. Mijzi, Jahanāt, Rahbah, Heil Islāt, Farfār, Ghaiz, and Lihbān; also the following villages in Wādi Beni 'Umr el-Gharbi: Heil, Shuweimarah, 'Aqrabīyah, Rahab, Dhabyān, and Beidha; also Hībi in Wādi Sarrāmi.

In Bātinah their settlements are at Sīb, Ghadhfān, and Hadd in the sub-vilayet of Sohār, at Harmūl, Nabar, Asrār Beni 'Umr, Umm el-'Inah, and Hameirah in the sub-vilayet of Liwa; and at Bileidah in the sub-vilayet of Shinās. Other settlements are at Ghashab and Felej el-'Āli in Wādi Fara'; at Hayyāl in Wādi el-Kebīr; and at Shareijah in Jebel Akhdhar. Ghadhfān is their principal place in the north and Lihbān in the south.

They must not be confounded with a similarly named section of the Beni Battāsh.

They are always at feud with their neighbours the Hāwāsinah and the Maqābīl

206. *Beni Waheib* (sing. *Waheibi*).

A tribe of the Oman Sultanate, numbering 3,500 souls; Ibadhi in religion and Hināwi in politics; scattered over the Muscat district, and not elsewhere except at Daghmar and Quryāt (60 hours). In the Muscat district their settlements are: in Wādi Mijlās and its tributaries at La'bān (40 houses), Sālifah (30), Būlīdah (25), Habūbīyah (160), Mizra' Sumeir (20), Mizra' Baleil (15), Heithadh (30), Fayādh (20), and Heifal (15); in Wādi Maih and its tributaries, at Dhahr Sidrah (30), Tuyān Jahlūt (40), Sa'ādi (60), Maheidith (20), Rākil Milh (30), Mandharīyah (20), Mahā'il (25), Tawīlah (30), and Hājir (30); on the coast at Bistān (20), and Yiti (20); and at Wateyyah (6), Ruwi (25), and Muscat town (45).

Besides these settled members there are two sections of Bedouins viz. Kawāsib (25 families) and Shabūl (35 families).

207. Āl Wahībah (sing. Waheibi).

A very important tribe of the Sharqīyah and Ja'lān districts in the Oman Sultanate, almost entirely Bedouin, and enjoying at present (1905) a high position in the tribal system. They number about 13,000 souls. Ibadhi in religion and Hināwi in politics. The sedentary members occupy the villages of Sadeirah and Aflāj and part of the town of Mudheibi in the Baldān el-Habūs division of Sharqīyah ; they are found also on the SE. coast as far north as Ras Sheiblah (20 houses), and as far south as Ras Sarāb ; settlements of them exist at Majiz el-Wahībah (100) and Laghshībah (20) in Bātinah, at 'Adeibah (15) and Ghubrah (30) in Muscat ; and at Ghāllah (10) in Wādi Bōshar.

The Āl Wahībah are warlike, but though always ready to fight for plunder they are not unpleasant in ordinary dealings. They own the fastest camels in Oman and practically no date-groves or villages. This combination makes them most elusive enemies. They have a bitter feud with the Jannabah and sometimes among the Hikmān of Mahōt Parties of them regularly visit the Sheikh of Abu Dhabi and receive presents from him. The majority of the nomads are purely pastoral but a few on the SE. coast are expert fishermen.

They are divided into many sections under six large, but apparently nameless groups :

Groups of sections and fighting strength (1905).

Group I
'Asākirah
Barātamīn (60)
Hāl Bu Ghafeilah, 70
Āl Bu Hidai, 70
Aulād el-Jahāmah, 60
Hāl Khamīs, 60
Likānīn
Mabābisah
Madhākīr, 70
Hāl Mūnis, 60
Muwāfid
Beni Na'mān, 60
Shalālibah, 50
Aulād 'Umr, 80

Group II
'Asāsif. 100
Āl Badr, 100
Jahāfif, 80
Karāhinah
Hāl Bu Ma'mar
Mughā'irah, 200
Shuwālīl, 150
Suweid

Group III
Hatātimah
Madhāwirah, 200
Mufanaj
Hāl Muharram
Hāl Mushīn

Group IV
Hāl Hadām
Aulād el-Hindi
Jidālah, 200

Group V
Hāl Badr, 100
Yāl Gharīb
Hāl Hindi, 60
Hāl Mahāsib
Hāl Sinā'u

Group VI
Marāmihah, 250

208. Warūd (sing. Wardi).

A tribe of the Oman Sultanate, numbering 200 souls; Ibadhi in religion and Hināwi in politics, though formerly Ghāfiri ; settled at Samad in Sharqīyah and dependent on the Habūs.

209. *Washāhāt* (sing. *Washāhi*).

A tribe of the Oman Sultanate, numbering 850 souls; in religion, mostly Ibadhi, with some Shafei; in politics mostly Hināwi, with some Ghāfiris. Settled at Tameit, Mushabbah, and 'Ajīb in Wādi Hatta and at Aswad in Wādi el-Qōr.

210. *Ya'āqīb* (sing. *Ya'qūbi*).

A tribe of the Oman Sultanate, numbering 3,500 souls; of Yemeni origin, but now Ghāfiri in politics and Sunni in religion. Settled at 'Ibri, in Dhāhirah.

211. *Ya'āribah* (sing. *Ya'rabi*).

A tribe of the Oman Sultanate, numbering 800 souls; Ghāfiri in politics and Ibadhi in religion. Settled at Nakhl, Tuweyyah, Tīkhah, and Hazam. They were once important, and supplied the rulers of Oman from A.D. 1625 to 1744. They have no influence now.

212. *Yahāmidah* (sing. *Yahmadi*).

A tribe of the Oman Sultanate, numbering 300 souls; Ghāfiri in politics and Ibadhi in religion. Settled in Sohār town and Nakhl.

213. *Beni Yās.*

One of the most compact and powerful tribes of Trucial Oman; their range is practically co-extensive with the territories of the Sheikh of Abu Dhabi, the basis of whose power they are.

Nomad. The Beni Yās nomads, numbering about 2,000 souls, are all in the Abu Dhabi principality. Their favourite pastures are in Beinūnah, a tract of the Dhafrah district.

Settled. The non-nomads number in all about 12,000; of whom about 8,000 are settled in the Abu Dhabi principality, about 2,000 in Dibai territory, and the rest outside Oman, viz.: 1,200 in Hanjām Island, 600 in Bahrein, 200 on Tārūt Island, and over 100 in Qatar.

In Abu Dhabi town they number 2,800 souls, and in Dibai they occupy 440 houses. Here, on the coast, they are engaged in pearl-fishing and navigation.

Inland, in Dhafrah, they number 5,100 souls and hold all the permanent settlements. [The only other tribe to be seen in Dhafrah is the Mansūri (Manāsīr), and they only come to summer in the Līwah subdivision.] Here the Beni Yās are semi-civilized, living in huts of date-sticks and leaves, owning date plantations individually (not collectively as do the Manāsīr) and trading and corresponding with Abu Dhabi and even Dibai. Their main industry is date-growing, but some of them take a share in pearl-fishing and own a number of boats which are kept at Bandar Radeim, Khōr Mugheirah, and Bandar Mirfah. The pearl-fishers pay dues and the date-growers pay 2,500 dollars a year as agricultural taxes to the Abu Dhabi Sheikh. Although, at times, sections of the tribe in the principality have evinced a disposition to hive off (as did the Āl Bu Falāsah section who now live in Dibai), the tribe as a whole is well-affected and faithful to the Sheikh, and he is himself one of their number (Āl Bu Falāh section).

The Beni Yās are of the Hināwi political faction and differ from most of their neighbours in being, wherever they occur, Maliki Sunnis and not Hināwi. They had in 1905 no special relations of friendship or enmity with adjoining tribes; at that time the following were their tribal sections :

Sections.	Sub-sections.
Āl Falāh	Āl Saʻdūn.
Āl Bu Falāh (the Sheikh of Abu Dhabi belongs to this section).	
Āl Bu Falāsah	Mijardah. Rawāshid. Yideiwāt or Līdeiwāt.
Āl Bu Hamīr.	
Hawāmil.	
Mahāribah.	
Mazāriʻ.	
Qaneisāt.	
Qasal.	
Qubeisāt.	
Qumzān.	
Rumeithāt.	
Sabā'is.	
Beni Shikr.	
Āl Sultān.	

A few others not definitely ascertained.

214. *Zaʻāb* (sing. *Zaʻābi*).

A tribe of Oman, numbering 4,500 souls, of whom 3,300 are in Trucial Oman and 1,200 in the Sultanate. They are Hanbali in religion and Hināwi in politics; settled at Jezīrat el-Hamra (500 houses), and Khōr Kalba (150) in the Shārjah principality; at Saham town, Qasbiyat ez-Zaʻāb, Abu Dhurūs, and Bu Baqarah, in the Sultanate of Oman. Some of them own date-groves at the village of Khatt in the Jiri plain, and go there in the hot weather.

215. *Zafeit* (sing. *Zafeiti*).

A tribe of the Oman Sultanate numbering 250 souls, all Bedouins of the Dhāhirah district, Ghāfiri in politics and in religion Ibadhi.

216. *Zahūm* (sing. *Zahmi*).

A tribe of Trucial Oman, numbering 100 souls, settled at Sīji in Wādi Hām where they have 20 houses, 2,000 date-palms and some livestock. They are claimed by some to belong to the Sharqiyīn, but their settlement at Sīji is separate and the claim has not been allowed.

217. *Zarrāf* (sing. *Zarrāfi*).

A tribe of the Oman Sultanate, numbering 200 souls, Ghāfiri in politics and Sunni in religion, settled at Arbaq and Shateifi in the Muscat district. They are merchants and sailors.

218. *Zatūt* (sing. *Zutti*).

A non-Arab tribe of Oman, numbering 1,000 souls, settled in various parts, chiefly at Bireimi, Muscat town, Matrah and Nakhl. They are generally Ibadhi in religion and apparently have a language of their own. Some say they are a branch of the Sulubba, others connect them with the Indian Jāts. They marry among themselves and are farriers, goldsmiths, blacksmiths, armourers, carpenters, pedlars. Their women dance for payment but are not immoral. The levirate law obtains among them. They are despised but not molested by the Arabs, who value them for their services.

219. *Beni Zīd* (sing. *Zīdi*).

A tribe of the Oman Sultanate, numbering 1,000 souls, Ibadhi in religion and Hināwi in politics; settled at Fida in Wādi Dhank in Dhāhirah.

220. *Zikāwinah* (sing. *Zikwāni*).

A tribe of the Oman Sultanate numbering 300 souls; Ibadhi in religion and Hināwi in politics; settled at Samad in Sharqīyah.

SEDENTARY TRIBES OF THE CENTRE

1. 'A'id.

SETTLED members of 'A'īd are reported at Hareimlah in 'Āridh, and at 'Adhār, Dilam, Suleimīyah (or Salāmīyah), and Yemāmah in Kharj, where they form the principal non-Bedouin tribe of the district.

2. Anazah.

Communities of this important group (see p. 104) are found in the following places in Nejd: (a) in 'Āridh, at Barrah, Hareimlah and Malham in Mahmal; at Bātin esh-Shuyūkh, Manfūhah and Riyādh in Wādi Hanīfah; and at Dhrumah (Ifqahha tribe), and the villages of Mizāhmīyah and Rōdhah in the Dhrumah district; (b) in Harīq, at Harīq town (Hazāzinah sub-tribe of the Ruweilah) and Mufeijir (same sub-tribe); (c) in Hautah, at Hautah town and Hilwah, at both of which places they are of the Dā'ūd tribe; (d) in Aflāj, at Raudhah (Ijdeimāt tribe); (e) in Sedeir, at Dākhilah (Āl Bu Rabā' tribe), Dhalmah ('Askar tribe), Harmah, Ijwei, Janūbīyah, Khīs, Mejma' ('Askar and Haweidi tribes), Ruweidhah, Samnān near Zilfi (Haweishān tribe), and Tuweim; (f) in Qasīm, at Aneizah, Boreidah, Dhalfa'ah, Dharās, 'Ain Ibn-Faheid, Ghāf near Boreidah, Khabrah, Khadhar, Mureid Seyyid, Quseibah, Rass, Raudhat er-Rubei'a, Seib, Shahībīyah, Shiqqah, Ta'ammīyah, Watāt and Wathāl. In the Wādi Sebei', Anazah are reported at Khurmah and Raudhah, and they are also said to be found in Kharj.

In Jebel Shammar settled Anazah live in Beidha Nethīl (?), Ghazālah, and Jauf el-'Amr.

3. Ashrāf.

A few settlements of Ashrāf from the Hejaz (cf. p. 157 f.), are found in Nejd in the following places : in Harīq, at Na'ām ; in Aflāj, at Leilah and Seih ; in Wadyān Dawāsir, at Sabhah.

4. Ateibah.

Communities of Ateibah (see p. 125) exist in 'Āridh, at Banbān, Barrah, and Rghabah ; in Sedeir, at Ilaqah, Iqlah, and Zilfi ; in Qasīm, at Qasr ibn-'Aqeyyil, Athlah, Basr, Bukeirīyah, Ahlab ed-Dūd, 'Ain Ibn-Faheid, Ghāf, Ghammāsh, Heid, Jan'i, Mudhnib (?), Nafi, Quwei'ah, Seib, and Wudhākh.

5. Buqūm.

This tribe, which is intimately connected with the Sebei' and Sahul (see p. 130), is said to be represented among the inhabitants of the villages of Rumadān and Turabah in the district of Wādi Sebei'.

6. Dawāsir.

This widely diffused tribe, which has almost ceased to be Bedouin (see p. 131), is settled in various districts of Nejd; the Saleyyil and Wādi Dawāsir divisions of Wadyān Dawāsir belong almost entirely to them. In Aflāj they occupy the following places: Badī', Haddār, Hamar, Kharfah, Marwān, Rajeijīyah, Raudhah, Wasīt, and Wuseilah. In 'Āridh, Dawāsir are found in the following places in Mahmal: Bīr, Dqalah, Hasi, Jarīnah, Malham, Sufurrah, and Thādiq; and in Wādi Hanīfah at 'Ammārīyah, Dar'īyah, and Manfūhah; they also occur in Dhrumah and Mizāhmīyah. Their settlements in Kharj are at Dilam, Suleimīyah, and Yemāmah; in Harīq-Hautah at Harīq town, Hautah town, and Hilwah; in Woshm, at Marāt; in Sedeir, at 'Audah, Ghāt, Hasūn, Jalājil, Ma'āshibah, Raudhah, Ruweidhah, and Zilfi; in Qasīm, at Hatān, Huweilān, Quwei'ah, and Shamāsīyah. In the district of Wādi Sebei' and Wādi Turabah, they are settled in Hazam, Khurmah, Raudhah, Rumadān, and Suweyyid.

Beyond the limits of Nejd, Dawāsir are found in great numbers in Bahrein, whither they immigrated in 1845, after first settling in Zakhnunīyah Island. Offshoots of this community are found in the Persian coast-district of Dashtistān, in Chāh Kūtah and its dependent villages, and at the village of Jazīrah in Bushire harbour. A few households are also settled at Dōhah in Qatar, and in Koweit town.

It is possible that the Āl Breik are not to be regarded as a main tribe of the Dawāsir, since by some authorities they are classified in the Misā'irah group. In the following table of the Dawāsir only those clans are included whose places of settlement have been ascertained.

DAWĀSIR

Tribe.	Sub-Tribe.	Clan.
ĀL BREIK, at Nuweimah		
ĀL HASAN	'Ammār	'Ajlān (or 'Ajālīn), at Leilah in Aflāj.
		Buras (or Āl Abu Ras), at Leilah.
		Huqbān, at Raudhah and Wāsit in Aflāj; at Kamidah in Wadyān Dawāsir.
		Idghamah, at Rajeijīyah in Aflāj.
		Ishkarah, at Badī', Hamar and Wuseilah in Aflāj; at Dārsah in Wādi Dawāsir. The clan includes two families known as the Āl Bu 'Ali and Harāthmah.
		Māna', at Aseil in Wadyān Dawāsir; at Leilah.
		Mubārak, at Raudhah.
		Qainān, one of the largest clans of the 'Ammar; settlements not ascertained.
		Sa'd, at Aseil.
		Sukhābirah, at Badī'.
	Farjān	'Arfaj, at Wuseilah.
		Badrāni, at Bir in 'Āridh.
		Bidārīn (possibly to be identified with Badrāni), at Jalājil and Zilfi in Sedeir.
		Hamdān, at Leilah.
		Jadhālīn, at Leilah.
MAKHĀRĪB or MAKHĀRĪM, at Ma'talah in Wādi Dawāsir and elsewhere.		

Tribe.	Sub-Tribes.	Sub-Tribes (cont.).
MISĀ'IRAH	*Al Abu el-Hasan*, at Quweiz in Wadyān Dawāsir. *Al Bu Sabbā'*, at Nazwah in Wadyān Dawāsir. *Al Rishdān*, at Ruweisah in Wādi Dawāsir. *Hanābijah*, at Bilād el-Hanābijah in Wādi Dawāsir.	*Inteifāt*, at Haddar in Aflāj. *Sharāfah*, at Sabhah and Thamāmīyah in Wādi Dawāsir. *'Uweidhāt*, at Thamāmīyah. *'Uweimir*, at Huweizah in Wādi Dawāsir.
RIJBĀN, at Dām in Wadyān Dawāsir and elsewhere.	*Khatātibah*, at Muqābil in Wādi Dawāsir.	
SUHABAH		
WIDĀ'ĪN	*'Areimah*, at Bilād Al Hāmid in Wādi Dawāsir. *Dawwās*, at Mathnah in Sāleyyil. *Al Dhuwayyān*, at Bilād Āl Dhuwayyān and Khataijān in Saleyyil. *Farrāj*, at Kheirān in Saleyyil. *Al Hāmid*, at Bilād Āl Hāmid in Wādi Dawāsir. *Al Haneish*, at Dahlah in Saleyyil. *Hijji*, at Tamnah in Saleyyil; at Leilah in Aflāj. *Al 'Isa*, at Thādiq in 'Āridh. *Jibārin* (or *Al Jābir*) at Leilah.	*Khadhrān* (owners of Shutbah in Aflāj, but have not permanently settled there). *Khamāsīn*, at Mishrif in Wādi Dawāsir. *Midbal* (or Midābilah), at Dhrumah in 'Āridh. *Al Mohammed*, at Bilād Āl Mohammed in Saleyyil. *Al Nāhish*, at Fara'ah in Wādi Dawāsir. *Al Suweilim*, at Thādiq in 'Āridh; at Muqābil in Saleyyil. *'Umūr*, at Kabkābīyah and Tamrah in Saleyyil. *Walāmin*, at Nafjān in Wādi Dawāsir.

7. Fadhūl.

This tribe, connected by vague tradition with the Beni Lām, is represented in the following parts of Nejd : in 'Āridh, at Bīr, Jarīnah, Mahriqah, Malham (Fadhl and Kathīr sub-tribes), Malqa, 'Audah, and Dhrumah ; in Harīq, at Harīq town ; in Hautah, at Hautah town (Āl Tālib and Kathrān sub-tribes) ; in Aflāj, at 'Amār (Mugheirah sub-tribe), Leilah, Raudhah (Mugheirah sub-tribe), and Umm Shinādhir ; in Sedeir, at 'Asheirah, 'Attār, Mejma' (Fadhl and Kathīr sub-tribes), Tuweim and Zilfi. The Fadhūl are a tribe of considerable size, but they do not appear to be found outside the limits of Nejd.

8. Beni Hajar.

Small settlements of Beni Hajar, now altogether unconnected with the Bedouin tribe of that name (see p. 141), occur in Aflāj at Wuseilah, and in 'Āridh at Hareimlah and Thādiq. Arabs claiming to be Beni Hajar are found on the Persian coast, e.g. in the Rūd-hilleh district.

9. Harb.

Settled members of this tribe (see p. 123) are found in 'Āridh at Rghabah, in the Wādi es-Sirr at Barrūd, and in Sedeir at Samnān near

Zilfi. Some inhabitants of villages in Qasīm claim to be of Harb descent, especially at Basr, Bukeirīyah, 'Ain Ibn Faheid, Hamar, Hilālīyah, Jau'i, Mureid Seyyid, Nabhānīyah, Qaryah, Quwei'ah, Sheihīyah, Shiqqah, Subeih, and Ummahāt ez-Ziyābah.

10. *Hawāzin.*

In Jebel Shammar at Jauf, Beidha Nethīl, Sakākah and Teima, and in Nejd at Ghāt (in Sedeir) are settled inhabitants of this name, whose position has given rise to discussion. They would appear to be of Hawāzin descent, though members of the Huteim and Harb tribes; but their connexion with the Hawāzin of Koweit is still a matter of uncertainty (see p. 146).

11. *Huteim.*

Settled Huteim are said to dwell at Ghazālah, and Mustajiddah in Jebel Shammar, and at Hāyat, between Mustajiddah and Kheibar. In the Wādi es-Sirr they are reported at 'Ayūn es-Suweina' and Feidhah. The tribe is closely related to the Sherārāt (see p. 145).

12. *Beni Khadhīr.*

This name is used to describe a large body of inferior non-Arab tribes in Nejd, who cultivate the soil for Arab masters; they seldom own land themselves, but the Qasīm, who are Beni Khadir, are said to do so at Seih in Aflāj. Beni Khadhīr are settled in the following places: in 'Āridh, at Hareimlah, Jarīnah, Malham (Hadhaid, Hamadāt, Muhārib and Marshūd tribes), Rghabah, Salbūkh, Sedūs and Thādiq (Rabeyya, Jidā'ah, Mizei'al, and Jamei'ah tribes); in Mahmal, and at Jabeilah, Malqa, 'Ammārīyah, Ilb, 'Audah, Dar'īyah, 'Araj, Bātin esh-Shuyūkh, Riyādh, Manfūhah, Masni and Hā'ir on Wādi Hanīfah; in Kharj, at 'Adhār, Dilam, Na'ajān and Suleimīyah; in Harīq, at Harīq town and Mufeijir; in Hautah, at Hautah town, Hilwah, Quwei, and Wuseitah; in Aflāj, at 'Amār, Badī', Haddār, Haradhah, Kharfah, Leilah, Rajeijīyah, Raudhah, Seih, Shutbah, Stārah, Wāsit, and Wuseilah; in Sedeir, at 'Asheirah, 'Attār, 'Audah, Dākhilah, Ghāt, Harmah, Hasūn, Hautah, Jalājil, Janūbīyah, Khatāmah, Khīs, Mejma', Raudhah, Ruweidhah, Tameir, Tuweim and Zilfi (Beni 'Atij and Natāqah tribes). Beni Khadhīr are also said to be settled at Quwei'īyah in the south-western desert.

13. *Beni Khālid.*

Allusion has already been made to the widely-scattered settlements of this tribe (see pp. 139–40); the following are localities in which their presence is reported in Nejd: in 'Āridh, at Malham (Qammāz sub-tribe); in Sedeir, at Zilfi (Dūshān and Hamrān sub-tribes); in Qasīm, at Aneizah, Quseibah, and perhaps at Khabb and Qisei'ah; at Quwei'īyah in the south-western desert there are said to be members of a sub-tribe known as 'Arāfah. In the following table of the settled Beni Khālid, which is not exhaustive, sub-tribes and clans are included from the Gulf Coast ; for the nomadic sections of the tribe see p. 140.

BENI KHĀLID

Sub-Tribe.	Clan.	
'AMA'IR	Dawāwdah	A few at Yasrah in Bahrein and at 'Anik in the Qatīf Oasis.
	Al Hasan	A few in the islands of Musallamīyah and Jinnah.
	Al Khālid	On Musallamīyah Island ; the Sheikh of this clan is the Paramount Chief of the tribe.
	Al Razin	On Musallamīyah Island.
	Al Shāhīn	On Jinnah Island.
AL SUBEIH	Al Bū 'Ainein	Only in Qatar and Bahrein ; they are pearl-divers, pearl-merchants, and boatmen, and are now practically a separate tribe.
	Dhaheirāt	At Qasr Āl Subeih in Hasa.
	Had-hūd	At Qasr Al Subeih.
	Hameidāt	In Qatar and Bahrein ; they are now practically a separate tribe.
	Al Katab	In Hasa.
'ARAFAH		Reported at Quwei'īyah.
DŪSHAN		At Zilfi.
HAMRĀN		At Zilfi.
AL JABŪR		Half-settled, at Jishshah in the Hasa Oasis.
MUHASHĪR		Some on Musallamīyah ; a few at Koweit ; others (half-settled) at 'Anik in the Qatīf Oasis.
AL MIQDAM		At Kalābīyah in the Hasa Oasis.
QAMMAZ		At Malham.

14. *Muteir*.

Though the Muteir are essentially nomadic (see p. 138), communities are reported in the following localities of Nejd : in 'Āridh, at Dhrumah (of a sub-tribe called Nafīsah, said to belong to the Braih) ; in Woshm, at Jareifah ; in Sedeir, at 'Asheirah. Some of the inhabitants are said to be of Muteir blood in the following places in Qasīm, which district may perhaps be regarded as their principal seat : Bukhā'irīyah, Buteinnīyat, Ghāf near Boreidah, Hatān, Khabb, Khabb el-Qabar, Khudheirah, Mureid Seyyid, Rafi'ah, Raudhat el-Mahanna, Ta'ammiyah, Ummahāt ez-Ziyābah, Wahtān, and Qasr Zeid.

Muteir are also said to inhabit villages in the Wādi el-Mīyah tract of the Hasa province.

15. *Negroes*.

Full-blooded negroes dwell in some numbers in Jauf el-'Amr, and at Huweyyat beyond the western borders of Jebel Shammar. At Hāyat, also beyond the border, are about 100 houses of negroes and half-castes. In the southern districts of Nejd a strong infusion of negro blood is reported, and there are said to be many full negroes, especially in Aflāj and Wadyān Dawāsir.

16. *Qahtān.*

In the Central South this tribe is almost entirely nomadic (see p. 131), but communities of reputed Qahtān blood are ascribed to the following places in Nejd: in 'Āridh, at Malqa and Manfūhah; in Hautah, at Hautah town; in Sedeir, at Mejma', Raudhah, Zahlūlah, and Zilfi; in Qasīm, at Basr and Wahtān (Hatān); in SW. Nejd, at Quwei'īyah and Sha'arah.

17. *Sahul.*

The Sahul, connected with the Sebei', and possibly only a sub-tribe (see p. 130), are now more settled than nomadic. They are reported in the following places in Nejd: in 'Āridh, at Barrah, Malham, and Dhrumah; in Kharj, at Suleimīyah and Yemāmah; in Harīq, at Harīq town; in Hautah, at Hautah town; in Aflāj, at Harādhah ('Anājīd sub-tribe) and Stārah (Qubābinah sub-tribe).

18. *Sebei'.*

The home of this tribe is in the Wādi Sebei', between Woshm and N. Asir (see p. 130), but settled communities are widely distributed in Nejd, where they are found in the following places: (*a*) in 'Āridh, at 'Aweinidh, Barrah, Ghiyānah, Hareimlah, Hizwah, Malham (Āl Ibn Rashīd sub-tribe), Rghabah, Salbūkh, Sedūs, all in the Mahmal region; at 'Ammārīyah, Ilb, 'Audah, 'Arjah, Masāni', Hā'ir, all on Wādi Hanīfah, and at Dhrumah (Āl 'Abd el-'Azīz sub-tribe); (*b*) in Kharj, at Dilam and Yemāmah; (*c*) in Harīq, at Harīq town (Kathlān sub-tribe); (*d*) in Hautah, at Hautah town and Hilwah (Kathlān sub-tribe); (*e*) in Aflāj, at Leilah (Rashūl sub-tribe); (*f*) in Woshm, at Shaqrah (Sūdah sub-tribe) and Watheithīyah; (*g*) in Sedeir, at 'Attār, Ghāt, Harmah, Hautah, Khatāmah, Khīs, Mejma', and Ruweidhah; and (*h*) in Qasīm, at 'Aneizah, 'Aushazīyah (Matārīd sub-tribe), Badāyah and Wādi.

19. *Shammar.*

The Shammar are a powerful nomadic tribe (see p. 132), but they have settled communities in the following places in Jebel Shammar: 'Alaq (Aslam tribe), 'Aqdah, Beidha Nethīl, Bida', Feid, Ghazālah, Hā'il, Hafeinah, Hafnah, Jadhāmīyah, Kehāfah (Mas'ūd sub-tribe of the Aslam), Laqītah, Mūqaq, Mustajiddah, 'Odheim, Qasr er-Rabei'īyah, Sab'ān (a sub-tribe of the Aslam), Tābah, Teima, and Waqīd. In the Nefūd, Shammar are settled in Qana, and there are permanent military posts at the wells of Trobah and Hayyanīyah. In Nejd, inhabitants of reputed Shammar blood are found in the following places: in Qasīm, at 'Ayūn, Buteiniyāt, Ahlab ed-Dūd, Hamar, Qasr Sa'īd, Shiqqah, and Tanūmah ; and in Sedeir, at 'Areirah, Artawīyah, Athlah, 'Attār (Qidārah section) and Zilfi.

20. Sherārāt.

The Sherārāt, who are related to the Huteim (see p. 144), form a proportion of the population at Jauf el-'Amr.

21. Sunnā'

The Sunnā', forming the smiths' caste, are sometimes found settled in the villages of Nejd (see p. 145).

22. Beni Tamīm.

The Beni Tamīm (see above, p. 136), now entirely a settled tribe, form an important element of the fixed population in Nejd and Jebel Shammar ; in Qasīm the people may perhaps be assumed to be Tamīm where the presence of other tribes is not reported. Communities and smaller groups of Beni Tamīm are found in the following places in Nejd : in 'Āridh, at 'Ammārīyah, 'Arjah, Dar'īyah, Dhrumah, Hareimlah, Hizwah, Mahriqah, Manfūhah, Masāni', Riyādh, Sedūs, Sufurrah, Thādiq ; in Kharj, at 'Adhār, Dilam, Na'ajān, and Suleimīyah ; in Hautah, at Hilwah and Quwei' ; in Sedeir, at 'Asheirah, 'Audah, Dākhilah, Dhalmah, Harmah, Hasūn, Hautah, Jalājil, Janubīyah, Khatāmah, Khīs, Raudhah, Ruweidhah, Tameir, Tuweim, and Wushei ; in Qasīm, at Aneizah, Boreidah, and in all the oases ; in the Wādi es-Sirr, at Feidhah.

In Jebel Shammar, the presence of Beni Tamīm is noted at 'Alaq, Qasr el-'Ashruwāt, Feid, Mustajiddah, Sab'ān, Samīrah, and Sileimi.

The tribal organization of the Beni Tamīm has tended to disappear in the process of settlement. The principal sub-tribes, with their lines of distribution, are enumerated in the following table, which must not, however, be regarded as exhaustive :

BENI TAMIM

Sub-Tribes.	Sub-Tribes.	Sub-Tribes.
Husein.	Mājid.	Thamārah.
At Hautah in Sedeir.	At Thādiq in 'Āridh.	At Mejma'.
'Abd el-Jabbār.	Ibn Mu'ammar.	Tuweim.
At Dhalmah in Sedeir.	At Sedūs in 'Āridh.	In Kharj.
Al Mādhi.	Nawāsir.	Wahabah.
At Harmah and Raudhah in Sedeir.	At Dhrumah in 'Āridh ; at Hautah and Mejma' in Sedeir.	At Mejma'.
		Wahūb.
		At Riyādh.

23. Beni Zeid.

This settled tribe, connected by some authorities with the Beni Tamīm and by others with the Dawāsir, is found at Shaqrah and Washeiqir in Woshm. In the Wādi Turabah it is represented at Khurmah and Rumadān ; communities also occur at Quwei'īyah and Sha'arah in the tract between the above districts.

INDEX

In the alphabetical order of names no account is taken of the article (el, ed, edh, en, er, es, esh, et, eth, ez), of the prefixes ibn, bint, nor of the titles Bey, Emir, Effendi, Hajj, Pasha, Seyyid, Sheikh, Sultan.

Names commencing with Ahl, Āl, Beni, Jebel, Khōr, and Wādi will be found under the specific name.

Figures in heavy type indicate the page on which the fullest description of personalities will be found.

A

'Abābid tribe, 278.
'Abad, Yahya, 223.
'Abādilah family, genealogical tree, 7.
   el-'Abādilah, Hāzir, **14.**
'Abādilah, tribe of Oman, 278.
'Abādilah Ashrāf, clan, 3, 33, 157, 159.
'Abbād tribe, 151.
'Abbās house, 58, 59.
'Abbās, 'Ali ibn, **48,** 52.
   el-Faleiji, **91.**
'Abbās, Ibn, **24,** 29, 50, 160, 213, 236.
'Abbās, Mansūr ibn, **15.**
'Abbās, Sa'īd, **58,** 59.
'Abd ibn 'Abdullah, 159.
   el-'Āl ibn Ahmed el-Idrīs, 25.
   el-'Āl, Senussi ibn, 25.
   el-'Āl el-Idrīsi, Mustafa ibn, **24,** 25, 68.
   el-'Azīm house, 55.
   el-'Azīm, 'Ali, 55.
   el-'Azīz I, 95.
   el-'Azīz ibn 'Abd er-Rahmān [Ibn Sa'ūd], Emir of Nejd, 77, **84,** 86-8, 91, 93, 126, 138.
   el-'Azīz ibn 'Abdullah, 94.
   el-'Azīz, Hāmid ibn, **74.**
   el-'Azīz Hamūd, 91.
   el-'Azīz, Mit'ab ibn, 88, 92.
   el-'Azīz ibn Mohammed, 7, 25, 83, 87.
   el-'Azīz ibn Musheit, **24,** 26, 37, 39, 40, 188, 189, 205-7.
   el-'Azīz, Nūrah bint, **90,** 91-3.
   el-'Azīz, Sa'd ibn, 4.
   el-'Azīz ibn Sa'īd, **91.**
   el-'Azīz ibn Sālim ibn Bedr, **78.**
   el-'Azīz ibn Sa'ūd, 87, 140.
   el-'Azīz, Sa'ūd ibn : *see* Sa'ūd ibn 'Abd el-'Azīz.
   el-'Azīz ibn Suleim, 95.
   el-'Azīz Tayyār, **10.**
   el-'Azīz, Tūrki ibn, **86,** 87.
   el-Bāri ibn Ahmed, **44,** 47, 57.
   el-Emīr tribe, 28.
   el-Hādi, **26,** 189, 190.
   el-Hādi, Hasan, **65.**
   el-Hakk ibn Ahmed el-Idrīs, 25.
   el-Hamīd, Sultan, 9, 96, 220.
   el-Hamīd ibn Shā'if ibn Seif, **68,** 250.

'Abd, Husein ibn, 206, 207.
   ibn Ibrāhīm, 206, 207.
   el-Jebba ibn Ahmed el-Idrīs, 25.
   el-Kerīm house, 49, 53, 81.
   el-Kerīm, 'Abd el-Muhsin ibn, 134, 136.
   el-Kerīm ibn Fadl ibn 'Ali, **61,** 62, 246.
   el-Kerīm, Mohammed ibn, 134, 136.
   el-Khalīfah, **26.**
   el-Latīf Mandīl, **78.**
   el-Latīf Mizeini, **10,** 20.
   el-Majīd Fadl, **61,** 62.
   el-Mālik el-Khotib, **10.**
'Abd, Mohammed ibn, 174.
   el-Muhsin ibn 'Abd el-Kerīm, 134, 136.
   el-Muhsin ibn Assim, **10.**
   el-Muhsin el-Barakāti, 7, **8.**
   el-Muhsin el-Hadhdhāl, Fahd Bey ibn, **98,** 107, 110.
   el-Muhsin es-Sedeiri, Sa'd ibn, **96.**
   el-Muhsin Subhi, **10.**
   el-Mu'īn ibn 'Aun, Mohammed ibn, 3, 7, 40, 211.
   el-Mutallib family, 157.
   el-Mutallib, 7, 8.
   en-Nābi Kal Ewāz, **78.**
   en-Nebi Husein, **62,** 262.
   el-Qādir house, 46, 59.
   el-Qādir, 'Abdullah, **46.**
   el-Qādir, Mohammed ibn, **35.**
   el-Qādir Ambāri, **46.**
   el-Qādir el-Mekkawi, **62.**
   el-Qādir Sheibi, **19.**
   er-Rahīm, **74.**
   er-Rahmān, of Jiddah, **13.**
   er-Rahmān, of Ru'eis, **10.**
   er-Rahmān, 'Abd er-Razzāq ibn, **63.**
   er-Rahmān ibn Ahmed, 53.
   er-Rahmān, Ahmed ibn, 13, 52.
   er-Rahmān ibn 'Ā'idh, Nāsir ibn, 180, 182.
   er-Rahmān ibn 'Ā'idh, 'Abdullah ibn, 182.
   er-Rahmān ibn 'Ā'idh, 'A'idh ibn, 182.
   er-Rahmān ibn 'Ā'idh, Mohammed ibn, 182.
   er-Rahmān 'Arār ibn Nāsir, **30.**
   er-Rahmān Ba Juneid, **10.**
   er-Rahmān Bishna'q, **10.**

336

'Abd er-Rahmān el-Bura', Husein ibn, 223.
  er-Rahmān ibn Feisāl, 78, 86, 87.
  er-Rahmān ibn Husein, 263.
  er-Rahmān, Husein ibn, 263.
  er-Rahmān ibn Husein, Mohammed ibn, 54.
  er-Rahmān, Lutf ibn, 53.
  er-Rahmān, Mohammed ibn, 30, 35, 47, 59, 87, 171, 172, 180.
  er-Rahmān ibn Mufarrih, 182.
  er-Rahmān Ba Muharrem el-Hadhrami, 27.
  er-Rahmān ibn el-Qādhi, 182.
  er-Rahmān ibn Qasim, 63, 271.
  er-Rahmān, Sa'd ibn, 4, 84, 85, 87.
  er-Rahmān esh-Shāmi, Mohammed, 55.
  er-Rahmān esh-Shatri, 276.
  er-Ra'ūf Jamjūm, 10.
  er-Razzāq ibn 'Abd er-Rahmān, 63.
  er-Ru'b Shabein, 62.
  Sa'd 'Abd Nāsir 'Adāwi, 37.
Abd, Sa'īd ibn, 26, 39, 205, 207.
  el-Wadūd, 46.
  el-Wahhāb ibn Mohammed, 25.
  el-Wahhāb, Mohammed ibn, 83.
  el-Wahīd federation, 68.
  el-Wahīd Sultanate, 67, 68, 247.
'Abdah tribe, 95, 135.
  el-'Abdal, 'Abdu 'Ali, 51.
'Abdāli country, 61.
  Sultans, genealogical tree, 62.
  tribe, 61, 246.
'Abdallah Ba 'Imād, 270.
'Abdillah ibn Mohammed, 3, 7.
'Abdīyah bint 'Amr, 26, 36, 170.
'Abdu, 'Ali ibn, 28, 176.
  'Ali el-'Abdal, 51.
  Mohammed, 50.
'Abdu, Mohammed ibn, 28, 35, 176.
'Abd el-Majid, Sultan, 47
'Abdullah family, 253.
'Abdullah, 'Abd ibn, 159.
'Abdullah, 'Abd el-'Azīz ibn, 94.
  'Abd el-Qādir, 46.
  ibn 'Abd er-Rahmān ibn 'Ā'idh, 182.
  Abu Zenādah, 9.
  ibn Ahmed, 273.
  ibn 'Ali, 7, 26, 182.
'Abdullah, 'Ali ibn, of Bahrein, 79.
'Abdullah, 'Ali ibn, of the Juheinah, 7, 12, 15.
  'Ali Ridha (Riza), 9.
  ibn 'Askar, 94.
  Ba Haidarah, Fadl ibn, 64, 248.
  Ba Jubeir, 34.
  el-Badri, 46, 52.
  Badweilān, 30.
'Abdullah, Beni, tribe, 85.
  Beshir, 241.
  Pasha el-Bōni, 13, 46, 237, 239, 242.
  ed-Dīn ibn Ahmed, 66, 264.
  el-Gharbi, 228.
  ibn Ghazeilān, 46, 232.
  ibn Hamūd, 26, 207, 209, 210.
'Abdullah, Hasan, 239.
  ibn Hujahri, 160.
  ibn Humeid es-Sālimi, 71, 78, 81.
  ibn Husein, 3, 4, 5, 7, 23, 264.
  ibn 'Īsa, 63, 75.
  ibn el-Jalāl, 94.

'Abdullah ibn Jasīm eth-Thāni, 74.
  Jibāla, 53.
  Kauzi, 242.
  el-Khalīfah, 94.
  el-Kheimri, Sālim ibn, 81.
'Abdullah, Khōr, 76, 77.
  el-Khotib, Mohammed ibn, 52.
  el-Ma'an, 221.
  el-Mansūri, 45, 46.
  Mashhur, 224.
  el-Metā'ibah, 152.
  ibn Mifdhil, 181.
  ibn Milhem, 26, 163.
  ibn Mufarrih, 26, 180, 182.
  ibn Mughāthil, 28, 182.
  ibn Muhsin, 46, 58, 272.
'Abdullah, Muhsin ibn, 57, 234.
'Abdullah, Muqbil, 67, 265.
  ibn Muzerqah, 196.
  en-Nahāri, 240.
  ibn Nāsir, 93.
  ibn Nimshah, 183.
  el-Qasīm, 46.
  ibn Rashīd, 83, 87.
  ibn Rashīd el-Hāshimi, 78.
  ibn Rashīd, Mohammed ibn, 87, 92.
'Abdullah, Sa'd, 240.
  ibn Sa'īd, 94.
'Abdullah, Sālih ibn, of the 'Amūdi, 273.
'Abdullah, Sālih ibn, of Bālhāf, 68, 247.
'Abdullah, Sālih ibn, of the Upper 'Aulaqi, 69, 253.
  ibn Sālim, 294.
  ibn Salmān, 94.
  ibn Sana, 208.
  Sarrāj (Sa Rāj), 9.
  ibn Sa'ūd, 83, 85, 87.
  Serāji, 53.
'Abdullah, Seyyid, 59, 60.
'Abdullah, Sheikh, 75.
  esh-Sherif, of Ibha, 33.
'Abdullah, Sherif, of Kaukebān, 53.
  et-Tarāf, 233.
  Tawā'd, 9.
  ibn Telāl, 92.
'Abdullah, Telāl ibn, 87, 92.
  ibn Thawāb, 10.
'Abdullah, Tūrki ibn, 87.
  ibn 'Ubeid, 92.
  ibn Zāmil, 94.
  Zawāwi, 9.
Abeid, Sheikh, 253.
Abela Effendi, 245.
'Ābid el-Emīr tribe, 173.
'Ābid, Mohammed, 15.
'Abidah ('Ābidah) tribe, 36, 39, 188, 189.
el-'Ābidīn, Zein, 41, 200.
Abiyān, 66.
Abraham, the arch-patriarch, 102 ; descendants of, 103.
'Abriyīn tribe, 278.
'Abs, Beni, tribe, 23, 41, 51, 159, 160.
'Abshān, 'Ali ibn ('Ali Ghālib Bey), 28, 163, 164.
'Absi, Āl, tribe, 220.
Abu 'Adullah, 'Awad, 253.
  Aftān, 178.
  Ahmed, Husein, 65, 255.
  'Ali, 'Amr, 248.
  'Ali, Husein, 263.
  'Allāmah, 27.

Abu 'Arīsh, 22, 23.
'Atanah, Beit-'ali, **31,** 215, 216.
'Awad, Mohammed 'Ali, **66,** 248.
Bekr family, 277.
Bekr Khukūr (or Shakir ?), **10.**
Bureiz, tribe, 117.
Dhabi Settlement, 73, 86.
Dhabi, Sheikh of, 82, 143, 287, 292, 304, 311, 323, 324.
Dharā', Lizām, 138.
Dūsah, Mohammed, 181, 182.
Fadhl, Umm Heithami, 268.
Fārid, Umm Rūsas, 256.
Halīm, **27,** 32, 179.
Hamid, Ahl 'Ali, 257.
Harbah, 232.
el-Hasan, Mohammed, 25.
Hashar, Tāhir, 177, 178.
Jābir family, **97.**
Jerīdah, **11.**
Khurfān, Ismā'īl, 175.
Manāwir el-Husein, Sālim, 153.
Mandīl Hasan, **32,** 167.
Matīr, **35,** 160, 161.
el-Mejd house, 59.
Meshkūr, Fā'iz, 101.
Mismār, **35,** 212, 213.
Misudah, Mijāli, 268.
Mu'ammed, Ibrāhīm, **33,** 210.
Muhsin, 'Ali, 256.
Nā'ib, 230.
Numej, Mohammed, 157, 158.
Nuweibah, Mohammed, 30, 36, **55,** 59, 193.
Radīyah, 174.
Ruheihah tribe, 117.
Sa'īd, 'Amr, 248.
Sa'īd Ferhān, **97.**
Salām, Mohammed, **35,** 190, 192.
Sālih Freh, **97.**
Sārah, Āl Abu, family, 180, 182.
Shiha, Mohammed, 50.
Shihah, Hādi, 221.
Sittah, sub-tribe, 99.
Tālib, 167.
Tarash, Mohammed, 166.
Tayy, 'Audah, 17.
Tayy, Mohammed, 118.
Tayy, sub-tribe, 117.
Thālib, Nāsir, **68,** 255.
Zenādah, 'Abdullah, **9.**
'Abūd, Husein ibn, 192.
'Abūd section of the Ateibah, 127.
'Adāwi, 'Abd Sa'd 'Abd Nāsir, 37.
Aden, 23, 34, 43, 48, 49, 52, 54, 61–9, 80.
British Resident at, 38, 56, 64, 274.
Government, 49, 55.
hinterland, 42, 44, 49.
Protectorate, tribes of the, 246–72.
Treaty, 63, 68, 69.
'Adi, Beni, tribe, 278.
'Adwān tribe, 149–51.
Aflāh tribe, 220.
Afrir, Ahl, tribe, 63.
Aftān, Abu, 178.
Āgha Khān, of Bombay, 301.
Aghbein tribal division, 114.
Ahamda section of the Beni Sālim, 14.
Ahdal house, 31, 44, **47.**
el-Ahdal, Ahmed, 47.
el-Ahdal, 'Ali, 47.

Ahim, Āl, sub-tribe, 230.
Ahl : *see under specific name.*
Ahlās, Beni, tribe, 220.
el-Ahlāsi, Nāsir Husein, 220.
Ahmed, 'Abd el-Bāri ibn, **44,** 47, 57.
Ahmed ibn 'Abd er-Rahmān, **13,** 52.
Ahmed, 'Abd er-Rahmān ibn, 53.
Ahmed, 'Abdullah ibn, 273.
Ahmed, 'Abdullah ed-Dīn ibn, 66, 264.
'Abdullah el-Mekki, **27,** 28.
el-Ahdal, 47.
ibn Ahmed, **53.**
ibn 'Ali, 25.
Ahmed, 'Ali ibn, 50.
ibn 'Ali, 'Ali ibn, 246.
Ahmed, Asad Dhān ibn, **12.**
ibn 'Awad Budus, **63.**
Ba Hārūn, **11.**
Ba Zā'za, **13.**
Dabwān, 230.
ed-Dahyāni, **47,** 235.
Fad'il, 51.
ibn Fadl, **61,** 62.
Fadl, 'Ali ibn, **61,** 62.
Fadl, Fadl ibn, **61,** 62.
Ahmed, Fātimah bint, 248.
Feizi Pasha, 42, 48, 49, 84, 222.
Hādi Thawāb, Yahya 'Ali ibn, **41,** 159, 160.
ibn Hāmid, **27,** 160.
Ahmed, Hasan ibn, **65.**
el-Hayyāni, 32, 200, 203.
el-Heij, Hādi ibn, 28, **51,** 159, 187, 243.
el-Hezāzi, 8.
Hidiyān, Ghālib ibn, **65.**
Himādi, 'Ali ibn, 52.
ibn Husein, **47,** 234, 264.
Ahmed, Husein ibn, of Hūth, 52.
Ahmed, Husein ibn, of Khartūm, 54.
Ahmed, Husein ibn, of Qufl, 57.
Ahmed, Husein ibn, of Shūghrah, **65,** 66, 264, 265.
(Hamād) ibn Ibrāhīm, 33, **79.**
el-Idrīs, 25.
el-Idrīs, 'Abd el-'Āl ibn, 22, 25.
el-Idrīs, 'Abd el-Hakk ibn, 25.
el-Idrīs, 'Abd el-Jebba ibn, 25.
el-Idrīs, Mohammed ibn, 22, 25.
Ahmed, 'Imād ibn, 270.
Ahmed, 'Īsa ibn, **80.**
Ahmed, Ismā'il ibn, 52.
ibn Jābir II, 77, 78.
Jāhiz, **47,** 53.
el-Jahwashi, Mohammed ibn, 202.
Janāh, **27,** 187.
el-Jans, 237.
Ahmed, Khālid ibn, **73.**
Bey Khobami, Seyyid Miralai, **47.**
Khobami, Seyyid, 47.
Mab'ūth el-Kibsi, 235.
el-Madani, 229.
ibn Mansūr el-Kerīmi, **11.**
Marwa'i, 51.
Masāwah, **27,** 179.
Ahmed, Mohammed ibn, of the Ja'dah tribe, 176.
Ahmed, Mohammed ibn, of the 'Umr tribe, 168.
ibn Mohammed Abu Toqeiqah, **11,** 19.

Ahmed ibn Mohammed el-Kaukebāni, 234.
    ibn Mufarrih, 180.
    ibn Mufraj, 201.
    ibn Muhsin, **63**, 69, 263.
    el-Mullah, **11**.
    ibn Muqbil el-Wada'i, 238.
    ibn Muta'āli, **27**, 32, 199-201.
    Muthanna, **63**.
    Na'mān, **47**, 48, 56, 229, 265.
    Na'mān, Mohammed ibn, 265.
    Nāsir, **48**.
    Nāsir er-Rasūl, **48**.
Ahmed, 'Omar ibn, 276.
    ibn el-Qādhi, 182.
    ibn Qādim, 275, 276.
    ibn el-Qasīm, **48**, 58, 235.
Ahmed, Rashīd ibn, **74**.
    Sāfi, **11**.
    ibn Sa'īd (of the Azd tribe), 70.
    Sa'īd, of Hābil es-Sabt, 270.
    ibn Sālih, 240.
Ahmed, Sālih ibn, 271.
Ahmed, Seyyid, 22, 54, **60**, 241.
    ibn Sha'r, 186.
    esh-Sherā'i, 42.
    esh-Sherīf, **27**, 33.
    ibn Shiblān, 183.
    Sultān, 222.
    Tal'āt, **11**.
    ibn Tālib, Sālih ibn, **69**.
    et-Tarāf, Sa'd ibn, 233.
    Tewfik Pasha, **48**, 54.
    eth-Thanayyān, **94**.
    eth-Thāni, 75.
    ibn Tuqeiqah, 118.
    Umm Basūs, 270.
    ibn Umm Shi'bah, **27**, 181.
    Umm Tomi, 'Ali ibn, 269.
    Wahhās, 231.
    ibn Yahya, 46, **48**, 51.
Ahmed, Yahya ibn, of the Fadhā'il house, 57, **59**.
Ahmed, Yahya ibn, of the Jibāli house, 50.
Ahmed, Yahya ibn, of the Sherā'i house, **59**.
    Yahya Bahr, 47.
    ibn Yahya Fāri', **48**, 50, 228.
    Yahya Karāt, 50.
    Zeilah, **28**, 34.
Ahmednagar, 65, 66.
Ahnum, Wādi, sub-tribe, 50, 229.
Ahtalah, Ahl, tribe, 261.
'A'id tribe, 327.
Aida clan, 106.
'Ā'idh ibn 'Abd er-Rahmān ibn 'Ā'idh, 182.
    ibn 'Ali, 221.
    ibn Hasan, 195.
'Ā'idh, Hasan ibn 'Ali Mohammed ibn, 26, **32**.
    ibn Jabbār, **28**, 206, 208.
    Shuweit, 'Ali ibn, 230.
Aidin vilayet, 58.
'Ain, Wādi, 22, 243.
'Aish, 'Ali, 51.
'Ajalah, Sālih ibn, **40**, 171.
'Ajam, tribe of the Oman Sultanate, 278.
Ajam, Ahl, tribe of the Lower 'Aulaqi, 261.
'Ajārmah tribe, 151, 152.
'Ajeimi ibn Sa'dūn, 77, 79, 80, 88, **97**, 137.
'Ajeimi tribe, 99.
'Aji, Ibn, 173.
'Ajil, Ibn, 135.

'Ajmān, Ibn, 233.
'Ajmān tribe, 74, 77-80, 85, 96, 99, 140, 141.
Akaba, 17, 99.
Akābarah tribe, 273.
Akhdhar, Jebel, 71.
Āl : *see under specific name.*
'Alawi house, 51.
    ibn 'Ali, 269.
'Alawi, 'Ali ibn, **63**, 266, 267.
el-'Alawi, 'Ali ibn 'Abdullah ibn Sālim, **79**.
'Alawi, Fadl ibn, **64**.
'Alawi, Hasan, 50.
'Alawi tribe, 64, 67, 249.
'Alāyah, 34.
Aleppo, 97.
Alexandria, 13.
'Ali ibn 'Abbās, **48**, 52.
    el-'Abdal, 'Abdu, 51.
    'Abd el-'Azīm, 55.
    'Abd el-Qādir, Sālih Muhsin ibn, **19**.
    ibn 'Abdu, **28**, 176.
    ibn 'Abdullah, of the Juheinah, 7, **12**, 15.
    ibn 'Abdullah, of Bahrein, **79**.
'Ali, 'Abdullah ibn, 7, **26**, 182.
    ibn 'Abdullah ibn Sālim el-'Alawi, **79**.
    ibn 'Abshān ('Ali Ghālib Bey), **28**, 163, 164.
    Abu 'Awad, Mohammed ibn, **66**, 248.
    Abu Hamid, Ahl, 257.
    Abu Muhsin, 256.
    el-Ahdal, 47.
    ibn Ahmed, 50.
'Ali, Ahmed ibn, of Sabia, 25.
    ibn Ahmed ibn 'Ali, Sir, 246.
    ibn Ahmed Fadl, **61**, 62.
    ibn Ahmed Himādi, 52.
    ibn Ahmed Umm Tomi, 269.
'Ali, 'A'idh ibn, 221.
    ibn 'Ā'idh Shuweit, 230.
    'Aish, 51.
'Ali, Āl, tribe, 278.
    ibn 'Alawi, **63**, 266, 267.
'Ali, 'Alawi ibn, 269.
    ibn 'Ali es-Salāmi, 238.
    ibn 'Ali ez-Zindāni, **64**.
    'Amr, 251.
    el-Arhabi, 231.
    'Askar (Nāji), **63**, 67, 271.
    Ba Haidarah, **64**, 249.
    Ba Sālih Ba Rājih, 269.
    Ba Sālim, 270.
    ibn Badah, 94, **95**.
    Bedāwi, **28**, 222.
'Ali, Beni, tribe, 12, 279.
'Ali, Caliph, 3, 42, 157.
    Da'ām, 222.
    ed-Damaji, 223.
    ibn Dhāfir walad Dhāfir ibn Jāri, **28**, 212.
    Dhi'āb, Sultān ibn, 149, 151.
    Fad'il, 51.
    ibn Fayy, **29**, 185.
    Ghālib Bey : *see* 'Ali ibn 'Abshān.
    ibn el-Hādi, **49**, 58.
'Ali, Hādi, 245.
    Haidar Pasha (or Haidar 'Ali), **8-9, 11**.
    ibn Hamūd, **29**, 91, 93, 195, 196, 245.
    Harharah family, 270.
    ibn Hasan, 53.

'Ali, Hasan ibn, 25, 180, 182.
   ibn Hasan Abu Mejd, **59.**
   el-Hibshi, **11.**
   el-Himāzi, **59.**
   ibn Hizām, 224.
   Humādi, Fadl ibn, **64,** 265.
   ibn Husein, **5,** 6, 7.
'Ali, Husein ibn, of the 'Anazah, 221.
'Ali, Husein ibn, of Abu 'Arīsh, 22, 42.
'Ali, Husein ibn, Emir of Mecca : *see* Husein ibn 'Ali.
   ibn Huseini, 240.
'Ali, Ibn, of the 'Alaunah, **28.**
'Ali, Ibn, of the 'Abdah, 135.
   Ibrāhīm, 243.
'Ali, Ibrāhīm, 239.
   ibn Ismā'īl, Seyyid, **49,** 222.
   ibn Ismā'īl, Sherif, **49,** 53.
'Ali, Ismā'īl, 224.
   ibn 'Iteij, **29,** 206, 207.
   ibn Jabbār, **29,** 197.
'Ali, Jābir ibn, 92.
   Ja'far, **64.**
   Jibāla, 53.
   el-Khalīfah, 'Īsa ibn, **75,** 76, 78–80, 86.
   el-Khalīfah, Khālid ibn, **75.**
   ibn Khanfūr, **29,** 181.
   ibn Lāhik, 181, 182.
   Lāri, Mohammed, **15.**
   Latīfah, **12.**
'Ali, Lutf ibn, 53.
   ibn Ma'addi, **29,** 177, 178.
   ibn Mani, **64,** 265.
   el-Mansūr, 43, 45, 46.
   Maqla, **59.**
   Mauna es-Sakladi, 271.
   Ma'wad, 241.
   ibn Medīni, **29,** 34, 168.
   Midkorn, 202.
   Miqdād, 221, 222.
   ibn Mohammed, of the Balasmar tribe, **29,** 30.
   ibn Mohammed, of Hūth, 53.
   ibn Mohammed, of Madfa'ah, 165.
   ibn Mohammed, of Sabia, 25.
   ibn Mohammed ibn 'Abd el-Mu'īn, 7.
   ibn Mohammed ibn Ahmed, 22.
   ibn Mohammed ibn 'Ā'idh, Hasan ibn, 26, **32.**
   ibn Mohammed, Mohammed ibn, 25.
'Ali, Mohammed ibn, of the Ahl es-Sa'īdi, 248.
'Ali, Mohammed bin, of the Beni Bu 'Ali, 279.
'Ali, Mohammed ibn, of the Beni Kebīr, 171.
'Ali, Mohammed ibn, of the Ja'āfirah, **35,** 177.
   Mohammed Pasha, 33, 34.
   Mohammed, Ahl, tribe, 251.
   el-Morghāni, 22, 68.
   ibn Mubhi, **29,** 213.
   Muhsin Yahya, 235.
   ibn Muqdi, 176.
   Mūsa Khān, 71.
   Mustafa ibn Mohammed, 25.
   ibn el-Mutawakkil, 231.
   ibn Nāshir ibn Shā'if, **64,** 249.
   Nāsir el-Kamarāni, **49.**

'Ali, Nāsir ibn, 7, **8.**
   ibn Nāsir, 235.
   ibn 'Omar el-Ahdal, shrine of, 47.
   el-Qahm, **28,** 187.
'Ali, Qā'id ibn, 231.
   ibn Qasīm, 47, 51.
'Ali, Rahmah bint, 7.
   ibn Rā'ih, Mufti, **30,** 165.
   ibn Rashīd, 92.
   Ridha, 26, 170.
   ibn Rukwān, **30,** 194.
   Saghīr, 238.
   Sahil, 230.
   Sa'id Pasha, **49,** 54, 66, 67, 264.
   es-Salāmi, 'Ali ibn, 238.
   ibn Sālih, 227.
'Ali, Sālih ibn, 224, 230.
   ibn Sālih el-Hārithi, **79,** 80.
   ibn Seilah, 228.
'Ali, Seyyid, of the Jaraf tribe, 230.
'Ali, Seyyid, of Khamir, 54.
   esh-Shāmi, Mohammed ibn, **55,** 59.
   Sharkāsi, **12.**
   Shawi', 224.
   Sherā'i, Husein ibn, 52.
'Ali, Sherif, of Mecca, 11, 13, 20, 22, 127.
'Ali, Sherif, of Sa'dah, 58.
'Ali, Sherif, of San'ā, 59.
   ibn Suleimān esh-Sharqi, **97,** 111, 112.
'Ali, Suleimān ibn, **40,** 185, 186.
'Ali, Tahar ibn, **40,** 179.
   ibn Tāli', 198.
   Walad 'Ali ibn Murā'i, Mohammed ibn, **35,** 190, 191.
   Yahya el-Yemeni, **49,** 221, 234.
   ibn Yahya Fāri', 228.
   Yūsuf ibn Sālim el-Māliki, **11.**
   ibn Zāmil, 93.
   ez-Zindāni, 'Ali ibn, **64.**
   Allāmah, Abu, **27.**
'Alqam el-'Alein, tribe, 35.
   el-Hūl tribe, 160, 161.
   es-Sahil tribe, 27.
'Alwi sub-tribe, 77, 95.
el-'Alyān, Shadhli, 11, **19.**
'Amā'ir sub-tribe, 331.
'Amān el-Muqaddam, **12.**
'Amārāt tribe, 98, 99, 106, 107, 110.
Amarīyīn tribe, 50, 220.
Ambāri, 'Abd el-Qādir, **46.**
el-Amīn Bahr, 50.
Amīn el-Mekki, Mohammed Effendi, **16.**
Amīn Mohammed Pasha, 40.
Amīri tribe, 63, 68, 69, 249, 250.
'Ammān, Arabs of, independent tribes, 55, 153.
'Ammar, Ahl, tribe, 221.
'Ammar, Āl, tribe, 221.
'Amr, 'Abdīyah bint, **26,** 36, 170.
   Abu 'Ali, 248.
   Abu Sa'īd, 248.
   Akhu 'Abdīyah, Mohammed ibn, 170.
'Amr, 'Ali, 251.
'Amr, Beni, Asir tribe, 40, 161.
'Amr, Beni, section of the Harb, 5, 13, 18, 123, 124.
'Amr, Mohammed ibn, 26, **36.**
'Amr, Sālim ibn, **69,** 271.
'Amrān, 43.
'Amūdi tribe, 13, 273.
'Anazah ibn Asad, 104.

Anazah : Northern tribes, 4, 104-11 ;
  settled tribe of the Centre, 327 ;
  Yemen tribe, 221.
Aneizah, 89, 94-6.
Anīs tribe, 221, 222.
Ansāri, Barakāt, **13.**
Anwar Eshji, **12.**
'Anz, Dabwān ibn, 230.
'Aqad, Juheish ibn, **34,** 177.
'Aqrabi tribe, 64, 248.
'Arab (Makhlukh), Ras, 16.
Arab Party, 21.
'Arābah, Beni, tribe, 280
el-'Arabi, Mohammed, 25.
el-A'rāf, 'Othmān Pasha, 55.
'Arafah sub-tribe, 331.
'Arā'if : *see* Aulād Sa'ūd.
'Arāqi, 81.
'Arār house, **30.**
'Arār ibn Jāzi, 117, 118.
  ibn Nāsir, 193.
  ibn Nāsir, 'Abd er-Rahmān, **30.**
'Arfu'a : *see* Refa'i.
Argo (Arju), Island, 23, 24.
Arhab sub-tribe, 231.
el-Arhabi, 'Ali, 231.
'Āridh, 84.
'Ārif 'Areifān, Mohammed ibn, **16,** 18.
'Arjalah, Beni, sub-tribe, 229.
'Arjalah, Qasim, 229.
'Arjalah, Sālih, 229.
Armān, Ahl (division of the Oleh confedera
  tion), 266, 267, 268.
'Arubeij, Sa'd ibn, **18.**
'Arwāl, Ahl, tribe, 268.
'Asābili, 31, 40
Asad, 'Anazah ibn, 104.
Asad Dhān ibn Ahmed, **12.**
As'af, Sheikh, 19.
'Asākir clans, 255.
'Aseidān, Sa'īd ibn, **40,** 216, 217.
Asfān, 14.
'Asheish, Husein, 230.
A'shish house, 52.
Ashrāf clans, 9, 10, 13-18, 20, 40, 44, 49,
  157, 158, 327.
Ashūr, Mahmūd, **15.**
'Āsi ibn Ferhān, 134, 136.
'Asimah, Āl, sub-tribe, 29, 195, 196.
Asir, 5, 8, 22-42.
  district, tribes of the, 159-219.
  north-east borderland tribes, 130.
Asiri Qahtān tribes, 30, 36.
'Askar house, 94.
'Askar, 'Abdullah ibn, **94.**
'Askar (Nājib), 'Ali, **63,** 67, 271.
'Askar, Muhsin, 63, **67,** 271.
'Askar, Yahya ibn, 271.
'Asla, Āl, sub-tribe, 26, 28.
Aslam section of the Shammar, 89, 95, 135
Aslam, Beni, tribe, 28, 222.
Assīm, 'Abd el-Muhsin ibn, **10.**
'Atas Hadhrami, **12.**
Ateibah tribe, 3-5, 10, 14, 19, 84-6, 125-7,
  327.
'Ateifāt sub-tribe, 100, 109.
Athālif, 33.
Atif Jābir, Sālim Sālih ibn, 271.
'Atīfi sub-tribe, 269.
Atik, Ahl, tribe, 257.
'Atīyah, Beni, tribe, 119.

'Atīyah, Mohammed ibn, 119.
Atyuk, Mohammed, **66.**
'Audah, 117, 118.
'Audah Abu Tayy, 17.
'Audillah tribe, 62, 67, 68, 250, 251.
'Auf sub-tribe, 5, 10, 12-15, 124, 125.
'Auf, Beni, tribe, 280.
Aulād Āl Umm Husein, 197.
  el-'Alaunah, tribe, 28, 173, 174.
  el-Emīr Mohammed ibn 'A'idh family,
    39, 180, 182, 216.
  Hadīd tribe, 288.
  Kāsib tribe, 299.
  Kuleib tribe, 301.
  Mahriz tribe, 303.
  ibn Mufarrih clan, 26, 27, 180-2.
  Sa'ūd (or 'Arā'if), 84, 85, **86.**
'Aulaqi tribes, 44, 48, 55, 62, 65, 69, 257-61.
'Aulaqi (tribal confederation), 251-61,
'Aulaqi, Upper, Sultan of, 63, 250-6, 263.
'Aun er-Rafiq, 7,'31, 157.
Ausat family, 225.
'Awābi, 71.
Awābthah tribe, 273.
'Awad Abu 'Abdullah, 253.
  Budus, Ahmed ibn, **63.**
'Awad, Sir Ghālib ibn, **66.**
  ibn Haidarah, **64,** 267.
'Awad, " Jemadar ", 66.
  el-Ka'aiti, Ghālib ibn, 274, 277.
  el-Ka'aiti, Husein ibn, 277.
  el-Ka'aiti, Manassar ibn, 277.
  el-Ka'aiti, 'Omar ibn, **66,** 277.
'Awad, Mohammed ibn, 183.
'Awad, Sālih ibn, **69.**
  Salīmi, **12.**
el-'Awaj, Sālih, 233.
'Awajah, 47.
'Awāmir, Hadhramaut tribe, 273.
  Oman tribe, 280.
'Awānāt tribe, 281.
Aweni, Ahl, tribe, 267.
'Awwād ibn Kallāb, 152.
'Awwam, Beni, tribe, 222.
el-'Ayāshi, Jābir, **15.**
Ayyam, 46.
el-Ayyam, Qasīm, house of, 46.
Azah house, 52.
Azani, Ahl, tribe, 262.
Azd tribe, 70.
'Azīz, Āl (or 'Ayāl), tribe, 281.
'Azīz, Beni, tribe, 223.
'Azīz, Mansūr ibn, 36, 182.
'Azīz, Mohammed ibn, **36,** 181.
'Azīz ibn Musheit, **30,** 35, 171, 172.
Azraqi section of the Amīri, 65.
Azza, Sherifah, 157.
'Azzām, Beni, tribe, 281.
'Azzām, Walad, 144.

B

Ba Feyyād, Ahl, tribe, 255.
  Hadah, Ahl, tribe, 255.
  Haidar, Mohammed Sa'īd, **37.**
  Haidarah, 'Ali, **64,** 249.
  Hakīm, **49.**
  Hārūn, Ahmed, **11.**
  'Imād, 'Abdallah, 270.
  Jubeir, 'Abdullah, 34.

Ba Jubeir, Mohammed, 34.
Jubeir, 'Omar, 34.
Jubeir, Sālim, 34.
Jubeir, firm of, **34**, 38.
Juneid, 'Abd er-Rahmān, **10**.
Kāzim tribe, 259.
Krad, Ahl, tribe, 260.
Kunnāshi, Ahl, tribe, 267.
La Rāj, **12**.
Leil, Ahl (division of the Oleh confederation), 64, 266, 267.
Muharrem el-Hadhrami, 'Abd er-Rahmān, **27**.
Nāji' Hadhrami house, **13**.
Nāsir, Murshid, 270.
Ras, Ahl, tribe, 258.
Sabrein Hadhrami, **13**.
Sālih Ba Rājih, 'Ali, 269.
Sālim, 'Ali, 270.
Selāhah, Ahl, tribe, 260.
Thobān, Ahl, tribe, 258.
Zā'za house, **13**.
Zā'za, Ahmed, **13**.
Badā'ah tribe, 281.
Badah, 'Ali ibn, 94, **95**.
Badar, Āl, tribe, 282.
Badri house, 46, 52.
el-Badri, 'Abdullah, **46,** 52.
Badweilān, 'Abdullah, 30.
Badweilān, Bukr, 30.
Badweilān, firm of, **30**.
Baghdad, 76, 89, 98.
Bahan, Ahl, tribe, 261.
Bahārinah tribe, 282.
Bahlah, 81.
Bahr Ibn Sekeinah tribe, 38, 162, 201.
Bahrān, Mash'ad ibn, **34,** 169.
Bahrān, Sheikh, **30,** 215.
Bahrein, 75, 76, 78–80, 86, 96.
Ruler of, **75.**
Bahri, Beni, tribe, 282.
Bahtīn, 3.
Bairām Bey, **49.**
Bājil, Kaimmakam of, 223.
Bakhīt, Murzut ibn, 175.
Bakri, Ibn, **30,** 179.
Bal Hārith tribe, 63, 69, 255, 262, 263.
Balahmar tribe, 28, 162–4.
Balaksah, Sabt, **68.**
Balasmar tribe, 29, 30, 164, 165.
Bal'aryān tribe, 164.
Bālhāf Sultanate, 68, 247, 275.
Baliana, 20.
Balūchi (or Balūsh) tribe, 282.
Balūs, 32.
Bamar, Sālim, 273.
Bandar Shuweikh, 76.
Zobeir, 76.
Barak, Ahl, tribes, 32, 36, 165–7.
el-Barak, Hāmid Ibag 'Alawi, 68.
el-Barak, Mas'ūd, **55,** 226, 227.
Barakāt Ansāri, **13.**
ibn Mohammed Abu Numej, 158.
el-Barakāti, 'Abd el-Muhsin, 7, **8.**
Barghāsh ibn Hamūd, 137.
ibn Sa'īd ibn Sultān, 72.
et-Tuwālah, Dhāri ibn, **95.**
Barkah, 71, 72.
Barrīyah tribe, 138, 139.
Bāshir el-Farūj, 153.
el-Turmān, 153.

Basra, 76, 80, 86, 89, 97.
Battāsh, Beni, tribe, 70, 72, 81, 283.
Battāsh, Derwīsh, 269.
Bawārih tribe, 284.
Bayāsirah tribe, 284.
Bedāwi, 'Ali, **28,** 222.
el-Bedāwi, Ghālib, **13.**
el-Bedāwi, Mohammed 'Ali, 12, 13, **15,** 121.
Bedr ibn Telāl, 92.
Bedu, Ahl, tribe, 261.
Bedūr, tribe, 99.
Beersheba, 98.
Behari, Wādi, 63.
Beida Sultanate, 66, 262.
district, 44.
tribe, 62, 262.
Beihān, Sherif of, 54, 63, 255.
tribe, 69, 262, 263.
Beihān ed-Daulah, 66.
Beirut, 94.
Beishi, Āl, 63.
Beit-'ali Abu 'Atanah, **31,** 215, 216.
Beit el-Faqīh, 56, 59.
el-Faqīh, Seyyids of, **50.**
el-Felej, 71.
Jashīsh, 50.
Sherāf ed-Dīn family, 234.
el-Beit, Sherif, 276.
Bekhīt, Sheikh, 159.
Bekīl tribe, 44, 52, 231–3. See Hāshid wa Bekīl.
Bekr, Abu, family, 277.
Belā'ir, tribe, 29, 33, 34, 167, 168.
Belqa district, 149–53.
Belqawīyah tribe, 149–53.
Beneyton, M., 56.
Beni : see under specific name.
Berqah section of the Ateibah, 126, 127.
Beshīr, 'Abdullah, 241.
Bidāh tribe, 284.
Bidbid, 71.
Bidūwāt tribe, 284.
Bijad, Beni, sub-tribe, 40, 205, 206, 208.
Billi tribe, 4, 5, 20, 119, 120.
Bir 'Ali, 69.
el-Māshi, 15.
Raha, 12.
Birk, Ahl, section of the Beni Hilāl, 28, 35.
Birkān tribe, 251.
Bīshah, 5, 11, 34, 41.
Bisharra family, **97,** 115.
Bīshat ibn Salīm sub-tribe, 35, 190, 191.
Bishna'q, 'Abd er-Rahmān, **10.**
Bishr, Beni, tribe, 26, 36, 89, 106, 189, 190.
Bombay Government, 65.
el-Bōni, 'Abdullah Pasha, **46,** 237, 239, 242.
Boreidah, 84, 89, 91, 94, 95.
Bōshar, Āl, tribe, 284.
Breik, Āl, tribe, 328.
British Government, 9, 71, 74, 75, 80, 86.
navy, 73, 74.
troops, 74, 77, 79.
Bruhīmi, sub-tribe, 269.
Bu Ahmed, Husein, 258.
'Ali, Beni, tribe, 71, 279.
'Amīm, Āl, tribe, 280.
Bekr, Ahl, tribe, 71.
Bekr ibn Nāsir, 257.
Bul, Ahl, tribe, 261.
Felāsah clan, 73.

Bu Hasan, Beni, tribe, 290.
'Isa, Āl, tribe, 294.
Kelbi, Āl, tribe, 299.
Khareiban, Āl, section of the Na'īm, 308.
Maheir, Āl, tribe, 302.
Qarein, Āl, tribe, 310.
Rasheid, Āl, tribe, 312.
Sa'īd, Āl, tribe, 70, 315.
Sālih, Manāsir, 252.
Shāmis, Āl, section of the Na'īm, 308.
Tahif, Ahl, tribe, 251.
el-Bukheit, Nahār, 151.
Bukr Badweilān, 30.
el-Hādhin, Ahl, tribe, 251.
Bulqarn esh-Shām, tribe, 34, 169.
el-Yemen, tribe, 35, 169.
Bunder ibn Telāl, 92.
Bunyar, Ahl, tribe, 62, 262.
Buqūm tribe, 130, 327.
Bura' tribe, 223.
Burt, Husein, 222.
Buti ibn Suheil, 73.
Butūn tribe, 138.

C

Cairo, 22, 41, 83, 87, 94.
Canning, Lord, 70.
Caprotti, Giuseppe, **50**.
Christian tribes of the Kerak-Shōbak district, 155.
Coccali, Demetrius, **50**.
Committee of Union and Progress, 6, 8, 9, 14.
Constantinople, 3, 6, 8, 9, 14, 28, 29, 31, 33, 35, 36, 38, 40, 43, 47, 76, 89, 91, 94, 96, 97.
Cox, Sir P., 77, 85.
Crawford, Captain, 38.
Cyrenaica, 22.

D

Da'ām, 'Ali, 222.
Dabwān, Ahmed, 230.
Dabwān ibn 'Anz, 230.
Daghmar, 71.
Daghshar, Sheikh, **50**, 220.
Dahāminah tribe, 285.
Dahāmishah sub-tribe, 99.
Dahāmsh, 113.
Dahanah desert, 77.
Daheilāt tribe, 285.
Dahlān, 47.
Dahr plateau, 62.
Dahrān, 30.
Dahyān, 55.
Dahyān, Ismā'īl ibn, 127.
ed-Dahyāni, Ahmed, **47**, 235.
Dajhid, Rājib ibn, 175.
Dakar, Ahl, tribe, 259.
Dalālil tribe, 285.
Damaj, Āl, tribe, 223.
ed-Damaji, 'Ali, 223.
Damascus, 6, 8, 17, 83, 89, 91, 94, 98-101.
Danān, Seyyids of, **50**.
Dara'īn section of the Ateibah, 127.
Darajah, 30.
Darāmikah tribe, 285.

Darān, Hamūd ibn, 127.
Darb, 33.
Dareija, 56.
Dar'īyah, 83.
Darū' tribe, 285.
Dawakah tribe, 286.
Dawākhilah, 3.
Dawāsir (Dosiri) tribe, 80, 85, 131, 328, 329.
Dāwud, Beni, tribe, 286.
Daya', Ahl, tribe, 259.
Dein tribe, 273.
Deiri, 69.
Deiri Muflahi section of the Amīri, 64, 65.
Demān, Ahl, tribe, 251.
Derwīsh Battāsh, 269.
ed-Derwish, Feisāl ibn Sultān, 77, **95**, 138, 139.
Derwīsh, Mustafa, **18**.
Derwīsh, Seyyid, **31**.
Dhaba, 11.
Dhabābihah tribe, 286.
Dhabi, Abu : see Abu Dhabi.
Dhāfir ibn Jāri, 'Ali Bey ibn Dhāfir Walad, **28**, 212.
Dhafīr (or Dhufīr) tribe, 88, 89, 99, 136-8.
Dhahbān, 24, 26.
Dhahi, 47.
Dhahūl tribe, 286.
Dhahūriyīn tribe, 286.
Dhakīr ibn Sha'r, **31**, 185, 186.
Dhāla, 67.
Emir of, 63, 65, 68, 69, 249.
Dhālim el-Hāshir, Beni, sub-tribe, 41, 199, 202.
Dhāmbari tribe, 69, 264.
Dhana Kuheil section of the Fed'ān, 98, 110.
Majīd section of the Fed'ān, 110.
Muslim tribes, 109.
'Ubeid tribes, 110.
Wā'il tribes, 110.
Dharāniq tribe : see Zaranik.
Dhāri ibn Barghāsh et-Tuwālah, **95**.
Dhāri ibn Fahd ibn 'Ubeid er-Rashīd, **90**, 92.
et-Tuwālah, 89, 135.
Dhawi Barakāt clan, 32, 158, 167.
Hasan clan, 36, 38, 158, 174, 175.
Surur tribe, 129, 158.
Zeid clan, 3, 8, 9, 11, 157.
Dhi'āb ibn Fahhād ibn Tūrki, **72**.
edh-Dhi'āb, Hasan, **14**.
Dhibin, 59.
Dhimrah, 62.
Dhōfir, 57.
Dhu Fāri' sub-tribe, 46, 48, 50, 226, 228.
Ghazeilān sub-tribe, 46.
Husein tribe, 47, 57, 234.
Mohammed sub-tribe, 47, 231, 232.
'Udhrah tribe, 55, 58, 226, 227.
Dhubi tribe, 68, 69, 271.
Dhufīr tribe : see Dhāfir.
Dhuh, Sa'd ibn, **39**, 178, 179.
Dhuleim, Ferdān ibn, **31**, 192.
Dhuleim, Mohammed ibn, 26, 30-2, **36**, 39, 187, 188, 191-3.
Dhuleim ibn Sha'r, 36, 193.
Dhur'ān, 49.
Kaimmakam of, 221.
Dhuwāhir section of the Beni Sālim, 15.
Dibai, 73, 74.
Diban, Seif, 269.

Didi house, 52.
ed-Dīn house, 53.
ed-Dīn, Beit Sherāf, family of, 234.
ed-Dīn Bey, Muhyi, **38.**
ed-Dīn, Hāfiz, house of, 53, 55, 59.
ed-Dīn el-Mutawakkil : *see* Yahya ibn Mohammed ed-Dīn.
Pasha, Sa'd, **9.**
Dirhem ibn Yahya Fāri', 48, **50,** 226, 228.
Diyān, Ahl, sub-tribe, 248.
Dōhah, 74, 75.
Doreihimi, 47.
Dosiri tribe : *see* Dawāsir.
Dubeini, sub-tribe, 269.
Dukhān, Sherif, 129.
Duleim, tribe, 97, 98, 111, 112.
ed-Dureib, Āl, tribe, 26, 36, 170.
Dūs, 39.
Dūshān sub-tribe, 331.

E

Egypt, 3, 4, 6, 8, 37, 42, 73, 83.
El : *see under specific name.*
Elhīn section of the Ahl Armān, 63, 267.
Elhīn, Ahl, section of the 'Audillah, 251.
Elias 'Osman, 245.
Emīn Pasha, Mohammed, 161.
Emīr esh-Shibi, 233, 235.
Enver Pasha, 6, 43.
Eritrea, Governor of, 50.
Eshji, Anwar, **12.**
Eshref Bey, 9, 89.
Euphrates caravan road, 97.
River, 98.
Valley, 89.
Ewāz, 'Abd en-Nābi Kal, **78.**

F

Fadhā'il house, 59.
Fadhl, Sir Ahmed, 249.
Fadhli tribe, 40, 64, 65, 264, 265.
Fadhūl tribe, 130, 329.
Fad'il, Ahmed, 51.
Fad'il, 'Ali, 51.
Fad'il, Yahya, 51.
Fadl, 'Abd el-Majīd, **61, 62.**
ibn 'Abdullah Ba Haidarah, **64,** 248.
ibn Ahmed Fadl, **61,** 62.
Fadl, Ahmed ibn, **61,** 62.
ibn 'Alawi, **64.**
ibn 'Ali, 'Abd el-Kerīm ibn, **61,** 62, 246.
ibn 'Ali Humādi, **64,** 265.
Fadl, Muhsin ibn, **61,** 62.
Faham, Beni, tribe, 127.
Fahd ibn 'Abd el-Muhsin el-Hadhdhāl, **98,** 107, 110.
Fahd, Feisāl ibn, **90,** 92.
ibn Jābir, 92.
Fahd, Sheikh, 141.
ibn 'Ubeid, 92.
Fahhād ibn Jābir, 92.
ibn Ma'mir, **95.**
Fahhād, Sheikh, 86.
ibn Tūrki, 72.
ibn Tūrki, Dhi'āb ibn, **72.**
ibn 'Ubeid, 92.

Fa'i ibn Hasan, 166.
Fā'iz Abu Meshkūr, Telāl ibn, 98, **101,** 113, 116.
ibn Sa'īd, **31,** 40, 211, 212.
Walad Fā'iz ibn Qurūm, Sa'īd ibn, 31, **40,** 211, 212.
Fā'iz, Yahya ibn, **41,** 207, 209.
ez-Zogheibi, **13.**
Fakhīrah, Mohammed Suleimān, **56.**
Fakkān, Khōr, settlement, 74.
el-Faleiji, 'Abbās, **91.**
Fantās, 78.
el-Fāqih, Beit, Seyyids of, **50.**
el-Faqīr, Shahāb, 109.
el-Farah, Tāhir Husein, 221.
Faraj ibn Sa'īd, **31,** 40, 211, 212.
Fārid family, 254.
Fārid, Muhsin ibn, **67,** 254, 257.
Fāris, Āl, tribe : *see* Fawāris.
Fāris, Mish'al ibn, 134.
Fāris ibn Sufūq, 134.
el-Farūj, Bāshir, 153.
Fasīkh, Hasan, 184.
Fathan, Ahl, tribe, 268.
Fat-hi ed-Dīn, Ibrāhīm ibn, **33.**
Fātimah bint Ahmed, 248.
bint Mohammed, 25, 90, 91, 96.
the Prophet's daughter, 3, 42, 118, 157.
Fātimah, Wādi, 3.
Fawāris (or Āl Fāris) tribe, 286.
Fawwāz ibn Telāl, **98,** 113, 114.
Fayy, 'Ali ibn, **29,** 185.
Fayy, Mohammed ibn, 176.
Fazāra' tribe, 287.
Fed'ān tribe, 106, 107, 110.
Feihān ibn Muheyya, 126.
el-Feir, Hamzah, **14.**
Feisāl, 'Abd er-Rahmān ibn, 78, **86,** 87.
Feisāl, Emir, 95, 96.
ibn Fahd, **90,** 92.
Feisāl, Hāmid ibn, **72.**
ibn Husein, **6,** 7, 9, 10, 15.
ibn Jābir, 92.
Feisāl, Mohammed ibn, **71,** 72, 87.
Feisāl, Nādir ibn, **71,** 72.
Feisāl, Sālim ibn, **72.**
Feisāl, Sa'ūd ibn, 86, 87.
ibn Sultān ed-Derwīsh, 77, **95,** 138, 139.
Feisāl, Teimur ibn, **71,** 72, 75, 79.
ibn Tūrki, 72, 78, 80–3, 87, 294.
Feisāl, Zeid ibn, 157.
Feizi Pasha, Ahmed, 42, 48, 49, 84, 222.
el-Fejīh, Sheikh, 195.
Ferdān ibn Dhuleim, **31,** 192.
Ferhān, Abu Sa'id, **97.**
Ferhān, 'Āsi ibn, 134, 136.
Ferhān, Humeidi ibn, 134.
Ferhān ibn Sufūq, 134.
Fez, 22.
Fileit, Beni, tribe, 287.
Firshah clan, 29.
Fitim ibn Muhsin, **13.**
French Government, 71.
Railway Survey, 56.
Fujeirah settlement, 74, 296.
el-Fuleiti, Humeid, **80.**
Fuqara sub-tribe, 105.
Furn, Sheikh, 10, **13.**
Futeisāt tribe, 287.
Fuzān, Husein ibn, **14.**

G

Garābih tribe, 223.
Gaza, 100.
Ghadīr-Rābugh, 5.
Ghafalah, Bedouin tribe of Trucial Oman, 287.
    tribe of Bātinah, 287.
Ghafeilāt tribe, 287.
Ghāfiri tribe, 82.
Ghai Melān, Ahl, tribe, 251.
Ghaili house, 54.
Ghaith, Beni, tribe, 287.
Ghalbah (Huseinīyah) house, 33.
Ghālib house, 58, 157.
Ghālib ibn Ahmed Hidiyān, Naqīb, **65**.
    ibn 'Awad, Sir, **66**.
    ibn 'Awad el-Ka'aiti, 274, 277.
    el-Bedāwi, **13**.
    el-Hādī, Imam, 42, 51.
Ghālib, Hamād ibn, **51**, 58.
    ibn Mit'ab el-Qanj, **98**, 114.
    ibn Muhsin 'Abd el-Kathīri, Mansūr ibn, **66**.
    Pasha, 5.
Ghālib, Sālih ibn, **66**.
Ghamar, Āl, sub-tribe, 37, 205, 206, 208.
Ghāmid country, 32, 40.
    tribe, 30, 35. 170–2.
Ghanamāt tribe, 153.
Ghaneim, Beni, sub-tribe, 17–19.
Ghaneim, Sa'd ibn, 122.
el-Ghānim, Khalīl, 174.
Ghannam, Shammakh ibn, Sheikh, **69**, 263.
el-Gharāmil, 'Ubeid, 96.
el-Gharbi, 'Abdullah, 228.
Gharbi, Seyyids of, **50**.
Ghāt, 96.
Ghawāmah tribe, 152.
Ghawānimah tribe, 28, 173, 174.
Ghawārib tribe, 287.
Ghaza ibn Shuqeir, 139.
el-Ghazalān, Mohammed, 87.
Ghazāzah, 98.
Ghazeilān, 'Abdullah ibn, **46**, 232.
Ghill, Beni, tribe, 223.
el-Ghindi, 'Izzet Bey, 23.
Ghiyādh tribe, 112.
Ghizah : see Saft el-Laban.
Ghōr, The, 101.
Ghufl tribal division, 114.
Ghurbān, 50, 58.
    Seyyids of, **50**.
Ghuzeil, Nāsir ibn, 129.
Goguyer, firm of, **79**.
Great Britain : see British Government.
Gulf Coast, 70–83.
Gwādar, 72.

H

Habashi, Āl, clan, 39, 179.
Habashi, Jebel, 48, 56.
Habbān Sultanate, 68, 247, 252, 254.
Habil, 22, 175.
Habūr, 57.
Habūs tribe, 287.
Hadādabah tribe, 288.
Hadādīyah, 47.
Haddād house, 57.
Hadhdhāl, Ibn, 108, 117.

Hādhīn, Ahl, tribe, 251.
Hādhinah, Khalīfah of, 256.
Hadhram (or Hadharmi) Beni, tribe, 288.
Hadhramaut, tribes of the, 13, 48, 61–9, 273–7.
el-Hadhramauti, Sālih el-Bedāwi, **68**.
Hadhrami family, 37.
el-Hadhrami, 'Abd er-Rahmān Ba Muharrem, **27**.
Hadhrami, 'Atas, **12**.
Hadhrami, Ba Nāji', house of, **13**.
Hadhrami, Ba Sabrein, **13**.
Hadhrami, Muharraj Baishi, **17**.
Hādi house, 49, 55.
Hādi Abu Shihah, 221.
    ibn Ahmed el-Heij, 28, **51**, 159, 187, 243.
    'Ali, 245.
el-Hādi, 'Ali ibn, **49**, 58.
el-Hādi, Ghālib, 42, 51.
Hādi 'Īsa, 52.
Hādi Lidin Allah house, 43, **46**.
el-Hādi, Mohammed ibn, **55**, 243.
Hādi Rizk, 50.
el-Hādi, Yahya ibn, **55**, 242.
el-Hādi, Yahya, 42.
Hadīthah, Sheikh, 114.
Hadīyah, Beni, sub-tribe, 319.
Hādiyin tribe, 288.
Hāfiz ed-Dīn house, 53, 55, 59.
Haidar 'Ali : see 'Ali Haidar Pasha.
Haidar Bey, **31**.
Haidarabad, Nizam of, 66.
Haidarah, Ahl, tribe, 261.
Haidarah, 'Awad ibn, **64**, 267.
Haidarah Mansūr, Ahl, tribe, 265.
Hā'il, 9, 83, 87–91, 95, 96.
    Emir of, 91, 94, 138.
Haiwāt tribe, 98, 99.
Hajar, 60, 81.
    Seyyids of, **51**.
Hajar, Beni, tribe, 85, 141, 142, 329.
Hajarein, 66.
Hajarīyah, Kaimmakam of, 47.
    tribe, 265.
Hājir, Beni, tribe : see Hajar, Beni.
Hajj, the, 16–19, 48.
Hajj el-Kabs, 242.
Hajj Railway, 97, 101.
Hajjah, Kaimmakam of, 224, 237, 245.
    tribe, 224.
Hajjāj sub-tribe, 100.
Hajriyīn tribe, 288.
Hajūr, 59, 223, 225, 227, 230, 233, 235–6, 239, 242.
Hakaba, 63, 263.
Hākim, Ba, **49**.
    ibn Muheid, **98**, 107, 108, 110.
    ibn Qeishīsh, 107, 110.
Halālamah tribe, 289.
Hali, 31, 32, 36.
Hali, Ahl, tribes, 28, 36, 172–4.
Halīl Bey, 51.
Halīm, Abu, 27, **32**, 179.
Halreish, Sheikh, 274.
Hamad, Āl, tribe, 289.
Hamād ibn Ghālib, **51**, 58.
Haya, 95.
    ibn Mohammed el-Khalīfah, Khalīfah ibn, **76**.
Hamād, Mohammed ibn, **16**.

Hamād, of San'ā, Sherif of Kaukebān, 53.
  es-Sūfi, **98.**
  ez-Zogheibi, Murshid ibn, **18.**
Hamdān ibn Nāsir, 79.
  ibn Zeid el-Khalīfah, **73.**
Hamdān tribes, 224.
  esh-Shām tribe, 224.
  el-Yemen tribe, 224.
Hāmed, Ahl, tribe, 258.
el-Hamīd, 'Abd, Sultan, 9, 96, 220.
Hāmid ibn 'Abd el-'Azīz, **74.**
Hamid, Ahl, tribe, 261.
Hāmid, Ahmed ibn, **27,** 160.
Hamīd, Beni, tribe, 289.
Hāmid ed-Dīn, Yahya, 42, 45.
Hāmid ibn Feisāl, **72.**
Hamīd el-Ghābir, Qasīm ibn, **68,** 250, 251.
Hāmid Ibag 'Alawi el-Barak, 68.
Hāmid ibn 'Īsa, **75.**
Hāmid ibn Nāsir Bu Kateyyan, **65,** 247.
Hamid, Nasr, 248.
Hāmid ibn el-'Uteir, **65,** 263.
Hamīm tribe, 289.
Hamim, Āl, tribe, 274.
Hammād, Beni, tribe, 289.
Hammām, Ahl, sub-tribe, 65, 254, 255, 258, 259.
Hammāmīd sub-tribe, 100.
Hamra, 15.
Hamrān sub-tribe, 331.
Hamri, 57, 58.
Hamrīyah, 74.
Hamsa ibn Mohammed, 130.
Hamūd, 'Abd el-'Aziz, 91.
Hamūd, 'Abdullah ibn, **26,** 207, 209, 210.
Hamūd, 'Ali ibn, **29,** 91, 93, 195, 196, 245.
Hamūd, Barghāsh ibn, 137.
  ibn Darān, 127.
Hamūd, Majīd ibn, 92.
  ibn Mohammed, 240.
Hamūd, Mohammed ibn, 92, 93.
Hamūd, Mudhi bint, 92.
  ibn Nāsir, **57.**
  Pasha, **51,** 235.
  er-Rashīd, Sultān ibn, 88, 92.
Hamūd, Sa'ūd ibn, 88, 92.
Hamūd, Selīm ibn, 92.
Hamūd Pasha, Sherif, 51, 243.
  Sirdāb, **32,** 33.
  es-Subhān, 90, 92, 93.
  ibn Subhān, 88.
  ibn Suweit, 88, **99,** 137, 138.
  ibn 'Ubeid, 88, 92.
Hamūd, 'Ubeid ibn, 92.
Hamumi tribe, 274.
Hamyār ibn Nāsir, **79.**
Hamzah el-Feir, **14.**
Hanādhilah tribe, 289.
Hanash, Ahl, tribe, 64, 267.
Hanash, Mohammed ibn, 203.
Hanash, Mohammed ibn, 128.
Hanīfah, Wādi, 83, 95.
Harajah, 36.
Harām el-Mekki, 19.
Harāsis tribe, 289.
Harāz, 54, 237.
Harb tribe, 4, 5, 10, 13, 14, 17, 18, 20, 85, 123-5, 329.
Harbah, Abu, 232.
Hareimlah, 83.

Harib, 54.
  Sherif of, **65.**
Harīq, 86.
Harīr, Jebel, 63.
Hārith, Āl, sub-tribe, 37, 195, 196.
el-Hārithi, 'Īsa ibn Sālih, 79, **80.**
Harrās, Beni, tribe, 289.
Hārūn er-Rashīd, 145.
Hasa, 73, 74, 76, 78, 83, 84, 86, 91.
Hasan 'Abd el-Hādi, **65.**
  'Abdullah, 239.
  Abu Mandīl, **32,** 167.
  Abu Mejd, 'Ali ibn, **59.**
  ibn Ahmed, **65.**
  Ahmed es-Sulh, 223.
Hasan, 'Ā'idh ibn, 195.
Hasan, Āl, tribe, 328.
  'Alawi, 50.
  ibn 'Ali, 180, 182.
Hasan, 'Ali ibn, 53.
  ibn 'Ali, 25.
  'Ali, firm of, 52, **65.**
  ibn 'Ali Maqla, Husein ibn, **59.**
  'Ali, Mohammed 'Abdullah ibn, 65.
  ibn 'Ali ibn Mohammed ibn 'Ā'idh, 26, **32.**
  'Ali Thawāb, 160.
  ibn el-'Aud, Mohammed ibn, **36,** 175.
Hasan, Beni: Asir tribe, 32, 38, 175; Belqa tribe, 150, 152; Hadhramaut tribe, 274; Oman tribe, 290.
  edh-Dhi'āb, **14.**
Hasan, Fa'i ibn, 166.
  Fasīkh, 184.
Hasan, Hayāzah ibn, 167.
  el-Hijam, 47.
Hasan, Husein ibn, 45, 222.
  ibn Jād, 118.
  ibn Khidhr, **32,** 218.
  el-Makrami, 54.
  ibn Matar, **32,** 214.
  ibn Mohammed Abu Numej, 158.
Hasan, Mohammed ibn, of the Āl Ikhtarsh, 176.
Hasan, Mohammed ibn, of the Beni Hilāl, **36.**
Hasan, Mohammed ibn, of Ibha, 38.
Hasan, Mohammed, of Ta'izz, **56,** 265.
Hasan, Muhsin ibn, 11, 16, 17, 53, **57.**
Hasan, Muqbil, 269.
Hasan, Mūsa, **38,** 175.
el-Hasan, Mustafa, 25.
Hasan Nāsir ibn Dhi'āb, **14.**
  Nāsir, Husein ibn, 14.
Hasan, Nimrūd, 97.
  ibn Qasīm Zeid, **51,** 52.
  Riza Bey,134.
  Rumāh, Mohammed ibn, 238.
  es-Sa'īd, **32,** 175.
  esh-Sherīf, 33.
  Shijeifi, 174.
  es-Sujaf, Ibrāhīm, 238.
Hasan, Suleimān ibn, of Ibha, 38.
Hasan, Suleimān ibn, of Mahad, 220.
Hasanah tribe, 83, 268.
Hashābirah tribe, 46, 224.
Hashābiri, 46, 47.
Hashāl, Ibn, 207.
Hashāsh, Mohammed ibn, 192.
Hashbal, Sa'īd ibn, **40,** 206, 208.

Hasheish, Beni, tribe, 224.
Hāshid tribe, 44, 46-8, 51, 54, 57-9, 226-31.
Hāshid wa Bekīl confederation, 225-33.
Hāshim, Beni, tribe : *see* Hishm.
Hāshim house, 55.
el-Hāshimi, Qasim, 241.
Hasrīt tribe, 290.
Hātim, Ahl, tribe, 268.
Haurah, 66, 69.
Haushabi tribe, 56, 64, 265.
Hautah, 86.
Hawāl, Beni, tribe, 291.
Hawāsh, Sheikh, 167.
Hawāshim tribe, 291.
Hawāsinah tribe, 291.
Hawāzin tribe, 77, 146, 147, 330.
Hāwi, Ibn, 147.
Haya, Beni, tribe, 291.
Haya, Hamād, 95.
Haya, Ibn, **95.**
Haya, Sālih, 95.
Hayāzah ibn Hasan, 167.
Hayāzah, Mohammed ibn, **38,** 166.
el-Hayyāni, Ahmed, 32, 200, 203.
Haza Qasīm, 269.
Hazam, 79.
Hazem, Sheikh, **14.**
Hāzir el-'Abādilah, **14.**
Hazm ibn Hithlein, Mohammed ibn, 141.
Heidān, 55.
Heidīyah ibn Ahmed, 264.
Heif, Husein ibn, **32,** 190, 191.
ibn Nāsir, 207, 209.
Heif, Nāsir ibn, **39,** 207, 209.
el-Heij, Hādi ibn Ahmed, 28, 51, 159, 187, 243.
el-Heij, Ibn : *see* Hādi ibn Ahmed el-Heij.
Heil, 71.
Heima, 54.
Hejaz, 3-21, 46, 89 ; Southern, minor tribes of, 5, 127-30.
Railway, 4, 6, 94, 100.
revolt, 23.
Heqeish sub-tribe, 114.
el-Hersi, Idrīs, 25.
el-Hezāzi, Ahmed, 8.
Hibah, Beni, tribe, 233.
Hibah Murrah, Sheikh, 239.
Hibshi family, 15.
el-Hibshi, 'Ali, **11.**
el-Hijam, Hasan, 47.
Hijra (in Hajūr), Seyyids of, **51.**
Hikmān tribe, 291.
Hikmi, Ibn, 47.
Hilāl, Beni : Asir tribe, 28, 33, 35, 36, 175, 176 ; Oman tribe, 292.
Hilmi Pasha, 51.
Himāzi house, 59.
el-Himāzi, 'Ali, **59.**
Himeyid, Ibn, 126.
Himrān sub-tribe, 58, 226, 227.
Hina, Beni, tribe, 292.
Hinādīs tribe, 292.
Hināwi tribes, 82.
Hindīyah Escape, 98.
Hirth tribe, 292.
Hishm (or Beni Hāshim) tribe, 293.
Hisn, Lāhik ibn, 182.
Hīt, 100.
Hithlein family, 79, 141.
Hithlein, Theidān ibn, **79,** 80, 141.

Hizām, 'Ali ibn, 224.
ibn Qā'id et-Tawāfi, 239.
ibn Qasīm, 228.
es-Sayādi, 243.
Hodeidah, 27, 44, 49, 57-9, 65.
Seyyids (Chief Munsībs) of, **51.**
Hofūf, 84, 96.
Hubeish, Beni, tribe, 233.
Hudheil tribe, 5, 127.
Hufāsh tribe, 234.
el-Hufdhi, Ibrāhīm, **33,** 199.
Hujahri, 'Abdullah ibn, 160.
Humeid el-Fuleiti, **80.**
Humeid, Nāsir ibn, **81.**
Humeid es-Sālimi, 'Abdullah ibn, 71, **78**, 81.
Humeidah tribes : Asir, 36, 165, 166 ; Northern, 115-17.
Humeidi ibn Ferhān, 134.
Humeidi tribe, 270.
Humeitah, Husein ibn, **99.**
Huneish house, 52.
Husein ibn 'Abd, 206, 207.
Husein, 'Abd en-Nebi, **62.**
ibn 'Abd er-Rahmān, 263.
Husein, 'Abd er-Rahmān ibn, 263.
ibn 'Abd er-Rahmān el-Bura', 223.
Husein, 'Abdullah ibn, 3, 4, **5,** 7, 23, 264.
Abu Ahmed, **65,** 255.
Abu 'Ali, 263.
ibn 'Abūd, 192.
ibn Ahmed, of the Ahl Hammām, **65,** 66, 264, 265.
ibn Ahmed, of Hūth, 52.
ibn Ahmed, of Khartūm, 54.
ibn Ahmed, of Qufl, 57.
Husein, Ahmed ibn, **47,** 234, 264.
Husein ibn 'Ali, Emir of Mecca, **3-5,** 7, 8, 11, 16-21, 23, 29-32, 36, 37, 40, 43, 44, 51, 84, 85, 88, 89, 100, 126, 128-30, 157, 180, 193, 205, 207, 214, 216, 228.
ibn 'Ali, of Abu 'Arīsh, 22, 42.
ibn 'Ali, of the 'Anazah, 221.
Husein, 'Ali ibn, **5,** 6, 7.
ibn 'Ali ibn Lāhik, 181, 182.
ibn 'Ali Sherā'i, 52.
'Asheish, 230.
ibn 'Awad el-Ka'aiti, 277.
Husein, Beni, tribe, 234.
Bey (Tal'āt Husni), **51.**
Bu Ahmed, 258.
Burt, 222.
Husein, Feisāl ibn, **6,** 7, 9, 10, 15.
ibn Fuzān, **14.**
ibn Hasan, 45, 222.
ibn Hasan ibn 'Ali Maqla, **59.**
ibn Hasan Nāsir, 14.
ibn Heif, **32,** 190, 191.
ibn Humeitah, **99.**
ibn Ismā'īl, 235.
el-Jinni, 52.
ibn Mekki, **33.**
Merza', 223.
ibn Mohammed ibn 'Abd el-Mu'īn, Emir, 7.
ibn Mohammed, Sherif of Hūth, 52.
ibn Mubārak, 4, 11, **14,** 16, 18.
el-Mudmāni, 236.
en-Na'āmi, **32,** 200.
Nesīt, Mohammed Effendi, **16.**
Husein, Sa'd ibn, **39,** 205, 207.

Husein, Salīm, **69**, 264.
Husein, Seyyid, of Hūth, 53.
Husein, Sherif, of San'ā, 59.
  ibn Thawābah, 52, 234.
Husein, Zeid ibn, 7, **8**, 11, 16, 19.
Husein Effendi Walad Muzeiqah Julas, **33**, 36, 181.
Huseini, 'Ali ibn, 240.
Huseinīyah, 56.
Huteim tribe, 89, 145, 147, 330.
Hūth, 46–9, 51, 57, 59.
  Seyyids of, **52**.
  Sherifs of, **52**.
Huwāfah sub-tribe, 18, 124.
Hūwalah tribe, 294.
el-Huweifi, Sa'd, **18**, 124.
Huweitāt tribe, 11, 17, 99, 117, 118.
Huyūd tribe, 294.

I

Ibha, 4, 23, 24, 26–9, 31–3, 36–40.
  Sherifs of, **33**.
Ibha-Muhā'il road, 37.
Ibha-Tā'if road, 40.
Ibrāhīm, 'Abd ibn, 206, 207.
  Abu Mu'ammed, **33**, 210.
Ibrāhīm, Ahmed (Hamād) ibn, 33, **79**.
  'Ali, 239.
Ibrāhīm, 'Ali, 243.
  ibn Fat-hi ed-Dīn, **33**.
  Hasan es-Sujaf, 238.
  el-Hufdhi, **33**, 199.
  el-Maqbūl, 47.
  Muhsin er-Rusās, 52, 232.
  ibn Muta'āli, 27, **33**, 199, 201, 202.
  Nā'ib el-Harām, **15**.
  ibn Nāsir, 93.
  Pasha, 83.
Ibrāhīm, Sa'īd ibn, 79.
  Sirhān, **34**.
  es-Subhān, 79, 90, 91, 93.
el-Idrīs, Ahmed, 25.
Idrīs el-Hersi, 25.
Idrīsi country, 51.
  family 22 ; genealogical tree, 25.
  Principate, **22–4**.
el-Idrīsi, Mohammed ibn 'Ali, 4, 16, **22–4**, 26–39, 41, 44, 46–8, 51, 54–7, 68, 85, 128, 159, 161–71, 173, 174, 176, 177, 179–81, 184, 186–8, 190–5, 199–201, 203–7, 210–16, 218–20, 225, 234, 235, 239, 240, 242–4.
Ikhtarsh sub-tribe, 36, 176.
'Imād ibn Ahmed, 270.
Indian Government, 70, 73–6, 84, 85.
  troops, 71.
'Irāq, 95, 97.
Irbe'a, Selīm Abu, **100**.
Irka, 63.
'Isa, 'Abdullah ibn, **63**, 75.
  ibn Ahmed, **80**.
  ibn 'Ali el-Khalīfah, **75**, 76, 78–80, 86.
'Isa, Beni, tribe, 294.
'Isa, Hādi, 52.
'Isa, Hāmid ibn, **75**.
'Isa, Mohammed ibn, **75**.
  ibn Sālih el-Hārithi, 79, **80**.
  Zeilah, 28, 34.
'Isa sub-tribe, 112.

Isba'i, Āl, tribe, 36, 165, 167.
Is-hāq house, 53.
Is-hāq, Mohammed ibn, 53.
Is-hāq ibn Muzellaf, **34**, 214.
Ismā'īl Abu Khurfān, Sherif, 175.
  ibn Ahmed, 52.
  'Ali, 224.
Ismā'īl, 'Ali ibn, Seyyid, **49**, 222.
Ismā'īl, 'Ali ibn, Sherif, **49**, 53.
Ismā'īl, Beni, tribe, 235.
  ibn Dahyān, 127.
Ismā'īl, Husein ibn, 235.
  el-Makrami, **54**, 244.
  ibn Mubārak, **15**.
Ismā'īliyah sect, 54.
Iswad, Ahl, 68.
Italians, 43.
'Iteij, 'Ali ibn, **29**, 206, 207.
Ithwel, Wādi, 16.
Izki, 71, 80.
Izzān Sultanate, 67, 247.
'Izzedīn house, 33.
'Izzet Bey el-Ghindi, 23.
'Izzet Pasha, 43, 50, 54, 242.

J

Ja'āfirah tribe, 32, 35, 177.
Jabbār, 'Ā'idh ibn, **28**, 206, 208.
Jabbār, 'Ali ibn, **29**, 197.
Jābir family, **97**, 115.
Jābir, Ahmed ibn, 77, 78.
Jābir ibn 'Ali, 92.
  el-Ayāshi, **15**.
Jābir, Beni, 294.
Jābir, Fahd ibn, 92.
Jābir, Fahhād ibn, 92.
Jābir, Feisāl ibn, 92.
Jābir ibn Mubārak ibn Sōbah el-Khalīfah, Sultan of Koweit, **77**, **78**, 79, 80, 85, 97, 115, 137, 138, 141, 147.
Jābir, Selīm Abu, **97**.
Jābir, Suleim ibn, 92.
Jābir, Telāl ibn, 92.
Jābiri tribe, 274.
Jabr, Beni, sub-tribe, 233.
Jabūr tribe, 296.
Jabūr, Āl, sub-tribe, 331.
Jacob, Colonel, 38, 56, 57, 59.
Jād, Hasan ibn, 118.
Jada tribe, 274.
Ja'dah tribe, 176.
Jadgāl (or Zidjāl) tribe, 296.
Jadīnah, Ahl, tribe, 267.
Ja'far, 'Ali, **64**.
Ja'far Pasha, **9**.
Ja'far tribe, 294.
Ja'far, Seyyid, 270.
Jaghbūb, 22.
Jahādhim tribe, 296.
Jahāwar tribe, 296.
Jahawashah clan, 114.
Jāhiz house, 47, 53.
Jāhiz, Ahmed, **47**, 53.
Jalājil, 89, 91.
el-Jalāl, 'Abdullah ibn, **94**.
Ja'lān, Emir of, 79.
Jāmi' tribe, 51, 235.
el-Jamrah, Muhsin, 224.
Janāh, Ahmed, **27**, 187.
Jandal, Ibn, 109.

Jannabah tribe, 296.
Jannah, 31, 38.
el-Jans, Ahmed, 237.
Jaraf tribe, 230.
Jarbu, Ibn, 276.
Jasim eth-Thāni, 'Abdullah ibn, **74**
  eth-Thāni, Khalīfah ibn, **75**.
Jasīm, Sheikh, 74, **80**.
Jauf, 47, 57, 87, 89, 100.
Jauz Belā'ir : *see* Jōz Belā'ir.
Jawāsim tribe : *see* Qawāsim.
Jāzi, 'Arār ibn, 117, 118.
Jāzi, Beni, sub-tribe, 117.
Jebāli house, 50, 60.
Jebāli, Āl, tribe, 36, 165–7.
el-Jebāli, Yahya, **60**.
Jebel Qurishi, Ma'az ibn, 221.
Jebel : *see under specific name.*
Jebelīyah (or Zobeid) confederation of
  tribes, 112.
Jebrīn, Ibn, 135.
Jeilāni house, 53.
Jeis ibn Mas'ūdi, sub-tribe, 27, 33, 199, 200, 202.
Jeizān, 22, 28, 33, 34, 37, 38, 41.
Jelājilah tribe, 296.
Jeleid, Sheikh, 192.
Jemāl Pasha, 6, 97, 111.
Jemālileil family, 15.
Jemīmah, Emir of, 48.
  tribe, 235.
Jerba, Ibn, 132.
Jerba, Sufūq ibn, 134.
Jerīdah, Abu, **11**.
Jerūd, 99.
Jerūdi, Mohammed Pasha, **99**.
Jezāb, 63.
Jezīrat el-Hamra, 74.
Jibāla house, 53.
Jibāla, 'Abdullah, 53.
Jibāla, 'Ali, 53.
Jibārah es-Sirāsiri, Mohammed ibn, **16**.
Jibuti, 37, 67.
Jiddah, 4, 8–10, 12, 13, 15–21, 23, 30, 34, 38.
el-Jifri, Seyyid, **34**.
Jihād, 18, 43, 80.
Jihāf, Jebel, 65, 67.
el-Jihāl, Āl, sub-tribe, 190, 191.
Jilūd, Sheikh, 193.
el-Jinni house, 52.
el-Jinni, Husein, 52.
Jissās tribe, 297.
Jīzah, 97, 101.
  Kaimmakam of, 98, 114.
Jōz (Jauz) Belā'ir, 29.
Jōz el-Ja'āfirah, 35.
Jubeir Ba, firm of, **34**, 38.
Jubūr tribal division, 114.
Judallah, Sherif, 129.
Juhadlah tribe, 5, 127.
Juheinah tribe, 4, 5, 13, 15, 17–19, 119–23.
Juheish ibn 'Aqad, **34**, 177.
Jukhādir, Nūr, **18**.
Juma Pasha, Mansūr ibn, **81**.
Jumā'ah, Beni, tribe, 30, 47, 235.
Jum'ān, Rāshid ibn, **39**, 216, 217.
Jum'ān ibn Safīq, 236.
Jumbra, 95.
Jūnah, Beni, sub-tribe, 199, 200, 202.
Jurabi sub-tribe, 270.
Jurba, 63.

K

Ka'ab, Beni, tribe, 297.
Ka'aiti, 66.
Ka'aiti family, **66**, 67–9, 274, 277.
Ka'bah, the, 19.
el-Kabb, Khōr, 76.
el-Kabs, Hajj, 242.
Kabsi, Seyyid, **53**.
Kadri, Qasīm ibn Seyyid Imām, **81**.
Kaheil, Beni, tribe, 298.
Kal Ewāz, 'Abd en-Nābi, **78**.
Kalba, Khōr, 70, 73.
Kallāb, 'Awwād ibn, 152.
Kam'ālah tribe, 235.
el-Kamarāni, 'Ali Nāsir, **49**.
el-Kamarāni, Mohammed, 233.
Kameirah, 56.
Karab, Ahl, tribe, 65, 247, 255.
Karlah, Ahl, tribe, 260.
Kasha', 64.
Kathīr, Āl, tribe, 299.
Kathīri, Mansūr, 275.
Kathīri tribe, 44, 66, 274.
Kaukebān, 49.
  Emir of, 48, 52, 234.
  Sherifs of, **53**.
Kauzi, 'Abdullah, 242.
Kebir, Beni, sub-tribe, 35, 172.
Kelbān, Beni, tribe, 298.
Keleib, Beni, tribe, 298.
Kenāwuz, Mudir of, 242.
Kerak district, tribes of, 101, 154–6.
Kerbela, 83, 98.
el-Kerīm, 'Abd, house of, 49.
Khabb, 52.
Khadān ibn Mohammed, **34**, 212, 213.
Khadhīr tribal division, 114.
Khadhīr, Beni, tribe, 330.
Khailan Abu Tayy, Mohammed ibn, **17**.
Khair, Mu'ādi ibn, **38**, 219.
Khālid ibn Ahmed, **73**.
  ibn 'Ali el-Khalīfah, **75**.
Khālid, Beni, tribe, 77, 81, 139, 140, 300, 330, 331.
  ibn Mohammed, 77.
Khālid, Sagar ibn, 73.
Khālid, Sakhr ibn, 231.
Khalīfah family, 75 ; genealogical tree, 77.
el-Khalīfah, 'Abd, **26**.
el-Khalīfah, 'Abdullah, **94**.
Khalīfah ibn Hamād ibn Mohammed el-Khalīfah, **76**.
el-Khalīfah, 'Isa ibn 'Ali, **75**, 76, 78–80, 86.
Khalīfah ibn Jasīm eth-Thāni, **75**.
el-Khalīfah : *see* Jābir ibn Mubārak.
Khalīfah tribe, 255.
Khalīl el-Ghānim, 174.
Khālis : *see* Khuleis.
Khamārah tribe, 300.
Khameyyis, Āl, tribe, 300.
Khamir, 43, 48, 58.
  Seyyids of, **54**.
Khamīs 'Abidah, 39.
  Musheit, 24, 29.
Khamīsīn tribe, 177.
Khāmmārah, Beni, tribe, 300.
Khanfūr, 'Ali ibn, **29**, 181.
Kharif sub-tribe, 231.
Kharīfōt, 70.
Khārijīyah, 76.

Kharj, 86.
Khartūm, 49, 58.
　Seyyids of, **54.**
Kharūs, Beni, tribe, 300.
el-Kharūsi, Sālim ibn Rashīd, 70, 71, 78, 81.
Khath'am tribe, 34, **177.**
Khaulān tribes : esh-Shām, 236 ; et-Tawāl, 235, 236.
Khaura, 63.
Khaz'al, Sheikh, 78.
Khazam, Beni, tribe, 301.
Khazeimāt tribe, 301.
Khazeir tribe, 301.
el-Kheimah, Ahl Ras, tribe, 73, 74, 300.
Kheirah, Ibn, **34,** 168.
Kheirān tribe, 236.
Khidhr, 99.
Khidhr, Hasan ibn, **32,** 218.
Khirshān house, 36.
Khirshān, Mohammed ibn, **36.**
Khiyar sub-tribe, 230.
Khobami, 47.
Khobami, Ahmed, 47.
Khobami, Ahmed Bey, **47.**
Khōjah (or Lawātiyah) tribe, 301.
Khōr : *see under specific name.*
Khoreibah Pass, 63.
Khotab, Beni, tribe, 236.
el-Khotib, 'Abd el-Mālik, **10.**
Khudra, Mufti ibn, 178.
Khukūr, Abu Bekr, **10.**
Khuleis (Khālis), 10.
Khurshān tribal division, 114.
Khuzām sub-tribe, 120.
Kiamil Pasha, 3.
Kibs, 48.
Kibs family, 235.
el-Kibsi, Ahmed Mab'ūth, 235.
Kifa, Jebel, 65.
Kinānah tribe, 28, 173, 174.
Kokha tribe, 237.
el-Kortadi, Mohammed, 25.
Koweit, 76–9, 83–7, 89, 90, 94, 95, 99.
　British Resident at, 96.
　Sultanate of, **76–82.** *See* Jābir ibn Mubārak.
Kufra, 22.
Kunūd tribe, 301.
Kurkmān, Nāsir ibn, **39,** 207, 209.

L

La Rāj, Ba, **12.**
La'ah, 49.
Lahak, Ahl, tribe, 260.
Lahej, 56, 61, 62, 65–8.
　Sultan of, 52, 55, 64, 246.
Lāhik, 'Ali ibn, 181, 182.
Lāhik ibn Hisn, 182.
Lahīyah : *see* Loheia.
Lakmūsh sub-tribe, 68, 247.
Lamak, Beni, tribe, 302.
Laqīt, Ahl, tribe, 259.
Lāri, Mohammed 'Ali, **15.**
Lasfar, 34.
Latīfah, 'Ali, **12.**
Laudar : *see* Loder.
Lawātiyah tribe : *see* Khōjah.
Leachman, Captain, 86, 94, 96.

Leimūn, Wādi, 3.
Leinah, 89.
Leshar, Ahl, tribe, 261.
Lingeh, 78.
Līth, 4, 12, 18, 23, 32, 36, 38.
Lizām Abu Dharā', 138.
Loder (Laudar), 68.
Loheia (Lahīyah), 22, 23, 36, 46, 58.
　Kaimmakam of, 51, 235, 243.
el-Luf, Qā'id, 237.
Luqwa house, 53, 57.
Lutf ibn 'Abd er-Rahmān, 53.
　ibn 'Ali, 53.
　Sāri, **54,** 229.
　ez-Zubeir, 241.
Luxor, 15, 22, 24.

M

Ma'addi, 'Ali ibn, **29,** 177, 178.
Ma'addi ibn Khair, 219.
Ma'ān, 99.
Ma'an family, 252, 254.
el-Ma'an, 'Abdullah, 221.
Ma'an, Ahl, tribe, 67, 68, 254, 256–8.
Ma'āwal tribe, 302.
Ma'āwal, Wādi, 80.
Ma'az ibn Jebel Qurishi, 221.
Mabīth, Ahl, tribe, 259.
Mabkhūt, Nāsir ibn, 46, 47, 50, 51, 54, 55, **57,** 58, 60, 223–32, 234.
Madān, Emir of, 58.
el-Madani, Ahmed, 229.
Mādeba, 101 ; Arabs of (independent tribes), 153.
Madfa'ah, 29.
Madhaji, Ahl, tribe, 257.
Maflahi tribe, 63, 271.
Mahallah, 3.
Mahārah tribe, 302.
Mahārib tribe, 302.
Mahāriq tribe, 303.
Mahārizah tribe, 303.
Mahāthil, Ahl, tribe, 267.
Mahd ibn Sa'ūd, **96.**
Mahdi, Āl, tribe, 128, 129.
Mahdi, Seyyid, 52.
Mahmūd Āshūr, **15.**
　ibn Mohammed, **61.**
　Nāzim (Nādim) Pasha, 43, 44, 49, **54,** 58.
Mahmūd, Seyyid, 240.
Mahras, tribe, 303.
Mahweit tribe, 237.
Ma'id el-Moghrabi, Sālih ibn, **58,** 226, 227
Majālibah tribe, 303.
Majīd, 'Abd el-, 47.
Majīd ibn Hamūd, 92.
Majīd, Ibn, of the Muhallaf tribe, 109.
　ibn Sa'īd ibn Sultān, 70, 72.
Ma'jil, Ibn, 109.
Makalla, 66, 68.
　Sultan of, 273–7.
Makārimah tribe, 237.
Makhārīb (or Makhārīm) tribe, 328.
Makhdūmi tribe, 270.
Makhtūm, Sa'īd ibn, **73.**
Makrahah, Ahl, tribe, 258.
Makrami family, 237, 244.
el-Makrami, Hasan, 54.

el-Makrami, Ismā'īl, **54,** 244.
el-Makrami, Mohammed, 54.
Malhah, 33.
Mālik, Beni, tribes : Asir, 29, 39, 177-9 ; Bekīl, 233 ; Hejaz, 129 ; Juheinah, 121, 122.
Ma'mir family, 95.
Ma'mir, Fahhād ibn, **95.**
el-Mamūn, Mohammed, 25.
Mana, Ahl, tribe, 260.
Manādharah tribe, 303.
Manāhil tribe, 275.
Manāmah, British Resident at, 75.
Manāri tribe, 46, 237.
Manas, Ahl, tribe, 261.
Manāsīr Bu Sālih, tribe, 252.
Manāsīr tribe, 85, 143, 303.
Manassar ibn 'Awad el-Ka'aiti, 277.
Manāwarah tribe, 304.
Mandīl, 'Abd el-Latīf, **78.**
Mani, 'Ali ibn, **64,** 265.
Mansūr ibn 'Abbās, **15.**
Mansūr, Ahl, tribe, 260.
el-Mansūr, 'Ali, 43, 45, 46.
Mansūr ibn 'Azīz, 36, 182.
   ibn Ghālib ibn Muhsin 'Abd el-Kathīri, **66.**
   ibn Ghālib, Mohassim ibn, 66.
   ibn Juma Pasha, **81.**
   Kathīri, 275.
   el-Kerīmi, Ahmed ibn, **11.**
   el-Kerīmi, Muhsin ibn, **17.**
el-Mansūr, Mohammed, 42.
Mansūr el-Qasim, 42.
el-Mansūri, 'Abdullah, 45, **46.**
Mansūri sub-tribe, 69, 269.
Mansūrīyah, 47.
Maqābil tribe, 304.
Maqānnah tribe, 304.
el-Maqbūl, Ibrāhīm, 47.
Maqbūl, Sheikh, 176.
Maqla house, 59.
Maqla, 'Ali, **59.**
Marar tribe, 304.
Marāshdah tribe, 153.
Marāziq tribe, 304.
Māreb, Sherifs of, **54,** 63, 65.
Marhab, Beni, tribe, 237.
Marūmi, Ahl, tribe, 267.
Marwa', 34, 44, 47.
Marwa'i, Ahmed, 51.
Marwān, Beni, tribe, 23, 30, 179.
Marzūq (Merzoq), Ahl, tribe, 251.
Masā'īd tribe, 106, 112.
Masākirah tribe, 305.
Masālihah tribe, 305.
Masār tribe, 237.
Masārihah tribe, 27, 32, 39, 41, 179.
Masāwah, Ahmed, **27,** 179.
Mash'ad ibn Bahrān, **34,** 169.
Mashāfirah tribe, 305.
Mashā'ikh tribe, 305.
Mashārifah tribe, 305.
Mashārij, 69.
Mashhur, 'Abdullah, 224.
Ma'sir, Misfir ibn, 196.
Masīs, Nā'if ibn, 139.
Masrūh sub-tribe, 10, 14, 16, 17, 123-5.
Mastūr, Sherif, **38.**
Mastūrah, 10.
Mas'ūd el-Barak, **55,** 226, 227.

Mas'ūd, Ibn, 221.
Mas'ūd es-Suweilim, **96.**
Mas'ūd tribe, 135.
Masyūghah, Sālim ibn, 117.
Matar, Beni, tribe, 237.
Matar, Hasan ibn, **32,** 214.
Matārīsh tribe, 305.
Matīr, Abu, **35,** 160, 161.
Matosalah, Ahl, tribe, 258.
Matrah, 71.
Maur, Wādi, 46, 51.
Mausata tribe, 63, 67, 271.
Ma'wad, 'Ali, 241.
Mawāhib tribe, 119, 120.
Māwiyah, 49, 52, 56.
"Māwiyah": *see* Mohammed Nāsir Muqbil.
Māwiyah tribe, 266.
Mazāri' tribe, 306.
Mecca, 3-6, 9-16, 18-22, 31, 37, 40, 48, 91, 100.
   Emirate of, **3-8** ; Ruling Sherifial ('Abādilah) family, genealogical tree, 7. *See* Husein ibn 'Ali.
Medā'in Sālih, 94.
Medāni family, 11, 15.
Medina, 4-6, 8-20, 100.
   Seyyids of, **15.**
Medīnat esh-Shāhid, 60.
Medīni, 'Ali ibn, **29,** 34, 168.
Mehājir, Ahl (group of tribes), 254, 258, 259.
Mehwari, Ahl, tribe, 267.
Meimūn, Beni, 124.
el-Mejd, Abu, house, 59.
Mejlis Belediyah, 27, 29, 37.
Mejma', 84, 85, 94.
Mekhādir tribe, 238.
el-Mekkawi, 'Abd el-Qādir, **62.**
el-Mekki, Ahmed 'Abdullah, **27,** 28.
Mekki, Husein ibn, **33.**
Melāhah, 28.
Menākhah, 49, 54.
   Kaimmakam of, 56, 238, 240.
Merāziq, Ahl, tribe, 259.
Merqūshi (Markashi) tribe, 264, 265.
Merza', Husein, 223.
Mesālikh sub-tribe, 100.
Mesopotamia, 99.
Mesrūh tribe, 238.
Meswar, 30.
   Seyyids of, **55.**
el-Metā'ibah, 'Abdullah, 152.
Metwah tribe, 238.
Meyāsir tribe, 268.
Midhat Pasha, 76.
Mīdi, 20, 22, 30, 34, 37, 40.
Midianite Huweitāt, the, 19.
Midkom, 'Ali, 202.
Mifdhil, 'Abdullah ibn, 181.
Mihah, Yahya, **41,** 179.
Mijāli Abu Misudah, 268.
Mikhlāf el-Yemen, 27.
   Emir of, 37, 204.
Milhān, Ahl, tribe, 238.
Milhem, 'Abdullah ibn, 26, 163.
Milhem, Sa'ūd ibn, 109.
Minbah, Beni, clan, 39, 179.
Minīf, Ibn, 275.
el-Miqātah, 10.
Miqdād, 'Ali, 221, 222.
Miqdām, Āl, sub-tribe, 331.

Misā'irah tribe, 329.
Misān, Mohammed ibn, 233.
Misfir ibn Ma'sir, 196.
Mish'al ibn Fāris, 134.
  ibn Mit'ab, 92.
Mishāqisah tribe, 306.
Misheri tribe, 251.
Mismār, Abu, **35,** 212, 213.
Mit'ab ibn 'Abd el-'Azīz, 88, 92.
Mit'ab, Mish'al ibn, 92.
Mit'ab, Mohammed ibn, 92.
  el-Qanj, 114.
  el-Qanj, Ghâlib ibn, **98,** 114.
Miyāyihah tribe, 306.
Mizeini, 'Abd el-Latīf, **10,** 20.
Mo'ayyad house, 60.
el-Mo'ayyadi, Yahya, **60.**
Mocha, 50.
  Kaimmakam of, 245.
Mocha-Ta'izz route, 52.
Modhiq (Medeiq), 18, 124.
Mohammarah, 78.
Mohammed ibn 'Abd, 174.
  'Abd el-'Azīz, 7.
Mohammed, 'Abd el-'Azīz ibn, 25, 83, 87.
  ibn 'Abd el-Kērim, 134, 136.
  ibn 'Abd el-Mu'īn, 'Ali ibn, 7.
  ibn 'Abd el-Mu'īn ibn 'Aun, 3, 7, 40, 211.
  ibn 'Abd el-Qādir, **35.**
  ibn 'Abd er-Rahmān, 30, **35,** 47, 59, 87, 171, 172, 180.
  ibn 'Abd er-Rahmān ibn 'Ā'idh, 182.
  ibn 'Abd er-Rahmān ibn Husein, **54.**
  'Abd er-Rahmān esh-Shāmi, **55.**
  ibn 'Abd el-Wahāb, 83.
Mohammed, 'Abd el-Wahhāb ibn, 25.
Mohammed, 'Abdillah ibn, 7.
  ibn 'Abdu, 28, **35,** 176.
Mohammed, 'Abdu, 50.
  'Abdullah ibn Hasan 'Ali, 65.
Mohammed, 'Abdullah ibn, 3, 7.
  ibn 'Abdullah el-Khotib, 52.
Mohammed 'Abdullah, Mohammed ibn, **67,** 68, 251.
  ibn 'Abdullah ibn Rashīd, 87, 92.
  'Ābid, **15.**
  Abu Dūsah, 181, 182.
  Abu el-Hasan, 25.
  Abu Nunej, 157, 158.
  Abu Nunej, Barakāt ibn, 158.
  Abu Nunej, Hasan ibn, 158.
  Abu Nuweibah, 30, 36, **55,** 59, 193.
  Abu Salām, **35,** 190, 192.
  Abu Shiha, 50.
  Abu Tarash, 166.
  Abu Tayy, 118.
  Abu Toqeiqah, Ahmed ibn, **11,** 19.
  ibn Ahmed, of the Ja'dah tribe, 176.
  ibn Ahmed, of the 'Umr tribe, 168.
  ibn Ahmed, 'Ali ibn, 22.
  ibn Ahmed el-Idrīs, 22, 25.
  ibn Ahmed el-Jahwashi, 202.
  ibn Ahmed Na'mān, 265.
  ibn 'Ali, of the Ahl es-Sa'īdi, 248.
  ibn 'Ali, of the Beni Bu 'Ali, 279.
  ibn 'Ali, of the Beni Kebīr, 171.
  'Ali, of Egypt, 3.
  'Ali, of Fez, 22.
  ibn 'Ali, of the Ja'āfirah, **35,** 177.

Mohammed, 'Ali ibn, of the Balasmar tribe, **29, **30.
Mohammed, 'Ali ibn, of Hūth, 53.
Mohammed, 'Ali ibn, of Madfa'ah, 165.
Mohammed, 'Ali ibn, of Sabia, 25.
  'Ali Abu 'Awad, **66,** 248.
  'Ali el-Bedāwi, 12, 13, **15,** 121.
  ibn 'Ali el-Idrīsi : *see* Idrīsi.
  'Ali Lāri, **15.**
  ibn 'Ali ibn Mohammed, 25.
  'Ali Pasha, 27, 33, 34.
  'Ali Sebāk, 218.
  ibn 'Ali esh-Shāmi, **55,** 59.
  ibn 'Ali Walad 'Ali ibn Murā'i, **35,** 190, 191.
  Effendi Amīn el-Mekki, **16.**
  Amīn Pasha, 40, 161.
  ibn 'Amr, 26, **36.**
  ibn 'Amr Akhu 'Abdīyah, 170.
  el-'Arabi, 25.
  ibn 'Ārif 'Areifān, **16,** 18.
  ibn 'Atīyah, 119.
  Atyuk, **66.**
  ibn 'Awad, 183.
  ibn 'Azīz, **36,** 181.
  Ba Jubeir, 34.
Mohammed, Beni, tribes : Asir, 179 ; Yemen, 46, 238.
  Bu Hamid, Ahl, tribe, 258.
  ibn Dhuleim, 26, 30–2, **36,** 39, 187, 188, 191–3.
  Emir : *see* Mohammed er-Rashīd.
Mohammed, Fātimah bint, 25, 90, 91, 96.
  ibn Favy, 176.
  ibn Feisāl, **71,** 72, 87.
  el-Ghazalān, 87.
  ibn el-Hādi, **55,** 243.
  ibn Hamād, **16.**
  Hāmid ed-Dīn el-Mutawakkil : *see* Yahya ibn Mohammed.
Mohammed, Hamsa ibn, 130.
  ibn Hamūd, 92, 93.
Mohammed, Hamūd ibn, 240.
  ibn Hanash, of the Umm Bina, 203.
  ibn Hanash, of the Juhadlah, 128.
  ibn Is-hāq, 53.
  ibn Hasan, of the Āl Ikhtarsh, 176.
  ibn Hasan, of the Beni Hilāl, **36.**
  ibn Hasan, of Ibha, 38.
  Hasan, of Ta'izz, **56,** 265.
  ibn Hasan ibn el-'Aud, **36,** 175.
  Hasan, Mohammed ibn, 48.
  ibn Hasan Rumāh, 238.
  ibn Hashāsh, 192.
  ibn Hayāzah, **36,** 166.
  ibn Hazm ibn Hithlein, 141.
Mohammed, Husein ibn, Emir, 7.
Mohammed, Husein ibn, Sherif, 52.
  Effendi Husein Nesīf, **16.**
  ibn 'Isa, **75.**
  ibn Ismā'īl, 235.
  el-Jābi, Murshid ibn, 240.
  Pasha Jerūdi, **99.**
  ibn Jibārah es-Sirāsīri, **16.**
  el-Kamarāni, 233.
Mohammed, Khadān ibn, **34,** 212, 213.
  ibn Khailān Abu Tayy, **17.**
Mohammed, Khālid ibn, 77.
  ibn Khirshān, **36.**
Mohammed el-Kaukebāni, Ahmed ibn, 234.
  el-Kortadi, 25.

Mohammed, Mahmūd ibn, **61**.
  el-Makrami, 54.
  el-Mamūn, 25.
  el-Mansūr, 42.
  ibn Misān, 233.
  ibn Mit'ab, 92.
  ibn Mohammed 'Abdullah, **67**, 68, 251.
  ibn Mohammed Hasan, 48.
  el-Morghāni, 22.
  ibn Muharrak, **37**.
  ibn Mūsa, 203.
Mohammed, Mūsa, 50.
  ibn Musa'i, **37**, 187.
  ibn Musā'idi, 184.
  ibn Musallat, **37**, 182, 183.
  el-Mushādi, Yahya ibn, 50.
  ibn Muta'āli, 202.
  el-Mutawakkil Muhsin, 45, 46, 55, 59.
  el-Mutawakkil Seif el-Islām, **55**.
  el-Mutawakkil Seif el-Khulufah, 46, 48, **55**, 59.
  ibn Muthanna, 271.
  ibn Muzhar, **37**, 198.
Mohammed, Nasīb ibn, **81**.
  ibn Nāsir, 79.
Mohammed, Nāsir ibn, 3, **18**.
  Nāsir Muqbil (" Māwiyah "), 49, **56**, 58, 265, 266, 306.
  en-Niha, 237.
  Nūr, **17**.
  Nūri Bey, **56**.
  ibn Nuweibah, 36, **55**.
  ibn Qasīm, 129.
Mohammed, Qasīm ibn, **55**.
Mohammed, Qasr 'Ali ibn, 32.
  er-Rashīd, Emir, 88, 90, 91, 93, 96, 123, 137.
  ibn Rashīd, 74, 83, 92.
  ibn Sa'īd, 128.
el-Mohammed, Sa'īd, **96**.
Mohammed Sa'īd Ba Haidar, **37**.
  ibn Sa'īdah, 107.
  ibn Sālih, of the Beni Ghaneim, **17**, 18.
  Sālih, of Jeizān, 28, **37**.
  Sālih el-Akhram, **67**, 265.
  Sālih Ja'far, 64.
  Sālih Sheibi, **19**.
  Sālih, Sa'd ibn, 17, **19**.
  ibn Sa'ūd, 83, 87, 96.
Mohammed, Sa'ūd ibn, 77.
Mohammed, Seyyid, 54.
  ibn Shāhir, **37**, 195, 196.
Mohammed, Sheikh of Tadmor, **100**.
  esh-Sherīf, 25, 33.
  ibn Shuweil, 191.
  Sibsib, 241.
  ibn Sōbah II, 77.
  Suleimān Fakhīrah, **56**.
Mohammed, Sultān ibn, 7.
  Tahar, of Jebel Jihāf, **67**.
  Tahar, of the Sabia district, **37**.
  et-Tawāl, Sālih ibn, 236.
  et-Tawil, **16**.
  et-Tayyār, 109.
  ibn Telāl, 92.
  ibn Tūrki, 71, **72**.
  ibn Tūrki ibn Mijlād, **99**, 110.
  ibn 'Urūr, **37**, 206, 208.
  Yahya, 58.

Mohammed, Yahya ibn, 53.
  ibn Yahya el-Ahdal, 47.
  Yahya Ba Sāhi, 23, 34, **37**, 68, 204.
  Yahya el-Hibah Fashīk, **56**, 57, 59, 245.
  Ya'qūb, 270.
  Zeid, of the Jāmi', 235.
  ibn Zeid, of the Munjahah, 185.
Mohammedīn tribe, 275.
Mohannah, Tahar ibn, **20**.
Mohassim ibn Mansūr ibn Ghālib, 66.
Morghāni family, 24.
el-Morghāni, 'Ali, 22, 68.
Moslems, 8, 43, 81, 155, 156.
Mosul, 51, 98.
Mu'ādi ibn Khair, **38**, 219.
Mu'āfa Sherāf, 239.
Mubārak, Husein ibn, 4, 11, **14**, 16, 18.
Mubārak, Ismā'īl ibn, **15**.
Mubārak, Jābir ibn, 79.
Mubārak, Nāsir ibn, 77, 78.
Mubārak, Sālim ibn, 77, **78**.
  ibn Sōbah el-Khalifah, Jābir ibn : *see* Jābir ibn Mubārak.
  ibn Sōbah, 76, 77, 85, 96.
Mubhi, 'Ali ibn, **29**, 213.
Mudhar, 113, 137.
Mudhi bint Subhān, 88, 90, **91**, 92, 93.
  bint Hamūd, 92.
Mudhīq, 32, 190.
el-Mudmāni, Husein, 236.
Mufarrih, 'Abd er-Rahmān ibn, 182.
Mufarrih, 'Abdullah Bey ibn, **26**, 180, 182.
Mufarrih, Ahmed ibn, 180.
Mufarrih, Sa'd ibn, 182.
Mufarrih, Sheikh, 180.
Muflahi clan, 69, 250.
Mufraj, Ahmed ibn, 201.
Mughāthil, 'Abdullah ibn, **26**, 182.
Mugheid, Beni, tribe, 26, 27, 29, 32, 33, 36, 37, 39, 179-84.
Muhā'il, 24, 31, 37, 40.
Muhallaf tribe, 109.
Muharraj Baishi Hadhrami, **17**.
Muharrak house, 37.
Muharrak, Mohammed ibn, **37**.
Muharraq Island, 75.
Muharrem Effendi, **38**.
Muhāshir sub-tribe, 331.
Muhāsin Effendi, **38**.
Muheid, Hākim ibn, **98**, 107, 108, 110.
Muheyya, Feihān ibn, 126.
Muhsin ibn 'Abdullah, **57**, 234.
Muhsin, 'Abdullah ibn, **46**, 58, 272.
Muhsin, Ahmed ibn, **63**, 69, 263.
  'Askar, 63, **67**, 271.
  ibn Fadl, **61**, 62.
  ibn Fārid, **67**, 254, 257.
Muhsin, Fitim ibn, **13**.
  ibn Hasan, 11, 16, 17, 53, **57**.
Muhsin, Imam, 237, 244.
  el-Jamrah, 224.
  ibn Mansūr el-Kerīmi, 5.
  el-Muntaser, Yahya ibn, **59**.
  el-Qaramāni, 231.
  ibn Sālih, **67**, 247, 254.
  Yahya, 'Ali, 235.
Muhyi ed-Dīn Bey, **38**.
Mujāhid house, 54.
el-Mujalli, Sālih, 154.
Mujarri ibn Sa'id, **35**, 169.
Mukarram, Yahya 'Abdullah, **59**.

Mukhalad sub-tribe, 120.
Mukhtār Pasha, 23, 49, 225, 234, 237, 238, 244.
Mu'luq, 51.
el-Mullah, Ahmed, 11.
Mumtaz Bey, 9.
Munāsar Saghīr, 57, 245.
el-'Useimi, 228.
Munīrah, 47.
Munīsh, firm of, 38.
Munjahah tribe, 29, 33, 184, 185.
Muntaser house, 59.
Muntefiq tribe, 77, 88, 89, 97, 99, 136, 137.
el-Muqaddam, 'Amān, 12.
Muqātil tribe, 238.
Muqbil 'Abdullah, 67, 265.
    Hasan, 269.
Muqbil, Mohammed Nāsir, 49, 56, 58, 265, 266, 306.
    Nāji', 67.
el-Wada'i, Ahmed ibn, 238.
Muqdi, 'Ali ibn, 176.
Muqfa', 47.
Murrah, Ahl, tribe, 84-6, 142, 143.
Murrah, Beni, tribe, 238, 239.
Murrah, Hibah, 239.
Murran, Beni, tribe, 239.
Murshid Ba Nāsir, 270.
    ibn Hamād ez-Zogheibi, 18.
    ibn Mohammed el-Jābi, 240.
Murzut ibn Bakhīt, 175.
Mūsa, Āl, tribe, 31, 37, 40, 185, 186.
Mūsa ibn 'Ali, Āl, tribe, 36, 165, 166.
Mūsa, Beni, sub-tribe, 122, 123.
Mūsa Hasan, 38, 175.
    Khān, 'Ali, 71.
    Mohammed, 50.
Mūsa, Mohammed ibn, 203.
    ibn Mushāfi, 178.
    ibn Sherein, 181.
Mūsabein tribe, 255, 266.
Musa'i, Mohammed ibn, 37, 187.
Musā'idi, Mohammed ibn, 184.
Musallamīyah Bay, 77.
Musallat, Mohammed ibn, 37, 182, 183.
Musandam, Ras, 73.
Musawwa', 13.
Muscat, 71, 80-2.
    British Resident at, 78-80.
Muscat (Oman), Sultanate of, 70-2;
    Sultans (Seyyids) since the beginning of the nineteenth century, genealogical tree, 72. See Teimur ibn Feisāl.
Museilihi house, 58.
Mushāfi, Mūsa ibn, 178.
Musheit, 'Abd el-'Azīz ibn, 24, 26, 37, 39, 40, 188, 189, 205-7.
Musheit, Āl, sub-tribe, 39, 205, 207.
Musheit, 'Azīz ibn, 30, 35, 171, 172.
Muslih, Sālih ibn, 58, 226, 227, 241.
Musnid ibn Telāl, 92.
Mustafa ibn 'Abd el-'Āl el-Idrīsi, 24, 25, 68.
    Derwīsh, 18.
    el-Hasan, 25.
    ibn Mohammed, 'Ali, 25.
Mustafa, Sa'īd ibn, 25.
Mustafa, Seyyid, 27, 28, 36, 37, 38, 162, 163, 199, 201.
Mustur, Sherif, 175.
Muta'āli, Ahmed ibn, 27, 32, 199-201.

Muta'āli, Ibrāhīm ibn, 27, 83, 199, 201.
Muta'āli, Mohammed ibn, 202.
Mutakir house, 51.
el-Mutallib, 'Abd, 7, 8, 157.
Mu'taridh, 51.
Mutarrifi tribe, 270.
el-Mutawakkil, 'Ali ibn, 231.
el-Mutawakkil, Mohammed, 55.
el-Mutawakkil Muhsin, Mohammed, 45, 46, 55, 59.
Muteir tribe, 77, 84, 85, 88, 138, 139, 331.
Muthanna, Ahmed, 63.
Muthanna, Mohammed ibn, 271.
Muthanna, 'Omar ibn, 271.
Mutlaq, Sa'd ibn, 289.
Mutlaq, Sheikh, 289.
Muwālik tribe, 307.
Muwālikh tribe, 307.
Muzeiqah Julas, Husein Effendi Walad, 83, 36, 181.
Muzellaf, Is-hāq ibn, 34, 214.
Muzerqah, 'Abdullah ibn, 196.
Muzhar, Mohammed ibn, 37, 198.

N

Na'ab (or Nu'abah) Beni, tribe, 307.
Na'āmi house, 27, 32.
en-Na'āmi, Husein, 32, 200.
Nabāhinah tribe, 307.
Nabhān, Sheikh, 81.
Nādir ibn Feisāl, 71, 72.
Nafārīn sub-tribe, 127.
Nafura of Nejrān, 140.
Nahad tribe, 275.
Nahār el-Bukheit, 151.
en-Nahāri, 'Abdullah, 240.
Nahās sub-tribe, 28, 205, 206, 208.
Nā'ib, Abu, 230.
Nā'ib el-Harām, Ibrāhīm, 15.
Nā'if ibn Masīs, 139.
    ibn Shahawān, 152.
    ibn Telāl, 92.
Nā'if, Telāl ibn, 92.
Na'īm tribe, 307.
Naimi, Sultān Mohammed ibn, 82.
Nāja' clan, 79, 141.
Najamāt sub-tribe, 98.
Nāji' 'Ali 'Askar, 271.
Nāji', Muqbil, 67.
Nāji' ibn Yahya, 232.
Nājih, Āl, sub-tribe, 180-2.
Naj'u tribe, 33, 37, 186.
Nakhlein fort, 69.
Na'mān, Ahmed, 47, 48, 56, 229, 265.
Na'mān, Beni, tribe, 307.
Namas, 28.
Naqbiyīn tribe, 308.
Nashar, Beni, tribe, 27, 28, 41, 187.
Nāshir ibn Shā'if, 'Ali ibn, 64, 249.
Nasīb ibn 'Abd er-Rahmān ibn 'Ā'idh, 180, 182.
    ibn Mohammed, 81.
Nāsir, 'Abd er-Rahmān 'Arār ibn, 30.
Nāsir, 'Abdullah ibn, 93.
    Abu Katevyān, Hāmid ibn, 99, 247.
    Abu Thālib, 68, 255.
Nāsir, Ahmed, 48.
Nāsir, Āl Bin, tribe, 309.
    ibn 'Ali, 7, 8.

Nāsir, 'Ali ibn, 235.
Nāsir, 'Arār ibn, 193.
Nāsir, Bu Bekr ibn, 257.
    ibn Dhi'āb, Hasan, 14.
    ibn Ghuzeil, 129.
Nāsir, Hamdān ibn, 79.
Nāsir, Hamūd ibn, 57.
Nāsir, Hamyār ibn, 79.
    ibn Heif, 39, 207, 209.
Nāsir, Heif ibn, 207, 209.
    ibn Humeid, 81.
    Husein el-Ahlāsi, 220.
Nāsir, Husein ibn Hasan, 14.
Nāsir, Ibrāhīm ibn, 93.
    el-Kamarāni, 'Ali, 49.
    ibn Kurkmān, 39, 207, 209.
    ibn Mabkhūt, 46, 47, 50, 51, 54, 55, 57, 58, 60, 223-32, 234.
    ibn Mohammed, 3, 18.
Nāsir, Mohammed ibn, 79.
    ibn Mubārak, 77, 78.
Nāsir Muqbil, Mohammed, 49, 56, 58, 265, 266, 306.
    ibn Nāsir, 57.
    ibn Rawwāf, 129.
Nāsir, Sa'd ibn, 182.
    ibn Salāmah, 93.
    ibn Sālih, 68, 247.
    ibn Shāhin et-Tawār, 74.
    ibn Shā'if ibn Seif, 68, 250.
    ibn Shākir el-'Abādilah, 18.
    ibn Sherein, 181.
    ibn Suleimān Siyabi, 81.
Nāsir, Yahya, 271.
Nāsir, Yahya 'Arār ibn, 30, 240.
Nasiyīn, Ahl, tribe, 68, 255.
Nasr Abu Thālib, 255.
Nasr Hamīd, 248.
Nawāfil tribe, 309.
Nawār tribe, 146, 147.
Nawāshirah tribe, 29, 34, 168.
Nawwāf ibn Nūri esh-Sha'lān, 6, 95, 100, 106.
Nawwāf, Sultān ibn, 100.
Nāzim Bey, 57, 97, 111, 134.
    Pasha, Mahmūd, 43, 44, 49, 54, 58.
Nebi Sālih Island, 75.
Nefūd, southern and eastern, 87.
Negroes of the Centre, 331.
Nehar ibn Telāl, 92.
Nejd, 73, 78, 83, 84, 86-9, 95.
    British Resident at, 84.
Nejd, Emirate of [Ibn Sa'ūds], 83-6. See 'Abd-el-'Azīz ibn 'Abd er-Rahmān.
Nejef, 89.
Nejrān, Emir of, 54, 244.
Nesīf, 'Omar, 16.
Nidābiyīn tribe, 81, 309.
Nidheiriyīn tribe, 309.
en-Niha, Mohammed, 237.
Nihim sub-tribe, 233.
Nimrūd Hasan, 97.
Nimshah, 'Abdullah ibn, 183.
Nisāb, 63, 65.
    Sultan of, 253-6, 262.
Nizār family, 144.
Nizwa, 71.
Non-Bedouin nomads, 144-8.
Noweidis et-Timyāt, 134.
Nu'a tribe, 275, 276.
Nu'abah tribe : see Na'ab, Beni

Nūbat es-Suwah, 66.
Numan tribe, 276.
Numej, Abu, 157.
Nūr Jukhādir, 18.
Nūr, Mohammed, 17.
Nūrah bint 'Abd el-'Azīz, 90, 91-3.
Nūri Bey, Mohammed, 56.
    esh-Sha'lān, 4, 6, 87-90, 98, 100, 106-9.
    esh-Sha'lān, Nawwāf ibn, 6, 95, 100, 106.
Nuweibah, Mohammed Abu, 30, 59, 193.
Nuzlat el-Yemenīyah, 10.

O

'Odeid, 73, 86.
Oleh confederation of tribes, 63, 64, 266-8.
Oman, 43, 73, 81.
    Sultan of ; see Muscat ; Teimur ibn Feisāl.
    Sultanate, tribes of, 278-326.
'Omar ibn Ahmed, 276.
    ibn 'Awad el-Ka'aiti, 66, 277.
    Ba Jubeir, 34.
    ibn Muthanna, 271.
    Nesīf, 16.
    ibn Qahtān, 68, 69, 270, 271.
'Omar, Sālih ibn, 270, 271.
'Omar, Thābit ibn, 274, 275.
'Oqair, 78, 84, 86.
'Osman, Elias, 245.
'Othmān Pasha el-A'rāf, 55.
'Othmān, Sa'īd ibn, 40, 161.
'Othmān Siwādi, 39, 179.
Ottoman Government, 4, 9, 12, 17, 40, 56, 76, 81, 84, 88, 89, 97, 99, 100.
    Parliament, 6, 21, 35.
    Steamship Company, 11.
    troops. 47, 48, 64, 65, 74.
    Upper House, 8.

P

Pan-Arabists, 5, 9.
Pan-Islamism, 8, 9.
Pera, 38.
Persian Gulf, 65.
Persians, 78.
" Pirate Coast ", 73.
Port Sudan, 49.

Q

Qa'aiti, Āl, sub-tribe, 232, 233.
el-Qa'aiti, Yahya, 232.
Qābil, Suleimān, 20.
el-Qādhi, 'Abd er-Rahmān ibn, 182.
el-Qādhi, Ahmed ibn, 182.
Qadhīmah, 11, 16.
Qādim, Ahmed ibn, 275, 276.
Qā' el-Harf, 46.
Qafalīyah tribe, 239.
el-Qahm, 'Ali, 28, 187.
Qahtān family, 140, 144.
Qahtān, 'Omar ibn, 68, 69, 270, 271.
Qahtān, Sālih ibn, 69.
Qahtān tribes : Asir, 36, 187 ; Central South, 85, 131, 332.

Qā'id ibn 'Ali, 231.
　el-Luf, 237.
　et-Tawāfi, Hizam ibn, 239.
el-Qalam, Beit, tribe, 309.
Qammāz sub-tribe, 331.
el-Qanj, Mit'ab, 114.
Qara tribe, 309.
el-Qaramāni, Muhsin, 231.
Qāsid, Beni, tribe, 272.
Qasim, 3, 5, 6, 83, 84, 86, 89, 91, 94, 96.
Qasim house, 42, 43, 46, 48, 55, 58, 60.
Qasim, 'Abd er-Rahmān ibn, **63**, 271.
el-Qasim, 'Abdullah, **46**.
el-Qasim, Ahmed ibn, **48**, 58, 235.
Qasim, 'Ali ibn, 47, 51.
　'Arjalah, 229.
　el-Ayyam house, 46.
　ibn Hamid el-Ghābir, **68**, 250, 251.
　el-Hāshimi, 241.
Qasim, Haza, 269.
Qasim, Hizam ibn, 228.
el-Qasim, Mansūr, 42.
Qasim ibn Mohammed, **55**.
Qasim, Mohammed ibn, 129.
　Seifi, 236.
　ibn Seyyid Imām Kadri, **81**.
　Shebīb, 229.
Qasim, Tālib ibn, 159.
　ibn Yahya, 239.
Qasim Zeid, Hasan ibn, **51**, 52.
Qasr 'Ali ibn Mohammed, 32.
Qa'tabah, 56.
　Kaimmakam of, 58, 221, 242.
Qatan, 66.
El-Qatar, 84, 86.
el-Qatar Peninsula, Ruler of, **74**.
Qateit tribe, 310.
Qatif, 78, 81, 84, 94.
Qa'ūd sub-tribe, 205, 206, 208.
Qawā'id tribe, 310.
Qawāsim (or Jawāsim) tribe, 73, 310.
Qeis, Beni, tribes: Asir, 35, 190, 192;
　　Yemen, 46, 239.
el-Qeishi, Yahya, 242.
Qeishīsh, Hākim ibn, 107, 110.
Qibli, Ahl, 103, 119.
Qishn, Sultan of, 63.
Qitab, Beni, tribe, 311.
Qoreish tribe, 3, 19.
Qrein Inlet, 76.
Qu'ād, Ibn, 111, 112.
Qudāsh house, 53.
Qufl, 48, 59.
　Markaz of, 223.
　Seyyids of, **57**.
Quhrah tribe, 239.
Qunfudah, 4, 13, 16, 18, 20, 22, 23, 27, 28,
　　30-2, 34, 35, 37-40.
Qurūm family, 211, 212.
Quryāt, 71.
El-Qūs house, 52.
Qutābah, Beni, sub-tribe, 33, 199, 201.
Quteibi tribe, 64, 67, 265.
Quti', 47.

R

Rabī'ah, 104, 137.
　Mujātirah tribe, 194.
　wa Rufeidah tribe, 29, 37, 195.

Rabī'at esh-Shām sub-tribe, 195, 196.
　et-Tahāhīn tribe, 194.
　el-Yemen tribe, 29, 197, 198.
er-Rabīz, Ahl, tribe, 259.
Rābugh, 11, 14-16, 18.
Rada'ah tribe, 240.
Radeināt tribe, 311.
Radfān, 64, 69.
Radīyah, Abu, 174.
er-Rafadi, Sājir, 111.
er-Rafīq, 'Aun, 7, 31, 157.
Ragheb Bey, 44, **57**.
Rahalah, sub-tribe of the Beni Sālim, 12, 124.
Rahānimah tribe, 240.
Rāhat es-Senhān, 31.
Rahbiyīn tribe, 311.
er-Rahīm, 'Abd, **74**.
Rahmah bint 'Ali, 7.
er-Rahmān, 'Abd, of Jiddah, **13**.
　'Abd, of Ru'eis, **10**.
　see 'Abd el-'Aziz.
Rā'ih, 'Ali ibn, **30**, 165.
Rajājil, 88, 91, 94, 96.
Rājib ibn Dajhid, 175.
Rājih, Sheikh, 242.
Ramāh tribe, 312.
Raqād, Beni, tribe, 312.
Raqād, Sa'd, 153.
Ras el-Jebel Peninsula, 73, 74.
Rashīd family, 88; genealogical tree, **92**
Rashīd, 'Abdullah ibn, 83, 87.
　ibn Ahmed, **74**.
Rashīd, Ali ibn, 92.
Rāshid (or Rawāshid), Beni, tribe, 312.
er-Rashid, Dhāri ibn Fahd ibn 'Ubeid, **90**, 92.
er-Rashīd, Hārūn, 145.
　el-Hāshimi, 'Abdullah ibn, **78**.
Rashīd, Ibn: see Sa'ūd ibn 'Abd el-'Aziz.
Rāshid ibn Jum'ān, **39**, 216, 217.
Rashīd el-Kharūsi, Sālim ibn, 70, 71, 78, **81**.
er-Rashīd, Mohammed, 88, 90, 96, 137.
Rashīd, Mohammed ibn, 74, 83, 92.
er-Rashīd, Refa'āya, **18**.
er-Rashīd, Sultān, 91, 93.
Rashīd ibn Sumeir, **100**, 109.
Rashīd, 'Ubeid ibn, 92.
Rashīds, Ibn: see Shammar, Jebel.
Rasīb, Beni, tribe, 312.
Rassite family, 42.
er-Rasūl, Ahmed Nāsir, **48**.
Ra'ūf Pasha, 23.
Rawāshid, Beni, tribe: see Rāshid.
Rawwāf, Nāsir ibn, 129.
Rayyān, Wādi, 3.
Razah, Ahl, tribe, 240.
Razah, Jebel, 30.
Red Sea, 20, 83.
　Lighthouse Administration, 50.
　Patrol, 14, 18.
Refa'āya, Rashīd, **18**.
Refa'i ('Arfu'a), sub-tribe, 18, 121.
Reimah, Ahl, tribe, 240.
Reish tribe, 37, 198.
Rhodes, 49.
Ridha (Riza), 'Abdullah 'Ali, **9**.
Ridha (Riza), 'Ali Bey, 26, 170.
Ridha (Riza), Zeini 'Ali, house of, **21**.
Rifā', 76.
Rijāl, 23, 33, 41.

Rijāl el-M'a tribes, 27, 32, 33, 38, 41, 198-203.
Rijbān tribe, 329.
Riyādh, 74, 83, 84, 86, 90, 94, 95, 99.
  Emirs of : see Nejd, Emirate of.
Riyām, Beni, tribe, 81, 312.
Riyāyisah tribe, 313.
Riza : see Ridha.
Riza Bey, Hasan, 134.
Rizk, Hādi, 50.
Rostāq, 70, 79.
Ruba' el-Khāli, 65.
Ru'eis, 10.
Rufādah, Suleimān Afnān, 15, 16, **20**, 120.
Rufeidat esh-Shām, sub-tribe, 195, 196.
  el-Yemen tribe, 32, 35, 36, 190-2.
Rukwān, 'Ali ibn, **30**, 194.
Rumādi, 97.
Rumāh, Ibn, 238.
Rumāh, Mohammed ibn Hassan, 238.
Rumei'ān, Āl, sub-tribe, 39, 179.
Rumeilah, 75.
Rūqah section of the Ateibah, 126.
Rusās house, 48, 52.
er-Rusās, Ibrāhīm Muhsin, 52, 232.
Rusheid, Āl, sub-tribe, 29, 205-8.
Ruwāhah, Beni, tribe, 313.
Ruweilah tribe, 88, 98, 100, 105, 106, 109, 149.

S

Sa'ādiyīn tribe, 315.
Sa'ar tribe, 276.
es-Sabān, Surūr, **20**.
Sabia (Sabīyah), 22-4, 27, 30, 33, 34, 41, 51.
Sabia, Ahl (Sabīyah), tribe, 203-5.
Sabrein Hadhrami, Ba, **13**.
Sabt Balaksah, **68**.
Sa'd ibn 'Abd el-Muhsin es-Sedeiri, **96**.
  ibn 'Abd er-Rahmān, 4, 84, 85, 87.
    'Abdullah, 240.
  ibn Ahmed et-Tarāf, 233.
  ibn 'Arubeij, **18**.
Sa'd, Beni, tribe, 129, 130, 314.
  ibn Dhuh, **39**, 178, 179.
  ed-Dīn Pasha, **9**.
  ibn Ghaneim, 122.
  ibn Husein, **39**, 205, 207.
  el-Huweifi, **18**, 124.
  ibn Mohammed Sālih, 17, **19**.
  ibn Mufarrih, 182.
  ibn Mutlaq, 289.
  ibn Nāsir, 182.
  Raqād, 153.
  ibn Sa'd, 223.
  ibn Sa'ūd, 87.
  ibn Suleim, **39**, 188, 189.
Sa'dah town, 42, 47, 49, 55.
Sa'dah clan of the Nawāshirah, 29.
Sa'dah, Sherifs of, 58.
Sādah family, 263.
Sadān, Wādi, 57.
Sa'dat en-Na'āmiyah family, 200.
Sadda, 60.
Sa'dūn, 'Ajeimi ibn, 77, 79, 80, 88, **97**, 137.
Sa'fān, Beni, tribe, 240, 241.
Sāfi family, 15.
Sāfi, Ahmed, **11**.
Safiq, Jum'ān ibn, 236.

Saft el-Laban (Jīzah), 8.
Safwān, 79, 80, 89.
Sagar ibn Khālid, 73.
Sagar, Sheikh, 74.
Saghīr, 'Ali, 238.
Saghīr, Ibn, 173.
Saghīr, Munāsar, **57**, 245.
Saghīr, Yahya, **41**, 187.
Sahār, 36.
  tribe, 241.
Sahil, 'Ali, 230.
Sahul tribe, 84, 85, 130, 332.
Sa'īd 'Abbās, **58**, 59.
  ibn 'Abd, 26, **39**, 205, 207.
Sa'īd, 'Abd el-'Azīz ibn, **91**.
Sa'īd, 'Abdullah ibn, 94.
  Effendi Abu Ras, **39**.
Sa'īd, Ahl, tribes : Lower 'Aulaqi, 266;
  division of the Oleh confederation, 267, 268.
Sa'īd, Ahmed ibn, of the Azd tribe, 70.
Sa'īd, Ahmed, of Hābil es-Sabt, 270.
  ibn 'Aseidān, **40**, 216, 217.
  Ba Haidar, Mohammed, **37**.
  ibn Fā'iz Walad Fā'iz ibn Qurūm, 31, **40**, 211, 212.
Sa'īd, Fā'iz ibn, **31**, 40, 211, 212.
Sa'īd, Faraj Bey ibn, **31**, 40, 211, 212.
  Ferhān, Abu, **97**.
es-Sa'īd, Hasan, **32**, 175.
Sa'īd ibn Hashbal, **40**, 206, 208.
  ibn Ibrāhīm, 79.
  ibn Makhtūm, **73**.
  el-Mohammed, **96**.
Sa'īd, Mohammed ibn, 128.
Sa'īd, Mujarri ibn, **35**, 169.
  ibn Mustafa, 25.
  ibn 'Othmān, **40**, 161.
  Pasha, **58**, 271, 272.
  Pasha, 'Ali, 48, **49**, 54, 66, 67, 264.
  ibn Suleimān, 275.
Sa'īd, Suleimān ibn, **20**.
  ibn Sultān ibn Ahmed ibn Sa'īd, 70, 72.
  ibn Sultān, Barghāsh ibn, 72.
  ibn Sultān, Majīd, 70, 72.
  ibn Sultān, Tūrki ibn, 70, 72, 294.
Sa'īd, Thuweini ibn, 72.
Sa'īdah, Mohammed ibn, 167.
Sā'idah tribe, 315.
es-Sa'īdi, Ahl, tribe, 66, 248, 255.
Sa'īdi plain, 68.
Sājir er-Rafadi, 111.
Sakhr, eponymous founder of the Beni Sakhr, 113, 115.
Sakhr, Beni, tribe, 98, 101, 113-16, 149.
Sakhr ibn Khālid, 231.
es-Sakladi, 'Ali Mauna, 271.
Salāmah ibn Subhān, 93.
Salām, Mohammed Abu, **35**, 190, 192.
Salāmah, Nāsir ibn, 93.
Salāmah, Subhān ibn, 93.
Salāmiyīn tribe, 316.
Salātinah tribe, 316.
Saleimiyīn tribe, 315.
Saleitah tribe, 114, 116.
Sālih family, 252.
Sālih ibn 'Abdullah, of the 'Amūdi, 273.
  ibn 'Abdullah, of Bālhāf, **68**, 247.
  ibn 'Abdullah, of the Upper 'Aulaqi, **69**, 253.
  ibn Ahmed, 271.

Sālih, Ahmed ibn, 240.
  ibn Ahmed ibn Tālib, **69**.
Sālih ibn 'Ajalah, **40,** 171.
  el-Akhram, Mohammed, **67,** 265.
  ibn 'Ali, 224, 230.
Sālih, 'Ali ibn, 227.
  'Arjalah, 229.
  ibn 'Awad, **69**.
  el-'Awaj, 233.
  el-Bedāwi el-Hadhramauti, **68**.
  Freh, Abu, **97**.
  ibn Ghālib, **66**.
  el-Hārithi, 'Ali ibn, **79,** 80.
  el-Hārithi, 'Isa ibn, 79, **80**.
  Haya, 95.
  Ja'far, Mohammed, 64.
  ibn Ma'id el-Moghrabi, **58,** 226, 227.
  ibn Mohammed et-Tawāl, 236.
Sālih, Mohammed ibn, of the Beni Ghaneim, **17,** 18.
Sālih, Mohammed, of Jeizān, 28, **37**.
  Muhsin ibn 'Ali 'Abd el-Qādir, **19**.
Sālih, Muhsin ibn, 67, 247, 254.
  el-Mujalli, 154.
  ibn Muslih, **58,** 226, 227, 241.
Sālih, Nāsir ibn, **68,** 247.
  ibn 'Omar, 270, 271.
  ibn Qahtān, **69**.
Sālih, Qā'id, **58**.
  ibn Selīm ibn Qutam, 276.
  Shadli, **58**.
  Sheibi, Mohammed, **19**.
  ibn Subhān, 93.
  es-Subhān, Sa'ūd ibn, 88, **91,** 92, 93.
  ibn Yahya Hizām, 242.
Sālih, Yahya ibn, **69**.
  ibn Zāmil, 96.
Sālim, 'Abdullah ibn, 294.
  ibn 'Abdullah el-Kheimri, **81**.
  Abu Manāwir el-Husein, 153.
  el-'Alawi, 'Ali ibn 'Abdullah ibn, **79**.
  ibn 'Amr, **69,** 271.
  Ba Jubeir, 34.
  Bamar, 273.
  ibn Bedr, 'Abd el-'Azīz ibn, **78**.
Sālim, Beni, sub-tribe, 10, 12, 14. 15, 18, 123, 124.
  ibn Feisāl, **72**.
  Husein, **69,** 264.
  el-Māliki, 'Ali Yūsuf ibn, **11**.
  ibn Masyūghah, 117.
  ibn Mubārak, 77, **78**.
  Qahtān, Yūsuf ibn, **21**.
  ibn Rashīd el-Kharūsi, 70, 71, 78, **81**.
  Sālih ibn 'Atif Jābir, 271.
  ibn Sultān, **74**.
  ibn Thuweini, 72.
Salīm, Yahya ibn, 181, 182.
  ibn Zāmil, 93.
Salīmi, 'Awad, **12**.
Salīyah, Sheikh, **19**.
Salmān, 'Abdullah ibn, **94**.
Salt, 97.
Sāmi Pasha, 17, 98, 100, 106, 114, 118, 154.
Samīd tribe, 138.
San'ā, 23, 39, 42–4, 46–8, 50, 51, 53–5, 58, 60.
  Imam of, 271.
  Imams of, previous to the reigning dynasty, genealogical tree, **45**.
  Seyyids of, **58**.
  Sherif of, 58.

Sana, 'Abdullah ibn, 208.
Sanhut, Sultān ibn, 127.
Saqāf, Seyyid, **19**.
Saqra sub-tribe, 100.
Sara' house, 53.
Sārah, Āl Abu, family, 180, 182.
Sareiriyīn tribe, 316.
Sāri house, 53.
Sāri, Lutf, **54,** 229.
Sāri tribe, 241.
Sārikh, Beni, tribe, 316.
Sarīr, 64.
Sarrāj (Sa Rāj), 'Abdullah, **9**.
Sarwi, Sheikh, **40,** 215.
Sa'ūd family, genealogical tree, **87**.
Sa'ūd ibn 'Abd el-'Azīz, Emir of Jebel Shammar [Ibn Rashīd], 3, 4, 6, 9, 17, 73–9, 83–6, **88–90,** 91, 92–6, 99, 100, 105, 107, 130–4, 136–8, 141–5.
Sa'ūd, 'Abd el-'Azīz ibn, 87, 140.
Sa'ūd, 'Abdullah ibn, 83, 85, 87.
Sa'ūd, Aulād, 84, 85, **86,** 126.
  ibn Feisāl, 86, 87.
  ibn Hamūd, 88, 92.
Sa'ūd, Ibn : see 'Abd el-'Azīz ibn 'Abd er-Rahmān.
Sa'ūd, Mahd ibn, **96**.
  ibn Milhem, 109.
  ibn Mohammed, 77.
Sa'ūd, Mohammed ibn, 83, 87, 96.
Sa'ūd, Sa'd ibn, 87.
  ibn Sālih es-Subhān, 88, **91,** 92, 93.
Sa'ūd, Tūrki ibn, 89.
Sa'ūdīn sub-tribe, 99.
Sa'ūds, Ibn : see Nejd, Emirate of.
es-Sayādi, Hizām, 243.
Sebāk, Mohammed 'Ali, 218.
Sebei' tribe, 84, 85, 130, 332.
Sedeir, 5, 6, 84, 85, 91, 94, 96.
Seibān tribe, 276.
Seif 'Abd el-Hādi, Shā'if ibn, 250.
  Diban, 269.
  el-Islām : see Mohammed el-Mutawakkil.
  el-Khulufah : see Mohammed el-Mutawakkil.
Seif, Shahīr ibn, **69,** 269.
  ibn Shā'if ibn Seif, **68,** 250.
  ibn Sultān, 70.
Seifi, Qasīm, 236.
Seilah, 'Ali ibn, 228.
Sekeinah, Bahr Ibn, 38, 162, 201.
Selīm Abu Irbe'a, **100**.
  Abu Jābir, **97**.
  ibn Hamūd, 92.
  ibn Qutam, Sālih ibn, 276.
Selmah, Jebel, 86.
Selqa tribe, 111.
Semā'il, 71, 81.
Senhān el-Hibāb tribe, 31, 36, 192, 193.
Senhān ez-Zeidi tribe, 241.
Senussi, Sheikh, 22, 25, 43.
Serāji house, 53.
Serāji, 'Abdullah, 53.
Serbih tribe, 242.
Serdīyah tribe, 98, 114.
Settled tribes of the Centre, 327–33.
Seyah, Āl, 35.
Seyyūn, 66.
Seyyūn and Terīm, Sultan of, 273, 274.

Sha'af Rashhah, sub-tribe, 26, 205, 207, 209.
Yarimah wa Khutab, sub-tribe, 190-2.
esh-Shā'ah, Ahl, tribe, 251.
Sha'bān, 176.
Shabein, 'Abd er-Ru'b, **62.**
Shabūl tribe, 316.
Shabwah, 65.
Shadhli el-'Alyān, 11, **19.**
Shadli, Sālih, **58.**
Shafei Madrasah, or College (Yemen), 46.
Shahāb el-Faqīr, 109.
Shahāb sub-tribe, 199, 203.
Shahā'irah tribe, 316.
Shahawān, Nā'if ibn, 152.
Shaheim, Beni, tribe, 316.
Shāhin et-Tawār, Nāsir ibn, 74.
Shāhir, Mohammed ibn, **37,** 195, 196.
Shahir ibn Seif, **69,** 269.
Shahrān tribe, 11, 24, 26, 28, 29, 33, 37, 39-41, 205-10.
Shahūm, Beni, tribe, 317.
Shā'if family, 225.
  ibn Seif 'Abd el-Hādi, 250.
  ibn Seif, 'Abd el-Hamid ibn, **68,** 250.
  ibn Seif, Nāsir ibn, **68,** 250.
  ibn Seif, Seif ibn, **68,** 250.
  esh-Shā'if, Yahya ibn Yahya, **60,** 232.
Shā'if section of the Bekil, 60.
Sha'ir, Ahl, tribe, 242.
Shakeil, Beni, tribe, 317.
Shakespear, Captain, 84, 86, 89-91, 94, 95, 100, 148.
Shakhārīyīn tribe, 317.
Shākir el-'Abādilah, Nāsir ibn, **18.**
  ibn Zeid ibn Fawwāz el-'Abādilah, **19.**
Shakūr tribe, 317.
esh-Sha'lān, Nūri, 4, 6, 87-90, 98, **100,** 106-9.
Shalāwah tribe, 130.
Shamāliyah, 95.
Shamar tribe, 242.
Shameili, Beni, tribe, 317.
Shāmi house, 59.
esh-Shāmi, Sheikh, **59,** 245.
Shamma, Ahl, tribe, 259.
Shammakh ibn Ghannam, **69,** 263.
Shammar family, 88.
  tribes, 89-91, 99, 132-6, 333; Irāq, 136; Jebel Shammar, 132, 133; Jezirah, 132, 134, 136; Nejd, 135.
Shammar, Jebel, 83, 85-9.
  Emirate of [ibn Rashīds], **87-91,** 132.
Shamrān tribe, 214.
  esh-Shām sub-tribe, 32, 214.
  et-Tihāmah sub-tribe, 34, 214.
  el-Yemen, see Shamrān et-Tihāmah.
Shamūs tribe, 317.
Shanbar, Sherif, **40.**
Shāqōsh sub-tribe, 317.
Shaqrah (Woshm), 96.
Sha'r, Ahmed ibn, 186.
Sha'r, Dhakir ibn, **31,** 185, 186.
Sha'r, Dhuleim ibn, 36, 193.
Sharā'inah tribe, 317.
Shārjah, 73, 74.
  British Resident at, 73.
  Sheikh of, **73,** 296.
Sharkāsi, 'Ali, **12.**
esh-Sharqi, Suleimān, 111.

Sharqiyīn tribe, 318.
Sharūq tribe: see Shurūj.
Shateir, Beni, sub-tribe, 319.
esh-Shatri, 'Abd er-Rahmān, 276.
Shatt el-'Arab, 89.
Shawābkah tribe, 150, 152, 153.
Shawāfi' tribe, 318.
Shawahlah clan, 10.
Shawākrah tribe, 153.
Shawāmis tribe, 318.
Shawi', 'Ali, 224.
Shāwīsh, Sheikh, 18.
Shebib, Qasim, 229.
Shefiq Pasha, Suleimān, 33.
Shehārah, 43, 48, 52, 55, 59.
Shehāri house, 42, 43, 55, 59.
Shehat Effendi, 54.
Sheiba, battle of, 97.
Sheibi house, **19.**
Sheibi, 'Abd el-Qādir, **19.**
Sheibi tribe, **69,** 271.
Sheikh 'Othmān, 65.
Sheikh Sa'īd, 48.
Sheiri clan, 63.
esh-Sheiri, Yahya Walad, 199.
Shemlān, Ibn, 274.
Shemsān tribe, 242.
Shenabrah clan, 40, 129, 158.
Sheradra, 53.
Sherāf, Mu'āfa, 239.
esh-Sherā'i, Ahmed, 42.
Sherārāt tribe, 144, 147, 333.
Sherāri house, 53, 59.
Shereif tribe, 36, 193.
Sherein, Mūsa ibn, 181.
Sherein, Nāsir ibn, 181.
Sherī'ah, the, 44.
esh-Sherīf, 'Abdullah, of Ibha, 33.
esh-Sherīf, Ahmed, **27,** 33.
esh-Sherīf, Hasan, 33.
esh-Sherīf, Mohammed, 25, 33.
Sherif ed-Dīn house, 53.
  ibn 'Izzedin house, 33.
Sherifial ('Abādilah) family of Mecca, genealogical tree, 7.
  Revolt, 49.
Shiah, the, 54.
Shi'bah, Beni, tribe, 33, 210.
Shibām, 49, 66.
esh-Shibi, Emīr, 233, 235.
Shiblān, Ahmed ibn, 183.
Shiheir, 66.
Shihir, Beni, tribe, 211-13.
  esh-Shām, Beni, sub-tribe, 31, 40, 211, 212.
  et-Tihāmah, Beni, sub-tribe, 34, 35, 212, 213.
  el-Yemen, Beni, sub-tribe, 28, 212, 213.
Shihūh tribe, 318.
Shij, 40, 161.
Shija'fah, 30.
Shijeifi, Hasan, 174.
esh-Shimāl, Ahl, 103, 104, 113, 119, 123, 137, 147.
Shiyābinah tribe, 320.
Shiyādi tribe, 320.
Shōbak district, tribes of, 154-6.
  Kaimmakam of, 154.
Shūghrah, 65, 66.
Shujeifi district, 47.

Shuqaiq, 24, 29, 37.
esh-Shuqaiq, Ahl, tribe, 213.
Shuqeir, Ghaza ibn, 139.
Shurmān, Kaimmakam of, 56.
Shurūj (or Sharūq) tribe, 320.
Shuweil, Mohammed ibn, 191.
Shuweini, Ahl, tribe, 267.
Shweihiyīn tribe, 298, 320.
Sīb, 72, 78.
Sibā' (Sba) tribe, 106, 107, 111.
Sibsib, Mohammed, 241.
Sifrān clan, 80.
Sihāf section of the 'Auf sub-tribe, 14, 125.
Sijah, 26.
Sinai, 4, 97–101.
Sinān, Beni, tribe, 320.
Sinjārah (tribe), 95, 135.
Sirdāb, Hamūd, **32,** 33.
Sirhān, Ibrāhīm, **34.**
Sirhān tribe, 151.
Sirhān, Wādi, 100.
Sitrah Island, 75, 76.
Siwādi, 'Othmān, **39,** 179.
Siyābiyīn tribe, 320.
Smyrna, 58.
Söbah II, Mubārak ibn, 76, 77, 85, 96.
Socotra, 63, 80.
Sohār, 70, 82.
Soma (Sauma'ah), 62, 63.
Somali Mullah, 24.
Subeih, Āl, sub-tribe, 331.
Subeihi tribe, 64, 69, 268–70.
Subh clan, 10.
Subh, Beni, tribe, 320.
Subhān family, 88 ; genealogical tree, 93.
Subhān, Hamūd ibn, 88.
Subhān Ibn, 93.
es-Subhān, Hamūd, 90, 92, 93.
es-Subhān, Ibrāhīm, 79, 90, 91, 93.
Subhān, Mudhi bint, 88, 90, **91,** 92, 93.
  ibn Salāmah, 93.
Sūbhan, Salāmah ibn, 93.
Subhān, Sālih ibn, 93.
es-Subhān, Sa'ūd, 88, **91,** 92, 93.
es-Subhān, Zāmil, 88, 91, 93.
Subhi, 'Abd el-Muhsin, **10.**
Sudan, 23, 24.
Sūdān tribe, 321.
Suez, 13.
es-Sūfi, Hamād, **98.**
Sufūq, Fāris ibn, 134.
Sufūq, Ferhān ibn, 134.
Sufūq ibn Jerba, 134.
Sufyān sub-tribe, 228.
Suhabah tribe, 329.
Suheil, Buti ibn, 73.
Sulābah, see Sulubba.
Suleil, Beni, tribe, 46, 242.
Suleim, ancestor of the Sherārāt, 144.
Suleim, 'Abd el-'Azīz ibn, 95.
Suleim ibn Jābir, 92.
Suleim, Sa'd ibn, **39,** 188, 189.
Suleimah, Emir of, 53.
  section of the Hāshid, 54, 226, 229.
Suleimān Afnān Rufādah, 15, 16, **20,** 120.
Suleimān, Ahl, tribe, 258.
  ibn 'Ali, **40,** 185, 186.
  ibn Hasan, of Ibha, 38.
  Hasan, of Mahad, 220.

Suleimān Qābil, **20.**
  ibn Sa'īd, **20.**
Suleimān, Sa'īd ibn, 275.
  esh-Sharqi, 111.
  esh-Sharqi, 'Ali, **97,** 111, 112.
Shefiq Pasha, 33.
Suleimān, Sheikh, 85, 86.
  ibn 'Ubeid, 92.
Siyabi, Nāsir ibn, **81.**
es-Sulh, Hasan Ahmed, 223.
Sultān ibn Ahmed ibn Sa'īd, Sa'īd ibn, 70, 72.
  ibn 'Ali Dhi'āb, 149, 151.
  ed-Derwīsh, Feisāl ibn, 77, **95,** 138, 139.
  ibn Hamūd er-Rashīd, 88, 92.
  ibn Mohammed, 7.
  Mohammed ibn Naimi, **82.**
  ibn Nawwāf, 100.
  er-Rashīd, 91, 93.
Sultān, Sālim ibn, **74.**
  ibn Sanhut, 127.
Sultān, Seif ibn, 70.
Sultān, Sheikh, of Safwān, 79, **80.**
  ibn Telāl, 92.
Sulubba tribe, 145, 147.
Sumeir, Ibn, 105, 108.
Sumeir, Rashīd ibn, **100,** 109.
Summān Steppe, 77.
Sunnā' tribe, 145–7, 333.
Sūq el-Khamīs, 54.
  esh-Shuyūkh, 99.
Sūr, 71, 80.
Sur', Beni, sub-tribe, 231.
Surūr es-Sabān, **20.**
Surur, Sherif, 158.
Suwālih tribe, 321.
Suwāwifah, tribe, 321.
Suweilim, Ibn, 95, 96.
es-Suweilim, Mas'ūd, **96.**
Suweirqīyah, 13.
Suweit, Hamūd ibn, 88, **99,** 137, 138.
Syria, 4–6, 9.
Syrian desert, region of, 97–101.

T

Tadmor, Mudir of, 100.
Tafilah, Arabs of, 156.
Tahar ibn 'Ali, **40,** 179.
Tahar, Mohammed, of Jebel Jihāf, **67.**
Tahar, Mohammed, of the Sabia district, **37.**
  ibn Mohannah, **20.**
Tāhir Abu Hashar, 177, 178.
  Husein el-Farah, 221.
Tahnūn ibn Zeid, 73.
Tā'if, 3, 4, 6.
Ta'izz, 42, 47–9, 52, 56.
Tal'āt, Ahmed, **11.**
Tal'āt Husni : see Husein Bey.
Tāli', 'Ali ibn, 198.
Tālib ibn Qasīm, 159.
Tamīm, Beni, tribe, 136, 333.
Tamīmi tribe, 276.
Tamlah, 49.
Taneij tribe, 321.
Tanūf, 70, 81.
  Imam of, 78.
et-Tarāf, 'Abdullah, 233.

et-Taráf, Sa'd ibn Ahmed, 233.
Tarif, Beni, tribe, 117.
Tarūt (Miniat el-Kamh), 8.
Tatimmaha tribe, 321.
Tauqah tribe, 135, 136.
Tawā'd, 'Abdullah, **9**.
et-Tawālah, Dhāri, 135.
Tawāyah section of the Huweitāt, 17.
et-Tawil, Mohammed, **16**.
Tayya, Wādi, 37.
Tayyār, 'Abd el-'Aziz, **10**.
et-Tayyār, Mohammed, 109.
Teima, 87, 89.
Teimur ibn Feisāl, Sultān of Oman, **71,** 72, 75, 79.
Teiwānīyah tribe, 321.
Telāl ibn 'Abdullah, 87, 92.
Telāl, 'Abdullah, 92.
Telāl, Bedr ibn, 92.
Telāl, Bunder ibn, 92.
  ibn Fā'iz Abu Meshkūr, 98, **101,** 113, 116.
Telāl, Fawwāz ibn, **98,** 113, 114.
  ibn Jābir, 92.
Telāl, Mohammed ibn, 92.
Telāl, Musnid ibn, 92.
  ibn Nā'if, 92.
Telāl, Nā'if ibn, 92.
Telāl, Nehar ibn, 92.
Telāl, Sultān ibn, 92.
Terābin tribe, 98.
Terīm, 66.
Tewfik Pasha, Ahmed, **48,** 54.
Thābit ibn 'Omar, 274, 275.
  ibn Yahya Dugheish, 231.
Thalah, 49.
Thameirāt tribe, 322.
Thāmir, *jidd* of the Dhuleim, 111.
eth-Thanayyān, Ahmed, **94**.
Thanayyān, Ibn, 94, 96.
eth-Thāni, Ahmed, 75.
Thaqīf, Beni, tribe, 129.
Thawāb, 'Abdullah ibn, **10**.
Thawāb, Hasan 'Ali, 160.
Thawābah, Husein ibn, 52, 234.
Theidān ibn Hithlein, **79,** 80, 141.
Thulam tribe, 100.
Thuweini ibn Sa'īd, 72.
Thuweini, Salīm ibn, 72.
Thuwwah, Beni, tribe, 40, 215.
Tihāmah, 37, 42, 44, 47, 56.
et-Timyāt, Noweidis, 134.
Tneib, 97.
Toweiq (Tuweiq), genealogy of, 113.
Tripolitan War : *see* Turco-Italian War.
Trucial Chiefs, **73,** 74.
  Coast, 84.
Tubeiq, Jebel, 101.
Tulūh sub-tribe, 100.
Tūmān section of the Shammar, 95.
Tuqeiqah, Ahmed ibn, 118.
Turco-Italian War, 13, 23, 27, 50, 51.
Tūrki ibn 'Abd el-'Azīz, **86,** 87.
  ibn 'Abdullah, 87.
Tūrki, Fahhād ibn, 72.
Tūrki, Feisāl ibn, 72, 78, 80-3, 87, 294.
  ibn Mijlād, Mohammed ibn, **99,** 110.
Tūrki, Mohammed ibn, 71, **72**.
  ibn Sa'īd ibn Sultān, 70, 72, 294.
  ibn Sa'ūd, 89.
Turkīyah, **96**.

Turks, 4–6, 10, 12, 14, 15, 17–20, **22–4,** 26–9, 31–3, 36, 38–44, 46–8, **51–9,** 62, 64, 66–9, 74–6, 79, 80, 84, **85,** 87, 89, 98–101.
el-Turmān, Bāshir, 153.
Tuweiq : *see* Toweiq.

U

'Ubāl, 47.
'Ubeid, 'Abdullah ibn, 92.
'Ubeid, Fahd ibn, 92.
'Ubeid, Fahhād ibn, 92.
  el-Gharāmil, 96.
  ibn Hamūd, 92.
  ibn Rashīd, 92.
'Ubeid, Hamūd ibn, 88, 92.
  er-Rashīd, Dhāri ibn : *see* Dhāri.
'Ubeid, Suleimān ibn, 92.
'Ubeid, Zeid ibn, 92.
el-'Ūd, Ahl, tribe, 243.
'Udhāqah, Emir of the, 55, 243.
Udhāqah tribe, 243.
'Umeir, Āl, tribe, 322.
Umlejh, 13, 17, 19.
Umm Bina sub-tribe, 199, 203.
  Basūs, Ahmed, 270.
  Bushti, Ahl, tribe, 261.
  Heithami Abu Fadhl, 268.
  Husein, Aulād Āl, 197.
  Jallah, 33.
  Jerei'āt, Āl, sub-tribe, 180, 181, 183.
  Manādhir clan, 36.
  el-Qaiwein settlement, 74.
  el-Qaiwein, Sheikh of, 311.
  Qasr, 76.
  Rusās Abu Fārid, 256.
  Sherāf, Āl, sub-tribe, 180, 181, 183.
  Shi'bah, Ahmed ibn, **27,** 181.
  Wādi Malah, Āl, sub-tribe, 29, 37, 180–3.
'Umr section of the Belā'ir, 168.
'Umr, Beni, tribe of the Oman Sultanate, 322.
'Unqān, 48.
'Uqeil tribe, 147, 148.
Urum Kundum, 97.
'Urūr, Mohammed ibn, **37,** 206, 208.
Useidah tribe, 114.
el-'Useimi, Munāsar. 228.
el-'Uteir, Hāmid ibn, **65,** 263.
'Utūb tribe, 75.

V

Vlach, von, of Bahrein, 90.

W

Wadā'ah tribe, 36, 193, 194.
Wādi : *see under specific name.*
el-Wādi, Ahl, sub-tribe, 230.
Wādi Jeizān, Ahl, tribe, 34.
el-Wadūd, 'Abd, **46**.
Wahab, Beni, sub-tribe of the Wuld 'Ali, 105.
Wahabism, 83.
Wahabites, the, 73, 74.
Wahāsha sub-tribe, 270.

Waheib, Beni, tribe, 322.
Wahhāb, Beni, sub-tribe of the Shahrān, 26, 39, 41, 205, 206, 209.
Wahhās, Ahmed, 231.
Wahībah, Āl, tribe, 323.
Wahīdis, the, 69.
Waht, 62.
Wā'il, 104.
Walad 'Azzām, 144.
Waqf, 16.
Wardah, Ibn, 147.
Warūd tribe, 323.
Washāhāt tribe, 324.
Waslallah ibn Wasim, **20**.
Wasm, 29.
el-Wāzi, Āl, sub-tribe, 180, 181, 183.
Wa'zāt tribe, 23, 51, 243.
Weimān, Āl, sub-tribe, 180, 181, 184.
Wejh, 17, 20.
Widā'in tribe, 329.
Willcocks, Sir W., 107.
Wilson, Colonel, 8, 9, 19.
Wuld 'Ali tribe, 4, 100, 105, 109.

Y

Ya'āqīb tribe, 324.
Ya'āribah tribe, 324.
Ya'bir tribe, 243.
Yadūdah, 97.
Yāfa', Lower, 65, 272.
 Upper, 63, 68, 69, 270, 271.
Yāfa' tribe, 277.
Yahāmidah tribe, 324.
Yahāwi, Ahl, tribe, 261.
Yahya 'Abad, 223.
 'Abdullah Mukarram, **59**.
 el-Ahdal, Mohammed ibn, 47.
 ibn Ahmed, of the Fadhā'il house, 57, **59**.
 ibn Ahmed, of the Jebāli house, 50.
 ibn Ahmed, of the Sherā'i house, **59**.
 ibn Ahmed ez-Zawari, 52.
Yahya, Ahmed ibn, 46, **48**, 51.
 'Ali ibn Ahmed Hādi Thawāb, **41**, 159, 160.
 'Arār ibn Nāsir, **30**, 240.
 ibn 'Askar, 271.
 Ba Sāhi, Mohammed, 23, 34, **37**, 68, 204.
 Bahr, Ahmed, 47.
 Dugheish, Thābit ibn, 231.
 Fad'il, 51.
 ibn Fā'iz, **41**, 207, 209.
 Fāri', Ahmed ibn, **48**, 50, 228.
 Fāri', 'Ali ibn, 228.
 Fāri', Dirhem ibn, 48, **50**, 226, 228.
 el-Hādi, 42.
 ibn el-Hādi, **55**, 242.
 Hāmid ed-Dīn, 42, 45.
 ibn Hamza house, 49.
 el-Hibah Fashīk, Mohammed, **56**, 57, 59, 245.
 Hizām, Sālih ibn, 242.
 el-Jebāli, **60**.
 Karāt, Ahmed, 50.
 Mihah, **41**, 179.
 el-Mo'ayyadi, **60**.
 ibn Mohammed, 53.

Yahya ibn Mohammed Hāmid ed-Dīn el-Mutawakkil, Imam of Yemen, 4, 23, 42, **43–4**, 45, 47–55, 57, 59, 79–81, 220–31, 234–8, 240–3, 245, 262.
 ibn Mohammed el-Mushādi, 50.
Yahya, Mohammed, 58.
 ibn Muhsin el-Muntaser, **59**.
Yahya, Nāji' ibn, 232.
 Nāsir, 271.
 el-Qa'aiti, 232.
 el-Qeishi, 242.
Yahya, Qasīm ibn, 239.
 Saghīr, **41**, 187.
 ibn Sālih, **69**.
 ibn Salīm, 181, 182.
Yahya, Seyyid, 53.
 esh-Sherīf, 33.
 Walad esh-Sheiri, 199.
 ibn Yahya esh-Shā'if, **60**, 231.
 el-Yemeni, 'Ali ibn, **49**, 221, 234.
Yahya, Zeid ibn, **52**, 60.
Yāl 'Abd es-Salām tribe, 316.
 Breik tribe, 285.
 Jarād tribe, 297.
 Khamīs tribe, 300.
 Sa'd tribes : Ghāfiri, 315 ; Hināwi, 314.
 Shabīb tribe, 316.
Ya'lah, Beni, tribe, 30, 31, 215.
Yām tribes, 54, 57, 244.
Yambo', 4, 8–10, 12, 15, 19.
 el-Bahr : see Yambo'.
 en-Nakhl, 15, 16.
Ya'qūb, Mohammed, 270.
Yās, Beni, tribe, 324.
Yazā'ida tribe, 153.
Yazīd, Ahl, sub-tribe of the Ahl es-Sa'idi, 66, 248.
Yazīd, Āl, sub-tribe of the Beni Mughed, 26, 180, 182.
Yemen, 9, 22, 23, 42–60, 67, 83.
 district, tribes of the, 220–45.
 Imamate of, **42–4**. See Yahya ibn Mohammed Hāmid ed-Dīn.
el-Yemen, Mikhlāf, Emir of, 37, 204.
Yerīm, 60.
Yeshbum valley, 67.
Yinfa'ah, Āl, sub-tribe, 26, 33, 205, 207, 210.
Yūb, Beni, tribe, 262.
Yūsuf ibn Sālim Qahtān, **21**.

Z

Za'āb tribe, 325.
Zafeit tribe, 325.
Zāfir, Beni, tribe, 244.
Zagārit tribe, 135.
Zahrān tribe, 39, 40, 216, 217.
Zahūm tribe, 326.
Zakari Bey, 222.
Za'liyah tribe, 46, 244.
Zāmil, 'Abdullah ibn, **94**.
Zāmil, 'Ali ibn, 93.
Zāmil, Sālih ibn, 96.
Zāmil, Salīm ibn, 93.
Zāmil es-Subhān, 88, 91, 93.
Zaranik (Dharāniq) tribe, 44, 56, 57, 59, 245.
Zarrāf tribe, 326.

Zatût tribe, 326.
Zauba' (Zoba) tribe, 135.
ez-Zawari, Yahya ibn Ahmed, 52.
Zāwāwi, 'Abdullah, **9.**
Zeben sub-tribe, 114.
Zebîd, 13, 26, 41, 46, 56.
   Seminary of, 22.
Zeid house, 51, 52, 157.
Zeid el-'Alauni clan, 5.
Zeid, Beni, tribe, 32, 47, 217, 218, 333;
   Northern, 217, 218; Southern, 218.
Zeid, Dhawi, family, 3, 9.
   ibn Fawwāz el-'Abādilah, Shākir ibn, **19.**
   ibn Feisāl, 157.
   ibn Husein, 7, **8,** 11, 16, 19.
   el-Khalīfah, Hamdān ibn, **73.**
Zeid, Mohammed, of the Jāmi', 235.
Zeid, Mohammed, of the Munjahah, 185.
Zeid, Tahnūn ibn, 73.
   ibn Yahya, 52, **60.**
   ibn 'Ubeid, 92.
Zeidi districts, 44.
Zeidīn, Beni, sub-tribe, 199, 200, 203.

Zeidism, 42.
Zeidist dynasty, 42.
Zeidīyah, 47.
   Kaimmakam of, 46, 242.
Zeilah, Ahmed, **28,** 34.
Zeilah, 'Isa, 28, **34.**
Zein el-'Ābidīn, 26, **41,** 201.
Zeini 'Ali Ridha (Riza) house, **21.**
Zeinia, 22, 24.
Zid, Beni, tribe, 326.
Zidjal tribe: *see* Jadgal.
Zikāwinah tribe, 326.
Zilfi, 94, 95.
Zindāni family, 67.
ez-Zindāni, 'Ali ibn 'Ali, **64.**
Zobeid, sub-tribe of the Harb, 4, 11, 16, 20, 38, 124, 125, 218, 219.
Zobeid confederation: *see* Jebelīyah.
Zobeir, 89.
ez-Zogheibi, Fā'iz, **13.**
Zohir, Wādi, 48.
Zōra, 74.
ez-Zubeir, Lutf, 241.
Zufar, Seyyids of, **60.**
Zufeir tribe, 245.

ARABIA PAST AND PRESENT

ANNALS OF OMAN
Sirhan ibn Sirhan

ARABIA IN EARLY MAPS
G.R. Tibbetts

ARABIAN GULF INTELLIGENCE
comp. R.H. Thomas

ARABIAN PERSONALITIES OF THE
EARLY TWENTIETH CENTURY
introd. R.L. Bidwell

DIARY OF A JOURNEY ACROSS ARABIA
G.F. Sadleir

THE GOLD-MINES OF MIDIAN
Richard Burton

HA'IL: OASIS CITY OF SAUDI ARABIA
Philip Ward

HEJAZ BEFORE WORLD WAR I
D.G. Hogarth

HISTORY OF SEYD SAID
Vincenzo Maurizi

KING HUSAIN & THE KINGDOM OF HEJAZ
Randall Baker

THE LAND OF MIDIAN (REVISITED)
Richard Burton

MONUMENTS OF SOUTH ARABIA
Brian Doe

OMANI PROVERBS
A.S.G. Jayakar

SOJOURN WITH THE GRAND SHARIF OF MAKKAH
Charles Didier

TRAVELS IN ARABIA (1845 & 1848)
Yrjö Wallin

TRAVELS IN OMAN
Philip Ward

LIBYA PAST AND PRESENT

APULEIUS ON TRIAL AT SABRATHA
Philip Ward

THE LIBYAN CIVIL CODE
I.M. Arif & M.O. Ansell

LIBYAN MAMMALS
Ernst Hufnagl

THE LIBYAN REVOLUTION
I.M. Arif & M.O. Ansell

MOTORING TO NALUT
Philip Ward

SABRATHA
Philip Ward

TRIPOLI
Philip Ward

OLEANDER TRAVEL BOOKS

THE AEOLIAN ISLANDS
Philip Ward

ALBANIA: A TRAVEL GUIDE
Philip Ward

BANGKOK: PORTRAIT OF A CITY
Philip Ward

COME WITH ME TO IRELAND
Philip Ward

JAPANESE CAPITALS: NARA, KYOTO, TOKYO
Philip Ward

ROSSYA: THE TRANS-SIBERIAN EXPRESS
Michael Pennington

TOURING CYPRUS
Philip Ward

OLEANDER MODERN POETS

CONTEMPORARY GERMAN POETRY
comp. Ewald Osers

THE HIDDEN MUSIC
Östen Sjöstrand

A HOUSE ON FIRE
Philip Ward

IMPOSTORS & THEIR IMITATORS
Philip Ward

LOST SONGS
Philip Ward

ONCE OFF (Lenier poems)
Royal College of Art

RAIN FOLLOWING
Sue Lenier

THE SCANDALOUS LIFE OF CÉSAR MORO
César Moro

SWANSONGS
Sue Lenier

UNDERSEAS POSSESSIONS
Hans-Juergen Heise

OLEANDER LANGUAGE AND LITERATURE

THE ART & POETRY OF C.-F. RAMUZ
David Bevan

BIOGRAPHICAL MEMOIRS OF
EXTRAORDINARY PAINTERS
William Beckford

CELTIC: A COMPARATIVE STUDY
D.B. Gregor

FRENCH KEY WORDS
Xavier-Yves Escande

FRIULAN: LANGUAGE & LITERATURE
D.B. Gregor

GREGUERÍAS: Wit and Wisdom of
R. Gómez de la Serna

INDONESIAN TRADITIONAL POETRY
Philip Ward

A LIFETIME'S READING
Philip Ward

MARVELL'S ALLEGORICAL POETRY
Bruce King

ROMAGNOL: LANGUAGE & LITERATURE
D.B. Gregor

ROMONTSCH: LANGUAGE & LITERATURE
D.B. Gregor

OLEANDER GAMES AND PASTIMES

CHRISTMAS GAMES FOR ADULTS
AND CHILDREN
Crispin DeFoyer

DARTS: 50 WAYS TO PLAY THE GAME
Jabez Gotobed

DICE GAMES NEW AND OLD
W.E. Tredd

ENLIGHTENMENT THROUGH THE ART
OF BASKETBALL
Hirohide Ogawa

ENNEAGRAMS: NINE-LETTER WORD GAME
Ian D. Graves

PUB GAMES OF ENGLAND
Timothy Finn

SUMMER GAMES FOR ADULTS
AND CHILDREN
Hereward Zigo

THE OLEANDER PRESS

COASTAL FEATURES OF
ENGLAND AND WALES
J.A. Steers

A DICTIONARY OF COMMON FALLACIES
Philip Ward

THE GERMAN LEFT SINCE 1945
W.D. Graf

INDONESIA: A BIBLIOGRAPHY OF
BIBLIOGRAPHIES
J.N.B. Tairas

JAN VAN RYMSDYK: MEDICAL BOOK
ILLUSTRATOR
J.L. Thornton

THE LIFE AND MURDER OF
HENRY MORSHEAD
Ian Morshead

MEDICAL BOOK ILLUSTRATION:
A SHORT HISTORY
J.L. Thornton & C. Reeves

THE SMALL PUBLISHER
Audrey & Philip Ward